T0203024

Lecture Notes in Computer Science

Lecture Notes in Artificial Intelligence   14736

Founding Editor

Jörg Siekmann

Series Editors

Randy Goebel, *University of Alberta, Edmonton, Canada*
Wolfgang Wahlster, *DFKI, Berlin, Germany*
Zhi-Hua Zhou, *Nanjing University, Nanjing, China*

The series Lecture Notes in Artificial Intelligence (LNAI) was established in 1988 as a topical subseries of LNCS devoted to artificial intelligence.

The series publishes state-of-the-art research results at a high level. As with the LNCS mother series, the mission of the series is to serve the international R & D community by providing an invaluable service, mainly focused on the publication of conference and workshop proceedings and postproceedings.

Helmut Degen · Stavroula Ntoa
Editors

Artificial Intelligence in HCI

5th International Conference, AI-HCI 2024
Held as Part of the 26th HCI International Conference, HCII 2024
Washington, DC, USA, June 29 – July 4, 2024
Proceedings, Part III

 Springer

Editors
Helmut Degen
Siemens Corporation
Princeton, NJ, USA

Stavroula Ntoa
Foundation for Research
and Technology – Hellas (FORTH)
Heraklion, Crete, Greece

ISSN 0302-9743   ISSN 1611-3349 (electronic)
Lecture Notes in Artificial Intelligence
ISBN 978-3-031-60614-4   ISBN 978-3-031-60615-1 (eBook)
https://doi.org/10.1007/978-3-031-60615-1

LNCS Sublibrary: SL7 – Artificial Intelligence

This Springer imprint is published by the registered company Springer Nature Switzerland AG
The registered company address is: Gewerbestrasse 11, 6330 Cham, Switzerland

If disposing of this product, please recycle the paper.

Foreword

This year we celebrate 40 years since the establishment of the HCI International (HCII) Conference, which has been a hub for presenting groundbreaking research and novel ideas and collaboration for people from all over the world.

The HCII conference was founded in 1984 by Prof. Gavriel Salvendy (Purdue University, USA, Tsinghua University, P.R. China, and University of Central Florida, USA) and the first event of the series, "1st USA-Japan Conference on Human-Computer Interaction", was held in Honolulu, Hawaii, USA, 18–20 August. Since then, HCI International is held jointly with several Thematic Areas and Affiliated Conferences, with each one under the auspices of a distinguished international Program Board and under one management and one registration. Twenty-six HCI International Conferences have been organized so far (every two years until 2013, and annually thereafter).

Over the years, this conference has served as a platform for scholars, researchers, industry experts and students to exchange ideas, connect, and address challenges in the ever-evolving HCI field. Throughout these 40 years, the conference has evolved itself, adapting to new technologies and emerging trends, while staying committed to its core mission of advancing knowledge and driving change.

As we celebrate this milestone anniversary, we reflect on the contributions of its founding members and appreciate the commitment of its current and past Affiliated Conference Program Board Chairs and members. We are also thankful to all past conference attendees who have shaped this community into what it is today.

The 26th International Conference on Human-Computer Interaction, HCI International 2024 (HCII 2024), was held as a 'hybrid' event at the Washington Hilton Hotel, Washington, DC, USA, during 29 June – 4 July 2024. It incorporated the 21 thematic areas and affiliated conferences listed below.

A total of 5108 individuals from academia, research institutes, industry, and government agencies from 85 countries submitted contributions, and 1271 papers and 309 posters were included in the volumes of the proceedings that were published just before the start of the conference, these are listed below. The contributions thoroughly cover the entire field of human-computer interaction, addressing major advances in knowledge and effective use of computers in a variety of application areas. These papers provide academics, researchers, engineers, scientists, practitioners and students with state-of-the-art information on the most recent advances in HCI.

The HCI International (HCII) conference also offers the option of presenting 'Late Breaking Work', and this applies both for papers and posters, with corresponding volumes of proceedings that will be published after the conference. Full papers will be included in the 'HCII 2024 - Late Breaking Papers' volumes of the proceedings to be published in the Springer LNCS series, while 'Poster Extended Abstracts' will be included as short research papers in the 'HCII 2024 - Late Breaking Posters' volumes to be published in the Springer CCIS series.

I would like to thank the Program Board Chairs and the members of the Program Boards of all thematic areas and affiliated conferences for their contribution towards the high scientific quality and overall success of the HCI International 2024 conference. Their manifold support in terms of paper reviewing (single-blind review process, with a minimum of two reviews per submission), session organization and their willingness to act as goodwill ambassadors for the conference is most highly appreciated.

This conference would not have been possible without the continuous and unwavering support and advice of Gavriel Salvendy, founder, General Chair Emeritus, and Scientific Advisor. For his outstanding efforts, I would like to express my sincere appreciation to Abbas Moallem, Communications Chair and Editor of HCI International News.

July 2024   Constantine Stephanidis

HCI International 2024 Thematic Areas
and Affiliated Conferences

- HCI: Human-Computer Interaction Thematic Area
- HIMI: Human Interface and the Management of Information Thematic Area
- EPCE: 21st International Conference on Engineering Psychology and Cognitive Ergonomics
- AC: 18th International Conference on Augmented Cognition
- UAHCI: 18th International Conference on Universal Access in Human-Computer Interaction
- CCD: 16th International Conference on Cross-Cultural Design
- SCSM: 16th International Conference on Social Computing and Social Media
- VAMR: 16th International Conference on Virtual, Augmented and Mixed Reality
- DHM: 15th International Conference on Digital Human Modeling & Applications in Health, Safety, Ergonomics & Risk Management
- DUXU: 13th International Conference on Design, User Experience and Usability
- C&C: 12th International Conference on Culture and Computing
- DAPI: 12th International Conference on Distributed, Ambient and Pervasive Interactions
- HCIBGO: 11th International Conference on HCI in Business, Government and Organizations
- LCT: 11th International Conference on Learning and Collaboration Technologies
- ITAP: 10th International Conference on Human Aspects of IT for the Aged Population
- AIS: 6th International Conference on Adaptive Instructional Systems
- HCI-CPT: 6th International Conference on HCI for Cybersecurity, Privacy and Trust
- HCI-Games: 6th International Conference on HCI in Games
- MobiTAS: 6th International Conference on HCI in Mobility, Transport and Automotive Systems
- AI-HCI: 5th International Conference on Artificial Intelligence in HCI
- MOBILE: 5th International Conference on Human-Centered Design, Operation and Evaluation of Mobile Communications

List of Conference Proceedings Volumes Appearing Before the Conference

47. LNCS 14730, HCI in Games: Part I, edited by Xiaowen Fang
48. LNCS 14731, HCI in Games: Part II, edited by Xiaowen Fang
49. LNCS 14732, HCI in Mobility, Transport and Automotive Systems: Part I, edited by Heidi Krömker
50. LNCS 14733, HCI in Mobility, Transport and Automotive Systems: Part II, edited by Heidi Krömker
51. LNAI 14734, Artificial Intelligence in HCI: Part I, edited by Helmut Degen and Stavroula Ntoa
52. LNAI 14735, Artificial Intelligence in HCI: Part II, edited by Helmut Degen and Stavroula Ntoa
53. LNAI 14736, Artificial Intelligence in HCI: Part III, edited by Helmut Degen and Stavroula Ntoa
54. LNCS 14737, Design, Operation and Evaluation of Mobile Communications: Part I, edited by June Wei and George Margetis
55. LNCS 14738, Design, Operation and Evaluation of Mobile Communications: Part II, edited by June Wei and George Margetis
56. CCIS 2114, HCI International 2024 Posters - Part I, edited by Constantine Stephanidis, Margherita Antona, Stavroula Ntoa and Gavriel Salvendy
57. CCIS 2115, HCI International 2024 Posters - Part II, edited by Constantine Stephanidis, Margherita Antona, Stavroula Ntoa and Gavriel Salvendy
58. CCIS 2116, HCI International 2024 Posters - Part III, edited by Constantine Stephanidis, Margherita Antona, Stavroula Ntoa and Gavriel Salvendy
59. CCIS 2117, HCI International 2024 Posters - Part IV, edited by Constantine Stephanidis, Margherita Antona, Stavroula Ntoa and Gavriel Salvendy
60. CCIS 2118, HCI International 2024 Posters - Part V, edited by Constantine Stephanidis, Margherita Antona, Stavroula Ntoa and Gavriel Salvendy
61. CCIS 2119, HCI International 2024 Posters - Part VI, edited by Constantine Stephanidis, Margherita Antona, Stavroula Ntoa and Gavriel Salvendy
62. CCIS 2120, HCI International 2024 Posters - Part VII, edited by Constantine Stephanidis, Margherita Antona, Stavroula Ntoa and Gavriel Salvendy

https://2024.hci.international/proceedings

Preface

The 5th International Conference on Artificial Intelligence in HCI (AI-HCI 2024), an affiliated conference of the HCI International conference, aimed to bring together academics, practitioners, and students to exchange results from academic and industrial research, as well as industrial experiences, on the use of artificial intelligence (AI) technologies to enhance human-computer interaction (HCI).

The rapid progress of AI, witnessing advancements across numerous domains, has transformed it from a research and academic field to a service available to the wide public, a landmark which has been recently achieved. In this rapidly evolving context, Human-Centered Artificial Intelligence has garnered the interest of researchers and scholars, emphasizing the seamless integration of AI technologies into human activities through well-planned design and development, and the prioritization of human values and well-being. Submissions explored user requirements and perceptions of AI systems, discussed evaluation aspects, and proposed frameworks to foster user participation in AI decision-making. Furthermore, papers delved into issues related to explainability and transparency, encompassing user studies, design principles, frameworks for explainable AI, and approaches to explanations of neural networks. Trust in AI and ethical considerations have constituted inspiring avenues of research, with contributions investigating issues related to fair representations, bias identification, responsible AI and the role of designers, ethical constraints, as well as trust formation and repair. Further, contributions included in the proceedings also addressed the role of AI systems in HCI. From methods to design AI systems to the use of AI tools in design, authors have illuminated the interplay between these two fields offering rich insights into aspects such as co-creation, interaction design, evaluation, but also information uncertainty, human annotation, emotion recognition, and gamification. Finally, numerous papers have explored application domains within the realm of AI in HCI across various contexts, such as immersive environments, industrial AI, e-Commerce, cultural heritage and learning. As editors of the proceedings of AI-HCI 2024, we are proud to present this outstanding collection of research contributions, which demonstrate the intricate interplay between AI and HCI and how they are shaping our future technological environments.

Three volumes of the HCII 2024 proceedings are dedicated to this year's edition of the AI-HCI conference. The first focuses on topics related to Human-Centered Artificial Intelligence, Explainability and Transparency, and AI Systems and Frameworks in HCI. The second focuses on topics related to Ethical Considerations and Trust in AI, Enhancing User Experience Through AI-Driven Technologies, and AI in Industry and Operations. Finally, the third focuses on topics related to Large Language Models for Enhanced Interaction, Advancing Human-Robot Interaction Through AI, and AI Applications for Social Impact and Human Wellbeing.

The papers in the AI-HCI 2024 volumes were accepted for publication after a minimum of two single-blind reviews from the members of the AI-HCI Program Board or, in some cases, from members of the Program Boards of other affiliated conferences. We would like to thank all of them for their invaluable contribution, support, and efforts.

July 2024

Helmut Degen
Stavroula Ntoa

5th International Conference on Artificial Intelligence in HCI (AI-HCI 2024)

The full list with the Program Board Chairs and the members of the Program Boards of all thematic areas and affiliated conferences of HCII 2024 is available online at:

http://www.hci.international/board-members-2024.php

HCI International 2025 Conference

The 27th International Conference on Human-Computer Interaction, HCI International 2025, will be held jointly with the affiliated conferences at the Swedish Exhibition & Congress Centre and Gothia Towers Hotel, Gothenburg, Sweden, June 22–27, 2025. It will cover a broad spectrum of themes related to Human-Computer Interaction, including theoretical issues, methods, tools, processes, and case studies in HCI design, as well as novel interaction techniques, interfaces, and applications. The proceedings will be published by Springer. More information will become available on the conference website: https://2025.hci.international/.

General Chair
Prof. Constantine Stephanidis
University of Crete and ICS-FORTH
Heraklion, Crete, Greece
Email: general_chair@2025.hci.international

https://2025.hci.international/

Contents – Part III

Advancing Human-Robot Interaction Through AI

Large Language Models for Enhanced Interaction

Enhancing Relation Extraction from Biomedical Texts by Large Language Models

Masaki Asada$^{(\boxtimes)}$ (ID) and Ken Fukuda (ID)

National Institute of Advanced Industrial Science and Technology (AIST), Tokyo, Japan
{masaki.asada,ken.fukuda}@aist.go.jp

Abstract. In this study, we propose a novel relation extraction method enhanced by large language models (LLMs). We incorporated three relation extraction models that leverage LLMs: (1) relation extraction via in-context few-shot learning with LLMs, (2) enhancing the sequence-to-sequence (seq2seq)-based full fine-tuned relation extraction by CoT reasoning explanations generated by LLMs, (3) enhancing the classification-based full fine-tuned relation extraction by entity descriptions that are automatically generated by LLMs. In the experiment, we shot that in-context few-shot learning with LLMs suffers in biomedical relation extraction tasks. We further show that entity explanations that are generated by LLMs can improve the performance of the classification-based relation extraction in the biomedical domain. Our proposed model achieved an F-score of 85.61% on the DDIExtraction-2013 dataset, which is competitive with the state-of-the-art models.

Keywords: Biomedical relation extraction · DDI extraction · Large language models

1 Introduction

Relation extraction (RE) is the natural language processing task of automatically extracting important relations between named entities in the text. One of the applications of relation extraction is automatic database completion and expansion. In order to construct databases from textual resources so that humans can easily access important information, it is necessary to comprehensively read a bunch of documents, which requires a large amount of manual cost. The research on relation extraction from texts is crucial in terms of achieving advanced human-computer interactions.

Relation extraction from biomedical texts is vital research to help biomedical experts. One of the tasks is extracting drug-drug interactions from texts. Drug-drug interaction (DDI) is defined as a change in the effects of one drug by the presence of another drug [4]. In order to practice "evidence-based medicine" [16] and prevent accidents caused by drugs, it is important to extract knowledge about DDIs from pharmaceutical papers comprehensively. Automatic

H. Degen and S. Ntoa (Eds.): HCII 2024, LNAI 14736, pp. 3–14, 2024.
https://doi.org/10.1007/978-3-031-60615-1_1

DDI extraction can greatly benefit the pharmaceutical industry, providing an interesting way of reducing the time spent by healthcare professionals reviewing the medical literature.

Classification-based supervised methods [14,17] have been conventionally adopted for information extraction from biomedical texts, however, with the success of large language models (LLMs), prompt-tuning-based information extraction methods [6] have been started to be studied. In prompt-tuning methods, the input sentence and the prompt, which is an instruction text for the target downstream task, are fed into the LLM, and then the LLM predicts the entities and relations between these entities. In recent years, research on prompt-tuning has drawn more and more attention, and various methods such as in-context learning [15] and instruction tuning [9] have been proposed. Because of the extremely large number of parameters in the LLM, it is not realistic to update the entire model parameters by supervised learning. Instead, a few-shot learning approach with only a few supervised examples, or a zero-shot learning approach with no supervised examples is commonly used to predict answers.

The critical issue is that despite the success of LLMs in generative tasks such as summarization and question answering, LLMs do not significantly improve performance on the information extraction task. According to the previous surveys [6,7], the GPT-3.5 model, which has 355B parameters, underperformed traditional classification-based state-of-the-art methods on several biomedical named entity recognition and relation extraction tasks. Furthermore, the GPT-4 model, which has an even larger model size, underperforms the method with fully supervised PubMedBERT [11], which has only 110 M parameters. These results show that the existing prompt-based few-shot and zero-shot learning with LLMs is not effective in the information extraction task in the biomedical domain.

In this study, we propose a novel information extraction method enhanced by LLMs. The overview of our proposed method is shown in Fig. 1. We investigated three DDI extraction methods that leverage LLMs. In the first method, we investigate the ability to extract DDIs in a few-shot learning setting via an extremely large-sized language model Gemini-Pro [20]. In the second method, we enhance the seq2seq-based full fine-tuned DDI extraction by CoT reasoning explanations generated by Gemini-Pro. In the third method, we enhance the classification-based full fine-tuned DDI extraction by drug entity descriptions that are automatically generated by Gemini-Pro. Our contributions are summarized as follows:

- We propose three DDI extraction methods that leverage the benefit of LLMs.
- Experimental results on the DDIExtraction-2013 dataset show that the entity descriptions that are generated by LLMs can boost the performance of the classification-based DDI extraction method, achieving significant F-score improvement.

Relation extraction from biomedical texts

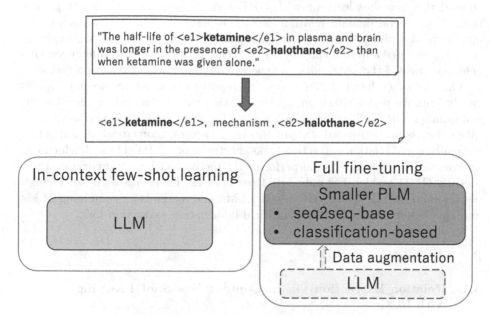

Fig. 1. An Overview of relation extraction methods with LLMs.

2 Related Work

Extracting information from biomedical literature is an important NLP task that can convert unstructured text data such as academic papers and web articles to structured data that can be easily accessed by humans. One of the target tasks is drug-drug interaction (DDI) extraction from the literature. The definition of DDI is broadly described as a change in the effects of one drug by the presence of another drug [4]. The detection of DDIs is an important research area in patient safety since these interactions can become very dangerous and increase healthcare costs. The DDIExtraction-2013 [18] dataset was constructed to promote automatic DDI extraction from the literature via machine learning methods.

On the DDI extraction task, classification-based methods using encoder-only relatively small pre-trained language models (PLMs) have shown high performance. PLMs in the biomedical domain such as BioBERT [13], SciBERT [5] and PubMedBERT [11] have been adopted for the DDI extraction task. Methods combining PLMs with information from external drug databases, e.g., Drug-Bank [22] have been proposed and it has been reported that using information from external databases improves the extraction performance rather than considering only the context [1–3].

In the general domain of relation extraction, REBEL [12], which adopted seq2seq-based PLMs showed higher performance than existing pipeline-based methods on joint extraction of entities and relations. Wadhwa et al. [21] firstly showed that few-shot learning with GPT-3 yields near state-of-the-art performance on general domain relation extraction datasets and then proposed the approach of training Flan-T5 with Chain-of-Thought (CoT) style "explanations" (generated automatically by GPT-3) that support relation inferences; this achieved state-of-the-art results on general domain relation extraction tasks.

On the other hand, Chen et al. [8] reported that LLMs do not significantly improve performance on the information extraction task in the biomedical domain. GPT-3.5 model, which has 355B parameters, underperformed traditional classification-based state-of-the-art on several biomedical named entity recognition and relation extraction tasks. Furthermore, GPT-4 model, which has an even larger model size, underperforms the method with fully supervised PubMedBERT [11], which has only 110M parameters. There has been not enough discussion regarding the effectiveness of LLMs, and methods for combining LLMs and smaller-size PLMs on the biomedical information extraction task.

3   Method

3.1   Relation Extraction via In-Context Few-Shot Learning with LLMs

We adopt forms of instructional in-context few-shot prompting to Gemini-Pro [20]. Figure 2 shows the instructional prompt and examples ("shots") for the input of LLMs. In this method, we verify two approaches: Direct prompting, which predicts the relation type directly from the instructional prompt and a few examples, and chain-of-thought prompting, which predicts the relation type after predicting an explanation of two entities.

Direct Prompting. To construct prompts for relation extraction, we use the prompt that defines the types of relations and instructs LLMs to predict the correct relation type from the given texts, as shown in Fig. 2 A. Special tokens (`<e1>`, `</e1>`, `<e2>`, `</e2>`) are used to clarify which of the drugs in the sentence are targeted. Example sentences are selected from the training dataset of the relation extraction corpus. Among them, we select the sentences that appeared within the annotation guideline for dataset construction, because we consider these examples to be representative of their relation types.

Chain-of-Thought Prompting. In chain-of-thought (CoT), the prompt instructs LLMs to first generate an explanation of entities and then predict the relation type, rather than directly predict the relation types. Examples for the few-shot learning are selected in the same way as in the Direct prompting method, and an explanation of each sentence is added, as shown in Fig. 2 B. As explanations, we adopt the text that describes the relation between entities in the annotation guideline.

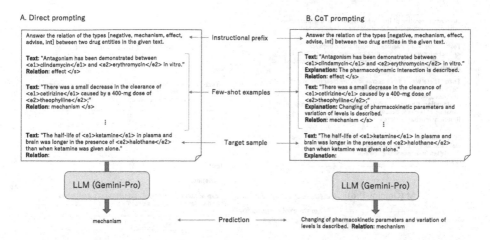

Fig. 2. Model overview of in-context few-shot learning with LLMs.

3.2 Seq2seq-Based Relation Extraction Enhanced by LLMs

We applied the method [21] of using LLMs for data augmentation in full fine-tuning of relation extraction with seq2seq-based PLMs to the biomedical domain. Figure 3 shows the overview of the method. In this method, relatively small-size PLMs with less than 1B parameters are fine-tuned on the whole training dataset. The relation labels are generated by the seq2seq model, and we add CoT style explanations generated automatically by LLMs that support relation inferences in fine-tuning on training dataset. Firstly we prepare the CoT style explanations for all examples of the training dataset, by feeding the instructional prompt and examples as shown in the left part of Fig. 3. Then we fine-tune seq2seq PLMs on gold relation labels and explanations generated by LLMs, as shown in the right part of Fig. 3.

3.3 Classification-Based Relation Extraction Enhanced by LLMs

We propose a classification-based relation extraction method that is enhanced by LLMs. In this approach, input sentences are converted into a pooled representation by the encoder-only PLMs, and resulting vectors are converted into the dimension of the number of relation labels for multi-class classification. We utilize LLMs for augmenting the information of entities in full fine-tuning with PLMs. Specifically, for the two entities in the sentence, descriptions of entities are generated in advance by LLMs with the prompt ''Please provide a short description on <ENTITY> in one sentence.'', as shown in Fig. 4. The input sentence, the first entity description, and the second entity description are given to the PLMs. Three output vectors are concatenated and finally, the resulting vector is fed to the linear layer for dimension conversion. We prepare the separated two PLMs, one for the input sentences, and the other for entity descriptions.

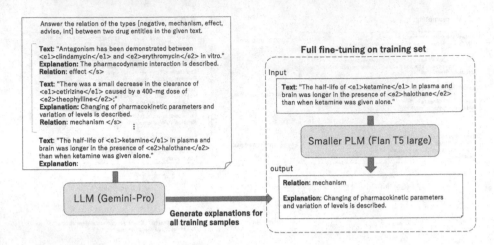

Fig. 3. Model overview of seq2seq-based relation extraction enhanced by LLMs.

4   Experimental Settings

4.1   DDI Extraction Task Settings

We followed the DDIExtraction-2013 [18] shared task settings. This dataset is composed of input sentences containing the drug mention pair, and the following four DDI types are annotated to each drug pair.

- *Mechanism*: This type is assigned when a pharmacokinetic interaction is described in an input sentence.
- *Effect*: This type is assigned when a pharmacodynamic interaction is described in an input sentence.
- *Advice*: This type is assigned when a recommendation or advice regarding the concomitant use of two drugs is described in an input sentence.
- *Interaction* (*Int.*): This type is assigned when the sentence states that interaction occurs and does not provide any detailed information about the interaction.

Table 1 shows the statistics of DDI extraction dataset. We can see that the dataset is highly imbalanced, there are roughly six times the number of pairs not mentioning a relation (negative pairs) than the pairs mentioning a relation (positive pairs). Since no validation set splitting is provided by the official dataset, we split the training data into a smaller training set and validation set to perform hyper-parameter tuning. After determining the hyper-parameters, we re-trained the model on the whole training set and evaluated the model on the test set.

4.2   LLMs and Prompts

We adopted Gemini-Pro [20] as a LLM. Gemini-Pro is a performance-optimized model in terms of cost as well as latency that delivers significant performance

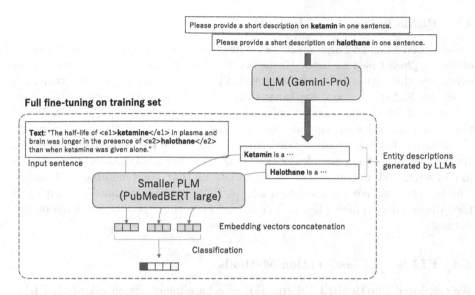

Fig. 4. Model overview of classification-based relation extraction enhanced by LLMs.

Table 1. The statistics of DDIExtraction-2013 dataset

	Train	Test
Documents	714	191
Sentences	6,976	1,299
Total drug pairs	27,792	5,716
Positive drug pairs	4,021	979
Mechanism	1,319	302
Effect	1,687	360
Advice	826	221
Interaction	189	96
Negative drug pairs	23,771	4,737

across a wide range of tasks. In the evaluation results on the series of text-based academic benchmarks covering reasoning, reading comprehension, STEM and coding, Gemini-Pro showed higher performance than GPT-3.5. We obtained the output from Gemini-Pro via Google AI API[1]. If the model generated text that did not match any relation label name, it was assumed to predict the negative relation.

To prepare the prompts for few-shot learning, we selected 14 examples from the annotation guideline[2] of the DDIExtraction-2013 dataset. The explanations for CoT reasoning are also extracted from the annotation guideline.

---

[1] https://ai.google.dev/.
[2] https://hulat.inf.uc3m.es/DrugDDI/annotation_guidelines_ddi_corpus.pdf.

4.3   PLMs for Seq2seq Methods

We adopted Flan-T5 Large [9] model, which has 783M parameters, as a baseline
of the seq2seq-based method. In the seq2seq-based DDI extraction, the model
generates the output in the form of `Relation: xxx`, and the model with CoT
generates `Relation: xxx Explanation: xxx`. The generated explanation part
is not used for the evaluation, only the generated relation type is used. When
the model generates an output that does not match any of the relation types,
We assume that the negative label is predicted. Flan-T5 model parameters are
trained on all training samples of the DDIExtraction-2013 dataset. Besides, the
model with CoT is trained on the explanations that are generated by Gemini-
Pro in advance. We set the beam size as 5 for the generation. We employed
the Adafactor optimizer [19], and tuned hyper-parameters on the development
dataset.

4.4   PLMs for Classification Methods

We employed PubMedBERT Large [11] as a baseline of the encoder-only PLMs
for classification-based relation extraction. We employed the Adafactor optimizer [19] and tuned hyper-parameters on the development dataset. Our significance tests are based on the permutation test [10]. We set the number of shuffles
to 5,000.

5   Results and Discussions

5.1   In-Context Few-Shot Learning-Based Relation Extraction
by LLMs

Table 2 shows the performance comparison among the traditional classification-
based method and few-shot in-context learning methods via Gemini-Pro with
and without CoT. As shown in Table 2, few-shot in-context learning via Gemini-
Pro showed quite low performances compared to the classification-based method
with smaller PLM (PubMedBERT-Large). The model with CoT showed a higher
F-score than the direct prompting model, but the performance is still much lower
than the fully fine-tuned PubMedBERT. These results are consistent with the
report [6] that have validated GPT-3.5 in other biomedical relation extraction
datasets, indicating that while LLMs have reasonable text generation capacity, it
is difficult to correctly predict relations between entities from few-shot samples.

We performed further analysis on the predicted relation labels by LLMs.
Figure 5 shows the normalized confusion matrix of the gold labels and predictions from Gemini-Pro with and without CoT. Each row of the matrix shows
the distribution of the label predictions by the model for each gold label, and
the scale is normalized. The diagonal components of the matrix indicate the
samples that are correctly predicted, which means the darker color of all diagonal elements indicates higher model performance. As shown in Fig. 5, there are
many positive relation instances incorrectly predicted as negative relations on

Table 2. The performance of DDI extraction on in-context few-shot prompt learning methods

Approach	Method	P	R	F(%)
Classification	PubMedBERT	83.41	84.26	83.84
In-context prompting	Gemini	13.55	26.65	17.96
	Gemini CoT	13.06	42.49	19.99

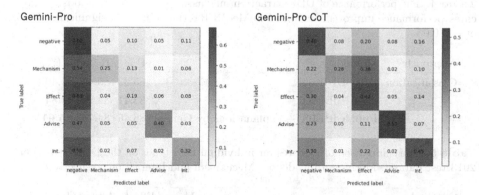

Fig. 5. Normalized confusion matrix of the labels and predictions from Gemini-Pro with and without CoT.

the model of Gemini-Pro without CoT. In the Gemini-Pro with CoT model, there are fewer cases of incorrectly predicting positive relations as negative relations, however, there are more cases of incorrectly predicting negative relations as positive relations. These results show that it is difficult for LLMs-based in-context few-shot learning to predict correct relation labels on a highly imbalanced relation extraction dataset.

5.2 Seq2seq-Based Relation Extraction Enhanced by LLMs

Table 3 shows the F-score comparison with baseline models and seq2seq-based models. Seq2seq-based Flan-T5 backboned DDI extraction model showed 82.25% of the F-score, which is lower than the classification-based baseline mode. In particular, the precision score is much lower than the classification-based method. The CoT model with the explanations generated by Gemini-Pro showed a lower F-score than the model without CoT.

5.3 Classification-Based Relation Extraction Enhanced by LLMs

Table 4 shows the F-score comparison between the baseline model, the model with entity explanations by Gemini-Pro, and state-of-the-art method HKG-DDIE [2] that utilizes the heterogeneous knowledge graphs information into DDI extraction task. By using the entity explanations that are generated by

Table 3. The performance of DDI extraction on seq2seq-based methods

Approach	Method	P	R	F(%)
Classification	PubMedBERT	83.41	84.26	83.84
Seq2seq	Flan T5	79.69	84.98	82.25
	Flan T5 + CoT by Gemini	78.13	83.04	80.53

Table 4. The performance of DDI extraction on classification-based methods. * indicates performance improvement from PubMedBERT (baseline) at a significance level of $p < 0.05$

Approach	Method	P	R	F (%)
Classification	HKG-DDIE [2]	85.32	85.49	85.40
	PubMedBERT	83.41	84.26	83.84
	PubMedBERT + explanations by Gemini	86.45	84.78	**85.61**[*]

Table 5. The comparison of F-scores for individual DDI types on the DDIExtraction-2013 test dataset. Mech. and Int. denote Mechanism and Interaction, respectively.

Method		Mech.	Effect	Advise	Int.
PubMedBERT	P	85.07	79.69	88.18	79.06
	R	88.74	87.22	94.57	35.41
	F	86.87	83.28	**91.26**	48.92
PubMedBERT + explanations by Gemini	P	87.94	83.64	89.38	85.18
	R	89.40	86.66	91.40	47.91
	F	**88.66**	**85.12**	90.38	**61.33**

Gemini-Pro, the F-score improved by 1.77 pp, showing significant performance improvement on the permutation test. Table 5 shows the performance comparison for individual DDI types. The model with entity explanations showed higher performance than the baseline model on the relation labels of *Mechanism*, *Effect*, and *Interaction*, while showing lower performance on *Advise* relation type. In particular, our proposed model improved the 12.41 pp F-score on Interaction type. These results show the effectiveness of leveraging LLMs for classification-based DDI extraction methods.

6   Conclusion

In this paper, we proposed three methods that leverage LLMs for the DDI extraction task. We showed that in-context few-shot learning with LLMs suffers in biomedical relation extraction tasks, which is also consistent with previous reports. We then investigated the seq2seq-based relation extraction in the biomedical domain. Seq2seq-based models showed a lower F-score, which lies in the low precision score. We added CoT explanations generated by LLMs to seq2seq-based models, but the model CoT explanations do not improve the DDI extraction performance. We further showed entity explanations that are generated by LLMs can improve the performance of the classification-based relation extraction method on the DDIExtraction-2013 task.

References

1. Asada, M., Miwa, M., Sasaki, Y.: Enhancing drug-drug interaction extraction from texts by molecular structure information. In: Gurevych, I., Miyao, Y. (eds.) Proceedings of the 56th Annual Meeting of the Association for Computational Linguistics (Volume 2: Short Papers), pp. 680–685. Association for Computational Linguistics, Melbourne, Australia (Jul 2018). https://doi.org/10.18653/v1/P18-2108, https://aclanthology.org/P18-2108
2. Asada, M., Miwa, M., Sasaki, Y.: Integrating heterogeneous knowledge graphs into drug-drug interaction extraction from the literature. Bioinformatics 39(1), btac754 (2022). https://doi.org/10.1093/bioinformatics/btac754
3. Asada, M., et al.: Using drug descriptions and molecular structures for drug-drug interaction extraction from literature. Bioinformatics 37(12), 1739–1746 (2020). https://doi.org/10.1093/bioinformatics/btaa907
4. Baxter, K., Preston, C.L.: Stockley's Drug Interactions, vol. 495. Pharmaceutical Press, London (2010)
5. Beltagy, I., et al.: SciBERT: a pretrained language model for scientific text. In: Proceedings of EMNLP-IJCNLP 2019, pp. 3615–3620. Hong Kong, China (Nov 2019)
6. Chen, Q., et al.: An extensive benchmark study on biomedical text generation and mining with ChatGPT. Bioinformatics 39(9), btad557 (2023). https://doi.org/10.1093/bioinformatics/btad557
7. Chen, Q., et al.: Large language models in biomedical natural language processing: benchmarks, baselines, and recommendations. arXiv preprint arXiv:2305.16326 (2023)
8. Chen, Y.: Incomplete utterance rewriting as sequential greedy tagging. In: Rogers, A., Boyd-Graber, J., Okazaki, N. (eds.) Findings of the Association for Computational Linguistics: ACL 2023, pp. 7265–7276. Association for Computational Linguistics, Toronto, Canada (Jul 2023). https://doi.org/10.18653/v1/2023.findings-acl.456, https://aclanthology.org/2023.findings-acl.456
9. Chung, H.W., et al.: Scaling instruction-finetuned language models (2022)
10. Fisher, R.A., et al.: The design of experiments (1937)
11. Gu, Y., et al.: Domain-specific language model pretraining for biomedical natural language processing. ACM Trans. Comput. Healthc. (HEALTH) 3(1), 1–23 (2021)
12. Huguet Cabot, P.L., Navigli, R.: REBEL: relation extraction by end-to-end language generation. In: Moens, M.F., Huang, X., Specia, L., Yih, S.W.t. (eds.) Findings of the Association for Computational Linguistics: EMNLP 2021, pp. 2370–2381. Association for Computational Linguistics, Punta Cana, Dominican Republic (Nov 2021). https://doi.org/10.18653/v1/2021.findings-emnlp.204, https://aclanthology.org/2021.findings-emnlp.204
13. Lee, J., et al.: BioBERT: a pre-trained biomedical language representation model for biomedical text mining. Bioinformatics 36(4), 1234–1240 (2019). https://doi.org/10.1093/bioinformatics/btz682

14. Liu, S., et al.: Drug-drug interaction extraction via convolutional neural networks. Comput. Math. Methods Med. 2016 (2016)
15. Radford, A., Wu, J., Child, R., Luan, D., Amodei, D., Sutskever, I., et al.: Language models are unsupervised multitask learners. OpenAI blog **1**(8), 9 (2019)
16. Sackett, D.L.: Evidence-based medicine. In: Seminars in Perinatology, vol. 21, pp. 3–5. Elsevier (1997)
17. Sahu, S.K., Anand, A.: Drug-drug interaction extraction from biomedical texts using long short-term memory network. J. Biomed. Inform. **86**, 15–24 (2018)
18. Segura-Bedmar, I., Martínez, P., Herrero-Zazo, M.: SemEval-2013 task 9 : extraction of drug-drug interactions from biomedical texts (DDIExtraction 2013). In: Manandhar, S., Yuret, D. (eds.) Second Joint Conference on Lexical and Computational Semantics (*SEM), vol. 2: Proceedings of the Seventh International Workshop on Semantic Evaluation (SemEval 2013), pp. 341–350. Association for Computational Linguistics, Atlanta, Georgia, USA (Jun 2013). https://aclanthology. org/S13-2056
19. Shazeer, N., Stern, M.: Adafactor: adaptive learning rates with sublinear memory cost. In: Dy, J., Krause, A. (eds.) Proceedings of the 35th International Conference on Machine Learning. Proceedings of Machine Learning Research, vol. 80, pp. 4596–4604. PMLR (10–15 Jul 2018). https://proceedings.mlr.press/ v80/shazeer18a.html
20. Team, G., et al.: Gemini: a family of highly capable multimodal models (2023)
21. Wadhwa, S., Amir, S., Wallace, B.: Revisiting relation extraction in the era of large language models. In: Rogers, A., Boyd-Graber, J., Okazaki, N. (eds.) Proceedings of the 61st Annual Meeting of the Association for Computational Linguistics (Volume 1: Long Papers), pp. 15566–15589. Association for Computational Linguistics, Toronto, Canada (Jul 2023). https://doi.org/10.18653/v1/2023.acl-long.868, https://aclanthology.org/2023.acl-long.868
22. Wishart, D.S., et al.: DrugBank 5.0: a major update to the DrugBank database for 2018. Nucleic Acids Res. **46**(D1), D1074–D1082 (2017). https://doi.org/10.1093/ nar/gkx1037

Using a LLM-Based Conversational Agent in the Social Robot Mini

Iván Esteban-Lozano[1,2], Álvaro Castro-González[1]([⊠])(iD),
and Paloma Martínez[2](iD)

[1] Robotics Lab, Systems Engineering and Automation Department, Universidad Carlos III de Madrid, Avenue de la Universidad 30, Leganés 28911, Spain
100383779@alumnos.uc3m.es, acgonzal@ing.uc3m.es
[2] Computer Science Department, Universidad Carlos III de Madrid, Avenue de la Universidad 30, Leganés 28911, Spain
pmf@inf.uc3m.es

Abstract. Natural Language Processing has witnessed significant growth in recent years. In particular, conversational agents have improved significantly thanks to the proliferation of the Large Language Models (LLM). Conversational agents have already been integrated with smartphones, smart speakers, or social robots (SRs). Unlike the mentioned electronic devices, a social robot allows more active and closer user engagement due to the presence of a physical object with a lifelike appearance that is able to express emotions. Therefore, SRs represent an appealing platform for deploying a conversational agent. In the field of social robotics, the ability of robots to interact with humans has traditionally been limited by their verbal skills. Until recently, robots could only understand a limited set of human utterances using specific rules, and the utterances of the robots were pre-defined sentences crafted offline. These restrictions, on many occasions, lead to repetitive interactions, which could cause users to lose interest during prolonged engagement with the robot. In this paper, we propose to integrate into our social robot Mini a conversational agent based on LLM. We present a new robot skill that can maintain a natural and seamless conversation with the user on any desired topic. The obtained results show a high usability of the skill and a high-quality interaction.

Keywords: Social Robots · Large-Language Models · chatbot · Conversational Assistants · Conversational Agents

1 Introduction

Conversational agents have already been integrated into smartphones, smart speakers, or social robots (SRs). Unlike the mentioned electronic devices, a social robot allows more active and closer user engagement due to the presence of a physical *object* that can be seen and touched. Moreover, the lifelike appearance of an SR eases users to establish a more realistic and enduring connection. Also, its ability to interpret and express emotions through gestures and movement

H. Degen and S. Ntoa (Eds.): HCII 2024, LNAI 14736, pp. 15–26, 2024.
https://doi.org/10.1007/978-3-031-60615-1_2

provides a more complete and natural experience. Therefore, SRs represent an appealing platform for deploying a conversational agent.

A conversational agent, or chatbot, is defined as a software system created for natural language interaction with users [18]. In particular, conversational agents have improved significantly thanks to the recent proliferation of the Large Language Models (LLM from now on). These models can analyze and generate human-like text, making them versatile tools for a wide range of applications (machine translation, assistants and interactive conversational bots, sentiment analysis, and text classification, among others). LLMs can process and generate text that appears coherent and right to people, but it does not mean that LLMs have consciousness or understanding. The performance of most LLMs is due to transformer architecture [17] that has revolutionized language technologies together with the availability of large training datasets to build and adapt these models to different applications.

In the field of social robotics, the ability of robots to interact with humans has traditionally been limited by their verbal skills. Until recently, robots could only *understand* a limited set of human utterances using specific rules or grammar [4]. Additionally, the utterances of the robots were pre-defined sentences that were crafted offline. These restrictions, on many occasions, lead to repetitive interactions which could cause users to lose interest during prolonged engagement with the robot [15].

The proposal is to integrate into our social robot Mini a conversational agent based on a LLM. We aim to create a new robot skill that is capable of maintaining a natural and seamless conversation with the user on any desired topic. Thanks to it, we expect to achieve more natural and friendly interactions that help to engage the user in the robot interaction [7].

Mini is a social robot designed to support and accompany seniors in their daily lives. We expect that using the robot as a conversational agent will provide companionship to elders helping them combat loneliness. In addition, we believe that social robots able to interact in a human-like manner allow their users to train their memory and mental agility and even have a fun and joyful time with the robot every day.

The rest of the paper is structured as follows. In Sect. 2, we describe and present the most relevant concepts of Language Models. After, the proposed conversational agent is presented in Sect. 3. The integration of the conversational agent in the robot Mini comes next (Sect. 4). In the last part of the paper, Sect. 5 presents the results that have led us to the conclusions of Sect. 6.

2   A Short History of Language Models

Large Language Models are neural networks with millions of parameters that represent adjustable weights in the network that are optimized during training to predict the next word in a sequence of words. During training, understanding context, as well as the relationship of tokens in a text, is considered to pay attention to specific parts of the input that are relevant in making predictions.

These models arise from the field of Natural Language Processing (NLP) and are used for the purpose of understanding and producing natural language text. [12].

Language models have evolved greatly from the earliest to the present day. The first ones were statistical models, and their operation consisted of predicting words through the use of different statistical techniques. These had major limitations due to the limited predictive power of the statistical techniques used, the small size of the datasets used, and the limited computing power available in the 1990 s. At the turn of the century, neural networks began to be used for the purpose of making these predictions on text sequences. The learning of these networks was limited by the same factors as previous statistical models, the small dataset used, and the scarcity of computational resources, achieving unremarkable results. In the decade that followed, another type of neural network began to be used that was more suitable for this task: the Long short-term memory (LSTM) network. This type of network belongs to the Recurrent Neural Networks (RNN) and is focused on the processing of sequences [3]. Moreover, thanks to the constant development of computer hardware featuring a greater amount of computational resources and the emergence of the cloud, models were trained with larger datasets, and more robust models were created. The main problem that arose then was the memory limitation of these networks, causing failures in the processing of long texts and relating the context with previous fragments.

The latest breakthrough in NLP is the Transformer Networks used by the state-of-the-art LLMs. These neural networks have a large long-term memory, and this characteristic makes it possible to analyse longer text strings, unlike the neural networks previously used in this type of generative models. Moreover, due to the way these networks process the data, a better analysis of the relationships between words, sentences and even fragments at different levels is achieved. This feature allows the language model to improve the interpretation of the text, understanding the context and making it more similar to the interpretation of the human being himself [17].

There are three types of Transformer architectures:

- (a) encoder-decoder [17], where the self-attention mechanism tunes each token weigh depending on the context of the entire sequence, capturing relationships and dependencies between the different parts of the input. Encoder-decoder architectures are suitable for applications like machine translation, text summarization and question-answering systems. An example of this architecture is T5 [14].
- (b) the encoder-only model outputs vectors generated by the encoder that are used as input to a classifier to make predictions. Some applications are text classification and sentiment analysis; BERT architecture is an encoder-only model [8].
- (c) decoder-only models are used in text generation. They only take into account the previous tokens to predict the next token in a sequence; Open AI GPT (Generative Pretraining models) has adopted a decoder-only model

[13]. All these models can be tailored to specific tasks and domains. Recently, Zhao et al. have presented an extensive review of current LLMs [19].

LLMs are pre-trained models that can be used "off the shelf", but they might require further fine-tuning to enhance their capacity. Fine-tuning could be performed in two ways: training on additional data for adapting to different domains or using prompt engineering to improve the output of the model. Prompts are instructions that provide guidance during the text generation process that include detail and context to the input. There are several strategies like zero-shot, one-shot, and few-shot prompting depending on the number of examples (input-output) the user provides to the model. Moreover, some instructions or constraints can be provided to improve the prompt. Min et al. describe in detail several works applying pre-training and then fine-tuning, prompting, and text generation approaches [11]. Fine-tuning on additional data might require many annotated examples, could be expensive in computing resources, and it can increase the carbon footprint.

3   The Proposed System

The conversation agent proposed in this work is integrated into a social robot as part of one of the functionalities that this robot offers to its users. The robot interacts verbally with its users thanks to two modules: the Automatic Speech Recognition (ASR) module and the Text-to-Speech (TTS) module. Both modules are used as the interface between the user and the LLM that implements the conversational agent. The conversational flow starts either with the user's utterance, if the user takes the initiative, or with the robot's utterance, in case it takes the initiative. In case the user takes the first step, the robot collects this audio fragment through its microphones, and it is sent to the ASR engine. The ASR translates the audio signal into the corresponding text transcription, and this is input into an LLM. After processing the input, the LLM generates the response as a text that the TTS engine synthesizes, producing the robot's speech. This is a cyclical process that is repeated over time until the conversation is over. This process is shown in Fig. 1.

For the conversational agent, we have considered several LLM. After evaluating their performance, their inference time, and their cost, we opted to use GPT-3.5, in particular gpt-3.5-turbo. We set the *temperature* parameter to 0.3, which corresponds to a low degree of randomness in the output of the model, and used the OpenAI API to access this model online.

3.1   Prompting

In the context of Artificial Intelligence (AI), a prompt is an instruction that triggers a response from an AI model, allowing interaction between the user and the AI system. These models do not perform actions on their own but respond to instructions (prompts) provided by users. Prompting engineering, or simply

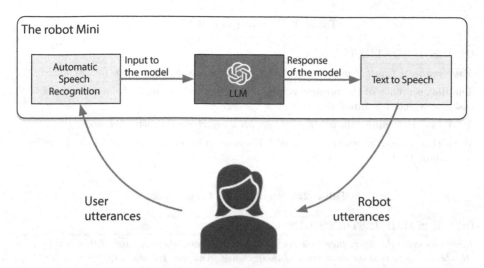

Fig. 1. Overview of the proposed conversational agent in the robot Mini

prompting, refers to the process of providing prompts to the generative AI system and is crucial to obtaining appropriate responses. The quality of the prompt can significantly influence the response generated by the AI. The quality of these prompts is critical for successful results.

Therefor, defining the right prompt for the task at hand is crucial. In our case, the prompt needs to clearly describe the task, i.e., operating as a conversational assistant, and the context, i.e., interacting with elderly people. Some general considerations for designing prompts include: describing tasks and context, generating short responses to speed up communication, adopting a familiar tone, and taking the initiative in the conversation [6].

In this work, we have followed an iterative process during the design of the final prompt for the model used in the conversational agent. After each iteration, the result was tested and compared with the model's responses to the same questions with the previous prompts. In this way, the prompt was adjusted after each iteration and tested again so that it was aligned with the objectives proposed for the assistant. The final prompt consists of three blocks included in Tables 1, 2, and 3:

1. Context block: Establishes the purpose of the assistant and its focus on older people, underlining the importance of natural and friendly conversations (see Table 1).
2. Instructions Block: Details specific instructions, from starting the conversation to answering questions and maintaining an appropriate tone (see Table 2).
3. Additional Information Block: Provides details about the attendee's purpose, priorities and general guidelines for positive interactions (see Table 3).

Table 1. Prompt Context block.

BLOCK 1: CONTEXT
Your name is Chatbot and you are a conversational support service for the elderly. \
The first sentence of the prompt is intended to enable the model to get a sense of the task for which it is intended.
Your task is to maintain a conversation on a selected topic with the user. \
With this second interaction, the model is able to know the context of the situation and adapt to it.

Table 2. Prompt Instructions block.

BLOCK 2: MAIN INSTRUCTIONS
First you greet the user, then you ask them how they are, then you ask if they want to start a conversation on a topic of their choice. And you tell them that if they want to change the subject at any time, all they have to do is let you know. \
After this brief introduction to the task to be carried out, the assistant is told how to carry out the first interaction with the user. The user is greeted with a first greeting, followed by a first wildcard question about his or her personal status in order to have a first topic to talk about. Subsequently, it is proposed to start a conversation on a topic and the user is told that he/she can change the topic at any time he/she wishes.
You wait for his response, and begin to engage him in a conversation through questions and answers on the subject.\
This indication provided to the model is the instruction for the model to start and maintain a conversation with the user on the topic proposed by the user, providing questions and answers on the topic.
Don't just wait for a response from the user, take the initiative in the conversation. \
The next instruction is of great importance as the robot has to be active in the conversation and with the user, in order to prolong the conversation so that it does not reach a point where it stops. The model has to achieve an interactive conversation on both sides.
You respond in a very brief, conversational, approachable and friendly style. \
The fifth proposal instructs the model to use a response style focused on achieving fluency and closeness in the conversation, which is of vital importance so that the conversation does not become tiresome for the user.
Don't focus on providing a lot of scientific data, but more on an informal and close conversation.\
Continuing with this trend of making the conversation fluid, the following instruction is included to emphasise to the model the type of interaction that is desired with the user and the importance of the conversation being informal and close so that the user feels comfortable and safe interacting with the robot.
Limit your answers to three sentences. \
The maximum length of the response is defined at the end of the instructions concerning the structure of the conversation. In this way, it is possible to make the conversation even more fluid, preventing the model's response from being too long and containing too much information that could saturate the user.

Table 3. Additional Prompt Instructions block.

BLOCK 3: ADDITIONAL INSTRUCTIONS
Some of the topics you can suggest to talk about with the user are: History, geography, art, literature, sports, talking about your life, practising languages. \
Finally, there are some topics that the assistant can talk about with the user, the central theme has to focus on talking about the user's life and the topics of the user's choice. Even so, there are some general topics about which the assistant can suggest a conversation to the user in case the user does not take the initiative.
Play a game proposed by you or by the user, some games can be: Guess the song, trivia questions or continue with the proverbs. \
Also, it is of great value the possibility for the wizard to propose the user to play a game to pass the time, such as those mentioned in the last lines of the code.

4   Integration into Mini

In this work, we have considered the social robot Mini (see Fig. 2). Mini is a desktop robot intended for seniors to accompany, support, and assist them in their daily activities [16]. It has been designed and built by the Robotics Lab, from Universidad Carlos III de Madrid. Mini is equipped with touch sensors to detect when and how it is touched, a microphone to capture its users' voice and other audio signals from the environment, and a tablet to extend the interaction capabilities of the robot. Besides, Mini can move its head, arms, and body, can change the color of its cheeks and beating heart, has a vumeter-like mouth, and has a pair of screen-based animated eyes.

Fig. 2. The social robot Mini

In terms of the software architecture, the robot Mini has five main elements (see Fig. 3): (i) the skills represent the repertoire of functionalities that are offered to Mini users; (ii) the Decision-Making System (DMS) selects the skill that needs to be activated at each moment depending on external (e.g. user preferences) and internal (e.g. internal motivations) events [10]; the HRI Manager orchestrates the multimodal human-robot interaction using Communicative Acts (CAs) that handle the exchange of information between Mini and a user [4]; (iv) the Perception System manages the low-level communication and configuration of the different sensors; and (v) the Expression System orchestrates the robot actuators to communicate a coherent multimodal message in a timely manner [5].

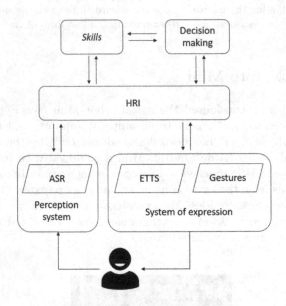

Fig. 3. Diagram of the Mini software architecture.

For this work, we have created a new skill for allowing Mini to operate as a conversational agent using verbal communication. This skill will be activated by the DMS and will request the HRI Manager to execute the proper CAs to give information to the user, to ask questions, or when waiting from some ipnut from the user.

Focusing on the Perception System, we have integrated the ASR engine from Google[1]. This is a grammar-free voice-to-text tool that is executed in the Google Cloud. This service provides a literal transcription of the user speech that will feed to our LLM.

In the Expression System, the robot utterances are generated by the commercial TTS ReadSpeaker[2]. In combination with the TTS, Mini accompanies its

---

[1] https://cloud.google.com/speech-to-text/.
[2] https://www.readspeaker.com.

utterances with non-verbal gestures that have been defined offline. During the operation of the conversational agent skill, the robot performs smooth random movements of its arms, head, and body in order to give Mini a lively appearance.

4.1 Design of the *Conversational Agent Skill*

The *Conversational Agent Skill* has been modeled as a state machine with four states: *greeting*, *conversation*, *continuing*, and *ending*. The flowchart is shown in Fig. 4.

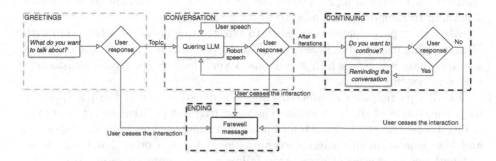

Fig. 4. Diagram of the Conversational Agent Skill.

When the DMS activates the skill, the skill initiates in the state *greeting*, where the robot asks the user what (s)he wants to talk about. After the user responds, the skill moves to *conversation* state. In this state, the transcription of the user's response provided by the ASR is input to the model, and the output is collected and synthesized by the TTS. Then, the user can continue the conversation with other response. This dialog continues until a certain number of turns, i.e. five turns, is reached. At this point, the skill advances to the *continuing* state, where the robot asks the user if (s)he wishes to continue the conversation. If the user answers no, it advances to the *ending* state, where the robot launches a farewell message, and the conversation ends. Otherwise, if the user replies affirmative, the robot reminds the user what they were talking about before the skill transits to the *conversation* state to continue the dialog.

It is important to mention that our skill can stop at any moment if the user does not want to continue or if the system does not receive a response (for example, if the user is gone).

5 Evaluation

We have evaluated the Conversational Agent Skill with 24 users (16 of them were male) interacting freely with the robot. Participants were faculty members and graduate students and 75% of them were between 23 and 27 years old.

Prior to the interaction with the robot, an experimenter presented Mini to the participants and they were informed of the skills and capabilities of Mini. They have also been informed of the data protection policy and have signed a consent form. Data collection was conducted in compliance with the Data Protection Regulations of Universidad Carlos III de Madrid.

During the evaluation, the participants were asked to keep a conversation with Mini about one topic that they decided following the interaction flow described in Fig. 4. Participants could stop the interaction at any moment.

After their interaction, participants completed the System Usability Scale questionnaire [2] to measure the perceived ease of use of the Conversational Agent Skill. The resulting SUS score was 78.5 points, which means good usability according to Bangor et al.'s adjective rating scale [1].

After that, participants were asked to rate the quality of the interaction with Mini, ranging from 0 (the lowest value) to 10 (the highest value). The obtained average value was 8.1, which represents a very high participants' satisfaction with our system.

Finally, participants completed two open questions about the positive and negative aspects of the interaction. The most frequent positive aspects were the ability to discuss any topic, Mini's spontaneity and coherence in its responses, and the generation of engaging conversations. On the other hand, the most frequent negative aspects were ASR failures, some unusual interactions, and delays in Mini's responses.

6   Conclusions

In this paper, we have presented a new skill that allows our social robot Mini to operate as a conversational agent. The core element of this skill is the GPT-3.5 LLM that has been integrated with the robot's software architecture. After evaluating the skill in real interactions, it has exceeded our initial expectations, standing out for the quality of conversations and its high usability. This implies a great opportunity to endow this kind of functionality in social robots that operate as companions for elderly people.

Although the positive results, we have observed some limitations. Using LLM in the cloud adds extra delays that might not be acceptable for a system interacting with humans in real time and requires a stable high-speed Internet connection. New research in reducing the size of LLM (small LLM) with fewer parameters offers new opportunities to get faster LLM and, additionally, with lower power consumption. Because of the extensive use of generative AI, recent small LLMs enhance ecological sustainability and reduce carbon footprint. Also, users have to be aware that the LLM output is not always correct and might suffer from "hallucinations". To cope with these problems, Retrieval-Augmented Generation (RAG) [9], a more sophisticated way of customizing generative LLMs, has emerged. RAG combines information retrieval with text generation, which helps to provide more accurate and contextually relevant answers. Concerning user interaction, some problems experienced by the participants were due to the limitations of the ASR in certain circumstances, such as very short sentences, noisy environments, or a limited range of operation of the robot's microphones.

Acknowledgments. This work was partially supported by ACCESS2MEET project (PID2020-116527RB-I0) supported by MCIN AEI/10.13039/501100011033/ and Madrid Regional Government (Comunidad de Madrid-Spain) under the Multiannual Agreement with UC3M in the line of Excellence of University Professors (EPUC3M17) and in the context of the V PRICIT (Regional Programme of Research and Techno-logical Innovation. This work has been supported by the Madrid Government (Comu-nidad de Madrid-Spain) under the Multiannual Agreement with UC3M ("Fostering Young Doctors Research", SMM4HRI-CM-UC3M), and in the context of the V PRICIT (Research and Technological Innovation Regional Programme). This work has been partially supported by the project "Robots sociales para mitigar la soledad y el ais-lamiento en mayores (SOROLI)", funded by Agencia Estatal de Investigación (AEI), Spanish Ministerio de Ciencia e Innovación (PID2021-123941OA-I00).

Disclosure of Interests. The authors have no competing interests.

References

1. Bangor, A., Kortum, P., Miller, J.: Determining what individual SUS scores mean: adding an adjective rating scale. J. Usability Stud. **4**(3), 114–123 (2009)
2. Brooke, J.: SUS: a 'quick' and 'dirty' usability scale. In: Jordan, P.W., Thomas, B., Weerdmeester, B.A., McClelland, I.L. (eds.) Usability Evaluation in Industry, vol. 21, pp. 189–194. Taylor and Francis (1996)
3. Dupond, S.: A thorough review on the current advance of neural network struc-tures. Annu. Rev. Control. **14**(14), 200–230 (2019)
4. Fernández-Rodicio, E., Castro-González, I., Alonso-Martín, F., Maroto-Gómez, M., Salichs, M.: Modelling multimodal dialogues for social robots using communicative acts. Sensors (Basel). **20**(12), 3440 (2020). https://doi.org/10.3390/s20123440
5. Fernández-Rodicio, E., Maroto-Gómez, M., Castro-González, I., Malfaz, M., Salichs, M.: Emotion and mood blending in embodied artificial agents: express-ing affective states in the mini social robot. Int. J. Soc. Robot. **14**(8), 1841–1864 (2022). https://doi.org/10.1007/s12369-022-00915-9
6. Fulford, I., Ng, A.: ChatGPT prompt engineering for developers (2023). https://www.deeplearning.ai/short-courses/chatgpt-prompt-engineering-for-developers/
7. Hameed, I.: Using natural language processing (NLP) for designing socially intel-ligent robots. In: 2016 Joint IEEE International Conference on Development and Learning and Epigenetic Robotics (ICDL-EpiRob), pp. 268–269 (2016). https://doi.org/10.1109/DEVLRN.2016.7846830
8. Kenton, J.D.M.W.C., Toutanova, L.K.: BERT: pre-training of deep bidirectional transformers for language understanding. In: Proceedings of NAACL-HLT, vol. 1, p. 2 (2019)
9. Lewis, P., et al.: Retrieval-augmented generation for knowledge-intensive NLP tasks. In: NIPS 2020: Proceedings of the 34th International Conference on Neural Information Processing Systems, pp. 9459–9474 (2020)
10. Maroto-Gómez, M., Castro-González, I., Castillo, J.C., Malfaz, M., Salichs, M.N.: An adaptive decision-making system supported on user preference predictions for human-robot interactive communication. User Model. User-Adap. Interact. **33**(2), 359–403 (2023). https://doi.org/10.1007/s11257-022-09321-2

11. Min, B., et al.: Recent advances in natural language processing via large pre-trained language models: a survey. ACM Comput. Surv. **56**(2), 140 (2023). https://doi.org/10.1145/3605943
12. Peng, B., et al.: RWKV: reinventing RNNS for the transformer era. arxiv preprint (2023)
13. Radford, A., Narasimhan, K., Salimans, T., Sutskever, I.: Improving language understanding with unsupervised learning. Technical report, OpenAI (2018)
14. Raffel, C., et al.: Exploring the limits of transfer learning with a unified text-to-text transformer. J. Mach. Learn. Res. **21**(1), 1–67 (2020)
15. Salcedo, J.S., Martínez, S.C., Montoya, J.C.C., Castro-Gonzalez, A., Salichs, M.A.: Modelos de lenguaje natural para robots sociales. XLIII Jornadas de Automática (2022).https://doi.org/10.17979/spudc.9788497498418.0828
16. Salichs, M.A., et al.: Mini: a new social robot for the elderly. Int. J. Soc. Robot **12**(6), 1231–1249 (2020). https://doi.org/10.1007/s12369-020-00687-0
17. Vaswani, A., et al.: Attention is all you need. In: Guyon, I., Luxburg, U.V., Bengio, S., Wallach, H., Fergus, R., Vishwanathan, S., Garnett, R. (eds.) 31st Conference on Neural Information Processing Systems (NIPS 2017)**30**. Curran Associates, Inc. (2017)
18. Wahde, M., Virgolin, M.: Conversational agents: theory and applications. arXiv arXiv:2202.03164 (2022). https://api.semanticscholar.org/CorpusID:246634059
19. Zhao, P., Jin, Z., Cheng, N.: An in-depth survey of large language model-based artificial intelligence agents. arXiv preprint arXiv:2309.14365 (2023)

A Proposal to Extend the Modeling Language for Interaction as Conversation for the Design of Conversational Agents

Ulisses da Silva Fernandes[ID], Bruno Azevedo Chagas[ID], and Raquel Oliveira Prates[(✉)][ID]

Federal University of Minas Gerais, Belo Horizonte, Minas Gerais 31270-901, Brazil
rprates@dcc.ufmg.br
https://dcc.ufmg.br/

Abstract. Conversational agents have become a topic of growing interest in recent years. Their increasing popularity offers opportunities and challenges for Human-Computer Interaction (HCI). Among them, there is a need for more research into whether existing HCI dialogue models apply to conversational agents. Our research focuses on MoLIC (Modeling Language for Interaction as Conversation), a design phase dialogue model based on Semiotic Engineering theory, which allows designers to represent interaction as conversations between a system and its users. Previous studies have pointed out MoLIC's limitations in modeling conversational agents. In this article, our goal is to propose and evaluate an extension to MoLIC to broaden its expressiveness and allow it to be applied to the context of conversational agents. We describe the new elements and adaptations proposed and illustrate how they can be used to model relevant aspects of conversational agents. To evaluate the extension proposed we conducted a case study, in which we applied the extended version of MoLIC in a reverse engineering modeling of an existing chatbot, the chatbot for the Superior Electoral Court (TSE) of Brazil. Our results show that the proposed extension was useful and necessary for describing the TSE's interaction model. This work brings research contributions to the field of HCI, and in particular to the research and development of conversational agents, as well as research on MoLIC and Semiotic Engineering.

Keywords: Intelligent Conversational Agents · Modeling Chatbots · Virtual Assistants · MoLIC · Semiotic Engineering

1 Introduction

Conversational agents have become a topic of increasing interest in recent years. Activated by text or voice commands from users, they are capable of responding appropriately to different types of conversations and can be used for personalized service, being available 24 h a day, reducing service and waiting times for users

H. Degen and S. Ntoa (Eds.): HCII 2024, LNAI 14736, pp. 27–46, 2024.
https://doi.org/10.1007/978-3-031-60615-1_3

[14]. Furthermore, they may have some level of autonomy, even if minimal, to assist and even guide users in the interaction. These technologies can be reactive or proactive, based on user input or changes in the environment and some are adaptive and capable of learning to deal with contextual information or consider user preferences [23].

The increasing popularity of conversational agents offers opportunities and challenges for Human-Computer Interaction (HCI) [12, 21]. The structure of the interaction in these systems can make it more difficult to explore them since there are many more interactive paths available in an interaction using natural language than in a graphical user interface [21]. Thus, there is a need for further investigation into whether existing HCI approaches apply to dialogue models and evaluation of communication between users and conversational agents [12].

Most existing studies on dialogue models for conversational agents are oriented to facilitate the implementation of systems and do not focus on interaction [10]. In a previous study [10], we identified a set of limitations in the applicability of MoLIC – a Modeling Language for Interaction as Conversation grounded on Semiotic Engineering theory – for expressing the interaction models of conversational agents. Therefore, in this article, our goal is to propose an extension to MoLIC to increase its expressiveness and allow its application to the context of conversational agents and to carry out a preliminary evaluation of the proposal.

To generate the proposal we conducted an iterative process to propose and evaluate new or adapted elements for MoLIC elements. The proposal took into account the communicative goal of MoLIC, and each change or new element was discussed by the researchers and applied to the situations described as limitations [10] to see if they would be able to solve the challenge identified. If the element was not able to satisfactorily model the issues in hand, a new iteration cycle discussing the proposed took place. Once a final set of adapted and new elements was defined, a new evaluation of the proposed set of extended elements for MoLIC was conducted by using the extended version of MoLIC. The case study conducted applied MoLIC in a reverse engineering modeling of an existing chatbot, the chatbot for the Superior Electoral Court (TSE) of Brazil. The decision to select a reverse engineering approach was to make sure the evaluation took into account real chatbot interactive paths (as opposed to a fictitious chatbot design scenario). Our results show that the proposed extension was useful and necessary in describing the TSE's chatbot interaction model.

This article is organized as follows: in Sect. 2 we present the work related to conversational agents and models proposed for them; then, in Sect. 3, we present MoLIC - its overall goal and its elements; in Sect. 4 we describe the limitations identified in the expressiveness of MoLIC for the context of conversational agents; Sect. 5 presents our extension proposal. Next, we present the initial evaluation of our proposal by analyzing its applicability to the TSE chatbot in Sect. 6. Finally, we present our final remarks and future work in Sect. 7.

2   Related Work

In this section, we present the main concepts of conversational agents and an overview of the main interaction models of this technology, describing their objectives and limitations.

2.1   Conversational Agents

In the literature, it is very common to come across different terminologies for this type of technology, such as conversational agents, chatbots, dialogue systems, and virtual assistants [17]. Although conversational agent and chatbot are the most common terms, it is not clear that there is an evident difference between these concepts. In this work we use these terms as synonyms and adopt the definition proposed in [17]: "Conversational agents or chatbots are software-based dialogue systems designed to simulate a human conversation process, processing and generating natural language data through a text or voice interface to help users achieve a specific objective or satisfy a specific need".

There have been several reviews of and proposed taxonomies for conversational agents. In a review of existing literature reviews on conversational agents, Motger et al. [17] have proposed a holistic taxonomy for the field. They have identified six main domains/research areas: Everyday Life (most common), Commerce, Business Support, Technical Infrastructure, Healthcare, and Education. As for the objectives, they are also divided into 6 groups: User Support, Information Request, User Involvement, Action Execution, User Training, and Information Collection.

From a technical perspective, Motger et al. [17] have classified conversational agents into two broad categories: deterministic - allows deterministic mapping between user inputs and responses from a closed data set; and based on Machine Learning (ML) - designed with an adaptive knowledge base and capable of processing and interpret user inputs, creating original outputs as responses to the inputs provided. These two approaches are complementary and the advantages and disadvantages of each can be used to choose the best one in a specific scenario. Hybrid approaches are also possible.

Interacting with conversational agents is significantly different from interacting with other types of technologies and presents new challenges for interaction design [3,12]. The focus shifts from designing a visual layout and functional interactive elements to designing the conversations that the agent can have with its users [12]. A book edited by Moore and Arar [15] discussed the concept of user experience design (UX) and some of the various nuances and complexities of interaction design with conversational agents. One of the points the authors draw attention to is that conversational interactions must be carefully designed through a "conversation first" approach that focuses mainly on the sequence and structure of statements and decision-making between agent and user since the visual elements of the interface play only a secondary role.

According to Valério et al. [21], a big difference between traditional GUI interfaces and conversational agents is how the technology is presented to the user. In the former, the interface depicts, through its elements (available instructions, buttons, options, etc.), the possible actions users can take. In the latter, the challenge lies in the fact that the technology is presented to the user sentence by sentence, step by step. Furthermore, conversational interfaces are also more open to variations in user input, since the range of users' expressions in natural language is unlimited, opening up a greater set of possibilities and interactive paths that the user could follow. Thus, conversational agents' communicability (i.e. a system's ability to convey to users who its intended users are, what goals it is intended for, and how to interact with it to achieve these goals [9]) is highly dependent on the dialogue flows available and explored by users [21].

In this article, our focus is to support designers to reflect and make decisions about the possible interaction paths, i.e. possible conversation flows between users and conversational agents. In the next subsection, we present a review of the models proposed in the literature for conversational agents.

2.2   Modeling Interaction in Conversational Agents

Despite the growing interest in interaction with conversational agents, there is no consolidated approach or consensus on how to design them [1,19]. One of the approaches being explored is interaction modeling, which can help designers explore solutions, conceive alternatives, and reflect on decisions before implementation [2]. However, research on interaction models of conversational agents is scarce, since most of the work we found investigates technical frameworks and AI techniques to support the development of conversational agents.

In [22], authors present guidelines on how to model a dialogue-based conversation with a chatbot and a framework built with Microsoft Conversational Services. The created framework provides functionality for dialogue modeling and administration of dialogue sessions, supporting issues related to both the design and use of chatbots.

In a similar direction, Pérez-Soler et al. [18] proposed to automate the task of designing and creating agents, using a dynamic modeling service based on a meta-model. Guzzoni et al., [13] presented a new architecture for developing intelligent assistants that provide a unified tool and approach for rapid application development incorporating natural language interpretation, dialogue management, plan execution, and web services integration. Valtolina and Neri [20] proposed a platform to support domain experts in creating bots through a graphical conversation flow editor. These works focus on supporting technical development and deployment, even when targeted at domain experts.

Castle-Green et al. [6] address differences between rule-based conversational agents (fragile, use decision trees, and require a lot of data) and corpus-based/ stochastic (use training data to learn). They bring up the challenges in using branching structures when designing conversational agents and indicate promising next steps in the research area, however, they do not present a proposal for a new tool or adaptation of an existing one to model the interactions of these technologies.

Focusing on interaction, Carlmeyer et al. [5] presented an initial interaction model for incremental presentation of information, including different timing strategies for presenting the next piece of information in a given task. The results led to the formulation of the interactive and incremental model that distinguishes between the dialogue and task levels, allowing a general description of the interaction. It also includes different user input modalities as well as the possibility to monitor task progress. A current limitation is that if a sub-task fails, the entire interaction fails. Therefore, a modeling tool that provides a complete view of the conversation with the conversational agent can be a solution to deal with this limitation, without compromising the modeling.

In a similar vein, Cambre and Kulkarni [4] considered how researchers and designers can build new and intuitive voice interfaces. Although the authors studied voice design techniques and pointed out opportunities for future studies, they did not present how to model conversational agent interactions.

Moore et al. [16] proposed a conversational UX framework called the Natural Conversation Framework (NCF), which is based on Conversational Analysis and provides a set of features to support the design of agent conversations. They also proposed the use of transcripts to represent and communicate conversational drawings as simple examples of representative dialogue in plain text, as in a film script. Although it appears to be powerful and useful at a lower level of conversation design abstraction, its approach does not cover a higher level of abstraction in interaction design, and it does not provide an overview of what could or should happen during the interaction.

Given the focus of the models presented and their limitations, in this work, we chose to investigate interaction modeling at a higher level of abstraction. Our goal is to allow designers of conversational agents to focus first on designing the user's possible conversations with the system, before defining its implementation and interface. Our goal is to support conversational agent designers in defining the possible conversational paths between users and the system, before defining its implementation and interface. To do so, we have investigated the use of MoLIC, as presented in the next section.

3   MoLIC

Conversational agents are part of an emerging technology and can be explored from different perspectives and theories. As discussed in the previous section, interaction modeling for conversational agents is still an unexplored field. Our goal was to investigate how to support designers in their conception of the possible communicative paths between users and conversational agents. Thus in our research, we chose to investigate how MoLIC (Modeling Language for Interaction as Conversation) could be used in this context.

MoLIC is based on Semiotic Engineering (SemEng) theory [9] - an HCI theory that perceives a system's interface as a meta-communication artifact, in which the system-user communication allows for a designer-to-user communication to take place. The system conveys a designer-to-user message about the designers' intent and design principles represented in the system and is called the *designer's deputy* for this reason. In this theoretical framework, MoLIC has been proposed to allow designers to model (all) the possible user interactions with the system [2,7,9].

As MoLIC considers the user-system interaction as a conversation, it was a natural candidate to be used in the context of conversational agents. In this direction, our first step was to investigate MoLIC's applicability in this context [10]. However, the results of these previous studies were that there were limitations when using MoLIC in this context. Next, we briefly present MoLIC, and in the next section, we present the challenges found regarding its applicability to conversational agents' context.

MoLIC is a language for modeling human-computer interactions as conversations [2,7,9]. Its goal is to allow for the representation of all possible paths that user-system conversations can take. It bridges the gap between the task model at the user goal level and the interface representation level, allowing designers to model what and how users will interact with the system, without committing to a particular interface design [2].

Through the interaction diagram, the designer represents the possible interactive paths, defining the scenes and dialogues that will be available in the system for users to achieve their objectives. Figure 1 on the left (I) shows a snippet of an example of a MoLIC model of a banking system, showing the main elements that make up the language [7]. On the right, Fig. 1 (II) depicts some of the main elements available in MoLIC.

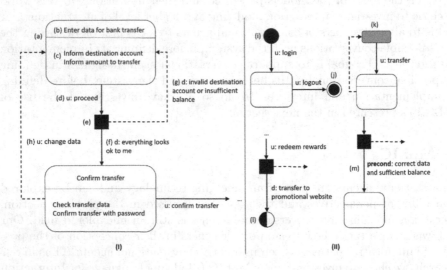

Fig. 1. (I) MoLIC modeling example. (II) Other elements of the MoLIC.

A **scene** (a) is a stage in the conversation between the user and the system about a specific topic. A scene is represented by a rectangle with rounded edges.

The **topic** of the scene is represented by a sentence at the top of the rectangle (b). **Dialogues** represent the content of the scene (c) and describe the different subtopics or parts of a scene, such as entering various data (destination account, amount to transfer, etc.). Scenes are articulated through turn-taking represented by **transitions** indicated in (d) by a directed solid line. Next to the line, the text represents who the utterer is ('u' for the user and 'd' for designer's deputy - *i.e.* system) and its content (e.g. "u: proceed"). The black box (e) represents textbfinternal system processes, which are hidden from users, In (f) we have a statement from the system, labeled 'd:', for example: "d: everything looks ok to me". The dashed line represents a **breakdown recovery transition**, i.e. a recovery path taken by the system or users when/if there is a breakdown in the communication process (as seen in (g) and (h), respectively).

Other elements of MoLIC are depicted in Fig. 1 (II): in (i) we have the **opening point** of the conversation while in (j) we have the **closing point**. In (k) we have **ubiquitous access**, which means "in any scene where users are, they can utter <speech>". In this example, ubiquitous access indicates that from any point in the system, users can say "u: transfer", which will take them to the scene related to transfers. It is important to note that once the conversation has started, users can change their minds and cancel the transfer, returning to the place where they were before. In (l) we have the representation of an **external interlocutor** who represents another system that will be activated or affected by the system being designed. Finally, in (m), we have the keyword '**precond**', which indicates the conditions that must be met for the related transition to occur.

After over 15 years since MoLIC's proposal [2], De Carvalho et al. [8] conducted a systematic literature review, analyzing the various contexts and different purposes for which MoLIC had been used. The authors concluded that MoLIC was a consolidated model in use by the HCI community, mainly in Brazil. A recent work [11] investigated the use of MoLIC in the design of Artificial Intelligence (AI) systems that considered people in the loop approach. Even though conversational agents can make use of AI, their focus was to express the participation of the AI's portion of the system in the user-system interaction, whereas ours is on the specific interactive paths that communication agents use in their interaction with users (independently of their technical approach).

4   MoLIC's Limitation to Represent Conversational Agents

In previous works, we have analyzed the applicability of MoLIC to the context of conversational agents [10] and identified 4 situations in which MoLIC presented limitations for modeling interaction in this context. These limitations were classified into four categories discussed in each of the following subsections.

4.1   Standardized Communication Snippets

In some situations, conversational agents can talk about different contents using the same communication structure. For example, if the chatbot presents a set of structured questions with their answers as a way of offering information to the user. In terms of representation in MoLIC for each of the topics, the structure of the communication represented would be the same, with only differences between the contents presented in each scene. The different interactive paths can be represented in MoLIC. However, if each structure or set of topics is large, representing all of them can generate an overloaded interaction diagram, making it difficult for designers to have a holistic view of the intended meta-communication.

4.2   Transfer of Responsibility / Interlocutor During Communication

In the analyses carried out, it was identified that, in some situations, the conversational agent transferred control to a third interlocutor who was not initially involved in the conversation.

1. Service Request: The conversational agent interacts with another system to request a service (e.g. send an email);
2. Responsibility Transfer: The conversational agent yields the floor (i.e. control) to another system, temporarily or permanently (e.g. if a conversational assistant transfers the control to Google Maps as a response to a user's request for information about a route);
3. Information Request: The conversational agent responds to the user's request for information with content generated by other systems (e.g. the agent presents the result of a mathematical calculation performed by the calculator application).

Regarding these three cases, cases 1 and 3 can be represented using MoLIC - "Point of contact with another system" (see element (l) of Fig. 1) (case 1), and indicating the source of the response as part of the response generated by the system after processing (case 3). However, for case 2 (responsibility transfer), MoLIC allows indicating how to transfer the conversation to another system but does not consider how to represent transferring it back to the agent, resuming the user-chatbot interaction.

4.3   Modeling Breakdown Recovery

Another limitation identified is related to the variety of types of communicative breakdowns that can occur when users interact with conversational agents. As these systems must deal primarily with open input, unexpected behaviors caused by the system's interpretation of the user's expression (in voice or written text) or its content should be considered. Thus, in the analysis carried out, six possible results of user-chatbot interaction were identified that designers could intend to represent in an interaction model:

1. The system correctly understands the user's request and returns the user's expected response;
2. The system understands the user's request, but identifies that relevant information is missing and asks the user additional questions to complete the information;
3. The system does not fully understand the user's request, but understands parts of it, and starts a conversation to clarify what the user wants to say;
4. The system does not understand the user's request, but is aware of the failure and asks the user to repeat or try an alternative message;
5. The system understands the user's request, but cannot satisfy it, and informs the user about it;
6. The system misunderstands the user's request and returns an incorrect response.

Regarding MoLIC, case 1 represents the expected flow of communication. Case 6, in turn, is not possible to model, as the system is not capable of identifying its own misunderstanding. However, cases 2 to 5 represent some type of recoverable breakdown in communication and it would be interesting to represent the different possibilities associated with each user interaction with the conversational agent.

4.4   Conversational Agents' Intelligence

In systems in which all its communicative paths have been previously defined and which have a limited set of questions and answers that they can understand, MoLIC can be used (even with the limitations described previously). However, intelligent systems bring new issues that would need to be considered when extending MoLIC: the system's autonomy, transparency, and explainability (i.e., the need for users to understand the system's logic and decisions) [11,23]. MoLIC uses the black box for processing, but it was designed for traditional systems. In AI-based conversational systems, the user's speech is just one of the inputs considered in generating the response. These systems were made to learn from the knowledge acquired from data from a set of users (machine learning) and the interaction must be designed to allow users to know what is happening during processing.

5   Extending MoLIC

To solve the limitations identified in MoLIC's applicability to conversational agents, in this article, we present our proposal to extend MoLIC to this context. Our methodology to propose new elements has been an iterative process to propose how to adapt existing MoLIC elements or propose new ones.

The proposal took into account the communicative goal of MoLIC, and each change or new element was discussed by a panel of 3 researchers who are experts in Semiotic Engineering and MoLIC. Once they believed the proposal was sound it was applied to the situations described as limitations [10] to see if they would be able to solve the challenge identified. If the element was not able to satisfactorily model the issues in hand, a new iteration cycle discussing the proposed element took place.

Finally, once a final set of adapted and new elements was defined, a new evaluation of the proposed set of extended elements for MoLIC was conducted in a case study (presented in Sect. 6). The case study conducted applied MoLIC in a reverse engineering modeling of an existing chatbot, the chatbot for the 2022 Brazilian Presidential elections made available by the Superior Electoral Court (TSE) of Brazil. The decision to select a reverse engineering approach was to make sure the proposed elements would be useful to model real chatbots (as opposed to a fictitious chatbot design scenario).

Next, we present the new elements proposed in our extension, which include new and adapted elements. For each element, we describe their purpose, and graphical representation and illustrate their use.

5.1   Template Element

In many conversational agents, different conversations can be presented to the user following the same structure, for example, in a "top 10 questions" on different topics. As described in Sect. 4.1, these excerpts present the same communication structure, but their contents are different. Therefore, we propose the template element that allows a representation of the communication structure in general, and then a more concise representation of each instance of this structure, indicating their specificities.

The proposed template element presents two levels of abstraction: the detailed level that presents the description of the communication structure (scenes, system processing, and transitions); and the abstract level that indicates which template is being created and the specific content that represents each instance. The abstract higher level would be included in the interactive diagram, and the detailed level would be represented separately. Figure 2 illustrates the representation of the template element for each level of abstraction - the abstract level (defined as level 1) indicates the template's representation to be used in the diagram model, while the detailed level (level 2) describes the section of an interactive path described by the template.

Note that at the abstract level, the template is represented by a gray box with a label in the upper left corner that contains the template type and the name of the instance being represented. In this gray template element box, the attributes' values necessary to define the instance being represented must be described. Furthermore, the element also features two small circles that represent the entry and exit points of the conversation flow. The template can provide more than one entry and exit point, in which case the circles can be numbered to indicate an association between an entry point and the exit.

The detailed level represents the expanded gray box. Thus, the top left corner contains the type of template being represented, while the white box in the top right corner contains the list of attributes that will be used to describe the

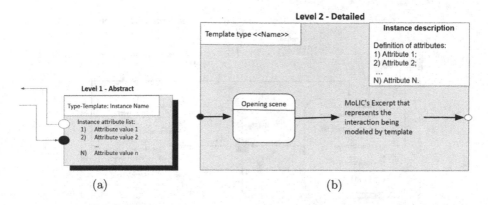

Fig. 2. Template element - (a) Abstract and (b) detailed levels.

instance (the value for each attribute will be defined in the gray box of the abstract level element when an instance of the template is used). Finally, circles represent at least one entry point (black circle) and one exit point of the template (white circle). In the gray area of the template, the diagram model represents the communicative structure being abstracted by the template, indicating in scenes, dialogues, or transitions which element will receive each attribute defined.

Applying the Template Element. The template element proposed can be used to solve two of the limitations presented in Sect. 4: Standardized Communication Snippets and Modeling Breakdown Recovery. In both cases, the template element is used to describe the communicative structure that will be reused for different contents in the case of Standardized Communication Snippets, and the interactive path required to recover from one of the breakdown cases, in the case of Modeling Breakdown Recovery.

To illustrate its use in the need to represent standardized communication snippets, we created a generic example that represents a question-and-answer template, which could be used in a conversational agent that provides health information. Figure 3 represents the detailed level describing the interaction of the template's questions and answers in general. In its turn, Fig. 4 illustrates the use of the abstract level of the question-and-answer template in a diagram model for a chatbot on health information.

Concerning the breakdown recovery modeling described in Sect. 4.3, the different breakdown cases may imply a different behavior pattern for the system to continue the interaction and recover from the breakdown. Thus, we identified that the proposed template element can also be used to represent the communication structure associated with each type of breakdown.

Figure 5 represents an excerpt from a model in which, in relation to the "Request Services" scene, the designer predicts that different types of breakdowns may occur and for each of them a different recovery strategy is modeled. Case 1 (in which the agent understands the user's request) and case 5 (in which the agent

38   U. S. Fernandes et al.

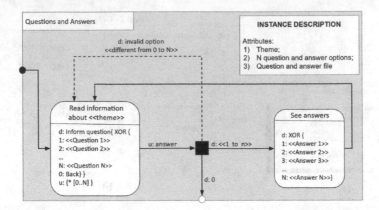

Fig. 3. Generic "Questions and Answers" Level 2 template for a healthcare chatbot.

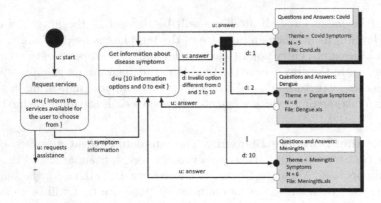

Fig. 4. Model of a healthcare chatbot with template.

realizes that it does not know how to respond to the request) are represented by the transition to the "View Response" scene and breakdown transition (dotted directed line) back to the "Request Services" scene respectively.

The breakdowns that represent cases 2 to 4 (in which the agent perceives the breakdowns and engages in other conversations with the user to recover from them), the user's interaction is taken to the template instance of the "Breakdown Recovery" template (indicated on the right side of Fig. 5)[1]. For each instance, the name of the instance (in the white rectangle on the upper left side), and the attributes (type of problem and the subject of the request) are represented. For reasons of space, we did not include the detailed level of the template, which describes the excerpt of the interaction model representing the defined structure of communication associated with each of these breakdowns. The template generates a revised response from the interaction that goes back to the system's

---

[1] Notice that as case 6 (system's misunderstanding) is not a situation designer would model it is not included in the example.

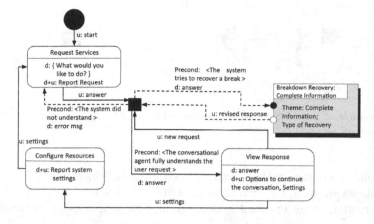

Fig. 5. Template Use for Breakdown Recovery cases.

processing element and will lead to either a successful response (proceeding to the "View Response" scene) or another breakdown (proceeding to case 5 – system is not able to respond – or looping to the "Breakdown Recovery" template again for cases 2 to 4).

5.2   Allowing for the Interaction with a Third-Party System

As discussed in Sect. 4.2, in some situations the conversational agent includes another system in the conversation, either to request a service or information or by transferring control of the conversation, temporarily or permanently, to it.

MoLIC 2.0 has the element "point of contact with another system" (see Fig. 1 "1") that represents the influence of the interaction model being represented in another system. Thus, this element can be used to represent the situation when the agent requests a third-party system to perform a service for the user.

However, MoLIC does not include the possibility to model a response from the third-party system, nor to model a temporary or complete transfer of responsibility to that system. Thus, we propose an adaptation, allowing transitions from the third-party system back to the model. Figure 6 illustrates 2 example cases showing the representation of the interaction with a third-party system. In case 1, when sending a request to the third-party system, the model indicates a transition from the system (i.e. feedback to the user) informing that the request was made. Case 2 illustrates the situation in which the model waits for feedback from the third-party system to continue the interaction. Notice that in this case, we have also included a representation for the new interlocutor - the third-party system "t" (see Fig. 6 - Case 2 - "t: Email sent!").

Finally, the situation in which the agent definitively transfers the conversation to another system and ends its interaction with the user cannot be represented in MoLIC 2.0. Thus, we created a new element "transfer to another system". The graphical representation of this element combines the graphical representation

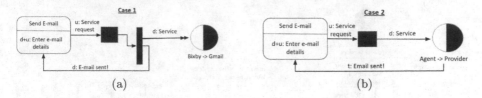

(a)   (b)

Fig. 6. Example of transfers to other systems using the MoLIC "point of contact with another system" element.

of the "point of contact with an external system" and "closing point" elements. Figure 7 shows an excerpt from a model in which the "View maps" scene transfers the conversation to an external system, ending its own conversation with the user.

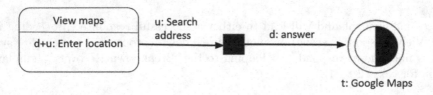

Fig. 7. Example of a model using the new "transfer to another system" element.

5.3   Adaptations to MoLIC 2.0 Elements

Intelligent systems introduce new types of interactions that need to be considered when modeling the interaction because of situations that did not exist in traditional system design, for instance, system autonomy enabling the system to start or finish a conversation at its "will" [23]. As we will see below, for the three cases of starting and ending conversations, we suggest small adaptations to the current version of MoLIC.

The **Opening Point** and **Closing Point** are Molic 2.0 elements that indicate the starting and ending points, respectively, of the user-system conversation. The transitions from the opening point to a scene, or from a scene to a closing point, usually are associated with a user utterance. However, conversational agents often take the initiative themselves to initiate or terminate the conversation (e.g. a chatbot interacts with a user on a website asking if they need any help). Thus, the adaptation is to allow the transition from/to an opening/closing point to be made by the system (and not only by users). Figure 8 depicts the possible interlocutors for the opening (Fig. 8a)/closing (Fig. 8b) points.

Another situation in which conversational agents often take the initiative to start a conversation is when, after an interaction (that has not been ended), the

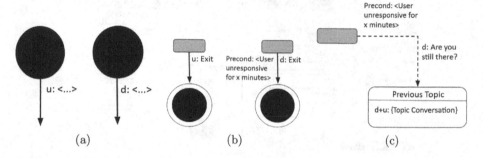

Fig. 8. Opening Point: (a) Utterance by user or system (new) (b) Closing Point: Utterance by user or system (new); (c) Modeling system's initiative to resume conversation.

user does not say anything to the agent for some time. In this case, some chatbots will send a message with the intent to resume the conversation. To account for this situation, we have proposed the use of the "ubiquitous access" element to indicate that the utterance could be emitted at any moment and the use of the dotted line for the transition to represent the system's attempt to recover the communication that was interrupted. This transition could have as a precondition that a specific period has elapsed since the previous communication, and its interlocutor is the system. Figure 8c shows the adapted use of the elements.

6 Initial Evaluation of Proposal

To evaluate our proposal, we selected a chatbot (different from those used in [10]) to assess whether the new and adapted elements would improve MoLIC's expressivity. As explained in Sect. 5, we reverse-engineered the interaction model of the selected conversational agent, analyzing the need for the new/adapted elements of the proposal, and whether any other limitations were noticed.

For our analysis, we selected the chatbot developed by the Superior Electoral Court (TSE)[2] for the presidential elections in Brazil in 2022 available for WhatsApp. The analysis was conducted by the 1st author, and the results were reviewed and discussed with the other 2 authors in October 2022. Once users add the chatbot's contact, they may start interacting by messaging the word "HI" to the chatbot. In response, the chatbot offers a short explanation of how to interact with it and a list of the available content. Among the possible interactions, the chatbot provides text instructions, radio buttons to choose options, buttons, and responds through texts, images, and even audio (see Fig. 9).

We identified that the TSE chatbot presents conversation patterns that are repeated in different contexts, which allowed us to apply the template element. A template to represent the question-and-answer interactions was modeled.

---

[2] https://www.tse.jus.br/comunicacao/noticias/2022/Abril/chatbot-tira-duvidas-do-tse-no-whatsapp-traz-novidades-para-as-eleicoes-2022. (Last visit: January 2024).

Fig. 9. Interaction screens with the TSE chatbot, 2022.

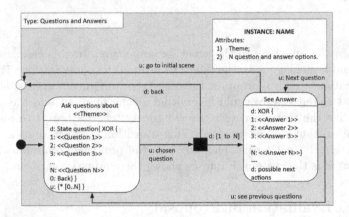

Fig. 10. Detailed level of the question-and-answer template for the TSE chatbot.

Figure 10 shows the detailed level of the question-and-answer template, whereas Fig. 11 illustrates an excerpt of the chatbot model that shows 2 instances of the question-and-answer template being used to represent the possibility of the user talking about the top 10 questions, or about acting as an officer during the election (officer's channel).

At different moments, the chatbot offered users the chance to move on and start interacting directly with other systems, namely the Electoral Justice Website or a site to verify fake news. Figure 12 on the left shows the chatbot's dialogue with the possibility to go to "boatos.org" and learn about/check the veracity of the information; and on the right the excerpt of the model indicating the different possibilities to transfer permanently to other systems. Figure 13 shows a situation in which the chatbot takes the initiative to end the conversation after the user is inactive for 20 min. Figure 13(a) shows the user-chatbot conversation, and Fig. 13(b) the excerpt of the model referring to that interactive path.

In our reverse-engineering of the TSE chatbot, we used some (but not all) of the new/adapted elements. As described in this section we used the template element, transfer (permanently) to a third-party element, and the system's

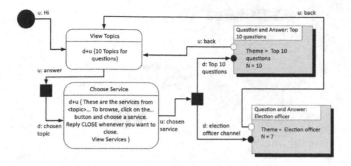

Fig. 11. Excerpt containing 2 instances of the question-and-answer template.

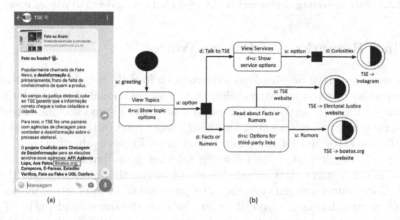

Fig. 12. Transfer to other systems (a) TSE chatbot screen; (b) Model excerpt.

initiative to end the interaction. The fact that these elements were necessary to model the TSE chatbot, indicates their usefulness in this context, and that our proposal extends the expressivity of MoLIC.

The fact that the other proposed elements/adaptations were not necessary in our modeling of the TSE chatbot does not mean they are not useful. It would not be expected that all conversational agents include all the communicative paths that can be expressed through our proposal. However, it does point to the need for a broader assessment of the proposal, that requires the analysis of a varied and larger set of conversational agents.

Finally, it is worth pointing out that we did not identify other specificities in representing interactive paths for conversational agents that could not be represented by our extended proposal of MoLIC.

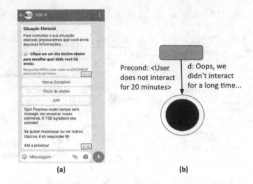

Fig. 13. Chatbot ending conversarion (a) TSE chatbot screen; (b) Model excerpt.

7   Final Remarks and Future Works

In this work, we have proposed an extension to MoLIC to solve its limitations in representing interactive paths relevant to conversational agents' interaction [10]. Our findings show that the proposal has allowed some specific aspects of this interaction to be represented for the chatbots used in the study identifying the limitations [10] and for the TSE chatbot used in our evaluation.

Thus, this work brings the following relevant contribution to HCI: (1) an increase in the community's knowledge about interaction modeling and the use of MoLIC for conversational systems; (2) a proposal of an interaction model that is useful in considering the overall communicative discourse, and paths of conversational agents, separately from its implementation [12,16]; (3) an extension of MoLIC's applicability and research [8].

As future steps, the consolidation of our extended MoLIC proposal requires further and broader evaluation of proposed elements and adaptations. Future evaluation should consider a larger number of chatbots, and also a more diverse set of chatbots regarding their domains, objectives, and technical perspective [17]. Furthermore, it is necessary to evaluate the proposal not only analytically, but also as part of a chatbot design process, as it is intended. One relevant aspect to consider is the fact that our extension has proposed the use of two levels of abstraction in the template element, which is new in MoLIC and can increase the complexity of the model and its use.

References

1. Adamopoulou, E., Moussiades, L.: An overview of chatbot technology. In: Maglogiannis, I., Iliadis, L., Pimenidis, E. (eds.) AIAI 2020. IAICT, vol. 584, pp. 373–383. Springer, Cham (2020). https://doi.org/10.1007/978-3-030-49186-4_31
2. Barbosa, S.D.J., de Paula, M.G.: Designing and evaluating interaction as conversation: a modeling language based on semiotic engineering. In: Jorge, J.A., Jardim Nunes, N., Falcão e Cunha, J. (eds.) DSV-IS 2003. LNCS, vol. 2844, pp. 16–33. Springer, Heidelberg (2003). https://doi.org/10.1007/978-3-540-39929-2_2

3. Brandtzaeg, P.B., Følstad, A.: Chatbots: changing user needs and motivations. Interactions **25**(5), 38–43 (2018). https://doi.org/10.1145/3236669
4. Cambre, J., Kulkarni, C.: Methods and tools for prototyping voice interfaces. In: Proceedings of the 2nd Conference on Conversational User Interfaces, pp. 1–4. CUI 2020, Association for Computing Machinery, New York, NY, USA (2020). https://doi.org/10.1145/3405755.3406148
5. Carlmeyer, B., Chromik, M., Wrede, B.: Interaction model for incremental information presentation. In: Proceedings of the 5th International Conference on Human Agent Interaction, pp. 335–339. HAI 2017, Association for Computing Machinery, New York, NY, USA (2017). https://doi.org/10.1145/3125739.3132582
6. Castle-Green, T., Reeves, S., Fischer, J.E., Koleva, B.: Decision trees as sociotechnical objects in chatbot design. In: Proceedings of the 2nd Conference on Conversational User Interfaces, pp. 1–3. CUI 2020, Association for Computing Machinery, New York, NY, USA (2020). https://doi.org/10.1145/3405755.3406133
7. Da Silva, B.S., Barbosa, S.D.J.: Designing human-computer interaction with molic diagrams-a practical guide. Monografias em Ciência da Computação **12**, 50 (2007)
8. De Carvalho, A.P., Pereira, F.H.S., Assunção, O.B., Pereira, A.F., Prates, R.O.: An analysis of MoLIC's consolidation. In: Proceedings of the 18th Brazilian Symposium on Human Factors in Computing Systems, pp. 1–15. IHC 2019, Association for Computing Machinery, New York, NY, USA (2019). https://doi.org/10.1145/3357155.3358461
9. De Souza, C.S.: The Semiotic Engineering of Human-Computer Interaction. MIT press (2005)
10. Fernandes, U.D.S., Barbosa, G.A.R., Chagas, B.A., Barbosa, G.D.J., Barbosa, S.D.J., Prates, R.O.: Lessons learned from modeling the interaction with conversational agents. Int. Des. Architect. **55**, 139–173 (2023). https://doi.org/10.55612/s-5002-055-007
11. Ferreira, J.J., Fucs, A., Segura, V.: Modeling people-AI interaction: a case discussion with using an interaction design language. In: Marcus, A., Wang, W. (eds.) HCII 2019. LNCS, vol. 11584, pp. 379–388. Springer, Cham (2019). https://doi.org/10.1007/978-3-030-23541-3_27
12. Følstad, A., Brandtzæg, P.B.: Chatbots and the new world of HCI. Interactions **24**(4), 38–42 (2017). https://doi.org/10.1145/3085558
13. Guzzoni, D., Baur, C., Cheyer, A.: Modeling human-agent interaction with active ontologies. In: The Association for the Advancement of Artificial Intelligence Spring Symposium: Interaction Challenges for Intelligent Assistants, pp. 52–59. AAAI, Vancouver, British Columbia, Canada (2007). http://www.aaai.org/Library/Symposia/Spring/2007/ss07-04-009.php
14. Laranjo, L., et al.: Conversational agents in healthcare: a systematic review. J. Am. Med. Inform. Assoc. **25**(9), 1248–1258 (2018). https://doi.org/10.1093/jamia/ocy072
15. Moore, R.J., Arar, R.: Conversational UX design: an introduction. In: Moore, R.J., Szymanski, M.H., Arar, R., Ren, G.-J. (eds.) Studies in Conversational UX Design. HIS, pp. 1–16. Springer, Cham (2018). https://doi.org/10.1007/978-3-319-95579-7_1
16. Moore, R.J., Szymanski, M.H., Arar, R., Ren, G.-J. (eds.): Studies in Conversational UX Design. HIS, Springer, Cham (2018). https://doi.org/10.1007/978-3-319-95579-7
17. Motger, Q., Franch, X., Marco, J.: Software-based dialogue systems: survey, taxonomy and challenges. ACM Comput. Surv. **55**, 1–42 (2022). https://doi.org/10.1145/3527450

18. Pérez-Soler, S., Guerra, E., de Lara, J.: Flexible Modelling using Conversational Agents. In: 2019 ACM/IEEE 22nd International Conference on Model Driven Engineering Languages and Systems Companion (MODELS-C), pp. 478–482. IEEE, Munich, Germany (2019). https://doi.org/10.1109/MODELS-C.2019.00076
19. Rapp, A., Curti, L., Boldi, A.: The human side of human-chatbot interaction: a systematic literature review of ten years of research on text-based chatbots. Int. J. Hum. Comput. Stud. **151**, 102630 (2021). https://doi.org/10.1016/j.ijhcs.2021.102630
20. Valtolina, S., Neri, L.: Visual design of dialogue flows for conversational interfaces. Behav. Inf. Technol. **40**, 1–16 (2021). https://doi.org/10.1080/0144929X.2021.1918249
21. Valério, F.A.M., Guimarães, T.G., Prates, R.O., Candello, H.: Chatbots explain themselves: designers' strategies for conveying chatbot features to users. J. Interact. Syst. **9**(3), 1 (2018). https://doi.org/10.5753/jis.2018.710
22. Wachtel, A., Fuchß, D., Schulz, S., Tichy, W.F.: Approaching natural conversation chatbots by interactive dialogue modelling & Microsoft LUIS. In: 2019 IEEE International Conference on Conversational Data Knowledge Engineering (CDKE), pp. 39–42. IEEE, San Diego, CA, USA (2019). https://doi.org/10.1109/CDKE46621.2019.00013
23. Meyer von Wolff, R., Hobert, S., Schumann, M.: How may i help you? - State of the art and open research questions for chatbots at the digital workplace. In: Proceedings of the 52nd Hawaii International Conference on System Sciences, pp. 95–104. HICSS, Hawaii (2019). https://doi.org/10.24251/HICSS.2019.013

Optimizing Conversational Commerce Involving Multilingual Consumers Through Large Language Models' Natural Language Understanding Abilities

Joseph Benjamin Ilagan(✉)🆔, Jose Ramon Ilagan🆔, Pia Ysabel Zulueta🆔, and Maria Mercedes Rodrigo🆔

Ateneo de Manila University, Quezon City, Philippines
{jbilagan,jrilagan,pzulueta,mrodrigo}@ateneo.edu
https://www.ateneo.edu

Abstract. Due to the emergence of natural language processing (NLP) interfaces, there has been growing intent to use conversational channels for commerce. Beyond customer service, NLP-enabled AI agents are being integrated into various steps of the order-to-cash (OTC) process. Social media and messaging platforms such as Facebook Messenger have become pivotal for businesses, especially during and after the COVID-19 pandemic, but adoption has been limited. In addition, attitudes towards fully-automated conversational agents (CA) have been mixed, and there is room for human involvement in transactional conversations. A distinguishing contribution of this research is leveraging the inherent capabilities of Large Language Models (LLMs) in handling multilingual conversations and extracting transactional details through named entity recognition (NER). The study describes a hybrid human-AI setup augmenting agents with an auto-agent leveraging LLMs' natural language understanding (NLU) capabilities, designed using the OTC process pattern applied to conversational UX frameworks. A prototype of the setup aims to streamline operations and reduce errors by enhancing the user experience during key OTC steps through improved conversational design. Recognizing the irreplaceable essence of human interaction, the hybrid *human-in-the-loop* approach was chosen, mitigating the impersonal nature of full automation. A prototype handling customers and humans augmented by LLMs for NER handling of transaction, customer, and product information was built. Sample synthetic bilingual conversations between customers and sales agents were generated using ChatGPT and fed into the system for evaluation.

Keywords: Conversational user experience · conversational commerce · Large language models · Natural language understanding · Named entity recognition · Generative AI · Co-pilots

1 Introduction

Conversational commerce (CC) is the human-like dialogue between a business (or brand) and a consumer through messaging apps, live chat, chatbots (or digital

H. Degen and S. Ntoa (Eds.): HCII 2024, LNAI 14736, pp. 47–59, 2024.
https://doi.org/10.1007/978-3-031-60615-1_4

assistants), and voice assistants [11, 21]. The purported benefits of CC include increased engagement, reduced cart abandonment, obtaining helpful feedback, boosted (online) sales, and building brand loyalty [11]. Due to the emergence of natural language processing (NLP) interfaces, there has been growing intent to use a conversational agent (CA) for commerce. Beyond customer service, NLP-enabled AI agents are being integrated into various *order-to-cash* (OTC) processes: order entry (including product or service search and selection), order fulfillment, invoicing, and payment collection.

Social media and messaging platforms such as Facebook Messenger have become pivotal for businesses, especially during and after the COVID-19 pandemic. Messaging platforms have been used for general customer service [7], including answering inquiries and discovering product or service preferences [4, 25]. In countries like the Philippines, using social media and messaging platforms such as Facebook Messenger has allowed businesses to reach customers quickly and remotely, especially during and after the COVID-19 pandemic [4].

However, adoption has been limited due to challenges like lack of standards, insufficient natural language understanding (NLU), lack of personalization, absence of human touch, support for local languages, difficulty handling complex dialogue, and operationalizing conversations. As such, humans are still involved [11, 21].

Recent developments in artificial intelligence hold promise in addressing some of these challenges. Generative artificial intelligence (GAI) generates content using probability and statistics derived through training from existing digital content (ex., text, video, images, and audio) [2]. A large language model (LLM) is a GAI and statistical model of tokens in the large public corpus of human-generated text [20]. Through training, LLMs understand and produce human-like language [6]. The tokens involved are words, parts of words, or individual characters, including punctuation marks. They are generative because one can sample and ask them questions [20]. GPT (Generative Pre-trained Transformer), an LLM-based system, is designed to generate sequences of words, code, or other data from statistical distributions derived from training, starting from a source input called the prompt [9]. GPT is based on the transformer architecture [8, 19, 22], which trains large amounts of publicly-available data. Aside from generating content, LLMs have demonstrated improved performance in NLP and NLU, whether in English or other languages [24], but still make mistakes when following user intent [15, 16]. While LLMs continue to improve, human involvement may still be needed, whether to be the main business agent or representative or to provide feedback for further training and fine-tuning [16]. Still, selective intent mining leveraging LLMs' capabilities in named entity recognition (NER) will be useful for an AI-powered auto agent assisting the human agent.

A distinguishing contribution of this research is leveraging the inherent capabilities of Large Language Models (LLMs) in handling multilingual conversations. Unlike earlier tools and techniques, LLMs' advanced NLU and named entity recognition (NER) capabilities were harnessed to extract transactional details from unstructured conversation texts. This enabled the automated structuring of transaction records for database entry, marking a significant departure from traditional methods. Online transactions already occur via messaging apps but predominantly with human agents involved. With their enhanced NLU and NER capabilities, LLMs promise to address these challenges more effectively. The scope of conversation types will be *service conversations* [14], where one party (the customer) seeks a product or service, and the other party (a representative of the organization) provides the product or service. Both parties involve real humans, with the automated AI-powered agent only as a co-pilot to the seller or provider.

1.1 Objectives and Research Questions

This paper explores designing, architecting, and evaluating CC systems leveraging LLMs with inherent multilingual pretraining. The study proposes a hybrid human-AI setup augmenting agents with an auto-agent leveraging LLM NLU, designed using the OTC process pattern applied to conversational UX frameworks.

RQ1) How may the LLMs be harnessed for their natural language understanding (NLU) and named entity recognition (NER) capabilities to extract transaction details automatically?

RQ2) How should the hybrid human-agent CC be evaluated for readiness to handle natural conversations?

The system aims to streamline operations and reduce errors by enhancing the experiences of customers and sales agents during key OTC steps. The hybrid approach was chosen to mitigate the impersonal nature of full automation by recognizing the irreplaceable essence of human interaction and not relying purely on automated agents [11].

2 Review of Related Literature

Conversational user experience (CUX) design is a new design discipline that utilizes natural language processing to provide meaningful user engagement experiences through emerging chatbots and virtual agent platforms [14]. Conversational designers must express the mechanics of human conversation, yet current patterns of visual UX do not help much with this articulation [14]. Aside from the accessibility of the messaging platform, factors like informativeness, assurance, and empathy play a significant role in the purchasing intent of the customers when using a messenger platform [4,21]. Regarding informativeness, the architecture and design aspects involving conversational UX must acknowledge that agent knowledge is as important as knowing what the customer requests [14]. Therefore, part of the architecture must include knowledge database management and retrieval mechanisms (Including product, product description, price, etc.). The Natural Conversational Framework (NCF) consists of "(1) an underlying interaction model, (2) a library of reusable conversational UX patterns, (3) a general method for navigating conversational interfaces, and (4) a novel set of performance metrics based on the interaction model" [14]. The intent of this study is not to develop a fully automated chatbot, so some of the work related to CUX cited earlier is not applicable. AI-based chatbots are also perceived to be impersonal, so humans are still involved [4,21]. Instead, the conversation setup in this study is based on the concept of *human in the loop* and *mutual handover* [18]: small tasks handled by the machine, with the option to escalate to humans for more complex tasks. More importantly, regardless of the level of involvement of automation or humans, a task-oriented dialogue system specifically handles transaction tasks modifying state background (ex., recording a sale) [18]. Unfortunately, most task-oriented dialogue systems are information-seeking based and have quite limited transaction-based support [18], so this study hopes to contribute more to the transactional aspects of dialogue systems.

The evaluation of the efficacy of LLMs in extracting transaction data from natural conversations will require the presence of such conversations for testing, but preparing these conversations manually may be costly and time-consuming, so *data augmentation*, that is, the generation of new data by transforming existing data based on some prior knowledge [5]. The idea of generating and simulating natural conversations as a large language model task is nothing new, as featured in [13]. A similar technique of simulating conversations through synthetic data with the aim of *realism* was also featured in a framework for conversational recommender systems (CRS) by [10]. Related to this, while few-shot learning may be employed, some of the innate characteristics of humans acquired through how LLMs are trained are based on the idea of *homo silicus* [12].

Finally, with a prompting pattern or technique known as chain-of-thought (CoT) [23], LLMs can be induced to produce smaller, intermediate building blocks before answering [17]. The CoT approach to prompting has been found to yield significant performance improvements over other ways of prompting, and this study shall follow a similar approach.

3   Method and Implementation

The pilot case followed the ordering of merchandise (clothing of different sizes) with the buyers and sellers from metropolitan areas in the Philippines as the intended commercial location context.

3.1   Technical Architecture

The auto agent prototype for the pilot case was implemented as a Phoenix LiveView web application, receiving updates from a Viber chatbot webhook and executing actions based on the webhook messages. The choice of Phoenix was attributed to Elixir's capability to handle soft real-time updates, allowing the research to focus on the behavior of the LLM over implementation intricacies. OpenAI's gpt-3.5-turbo model served as the LLM via OpenAI's HTTP API. Supporting technology included Caddy, utilized as a reverse proxy web server, and Postgres, employed as the Phoenix application's database within a Docker container. Initial evaluations used synthetic conversation scenarios generated by the LLMs, deferring the need for real conversation data and addressing ethics and data privacy concerns.

The evaluation of the system entails producing test multilingual conversation data, in this case, using the *taglish* (combination of English and *Tagalog*, a major local dialect in the Philippines). For this research, the approach used for data augmentation involving synthetic conversations is described in the following subsections.

3.2 Knowledge Base

A sample products table was generated manually for the pilot case to represent the standardized product catalog of a business. This database includes 20 rows. Each row represents one clothing product and contains the following attributes:

- Product ID (integer)
- Color (string)
- Name (string)
- UOM (string)
- Unit Price (integer)

3.3 Synthetic Customer Data Preparation

Five different Filipino customer personas were generated for the pilot case. GPT-4 was used to generate the personas. The basis of this approach is from [3] and [12].

The following properties were created for all five customer personas: *demographic attributes, preferred language (English, Tagalog, or Taglish), conversational style,* and *monthly disposable income (in Philippine Pesos)*.

This step involves having ChatGPT generate customer personas. Five personas were created for the initial round. ChatGPT will remember the personas in the session.

3.4 Synthetic Seller Persona Creation

One Filipino seller persona was created using a similar method to Sect. 3.3.
The following details were created for the seller persona:

- Demographic attributes
- Preferred language (English, Tagalog, or *Taglish*)
- Conversational style
- Monthly revenue in Philippine pesos

This step involves asking ChatGPT to generate a seller persona based on certain demographics and attributes, including conversational style, disposable income, etc.

3.5   Synthetic Sales Conversation Creation

Synthetic bilingual customer-initiated conversations were generated using Chat-GPT and fed into the system for evaluation. Customers personas were initiated through prompts based on work done in [1,3,12] on the premise that LLMs have innate knowledge about behaviors based on the way they have been trained through large bodies of text.

GPT-4 was instructed to generate synthetic conversations with four characteristics intended to simulate the interaction between the customer as an agent that expresses relatively unstructured instructions and the seller as an agent that will need to perform structured bookkeeping of transaction details:

– First, that a conversation between a customer and a seller can end with either a confirmed transaction or a mere inquiry.
– Second, that the seller must ask for a customer's desired products, their delivery address, and an explicit confirmation of their order before the seller can consider the transaction to be confirmed.
– Third, that the seller knows about their own product catalog, but that the customer does not necessarily know the product catalog.
– Fourth, that the customer may sometimes change their desired products mid-conversation.

4   Results

Five synthetic conversations were generated using the approach detailed in Sect. 3. In this pilot case, the LLM component of the system is not given any power to affect the conversation directly; it is instead used to do background analysis of the conversation as it occurs. Such soft real-time analyses may be used as a basis for triggering parameterized jobs (e.g., inserting a new transaction record into the database upon determination that a transaction was confirmed solely from the conversation history contents).

4.1   General Applied CoT Approach

One pattern that emerged during the development of the pilot case was a pattern following CoT. The following sections will illustrate the efficacy of treating steps in conversation history analysis as black-box functions that accept a conversation history as a string and return semi-structured data (in this paper, JSON) to use in traditional programming control flow. The primary aim of this pilot case is to explore the ability of LLMs to serve as the implementation details of these black-box functions.

4.2   Presence of Necessary Conditions

The entry function of the conversation analysis tool determined whether the conversation history, up to that point, had satisfied three conditions: first, that the customer had selected products; second, that the customer had given their delivery address; and third, that the customer had explicitly confirmed their order. The function returned one JSON object with three keys referring to these conditions as boolean values.

With this return data, decisions may be made regarding whether the assistant program should proceed to insert a record into a database, prompt the seller to ask for more information, and other relevant operations. In this pilot case, the second step involving 4.3 proceeds if all conditions are true.

4.3 Product Resolution

In this pilot case, the assistant program is also tasked to parse the conversation data, which is relatively unstructured, into structured or semi-structured records of which products in which quantities are part of the transaction.

The first function for this task generates a JSON list where each record represents one conceptual line item in the transaction. At this stage, the function is only tasked to parse the product details as the customer and/or seller expressed them in the conversation.

The second function resolves each line item generated by the first function to an actual product in the products table. It was found that the LLM (GPT-3.5-Turbo) only performed acceptably once each column of the products table used the same terminology as the prompt (e.g., once the column **UOM** in the products table was renamed to "Size"). Only once each line item from the first function has been resolved to a known product can the transaction data be inserted into the database.

The execution of the pilot case has uncovered a potentially challenging and important step in this workflow. In this pilot case, the products table was small enough to include whole in the prompt of the second function; in larger cases, a proper search solution and further decomposition of tasks and functions may become necessary. Product resolution may become the subject of future work.

4.4 Database Insertions

Generating SQL statements to insert a new transaction and its corresponding line items becomes trivial once the relevant product IDs have been parsed out of the unstructured conversation data. The pilot case program uses formatted strings to generate the necessary INSERT statements. A program to be used in production will more likely use parameterized queries to avoid SQL injection.

4.5 Sample Case

This portion of the paper is an illustration of one of the five synthetic conversations and the analysis that the pilot case system performs on the conversation.

Example 1. The following conversation is a synthetic conversation generated by GPT-4. This specific conversation was chosen to illustrate that the assistant program should be able to understand languages other than English in settings where other languages may be used. The original conversation includes emoji Unicode characters that were excluded in this document.

ELENA: Hi po! Tatanong lang po ako kung ano-anong klase ng damit ang meron kayo sa online shop ninyo?

MARIA: Hello po, ma'am Elena! Salamat po sa inyong pagtatanong. Mayroon po kaming iba't ibang uri ng damit, kabilang na ang silk shirts, polo shirts, at dresses. Meron din po tayong iba't ibang kulay at sizes. Ano po ba ang hinahanap ninyo na damit?

ELENA: Mga dresses po sana, yung mga bagay sa edad ko. Ano po ba ang available ninyo?

MARIA: Sigurado po akong mayroon tayong magugustuhan kayo, ma'am Elena. Mayroon po tayong "Sunday Dress" na puti and comes in sizes S, M, L, at XL, ito ay nasa 2450 PHP. At mayroon din po tayong "Cool Night Dress" na Midnight Blue, ito ay nasa 1990 PHP. Pareho po yung mga ito na babagay sa inyo.

ELENA: Yung Sunday Dress na puti po, gusto ko yun. Size M po ako.

MARIA: Magandang pumili po kayo, ma'am Elena! Ilan po ba ang gustong bilhin ninyo na Sunday Dress na puti, size M?

ELENA: Dalawa po sana. Pero teka, pwede rin ba malaman kung ano pa ang ibang kulay ng Sunday Dress?

MARIA: Pasensya na po, ma'am Elena, ngunit ang Sunday Dress po namin ay available lang sa kulay puti. Gusto pa rin po ba ninyo mag-order ng dalawang piraso?

ELENA: Ahh sige po, dalawang puting Sunday Dress na lang po, size M.

MARIA: Narinig ko po, dalawang Sunday Dress na puti, size M, para sa inyo. Para po matuloy natin ang order, pwede ko po bang malaman kung saan ito ipapadala o anong address?

ELENA: Sa Davao City po, pa drop off sa San Lorenzo Ruiz Gkk, Bacaca Road, El Rio Vista Village. Paki double-check yung order ko po ha? Dalawang puting Sunday Dress, size M.

MARIA: Tama po. Dalawang Sunday Dress na puti, size M na ipapadala sa address ninyo sa Davao City. Ang total po ay 4900 PHP. Kung tama na po ang lahat, pwede po bang i-confirm ninyo na gusto ninyong ituloy ang order na ito at ipapadala ko na po ito once may confirmation na?

ELENA: Sige na nga po, ituloy na natin. Iconfirm ko na po ang order. Salamat po.

MARIA: Maraming salamat po, ma'am Elena! Ipa-process ko na po yung order ninyo. Kung may iba po kayong tanong o kailangan, huwag po kayong mahiya na mag-message. Salamat po ulit sa inyong pagtitiwala!

Product Resolution. The first step in the product resolution workflow yields the following JSON from the conversation as shown in Listing 1.1.

Listing 1.1. Example JSON data for an order containing items.

```
{
    "items": [
        {
            "details": {
                "name": "Sunday Dress",
                "size": "M"
            },
            "quantity": 2
        }
    ]
}
```

The second step in the product resolution workflow resolves the data to a known SKU as shown in Listing 1.2.

Listing 1.2. JSON representation of an order with product ID and quantity.

```
{
    "items": [
        {
            "product_id": 10000009,
            "quantity": 2
        }
    ]
}
```

Generated SQL INSERT Statements. Passing the resolved product data and the conversation data (for additional details such as delivery address) through the approach described above results in the INSERT statements shown in Listing 1.3.

Listing 1.3. SQL commands for inserting a new transaction and its associated line items.

```
INSERT INTO app_transaction (created_timestamp,
    delivery_address) VALUES (NOW(), 'San_Lorenzo_Ruiz_Gkk
    ,_Bacaca_Road,_El_Rio_Vista_Village,_Davao_City')
    RETURNING id;

INSERT INTO line_item (created_timestamp, transaction_id,
    product_id, quantity) VALUES (NOW(), 1, 10000009, 2);
```

Assuming initially empty tables, these statements result in the tables as illustrated in Fig 1.

```
$ psql -U postgres

postgres=# SELECT * FROM app_transaction;
 id |       created_timestamp       |      delivery_address
----+------------------------------+----------------------------
  1 | 2024-01-31 03:25:06.156323+00 | San Lorenzo Ruiz Gkk, ...
(1 row)

postgres=# SELECT * FROM line_item;
 id | ... | product_id | quantity | transaction_id
----+-----+------------+----------+----------------
  1 | ... |  10000009  |    2     |              1
(2 rows)
```

Fig. 1. Postgres and SQL commands for retrieving transaction details and associated line items from a database.

4.6 Drawbacks and Limitations

If extended, the approach used in this pilot case may result in numerous calls to the LLM, where many of the calls include the whole conversation history. If used message-by-message, the number of calls to the LLM will be multiplied accordingly. The cost of calling available LLMs (i.e., in time, money, etc.) therefore becomes a consideration in whether this approach will be useful.

The specific approach used in the pilot case suffers from several limitations. First, the pilot case did not consider how to store session state (e.g., whether the current conversation session with the user already has an associated transaction row in the database). In a production-grade system, failure to consider session state may lead to critical errors such as duplicate transaction rows being inserted into the database. One possible solution is to include session data in the prompt alongside the conversation history and to edit the prompts to induce the LLM to consider the session data when making decisions. Second, the pilot case did not comprehensively consider safeguards for cases where the LLM incorrectly evaluates conversation data and thus mistakenly initiates side effects. One possible solution, consistent with the scope of the paper, is to require the seller and/or the seller's agent to confirm side effects (e.g., inserting a record into the database) before the side effects may be executed.

5 Discussions

RQ1) How may the LLMs be harnessed for their natural language understanding (NLU) and named entity recognition (NER) capabilities to extract transaction details automatically?

Development of the pilot case revealed that the CoT prompt engineering pattern, applied as chained black-box functions in an otherwise traditional server-side application, enables the structuring of data in unstructured conversation logs. LLMs are used in the implementation details of these black-box functions.

It was found that the best results were achieved when each function's scope was limited, but this results in a large amount of data transfer to the LLM, which may affect the economics of using this approach depending on which LLMs are available.

RQ2) How should the hybrid human-agent CC be evaluated for readiness to handle natural conversations?

The pilot case was executed on synthetic conversation data. It is a limitation of this paper that the prompts used to generate the synthetic conversations included broad instructions (e.g., the customer may not know the SKUs), which may have introduced bias that affects how well the synthetic conversations represent real conversations. Despite this limitation, the most prominent characteristic of conversational commerce, the weak structure (or lack of structure) in conversational data, was manifest in the synthetic conversations. The approach developed in the pilot case demonstrated an ability to handle such lack of structure, which is sufficient cause to perform future work to refine the approach on real conversation data.

6   Conclusion and Future Work

Transaction entities (products, quantities, prices) from early tests signify the effectiveness of the LLMs NER capabilities in capturing structured data needed to change database state automatically from unstructured chat transaction conversations. However, the scale of the tests performed in the pilot case was small. Future work may require more robust and more scalable methodologies than manual evaluation for evaluating the accuracy of LLM output, especially if real (and therefore potentially unlabeled) data is involved in future work.

After the initial evaluations using synthetic conversation scenarios generated by the LLMs, a significant direction for future work will be incorporating real human feedback. CRS and sentiment analysis will also be incorporated to further personalization and user satisfaction. While synthetic scenarios offer controlled, reproducible conditions and address ethics and data privacy concerns, they may not capture the full spectrum of human behavior and unpredictability. The anticipated outcomes encompass design guidelines, continuous model enhancement strategies, and best practices for integrating LLMs into hybrid human-AI frameworks, aiming to deliver natural CC experiences at scale across languages. While this paper touches upon technical implementation details, they are not its primary focus. These details will be discussed in subsequent papers as part of a larger project. Finally, any intermediate work will still involve humans-in-the-loop, and any attempts to transition to automated conversational agents shall be treated as an effort with a different research track.

Acknowledgments. We want to thank the Department of Quantitative Methods and Information Technology of the John Gokongwei School of Management, the Ateneo Laboratory fro Learning Sciences (ALLS), and the University Research Council of the Ateneo de Manila University for making our participation and future presentation of this study possible.

References

1. Aher, G.V., Arriaga, R.I., Kalai, A.T.: Using large language models to simulate multiple humans and replicate human subject studies. In: International Conference on Machine Learning, pp. 337–371. PMLR (2023)
2. Baidoo-Anu, D., Owusu Ansah, L.: Education in the era of generative artificial intelligence (AI): understanding the potential benefits of ChatGPT in promoting teaching and learning (2023). SSRN 4337484
3. Brand, J., Israeli, A., Ngwe, D.: Using GPT for market research (2023). SSRN 4395751
4. Casimiro, A.V., Chua, C., Pasquin, D.E., Grimaldo, J.R.: The relationship of Facebook messenger marketing to the purchasing intention of the consumers of Philippine MSMEs. J. Bus. Manag. Stud. 4(2), 262–276 (2022). https://www.al-kindipublisher.com/index.php/jbms/article/view/3189
5. Chen, J., Tam, D., Raffel, C., Bansal, M., Yang, D.: An empirical survey of data augmentation for limited data learning in NLP. Trans. Assoc. Comput. Linguistics 11, 191–211 (2023)
6. Cooper, G.: Examining science education in ChatGPT: an exploratory study of generative artificial intelligence. J. Sci. Educ. Technol. 32(3), 444–452 (2023)
7. Cui, L., Huang, S., Wei, F., Tan, C., Duan, C., Zhou, M.: Superagent: a customer service chatbot for e-commerce websites. In: Proceedings of ACL 2017, System Demonstrations, pp. 97–102 (2017)
8. Devlin, J., Chang, M.W., Lee, K., Toutanova, K.: Bert: pre-training of deep bidirectional transformers for language understanding. arXiv preprint arXiv:1810.04805 (2018)
9. Floridi, L., Chiriatti, M.: GPT-3: its nature, scope, limits, and consequences. Mind. Mach. 30, 681–694 (2020)
10. Friedman, L., et al.: Leveraging large language models in conversational recommender systems (2023). http://arxiv.org/abs/2305.07961, arXiv:2305.07961 [cs]
11. Hennigan, L.: What Is Conversational Commerce? (2023). https://www.forbes.com/advisor/business/conversational-commerce/
12. Horton, J.J.: Large language models as simulated economic agents: What can we learn from homo silicus? Technical report, National Bureau of Economic Research (2023)
13. Li, S., et al.: AutoConv: automatically generating information-seeking conversations with large language models. In: Proceedings of the 61st Annual Meeting of the Association for Computational Linguistics (Volume 2: Short Papers), pp. 1751–1762 (2023). https://doi.org/10.18653/v1/2023.acl-short.149, http://arxiv.org/abs/2308.06507, arXiv:2308.06507 [cs]
14. Moore, R.J., Arar, R.: Conversational UX design: an introduction. In: Moore, R.J., Szymanski, M.H., Arar, R., Ren, G.-J. (eds.) Studies in Conversational UX Design. HIS, pp. 1–16. Springer, Cham (2018). https://doi.org/10.1007/978-3-319-95579-7_1
15. Naveed, H., et al.: A Comprehensive Overview of Large Language Models (2023). http://arxiv.org/abs/2307.06435, arXiv:2307.06435 [cs]
16. Ouyang, L., et al.: Training language models to follow instructions with human feedback. Adv. Neural. Inf. Process. Syst. 35, 27730–27744 (2022)
17. Qin, C., Zhang, A., Zhang, Z., Chen, J., Yasunaga, M., Yang, D.: Is ChatGPT a general-purpose natural language processing task solver? (2023). https://doi.org/10.48550/arXiv.2302.06476, http://arxiv.org/abs/2302.06476

18. Quarteroni, S.: Natural Language Processing for Industry: ELCA's experience. Informatik-Spektrum **41**(2), 105–112 (2018). https://doi.org/10.1007/s00287-018-1094-1, http://link.springer.com/10.1007/s00287-018-1094-1, 22 citations (Crossref) [2023-12-18]
19. Rahaman, M.: Can ChatGPT be your friend? Emergence of entrepreneurial research. Emergence of Entrepreneurial Research (2023)
20. Shanahan, M.: Talking About Large Language Models (2023). https://doi.org/10.48550/arXiv.2212.03551, http://arxiv.org/abs/2212.03551
21. Sidlauskiene, J., Joye, Y., Auruskeviciene, V.: AI-based chatbots in conversational commerce and their effects on product and price perceptions. Electronic Markets **33**(1), 24 (2023). https://doi.org/10.1007/s12525-023-00633-8, https://doi.org/10.1007/s12525-023-00633-8, 1 citations (Crossref). Accessed21 Oct 2023
22. Vaswani, A., et al.: Attention is all you need. In: Advances in Neural Information Processing Systems, vol. 30 (2017)
23. Wei, J., et al.: Chain-of-thought prompting elicits reasoning in large language models (2023). https://doi.org/10.48550/arXiv.2201.11903, http://arxiv.org/abs/2201.11903, arXiv:2201.11903 [cs]
24. Winata, G.I., Madotto, A., Lin, Z., Liu, R., Yosinski, J., Fung, P.: Language Models are Few-shot Multilingual Learners (2021). http://arxiv.org/abs/2109.07684, arXiv:2109.07684 [cs]
25. Yandug, J.S.G., De Francia, D.M.B., Paulo, J.O.: Assessment and improvement of Facebook business platforms for SMEs in the Philippines. In: Proceedings of the International Conference on Industrial Engineering and Operations Management, Dubai, UAE (2020). http://www.ieomsociety.org/ieom2020/papers/363.pdf

A Map of Exploring Human Interaction Patterns with LLM: Insights into Collaboration and Creativity

Jiayang Li[(⊠)], Jiale Li, and Yunsheng Su

College of Design and Innovation, Tongji University, Shanghai, China
Jiayanglee0506@gmail.com

Abstract. The outstanding performance capabilities of large language model have driven the evolution of current AI system interaction patterns. This has led to considerable discussion within the Human-AI Interaction (HAII) community. Numerous studies explore this interaction from technical, design, and empirical perspectives. However, the majority of current literature reviews concentrate on interactions across the wider spectrum of AI, with limited attention given to the specific realm of interaction with LLM. We searched for articles on human interaction with LLM, selecting 110 relevant publications meeting consensus definition of Human-AI interaction. Subsequently, we developed a comprehensive Mapping Procedure, structured in five distinct stages, to systematically analyze and categorize the collected publications. Applying this methodical approach, we meticulously mapped the chosen studies, culminating in a detailed and insightful representation of the research landscape. Overall, our review presents an novel approach, introducing a distinctive mapping method, specifically tailored to evaluate human-LLM interaction patterns. We conducted a comprehensive analysis of the current research in related fields, employing clustering techniques for categorization, which enabled us to clearly delineate the status and challenges prevalent in each identified area.

Keywords: Artificial Intelligence (AI) · Human-AI Interaction (HAII) · HCI theory · large language model · Critical review

1 Introduction

large language model(LLM) have significantly enhanced AI systems, particularly in generation, general intelligence, continous learning, and intention understanding [1]. Over the past two years, there has been a rapid increase in the number of studies and novel application designs revolving around LLM-based systems [2]. Technical issues that previously plagued researchers have been effectively optimized or resolved with the advent of large language model [3].

J. Li and J. Li—Both authors contributed equally to this research.

H. Degen and S. Ntoa (Eds.): HCII 2024, LNAI 14736, pp. 60–85, 2024.
https://doi.org/10.1007/978-3-031-60615-1_5

Amid rapid AI development, human-AI interaction is also evolving. Since a multitude of LLM-based solutions and system designs have emerged, expanding existing HAII patterns [4]. However, comprehensive research on human interaction with LLM-based AI systems is lacking, as most HAII reviews focus broadly and overlook specific LLM applications.

In this paper, we introduce a 5 stages mapping pocedure which includes defining the perspective, identifying dimensions, associating relevant concepts within dimensions, establishing evaluation criteria based on concepts, scoring and clustering.

Following the pocedure, we selected 106 out of 1398 papers based on selection criteria that align with the general definition of Human-AI Interaction(HAII). We adopt the perspectives of collaboration and creativity, and establish dimensions of Human-AI Interaction and Implementation-Creation. We then gather concepts pertinent to these dimensions to formulate our evaluation criteria. Finally, we used manual scoring and machine clustering for mapping, leading to an Overview and Map of Human-LLM Interaction Research.

Our mapping shows 4 clusters of human-LLM interaction: Processing tool, Analysis assistant, Creative companion and Processing agent. Overall, key contributions of this article include a new mapping procedure for human-AI interaction and a comprehensive map guided by this procedure. We anticipate this map will outline the field's emerging areas, aiding in the evaluation of current LLM systems and identifying future challenges and directions.

2   Related Work

2.1   The Undergoing Change in HAII Driven by Large Language Model

The advent of LLM and related technologies has led to rapid advancements in AI capabilities, particularly in the areas of general knowledge, intent understanding, and creative abilities. This has significantly altered the patterns and processes by which people interact with AI systems built upon LLM.

General Intelligence—The Capability to Process Complex Tasks and the Ability for Continual Learning. Early artificial intelligence mainly relied on machine learning algorithms such as statistical models [5], with a general logic of constructing a model through learning from existing data to then infer about new data or samples [6]. These models, being trained on specific datasets, are typically constrained to the domain or task relevant to that data, acquiring new knowledge or learning new tasks depends on new training data and the retraining of the model [7]. Within this technical context, AI acts merely as a static tool [8], performing specific low-level tasks such as prediction and classification based on fixed, standardized input data, and then returning the analysis results to the user or to other modules within the system [9–12].

Unlike previous task-specific models and pre-trained models equipped with domain intelligence [2], LLM demonstrate advanced capabilities in various cognitive tasks due to their extensive training on diverse datasets and large parameter sets [13]. LLM can perform various low-level tasks in a generative manner, invoking different external tools [14] or knowledge [15] as needed. In this context, LLM can autonomously manage certain aspects of complex tasks [16], strategically utilizing their diverse abilities, and orchestrating these capabilities to execute high-level tasks [17], such as operating a software development studio entirely through AI [18]. Concurrently, LLM exhibit exceptional in-context learning [19] and few-shot learning capabilities [20], enabling them to continually learn during human interaction. This allows their collaborative abilities and responsibilities to grow and adapt dynamically [21]. Unlike previous Human-AI interaction patterns, where AI systems are often viewed as tools for processing fixed procedures, LLM can be seen as assistants or companions capable of continuous mutual learning and joint development [22].

Intention Understanding—Natural Language Based Interaction and Collaboration. Language and text serve as the primary carriers of information for human communication and collaboration [23]. The capability of AI systems to comprehend human natural language significantly impacts the pattern and efficiency of the interaction process. Prior to the introduction of language models [24], AI's capacity to process natural language was limited. Statistical models, such as the bag-of-words model [25], and early deep learning techniques were usually just capable of language embedding within certain corpora, unable to achieve an understanding and generation of complex semantics.

Users. With the development of self-supervised training [26], the concept of pre-trained models has been widely adopted in the field of natural language processing (NLP) [27]. From the word2vec [28] to BERT [29] and now the widely used GPT [30], AI's capability to understand language has continuously improved. Presently, large language model, trained on massive corpora, exhibit exceptional intent recognition and natural language interaction abilities. They can respond to human needs based on natural language prompts [31], which significantly lowers the barrier for human to engage in collaboration with AI. Nowadays, a considerable number of interaction systems based on natural language have been proposed [32]. It is observable that interactive collaboration based on natural language prompts is gradually becoming a mainstream and promising mode of human-AI interaction [33].

Creativity—The Ability to Create New Content. AIGC has received widespread attention in recent years, but it is not a novel application scenario for AI. As early as 1950, there were research focus on speech generation using the Hidden Markov Model (HMM) [34]. However, due to the limitations in AI's generative capabilities, early generation tasks primarily focused on text-based content creation [35]. With the advancement of computer vision technologies, generative tasks have progressively expanded into the realm of imagery. Notable examples like the Generative Adversarial Networks (GANs) [36] and the diffusion generative models [37]. At this stage of technology, AI is capable of performing various image adjustments, such as stylization and filtering.

In recent years, with the growth of data and model sizes, large language model have exhibited exceptional generative capabilities. They can integrate user instructions to produce creative textual and visual content [38], the quality and usability of which have significantly improved compared to traditional models [39]. Against this backdrop, many conventional creative processes have begun to incorporate AI for collaborative production, such as scriptwriting, copywriting, graphic design, 3D modeling, and more.

2.2   The Current Review of Human-AI Interaction

Different Understanding of A in HAII Review. Human-AI Interaction is a frequently discussed topic within the Human-Computer Interaction field, primarily focusing on the interaction process between human and AI system. To date, there have been many comprehensive review studies on Human-AI Interaction, but the "A" (AI) of interest in these studies can vary considerably depending on the technological and research context. In this article [40], the researchers categorizes AI systems based on user visibility into AI-infused system and backend algorithms, then specifically targeting user-facing systems. Some researchers discuss the prospects for collaboration between human and AI with general capabilities [41]. Additionally, many studies define their focus through distinct application scenarios. For instance, several papers concentrate on the medical domain within article [42–44], while others address the educational field [45,46], and yet another article [47] is centered on management application scenarios.

Current Mapping of HAII. Numerous review studies have utilized diverse mapping approaches to systematically organize the extensive literature on Human-AI Interaction. In this study [48], the authors categorize the literature based on two key dimensions: the state of AI as either in design or usage, and the degree to which AI is human-centered. Conversely, this paper [49] employs a clustering method and post-principal component analysis to categorize AI roles, focusing on human interaction and classifying AI into four distinct roles. The practice of defining and differentiating HAII research based on AI roles is prevalent in the HAII community. In this research [50], researchers defining four roles based on AI's communicative behavior. And in this work [51], Researchers define four AI roles based on the level of moral conflict encountered in human-AI interactions.

3   Method

This review focuses on the interaction patterns between human and large language model. Accordingly, we have selected papers that explicitly identify with and contribute to the paradigms and patterns of Human-LLM Interaction. The papers in this systematic review have been gathered since the release of LLM. We primarily used the Association for Computing Machinery Digital Library (ACM DL) as our source for finding relevant articles on Human-LLM Interaction.

Guided by this core concept, we conducted two rounds of literature screening, identifying 106 publications from an initial pool of 1398. We then employed a combination of manual scoring and machine clustering for mapping. In the mapping process, we adopted an approach similar to the one outlined in framework [48], determining the evaluation approach for Human-LLM interaction patterns through multiple workshop rounds. This included defining the map's perspectives, dimensions, concepts, and evaluation criteria. We applied these criteria to perform manual scoring and machine clustering of the literature. At last we defined the characteristics and differences of these clusters, which illustrated the current research distribution within this map.

3.1   Search and Selection

In the literature search phase, we used the following keywords:

("large-language model" OR "chatgpt" OR "gpt" OR "LLM") AND ("human" OR "user" OR "interaction" OR "human-centered ai" OR "co-creation" OR "coordination" OR "collaboration" OR "user experience" OR "UX" OR "interaction design" OR "prompt design" OR "user study" OR "user perception" OR "tool").

This resulted in a total of 1398 initial items from the ACM Digital Library. We also seek for more information on the criteria or process used to significantly narrow down the selection. For example, "Following two rigorous rounds of manual review", prioritizing relevance to Human-LLM Interaction patterns, we refined our selection to 106 pertinent articles(see Fig. 1).

In the first round of selection, our criteria were twofold: whether the article was published in international journals or major conference proceedings in the HCI field, and whether it focused on general interaction paradigms instead of specific application scenarios of LLM capabilities.

The second round of selection centered on whether the studies addressed user perspectives in the interaction process with LLM, rather than solely focusing on LLM-related technical applications. To achieve these objectives, we established the following criteria:

1. The article must be based on systems that involve interaction between human and LLM (including applications layered on LLM).
2. These articles must present at least one user study to ensure that the LLM-based system is directly user-facing.
3. These articles should not focus solely on LLM applications within a specific domain, but rather on the general modes of interaction between LLM and human.

3.2   Mapping

Throughout the mapping process, we primarily referenced the workflow of mapping methods by [48]. Considering that the existing mapping dimensions are

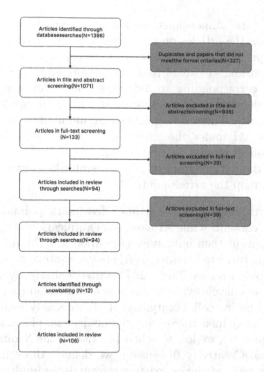

Fig. 1. Flow diagram of the database searches and article screenings.

not fully compatible, we need to summarize the article characteristics of articles included in review in order to propose new dimensions and mapping standards.

During the review and analysis of selected articles, we observed that in collaborative tasks involving human and AI, the main factors influencing the interaction patterns are the collaborative relationship between human and AI, as well as creative level of tasks undertaken by AI. Therefore, we drew upon Ding, Zijian, Chan, Joel's methodology [52] in studying Human-AI Interaction patterns. Collaboration and creativity are being chosen as the main perspectives for our mapping.

Building upon these two analytical perspectives [48,52], we contemplated which specific measurement dimensions could be used. We analyzed the characteristics of human involvement-AI autonomy and complexity-creativity of 110 selected articles. After thorough discussions, we ultimately established two evaluative dimensions: Human-AI and Implement-Creation.

1. Collaboration dimension corresponds to the Human-AI, reflecting the collaborative relationship and the decision-making dominance of human and AI.
2. Creativity dimension corresponds to Implement-Creation, measuring the type of tasks handled by AI in the collaboration process, to reflect AI's creative contribution in the system.

Upon determining these dimensions, we aimed to establish a set of mapping standards to position the articles on the corresponding coordinates. We defined the conceptual stages for each dimension after multiple rounds of discussion. In the Human-AI dimension, we categorized AI roles into four stages: tool, assistant, companion, agent, corresponding to four stages from human to AI decision-making. In the Implement-Creation dimension, we summarized three concepts: process, analysis, create. These conceptual stages aid in understanding the types of tasks handled by AI under the entire collaboration goal, facilitating more precise article classification and scoring criteria.

Next, based on these conceptual stages, we established criteria for each stage to more accurately map the articles onto the map.

1. In the Human-AI dimension, we defined five mark points(see Fig. 2), −2: Human produce content, while AI handles beautification and processing; −1: AI sparks the concept then human execute upon it; 0: human and AI inspire each other, taking turns to produce; 1: AI creates content, then human review, and AI refines based on feedback; 2: Executed entirely by AI without any human input. These levels evaluate the role and decision-making relationship of AI under the entire collaboration goal. To precisely evaluate articles at the same point, we refined the scoring to one decimal place. For instance, for articles with values −2, we located their position in the X range [−2.5, −1.5].

2. In the Implement-Creativity dimension, we defined three mark points (see Fig. 3), Organize and categorize existing information simply, 1: Organize and categorize given data; 2: Analysis and form opinions based on the given data; Generate new content based on given data. These dimensions evaluate the creativity of the task AI undertakes. By refining the scoring to one decimal place, we enhanced the precision of our evaluations, allowing for nuanced distinctions between articles that scored similarly. For instance, for articles with values −1, we located their position in the Y range [−1.5, −0.5].

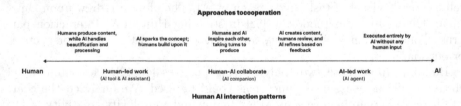

Fig. 2. Types of task division between human and AI in work.

Fig. 3. Innovation level of content produced through human-AI task.

We conducted three rounds of scoring for the 110 publications, with each round designed to incrementally refine and validate the objectivity of each article's score. The overall scores of the article (see Fig. 4).

We then used the K-means algorithm to cluster the 110 scored articles. We chose the k parameter as 4. This decision was based on the average deviation, which measures variability among the data, and the silhouette coefficient, an indicator of how similar an object is to its cluster compared to other clusters(see Fig. 5).

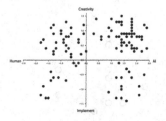

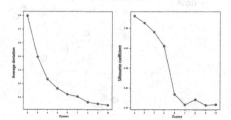

Fig. 4. The overall scores of the article in the map.

Fig. 5. Elbow (left) and silhouette (right) method for determining the optimal number of clusters.

4 Result

Based on our clustering, we defined four primary interaction pattern classifications between human and LLM: 1) Processing Tool, where LLM perform specific, directed tasks; 2) Analysis Assistant, providing analytical support to human input; 3) Processing Agent, engaging in more autonomous tasks with human; 4) Creative Companion, where LLM contribute creatively and collaborative in tasks.

4.1 Processing Tool

The articles labeled orange [53–59] (see Fig. 6), have the following characteristics. Regarding creativity, AI's role is confined to processing given data, lacking original creative input. It is usually responsible for static and specific tasks, processing data and producing outputs in a predetermined format, such as sequence-to-sequence, classification, recognition. From a collaborative standpoint, the work executed by AI and the result output mainly serve as raw material for human's decision-making or used as input for other modules. AI seldom takes the responsibility for decision-making while collaborating with human, it only provides inductions and summaries derived from the processing of existing data. In this scenario, human predominantly make decisions and form opinions, utilizing AI's

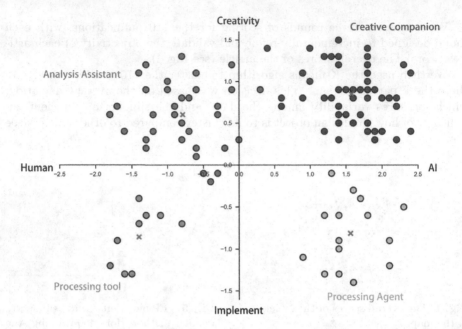

Fig. 6. Map of the feld of human-LLM interaction patterns. The chart displays the comparative volume of research papers in each sector.

work as a foundational basis. Therefore, we categorize the AI in this cluster as a Processing tool.

In this work [59], researchers employ large language model to facilitate user conversational interactions with smartphone interfaces. In terms of collaboration, LLM serve as tools for operation translation from natural language, while in creative aspects, the AI merely performs the function of mapping input data to a limited space of user interface actions. In study [53], the application of LLM focuses on traditional and task-specific functions like information retrieval, highlighting their potential in this domain. In study [58], AI-assisted treatment plans, while generated based on patient data, necessitate further evaluation and refinement by human physicians.

4.2   Analysis Assistant

The articles labeled red [60–95] (see Fig. 6), exhibit the following characteristics. From a collaborative perspective, the task of AI is not confined to summarizing data and returning processing result, rather, it involves formulating opinions based on provided information. AI's opinion would influence human, thereby aiding in collaboration decision-making. From a task creativity standpoint, AI-generated outcomes involve summarizing different perspectives and creatively interpreting the input data. There is a clear hierarchical and structural difference between AI system's input and output, the representation of input data in the output is highly abstract. Consequently, the work performed by AI exhibits a significant degree of creativity. In this cluster, AI functions as an Analysis assistant supporting human decision-making in collaboration, rather than merely serving as a tool.

In these studies [60–74], researchers discuss how human collaborate with AI in writing tasks, such as replying to emails or creating stories, AI would continously provide the reference or suggestion to facilitate human's writting. The following research [75–84] focuses on the interactive programming system that enables continuous mutual suggestions and pairs programming with human for programming tasks. Studies [85–93] delve into human reflection on AI-generated content and its capacity for inspiration, often focusing on Human-AI Interaction aspects like explainability and transparency. And these two studies [94, 95] in question are centered on the application scenarios of AI-assisted image creation, where individuals draw inspiration from designs generated by AI, and through providing feedback, collaborate with AI in the process of image creation.

4.3 Creative Companion

The articles labeled blue [96–142] (see Fig. 6), exhibit the following characteristics. From a collaborative perspective, AI is expected to handle more complex tasks and take on greater responsibility in decision-making. This primarily manifests in AI handling high-level tasks that require a combination of various specific skills working in concert. AI needs to independently decide when to utilize a particular skill at the right time. This also allows AI to reduce the dependency on human during task execution, granting it higher independence and autonomous decision-making authority. On the other hand, from a creative standpoint, human convey their ideas directly to large language model, which autonomously extend and create based on these inputs. AI will generate creations or answers based on the human's description, autonomously extending and interpreting these inputs. The content generated by AI could be inspirational, exhibiting elements of design and art.

In studies [96, 97], researchers explore AI's application in furniture, endowing it with autonomy and creativity to perceive events and generate content like diaries [96] and work suggestions [100]. In studies [98–121], they primarily presents chatbot that utilize natural language communication as their form of interaction to assist in responding to users' open-ended queries, such as psychological healing [98] and history learning [106]. In studies [122–136], AI systems are tasked with transforming input data into stylized and creative outputs, such as converting prose into Persian poetry [134], or generating comics from programming code [125]. The research in group [137–142] focuses on AI refining and elaborating on creative content from rough descriptions, such as generating complete game designs [137] or distilling literary ideas from existing articles [142].

4.4 Processing Agent

The articles labeled green [143–157] (see Fig. 6), exhibit the following characteristics. In the process of collaboration with human, AI will carry out a series of
complex tasks, leveraging its general capabilities for decision-making and task
processing. The system exhibits traits akin to a Creative Companion, implying
its ability to autonomously execute complex tasks and make decisions during key
collaborative phases. From a creative perspective, these tasks generally pertain
to the organization and descriptive summarization of data. The AI's output,
while only a summary of the input data, shows a higher complexity level than a
standard processing tool, though it does not exhibit additional creativity.

In this series of studies [143–154], AI operates with a high degree of autonomy in analyzing relevant information and summarizing content. This includes
tasks such as generating descriptive documents that outline human work [143],
selecting story endings from existing information [148], or presenting medical
papers interactively [146]. This research group utilizes AI to simulate user operations, including emulating user responses in completing questionnaires [155]
and mimicking user behavior within a search system [156].

5 Discussion

5.1 Mapping Methodology Based on Human and Algorithmic
       Approaches

This study uniquely contributes to both theoretical understanding and practical
applications in mapping Human-LLM Interaction patterns. In terms of mapping
methods, the scarcity of comprehensive review studies on Human-AI Interaction, particularly in the domain of interaction with LLM, results in a lack of
directly applicable mapping approaches in this field. Therefore, we developed
mapping methods specifically designed to capture the difference and complexities of human-AI interaction patterns. Our method consists of five steps: defining the perspective, identifying dimensions, associating relevant concepts within
dimensions, establishing evaluation criteria based on concepts, scoring and
clustering.

Firstly, our observations from the selected articles revealed two key influences
of LLM on HAII patterns: the relationship of Human-AI Collaboration and their
distinct task responsibilities. Hence, we chose collaboration and creativity as the
research perspectives for this review. Secondly, we identified studies on evaluating collaboration and creativity to determine the two evaluative dimensions:
Human-AI and Implement-Creation. Thirdly, upon the classification concepts
we found, combined with the characteristics of the selected articles and after
multiple rounds of discussion, we finalized the conceptual stages for each dimension. This process aids in a more intuitive understanding of different task states
at various stages and prepares specific standards for the two dimensions. Next,
through discussion and based on the different conceptual stages, we established

criteria for each stage, enabling us to more accurately map articles to their corresponding positions on the map. Finally, based on these scoring criteria, we conducted multiple rounds of scoring for the 110 selected articles and used the K-means algorithm for machine clustering, presenting an objective overview of the main type distributions in current research.

The conceptual stages we selected are partly similar to those defined in the source literature but are not completely identical. For instance, the definitions of AI tools and AI assistants, according to the former definition, AI tools are characterized as having low human involvement and low AI autonomy, and AI assistants are represented as having low human involvement and high AI autonomy. This aligns with our positioning of AI tools and AI assistants in the Human-AI dimension. While as we also consider the type of tasks each concept should handle in our definitions, AI tools in our study are involved in low-level tasks, whereas AI assistants handle the creation of viewpoints, which are relatively higher-level tasks. Our need to categorize conceptual stages into two distinct dimensions results in variations from the positions outlined in the referenced literature.

5.2   Differences Between Clusters

Building on our mapping and clustering results, we delved into a detailed analysis, focusing on the quantitative distribution and distinct characteristics of each cluster.

Research Interests. We analyzed the number of papers in each cluster and found that over three-quarters of the articles focused on AI's involvement in creative tasks(see Fig. 7).

Almost half of the papers were concentrated in the Creative companion cluster. This indicates that the AI systems based on large language model exhibit a heightened state of creativity and autonomy in task execution. This aligns with the current intuitive understanding that the performance enhancements of LLM compared to traditional AI are primarily evident in creativity and the execution of complex tasks. Therefore, more research interests are focusing on creative content generation, exploring how to grant AI more autonomy in decision-making within collaborative work with human.

Simultaneously, the tasks executed by AI are becoming more creative. This conclusion can be drawn from the observation that over three-quarters of the articles are concentrated in the clusters of Creative Companion and Analysis Assistant, both of which are positioned high on the creative dimension map. Compared to traditional AI tasks (such as classification, prediction, identification of given data), AI is now performing more creative tasks like image generation [135], scriptwriting [64]. AI, while operating within the framework of human guidance and requirements, goes beyond mere interpretation, creatively generating new content and insights."

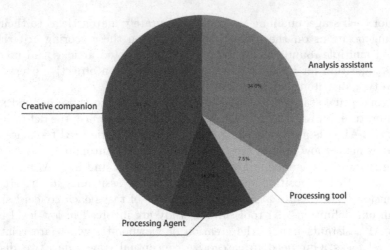

Fig. 7. The current research interests in the field of Human-LLM Interaction patterns.

Category Differences. To clarify the differences between similar or easily confused categories, we engaged in discussions to more precisely define their characteristics.

From the perspective of Collaboration, the differences between clusters cannot be simply summarized as the specific tasks AI performs. Rather, they are the relative relationship of these tasks to the overall collaborative goal, specifically manifesting in the extent to which AI's work influences decision-making in the collaborative process. Consider the scriptwriting task, for instance: in some studies [63], AI-generated scripts offer inspiration that human evaluate and potentially adopt in their writing. In other tasks, AI first collects human ideas or pre-work, and then generates the final script content [131]. Hence, in the latter case, the positioning on Collaboration mapping is closer to Human. These differences are mainly evident when comparing Creative Companion with Analysis Assistant.

We also find differences in the Collaboration dimension reflected in the complexity of tasks AI performs, such as AI's responsibilities in providing optimization suggestions to the system. Some works focus on using large language model to do the simple task like operation signal transformation [59]. Other works extend this technology to simulate and deduce a complex system behavior [156], where the latter handles more complex tasks and requires AI to exercise more autonomous decision-making and capacity planning, thus being mapped closer to AI on the Collaboration dimension. This difference is primarily manifested between Processing Tool and Processing Agent.

From a Creativity perspective, differences between categories stem not merely from the AI-generated content's structure or type but from the degree of creativity relative to the input. It is more about the degree of creativity in AI's output relative to the input it receives. For example, in code generation tasks, some works generate code based on detailed functional descriptions by professionals, translating from structural description like information in jupyter notebook to code [56]. Others generate code around human needs and abstract descriptions [78]. Compared to the former, the latter has more abstract input information, and the disparity between input and output data is more pronounced, thus being mapped closer to the Create in the Creativity dimension. This difference is evident between Analysis Assistant and Processing Tool.

The same difference can also be seen in different chatbots. In chatbots engaged in specific interactions with human, some are not restricted in their reference to external knowledge or context, conducting conversations on any subject with human [113]. In contrast, some chatbots are limited to explaining and describing given knowledge or documents [145]. Compared to the latter, the former produces content with higher degrees of freedom and is thus mapped closer to the Create position in the Creativity dimension. This difference is exemplified between Creative Companion and Processing Agent.

5.3   About the Vacancy in the Mapping

In our analysis, we identified a opbivous vacant space in the mapping (see Fig. 6). There are very few papers distributed within this area. Our explanation of this phenomenon is that the characteristics corresponding to the collaboration dimension in this interval $(-1, 1)$ require AI to provide continuous suggestions and participate in joint decision-making. Consequently, AI must focus on explaining its recommendations, prioritizing the transparency and interpretability of information. This necessitates that AI possesses a certain level of creative ability, such as generating explanations for its own work [148]. The task of providing explanations and clarifications inherently involves creativity, which accounts for the generally higher levels of creativity observed in AI personas within this specific interval.

5.4   Future Directions

As the understanding capabilities of large language model continue to improve, allowing for deeper comprehension of human expressions, the future will likely see LLM as companions in a wider array of specific application domains and collaborative tasks. Moreover, with the ongoing enhancement of LLM' generative abilities, their versatility, and transfer capabilities, the range of tasks in Human-LLM Interactions is set to expand, enabling LLM to undertake more creative work across various fields. In practical use, future interactions with large language model are expected to continue exhibiting the current three trends of task division:

1. Human-led tasks: Here, LLM primarily handle process execution and some decisions that are less critical to the overall task. human take charge of core decision-making and control the overall direction of the task.
2. Collaborative tasks: Both parties provide suggestions and jointly make decisions and execute the task.
3. AI-led tasks: Human mainly provide input, while the overall task is decided and executed by the LLM.

6   Limitation and Future Work

This article has certain limitations. During the literature search phase, we only organized articles published before July 2023. Given the rapid iteration of large language model related technologies, it is possible that new collaborative methods have emerged that were not included in this review. In the manual scoring phase, although the authors conducted three joint scoring sessions to be as objective as possible, manual analysis still retains a degree of subjectivity. To address this issue, future work could involve better integration of algorithms into the classification dimensions (such as using principal component analysis methods) to ensure a more objective assessment.

7   Conclusion

Interactions between human and AI are becoming increasingly common in today's society. This article organizes research related to Human-LLM Interaction modalities that have emerged since the advent of LLM. Adopting collaboration and creativity as research perspectives, it analyzes these articles from the Human-AI and Implement-Creation dimensions, constructing an overview and map of human-AI interaction research (HAII Research Overview and Map). On this basis, the study identified four main areas through machine clustering: Processing Tool, Analysis Assistant, Creative Companion, and Processing Agent. By conducting a secondary reading of articles within each cluster, we extracted the characteristics and research interests of each category and clarified the differences between them through discussion.

Overall, our review offers new perspectives and methods for understanding and evaluating Human-LLM Interaction patterns. It organizes existing research in the field based on this perspective, further classifies these studies through mapping, and clarifies the current status and challenges of each category.

Acknowledgments. This article received funding support from the Tongji University Graduate Important International Academic Conference Award Fund and the research project on key technologies of hydrogen energy town fuel cell integrated energy systems.

References

1. Chang, Y., et al.: A survey on evaluation of large language models. ACM Trans. Intell. Syst. Technol. **15**, 3641289 (2024)
2. Zhao, W.X., et al.: A survey of large language models. arXiv:2303.18223 [cs] (2023)
3. Min, B., et al.: Recent advances in natural language processing via large pre-trained language models: a survey. arXiv:2111.01243 [cs] (2021)
4. Hadi, M.U., et al.: A Survey on Large Language Models: Applications, Challenges, Limitations, and Practical Usage. preprint July 2023 (2023)
5. Muggleton, S.: Alan Turing and the development of artificial intelligence. AI Commun. **27**(1), 3–10 (2014)
6. Mahesh, B.: Machine Learning Algorithms -A Review (2019)
7. Niu, S., Liu, Y., Wang, J., Song, H.: A decade survey of transfer learning (2010–2020). IEEE Trans. Artif. Intell. **1**(2), 151–166 (2020). Conference Name: IEEE Transactions on Artificial Intelligence
8. Smith, R.G., Eckroth, J.: Building AI applications: yesterday, today, and tomorrow. AI Mag. **38**(1), 6–22 (2017). Number: 1
9. Pang, B., Lee, L., Vaithyanathan, S.: Thumbs up? Sentiment Classification using Machine Learning Techniques (2002). arXiv:cs/0205070
10. Li, J., Sun, A., Han, J., Li, C.: A survey on deep learning for named entity recognition. IEEE Trans. Knowl. Data Eng. **34**(1), 50–70 (2022). Conference Name: IEEE Transactions on Knowledge and Data Engineering
11. Full article: A survey of image classification methods and techniques for improving classification performance
12. Automatic Video Classification: A Survey of the Literature | IEEE Journals & Magazine | IEEE Xplore
13. Bubeck, S., et al.: Sparks of artificial general intelligence: early experiments with GPT-4. arXiv:2303.12712 [cs] (2023)
14. Qin, Y., et al.: Tool learning with foundation models. arXiv:2304.08354 [cs] (2023)
15. [2104.08164] Editing Factual Knowledge in Language Models
16. Zhou, D., et al.: Least-to-most prompting enables complex reasoning in large language models. arXiv:2205.10625 [cs] (2023)
17. [2303.17760] CAMEL: Communicative Agents for "Mind" Exploration of Large Language Model Society
18. Qian, C., et al.: Communicative Agents for Software Development. arXiv:2307.07924 [cs] (2023)
19. [2301.00234] A Survey on In-context Learning
20. Brown, T., et al.: Language models are few-shot learners. In: Advances in Neural Information Processing Systems, vol. 33, pp. 1877–1901 (2020)
21. [2301.02111] Neural Codec Language Models are Zero-Shot Text to Speech Synthesizers
22. Zheng, Q., et al.: Synergizing human-AI agency: a guide of 23 heuristics for service co-creation with LLM-based agents. arXiv:2310.15065 [cs] (2023)
23. Communication and collective action: language and the evolution of human cooperation - ScienceDirect
24. Jing, K., Xu, J.: A survey on neural network language models. arXiv:1906.03591 [cs] (2019)
25. Zhang, Y., Jin, R., Zhou, Z.-H.: Understanding bag-of-words model: a statistical framework. Int. J. Mach. Learn. Cybern. **1**(1), 43–52 (2010)
26. Technologies | Free Full-Text | A Survey on Contrastive Self-Supervised Learning

27. Pre-Trained Language Models and Their Applications - ScienceDirect
28. Using Word2Vec to process big text data | IEEE Conference Publication | IEEE Xplore
29. Devlin, J., Chang, M.-W., Lee, K., Toutanova, K.: BERT: pre-training of deep bidirectional transformers for language understanding. arXiv:1810.04805 [cs] (2019)
30. [1909.00512] How Contextual are Contextualized Word Representations? Comparing the Geometry of BERT, ELMo, and GPT-2 Embeddings
31. Cao, Y., et al.: A comprehensive survey of AI-generated content (AIGC): a history of generative AI from GAN to ChatGPT. arXiv:2303.04226 [cs] (2023)
32. Topsakal, O., Akinci, T.C.: Creating large language model applications utilizing LangChain: a primer on developing LLM apps fast. In: International Conference on Applied Engineering and Natural Sciences, vol. 1, pp. 1050–1056 (2023)
33. Why Johnny Can't Prompt: How Non-AI Experts Try (and Fail) to Design LLM Prompts | Proceedings of the 2023 CHI Conference on Human Factors in Computing Systems
34. Knill, K., Young, S.: Hidden Markov models in speech and language processing. In: Ide, N., Véronis, J., Young, S., Bloothooft, G. (eds.) Corpus-Based Methods in Language and Speech Processing. Text, Speech and Language Technology, vol. 2, pp. 27–68. Springer, Dordrecht (1997). https://doi.org/10.1007/978-94-017-1183-8_2
35. Iqbal, T., Qureshi, S.: The survey: text generation models in deep learning. J. King Saud Univ. - Comput. Inf. Sci. **34**(6, Part A), 2515–2528 (2022)
36. Goodfellow, I., Pouget-Abadie, J., Mirza, M., Bing, X., Warde-Farley, D., Ozair, S., Courville, A., Bengio, Y.: Generative adversarial networks. Commun. ACM **63**(11), 139–144 (2020)
37. Denoising Diffusion Probabilistic Models
38. Wu, Z., Ji, D., Yu, K., Zeng, X., Wu, D., Shidujaman, M.: AI creativity and the human-AI co-creation model. In: Kurosu, M. (ed.) HCII 2021. LNCS, vol. 12762, pp. 171–190. Springer, Cham (2021). https://doi.org/10.1007/978-3-030-78462-1_13
39. Zhang, C., et al.: A complete survey on generative AI (AIGC): is ChatGPT from GPT-4 to GPT-5 All You Need? arXiv:2303.11717 [cs] (2023)
40. Guidelines for Human-AI Interaction | Proceedings of the 2019 CHI Conference on Human Factors in Computing Systems
41. Future Trends for Human-AI Collaboration: A Comprehensive Taxonomy of AI/AGI Using Multiple Intelligences and Learning Styles
42. IJERPH | Free Full-Text | A Review on Human-AI Interaction in Machine Learning and Insights for Medical Applications
43. JMIR Human Factors - Human Factors and Technological Characteristics Influencing the Interaction of Medical Professionals With Artificial Intelligence-Enabled Clinical Decision Support Systems: Literature Review
44. Healthcare | Free Full-Text | On How Chronic Conditions Affect the Patient-AI Interaction: A Literature Review
45. Sustainability | Free Full-Text | Artificial Intelligence and Reflections from Educational Landscape: A Review of AI Studies in Half a Century
46. Bozkurt, A.: Unleashing the potential of generative AI, conversational agents and chatbots in educational praxis: a systematic review and bibliometric analysis of GenAI in education. Open Praxis **15**(4), 261–270 (2023)
47. Patil, R.S., Kulkarni, S.B., Gaikwad, V.L.: Artificial intelligence in pharmaceutical regulatory affairs. Drug Discovery Today **28**(9), 103700 (2023)

48. Capel, T., Brereton, M.: What is human-centered about human-centered AI? A map of the research landscape. In: Proceedings of the 2023 CHI Conference on Human Factors in Computing Systems, Hamburg Germany, April 2023, pp. 1–23. ACM (2023)
49. Kim, T., Molina, M.D., Rheu, M.(M.J.), Zhan, E.S., Peng, W.: One AI does not fit all: a cluster analysis of the Laypeople's perception of AI roles. In: Proceedings of the 2023 CHI Conference on Human Factors in Computing Systems, CHI '23, New York, NY, USA, April 2023, pp. 1–20. Association for Computing Machinery (2023)
50. Sundar, S.S., Lee, E.-J.: Rethinking communication in the era of artificial intelligence. Hum. Commun. Res. **48**(3), 379–385 (2022)
51. Bad machines corrupt good morals | Nature Human Behaviour
52. Mapping the Design Space of Interactions in Human-AI Text Co-creation Tasks - NASA/ADS
53. Penha, G., Palumbo, E., Aziz, M., Wang, A., Bouchard, H.: Improving content retrievability in search with controllable query generation. In: Proceedings of the ACM Web Conference 2023, WWW 2023, New York, NY, USA, April 2023, pp. 3182–3192. Association for Computing Machinery (2023)
54. Lu, X., Fan, S., Houghton, J., Wang, L., Wang, X.: ReadingQuizMaker: a human-NLP collaborative system that supports instructors to design high-quality reading quiz questions. In: Proceedings of the 2023 CHI Conference on Human Factors in Computing Systems, CHI 2023, New York, NY, USA, April 2023, pp. 1–18. Association for Computing Machinery (2023)
55. Lee, Y., Chung, J.J.Y., Kim, T.S., Song, J.Y., Kim, J.: Promptiverse: scalable generation of scaffolding prompts through human-AI hybrid knowledge graph annotation. In: Proceedings of the 2022 CHI Conference on Human Factors in Computing Systems, CHI 2022, New York, NY, USA, April 2022, pp. 1–18. Association for Computing Machinery (2022)
56. Mcnutt, A.M., Wang, C., Deline, R.A., Drucker, S.M.: On the design of AI-powered code assistants for notebooks. In: Proceedings of the 2023 CHI Conference on Human Factors in Computing Systems, CHI 2023, New York, NY, USA, April 2023, pp. 1–16. Association for Computing Machinery (2023)
57. Karinshak, E., Liu, S.X., Park, J.S., Hancock, J.T.: Working with AI to persuade: examining a large language model's ability to generate pro-vaccination messages. Proc. ACM Hum.-Comput. Interact. **7**(CSCW1), 1161–11629 (2023)
58. Yang, Q., et al.: Harnessing biomedical literature to calibrate clinicians' trust in AI decision support systems. In: Proceedings of the 2023 CHI Conference on Human Factors in Computing Systems, CHI '23, New York, NY, USA, April 2023, pp. 1–14. Association for Computing Machinery (2023)
59. Wang, B., Li, G., Li, Y.: Enabling conversational interaction with mobile UI using large language models. In: Proceedings of the 2023 CHI Conference on Human Factors in Computing Systems, CHI 2023, New York, NY, USA, April 2023, pp. 1–17. Association for Computing Machinery (2023)
60. Singh, N., Bernal, G., Savchenko, D., Glassman, E.L.: Where to hide a stolen elephant: leaps in creative writing with multimodal machine intelligence. ACM Trans. Comput.-Hum. Interact. (2022). Just Accepted
61. Bhat, A., Agashe, S., Oberoi, P., Mohile, N., Jangir, R., Joshi, A.: Interacting with next-phrase suggestions: how suggestion systems aid and influence the cognitive processes of writing. In: Proceedings of the 28th International Conference on Intelligent User Interfaces, IUI 2023, New York, NY, USA, March 2023, pp. 436–452. Association for Computing Machinery (2023)

62. Liu, Y., Mittal, A., Yang, D., Bruckman, A.: Will AI console me when i lose my pet? Understanding perceptions of AI-mediated email writing. In: CHI Conference on Human Factors in Computing Systems, New Orleans LA USA, April 2022, pp. 1–13. ACM (2022)

63. Shakeri, H., Neustaedter, C., DiPaola, S.: SAGA: collaborative storytelling with GPT-3. In: Companion Publication of the 2021 Conference on Computer Supported Cooperative Work and Social Computing, CSCW 2021, New York, NY, USA, October 2021, pp. 163–166. Association for Computing Machinery (2021)

64. Yuan, A., Coenen, A., Reif, E., Ippolito, D.: Wordcraft: story writing with large language models. In: 27th International Conference on Intelligent User Interfaces, Helsinki Finland, March 2022, pp. 841–852. ACM (2022)

65. Gero, K.I., Long, T., Chilton, L.B.: Social dynamics of AI support in creative writing. In: Proceedings of the 2023 CHI Conference on Human Factors in Computing Systems, CHI 2023, New York, NY, USA, April 2023, pp. 1–15. Association for Computing Machinery (2023)

66. Wu, T., Terry, M., Cai, C.J.: AI chains: transparent and controllable human-AI interaction by chaining large language model prompts. In: CHI Conference on Human Factors in Computing Systems, New Orleans LA USA, April 2022, pp. 1–22. ACM (2022)

67. Fu, L., Newman, B., Jakesch, M., Kreps, S.: Comparing sentence-level suggestions to message-level suggestions in AI-mediated communication. In: Proceedings of the 2023 CHI Conference on Human Factors in Computing Systems, CHI '23, New York, NY, USA, April 2023, pp. 1–13. Association for Computing Machinery (2023)

68. Kim, J., Suh, S., Chilton, L.B., Xia, H.: Metaphorian: leveraging large language models to support extended metaphor creation for science writing. In: Proceedings of the 2023 ACM Designing Interactive Systems Conference, DIS '23, New York, NY, USA, July 2023, pp. 115–135. Association for Computing Machinery (2023)

69. Buschek, D., Zürn, M., Eiband, M.: The impact of multiple parallel phrase suggestions on email input and composition behaviour of native and non-native English writers. In: Proceedings of the 2021 CHI Conference on Human Factors in Computing Systems, May 2021, pp. 1–13 (2021). arXiv:2101.09157 [cs]

70. Karolus, J., Feger, S.S., Schmidt, A., Woźniak, P.W.: Your text is hard to read: facilitating readability awareness to support writing proficiency in text production. In: Proceedings of the 2023 ACM Designing Interactive Systems Conference, DIS '23, New York, NY, USA, July 2023, pp. 147–160. Association for Computing Machinery (2023)

71. Goodman, S.M., et al.: LaMPost: design and evaluation of an AI-assisted email writing prototype for adults with dyslexia. In: Proceedings of the 24th International ACM SIGACCESS Conference on Computers and Accessibility, ASSETS '22, New York, NY, USA, October 2022, pp. 1–18. Association for Computing Machinery (2022)

72. Biermann, O.C., Ma, N.F., Yoon, D.: From tool to companion: storywriters want AI writers to respect their personal values and writing strategies. In: Proceedings of the 2022 ACM Designing Interactive Systems Conference, DIS '22, New York, NY, USA, June 2022, pp. 1209–1227. Association for Computing Machinery (2022)

73. Jakesch, M., Bhat, A., Buschek, D., Zalmanson, L., Naaman, M.: Co-writing with opinionated language models affects users' views. In: Proceedings of the 2023 CHI Conference on Human Factors in Computing Systems, CHI '23, New York, NY, USA, April 2023, pp. 1–15. Association for Computing Machinery (2023)

74. Bhavya, B., Xiong, J., Zhai, C.: CAM: a large language model-based creative analogy mining framework. In: Proceedings of the ACM Web Conference 2023, WWW '23, New York, NY, USA, April 2023, pp. 3903–3914. Association for Computing Machinery (2023)

75. Robe, P., Kuttal, S.K.: Designing PairBuddy-a conversational agent for pair programming. ACM Trans. Comput.-Hum. Interact. **29**(4), 34:1-34:44 (2022)

76. Ross, S.I., Martinez, F., Houde, S., Muller, M., Weisz, J.D.: The programmer's assistant: conversational interaction with a large language model for software development. In: Proceedings of the 28th International Conference on Intelligent User Interfaces, Sydney NSW Australia, March 2023, pp. 491–514. ACM (2023)

77. Robe, P., Kuttal, S.K., AuBuchon, J., Hart, J.: Pair programming conversations with agents vs. developers: challenges and opportunities for SE community. In: Proceedings of the 30th ACM Joint European Software Engineering Conference and Symposium on the Foundations of Software Engineering, ESEC/FSE 2022, New York, NY, USA, November 2022, pp. 319–331. Association for Computing Machinery (2022)

78. Jonsson, M., Tholander, J.: Cracking the code: co-coding with AI in creative programming education. In: Proceedings of the 14th Conference on Creativity and Cognition, C&C '22, New York, NY, USA, June 2022, pp. 5–14. Association for Computing Machinery (2022)

79. Weisz, J.D., et al.: Better together? An evaluation of AI-supported code translation. In: 27th International Conference on Intelligent User Interfaces, IUI '22, New York, NY, USA, March 2022, pp. 369–391. Association for Computing Machinery (2022)

80. Al Madi, N.: How readable is model-generated code? Examining readability and visual inspection of Github copilot. In: Proceedings of the 37th IEEE/ACM International Conference on Automated Software Engineering, ASE '22, New York, NY, USA, January 2023, pp. 1–5. Association for Computing Machinery (2023)

81. Jiang, E., et al.: Discovering the syntax and strategies of natural language programming with generative language models. In: Proceedings of the 2022 CHI Conference on Human Factors in Computing Systems, CHI '22, New York, NY, USA, April 2022, pp. 1–19. Association for Computing Machinery (2022)

82. Kazemitabaar, M., Chow, J., Ma, C.K.T., Ericson, B.J., Weintrop, D., Grossman, T.: Studying the effect of AI code generators on supporting novice learners in introductory programming. In: Proceedings of the 2023 CHI Conference on Human Factors in Computing Systems, CHI 2023, New York, NY, USA, April 2023, pp. 1–23. Association for Computing Machinery (2023)

83. Barke, S., James, M.B., Polikarpova, N.: Grounded copilot: how programmers interact with code-generating models. Proc. ACM Program. Lang. **7**(OOPSLA1), 7885–78111 (2023)

84. Liu, M.X., et al.: "What it wants me to say": bridging the abstraction gap between end-user programmers and code-generating large language models. In: Proceedings of the 2023 CHI Conference on Human Factors in Computing Systems, CHI '23, New York, NY, USA, April 2023, pp. 1–31. Association for Computing Machinery (2023)

85. Danry, V., Pataranutaporn, P., Mao, Y., Maes, P.: Don't just tell me, ask me: AI systems that intelligently frame explanations as questions improve human logical discernment accuracy over causal AI explanations. In: Proceedings of the 2023 CHI Conference on Human Factors in Computing Systems, CHI '23, New York, NY, USA, April 2023, pp. 1–13. Association for Computing Machinery (2023)

86. Gero, K.I., Liu, V., Chilton, L.: Sparks: inspiration for science writing using language models. In: Proceedings of the 2022 ACM Designing Interactive Systems Conference, DIS '22, pages 1002–1019, New York, NY, USA, June 2022. Association for Computing Machinery

87. Wang, Q., Madaio, M., Kane, S., Kapania, S., Terry, M., Wilcox, L.: Designing responsible AI: adaptations of UX practice to meet responsible AI challenges. In: Proceedings of the 2023 CHI Conference on Human Factors in Computing Systems, CHI '23, New York, NY, USA, April 2023, pp. 1–16. Association for Computing Machinery (2023)

88. Wallace, B., Hilton, C., Nymoen, K., Torresen, J., Martin, C.P., Fiebrink, R.: Embodying an interactive AI for dance through movement ideation. In: Proceedings of the 15th Conference on Creativity and Cognition, C&C '23, New York, NY, USA, June 2023, pp. 454–464. Association for Computing Machinery (2023)

89. Robertson, J., et al.: Wait, but why? Assessing behavior explanation strategies for real-time strategy games. In: 26th International Conference on Intelligent User Interfaces, IUI '21, New York, NY, USA, April 2021, pp. 32–42. Association for Computing Machinery (2021)

90. Guo, S., Zhang, S., Sun, W., Ren, P., Chen, Z., Ren, Z.: Towards explainable conversational recommender systems. In: Proceedings of the 46th International ACM SIGIR Conference on Research and Development in Information Retrieval, SIGIR '23, New York, NY, USA, July 2023, pp. 2786–2795. Association for Computing Machinery (2023)

91. Zamfirescu-Pereira, J.D., Wong, R.Y., Hartmann, B., Yang, Q.: Why Johnny can't prompt: how non-AI experts try (and fail) to design LLM prompts. In: Proceedings of the 2023 CHI Conference on Human Factors in Computing Systems, CHI '23, New York, NY, USA, April 2023, pp. 1–21. Association for Computing Machinery (2023)

92. Fraile Navarro, D., Kocaballi, A.B., Dras, M., Berkovsky, S.: Collaboration, not confrontation: understanding general practitioners' attitudes towards natural language and text automation in clinical practice. ACM Trans. Comput.-Hum. Interact. **30**(2), 291–2934 (2023)

93. Ruoff, M., Myers, B.A., Maedche, A.: ONYX: assisting users in teaching natural language interfaces through multi-modal interactive task learning. In: Proceedings of the 2023 CHI Conference on Human Factors in Computing Systems, CHI '23, New York, NY, USA, April 2023, pp. 1–16. Association for Computing Machinery (2023)

94. Huang, F., Schoop, E., Ha, D., Canny, J.: Scones: towards conversational authoring of sketches. In: Proceedings of the 25th International Conference on Intelligent User Interfaces, IUI '20, New York, NY, USA, March 2020, pp. 313–323. Association for Computing Machinery (2020)

95. van der Burg, V., de Boer, G., Akdag Salah, A.A., Chandrasegaran, S., Lloyd, P.: Objective portrait: a practice-based inquiry to explore AI as a reflective design partner. In: Proceedings of the 2023 ACM Designing Interactive Systems Conference, DIS '23, New York, NY, USA, July 2023, pp. 387–400. Association for Computing Machinery (2023)

96. Cho, H., Lee, J., Ku, B., Jeong, Y., Yadgarova, S., Nam, T.-J.: ARECA: a design speculation on everyday products having minds. In: Proceedings of the 2023 ACM Designing Interactive Systems Conference, DIS '23, New York, NY, USA, July 2023, pp. 31–44. Association for Computing Machinery (2023)

97. Rajcic, N., McCormack, J.: Message ritual: a posthuman account of living with lamp. In: Proceedings of the 2023 CHI Conference on Human Factors in Computing Systems, CHI '23, New York, NY, USA, April 2023, pp. 1–16. Association for Computing Machinery (2023)

98. Srivastava, A., Pandey, I., Akhtar, Md.S., Chakraborty, T.: Response-act guided reinforced dialogue generation for mental health counseling. In: Proceedings of the ACM Web Conference 2023, WWW '23, New York, NY, USA, April 2023, pp. 1118–1129. Association for Computing Machinery (2023)

99. Xiao, Z., Li, T.W., Karahalios, K., Sundaram, H.: Inform the uninformed: improving online informed consent reading with an AI-powered chatbot. In: Proceedings of the 2023 CHI Conference on Human Factors in Computing Systems, CHI '23, New York, NY, USA, April 2023, pp. 1–17. Association for Computing Machinery (2023)

100. Arakawa, R., Yakura, H., Goto, M.: CatAlyst: domain-extensible intervention for preventing task procrastination using large generative models. In: Proceedings of the 2023 CHI Conference on Human Factors in Computing Systems, Hamburg Germany, April 2023, pp. 1–19. ACM (2023)

101. Nguyen, T.-P., Razniewski, S., Varde, A., Weikum, G.: Extracting cultural commonsense knowledge at scale. In: Proceedings of the ACM Web Conference 2023, WWW '23, New York, NY, USA, April 2023, pp. 1907–1917. Association for Computing Machinery (2023)

102. Xu, W., Charles, F., Hargood, C.: Generating stylistic and personalized dialogues for virtual agents in narratives. In: Proceedings of the 2023 International Conference on Autonomous Agents and Multiagent Systems, AAMAS '23, Richland, SC, May 2023, pp. 737–746. International Foundation for Autonomous Agents and Multiagent Systems (2023)

103. Pang, X., Wang, Y., Fan, S., Chen, L., Shang, S., Han, P.: EmpMFF: a multi-factor sequence fusion framework for empathetic response generation. In: Proceedings of the ACM Web Conference 2023, WWW '23, New York, NY, USA, April 2023, pp. 1754–1764. Association for Computing Machinery (2023)

104. Xu, C., Li, P., Wang, W., Yang, H., Wang, S., Xiao, C.: COSPLAY: concept set guided personalized dialogue generation across both party personas. In: Proceedings of the 45th International ACM SIGIR Conference on Research and Development in Information Retrieval, SIGIR '22, New York, NY, USA, July 2022, pp. 201–211. Association for Computing Machinery (2022)

105. Zhao, X., Wang, L., He, R., Yang, T., Chang, J., Wang, R.: Multiple knowledge syncretic transformer for natural dialogue generation. In: Proceedings of The Web Conference 2020, WWW '20, New York, NY, USA, April 2020, pp. 752–762. Association for Computing Machinery (2020)

106. Pataranutaporn, P., et al.: Living memories: AI-generated characters as digital mementos. In: Proceedings of the 28th International Conference on Intelligent User Interfaces, IUI '23, New York, NY, USA, March 2023, pp. 889–901. Association for Computing Machinery (2023)

107. Si, W.M., et al.: Why so toxic? Measuring and triggering toxic behavior in open-domain chatbots. In: Proceedings of the 2022 ACM SIGSAC Conference on Computer and Communications Security, CCS '22, New York, NY, USA, November 2022, pp. 2659–2673. Association for Computing Machinery (2022)

108. Ye, C., Liao, L., Liu, S., Chua, T.-S.: Reflecting on experiences for response generation. In: Proceedings of the 30th ACM International Conference on Multimedia, MM '22, New York, NY, USA, October 2022, pp. 5265–5273. Association for Computing Machinery (2022)

109. Jo, E., Epstein, D.A., Jung, H., Kim, Y.-H.: Understanding the benefits and challenges of deploying conversational AI leveraging large language models for public health intervention. In: Proceedings of the 2023 CHI Conference on Human Factors in Computing Systems, CHI '23, New York, NY, USA, April 2023, pp. 1–16. Association for Computing Machinery (2023)
110. Zamfirescu-Pereira, J.D., et al.: Herding AI cats: lessons from designing a chatbot by prompting GPT-3. In: Proceedings of the 2023 ACM Designing Interactive Systems Conference, DIS '23, New York, NY, USA, July 2023, pp. 2206–2220. Association for Computing Machinery (2023)
111. Xygkou, A., et al.: The "Conversation" about loss: understanding how chatbot technology was used in supporting people in Grief. In: Proceedings of the 2023 CHI Conference on Human Factors in Computing Systems, CHI '23, New York, NY, USA, April 2023, pp. 1–15. Association for Computing Machinery (2023)
112. Scott, A.E., Neumann, D., Niess, J., Woźniak, P.W.: Do you mind? User perceptions of machine consciousness. In: Proceedings of the 2023 CHI Conference on Human Factors in Computing Systems, CHI '23, New York, NY, USA, April 2023, pp. 1–19. Association for Computing Machinery (2023)
113. Yin, C., Li, P., Ren, Z.: CTRLStruct: dialogue structure learning for open-domain response generation. In: Proceedings of the ACM Web Conference 2023, WWW '23, New York, NY, USA, April 2023, pp. 1539–1550. Association for Computing Machinery (2023)
114. Niwa, M., Masai, K., Yoshida, S., Sugimoto, M.: Investigating effects of facial self-similarity levels on the impression of virtual agents in serious/non-serious contexts. In: Proceedings of the Augmented Humans International Conference 2023, AHs '23, New York, NY, USA, March 2023, pp. 221–230. Association for Computing Machinery (2023)
115. He, W., et al.: Unified dialog model pre-training for task-oriented dialog understanding and generation. In: Proceedings of the 45th International ACM SIGIR Conference on Research and Development in Information Retrieval, SIGIR '22, New York, NY, USA, July 2022, pp. 187–200. Association for Computing Machinery (2022)
116. Sharma, A., Lin, I.W., Miner, A.S., Atkins, D.C., Althoff, T.: Towards facilitating empathic conversations in online mental health support: a reinforcement learning approach. In: Proceedings of the Web Conference 2021, WWW '21, New York, NY, USA, June 2021, pp. 194–205. Association for Computing Machinery (2021)
117. Elgarf, M., Zojaji, S., Skantze, G., Peters, C.: CreativeBot: a creative storyteller robot to stimulate creativity in children. In: Proceedings of the 2022 International Conference on Multimodal Interaction, ICMI '22, New York, NY, USA, November 2022, pp. 540–548. Association for Computing Machinery (2022)
118. Hada, D.V., Vijaikumar M., Shevade, S.K.: ReXPlug: explainable recommendation using plug-and-play language model. In: Proceedings of the 44th International ACM SIGIR Conference on Research and Development in Information Retrieval, SIGIR '21, New York, NY, USA, July 2021, pp. 81–91. Association for Computing Machinery (2021)
119. Social Simulacra: Creating Populated Prototypes for Social Computing Systems | Proceedings of the 35th Annual ACM Symposium on User Interface Software and Technology. Archive Location: world
120. Cao, Q., Chen, X., Song, R., Jiang, H., Yang, G., Cao, Z.: Multi-modal experience inspired AI creation. In: Proceedings of the 30th ACM International Conference on Multimedia, MM '22, New York, NY, USA, October 2022, pp. 1445–1454. Association for Computing Machinery (2022)

121. Liu, Y., Huang, Q., Li, J., Mo, L., Cai, Y., Li, Q.: SSAP: storylines and sentiment aware pre-trained model for story ending generation. IEEE/ACM Trans. Audio Speech Lang. Process. **30**, 686–694 (2022)

122. Ashby, T., Webb, B.K., Knapp, G., Searle, J., Fulda, N.: Personalized quest and dialogue generation in role-playing games: a knowledge graph- and language model-based approach. In: Proceedings of the 2023 CHI Conference on Human Factors in Computing Systems, CHI '23, New York, NY, USA, April 2023, pp. 1–20. Association for Computing Machinery (2023)

123. Laban, P., Ye, E., Korlakunta, S., Canny, J., Hearst, M.: NewsPod: automatic and interactive news podcasts. In: 27th International Conference on Intelligent User Interfaces, Helsinki Finland, March 2022, pp. 691–706. ACM (2022)

124. Khanmohammadi, R., Mirshafiee, M.S., Rezaee Jouryabi, Y., Mirroshandel, S.A.: Prose2Poem: the blessing of transformers in translating prose to Persian poetry. ACM Trans. Asian Low-Resource Lang. Inf. Process. **22**(6), 1701–17018 (2023)

125. Suh, S., Zhao, J., Law, E.: CodeToon: story ideation, auto comic generation, and structure mapping for code-driven storytelling. In: Proceedings of the 35th Annual ACM Symposium on User Interface Software and Technology, UIST '22, New York, NY, USA, October 2022, pp. 1–16. Association for Computing Machinery (2022)

126. Jones, M., Neumayer, C., Shklovski, I.: Embodying the algorithm: exploring relationships with large language models through artistic performance. In: Proceedings of the 2023 CHI Conference on Human Factors in Computing Systems, CHI '23, New York, NY, USA, April 2023, pp. 1–24. Association for Computing Machinery

127. Rajcic, N., McCormack, J.: Mirror ritual: an affective interface for emotional self-reflection. arXiv:2004.09685 [cs] (2020)

128. Liu, V., Qiao, H., Chilton, L.: Opal: multimodal image generation for news illustration. In: Proceedings of the 35th Annual ACM Symposium on User Interface Software and Technology, UIST '22, New York, NY, USA, October 2022, pp. 1–17. Association for Computing Machinery (2022)

129. Huynh, L., Nguyen, T., Goh, J., Kim, H., Hong, J.B.: ARGH! automated rumor generation hub. In: Proceedings of the 30th ACM International Conference on Information & Knowledge Management, CIKM '21, New York, NY, USA, October 2021, pp. 3847–3856. Association for Computing Machinery (2021)

130. Lee, Y., Kim, T.S., Kim, S., Yun, Y., Kim, J.: DAPIE: interactive step-by-step explanatory dialogues to answer children's why and how questions. In: Proceedings of the 2023 CHI Conference on Human Factors in Computing Systems, CHI '23, New York, NY, USA, April 2023, pp. 1–22. Association for Computing Machinery (2023)

131. Lee, M., Liang, P., Yang, Q.: CoAuthor: designing a human-AI collaborative writing dataset for exploring language model capabilities. In: CHI Conference on Human Factors in Computing Systems, New Orleans LA USA, April 2022, pp. 1–19. ACM (2022)

132. Chung, J.J.Y., Kim, W., Yoo, K.M., Lee, H., Adar, E., Chang, M.: TaleBrush: sketching stories with generative pretrained language models. In: Proceedings of the 2022 CHI Conference on Human Factors in Computing Systems, CHI '22, New York, NY, USA, April 2022, pp. 1–19. Association for Computing Machinery (2022)

133. Yanardag, P., Cebrian, M., Rahwan., I.: Shelley: a crowd-sourced collaborative horror writer. In: Proceedings of the 13th Conference on Creativity and Cognition, C&C '21, New York, NY, USA, June 2021, pp. 1–8. Association for Computing Machinery (2021)

134. Chiou, L.-Y., Hung, P.-K., Liang, R.-H., Wang, C.-T.: Designing with AI: an exploration of co-ideation with image generators. In: Proceedings of the 2023 ACM Designing Interactive Systems Conference, DIS '23, New York, NY, USA, July 2023, pp. 1941–1954. Association for Computing Machinery (2023)

135. Liu, V., Vermeulen, J., Fitzmaurice, G., Matejka, J.: 3DALL-E: integrating text-to-image AI in 3D design workflows. arXiv:2210.11603 [cs] (2023)

136. Brie, P., Burny, N., Sluÿters, A., Vanderdonckt, J.: Evaluating a large language model on searching for GUI layouts. Proc. ACM Hum.-Comput. Interact. **7**(EICS), 178:1-178:37 (2023)

137. Lanzi, P.L., Loiacono, D.: ChatGPT and other large language models as evolutionary engines for online interactive collaborative game design. In: Proceedings of the Genetic and Evolutionary Computation Conference, GECCO '23, New York, NY, USA, July 2023, pp. 1383–1390. Association for Computing Machinery (2023)

138. Co-Writing Screenplays and Theatre Scripts with Language Models: Evaluation by Industry Professionals | Proceedings of the 2023 CHI Conference on Human Factors in Computing Systems. Archive Location: world

139. Dang, H., Goller, S., Lehmann, F., Buschek, D.: Choice over control: how users write with large language models using diegetic and non-diegetic prompting. In: Proceedings of the 2023 CHI Conference on Human Factors in Computing Systems, April 2023, pp. 1–17 (2023). arXiv:2303.03199 [cs]

140. Tholander, J., Jonsson, M.: Design ideation with AI - sketching, thinking and talking with generative machine learning models. In: Proceedings of the 2023 ACM Designing Interactive Systems Conference, DIS '23, New York, NY, USA, July 2023, pp. 1930–1940. Association for Computing Machinery (2023)

141. Chen, X."A"., et al.: Marvista: exploring the design of a human-AI collaborative news reading tool. ACM Trans. Comput.-Hum. Interact. **30**(6), 1–27 (2023)

142. Metzler, D., Tay, Y., Bahri, D., Najork, M.: Rethinking search: making domain experts out of dilettantes. ACM SIGIR Forum **55**(1), 13:1-13:27 (2021)

143. Wang, A.Y., et al.: Documentation matters: human-centered AI system to assist data science code documentation in computational notebooks. ACM Trans. Comput.-Hum. Interact. **29**(2), 17:1-17:33 (2022)

144. Alonso del Barrio, D., Gatica-Perez, D.: Framing the news: from human perception to large language model inferences. In: Proceedings of the 2023 ACM International Conference on Multimedia Retrieval, ICMR '23, New York, NY, USA, June 2023, pp. 627–635. Association for Computing Machinery (2023)

145. Petridis, S., et al.: AngleKindling: supporting journalistic angle ideation with large language models. In: Proceedings of the 2023 CHI Conference on Human Factors in Computing Systems, CHI '23, New York, NY, USA, April 2023, pp. 1–16. Association for Computing Machinery (2023)

146. August, T., Wang, L.L., Bragg, J., Hearst, M.A., Head, A., Lo, K.: Paper plain: making medical research papers approachable to healthcare consumers with natural language processing. ACM Trans. Comput.-Hum. Interact. (2023). Just Accepted

147. Sun, J., et al.: Investigating explainability of generative AI for code through scenario-based design. In: 27th International Conference on Intelligent User Interfaces, Helsinki Finland, March 2022, pp. 212–228. ACM (2022)

148. Zhou, M., Huang, M., Zhu, X.: Story ending selection by finding hints from pairwise candidate endings. IEEE/ACM Trans. Audio Speech Lang. Process. **27**(4), 719–729 (2019)

149. Shen, J., Yang, B., Dudley, J.J., Kristensson, P.O.: KWickChat: a multi-turn dialogue system for AAC using context-aware sentence generation by bag-of-keywords. In: 27th International Conference on Intelligent User Interfaces, Helsinki Finland, March 2022, pp. 853–867. ACM (2022)

150. Li, L., Zhang, Y., Chen, L.: Personalized prompt learning for explainable recommendation. ACM Trans. Inf. Syst. **41**(4), 1031–10326 (2023)

151. Xue, W., et al: PrefRec: recommender systems with human preferences for reinforcing long-term user engagement. In: Proceedings of the 29th ACM SIGKDD Conference on Knowledge Discovery and Data Mining, KDD '23, New York, NY, USA, August 2023, pp. 2874–2884. Association for Computing Machinery (2023)

152. Liao, Q.V., Subramonyam, H., Wang, J., Wortman Vaughan, J.: Designerly understanding: information needs for model transparency to support design ideation for AI-powered user experience. In: Proceedings of the 2023 CHI Conference on Human Factors in Computing Systems, CHI '23, New York, NY, USA, April 2023, pp. 1–21. Association for Computing Machinery (2023)

153. Zhang, X., Li, J., Chi, P.-W., Chandrasegaran, S., Ma, K.-L.: ConceptEVA: concept-based interactive exploration and customization of document summaries. In: Proceedings of the 2023 CHI Conference on Human Factors in Computing Systems, CHI '23, New York, NY, USA, April 2023, pp. 1–16. Association for Computing Machinery (2023)

154. Wang, Y., Shen, S., Lim, B.Y.: RePrompt: automatic prompt editing to refine AI-generative art towards precise expressions. In: Proceedings of the 2023 CHI Conference on Human Factors in Computing Systems, CHI '23, New York, NY, USA, April 2023, pp. 1–29. Association for Computing Machinery (2023)

155. Hämäläinen, P., Tavast, M., Kunnari, A.: Evaluating large language models in generating synthetic HCI research data: a case study. In: Proceedings of the 2023 CHI Conference on Human Factors in Computing Systems, CHI '23, New York, NY, USA, April 2023, pp. 1–19. Association for Computing Machinery (2023)

156. Sekulić, I., Aliannejadi, M., Crestani, F.: Evaluating mixed-initiative conversational search systems via user simulation. In: Proceedings of the Fifteenth ACM International Conference on Web Search and Data Mining, WSDM '22, New York, NY, USA, February 2022, pp. 888–896. Association for Computing Machinery (2022)

157. Le, T., Tran-Thanh, L., Lee, D.: Socialbots on fire: modeling adversarial behaviors of socialbots via multi-agent hierarchical reinforcement learning. In: Proceedings of the ACM Web Conference 2022, WWW '22, New York, NY, USA, April 2022, pp. 545–554. Association for Computing Machinery (2022)

The Use of Large Language Model in Code Review Automation: An Examination of Enforcing SOLID Principles

Gustavo F. Martins[1]([✉]), Emiliandro C. M. Firmino[1], and Vinicius P. De Mello[2]

[1] SW Development – SIDIA Institute of Science and Technology, Manaus, AM, Brazil
{gustavo.freitas,emiliandro.firmino}@sidia.com
[2] UX and Design – SIDIA Institute of Science and Technology, Manaus, AM, Brazil
vinicius.mello@sidia.com

Abstract. Within the ever-evolving domain of software development, the practice of having teams located in different geographical locations presents distinct obstacles, including disparate time zones, language hurdles, and differing degrees of experience. This paper presents a novel approach to address these difficulties by using an automated GitHub bot that utilizes Large Language Models (LLMs) to enforce SOLID principles during code reviews. This bot, which incorporates advanced models such as OpenAI's GPT-4 and the locally deployable Mixtral, has the objective of delivering immediate and practical feedback. Its purpose is to improve the quality of code and make learning easier for developers, particularly those who are new to programming. The bot's structure enables effortless incorporation into GitHub, utilizing LLMs to examine code modifications and offer observations regarding adherence to SOLID principles. An important characteristic of this method is the incorporation of Mixtral, which may be operated on-site, providing advantages in terms of data confidentiality and operational adaptability, essential for global enterprises with strict privacy demands. Here, we explores the bot's architecture, its incorporation with LLMs, and its capacity to revolutionize code reviews by offering a secure, efficient, and instructive instrument for geographically dispersed software development teams.

Keywords: SOLID · LLM · Code Review

1 Introduction

In the current landscape of software development, the trend of geographically dispersed teams has become the norm rather than the exception. This global collaboration model introduces a unique set of challenges, including but not limited to, disparate time zones, language barriers, and diverse levels of expertise among team members. In this context, automation, particularly in code reviews, emerges as a crucial strategy for upholding code quality and ensuring adherence to established design principles. Among these, the SOLID principles stand out as

H. Degen and S. Ntoa (Eds.): HCII 2024, LNAI 14736, pp. 86–97, 2024.
https://doi.org/10.1007/978-3-031-60615-1_6

a cornerstone in Object-Oriented Programming (OOP), providing a foundation for creating code that is both maintainable and scalable. However, the manual enforcement of these principles during code reviews can be a daunting and time-consuming task, requiring a deep understanding of the principles involved.

Addressing these challenges, this study introduces an automated code review bot that leverages a range of Large Language Models (LLMs), including but not limited to OpenAI's GPT-4 and Mixtral. This approach not only facilitates real-time adherence to SOLID principles during code reviews but also overcomes language barriers and provides instant feedback to globally distributed teams. Moreover, it serves as a valuable educational resource for novice developers, enhancing their understanding and application of key design principles. The paper elaborates on the bot's architecture, its integration with multiple LLMs, and the implications of such a system, setting it in contrast with existing code review solutions to underline its unique advantages and potential limitations. Through a detailed exploration of the necessity for such an innovation and a comprehensive review of the relevant literature, this analysis aims to foster a dialogue on the automation of SOLID principle enforcement in code reviews and the broader application of LLMs in software development.

2   Background

In this section, we provide an extensive overview of the fundamental concepts upon which our research is founded. We begin by analyzing the significance of code reviews in software development and their associated benefits and difficulties. Next, we examine the SOLID principles and stress their importance in object-oriented programming. Then, we examine the Language Model technology, discussing its current applications and potential uses in software development, namely code review. Finally, we discuss the use of bots in code development and review processes, laying the groundwork for a discussion regarding the integration of LLMs with these bots to improve code review.

2.1   Code Reviews

Code reviews are an essential aspect of software development teams, whether they use waterfall models or agile methodologies. They serve as a checkpoint to ensure that the code conforms to the established standards, is well-structured, readable, and error-free. In addition to enhancing code quality, code reviews promote learning and knowledge sharing, allowing developers to gain insights from their peers [6]. However, human-driven code reviews have disadvantages, including time-intensiveness, inconsistent feedback due to varying levels of expertise, and the possibility of bias.

2.2   SOLID Principles

The SOLID principles, introduced by Robert C. Martin [4], are a set of five design principles intended to make software designs more comprehensible, flexible, and maintainable. When adhered to, these principles reduce code odors, improve readability, and facilitate maintenance and scalability. The fundamentals, in summary, are:

- The Single Responsibility Principle (SRP): states that a class should have only one reason to change.
- Open-Closed Principle (OCP): Entities in software should be open to extension but closed to modification.
- Liskov Substitution Principle (LSP): Subtypes must be interchangeable with their base types without compromising the program's correctness.
- Interface Segregation Principle (ISP): Clients should not be required to rely on interfaces that they do not employ.
- Dependency Inversion Principle (DIP): High-level modules should not rely on low-level modules; instead, both should rely on abstractions.

2.3   Large Language Model Technology

In recent years, LLMs technology has seen significant advancements [8]. An LLM is, at its core, a form of artificial intelligence that comprehends, generates, and evaluates text. It has been trained on a large corpus of text data and can make context-based predictions. When applied to software development, particularly code reviews, LLMs hold great promise. They can evaluate code submissions automatically, identify deviations from norms, and provide useful feedback. Using LLMs effectively in code review processes does not come without obstacles, such as understanding programming nuances, context, and adapting to various coding styles and standards [3].

2.4   Mixtral LLM

Mixtral is a cutting-edge LLM framework distinguished by its flexibility and adaptability, particularly in enterprise environments [2]. A standout feature of Mixtral is its capability to be deployed locally within an organization's private infrastructure. This local deployment option addresses significant concerns related to data privacy, security, and compliance that are paramount in sensitive or regulated industries. By running Mixtral locally, organizations can leverage the powerful AI-driven insights and automation typical of LLMs while retaining full control over their data. This ensures that proprietary information, sensitive data, and intellectual property remain within the secure confines of the organization's network, mitigating risks associated with data breaches or unauthorized access. Furthermore, local deployment can enhance performance and reduce latency by eliminating the need for data to traverse external networks, making Mixtral a versatile solution for businesses seeking to harness the benefits of AI without compromising on security or compliance.

2.5   Role of Bots in Code Development and Review

The use of automated bots in software development and code review processes has become widespread. They assist with repetitive tasks, execute tests, verify style compliance, and even identify potential performance issues [10]. While their current application offers a number of advantages, such as time savings and fewer manual errors, there is room for improvement and evolution. The incorporation of LLMs can provide bots with a deeper understanding of context and improved feedback delivery, thereby enhancing their performance in the code review process.

2.6 Benefits for Large Global Development Teams

The utility of the proposed LLM-based code review bot for large global development teams is one of its significant benefits. In multinational corporations, teams frequently span multiple time zones and consist of members from diverse cultural backgrounds who speak different languages [5]. In such circumstances, the asynchronous nature of code review can be especially advantageous.

With the proposed bot, developers can submit pull requests at any time without coordinating with a reviewer in a different timezone, thereby reducing bottlenecks and increasing productivity. In addition, the bot's ability to provide feedback in multiple languages (a feature inherent to advanced LLMs) can help international teams overcome language barriers. By enforcing SOLID principles, it provides a shared quality standard to which all developers, regardless of location, can adhere to.

3 Related Works

The incorporation of LLMs in code development and review processes has been the focus of various recent studies. In this section, we present some related works done in this regard. A summary of the related work can be found in Table 1.

Table 1. Comparison of the main aspects of each related work

Reference	Main Focus	Methodology	Findings
[11]	Evaluation of LLMs	Benchmarks	– LLM size is not the sole performance factor – Combined training on code and natural language is beneficial.
[9]	Code review bots	Data analysis	– Increased merged pull requests – Possible maintenance challenges due to increased contributions.
[1]	Review Bot tool	User study	– Improved code review quality – Effective reviewer recommendation.
[7]	ChatGPT for SE tasks	Experiment	– Excelled in log summarization, code clone detection – Average performance in code review generation – Struggled with tasks requiring deeper code comprehension

3.1 A Systematic Evaluation of Large Language Models of Code

[11] provides a comprehensive evaluation of the performance of various large language models (LLMs) when applied to code-related tasks. The authors benchmark and compare models such as Codex, GPT-J, GPT-Neo, GPT-NeoX-20B,

and their own model, PolyCoder, on a variety of tasks, including code completion, code synthesis from natural language descriptions, and code perplexity in numerous programming languages.

The paper demonstrates that the size of the model is not the only significant factor for these tasks. A smaller model (Codex 300M) outperformed all other models in the HumanEval benchmark, indicating that there is significant room for improvement in open-source models using methods other than simply increasing model size. In fact, the authors suggest that the superior performance of GPT-Neo over PolyCoder in certain languages suggests that training on natural language text and code can be advantageous for code modeling.

The paper provides insights regarding the use of LLMs for a bot reviewer. LLMs such as GPT-4 may be a better option for a review bot because they can potentially be trained on both natural language and code, resulting in a more comprehensive understanding of the code and any associated documentation or comments. In addition, because these models are capable of code synthesis from natural language descriptions, they could be useful during code reviews for providing recommendations.

3.2 Effects of Adopting Code Review Bots on Pull Requests to OSS Projects

[9] examines the effects of adopting code review bots into the pull request workflow of open source software (OSS) projects. The researchers analyze data from 1194 OSS projects hosted on GitHub, focusing on the differences between merged and non-merged pull requests prior to and after the implementation of a code review bot.

The study indicates that implementing such a code review bot may lead to increased merged pull requests, suggesting faster and better feedback. While not directly addressing LLMs or SOLID principles in code review, the study implies the potential of LLMs in enhancing bot capabilities, such as identifying SOLID principle violations, possibly influencing the uptick in merges.

3.3 Reducing Human Effort and Improving Quality in Peer Code Reviews Using Automatic Static Analysis and Reviewer Recommendation

[1] proposes a tool called Review Bot to assist in reducing human effort in peer code reviews. Automatic static analysis is incorporated into the code review procedure by the tool. It uses output from multiple static analysis tools to automatically publish reviews. Through a user study, this paper demonstrates that integrating static analysis tools into the code review process can enhance the quality of code reviews. The Review Bot also includes an algorithm for recommending reviewers, which aims to simplify the process of identifying suitable reviewers for a large project.

The application of Large Language Models (LLMs) in code review is consistent with the standard procedure of utilizing automated tools for this purpose.

Similar to how the Review Bot identifies code issues through static analysis, an LLM-based bot could be developed to detect violations of the SOLID principles. Furthermore, the integration of the Review Bot's approach to recommending reviewers on the basis of previous line changes into an LLM-based system could facilitate the identification of reviewers who possess expertise or prior interactions with the particular code being evaluated.

3.4 ChatGPT: A Study of Its Utility for Common Software Engineering Tasks

[7] examines the potential applications of ChatGPT (Chat Generative Pre-trained Transformer) for common software engineering tasks. The authors conducted an experiment with fifteen pervasive software development tasks and evaluated ChatGPT's utility for these tasks. They computed the accuracy of ChatGPT for each task by comparing its output to that of human experts and/or cutting-edge tools.

The paper demonstrates that ChatGPT excels at log summarization, anaphora resolution, code summarization (method name generation), and code clone detection. However, its performance for tasks such as commit message generation, code review generation, natural language code search, and merge conflict resolution was only average. The paper further suggests the model's performance on code review tasks was only average. This may suggest that, although LLMs can provide some assistance with code review, their effectiveness may be limited. The SOLID principles are not explicitly mentioned in the paper, but given Chat-GPT's performance on the tasks evaluated, it may be reasonable to anticipate similar difficulties when applying LLMs to SOLID principle checks.

3.5 Insights and Implications for LLM-Based Code Review

The review of related works reveals a number of insightful observations regarding the application of automated tools and LLMs in code review. [11] demonstrate that although LLMs perform well in a variety of tasks, their efficacy is not universally superior, emphasizing the need for task-specific evaluations. Our proposal to investigate the use of an LLM-based bot for enforcing SOLID principles relies heavily on this finding.

[9] and [1] provide empirical evidence regarding the influence of automated review tools on code review workflows, demonstrating a generally positive effect. These findings encourage the investigation of LLMs' potential to further improve the quality of code review. Nevertheless, [7] indicates that our proposal may face obstacles regarding the efficacy of LLMs for basic coding tasks.

4 Proposed Concept

At the heart of our proposed solution is a bot designed to facilitate the code review process by offering real-time guidance on adherence to SOLID principles during PRs. This bot springs into action upon the initiation of a PR through a webhook, meticulously analyzing the proposed code changes.

Uniquely, this bot harnesses the power of various LLMs, including OpenAI's GPT-4 and potentially locally deployable models like Mixtral, to dissect and evaluate code. These models, particularly GPT-4, have been trained on an extensive corpus of internet text, including a significant emphasis on programming languages and coding patterns. This training enables the bot to adeptly identify deviations from SOLID principles and suggest enhancements.

The process begins with the bot parsing the submitted code into digestible fragments, each of which is then evaluated by the chosen LLM. This evaluation aims to unearth any SOLID principle violations and to generate constructive feedback. The accumulated insights are then systematically integrated into the PR in the form of comments. This not only makes the feedback readily accessible to developers but also ensures that it can be immediately leveraged to refine the code.

It's important to underscore that the intention behind this bot is not to supplant human reviewers but to augment their efforts. By automating the preliminary review stages and ensuring a laser focus on critical design principles, the bot empowers human reviewers to dedicate more attention to the code's logic and other essential facets, thereby enhancing the overall quality and maintainability of the software.

4.1   Proposed Architecture and Integration

The architecture of our proposed bot is designed to be modular and scalable, consisting of several key components that work in concert to ensure seamless integration and effective analysis.

- **Integration of GitHub**: This element connects the bot to the GitHub environment. It serves two purposes. On the one hand, it monitors GitHub for events (such as the submission of a new PR), initiates the code analysis process, and notifies the Code Analysis Layer of code changes. In contrast, it posts the processed results from the Code Analysis Layer as comments on the PR. It is designed to communicate seamlessly with the GitHub API, allowing the bot to operate effectively within the GitHub ecosystem.
- **LLM Interface**: At the core of the bot's functionality is the interface to various LLMs, including GPT-4 and Mixtral. This interface is crucial for tapping into the advanced natural language understanding and code analysis capabilities of these models. It receives parsed code segments from the Code Analysis module, subjects them to in-depth analysis, and generates detailed feedback on the code's adherence to SOLID principles, along with suggestions for improvement.
- **Code Analysis Module**: This component is the analytical powerhouse of the bot, where the intricate process of code review is orchestrated. It accepts code changes from the GitHub Integration module, breaks them down into analyzable segments, and manages the interactions with the LLM Interface.

Upon receiving the analysis from the LLM Interface, this module applies additional processing to distill the insights into clear, concise, and actionable feedback. This feedback is then relayed back to the GitHub Integration module for publication on the relevant PR, thereby closing the loop and ensuring that developers receive timely and constructive guidance on their code.

Fig. 1. Component Diagram of the Proposed GitHub Bot for Code Review Automation.

The Fig. 1 depicts the components of the proposed system for automating code reviews. When a new pull request is created or an existing PR is modified on GitHub, a cyclical process is initiated. The Code Analysis Layer receives the extracted changes from the GitHub Integration Layer, which is responsible for interacting with the GitHub platform. This layer converts code changes into a format that can be analyzed by the LLM. Once the analysis is complete, the API returns results that include potential violations of the SOLID principle and suggestions for improvement. The Code Analysis Layer transforms these results into a developer-friendly, human-readable format. The results are then sent back to the GitHub Integration Layer, which adds the comments to the corresponding PR. Any changes to the PR will cause the bot to re-evaluate the code and update the comments as required. This flow is shown in Fig. 2.

4.2 Usage of the Proposed Bot

The bot is intended to be a seamless addition to the developer's workflow. Once integrated into a GitHub repository, the bot is automatically activated whenever a pull request is created. There are no additional steps required for developers to initiate the bot's review.

Once the automated system has concluded its analysis of the PR, it proceeds to publish its comments directly on the PR. The following observations highlight possible deviations from the SOLID principles in the modified code and propose recommendations for improvements. The feedback provided can be utilized by the developers to enhance the code's quality prior to a human review of the pull request. This practice not only guarantees that the code follows essential design principles, but also functions as an educational resource to assist developers in gaining a deeper understanding of the SOLID principles and their practical implementation in code.

Fig. 2. Simplified Flow Diagram of the Proposed GitHub Bot, a Continuous Analysis Cycle.

5   Impact Analysis

Our proposed code review bot is fundamentally distinct from existing solutions in its approach to code review and emphasis on SOLID principles enforcement as we analyse in this section.

5.1   Comparison with Existing Solutions

Unlike the work done by Xu et al. [11], our proposed bot takes advantage of LLMs' ability to comprehend both natural language and code. In addition, the evaluation of adherence to SOLID principles necessitates a deeper comprehension of the code's structure and design, which may prove difficult for even the most advanced LLMs. However, this is a niche that requires additional research, and our work aims to contribute to this field.

The paper by Wessel et al. [9] highlights the positive effect of code review bots on the efficiency of OSS projects. In addition to increasing productivity, our bot aims to improve code quality by highlighting places where SOLID principles are violated. It is hoped that by addressing these violations, we can avoid a portion of the maintenance burden that code review bots may introduce.

Meanwhile, Balachandran [1] illustrates the advantages of automated code review with static analysis. Our bot shares the goal of reducing human effort, but aims to supplement static analysis with LLMs' comprehension abilities. This dual approach could result in recommendations that are more precise and sensitive to context.

And finally, we try to minimize the issues identified by Sridhara et al. [7] by concentrating on a specific area we hope to enhance its performance in this task, building upon the average performance of LLMs in code reviews.

5.2   Potential Benefits

This proposal suggests a GitHub bot that uses Large Language Models to improve the code review process significantly. The bot automates many aspects of code reviews, providing quick feedback and freeing up human reviewers to focus on more complex code. It applies SOLID principles, which are fundamental in object-oriented programming, to prevent design issues and improve code durability and strength.

Table 2. Key benefits of the proposed bot

Benefit	Description
Enhanced Code Quality	By enforcing SOLID principles, we aim to improve the overall quality of code in the projects.
Time Efficiency	The bot can assist in identifying SOLID principles violations, potentially saving review time.
Educational	The bot could serve as an educational tool for developers unfamiliar with SOLID principles

Additionally, the incorporation of locally deployable LLMs, such as Mixtral, introduces a new dimension of benefits, particularly in terms of data security and operational flexibility. This feature is especially relevant for organizations with stringent data governance and privacy policies, as it allows sensitive code to be analyzed without leaving the corporate network. The bot thus not only acts as a powerful educational tool for developers, particularly beginners, by providing instant, consistent feedback on SOLID principles but also ensures a secure and adaptable code review environment. This adaptability is crucial for maintaining high coding standards, particularly in large or geographically distributed teams. The main benefits of this innovative review bot are summarized in Table 2, highlighting its potential to revolutionize the code review process.

5.3   Challenges and Limitations

The deployment and effective operation of our proposed bot, despite its numerous benefits, are not without challenges and limitations. One of the primary challenges lies in the bot's ability to achieve a deep and nuanced understanding of code context and complex design principles such as SOLID. These principles are characterized by their complexity and the subtlety with which they must be applied, posing a significant challenge for current LLMs that may not always possess the requisite depth of understanding akin to that of a seasoned developer. Such a gap in understanding can lead to instances of false positives, where the bot flags issues that do not exist, or false negatives, where actual issues go undetected. These inaccuracies could compromise the bot's reliability and efficiency, potentially leading to additional work or overlooked problems that could affect the overall quality of the code review process.

Moreover, while LLMs, including GPT-4 and models like Mixtral, have shown remarkable proficiency in various tasks, they inherently operate based on patterns learned from their training data. This method of operation means they lack the human-like capacity to genuinely understand or reason about code in the way a human developer might, particularly when it comes to applying the nuanced and context-dependent SOLID principles. This limitation underscores the need for careful consideration and possibly supplementary mechanisms to mitigate the impact of these constraints on the bot's performance in enforcing these principles effectively.

6   Conclusion

In this paper, we have introduced a novel approach to automating the code review process through a GitHub bot that enforces SOLID principles, harnessing the advanced capabilities of Large Language Models. Our bot's dedication to improving specific facets of code quality positions it as a significant enhancement to the conventional code review paradigm.

The impact of existing code review bots on the software development workflow is undeniable, contributing positively to the efficiency and quality of open-source projects. Yet, many of these existing solutions may not fully capitalize on the potential of LLMs or adequately enforce critical best practices, such as SOLID principles adherence. Our proposed bot seeks to fill this gap by employing not only GPT-4 but also incorporating the option for locally run LLMs like Mixtral. This inclusion not only leverages the analytical prowess of LLMs to scrutinize code against SOLID principles but also introduces the benefits of enhanced data security and operational flexibility inherent to local deployments. The anticipated advantages of this approach include not only improved code quality and time efficiency but also significant educational benefits for developers, particularly in reinforcing best coding practices.

While the proposal outlined in this paper remains theoretical at this stage, we are optimistic about its potential for practical application and its subsequent impact on the automation and efficacy of code review processes. It is our hope that this initiative will lay the groundwork for further exploration and innovation in the domain, especially in the context of employing LLMs like Mixtral to enforce and uphold stringent code quality standards.

References

1. Balachandran, V.: Reducing human effort and improving quality in peer code reviews using automatic static analysis and reviewer recommendation. In: 2013 35th International Conference on Software Engineering (ICSE), pp. 931–940. IEEE (2013)
2. Jiang, A.Q., et al.: Mixtral of experts. arXiv preprint arXiv:2401.04088 (2024)
3. Kojima, T., Gu, S.S., Reid, M., Matsuo, Y., Iwasawa, Y.: Large language models are zero-shot reasoners. Adv. Neural. Inf. Process. Syst. **35**, 22199–22213 (2022)

4. Martin, R.C.: Agile Software Development: Principles, Patterns, and Practices. Prentice Hall PTR (2003)
5. McDonough, E.F., Kahn, K.B., Griffin, A.: Managing communication in global product development teams. IEEE Trans. Eng. Manage. **46**(4), 375–386 (1999)
6. Sadowski, C., Söderberg, E., Church, L., Sipko, M., Bacchelli, A.: Modern code review: a case study at google. In: Proceedings of the 40th International Conference on Software Engineering: Software Engineering in Practice, pp. 181–190 (2018)
7. Sridhara, G., Mazumdar, S., et al.: ChatGPT: a study on its utility for ubiquitous software engineering tasks. arXiv preprint arXiv:2305.16837 (2023)
8. Wei, J., et al.: Emergent abilities of large language models. arXiv preprint arXiv:2206.07682 (2022)
9. Wessel, M., Serebrenik, A., Wiese, I., Steinmacher, I., Gerosa, M.A.: Effects of adopting code review bots on pull requests to OSS projects. In: 2020 IEEE International Conference on Software Maintenance and Evolution (ICSME), pp. 1–11. IEEE (2020)
10. Wyrich, M., Bogner, J.: Towards an autonomous bot for automatic source code refactoring. In: 2019 IEEE/ACM 1st International Workshop on Bots in Software Engineering (BotSE), pp. 24–28. IEEE (2019)
11. Xu, F.F., Alon, U., Neubig, G., Hellendoorn, V.J.: A systematic evaluation of large language models of code. In: Proceedings of the 6th ACM SIGPLAN International Symposium on Machine Programming, pp. 1–10 (2022)

LLM Based Multi-agent Generation of Semi-structured Documents from Semantic Templates in the Public Administration Domain

Emanuele Musumeci[1]([✉])(iD), Michele Brienza[1]([✉])(iD), Vincenzo Suriani[1]([✉])(iD), Daniele Nardi[1](iD), and Domenico Daniele Bloisi[2]([✉])(iD)

[1] Department of Computer, Control, and Management Engineering, Sapienza University of Rome, Rome, Italy
`{musumeci,brienza,suriani,nardi}@diag.uniroma1.it`
[2] UNINT Univeristy, Via Cristoforo Colombo, 200, 00147 Rome, Italy
`domenico.bloisi@unint.eu`

Abstract. In the last years' digitalization process, the creation and management of documents in various domains, particularly in Public Administration (PA), have become increasingly complex and diverse. This complexity arises from the need to handle a wide range of document types, often characterized by semi-structured forms. Semi-structured documents present a fixed set of data without a fixed format. As a consequence, a template-based solution cannot be used, as understanding a document requires the extraction of the data structure. The recent introduction of Large Language Models (LLMs) has enabled the creation of customized text output satisfying user requests. In this work, we propose a novel approach that combines the LLMs with prompt engineering and multi-agent systems for generating new documents compliant with a desired structure. The main contribution of this work concerns replacing the commonly used manual prompting with a task description generated by semantic retrieval from an LLM. The potential of this approach is demonstrated through a series of experiments and case studies, showcasing its effectiveness in real-world PA scenarios.

Keywords: Human-Centered AI · Public Administration · Task optimization

1 Introduction

Document creation is a typical task in the Public Administration (PA) setting, requiring repetitive sub-tasks that offer the potential for automation. For instance, when writing official certificates required in public offices, the required personal information from the requesting user is often very schematic and constitutes only a small percentage of the text present in the document.

H. Degen and S. Ntoa (Eds.): HCII 2024, LNAI 14736, pp. 98–117, 2024.
https://doi.org/10.1007/978-3-031-60615-1_7

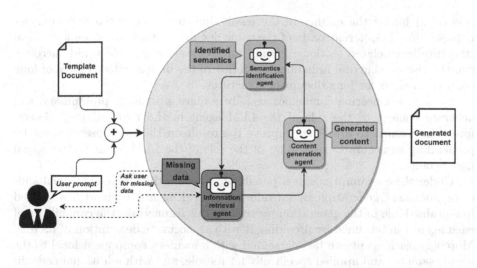

Fig. 1. The presented multi-agent architecture with the LLMs used in prompt engineering and multi-agent fashion for generating new documents.

The use of pre-made document templates manages only marginally to reduce the effort spent and applies only to rigidly structured documents, where the semantics of missing information can be perfectly defined in the templates themselves. Automation of the writing of this kind of document, which amounts to field-filling, is straightforward.

Instead, semi-structured documents offer a flexible format, in which missing information cannot be clearly tagged and is usually determined by the semantics of the surrounding context. For instance, standard fields like the current date can appear in different positions in the document with no pre-defined criteria.

Producing this kind of document requires additional effort to adapt their flexible structure to the current use case and the available and required information, with additional effort to recover missing information. The semantics associated with the necessary information require some contextual knowledge, which can be gained by the surrounding context and sometimes the overall semantics of the whole document. For instance, different terms can be used for the qualification of the same field: e.g. "Invoice," "Invoice No." "Bill" and "Purchase Order" can all label the same information (the invoice number). For this reason, structure and semantics in a semi-structured document are usually intertwined, and developing an efficient document generation pipeline that can run for a wide variety of documents is a very challenging task.

On these premises, the specific task of adapting semi-structured document templates can be supported by the use of Artificial Intelligence and in particular Language Models, to reduce the time spent automating the process and as a means to improve the generality of the automatic approach.

A straightforward solution could be to generate and therefore refine a document in several incremental steps, with a separate prompt for each one, but this could hinder the quality of the result due to the potential dependencies between data in different parts of the same document, that might be located in structurally unrelated sections. A fully unsupervised approach would therefore run the risk of incurring in hallucination due to the limited effectiveness of long context windows for long document structures.

Prompt engineering guidelines usually require providing preliminary and accurate context to the role of the LLM agent in the required task. Therefore it is possible to alter and improve the result on the same user request by prepending an accurate description of the role of the LLM agent to the actual user prompt.

Under these assumptions, it is possible to improve the incremental trial-and-error document generation by introducing several agents, each with a defined fine-grained role in the generation process. In this framework, the capabilities of each agent can be tuned by providing it with an accurate description of its role. Moreover, each agent can be augmented with a memory component local to the agent, sampled and applied specifically for its role, and with additional capabilities that compensate for the lacks of Language Models, such as interaction with the World Wide Web in real-time, access to private custom knowledge bases and information feeds to enhance agents with domain-specific knowledge, or the execution of specialized code as in a Function-as-a-Service framework. This kind of architecture is perfectly compatible with the emergent AI-as-a-Service (AIaaS) paradigm [3].

The multi-agent process assists the user by iteratively refining the prompt with the guidance of a pre-existing structure extracted from similar documents. Then, context-specific prompts are provided to the various agents during the process, depending on their specific role and the original document structure, with little to no human supervision. Interaction between the agents, which is conversational in nature, can include direct interaction with the user in cases in which intervention is needed.

We present a workflow and interaction framework for the LLM-assisted multi-agent generation of a semi-structured document in the PA domain, with limited human supervision. We then show the prompt refinement process necessary to obtain the required results for each specific agent role in the current workflow. The code and the additional results obtained from this work can be found at the following webpage https://sites.google.com/uniroma1.it/multi-agent-documentgeneration/home-page.

The remainder of the paper is organized as follows. Section 2 contains a description of the state of the art. Section 3 presents the description of the workflow and interaction framework. The prompt refinement process is then shown in Sect. 4. Finally, conclusions are drawn in Sect. 5.

2   Related Work

Since their release to the public, Large Language Models (LLMs) have shown great potential for a wide range of daily tasks [10]. In particular, their capabilities in document editing and generation use-cases offer great potential for their successful application to the PA domain. Most LLMs have shown greater performance in zero-shot [5] and in particular few-shot [4] tasks, where examples of acceptable results are provided along with the instructions for the task to be executed.

It has been shown that better results can be obtained by applying guidelines for prompt engineering [16]. Usually, when a human is involved, the prompt refinement becomes a trial-and-error process, by improving the final result by incremental changes to the initial prompt, based on the generated output.

Prompt engineering proved to be a crucial step both for the average and advanced users in applications of LLMs to the production of semi-structured documents, where the original structure requires subsequent adaptations through a trial-and-error process. Through prompt engineering, it is possible to improve the quality of the output obtained and especially its compliance with contextual specifications regarding the required content and style. For this reason, the main challenge of allowing PA entities to successfully integrate LLMs in their workflows is to enable the inexperienced user to create efficient prompts and to minimize the time spent improving the task description provided as a prompt to the Large Language Model.

As a trade-off for their versatility, LLMs incur in the problem of hallucination, causing results to be skewed and inaccurate or biased with respect to the original requests, especially with longer context windows. In the document generation task, especially for the generation of longer documents, prompts might tend to be long and rich in information, with the risk of causing hallucinations.

2.1 LLMs in the PA Domain

The integration of Large Language Models (LLMs) in automating document generation processes, particularly in the domain of PA, has seen significant interest due to the amount of document manipulation required in this domain. Some works are helping in information extraction from those documents, for example, when dealing with extracting and classifying relations from tenders of the PA [12].

Prior studies are nowadays predominantly focused on leveraging LLMs for structured data extraction, text summarization, and content customization [7] to enhance administrative efficiency and user engagement. Prompt engineering has shown relevant results in improving the LLM's generation capabilities [16], and, with guiding principles, LLMs can meet requirements and allow for enhanced quality in response [1].

An approach for information extraction for unstructured documents is presented in [9], where an embedding-based retrieval system with LLM is used for effective agriculture information extraction from unstructured data. The system features an embedding-based retrieval system along with LLM question-answering to automatically extract entities and attributes from the documents, and transform them into structured data.

When dealing with novel documents, also Retrieval-augmented generation (RAG) approaches allow large language models (LLM) to retrieve relevant knowledge, showing promising potential in mitigating LLM hallucinations and enhancing response quality, and, chance, facilitating the adoption of LLMs in practice [2]. However, existing RAG systems are often inadequate in answering multi-hop queries, which require retrieving and reasoning over iteratively. An improvement of this technology has been proposed in [14] where multi-hop reasoning steps are introduced in the RAG system.

The difficulties are even more common when dealing with the application of LLMs in generating semi-structured documents from semantically similar examples. This remains relatively unsolved and they still struggle with tasks that require generating complex, structured outputs [13]. This gap is primarily due to the inherent complexity of semi-structured documents, which defy conventional template-based approaches. Several approaches have been proposed to handle them. A notable example is represented by [15], where Chain-Of-Thought is presented as a series of intermediate reasoning steps that significantly improve the ability of large language models to perform complex reasoning. In particular, it is shown how such reasoning abilities emerge naturally in sufficiently large language models.

A closer step in the generation of semi-structured documents is represented by the Directional Stimulus Prompting Technology [8], where the LLM output is conditioned to generate desired outcomes, such as including specific keywords. The research on semantic understanding and context-aware generation provides foundational insights but stops short of addressing the specific challenges posed by semi-structured documents in PA.

Furthermore, the Artificial Intelligence as a Service ('AIaaS') trend [3] is going to play a growing role in society's technological infrastructure, enabling, facilitating, and underpinning functionality in many applications. AIaaS providers therefore hold significant power at this infrastructural level and with the upcoming legislation in Europe, their role can easily be diffused in the workflow of the public offices. The *AIaaS* approach aligns also with our proposed multi-agent approach in document generation tasks. The multi-agent approach has been demonstrated to improve problem-solving in overcoming the limitations of individual models [11]. In the PA domain, this distributed approach offers modularity and scalability, potentially suitable for handling various document types and complexities within PA settings.

In summary, while the literature provides valuable perspectives on the capabilities and applications of LLMs in various contexts, our work contributes a novel methodology and interaction framework for the LLM-assisted semi-structured document generation in PA, including multi-agent assistance in document generation and paving the way for further innovation and exploration in this domain.

3 Proposed Approach

The usual interaction model between an LLM and an inexperienced user for document generation features a trial-and-error process, aimed at refining the prompt until a satisfying result is reached. Longer prompts are required for longer documents, making it even more difficult to obtain a satisfying result. Moreover, in detail-rich documents, the performance of LLM agents is bound to decrease when document generation requires many tasks to be completed.

Given the requirement for user supervision in a trial-and-error process, we propose a different workflow aimed at minimizing user intervention. The proposed process, iterative in nature, follows the overall structure of a document template, which can be extracted from a pre-existing template document provided by the user as input.

The user is allowed to provide an initial prompt to describe the overall expected result. The initial prompt is then refined throughout iterations, to hold all the missing data required to generate the document, accumulating in the original prompt the outcomes of user interventions whenever requested by the agents. The *accumulated prompt* will serve as a data source throughout the document generation steps. Following the structure of the template document, the output document is then generated section-by-section, in reading order.

During the generic generation step, LLM agents are interrogated to solve fine-grained tasks depending on the availability of the information required to generate semantically suitable content for the current section, according to the semantics provided in the corresponding section in the template document. Each agent is instructed with a previously engineered prompt, describing its task, which is then completed by context-dependent information, depending on the semantics of the current section and the data extracted from the *accumulated prompt*.

The multi-agent framework allows specializing agents as much as necessary to prevent hallucinations, in sections where available contextual pieces of information are prone to provide undesired results (like what could happen in case the provided context is very short or the text is very schematic). Post-processing may be applied to improve the results, especially if a schematic output is expected, by explicitly asking the LLM agents to return specific tokens in case some conditions are met, as a way to force them to not hallucinate and comply with their role in the workflow. Detecting these tokens in the output may help in managing limit cases that would otherwise disrupt the workflow, improving the overall system robustness.

User intervention is required only in case the pieces of information retrievable from the *accumulated prompt* are not enough to comply with the semantics of the current document section, so the frequency of user intervention depends on the quality of the initial prompt. The advantage of this approach is that the *accumulated prompt* is used only as a data source: in this way, the agent tasked with extracting data from the prompt is less prone to hallucinate when the user prompt is not complete or clear. After user intervention, the new data provided by the user is added to the *accumulated prompt*, to be stored for future retrievals.

To ensure flexibility in the emulation of the original document template, the user is allowed to optionally skip the generation of a document section at any time, leaving the accumulated prompt unaltered. A representation of the workflow obtained according to this interaction model is shown in Fig. 2.

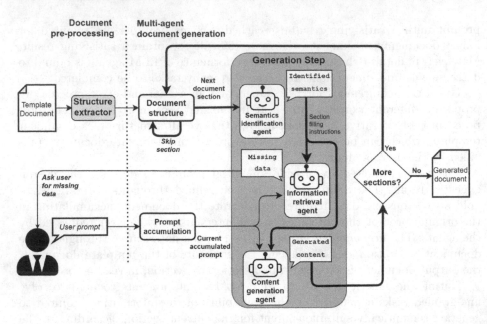

Fig. 2. Representation of our multi-agent architecture. The workflow for the generic generation step is highlighted by the bold black arrows.

Although our work focuses on the components atomically necessary to generate a document section-by-section, the presented interaction model allows the integration of additional agents to manage different aspects of document editing, depending on the level of structuring of the document and the level of expertise required by the specific task assigned to the agent.

3.1 Template Pre-processing

The document structure can be extracted on a format-dependent basis, using pre-existing tools. In our case, we used a REST API interface for cloud-based processing using the Adobe Extraction API[1], to extract bounding boxes and contents from figures, text blocks, and tables in the document. It is not important to deduce the field semantics at this stage as we only need structural cues for the next steps.

3.2 Multi-agent Interaction

The user is invited to provide an initial prompt giving an overall description and directives for the generated document, such as more general qualities like style or tone of the text or more specific information and data necessary for document generation. It is possible to leave the initial prompt empty, in which case the

---

[1] https://developer.adobe.com/document-services/docs/overview/pdf-extract-api/.

maximum level of user intervention will be required throughout the generation process.

The current workflow features a set of three LLM-based agents, each corresponding to a phase of the generic content generation step for a single document section, in order: *Section Semantics Identification, Information Retrieval, Content Generation.*

The *Section Semantics Identification* step is aimed at identifying the semantics of the current section from the document template. In case the template section contains tokens that need to be replaced in the current document section, which can appear as placeholders, such as "Name", "Surname", "Birthday", "City" or explicitly already populated with data, such as "John", "Doe", "01/01/1970", "Washington", the usual Natural Language Processing pipeline to perform Entity recognition and Semantic parsing on a sentence would generally require performing several preliminary tasks such as Part-of-Speech tagging, Named Entity Recognition, Relationship Extraction, before the actual semantic tagging of tokens, to build a semantic representation of the sentence good enough to extract the tokens of interest correctly. Using LLMs for this task allows instead exploiting their Commonsense Knowledge [6]. This step is therefore managed by the first LLM agent, the *Semantics Identification agent,* which autonomously identifies the semantics of the current section from the template document, identifying replaceable data in the provided template section.

The agent output is a list of directives and instructions on how to reproduce the semantics of the corresponding template, whenever the text allows deducing it, serving as instructions for the *Content Generation* phase, along with a list of identified replaceable data. In case the semantics of any of such data are identified, the list of instructions will contain directives on how to add them to the text generated for the corresponding section in the output document. Using only a schematic representation of the semantics as an output causes a degradation in the quality of the generated content downstream, therefore the instructions provided by the agent are discursive and verbose. The output of this phase will be provided to the *Information Retrieval agent,* to identify data required in the current section, and the *Content Generation agent,* enabling it to reconstruct the semantics of this template section in the output document.

It should be noted that the list of replaceable data might contain data that is already available in the accumulated user prompt as well as missing data. For this reason, the second phase, destined to *Information Retrieval,* is aimed at using the available information to retrieve the data specifically required by the current document section, according to the semantic cues previously extracted.

The second agent, the *Information Retrieval agent,* is specialized in extracting the required information from the accumulated prompt, which at the first step coincides with the initial prompt, and determining which data could not be retrieved. In case it is not possible to find all the required data (according to the instructions from the *Semantics Identification agent),* user intervention is required, to specify through a textual prompt the actual replacement values for the missing data. The result of this interaction is added to the *accumulated*

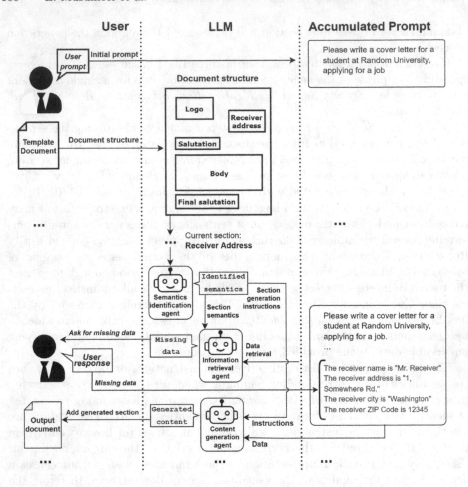

Fig. 3. Representation of a generation step instance. Notice how the *accumulated prompt* is enriched with the missing data provided by the user.

prompt, to be used by the *Content Generation agent* as a data source, or to be stored for the *Information Retrieval* phase of later iterations. Therefore, if the user decides not to specify some information, they will not be integrated into the result and will be ignored in the output content.

As a last step, during the *Content Generation* phase, the *Content Generation agent* is therefore instructed to generate the textual content for the current document section, using the *accumulated prompt*, now enriched with the required information, and the instructions coming from the *Semantics Identification agent*.

At the end, both an output document and a refined prompt are obtained. In particular, the refined prompt will contain all the missing data identified throughout the generation process. An example of a workflow instance is shown in Fig. 3.

3.3   Document Post-processing

During the document generation, only text content is processed, while the same structure of the original template document is used, including figures and other graphical elements, which can be skipped by the user during the generation process to avoid including them. Thanks to the modularity of this framework, additional agents can be added to improve the graphical appearance and improve its dependence on the context and the semantics of the user requirements, and additional processing steps can be added downstream to improve the graphical appearance of the result (for example by generating context-dependent images) but this is outside of the scope of the current work.

4   Experimental Evaluation

Agents were built using the latest OpenAI *GPT 3.5 Turbo* model (*gpt-3.5-turbo-1106*) with a context window of 16,385 tokens and a maximum of 4,096 output tokens.

Table 1. Agent task prompt refinement for Semantics Identification Agent, with template text " *Your name*".

Prompt engineering for the Semantics Identification Agent	
Template text: *Your Name*	
Agent task	**Agent answer**
You are an assistant helping to understand the structure content of a template document. Respond with the content that might be written in the document.	[Your Name]
	[Your Address]
	[City, State, Zip Code]
	[Email Address]
	[Phone Number]
You are an assistant helping to understand the structure content of a template document. Respond with the content that might be written in the document. Give just the action to do	Fill in your full legal name.
You are an assistant helping to understand the structure content of a template document. Respond with the content that might be written in the document. Give just the action to do. For example, if you read "Location", the output will be "Add the location"; if you read "Dear Someone", the output will be "Add salutation"	Add your full name

Experiments are aimed at designing an effective prompt for each agent, by performing a trial-and-error process to obtain a correct and contextually appropriate response from the LLMs.

The evaluation process tests the agents' ability to understand the assigned tasks, fine-tuning each agent's ability to conform to the expected outputs, given their specific role in the generation workflow.

The process of crafting an effective prompt that maximizes conformity of the output of a Large Language Model to the original requirements has the potential to dramatically improve the quality of the generated output, especially when this output is used in an intermediate step of a processing pipeline. The baseline version of the prompt point is obtained by following general prompt engineering guidelines [16], the most important one consisting of writing in a clear and imperative tone the task assignment for the LLM. Starting from the baseline and analyzing the response, it is then possible to refine the prompt in incremental steps, by adding instructions to force the model toward a more desirable output.

The most important undesirable behavior to keep under control is the chance for hallucination, which in this case can alter the data in the generated content and therefore provide false and unsatisfying textual content for the document section being generated.

Each prompt consists of two components: a "*system prompt*" containing the pre-assigned instructions used to inform the agent of its specific task, instructing it with its role and the guidelines for the generation of its output, and a "*context-specific prompt*", which contains the actual context-specific text for the current instance of the agent's task.

Obtaining a robustly engineered prompt requires careful tuning, considering the variety of possible inputs in a semi-structured document. On one hand, very schematic text consisting of single entities (such as "First name", "Last name" and other specific data) poses a challenge and requires more carefully engineered prompts. On the other hand, output should still be desirable in the case of less schematic, more discursive sections. The generic input for the generation step, which will be forwarded to the *Semantics identification agent*, is the textual content of the currently processed template document section, which is necessary to obtain semantic cues about the desired output text.

The output of the generation step coincides with the output from the *Content generation agent*.

4.1   Semantics Identification Agent

The *Semantics Identification agent* is tasked with producing a discursive and fluent explanation of the semantics of the current document section and most importantly of the instructions and directives for the generation of the content to be included in the output document, based on the expected semantics. To avoid hallucinations it is extremely important to have a non-schematic and unspecific description of the semantics of the current document section.

We show the prompt engineering process based on the answers of the same agent to different *system prompts*, progressively refined in incremental steps, for different template texts, in order of increasing verbosity of the *context-specific prompt* (therefore in decreasing order of schematism).

The first more schematic template text is "*Your name*", as could be found in any template document for a generic letter, in a field where the name of the user is required. The relevant results for this refinement process are provided in Table 1.

Table 2. Agent task prompt refinement for Semantics Identification Agent, with template text "*Dear Mr./Ms. (Lastname):*".

Prompt engineering for the Semantics Identification Agent	
Template text: *Dear Mr./Ms. (Lastname):*	
Agent task	**Agent answer**
You are an assistant helping to understand the structure content of a template document. Respond with the content that might be written in the document.	I hope this message finds you well. I am writing to inform you about the upcoming meeting scheduled for (date) at (time) in (location). The purpose of this meeting is to discuss (agenda items). Your presence and input at this meeting are crucial, so please make every effort to attend. If you are unable to attend, please notify me as soon as possible. Thank you for your attention to this matter, and I look forward to seeing you at the meeting.
You are an assistant helping to understand the structure content of a template document. Respond with the content that might be written in the document. Give just the action to do.	Insert the recipient's last name in the salutation.
You are an assistant helping to understand the structure content of a template document. Respond with the content that might be written in the document. Give just the action to do. For example, if you read "Location", the output will be "Add the location"; if you read "Dear Someone", the output will be "Add salutation".	Add salutation

The initial baseline version of the prompt describes the agent's task without specifying that the output should contain instructions on how to reproduce the semantics of the provided template text. The agent response is heavily affected by hallucinations, answering with plausible text for a generic letter, without giving a generic description of its semantics, clearly missing its objective. From the analysis of the answer, it can be assumed that the agent misinterprets the request "*Respond with the content that could be written*" as a request to provide the actual content of the generated document.

The addition of a clear instruction "*Give just the action to do*" in the second version of the system prompt definition gives the agent a clear explanation on how to perform its task. This sentence is crucial to improve the conformity of the agent's response to its original task, instructing it to provide a description of the action to perform to reproduce the semantics of the template section.

Table 3. Agent task prompt refinement for Semantics Identification Agent, with a long and very discursive template text.

Prompt engineering for the Semantics Identification Agent	
Template text: *First paragraphs : In your opening paragraph, concisely convey your enthusiasm for the role and the organization, while emphasizing your pertinent educational background. Aim to engage the reader's interest, prompting them to delve deeper into your resume. This section serves as a preview, showcasing your qualifications and setting the stage for the detailed skills and experiences outlined in your resume. Highlight your top skills that align with the job requirements, and showcase your familiarity with the organization by mentioning specific aspects such as their mission, ongoing projects, or strategic objectives, linking them to how your abilities and interests can add value to their team.*	
Agent task	**Agent answer**
You are an assistant helping to understand the structure content of a template document. Respond with the content that might be written in the document.	Dear [Hiring Manager's Name], I am writing to express my genuine enthusiasm for the [Job Title] position at [Organization Name]. With a strong educational background in [relevant field], I am confident in my ability to contribute to the success of your team. The innovative projects and strategic objectives of [Organization Name] resonate with my professional interests, and I am eager to bring my skills and expertise to support your mission. My top skills in [specific skills] and [specific skills] align closely
You are an assistant helping to understand the structure content of a template document. Respond with the content that might be written in the document. Give just the action to do.	Express enthusiasm for the role and the organization, emphasizing your educational background and top skills that align with the job requirements. Showcase your familiarity with the organization by mentioning specific aspects such as their mission, ongoing projects, or strategic objectives, and link them to how your abilities and interests can add value to their team.
You are an assistant helping to understand the structure content of a template document. Respond with the content that might be written in the document. Give just the action to do. For example, if you read "Location", the output will be "Add the location"; if you read "Dear Someone", the output will be "Add salutation".	Write an enthusiastic opening paragraph that emphasizes your relevant educational background and showcases your qualifications and skills that align with the job requirements. Mention specific aspects of the organization such as their mission, ongoing projects, or strategic objectives, and link them to how your abilities and interests can add value to their team

The relevant results for template text *"Dear Mr./Ms.(Lastname)"* are provided in Table 2. Here, the output to the second version of the prompt could be considered correct but it could be even more synthetic, considering that the optimal response would just be and instruction to *"Add a salutation"*.

Given that we aim to maintain the agent output as short and synthetic as possible, we found out that the result can be further improved by providing examples of correct and desirable outputs. This 'few-shot prompting' technique allows constraining the output to adhere as much as possible to a desirable format, furthermore improving the understanding of the agent on how to better perform in the assigned task. As seen in the third version of the prompt in Tables 1, 2 and 3 an addition of examples in the prompt makes it possible to obtain an answer that fits the desired requirements.

In particular, it should be noted how the tone of the agent's answer in 3 becomes increasingly descriptive and imperative, which is nearer to the required style, as the task prompt is refined.

Table 4. Agent task prompt refinement for Information retrieval.

Prompt Engineering for the Information retrieval Agent
Accumulated prompt: "My name is John Doe, i want write a letter for Random University, i am a student in Computer Science"
Section-specific task description: I want you to satisfy this instruction [Answer of the Semantics Identification Agent for section "*Your Name*"] What is the missing information?

Agent task	Agent answer
You are an assistant that has the purpose of searching which information is missing.The information that you have are **\<Accumulated prompt\>** If you have the information write the token [ALL_INFO]. **\<Section-specific task description\>**	The missing information is the full name of the university you want to write the letter to.
You are an assistant that has the purpose of searching which information is missing.The information that you have are **\<Accumulated prompt\>** Your output must be like this: the missing information to satisfy the request is INFORMATION_MISSING. If you have the information write the token [ALL_INFO]. Strictly respond with only the information that is missing. **\<Section-specific task description\>**	The missing information to satisfy the request is [ALL_INFO].

4.2   Information Retrieval Agent

The *Information Retrieval Agent* is tasked with retrieving information from the context initially provided by the user and progressively accumulated throughout iterations in the *accumulated prompt*, according to the instructions of the previous agent. The task description for this agent is obtained from the answer of the first agent as seen in Tables 4, 5 and 6.

The agent is instructed to return the [ALL_INFO] token to signal that it has managed to retrieve all the required information from the existing accumulated prompt.

In Table 4, when asked for the name using the baseline version of the prompt, the agent does not reply with the [ALL_INFO] token but requests further information, even though in the current *Accumulated prompt* the name of the user

Table 5. Agent task prompt refinement for Information retrieval.

Prompt Engineering for the Information retrieval Agent	

Accumulated prompt: "My name is John Doe, I want to write a letter for Random University, I am a student in Computer Science"

Section-specific task description:
I want you to satisfy this instruction
[Answer of the Semantics Identification Agent for section "*Dear Mr./Ms. (Lastname):*"]
What is the missing information?

Agent task	Agent answer
You are an assistant that has the purpose of searching which information is missing.The information that you have are <**Accumulated prompt**> If you have the information write the token [ALL_INFO]. <**Section-specific task description**>	The missing information is the specific name of the person to whom the letter is addressed. Typically, a salutation would include the recipient's name, such as "Dear [Recipient's Name]," or "To Whom It May Concern," if the specific
You are an assistant that has the purpose of searching which information is missing.The information that you have are <**Accumulated prompt**> Your output must be like this: the missing information to satisfy the request is INFORMATION_MISSING. If you have the information write the token [ALL_INFO]. Strictly respond with only the information that is missing. <**Section-specific task description**>	The missing information to satisfy the request are the salutation.

is already available, clearly deviating from the assigned task, while in Table 5, the agent erroneously replies to the baseline prompt with a further request for information, including context information that does not concern its task. The prompt is therefore refined by adding a clear example-based instruction ("*Your output must be like: ...*"), constraining the model to conform to a specific output format. Moreover, a reinforcement instruction is added to avoid hallucinations ("*Strictly respond with only the information that is missing.*").

A particularly interesting study case consists of using the engineered prompt and providing a text without a semantic value, such as a placeholder text:

Table 6. Agent task prompt refinement for Information retrieval, with a very long and discursive core section of the template document

Prompt Engineering for the Information retrieval Agent

Accumulated prompt: "My name is John Doe, I want to write a letter for Random University, I am a student in Computer Science"

Section-specific task description:
I want you to satisfy this instruction
[Answer of the Semantics Identification Agent for a verbose template body section]
What is the missing information?

Agent task	Agent answer
You are an assistant that has the purpose of searching which information is missing. The information that you have are <**Accumulated prompt**> If you have the information write the token [ALL_INFO]. <**Section-specific task description**>	The missing information includes your current level of education (e.g., undergraduate, graduate), any specific skills or experiences you want to highlight, and the specific job requirements or aspects of Random University with which you want your skills to align to.
You are an assistant that has the purpose of searching which information is missing. The information that you have are <**Accumulated prompt**> Your output must be like this: the missing information to satisfy the request is INFORMATION_MISSING. If you have the information write the token [ALL_INFO]. Strictly respond with only the information that is missing. <**Section-specific task description**>	The missing information to satisfy the request are the specific aspects of the organization such as their mission, ongoing projects, or any other relevant details.

Template text: *Lorem ipsum dolor sit amet, consectetur adipiscing elit...*

The template text is the placeholder text ("*Lorem Ipsum ...*") typically used to test graphical templates. The agent answer perfectly conforms to the prescribed task as this placeholder is usually found in the discursive sections of document templates:

Agent Answer: *The missing information to satisfy the request is the content of the main body of the document.*

4.3   Content Generation Agent

The *Content Generation Agent* is tasked with generating the text in the output document following the instructions of the other agents and using the information contained in the *accumulated prompt*.

The *system prompt* for this agent, as in the cases of the previous agents, contains clear instructions and constraints to obtain a desirable output. The baseline prompt is:

Agent task:
You are an assistant with the purpose of generating a document with the available information. You have the following information:
{Accumulated prompt}
For example, if you read "Add salutation name", write the salutation only.

where {Accumulated prompt} is the currently *accumulated prompt*.
With this baseline, the model tends to add initial greetings and a conclusion. This deviation from the original task could be solved by forbidding the addition of out-of-context information, by adding the following sentence

Remember that in an opening paragraph, it is absolutely forbidden to write "dear someone", or "sincerely" at the end of the document.

As for the previous agents, adding examples of the desired result drives the agent's output to the desired format.

4.4   Prompt-Engineered Results

Examples of a full processing iteration of template sections with the refined prompts are shown in Figs. 4 and 5.

Figure 4 in particular presents a case in which, thanks to the prompt engineering process, the *Content Generation agent* is able to retrieve the necessary data from the *accumulated prompt* without asking for user intervention, then using the instructions for the reproduction of the semantics of the document section, provided by the *Semantics Identification agent*, to generate a desirable result.

Figure 5 instead presents a case in which some missing information is detected, which requires user intervention to provide such missing data, which is then added to the *accumulated prompt*.

In both cases, a dramatic improvement in the quality of the agents' responses was obtained by adding examples for the structure of the expected result.

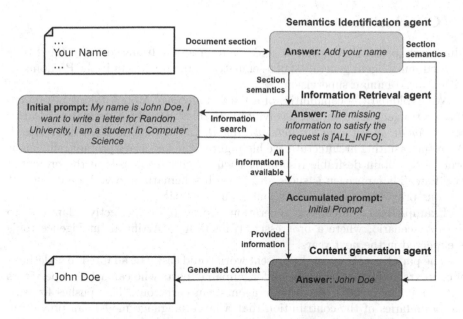

Fig. 4. Agent responses throughout a single generation step, starting from the template text: "*Your name*". The figure represents a single generation step for a section of the document, showing an example of successful generation using the engineered prompt. In this case all information is retrieved in the original user prompt, so no information is asked to the user.

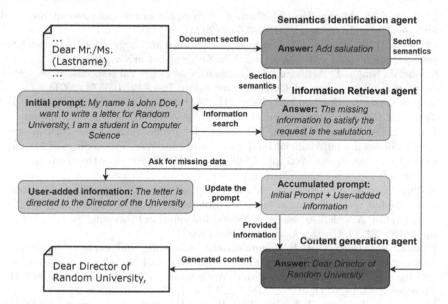

Fig. 5. Agent responses throughout a single generation step, starting from the template text: "*Dear Mr./Ms. (Lastname)*". In this case, user intervention is required to add missing information.

5   Conclusions

This work presents a workflow and an interaction framework for the LLM-assisted multi-agent generation of a semi-structured document in the PA domain, with limited human supervision.

We exploited the capabilities of a Large Language Model, taking advantage of a multi-agent architecture, involving three roles, namely, a *Semantics Identification Agent*, an *Information Retrieval Agent*, and, a *Content Generation Agent*. With the resulting architecture, we highlighted the necessary prompt refinement process to obtain desirable results for each specific agent role in the presented workflow. The approach is successful in both schematic and verbose document sections providing enough cues about their semantics.

Example-based document generation proves to be perfectly adaptable to the PA scenario, where a progressive transition to Artificial Intelligence tools is expected in the next years.

The paradigm shown in the present work could easily be adapted to a plethora of contexts, reducing the workload for human experts who can act as supervisors of the job that a pool of synthetic agents can carry out. This pushes forward the boundaries of the contribution that a large language model can provide in an office context and also represents a notable starting point for research in the field of multi-role architecture for everyday tasks.

References

1. Bsharat, S.M., Myrzakhan, A., Shen, Z.: Principled instructions are all you need for questioning LLaMA-1/2, GPT-3.5/4 (2024)
2. Chen, J., Lin, H., Han, X., Sun, L.: Benchmarking large language models in retrieval-augmented generation (2023). arXiv preprint arXiv:2309.01431
3. Cobbe, J., Singh, J.: Artificial intelligence as a service: legal responsibilities, liabilities, and policy challenges. Comput. Law Secur. Rev. **42**, 105573 (2021)
4. Hegselmann, S., Buendia, A., Lang, H., Agrawal, M., Jiang, X., Sontag, D.: TabLLM: few-shot classification of tabular data with large language models. In: Ruiz, F., Dy, J., van de Meent, J.W. (eds.) In: Proceedings of The 26th International Conference on Artificial Intelligence and Statistics. Proceedings of Machine Learning Research, vol. 206, pp. 5549–5581. PMLR (2023). https://proceedings.mlr.press/v206/hegselmann23a.html
5. Kojima, T., Gu, S.S., Reid, M., Matsuo, Y., Iwasawa, Y.: Large language models are zero-shot reasoners. In: Koyejo, S., Mohamed, S., Agarwal, A., Belgrave, D., Cho, K., Oh, A. (eds.) Advances in Neural Information Processing System, vol. 35, pp. 22199–22213. Curran Associates, Inc. (2022)
6. Krause, S., Stolzenburg, F.: Commonsense reasoning and explainable artificial intelligence using large language models. In: Nowaczyk, S., et al. (eds.) Artificial Intelligence, ECAI 2023 International Workshops. CCIS, vol. 1947, pp. 302–319. Springer, Cham (2024). https://doi.org/10.1007/978-3-031-50396-2_17
7. Li, J., Tang, T., Zhao, W.X., Nie, J.Y., Wen, J.R.: Pretrained language models for text generation: a survey (2022). arXiv preprint arXiv:2201.05273
8. Li, Z., Peng, B., He, P., Galley, M., Gao, J., Yan, X.: Guiding large language models via directional stimulus prompting (2023). arXiv preprint arXiv:2302.11520

9. Peng, R., Liu, K., Yang, P., Yuan, Z., Li, S.: Embedding-based retrieval with LLM for effective agriculture information extracting from unstructured data (2023). arXiv preprint arXiv:2308.03107

10. Radford, A., Wu, J., Child, R., Luan, D., Amodei, D., Sutskever, I., et al.: Language models are unsupervised multitask learners. OpenAI blog 1(8), 9 (2019)

11. Rasal, S.: LLM harmony: multi-agent communication for problem solving (2024). arXiv preprint arXiv:2401.01312

12. Siciliani, L., Ghizzota, E., Basile, P., Lops, P.: OIE4PA: open information extraction for the public administration. J. Intell. Inf. Syst. **62**, 273–294 (2024)

13. Tang, X., Zong, Y., Zhao, Y., Cohan, A., Gerstein, M.: Struc-bench: Are large language models really good at generating complex structured data? (2023). arXiv preprint arXiv:2309.08963

14. Tang, Y., Yang, Y.: MultiHop-RAG: Benchmarking retrieval-augmented generation for multi-hop queries (2024). arXiv preprint arXiv:2401.15391

15. Wei, J., et al.: Chain-of-thought prompting elicits reasoning in large language models. In: Koyejo, S., Mohamed, S., Agarwal, A., Belgrave, D., Cho, K., Oh, A. (eds.) Advances in Neural Information Processing Systems, vol. 35, pp. 24824–24837. Curran Associates, Inc. (2022)

16. White, J., et al.: A prompt pattern catalog to enhance prompt engineering with ChatGPT (2023). arXiv preprint arXiv:2302.11382

Enabling Human-Centered Machine Translation Using Concept-Based Large Language Model Prompting and Translation Memory

Ming Qian[1]([⊠]) and Chuiqing Kong[2]

[1] Charles River Analytics, Cambridge, MA 02138, USA
mqian@cra.com
[2] FreeLance Translator and Researcher, San Mateo, CA 94403, USA

Abstract. This study evaluates a novel human-machine collaborative machine translation workflow, enhanced by Large Language Model features, including pre-editing instructions, interactive concept-based post-editing, and the archiving of concepts in post-editing and translation memories. By implementing GPT-4 prompts for concept-based steering in English-to-Chinese translation, we explore its effectiveness compared to traditional machine translation methods such as Google Translate, human translators, and an alternative human-machine collaboration approach that utilizes human-generated reference texts instead of concept description. Our findings suggest that while GPT-4's discourse-level analysis and augmented instructions show potential, they do not surpass the nuanced understanding of human translators at the sentence-level. However, GPT-4 augmented concept-based interactive post-editing significantly outperforms both traditional methods and the alternative method relying on human reference translations. In testing English-to-Chinese translation concepts, GPT-4 effectively elucidates nearly all concepts, precisely identifies the relevance of concepts within source texts, and accurately translates into target texts embodying the related concepts. Nevertheless, some complex concepts require more sophisticated prompting techniques, such as Chain-of-Thought, or pre-editing strategies, like explicating linguistic patterns, to achieve optimal performance. Despite GPT-4's capabilities, human language experts possess superior abductive reasoning capabilities. Consequently, at the present stage, humans must apply abductive reasoning to create more specific instructions and develop additional logic steps in prompts, which complicate the prompt engineering process. Eventually, enhanced abductive reasoning capabilities in large language models will bring their performance closer to human-like levels. The proposed novel approach introduces a scalable, concept-based strategy that can be applied across multiple text segments, enhancing machine translation workflow efficiency.

Keywords: Human-centered Machine Translation · Human-Machine Collaboration · Translation Workflow · Concept-based Post-editing · Concept-based Translation Memory · Large Language Modeling · Prompt Engineering · Chain-of-Thought Prompting · Translation Concept · Automatic Post-editing · Few-shot Learning · Abductive Reasoning · Human-like Learning

H. Degen and S. Ntoa (Eds.): HCII 2024, LNAI 14736, pp. 118–134, 2024.
https://doi.org/10.1007/978-3-031-60615-1_8

1   Introduction

John McCarthy's insight, "To understand natural language is to understand the concepts in the language, not just the words," underscores the critical importance of comprehending the concepts expressed in texts. Recent advancements in generative Artificial Intelligence (GenAI), particularly through large language models (LLMs), like GPT-4, have demonstrated their effectiveness as machine translation tool in various studies and evaluations [1, 2]. Unlike traditional machine translation (MT) tools such as Google Translate, which rely solely on the source language text, GPT-4 possesses the ability to understand and follow instructions and can even learn from bilingual examples provided within the prompt. This capability enables GPT-4 to deliver translations that are more sensitive to context and accuracy, establishing it as a more adaptable and user-friendly option compared to conventional approaches.

1.1   Challenges in Traditional Machine Translation Within Human-Computer Interaction Contexts

Human-machine collaboration is essential in traditional machine translation (MT) to facilitate the correction of inaccuracies in MT-generated translations [3]. Human translators play a pivotal role by post-editing and refining MT results, contributing corrections that machines can then leverage to enhance their translation proficiency. This synergy between human expertise and machine learning significantly improves the reliability and accuracy of machine-translated text. However, the manual nature of MT post-editing renders it time-intensive and less cost-efficient. Automatic post-editing (APE) seeks to streamline this process by automatically enhancing the outputs of MT systems, drawing on the insights gained from previous human post-editing interventions on similar MT outputs [4]. A key metric in this context is the Translation Edit Rate (TER), which measures the edit distance between the machine's translation hypothesis and the human reference translation. In APE, the versions that have been post-edited serve as benchmarks for evaluation, as they are compared to the system's output or hypothesis. The TER score is determined by the edit distance between these two versions, offering a quantitative measure of the APE system's performance.

MT is often characterized by various levels of repetition, high volume, and the necessity to complete translations within tight deadlines [3]. The translation memory (TM) facilitates enhanced collaboration between human translators and MT tools. By leveraging previously human-edited translated texts, MT tools can generate translations that may subsequently be refined through human post-editing. These human edits are incorporated into the TM, enabling the machine to 'learn' new ways of translating. This iterative process contributes to the ongoing enhancement and precision of MT capabilities. The foundational element of building a TM is at the sentence level, with the primary technique for identifying correspondences in TM being string matching algorithms. These algorithms assess the similarity between the source text and the stored translation units. Matches found are typically classified into three categories: exact match (100%), nearly exact match (95%–99%), and fuzzy match (50%–94%) [5]. This systematization allows for a structured approach to improving translation quality over time [6].

In addition, MT often struggles to maintain the tone and style of the original text in the translated version because it faces challenges to understand cultural difference and semantic nuances between source and target language as well as translating colloquial phrases and idioms [7, 8].

1.2 Augmented Machine Translation via Large Language Model

The resolution to the previously mentioned constraints may be found in Generative Large Language Models (LLMs) like GPT-4. A prompt for an LLM is a meticulously designed input that steers the model towards generating precise, high-quality outputs. By employing prompt engineering, we can offer diverse instructions and bilingual text examples, thereby enabling new features for the workflow of human-machine collaboration (as depicted in Fig. 1).

1. *Pre-editing instructions* encompass writing style, tone, and various elements, which can be delineated through directives originating either from human translators or automated analyses of a source or reference text. Traditional machine translation tools lack support for this functionality.
2. *Interactive human-machine collaborative interactive post-editing*: A human post-editor can direct an APE agent through conceptual instructions and/or bilingual text examples showcasing the desired concept. For instance, an instruction to "convert the units of measure to metric from English (or imperial) units in the target text" would lead to the conversion of inches to centimeters and miles to kilometers in the resulting text. Multiple rounds of interaction can facilitate revisions targeting various concepts. While traditional MT tools support automatic post-editing that adapts based on human-edited content in the past and measures similarity through edit distance, they lack the capability to make inferences based on conceptual understanding.
3. *Concept-based APE memory*: In contrast to traditional APE systems, which store triplets consisting of the source text, the machine translation (MT) output, and the human post-edited version, concept-based post-editing memory also incorporates the concept description crafted by the human translator. This approach enhances segment matching by prioritizing concept similarity over mere string similarity.
4. *Concept-based translation memory*: Following a similar approach, traditional translation memory systems save the source text and the target text generated by machine translation (MT) plus human post-editing. Concept-focused translation memory goes a step further by incorporating the concept description too. This modification allows for segment matching to be evaluated based on concept similarity, moving beyond mere string similarity.

In this study, we assess the efficacy of directing translation output with concept-based GPT-4 prompts. Utilizing English-to-Chinese examples, we examine GPT-4's capacity to steer the generation of the target language in alignment with concepts outlined in both a discourse-level pre-editing guide and sentence-level interactive human-machine collaborated post-editing prompts (refer to Sect. 2). Conversely, with Chinese-to-English examples, we evaluate GPT-4's proficiency in elucidating translation concepts, assessing their relevance to source test segments, and accurately rendering these concepts in the target language (refer to Sect. 3). Findings and conclusions are summarized in Sect. 4.

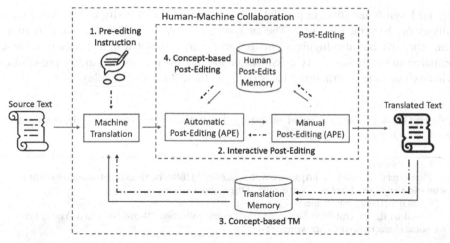

Fig. 1. Workflow of human-machine collaboration enhanced by LLM prompting features, highlighted with red text and arrows

2 Augmented Machine Translation via Concept-Driven Large Language Model Prompting

2.1 Motivation

Within the realm of English-to-Chinese translation related concepts, this section delves into the following research questions:

1. Does GPT-4 augmented MT outperforms traditional MT tool, such as Google Translate?
2. Which GPT-4-enabled augmented instructions yield the highest effectiveness and efficiency? We tested several types of instruction, including discourse-level style concepts, concept-based sentence-level post-editing, and GPT-4-augmented MT that incorporates human-generated translation references as part of the instruction.

  - For the source language, a social media discourse[1] was chosen to analyze the discourse-level writing style, and segments from this discourse were utilized for sentence-level experiments. The discourse was translated into Chinese by a translator certified by the American Translators Association, serving as the basis for providing a human-generated reference translation for one type of augmented instruction. The quality of various GPT-4-enhanced machine translation outputs was assessed by two professional English-to-Chinese translators using 5-point Likert scale ratings.

2.2 Augmented Instruction for Discourse-Level Style

LLMs have the capability to produce style analysis reports for narratives. Table 1 showcases an instance where ChatGPT is employed to generate a style analysis report for an

---

[1] https://www.thecut.com/2020/03/book-excerpt-samantha-irbys-wow-no-thank-you.html.

original English narrative. In parallel, two human translators performed a similar style analysis on the same discourse. The analysis generated by GPT-4 was not only more comprehensive but also highly accurate, and it was completed in a shorter timeframe compared to the human analysts. Subsequently, GPT-4 prompt can utilize pre-editing style analysis as its instructional basis (refer to Table 2 for an example).

Table 1. GPT-4 produced a report analyzing the discourse-level writing style, with entries identified by humans highlighted in bold.

User (Prompt)

Please read the story at **https://www.thecut.com/2020/03/book-excerpt-samantha-irbys-wow-no-thank-you.html** and derive a list of the author's writing style.

ChatGPT (Used Link Reader)

Based on the excerpt from Samantha Irby's essay collection "Wow, No Thank You.", here are some characteristics of her writing style:

1. Humorous and Self-deprecating: Irby often uses humor and self-deprecation to engage her readers. She makes fun of herself and her situations, which adds a light-hearted tone.
2. Conversational Tone: Her writing style is very conversational, feeling personal and relatable.
3. **Vivid Descriptions**: Irby uses vivid and detailed descriptions to paint a clear picture of her experiences. This helps to immerse the reader in her stories.
4. **Casual Language and Slang**: She uses casual language, slang, and colloquialisms, which contributes to the conversational and informal tone of her writing.
5. Honesty and Authenticity: Irby's writing is characterized by its honesty and authenticity. She doesn't shy away from discussing personal and sometimes uncomfortable topics.
6. Anecdotes: She uses anecdotes to illustrate points and make writing more relatable.
7. **Exaggeration for Effect**: Irby often uses exaggeration to emphasize her points.
8. Direct Address: She frequently addresses the reader directly, which helps to establish a connection between her and the reader.
9. Use of Rhetorical Questions: Irby often uses rhetorical questions to eng reader and encourage them to think more deeply about the topics she's discussing.
10. Pop Culture References: She incorporates pop culture references into her writing, which can make her work feel more current and relatable to a wide audience.

2.3 Augmented Instruction for Concept-Based Sentence-Level Post-editing

The sentence-level post-editing approach, rooted in a concept-based methodology, begins by applying a basic translation instruction to generate a preliminary translation. This is followed by the integration of human-crafted, concept-based instructions into the prompt in response to the issues observed in the initial rendition. This process

Table 2. The GPT-4 prompt employs pre-editing style analysis as its instructional basis.

Translate the following sentences to Chinese reflecting the following writing styles (if applicable): humorous, self-deprecating, conversational tone, vivid description, casual language and slang, honesty and authenticity, use of anecdotes, exaggeration for effect, direct address, use of rhetorical questions, and pop culture reference.

Original English: ...

The full translation to Chinese is:
... (GPT-4 output)

is designed to facilitate the creation of a refined and improved translation. Table 3 illustrates a GPT-4 prompt example for this approach. Multiple instructions can be given by humans to revise the target text based on different concepts.

Table 3. The GPT-4 prompt employs descriptions of concepts provided by humans to enhance machine translation revisions.

Translate the following text segment from English to Chinese:
Original English: ...
The Chinese translation is:
... 他的身高是5 英尺10 英寸 *(His height is 5 feet and 10 inches)*... [GPT-4 output]

Revise the translation to reflect the following concepts (descriptions provided by humans):

"convert the units of measure to the international System of Units (SI)"

The Revised Chinese translation is:

... 他的身高是 1.78 米 *(His height is 1.78 meters)*... [GPT-4 revised output]

2.4 Performance Evaluation

In reference [9], four methods were assessed for translating 20 text segments—extracted from the discourse mentioned in Table 1—from English to Chinese. The details of the experiments and results have already been published in [9], so here, we focus solely on presenting the performance outcomes in Fig. 2. This table displays the ratings given by two evaluators for (1) MT by Google Translate; (2) translation by a professional human translator; (3) GPT-4 augmented MT using writing style analysis for instruction; and (4) GPT-4 augmented MT with instructions based on human-generated reference translations. Overall, the human translation received the highest scores from expert evaluations. In contrast, GPT-4 enhanced translations, whether utilizing discourse-level style analysis or human-generated reference translations in the prompt, surpassed the performance of the basic MT provided by Google Translate.

The GPT-4 augmented instructions using discourse-level analysis have the potential to surpass traditional machine translation (MT) methods, yet they do not exceed the performance of human experts due to the latter's superior understanding at the sentence level. Additionally, it was observed that human experts performed better than GPT-4 augmented MT that used human-generated reference translations. In other words, translations done by humans alone outperformed those produced by combining human and AI efforts. This indicates that providing human-generated translations as additional context does not necessarily enhance AI-generated results to surpass expert human performance. Moreover, incorporating human-generated sentences for instructions or context is not practically viable for maintaining the cost-effectiveness of machine translation.

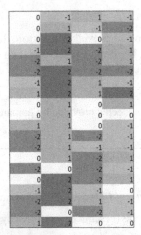 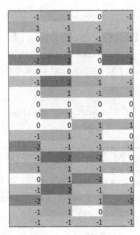

Fig. 2. Color-coded 5-point Likert scores were assigned by two evaluators across four categories: Google Translate, human expert, GPT-4 augmented MT using style analysis, and GPT-4 augmented MT using human-generated reference translations (due to space limitation, more details are provided in [9]). Two tables represent two evaluators, twenty rows represent the twenty examples, and four columns represent the four categories.

Ten examples, selected from the original 20 text segments, underwent testing for translation post-editing/revision, guided by concept-based instructions from human users. A selection of these concept-based revision instructions is provided below (for a comprehensive list of examples, refer to [9] due to space limitations):

1. The phrase should be revised to indicate that going outside is not necessary, rather than implying a perpetual state of staying indoors.
2. The expression "go dolphin" should be adapted to reflect cultural relevance since the concept of a school mascot, particularly "dolphin," may not resonate with Chinese audiences.
3. Instead of directly translating "go on like a house on fire," which may not convey the intended meaning in Chinese, a culturally equivalent idiom should be used.
4. For units of measure, conversions should be made from English units to metric units, which are familiar to Chinese receptors.

- Following the generation of the revised translations, the two evaluators were requested to provide evaluation rating scores for the following questions:

1. Does the revised translation adhere to the provided human guidelines?
2. Does the revised translation match the performance of the version created by a human expert?

Figure 3 displays the rating scores assigned by the two evaluators. Utilizing GPT-4, the augmented MT results demonstrate a strong adherence to human instructions, with the quality of these revised MT outputs nearing that of human experts. The concept-based method outperforms approaches that use human translation outcomes as a reference.

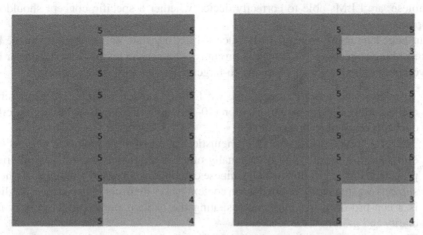

Fig. 3. Color scaled 5-point Likert rating scores were assigned by the two evaluators, captured in two columns to assess two aspects: the adherence of the revised translation to human guidance and its performance equivalence to versions produced by the human expert. Two tables represent the assessments of the two evaluators. Each table consists of ten rows, each corresponding to a different example.

The advantages of a concept-based approach are twofold:

1. Human guidance is provided at the sentence level, allowing for precise adjustments. The results showed that the approach outperforms traditional MT, and human-provided concept description outperforms human-provided reference translation in terms of guiding GPT-4 towards better translation quality.
2. The method is highly scalable; a single concept (such as converting to metric units instead of using English units) can be implemented across several sentences simultaneously. Additionally, concepts supported by descriptions and numerous bilingual examples can be stored in both post-editing memory and translation memory for future use, enabling concept-based memory systematization.

3 Assessing the Proficiency of Large Language Model in Applying Translation Concept

3.1 Motivation

Within the context of concepts related to Chinese-to-English translation, this section delves into the following research questions:

1. Can LLMs grasp translation concepts and rules? For instance, are LLMs capable of elucidating a translation concept with proficiency akin to that of a human?
2. Can large language models (LLMs) accurately identify when to implement translation concepts? For instance, when encountering a text in a source language such as Chinese, are LLMs able to correctly decide whether a specific concept should be applied?
3. Can large language models (LLMs) successfully translate into a target language by interpreting concepts outlined in the prompts, whether via textual instructions or by leveraging a small number of source-to-target examples (few-shot learning)?

- To address the research questions, we focused on ten essential concepts crucial to Chinese-to-English translation [10–13], aiming to capture domain-specific concepts relevant to this context.
- The term "pro-drop" describes a linguistic feature where a language permits the omission of subjects (and occasionally other pronouns) if they can be inferred pragmatically or grammatically. Chinese exemplifies a pro-drop language, where subjects are frequently omitted when context makes them clear. In contrast, English is a non-pro-drop language, necessitating the explicit presence of subjects for clarity and grammatical accuracy.
- The linguistic term "dislocation" describes the occurrence where the placement of words or phrases within a sentence varies considerably between two languages. This presents significant translation challenges, especially between languages with markedly different syntactic structures, such as Chinese and English.
- The concept of implicit conjunctions and the use of linking or transition words in Chinese contrasts with English. Chinese frequently omits conjunctions that are essen-tial in English, relying more on contextual cues and the logical flow inherent in sentence structure. For example, two clauses in Chinese might be juxtaposed without a con-junction, yet a native speaker can intuit their relationship through context.
- The practice of amalgamating clauses and brief sentences in Chinese to form an extended English sentence is noteworthy. English facilitates the construction of intri-cate sentences comprising several clauses, typically inter-connected by conjunctions, enabling the articulation of subtle nuances and conditional statements. In contrast, Chinese tends to emphasize succinctness and conciseness.
- Deverbalization, a key concept in translation studies, becomes especially pertinent when translating between languages with markedly different structures, such as from Chinese to English. This approach shifts focus from literal, word-for-word translation, which can result in un-natural or imprecise outcomes due to disparities

in gram-mar, syntax, and cultural nuances. Instead, deverbalization involves inter-preting the source text's meaning at a more abstract level, followed by articulating this understanding in the target language. This method allows for a translation that is not only linguistically accurate but also culturally and contextually resonant.

- Eliminating redundancy is a common practice in translating Chinese, enhances the readability and clarity of the target text. While some redundancies in Chinese may be necessary to emphasize meaning, many can be removed without loss of intent. This process ensures a more concise and coherent translation.
- Changing subject selection involves selecting a different subject than the one in the source text to enhance the readability and fluency of the English translation.
- Changing perspective in the context of translating from Chinese to English involves altering the viewpoint or approach when converting text from one language to the other. This is particularly important due to the substantial differences between Chinese and English in grammar, syntax, idiomatic expressions, and cultural nuances.
- Changing parts of speech is essential to faithfully convey the meaning of the original while ensuring adherence to English expressions, regardless of the corresponding parts of speech in Chinese.
- Cultural translation aims to retain the intended meaning of a culturally sensitive message while considering cultural differences, in order to avoid confusion that may result from a direct translation.

Two professional English-to-Chinese translators evaluated the outcomes of multiple GPT-4 augmented MT results by building consensus on 5-point Likert rating scores.

3.2 The Capability of LLMs to Elucidate Translation Concepts

GPT-4's knowledge of ten specific concepts was evaluated by presenting it with questions such as, "What is the concept of 'pro-drop' and 'non pro-drop' in the domain of Chinese-to-English translation?" Two human experts reviewed the responses produced by GPT-4 and reached a consensus using a 5-point Likert scale, ranging from very satisfied (2), somewhat satisfied (1), neither satisfied nor dissatisfied (0), somewhat dissatisfied (-1), to very dissatisfied (-2). This assessment aimed to gauge GPT-4's comprehension of these translation concepts. Figure 4 displays the Likert scores for the ten concepts, showing that GPT-4 exhibits a satisfactory understanding of most concepts, with the notable exception of the concept of dislocation.

| 2 | -1 | 2 | 2 | 2 | 2 | 1 | 1 | 2 | 2 |

Fig. 4. Likert scores based on consensus reached by two human evaluators on GPT-4's elucidation of translation concepts. A total of ten concepts were assessed, including: 1) Pro-drop; 2) Dislocation; 3) Implicit conjunctions and transition words; 4) Combining short Chinese sentences into longer English sentences; (5) Deverbalization; (6) Eliminating redundancy; (7) Changing subject selection; (8) Changing perspective; (9) Changing parts of speech; (10) Cultural translation.

3.3 Assessing the LLM's Proficiency in Identifying When to Apply Translation Concepts

For each concept, four examples were compiled, resulting in a total of 40 examples. The format for each prompt included an initial textual definition of the concept, succeeded by three examples demonstrating its application. This was followed by a test instance featuring a segment of text in the source language, Chinese. GPT-4 was then required to assign a score ranging from 0 to 100 for this segment, where a score of 0 implies the concept is entirely irrelevant to the translation of the test instance, and a score of 100 indicates the concept is critical. Should the score surpass 75, GPT-4 was further instructed to produce an English translation that incorporates the concept. Due to space reasons, Table 4 shows only one example for the concept of dislocation.

The purpose of this experiment was to evaluate GPT4's proficiency in precisely identifying the relevance of a concept within a Chinese sentence and its ability to generate an accurate translation into the target language that embodies the recognized concept. Figure 5 presents the classification scores, ranging from 0 to 100, obtained by GPT for ten concepts employing a 1-in-4 leave-one-out cross-validation (LOOCV) method. The findings show high accuracy, with all scores surpassing 80/100, indicating strong precision. An assessment of recall effectiveness is planned for subsequent analysis.

3.4   The Capability of LLM to Produce Target Translations that Reflect Relevant Concepts

Table 5 showcases the Likert scores assigned by human evaluators to the Chinese-to-English translations produced by GPT4. As outlined in Sect. 3.3, these translations were generated following prompts that included specific concepts along with three bilingual examples. GPT4's performance is noted to be proficient in six of the concepts. More remarkably, it shows a strong ability in accurately detecting and translating expressions that embody certain concepts effectively. Yet, it encounters difficulties with four others: deverbalization, changes in subject selection, perspective shifts, and alterations in parts of speech (Fig. 6).

- We have tested more sophisticated prompting techniques for concepts that perform poorly. For instance, one approach we experimented with was the Chain-of-Thought (CoT) prompting, which helps LLMs in following a reasoning process by breaking down concepts into smaller, more manageable steps.
- For example, related to the four instances pertaining to the subject changing selection concept.

  1. 资源环境约束边界临近，最典型的例
     子就是雾霾。(direct translation: The boundaries of resource and environmental constraints are approaching. The most typical example is smog.)
  2. 老年人本身的免疫功能就相对于年轻人要弱一些。(direction translation: The immune function of the elderly is weaker than that of the young.)
  3. 未来20年气候变化的威胁将超过恐怖主义。(direct translation: Climate change will be more of a threat than terrorism in the next 20 years.)
  4. 迁移的流向和形式也都发生了很大的变化。(direct translation: The flow and form of migration have also undergone great changes.)

Table 4. GPT-4 prompting and output visualized: the prompt, which includes a definition of the concept of dislocation and three examples of translations from source to target language, is displayed in black, whereas the responses generated by GPT-4 are highlighted in red.

The linguistic concept dislocation refers to the phenomenon where the positioning of words or phrases in a sentence differs significantly between two languages. This occurs frequently in Chinese-to-English translation, as certain Chinese sentences do not follow the "subject–verb–object" word order. This can pose challenges in translation, particularly between languages with distinct syntactic structures, like Chinese and English

Three examples are listed below to illustrate the Chinese-to-English translation that reflect the concept above:

Chinese: 常态化防控和应急处置放松了要求。
English: The requirements for daily prevention and control, as well as emergency response, have been relaxed.

Chinese: GDP 比重，非典时期才影响 26%，这(次)是占到 74%。
English: 26% of the GDP was affected during the SARS outbreak. But this time, the proportion is 74%.

Chinese: 我知道这个目标目前在国际上是很多国家所没有制定的。
English: I'm aware that many countries around the world have not yet set this goal.

If you are an expert-level translator, do you think we should apply the same concept on the following Chinese text segment?
Chinese: 当地语言以前中国公司不太注重。

Please give a score between 0 and 100 (0 means the concept definitely should not be applied on translating the sentence while 100 means that the concept definitely should be applied on translating the sentence.
If the score is above 75, what should be the proper translation reflecting the concept. Please generate a proper English translation reflecting the concept.

The concept of dislocation in translation, particularly between Chinese and English, is indeed crucial to consider due to the significant differences in syntactic structures between these languages. The examples you've provided illustrate how sentence structure in English often differs from Chinese, with the need to rearrange elements for clarity and coherence in English.

For the Chinese sentence "当地语言以前中国公司不太注重," applying the concept of dislocation would be highly relevant. I would give this a score of 90, indicating a strong necessity to apply this concept in translation. The sentence structure in Chinese is quite different from what would be considered clear and coherent in English.

A translation that reflects this concept of dislocation, ensuring the sentence is rearranged for clarity in English, would be:

"Previously, Chinese companies did not pay much attention to local languages."

In this translation, the subject ("Chinese companies") is moved to the beginning of the sentence to align with typical English sentence structure, where the subject often precedes the verb. This adjustment makes the sentence clearer and more natural in English.

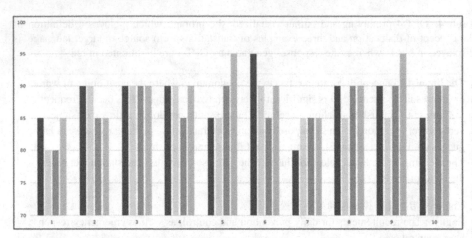

Fig. 5. Using a 1-in-4 leave-one-out cross-validation (LOOCV) approach, GPT-4 achieved scores higher than 80/100 across ten distinct linguistic concepts. These concepts are categorized into clusters as follows: 1) pro-drop, 2) dislocation, 3) implicit conjunctions and transition words, 4) merging short sentences in Chinese into longer English sentences, 5) deverbalization, 6) eliminating redundancy, 7) changes in subject selection, 8) shifts in perspective, 9) changes in parts of speech, and 10) cultural transitions.

1	2	2	2	2	2	-2	-1	-2	1
2	2	2	2	-2	2	-2	-2	2	-1
2	2	0	1	-2	2	2	2	1	2
-1	2	2	1	-2	2	-1	-2	-2	1

Fig. 6. Human evaluators assigned Likert scores to translations generated by GPT-4 from Chinese to English that incorporated instructions and few-shot examples related to specific concepts. Each column represents one concept: 1) prodrop, 2) dislocation, 3) implicit conjunctions and transition words, 4) merging short sentences in Chinese into longer English sentences, 5) deverbalization, 6) redundancy elimination, 7) subject selection changes, 8) perspective shifts, 9) part of speech changes, and 10) cultural transitions. For each concept, four translation outcomes (four rows in the table) were evaluated, employing the 1-in-4 LOOCV method

We noted that examples #2, #3, and #4 utilized the possessive particle "的" to connect two nouns, signifying possession or a relationship and necessitating a shift in the subject from one noun to another. In contrast, example #1 implied the use of the possessive particle to link two nouns. This variation could account for the inadequate performance observed in few-shot learning. To make the task more straightforward for GPT-4, we replaced the example #1 with another example in which the possessive particle was explicitly used.

1. 技术的进步极大地改变了我们的生活方式。(direct translation: The advancement of technology has greatly changed our way of life.)

2. 老年人本身的免
   疫功能就相对于年轻人要弱一些。(direction translation: The immune function of the elderly is weaker than that of the young.
3. 未来20年气候变化的威胁将超过恐怖主义。(direct translation: The threat of climate change will be more than terrorism in the next 20 years.)
4. 迁移的流向和形式也都发生了很大的变化。(The flow and form of migration have also undergone great changes.)

   We checked the 1-in-4 leave-one-out cross-validation (LOOCV) performance again. However, the outcomes were not satisfactory either. On several occasions, GPT4 did not utilize the two nouns linked by "的" but instead selected other nouns within the sentence. This necessitated our provision of comprehensive, step-by-step analyses for the few-shot examples included in the prompt, as illustrated in Table 5.

Table 5. Four instances related to the concept of changing subject selection, demonstrating how Chain-of-Thought (CoT) prompting facilitates reasoning through smaller, manageable steps.

迁移的流向和形式也都发生了很大的变化。 *Direct translation:* The direction and form of migration have also undergone significant changes. *The subject phrase:* The direction and form of migration ***Translation with alternative subject selection using the other noun in the subject phrase***: Migration was happening in different directions and ways.
技术的进步极大地改变了我们的生活方式。 *Direct translation*: The progress of technology has greatly changed our way of life. *The subject phrase*: The progress of technology ***Translation with alternative subject selection using the other noun in the subject phrase***: Technology have greatly advanced to change our way of life.
老年人本身的免疫功能就相对于年轻人要弱一些。 *Direct translation*: The immune function of elderly people is relatively weaker than that of younger people. *The subject phrase*: The immune function of elderly people ***Translation with alternative subject selection using the other noun in the subject phrase***: Unlike younger people, the elderly have weaker immune systems.
未来20年气候变化的威胁将超过恐怖主义。 *Direct translation*: The threat of climate change will exceed that of terrorism in the next 20 years. *The subject phrase*: The threat of climate change ***Translation with alternative subject selection using the other noun in the subject phrase***: In the next two decades, climate change will pose a greater threat than terrorism.

   The performance of the 1-in-4 leave-one-out cross-validation (LOOCV) is significantly enhanced by the detailed reasoning provided through the Chain-of-Thought (CoT) method. Nonetheless, its practical application is constrained by the necessity to deconstruct the original concept (altering subject selection) into a detailed, step-by-step reasoning process. Unlike human translators, who can adapt a concept across varied contexts by recognizing both explicit and implicit patterns and focusing on the core intent, the GPT-4-based few-shot approach depends on the identification of explicit patterns through detailed descriptions. For reasons of space, the CoT strategies for the other three concepts are not detailed here. Combining the CoT approach with a focus on making patterns more explicit could enhance cross-validation performance to acceptable levels.

- Abduction is an inference process that identifies the most plausible explanations for observed phenomena. Human language experts exhibit superior abduction skills compared to GPT-4. For instance:

1. They can discern that the use of explicit or implicit particles linking two nouns does not affect the application of the translation concept.
2. They can recognize, from few-shot examples, that changing the subject in a sentence beginning with "A's B" involves selecting A or B, and it is unlikely for other nouns in the sentence to be chosen.

In comparison, GPT-4 struggles with such abductive inference reasoning. As a result, human experts must engage in abduction to derive specific instructions (deductive rules) and develop step-by-step logic in example prompts (inference demonstration). This necessity complicates and extends the prompt engineering process. Enhancing abductive reasoning capability and performance in language models would make AI/ML learning systems more human-like.

4 Conclusions

Envisioning an enhanced human-machine collaborative workflow augmented by Large Language Model (LLM) prompting features, including pre-editing instructions, interactive human-machine collaborative post-editing, concept-based post-editing memory, and concept-based translation memory, we evaluate the effectiveness of steering translation output through concept-based GPT-4 prompts.

Utilizing English-to-Chinese examples, we examine GPT-4's capacity to steer the generation of the target language in alignment with concepts outlined in both a discourse-level pre-editing guide and sentence-level interactive human-machine collaborative post-editing prompts.

Instructions augmented by GPT-4 through discourse-level analysis show promise in outperforming traditional machine translation (MT) methods. However, they still fall short of matching the expertise of human translators, who possess a superior grasp of sentence-level nuances. Despite this, the GPT-4-augmented approach for concept-based post-editing, fostering a novel form of collaboration between humans and machines, surpasses both traditional MT and the other human-machine collaborative methods that rely on human-provided reference translations. This concept-based strategy offers significant scalability, allowing a single concept to be applied across multiple sentences at once. Furthermore, concepts, when supported by detailed descriptions and a wealth of bilingual examples, can be archived in both post-editing and translation memories. This facilitates the creation of a systematized concept-based memory framework, ready for future application and enhancing the efficiency of the MT workflow.

Utilizing Chinese-to-English examples, we evaluate GPT-4's proficiency in elucidating translation concepts, assessing their relevance to source test segments, and accurately rendering these concepts in the target language.

GPT-4 exhibits a satisfactory understanding of most concepts in terms of its ability to elucidate, and it can precisely identify the relevance of a concept within a source sentence. Furthermore, GPT-4 shows a strong ability to accurately translate into the target text that embody certain concepts effectively. However, for certain concepts, more sophisticated prompting techniques, such as the Chain-of-Thought (CoT), are required to break down the concepts into smaller, more manageable steps, and converting the original source text into more explicit form for analysis. Unlike human translators, who can adapt a concept across varied contexts by recognizing both explicit and implicit patterns and focusing on the core intent, the GPT-4-based approach depends on the identification of explicit patterns through detailed reasoning descriptions. Human language experts possess superior abductive reasoning capabilities compared to GPT-4. Consequently, at the present stage, humans must apply abductive reasoning to create more specific instructions and develop additional logic steps in prompts, which complicate the prompt engineering process. Eventually, enhanced abductive reasoning capabilities in large language models will bring their performance closer to human-like levels.

The proposed approach introduces a scalable, concept-based strategy that can be applied across multiple text segments simultaneously. Additionally, this method enables segment matching based on conceptual similarity, surpassing basic string similarity. It will enhance machine translation workflow efficiency significantly.

References

1. Jiao, W., Wang, W., Huang, JT., Wang, X., Tu, Z.P.: Is ChatGPT a good translator? Yes with GPT-4 as the engine (2023). arXiv preprint arXiv:2301.08745
2. Roman, K.: How GPT-4 Is Transforming the Language Service Industry: Benefits and Challenges. https://www.linkedin.com/pulse/how-gpt-4-transforming-language-service-industry-benefits-kotzsch/. Accessed 7 Feb 2024
3. O'Brien, S.: Translation as human–computer interaction. Transl. Spaces 1(1), 101–22 (2012)
4. Do, Carmo, F., et al.: A review of the state-of-the-art in automatic post-editing. Mach. Transl. 35, 101–143 (2021)
5. MemoqDocs: Match rates from translation memories and LiveDocs corpora. https://docs.memoq.com/current/en/Things/things-match-rates-from-translation-m.html. Accessed 12 Feb 2024
6. Christensen, T.P., Schjoldage, A.: Translation-memory (TM) research: what do we know and how do we know it? Hermes-J. Lang. Commun. Bus. 44, 89–101 (2010)
7. CSOFT International Blog Post: 5 Limitations of Machine Translation. https://blog.csoftintl.com/limitations-machine-translation/. Accessed 12 Feb 2024
8. Translation & Interpretation Services Blog Post: The Advantages and Disadvantages of Machine Translation. https://translationsandinterpretations.com.au/blog/the-advantages-and-disadvantages-of-machine-translation/. Accessed 12 Feb 2024
9. Qian, M., Wu, H.Q., Yang, L., Wan, A.: Augmented Machine Translation Enabled by GPT4: Performance Evaluation on Human-Machine Teaming Approaches. NLP4TIA (2023)

10. Bao, C.Y.: Class notes on Chinese-to-English translation. Advanced Translation and Interpretation Course. Translation and Interpretation Program, Middlebury Institute of International Studies (2022)
11. Chen, J.S.: Pro-drop parameter, Universal Grammar and second language acquisition of Chinese and English, Doctoral dissertation, UNSW Sydney (2001)
12. Chen, H.: Gaoji Hanying Fanyi [An advanced coursebook on Chinese-English translation], PEKING University Press (2009)
13. StiegelbauerT, L.R., Schawarz, N., Husar, D.B.: Three Translation Model Approaches. Studii de Ştiintă şi Cultură. **12**(3), 45–50 (2016)
14. Tan, X., Kuang, S., Xiong, D.: Detecting and translating dropped pronouns in neural machine translation. In: Tang, J., Kan, M.-Y., Zhao, D., Li, S., Zan, H. (eds.) NLPCC 2019. LNCS (LNAI), vol. 11838, pp. 343–354. Springer, Cham (2019). https://doi.org/10.1007/978-3-030-32233-5_27

Enhancing Large Language Models Through External Domain Knowledge

Laslo Welz[✉] and Carsten Lanquillon

Heilbronn University of Applied Sciences, Max-Planck-Str. 39, 74081 Heilbronn,
Germany
lawelz@stud.hs-heilbronn.de, carsten.lanquillon@hs-heilbronn.de

Abstract. Large Language Models (LLM) demonstrate promising
results in generating content with current fine-tuning and prompting
methods. Yet, they have limited application in industrial knowledge management or specific expert domains, due to weak factuality and safety-
critical hallucination. Therefore, it is necessary to enhance the language
model with external knowledge. The provision and representation of the
external knowledge holds several challenges and problems. This paper
proposes a human-centred LLM-based system architecture designed as
a modular extension, which improves the overall factuality of the generated output. Following a design science research approach, first the
problems and objectives of the research are identified. In the next step
the artifact is developed based on requirements deducted from literature.
Eventually, the functionality of the artifact is demonstrated as a proof-
of-concept in a case study. The research contributes an initial approach
for effective and grounded knowledge transfer, which minimizes the risk
of hallucination from LLM-generated content.

Keywords: Large Language Models · Expert Knowledge ·
Information Retrieval · Retrieval Augmented Generation

1 Introduction

Knowledge Management is a critical aspect of modern working environments.
The need for efficient knowledge transfer rises, especially between subject experts
and new employees [20]. For this task, expert systems using artificial intelligence
(AI) technologies have already been established in business applications [38,43]
and companies increasingly develop their own in-house [29] or domain specific
chatbots [47,49] as support for everyday work processes. The brain behind these
chatbots are large language models (LLMs), which are primarily based on the
transformer architecture [44]. LLMs can be used for supporting knowledge-
intensive tasks in various application areas, such as question answering, text
summarization and translation [2,20,26]. As the tasks get more complex, training methods and inference patterns for LLMs, like prompting must be established
more consistently and accurately [31]. Current research on combining different
prompting methods achieve near human level performance, but not on an expert

H. Degen and S. Ntoa (Eds.): HCII 2024, LNAI 14736, pp. 135–146, 2024.
https://doi.org/10.1007/978-3-031-60615-1_9

level [26]. Limitations on pre-training information and factual accuracy is an issue, when handling knowledge-intensive tasks [46]. Depleting long-term knowledge during model training is also an issue [51]. Nonetheless, it must be kept in mind that current models learn from public data sources and not from real understanding and knowledge. This poses the risk of fictional responses from the system, which is known as hallucination. The consequences are degrading trust in the model and raised safety concerns for real world applications [18]. LLMs are not the only providers of knowledge. External knowledge sources can help LLMs generate more grounded responses. Hence, the context in current conversations can be improved [35]. Companies facilitate their own knowledge as capital. Considering safeguards for protecting intellectual property rights is important for them before sharing their corporate knowledge assets to third party systems [37]. Developing hybrid approaches that complement existing LLMs with more comprehensive and factual knowledge is necessary [13].

A common paradigm for knowledge representation are knowledge graphs (KG) [12]. The use of KGs as an external knowledge source has already been discussed in prior research [20,30,52]. They achieve good results for low-scale domain-specific use cases, but pose limitations for large-scale applications with unstructured text sources [17]. Furthermore, building a KG from scratch is time-consuming and it lacks robustness in a continuous changing environment [52]. Concerning the last issue, Buhl et al. [3] propose a solution by accepting KG incompleteness. They design a human-in-the-loop approach using a chatbot interface that completes and validates the KG continuously through human feedback [3]. This framework is suitable for domain application, but becomes more complex with further automation.

It is desirable to overcome these issues and enable knowledge protective interactions with AI systems grounded on expert knowledge. As a solution, the design of a human-centred agent architecture is proposed that is suited for domain specific expert knowledge acquisition and validation. The agent acts as a modular add-on for a language model. Knowledge can be acquired in form of texts as well as documents and is stored in a separate knowledge base. Concerning data quality, the knowledge base acquisition layer filters data that might be incomplete, out-dated or originates from non-expert sources. Data augmentation is used to retrieve and manipulate knowledge fragments, so it can be provided in a readable response. To verify extracted knowledge, the answer corpus should contain additional metadata, such as document title, author, and date. A rule-based layer is implemented between the language model and the agent, deciding if it is necessary to access additional expert knowledge to satisfy the users intent.

This paper is structured by following the design science research approach by Peffers et al. [34] in its first four phases. Initially, the problem statement and research question is formulated. The validation of their significance for research is established through a systematic literature review [45]. The main research question will be addressed with the assistance of sub-questions derived through a deductive approach [28]. During the design phase, an artifact is introduced. To demonstrate the artifact as a proof of concept, a case study is conducted [9].

2   Problem Identification and Objectives

Factuality, in the context of LLMs, refers to the ability to generate contents based on credible sources and commonsense [46]. It is an important criteria with regard to knowledge transfer in a professional work environment. It is not yet explored how workers and businesses adopt and use LLMs. One key factor is the human confidence to use these models, without needing to verify the output through independent research [7]. Moreover, LLMs have limited abilities for generating precise domain-specific knowledge. Several techniques exist to supply the LLM with external knowledge [24,50] and improve factual knowledge output [21,46]. There are principals designed to identify factual inaccuracies, but they solely focus on a single aspect of intrinsic knowledge quality [4]. In comparison to LLM-generated knowledge, retrieved external knowledge is prone to low relevancy and coherency [4]. Retrieval-augmented generation (RAG) is an emerging discipline in the field of generative AI. It includes the following steps: Load data, split into smaller chunks, embed chunks into vectors, store and retrieve chunks for prompt generation [24]. Unlike retrieval-only models that are based on dialogue corpora, RAG models can ingest different forms of knowledge sources [25]. Although this approach is suitable to improve the factuality of LLM answer ability, it has some limitations. Missing or distracting information, as well as not recognizing misinformation by the model can result in fatal errors [46]. Instead of building an optimized model, a modular LLM-based agent framework is developed to minimize these weaknesses [46,48]. Therefore, the following research question must be answered: *How can a system architecture for an LLM-based application be designed and implemented, in which external expert knowledge is provided by a retrieval agent?* Three sub-questions have been identified based on the literature:

1. *How can factuality be validated during knowledge acquisition?* When building a knowledge base, data quality can be affected through low relevance, redundancy and missing sources [4,36]. It is important to define thresholds that filter out mistrustful data sources [4].
2. *How can metadata be supplied with the response?* The absence of uncertainty leads to a higher confidence in an LLM output [1]. Interpretation and explainability of the model output can be supported with appropriate source verification [33].
3. *How can a domain-specific interaction between LLM and retrieval model be established?* The external knowledge base can contain knowledge gaps [46]. Focusing on a domain-specific agent framework, it is necessary to set up interaction mechanics to reduce empty or hallucinated outputs.

3   Related Works

This paper builds upon other research contribution in the field of LLMs and external knowledge infusion. Peng et al. develop a modular LLM architecture that reduces hallucinations without compromising efficient response generation

[35]. They apply a knowledge consolidator based on the Bing Search API and store data in task-specific databases. The cached data is used to verify the responses from the connected LLM [35].

Up-to-date information sourced from the web is used by Lazaridou et al. to enhance LLM performance and increase factuality [23]. They utilize the Google Search API to aggregate and clean data from the top 20 results. The modified text is used for prompting the LLM and generating multiple answers. Additionally a re-ranking stage is deployed that generates a score to select the best generated answer. The authors suggest to focus on enhancing existing smaller models instead of creating larger models [23].

Shi et al. implement a retrieval-augmented LLM to enhance shared-decision making in a clinical context [40]. A knowledge base is established by creating a pre-processing pipeline for text documents. The LLM utilizes the knowledge base, if the base response is not sufficient for answering the user query. This is realized by a reasoning step, implemented with chain-of-thought prompting. The knowledge base validation is accomplished by a human-in-the-loop concept [40].

Another reasoning approach is used by the authors in [26] in their research about answering difficult real-world-based questions. They investigate the effect of grounding the LLM with external knowledge from Wikipedia in comparison to direct zero-shot prompting. The results indicate better interpretable outputs with augmented prompts [26].

Cui et al. apply a vector- and keyword-based retrieval method for LLMs to overcome inaccuracies with vector database retrieval [5]. They design a retrieval model based on BERT and Faiss to extract and rank the most relevant results. In a second step, fine-tuning is used to extract keywords from the user query. This enhances domain-specific responses, but also poses risks of missing generalization by the model [5].

4   Design and Development of the Artifact

In the following section the integration of an LLM-based agent architecture is explained. An expert system architecture serves as a base for the approach (see Fig. 1). Central component of the architecture is the knowledge base. Expert knowledge can be added to the knowledge base through the acquisition module. A user can enter a request in the user interface. The inference engine is the intelligence and handles requests from the user interface. It also engages with the knowledge base and passes results back to the user, based on the knowledge base query output.

4.1   Expert Knowledge Acquisition

Building a domain-specific expert knowledge base, it is expected to split incoming knowledge and text artefacts based on their quality. A pre-retrieval process step is implemented to enhance the data being loaded into the knowledge base [8]. Data quality criteria for structured data cannot be applied to unstructured

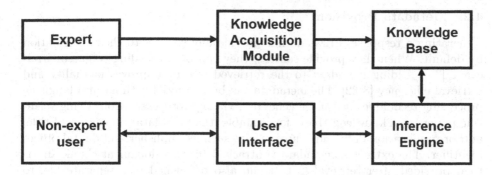

Fig. 1. Common expert system architecture based on [15]

text data, due to their complex syntax and semantics. From the data consumer point of view, the data must be "fit to use". There are different approaches to define text quality dimensions. One focuses on contextual, intrinsic, representational and accessibility metrics [42]. Similar dimensions are used to evaluate generated text from LLMs [4]. This evaluation taxonomy is adapted and applied to the knowledge acquisition module. There are four intrinsic evaluation aspects, which will be covered. These aspects focus on the internal properties of the acquired text documents, without reflecting on the impact on attached downstream tasks [4].

- *Factuality:* Factuality compares the comprised information with verified external evidence. Trustful sources, reviews and fact-checkers can indicate, if the data contains ground-truth knowledge. A good method to obtain trustful documents is to check their source origin. This can be accomplished via metadata extraction.
- *Relevance:* Relevance plays a role in either matching the user query with the desired output or incorporating only relevant domain knowledge. Keyword extraction can be helpful, to categorize knowledge. The keywords have to be matched if knowledge about one specific topic is collected. Matching can be achieved via 1:1 comparison or a fuzzy approach with semantic similarity.
- *Coherence:* Depending if the knowledge is composed of long-form text, coherence can be measured on sentence- or paragraph level. When acquiring fulltext documents, this quality aspect must not be checked. Coherence can decrease, if the text is chunked for retrieval processing. Therefore, the right chunking methods have to be applied to preserve coherence.

Informativeness: Informativeness refers to whether the acquired knowledge is novel or unexpected to the existing knowledge base. Since this is correlated with the relevancy aspect, it is sufficient to eliminate redundancy, before building the knowledge base.

4.2   Metadata Provision

Generating a response, LLMs do not provide any sources to their information by default. When they provide sources, they can be misleading, vague or irrelevant [36]. Adding metadata to the retrieved output improves factuality and retrieval efficiency [8,32]. The metadata can be extracted with natural language processing techniques or can be generated via keyword extraction. Using scientific papers as a knowledge base, for example, the metadata can consist of title, author, publication date and source origin, such as publisher and digital object identifier. The extracted metadata is attached to each document chunk and is then provided after retrieval [27]. It can also be cached in a separate file, to obtain information about the existing papers in the knowledge base more easily.

4.3   Prompt Generation

Missing information limits the ability of the LLM to generate qualitative content [46]. Furthermore, the LLM can be too superficial and lacks specific expert knowledge. This issue can be solved by either training the model to say "I do not know" [53], or provide alternative information sources [35]. In this context, the LLM primarily infers with the external knowledge base. In the event, that the external knowledge base is missing information or fails to retrieve any context, the blank output can be replaced with the LLM's knowledge. Applying different prompt templates based on query context, is the simple solution to create a custom output. Rule-based mechanics have to be implemented, to enhance the user interaction and unveil loopholes in the knowledge base. To improve knowledge handling, first the domain scope of the knowledge base needs to be defined. The user query can then be verified by keyword extraction, to decide if it fits the domain of the knowledge base. Using this approach, the LLM generates factual answers only for its defined domain.

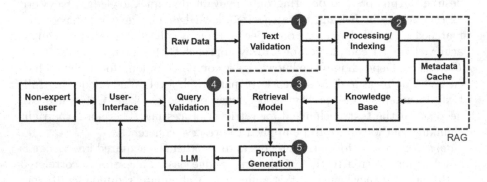

Fig. 2. LLM-based system architecture (own illustration).

5   Demonstration

This chapter presents the prototypical implementation of the architecture and its components. Furthermore, a case study is conducted to describe the process execution in detail.

5.1   Implementation

For implementing the system architecture as a prototype, the open-source framework DSPy from Stanford is used. It is suitable for developing and optimizing LLM pipelines with modular building blocks [22]. The framework consists of two main components: The retrieval model and the language model. By default, DSPy deploys ColBERTv2 as the retrieval component, which is a fast and effective pre-trained language model [39]. For production systems, fast execution times are an important factor for RAG [14]. The applied language model is Microsoft's Phi-2, a lightweight 2.7 billion parameter model, which scores promising benchmarks against much larger models [16]. The advantage of deploying a smaller model is that it can run on a single GPU. DSPy also offers an interface with OpenAI's GPT models. The overall framework, as well as various scripts for the data/knowledge pipeline and prompt generation are implemented in Python. To connect the retrieval model to the relevant documents, a TSV-file is created, which stores all document contents in a collection. The collection itself consists of multiple passages. Each passage represents a document chunk with the corresponding metadata from the initial document. Chunking is applied by a recursive text splitting method. The metadata is also separately stored in a JSON-file.

5.2   Case Study

The prototype is demonstrated based on a case study in the knowledge management context. Knowledge management is defined as the ability to organize knowledge and turn it into ideas or strategies [10]. It is widely adapted in many industries to achieve sustainable competitive advantages [41]. Knowledge is classified into different categories, either organizational, project, domain or user-specific [37]. This case study will focus on the domain knowledge, especially expert knowledge for one domain topic. Expert knowledge represents the expertise of administrators, scientists and technologists and has a high degree of codification [11]. Explicit knowledge can be found in spreadsheets, databases and information systems [41]. Unifying all the expert knowledge and make it searchable via an simple chat interface, can help to make knowledge-intensive tasks more efficient. The system architecture introduced above makes information more accessible for employees from work-floor up to management.

Within the scope of this case study, the implementation will be discussed in more detail following the three sub-questions presented in Sect. 2. The abstract functionality is shown in Fig. 2. Individual process steps are highlighted by the numerical description.

The data pipeline starts with processing and filtering the collected PDF-documents. From each document, the metadata is extracted. If no initial metadata file exists, the generated keywords from each document are saved in a list. Otherwise, the keywords will be matched against the existing keywords based on a similarity score. The selected document is rejected, if the score is lower than the threshold of 0.8, which indicates a low domain relevance. In addition, the information about the source in the metadata is checked. If the source is trustful, for example if it is a scientific database, the document is further processed. Otherwise, the document is discarded (*step 1*).

In the next processing step, the document text is cleaned with regular expression techniques, to make the subsequent retrieval more effective. Furthermore, the text is chunked into smaller passages of 512 tokens. For each passage, the corresponding metadata snippet is attached, so the metadata can be supplied with the retrieval model. After merging the text passage with the metadata, all rows are written into a single TSV-file, which acts as a knowledge base for the retrieval model (*step 2*).

Each row in the TSV-file represents a passage from the text collection. For indexing, the retrieval model takes a passage and transforms the text into vector representations through an embedding model. This allows a more efficient search. Next, the search module takes a query and the number of desired passages to retrieve. ColBERTv2 can retrieve multiple passages and ranks them based on relevance for the query (*step 3*). For minimizing context length, which is an important criteria for prompting, the number of extracted passages is set to 2. Two passages equals 1024 tokens, which is half of the maximal context length for the Phi-2 language model.

Before the actual prompt generation, the user query is analyzed for matching domain-specific keywords, which were defined in step 1. If the similarity score is too low, the LLM output generates an "out of domain" error message (*step 4*). A valid request triggers the retrieval sub-process and inserts the response into a prompt template. Each prompt template consists of the user query, an instruction text and the retrieved passages with the metadata. If the model retrieves an empty passage, an LLM-only prompt is triggered. The user gets informed about the retrieval error and receives a zero-shot LLM-generated knowledge output. No metadata will be supplied with the response. When a passage is received, the prompt template instructs the LLM to only use the passage content to generate an answer. The metadata is attached to the answer corpus in a formatted structure. As a third option, the answer generation is delimited and the LLM can extend the retrieved answer corpus with its own zero-shot attempt (*step 5*).

In summary, the case study demonstrates a novel approach on combining an expert-grounded knowledge base with an LLM to increase factuality. The rule-based mechanics for answer generation eliminates incomplete and incorrect outputs and enhances the user experience.

6   Discussion

Using the design science approach, a novel system architecture for LLM-based application with a retrieval agent has been implemented. The fundamental characteristics of the architecture have been deducted from established methodologies found in scientific literature. Additionally, the features were enhanced through own insights based on the three sub-questions identified as research gaps. The increasing research in this field and its importance for knowledge management in the industry emphasizes the significance of the contributions in this paper [6,8].

Filtering out non-domain-specific documents before ingesting them into the knowledge base, creates a dense expert knowledge foundation. The approach to select them on keyword similarity is a valid choice, but can be prone to overzealous filtering. Further, attaching the metadata directly to their respective passages is a simple solution for obtaining source-grounded content from the retrieval model. Using a rule-based approach for answer generation with the language model, shows that prompt templates can leverage the unique propositions of LLMs without the need of additional fine-tuning. Considering additional rules and edge cases, a reasoning-based approach should be considered.

Limitations. The biggest limitation of the proof of concept is the demonstration on a small-scale context. To further generalize the findings for possible RAG system implementations, bigger datasets have to be implemented. In addition, the DSPy framework is not fully utilized. It provides additional features, which could further optimize the LLM integration. Considering design configurations, the prototype does not enable accessing primary sources of the extracted documents, which restricts full factuality. Due to the fact that RAG is a fast developing research field, additional research and evaluation of the prototype have to be considered.

Future Works. The prompt generation opens up the possibility to integrate advanced prompting paradigms, like chain-of-thought. Then the model could iteratively assess, when to use expert knowledge best and when not. The system architecture could also be extended with a long-term memory module, which remembers past conversations. In a corporate context, additional user management could be implemented, to handle specific access and outputs to the knowledge base. Phi-2 achieves satisfactory performance, but bigger models, like Mixtral of Expert [19], extend the performance even more. Otherwise, it would be encouraging to focus on implementing smaller models, which get all their knowledge from external knowledge sources.

References

1. Augenstein, I., et al.: Factuality challenges in the era of large language models (2023). https://arxiv.org/abs/2310.05189
2. Bran, A.M., Cox, S., Schiller, O., Baldassart, C., White, A.D., Schwaller, P.: Augmenting large language models with chemistry tools (2023). https://arxiv.org/abs/2304.05376
3. Buhl, D., Szafarski, D., Welz, L., Lanquillon, C.: Conversation-driven refinement of knowledge graphs: true active learning with humans in the chatbot application loop. In: Degen, H., Ntoa, S. (eds.) HCII 2023. LNCS, vol. 14051, pp. 41–54. Springer, Cham (2023). https://doi.org/10.1007/978-3-031-35894-4_3
4. Chen, L., et al.: Beyond factuality: a comprehensive evaluation of large language models as knowledge generators (2023). https://arxiv.org/abs/2310.07289
5. Cui, J., Li, Z., Yan, Y., Chen, B., Yuan, L.: ChatLaw: open-source legal large language model with integrated external knowledge bases (2023). https://arxiv.org/abs/2306.16092
6. Earley, S.: What executives need to know about knowledge management, large language models and generative AI. Appl. Mark. Anal. **9**(3), 215–229 (2023)
7. Eloundou, T., Manning, S., Mishkin, P., Rock, D.: GPTs are GPTs: an early look at the labor market impact potential of large language models (2023). https://arxiv.org/abs/2303.10130
8. Gao, Y., et al.: Retrieval-augmented generation for large language models: a survey (2024). https://arxiv.org/abs/2312.10997
9. Gibbert, M., Ruigrok, W.: The "what" and "how" of case study rigor: three strategies based on published work. Organ. Res. Methods **13**(4), 710–737 (2010). https://doi.org/10.1177/1094428109351319
10. Gold, A.H., Malhotra, A., Segars, A.H.: Knowledge management: an organizational capabilities perspective. J. Manage. Inf. Syst. **18**(1), 185–214 (2001). http://www.jstor.org/stable/40398521
11. Harries, S.: Records Management and Knowledge Mobilisation: A Handbook For Regulation, Innovation and Transformation. Chandos Information Professional Ser. Elsevier Science, Burlington (2011)
12. Hogan, A., et al.: Knowledge graphs. ACM Comput. Sur. **54**(4), 1–37 (2021). https://doi.org/10.1145/3447772
13. Hu, X., Tian, Y., Nagato, K., Nakao, M., Liu, A.: Opportunities and challenges of chatGPT for design knowledge management. Procedia CIRP **119**, 21–28 (2023). https://doi.org/10.1016/j.procir.2023.05.001
14. Ilin, I.: Advanced RAG techniques - an illustrated overview (2023). https://pub.towardsai.net/advanced-rag-techniques-an-illustrated-overview-04d193d8fec6
15. Janjanam, D., Ganesh, B., Manjunatha, L.: Design of an expert system architecture: an overview. J. Phys. Conf. Ser. **1767**(1), 012036 (2021). https://doi.org/10.1088/1742-6596/1767/1/012036
16. Javaheripi, M., Bubeck, S.: Phi-2: the surprising power of small language models (2023). https://www.microsoft.com/en-us/research/blog/phi-2-the-surprising-power-of-small-language-models/
17. Ji, S., Pan, S., Cambria, E., Marttinen, P., Yu, P.S.: A survey on knowledge graphs: representation, acquisition, and applications. IEEE Trans. Neural Netw. Learn. Syst. **33**(2), 494–514 (2022). https://doi.org/10.1109/tnnls.2021.3070843
18. Ji, Z., et al.: Survey of hallucination in natural language generation. ACM Comput. Surv. **55**(12), 1–38 (2023). https://doi.org/10.1145/3571730

19. Jiang, A.Q., et al.: Mixtral of experts (2024). https://arxiv.org/abs/2401.04088
20. Kernan Freire, S., Foosherian, M., Wang, C., Niforatos, E.: Harnessing large language models for cognitive assistants in factories. In: Lee, M., Munteanu, C., Porcheron, M., Trippas, J., Völkel, S.T. (eds.) Proceedings of the 5th International Conference on Conversational User Interfaces, pp. 1–6. ACM, New York (2023). https://doi.org/10.1145/3571884.3604313
21. Khandelwal, U., Levy, O., Jurafsky, D., Zettlemoyer, L., Lewis, M.: Generalization through memorization: nearest neighbor language models (2020). https://arxiv.org/abs/1911.00172
22. Khattab, O., et al.: DSPy: compiling declarative language model calls into self-improving pipelines (2023). https://arxiv.org/abs/2310.03714
23. Lazaridou, A., Gribovskaya, E., Stokowiec, W., Grigorev, N.: Internet-augmented language models through few-shot prompting for open-domain question answering (2022). https://arxiv.org/abs/2203.05115
24. Lewis, P., et al.: Retrival-augmented generation for knowledge-intensive NLP tasks (2021). https://arxiv.org/abs/2005.11401
25. Li, H., Su, Y., Cai, D., Wang, Y., Liu, L.: A survey on retrieval-augmented text generation (2022). https://arxiv.org/abs/2202.01110
26. Lievin, V., Hother, C.E., Winther, O.: Can large language models reason about medical questions? (2022). https://arxiv.org/abs/2207.08143
27. Matricardi, F.: Metadata metamorphosis: from plain data to enhanced insights with retrieval augmented generation (2023). https://medium.com/mlearning-ai/metadata-metamorphosis-from-plain-data-to-enhanced-insights-with-retrieval-augmented-generation-8d1a8d5a6061
28. Mayring, P.: Qualitative content analysis. Forum Qual. Soc. Res. **1**(2) (2000). https://doi.org/10.17169/FQS-1.2.1089
29. McKinsey & Company: Meet Lilli, our generative AI tool that's a researcher, a time saver, and an inspiration (2023). https://www.mckinsey.com/about-us/new-at-mckinsey-blog/meet-lilli-our-generative-ai-tool
30. Moiseev, F., Dong, Z., Alfonseca, E., Jaggi, M.: Skill: structured knowledge infusion for large language models (2022). https://arxiv.org/abs/2205.08184
31. Mollick, E., et al.: Navigating the jagged technological frontier: field experimental evidence of the effects of AI on knowledge worker productivity and quality (2023). https://www.hbs.edu/ris/Publication%20Files/24-013_d9b45b68-9e74-42d6-a1c6-c72fb70c7282.pdf
32. OpenAI: chat GPT retrieval plug-in (2023). https://github.com/openai/chatgpt-retrieval-plugin
33. OpenAI: GPT-4 system card (2023). https://cdn.openai.com/papers/gpt-4-system-card.pdf
34. Peffers, K., Tuunanen, T., Rothenberger, M.A., Chatterjee, S.: A design science research methodology for information systems research. J. Manag. Inf. Syst. **24**(3), 45–77 (2007). https://doi.org/10.2753/MIS0742-1222240302
35. Peng, B., et al.: Check your facts and try again: improving large language models with external knowledge and automated feedback (2023). https://arxiv.org/abs/2302.12813
36. Peskoff, D., Stewart, B.: Credible without credit: domain experts assess generative language models. In: Proceedings of the 61st Annual Meeting of the Association for Computational Linguistics (Volume 2: Short Papers). Association for Computational Linguistics (2023). https://doi.org/10.18653/v1/2023.acl-short.37
37. Rezgui, Y.: Ontology-centered knowledge management using information retrieval techniques. J. Comput. Civ. Eng. **20**, 261–270 (2006)

38. Salvini, S., Williams, M.H.: Central knowledge management for expert systems. MAthl. Comput. Model. **16**(6), 137–144 (1992)
39. Santhanam, K., Khattab, O., Saad-Falcon, J., Potts, C., Zaharia, M.: ColBERTv2: effective and efficient retrieval via lightweight late interaction (2022). https://arxiv.org/abs/2112.01488
40. Shi, W., Zhuang, Y., Zhu, Y., Iwinski, H., Wattenbarger, M., Wang, M.D.: Retrieval-augmented large language models for adolescent idiopathic scoliosis patients in shared decision-making. In: Wang, M.D., Yoon, B.J. (eds.) Proceedings of the 14th ACM International Conference on Bioinformatics, Computational Biology, and Health Informatics, pp. 1–10. ACM, New York (2023). https://doi.org/10.1145/3584371.3612956
41. Si Xue, C.T.: A literature review on knowledge management in organizations. Res. Bus. Manag. **4**(1), 30 (2017). https://doi.org/10.5296/rbm.v4i1.10786
42. Sonntag, D.: Assessing the quality of natural language text data (2004). https://www.dfki.de/~sonntag/text_quality_short.pdf
43. Tripathi, K.P.: A review on knowledge-based expert system: concept and architecture. IJCA Spec. Issue Artif. Intell. Tech. Novel Approach. Pract. Appl. **4**, 19–23 (2011)
44. Vaswani, A., et al.: Attention is all you need. In: 31st Conference on Neural Information Processing Systems (NIPS) (2017)
45. vom Brocke, J., Simons, A., Niehaves, B., Reimer, K., Plattfaut, R., Cleven, A.: Reconstructing the giant: on the importance of rigour in documenting the literature search process. In: ECIS 2009 Proceedings, vol. 161 (2009)
46. Wang, C., et al.: Survey on factuality in large language models: knowledge, retrieval and domain-specificity (2023). https://arxiv.org/abs/2310.07521
47. Wang, D., et al.: DocLLM: a layout-aware generative language model for multimodal document understanding (2023). https://arxiv.org/abs/2401.00908
48. Wang, Y., et al.: RecMind: large language model powered agent for recommendation (2023). https://arxiv.org/abs/2308.14296
49. Wu, S., et al.: BloombergGPT: a large language model for finance (2023). https://arxiv.org/abs/2303.17564
50. Yogatama, D., de Masson d'Autume, C., Kong, L.: Adaptive semiparametric language models (2021). https://arxiv.org/abs/2102.02557
51. Yuan, Z., Hu, Songbu, Vulic, Ivan, Korhonen, A., Meng, Z.: Can pretrained language models (Yet) reason deductively? (2023). https://arxiv.org/abs/2210.06442
52. Zhang, B., Reklos, I., Jain, N., Peñuela, A.M., Simperl, E.: Using large language models for knowledge engineering (LLMKE): a case study on Wikidata (2023). https://arxiv.org/abs/2309.08491
53. Zhang, H., et al.: R-tuning: teaching large language models to refuse unknown questions (2023). https://arxiv.org/abs/2311.09677

ChatGPT and Language Translation

A Small Case Study Evaluating English – Mandarin Translation

Charles Woodrum[✉]

Boston, MA, USA
charles.a.woodrum@gmail.com

Abstract. ChatGPT and other Large Language Models (LLMs) have garnered immense attention since the first versions of ChatGPT were released. Language translation, meanwhile, has a storied history of evolving in response to ever-improving Machine Translation (MT). In the interest of comparing this new tool to existing human and Neural Machine Translation (NMT) tools, this study presents a focused examination of translation, comparing the ability of ChatGPT, Google Translate, and professional human translators to translate short English passages into Mandarin. This language pair was chosen to present maximum difficulty, with two very different languages, each with many native speakers and thus plenty of training data. The study's methodology was designed to ensure a comprehensive and unbiased comparison of methods. Five 250-word English passages were translated into Mandarin by three professional translators, Google Translate, and ChatGPT. Each of the translators were subsequently asked to rate the quality of the other translations on a scale of 0–100 and predict whether the translation was done by a human, ChatGPT, or Google Translate without knowing the origin of the translation. The results indicated that there is no statistically significant difference in the quality of translations among the three methods, underscoring the advanced capabilities of ChatGPT in providing translations comparable to that of professional human translators and Google Translate. Though this study was proof-of-concept in nature due to being limited by its small size (and thus it should not be taken as absolute evidence for the conclusions), it does highlight potential trends in the ever-increasing quality of machine translation. The methodology of the study offers a blueprint for more extensive research with more translators and more language combinations, presenting findings that suggest a narrowing gap between machine and human translation quality. This paper presents the findings of this study, outlines the process for more extensive research, and it hopes to offer insights for translators looking to respond to the ever-increasing abilities of AI translation tools.

Keywords: ChatGPT · Translation · Neural Machine Translation · NMT · Large Language Models · LLM · AI · Artificial Intelligence · Machine Translation · MT · Prompt Engineering · Fine Tuning

C. Woodrum—Independent Researcher.

H. Degen and S. Ntoa (Eds.): HCII 2024, LNAI 14736, pp. 147–157, 2024.
https://doi.org/10.1007/978-3-031-60615-1_10

1   Introduction

1.1   Historical Background - PreGPT

This paper was written nearly on the 70th anniversary of the beginning of machine translation, a field that arguably began with the rule-based machine translation of over 60 Russian sentences into English [1]. This 1954 experiment garnered significant attention and began the era of Rule-Based Machine Translation (RBMT). This saw the rise of programs like SYSTRAN in 1968 which compiled extensive dictionaries and sets of linguistic rules for language pairs to perform translation [2,3].

RBMT was eventually supplanted by Statistical Machine Translation (SMT) in the 1990s, which relied on the increasing abundance of data sets (large corpora translated from one language into another) to create statistical models of word and phrase correspondences between languages [4].

SMT was then followed by Neural Machine Translation (NMT) around the 2010s, aided by advancements in neural networks and increases in available data for training. The seminal development in this field was the sequence-to-sequence model (seq2seq) in 2014, which used Recurrent Neural Networks (RNN's) to process input and output sequences that varied in length [5]. NMT was further enhanced by the introduction of transformer models in 2017 by Vaswani. Transformer models rely on attention mechanisms, which focus on different parts of input data when producing output. In translation, this allows certain parts of input text to be weighted more than other parts. The transformer model also removes the RNN's need for recurrence and convolutions, which reduces training costs [6]. The transformer model is the foundation on which Large Language Models (LLMs) like ChatGPT would be built.

1.2   Background - LLMs and ChatGPT

ChatGPT-4, which was used to generate some of the text and translations in this study, is a Generative Pre-Trained Transformer (GPT) that has been optimised for general use in a chat setting. OpenAI, the company behind ChatGPT, was founded in December of 2015, but did not produce its first GPT, GPT-1, until June 2018. It was followed by GPT-2 in 2019 and GPT-3 in 2020 and has culminated in GPT-4 in 2023. Each iteration of their GPT came with increased performance and more parameters (117 million to 1.5 billion to 175 billion and beyond for GPT-4) [7–9]. Models like this with large training sets and high parameter counts that aim to achieve general-purpose or high-level language generation or understanding are termed Large Language Models (LLMs), and many have been produced to date (some of which are open source) by various organizations [11,12].

Advanced technical details on the architecture and inner workings of Chat-GPT are beyond the scope of this paper, but a high-level explanation will be provided so the reader has a clearer picture of what's going on. As its name suggests, a generative pre-trained transformer tries to generate text. Specifically, it tries to generate text based on a "prompt" - a set of text that is fed into the model that consists of user input. The prompt is broken up into "tokens", individual strings of characters that can be one or more characters in length. The tokens are then turned into numerical input into the model, which generates the optimal best token. Most explanations claim that the next token is the "most likely" one to come next, usually highlighting examples like: "peanut butter and" usually implies "jelly" as the next word. While statistical prediction provides a useful way of understanding the original premise, it is not the full picture. In fact, models trained only to do predictions fall short of the performance seen in ChatGPT. On top of the statistical predictions, the model is tuned with extensive human feedback to optimize its ability to complete text in a useful manner. These two steps seem to have generated the advanced abilities of ChatGPT [7–9].

1.3 ChatGPT and Translation

The data set used to train ChatGPT is not known publicly [10], though there has been informed speculation that it relies heavily on common crawl [13], a compendium of publicly available internet data in many languages that is about 45% English, which drastically outweighs the second most common language, standard German (6%). Chinese languages (including Mandarin, the target language for this study) makes up only 4.3% of common crawl. The 15th most common language, Indonesian, makes up less than 1% of the data set [14,15]. It is important to note that, though Common Crawl likely plays a strong role in the data set training OpenAI's GPTs, it must be noted that this is only informed speculation. Furthermore, ChatGPT is not trained to optimize for translation [10], so any exceptional ability with translation tasks is not automatically expected. This has, of course, not stopped anyone from requesting translations of all kinds from ChatGPT [16], nor has it stopped anyone from performing analysis on the translations done by ChatGPT (a simple search through Google Scholar will more than demonstrate this [17]). Analysis in these works typically focuses on scoring translation quality with technical measures, and it has resulted in Chat-GPT being rated among the top-performing models (competing directly with the state-of-the-art NMT tools for English<>German translation [18]) to being rated as quite inferior to human translation (being designated "not good" at translation of indigenous languages [19]).

2 Motivation and Methodology for This Study

2.1 Motivation

Though NMT methods can allow for fine tuning of models, they do not offer the ability of the translator to read a translation and communicate with the model regarding alternatives in phrasing, style, word choice, etc. This is in stark contrast with the abilities of an LLM chatbot, with which a translator (or layman) can converse and alter a translation. For example, the user could request that one word used frequently in the target language be replaced by another throughout the text and that the text be updated accordingly, and ChatGPT could seamlessly perform this update, though there's always the chance that errors can be generated.

With all the attention that has been paid to the quality of LLM translations, less attention, it seems, has been played to the interaction between translator and LLM. Can translators notice that text has been written by an LLM? Can they identify that a translation has been done by an LLM/NMT/human translator? How do they rate whole passages that are translated by these three methods? This study seeks to provide a framework for answering these questions, though it is limited in the strength of its conclusions by its small size. The methodology can be easily expanded to execute statistically powerful/conclusive experiments by large organizations who seek to characterize the quality of machine translations and the ability of general users and translators to do translation with LLMs.

2.2 Methodology

Five passages English passages of approximately 250 words were generated for translation purposes. Three were written by the author and two were written by ChatGPT. The dual-source generation was implemented to allow for exploration into two questions: can people correctly select which passages were written by ChatGPT and does ChatGPT translate passages that it wrote better than passages written by a human, all else being relatively equal? Passages were numbered randomly from 1–5 with no title and emailed to three professional translators. The translators were asked to list which, if any, of the passages they thought were generated by ChatGPT. The translators were then asked to translate the passages according to their normal workflow so long as they avoided using LLMs in the process, and to keep their work on these translations independent of the other translators, and to rank the translation difficulty from easiest to hardest for each of the five passages.

Once the translations were collected, ChatGPT generated translations of each passage with the prompt "*Translate the following passage into Mandarin:*" followed by the new line character "\n" and the passage in English. Another translation was generated with the prompt "*You are an English to Mandarin translator, translate the following English passage into the most accurate and natural Mandarin text that you can possibly produce:*" followed by the new line character twice (\n\n) and the passage in English. The inclusion of two different prompts is meant to explore the effect of prompt engineering on translation outcome, though any strong conclusions will require exploration with more data samples. Another translation was produced with Google Translate, which has used NMT for its translations for Chinese since 2016 [20].

Each of the passages were then emailed back to the translators along with 5 translations (2 from the other human translators, 2 from ChatGPT, and 1 from Google Translate). The translators were asked to rate the translation on a scale of 0 to 100, then make any comments on the translation, and then to decide whether or not the translation came from a human, NMT engine, or a Large Language Model.

ChatGPT was also asked 5 times in 5 separate chats to "Rank the following 5 passages from easiest to hardest to translate from English to Mandarin." followed by "Passage {passage number}:" followed by each passage in English in backtick marks. ChatGPT was also asked in five separate chats to determine which of the five passages it believed were generated using ChatGPT-4 with the prompt "Out of the five following passages, which do you think were generated by ChatGPT4. Don't give any long winded explanation; just give your best answer. I know it's hard." followed by "Passage {passage number}:" with the full passage in backtick marks. Such prompt engineering was needed to ensure that the LLM actually produced a response, since it had a tendency to not answer the question when asked to rank the passages more directly. ChatGPT was also asked, for each passage, to rank the translation from 0 to 100 and to determine whether or not the translation was generated from a human, NMT engine, or an LLM with the prompt "Given the following passage in English {Passage in English in backtick marks}, rank the following Mandarin translation from 0 to 100, then choose whether or not the translation came from a human, Google Translate, or ChatGPT-4. {Mandarin Translation in backtick marks}".

2.3   Examples

The following is a passage generated by ChatGPT in English

Cultural anthropology stands as a sentinel at the crossroads of human societies, offering insights into the diverse tapestry of cultures that populate our planet. This discipline delves into the complexities of social behavior, rituals, and belief systems, employing a nuanced lexicon that speaks to the intricacies of human interaction and societal constructs. Anthropologists engage in ethnographic research, a methodological cornerstone of the field, which involves immersive participation within the communities they study. This approach, known as participant observation, allows them to glean an insider's perspective (or an 'emic' viewpoint) on the dynamics of social structures, language, and cultural practices. For example, the exploration of kinship systems in different societies reveals the varying ways in which human relationships and familial responsibilities are perceived and organized.

The discipline also scrutinizes the effects of globalization on indigenous and local cultures. This includes examining how the infusion of modern technology and global media influences, and at times disrupts, traditional practices and values. This cultural interplay often leads to a hybridization of customs, though it can also contribute to the dilution or even loss of cultural uniqueness. Cultural anthropology, therefore, serves as a crucial interpretive tool in understanding the complex web of human societies. It challenges us to look beyond our own cultural norms and consider the diverse ways in which people around the world experience and interpret

C. Woodrum

their realities. Through its analytical lens, we gain a deeper appreciation for the rich variety of human life and the ongoing dialogue between tradition and modernity [21].

The following is a translation by a human translator [22]

文化人类学是人类社会交叉口的哨兵，展现我们地球上形形色色的文化的情况。文化人类学探究的是社会行为、仪式、信仰体系的复杂性，用细腻的语言描述人际交往和社会结构的错综复杂。人类学家进行的民族志研究是这一科学方法论的基石，需要亲身参与他们研究的社群。这种称为参与观察的方法让研究者以亲身经历者的角度（即"主位"视角）了解社会结构、语言、文化习俗动态。举例来说，研究不同社会的亲属体系能了解如何看待人类关系和家庭责任的及其组织方式。
文化人类学也研究全球化对土著和地方居民的影响，包括调查现代科技和全球媒体的融入如何在某些时候颠覆传统习俗和价值观。这种文化的相互作用通常会导致习俗混杂，不过也可能导致文化独特性淡化甚至消失。因此，文化人类学是用于理解人类社会复杂关系网的重要解释性工具，鼓励我们关注其他群体的文化规范，了解全球各地人民的经历，解读他们的现实生活。通过其分析视角，我们能更加感恩人类生活的丰富多样，以及传统和现代之间的持续碰撞。

The following is the same passage translated by Google Translate [23]

文化人类学是人类社会十字路口的哨兵，为我们这个星球上的多样化文化提供深入的见解。该学科深入研究社会行为、仪式和信仰体系的复杂性，采用细致入微的词汇来讲述人类互动和社会结构的复杂性。人类学家从事民族志研究，这是该领域的方法论基石，其中涉及他们所研究的社区的沉浸式参与。这种方法被称为参与观察，使他们能够收集内部人士对社会结构、语言和文化实践动态的观点（或"主位"观点）。例如，对不同社会中的亲属制度的探索揭示了人类关系和家庭责任被感知和组织的不同方式。该学科还审视全球化对土著和地方文化的影响。这包括研究现代技术和全球媒体的注入如何影响甚至有时破坏传统实践和价值观。这种文化相互作用常常导致习俗的混合，但也可能导致文化独特性的淡化甚至丧失。因此，文化人类学是理解人类社会复杂网络的重要解释工具。它挑战我们超越我们自己的文化规范，并考虑世界各地的人们体验和解释现实的不同方式。通过其分析镜头，我们对人类生活的丰富多样性以及传统与现代之间持续的对话有了更深刻的认识。

And the following is the passage translated by ChatGPT-4 [24].

文化人类学站在人类社会的十字路口，作为哨兵，提供了对我们星球上众多文化的多样性帷幕的洞察。这门学科深入探讨社会行为、仪式和信仰体系的复杂性，运用一种细腻的词汇表，表达了人际互动和社会结构的复杂性。人类学家从事民族志研究，这是该领域的方法论基石，涉及深入参与他们所研究的社区。这种方法，被称为参与观察，使他们能够洞察社会结构、语言和文化实践的内部视角（或"内视角"）的动态。例如，对不同社会中亲属制度的探索揭示了人际关系和家庭责任被感知和组织的不同方式。

该学科还审视全球化对原住民和当地文化的影响。这包括考察现代技术和全球媒体影响的融入如何影响，有时甚至扰乱传统习俗和价值观。这种文化交融通常导致习俗的混合，但也可能导致文化独特性的稀释甚至丧失。因此，文化人类学作为一个重要的解释工具，帮助我们理解人类社会复杂的网络。它挑战我们超越自己的文化规范，考虑世界各地的人们以不同的方式体验和解释他们的现实。通过其分析视角，我们对人类生活的丰富多样性以及传统与现代性之间的持续对话有了更深的欣赏。

Speakers of Mandarin and English may find an examination of these passages interesting.

3 Results

Since the sample size is so small for each question, full results will be reported for each question. In most cases, statistical analysis is possible but not powerful.

3.1 Classifying AI Generated Text

The first question asked of translators was to identify which of the passages were AI generated and which were human written. Translators were unable to do this, and whether the text was human or AI written had no effect on their predictions ($p > 0.99$) [26] Table 1.

Table 1. Contingency table on the translator's assessments of human vs AI written passages.

	Predicted AI Generated	Predicted Human Generated	Total
AI Generated	1	5	6
Human Generated	2	7	9
Total	3	12	15

Interestingly, ChatGPT-4 was also given the text and queried for it's take on which passages it generated, and, when evaluated as an ML model, performed very poorly with an F1 score of 9% [27]. This isn't necessarily surprising, since OpenAI's own AI detector was taken down due to low success [28] Table 2.

Table 2. Contingency table on ChatGPT's assessments of whether or not it wrote the passages. Note that it was queried multiple times in separate chats

	Predicted AI Generated	Predicted Human Generated	Total
AI Generated	1	11	12
Human Generated	9	9	18
Total	10	20	30

3.2   Human Ratings of Translation Quality

Translators were asked to rate the quality of translations between 0 for terrible and 100 for "perfect". The full results are found in Table 3 with a histogram of the values in Fig. 1

Table 3. Table of assessments of translation quality by human translators by passage. Note that the translators could not rate themselves, so there are two ratings for the human translators and three for the non-human methods. "ChatGPT 1" refers to the simple prompt introducing the translation task, and "ChatGPT 2" refers to the modified prompt attempting to improve performance.

Passage	Human 1	Human 2	Human 3	ChatGPT 1	ChatGPT 2	Google Translate	Average
1	82, 60	50, 80	95, 80	85, 72, 80	75, 73, 30	90, 82, 40	71.6
2	86, 90	95, 76	95, 90	85, 78, 70	90, 74, 70	85, 72, 70	81.7
3	82, 90	95, 86	95, 80	95, 75, 80	95, 76, 80	95, 88, 90	86.8
4	76, 85	90, 72	80, 70	80, 75, 75	98, 82, 85	95, 76, 80	81.3
5	84, 80	95, 74	95, 80	90, 75, 60	90, 72, 60	85, 80, 80	80
Average	81.5	81.3	86	78.3	76.7	80.5	≈80.5

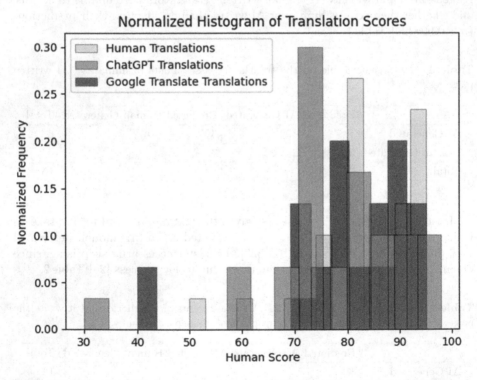

Fig. 1. A histogram of the human-generated scores of translations grouped by method of translation generation.

The average human translation scored 82.8/100, only slightly higher than ChatGPT with either prompt (78.3 and 76.7) and Google Translate (80.5). Using a two-sample t-test with level-of-significance 0.05, we see that there is no statistically significant difference between the mean human translation and the mean of all the ChatGPT translations (p = 0.082), nor is there a difference in translation ranking between humans and the NMT translations provided by Google translate (p = 0.55). There is also no statistically significant difference between the ChatGPT translations and the NMT (p = 0.48). There was also no statistically significant difference between the quality of ChatGPT translations with different prompts (p = 0.73) [26].

4 Conclusions

This study sought to evaluate the capabilities of ChatGPT in translating English passages into Mandarin and compare its performance to Google Translate and professional human translators. Along the way, the study also found that professional translators and ChatGPT were unable to identify AI-generated and human-written texts. This is, however, a well-established phenomenon. With regard to translation quality, it revealed that the line between human and machine translation is becoming narrow to the point of statistical insignificance, though it must be stated unequivocally that this study is too small for strong conclusions to be made regarding the field as a whole.

The comparable performance of ChatGPT and humans and NMT is remarkable, since ChatGPT is not optimized for translation but still delivered translations with a quality comparable to that of Google Translate and professional human translators. Attempting to correct for this with prompt engineering alone did not improve performance of translation, but it did not hurt it, either. It is therefore likely that more training data and/or fine-tuning may be necessary to augment ChatGPT's performance.

This study, though small, has a methodology that serves as a proof-of-concept for future research. It highlights the potential for larger-scale studies to further investigate the capabilities of AI in translation, emphasizing the need for more extensive research to draw stronger conclusions. More language combinations, more translators, and more data are ultimately needed. Other explorations, like fine-tuning ChatGPT with OpenAI's "Custom GPTs", will provide more opportunities for further research.

As AI technology in both NMT and Generative AI continues to advance, it is imperative for further research to explore these capabilities so that translators, business people, and the AI industry can gain insights into the future of translation and the changes that will bring to the translation industry.

Acknowledgement. The author would like to acknowledge the assistance of the Mandarin<>English translators Ming Qian, Chuiqing Kong, and Zhenhuan Lei. Without them this paper would not be possible. Special thanks also to Ming Qian for the invitation and suggestion for this work.

Conflicts. The author has no competing interests to declare that are relevant to the content of this article.

References

1. MacDonald, N.: Language translation by machine - a report of the first successful trial. Comput. Autom. **3**(2), 6–34 (1954)
2. Benjamins, J.: Early Years in Machine Translation: Memoirs and Biographies of Pioneers. John Benjamins Publishing Co., Amsterdam, Philadelphia (2000)
3. SYSTRAN: Company. https://www.systransoft.com/systran/. Accessed 16 Feb 2024
4. Brown, P., Pietra, S., Pietra, V., Mercer, R.: The mathematics of statistical machine translation: parameter estimation. Comput. Linguist. **19**(2), 263–311 (1993)
5. Sutskever, I., Vinyals, O., Le, Q.V.: Sequence to sequence learning with neural networks. In: Proceedings of the Conference on Neural Information Processing Systems (2014)
6. Vaswani, A., et. al.: Attention is all you need. In: Proceedings of the Conference on Neural Information Processing Systems (2017)
7. Karpathy, A., et. al.: Generative models. OpenAI Research. https://openai.com/research/generative-models. Accessed 26 Feb 2024
8. Wolfram S.: What is ChatGPT Doing ... and Why Does It Work? Stephen Wolfram Writings. https://writings.stephenwolfram.com/2023/02/what-is-chatgpt-doing-and-why-does-it-work/. Accessed 16 Feb 2024
9. Marr, B.: A short history of ChatGPT: a short history of ChatGPT: how we got to where we are today. Forbes. https://www.forbes.com/sites/bernardmarr/2023/05/19/a-short-history-of-chatgpt-how-we-got-to-where-we-are-today/?sh=761ad2d6674f. Accessed 16 Feb 2024
10. Achiam, J., et. al.: GPT-4 technical report. arXiv:2303.08774v4. Accessed 19 Dec 2023
11. Norouzi, A.: The list of 11 most popular open source LLMs of 2023. https://www.lakera.ai/blog/open-source-llms. Accessed 16 Feb 2024
12. The LLM Index by Sapling.ai. https://sapling.ai/llm/index. Accessed 16 Feb 2024
13. Layton, D.: ChatGPT - show me the data sources. https://medium.com/@dlaytonj2/chatgpt-show-me-the-data-sources-11e9433d57e8. Accessed 16 Feb 2024
14. CommonCrawl Homepage. https://commoncrawl.org. Accesssed 16 Feb 2024
15. Statistics of Common Crawl Monthly Archives: Distribution of Languages. https://commoncrawl.github.io/cc-crawl-statistics/plots/languages. Accessed 26 Feb 2024
16. Quillen, S.: How Many Languages Does ChatGPT Speak? https://sjquillen.medium.com/how-many-languages-does-chatgpt-speak-bf5cfc35a586. Accessed 16 Feb 2024
17. ChatGPT Translation Google Scholar Search Results. https://scholar.google.com/scholar?hl=en&as_sdt=0%2C36&q=ChatGPT+translation&oq=trans. Accessed 26 Feb 2024
18. Manakhimova, S., et. al.: Linguistically motivated evaluation of the 2023 state-of-the-art machine translation: can GPT-4 outperform NMT? In: Proceedings of the Eighth Conference on Machine Translation, Singapore, pp. 224–245. Association for Computational Linguistics (2023)

19. Stap, D., Araabi, A.: ChatGPT is not a good indigenous translator. In: Proceedings of the Workshop on Natural Language Processing for Indigenous Languages of the Americas (AmericasNLP), Toronto, Canada, pp. 163–167. Association for Computational Linguistics (2023)
20. Turovsky, B.: Found in translation: more accurate, fluent sentences in Google Translate. https://blog.google/products/translate/found-translation-more-accurate-fluent-sentences-google-translate/. Accessed 16 Feb 2024
21. OpenAI: ChatGPT Conversation. https://chat.openai.com. Accessed 28 Nov 2023
22. Translation by Chuiqing Kong, 07 December 2023
23. Google Translate translation. https://translate.google.com/. Accessed 28 Nov 2023
24. OpenAI: ChatGPT Conversation. https://chat.openai.com. Accessed 16 Feb 2024
25. OpenAI: ChatGPT Conversation. https://chat.openai.com, Accessed 16 Feb 2024
26. Casella, G., Berger, R.L.: Statistical Inference, 2nd edn. Duxbury, Pacific Grove, CA (2002)
27. Géron, A.: Hands-on machine learning with Scikit-Learn, Keras, and TensorFlow, 2nd edn. O'Reilly Media Inc., Sebastopol, CA (2019)
28. Kirchner, J.H., et. al.: New AI classifier for indicating AI-written text. https://openai.com/blog/new-ai-classifier-for-indicating-ai-written-text. Accessed 16 Feb 2024

Large Language Models for Tracking Reliability of Information Sources

Erin Zaroukian[✉] [iD]

DEVCOM Army Research Laboratory, Aberdeen Proving Ground, MD 21005, USA
erin.g.zaroukian.civ@army.mil

Abstract. Human decision makers track variability in the reliability of their information sources, such that human decision making can be modeled using a hierarchical gaussian filter [1]. This variability tracking can be utilized to infer the intentions of social information sources, akin to Theory of Mind (ToM), which describes the ability to ascribe mental states to others [2]. Meanwhile, Large Language Models (LLMs) have shown evidence of an emergent ToM as larger and larger models move toward producing human-like performance on false belief Theory of Mind tasks [3]. While LLMs have shown evidence of ToM, do they behave like humans in other inferential abilities? Specifically, can a sufficiently large language model track variability in information sources? Here, we conduct an experiment to address this question, finding modest success among LLMs in identifying simple patterns in longitudinal data from an information source and in providing responses consistent with detecting a change in that source's reliability. When more complex patterns are presented, however, the LLMs tested failed and overall provided responses that were non-human-like in a number of ways.

Keywords: Theory of Mind · Decision making · Large Language Models

1 Introduction

Successful human decision makers must consider the reliability of their information sources. For example, a party planner might need accurate weather predictions, and so if one source makes incorrect predictions more often than other sources, that source should be discounted or even ignored in their decision-making process. Furthermore, the reliability of an information source can change over time, such as a weather model that has high accuracy in the summer but performs more and more poorly as the weather cools. Human decision makers have been shown to track variability in the reliability of their information sources[1] such that human decision making can be modeled using a hierarchical gaussian filter [1]. This variability tracking can be utilized to infer the intentions of social information sources, akin to Theory of Mind (ToM).

---

[1] Diaconescu et al. demonstrate more successful tracking of changes in reliability from social sources, such as a weatherman, than from non-social sources, such as the output of a weather model [1].

H. Degen and S. Ntoa (Eds.): HCII 2024, LNAI 14736, pp. 158–169, 2024.
https://doi.org/10.1007/978-3-031-60615-1_11

ToM describes the ability to ascribe mental states to others [2], such that, for example, someone possessing ToM can recognize that another person may hold a false belief and be able to reasonably predict their behavior based on that false belief. This ability is classically assessed with tests like the Sally-Anne test, shown in Fig. 1, where Sally places a marble in a basket, but while she is away Anne surreptitiously moves the marble out of the basket and into a box. A test participant exercising ToM will expect Sally to hold a false belief about the marble's location such that she will look for her marble in the basket.

Fig. 1. The Sally-Anne false belief test as depicted in Baron-Cohen et al. (1985) [4].

Recent work by Kosinski shows evidence of the emergence of ToM in Large Language Models (LLMs) [3], where larger and larger models move toward producing human-like performance on false belief Theory of Mind tasks. This mirrors certain theories of ToM which tie its emergence in humans with our (ontogenetically or phylogenetically) increasing vocabularies and language abilities, and it provides an interesting alternative strategy to achieving computational ToM that avoids hardcoding specific abilities. In Kosinksi's work, some ToM ability appears to emerge in models with around 175 billion parameters, and performance comparable to that of a 6-year-old was achieved with GPT-4, which likely has trillions of parameters, and may have achieved this human-like ability by generalizing from sufficient similar tasks in their training.

While LLMs have shown evidence of ToM through false belief tasks, do they behave like humans in other inferential abilities? Specifically, can a sufficiently large language model track variability in information sources, as in Diaconescu's work [1]. This work presents a study to address this question.

2 Methods

This study explores LLM completions of 30 days of simple weather data of the form "On day X, the weatherman said it would be [sunny/rainy]. He was [correct/incorrect]." The data was Uniform (every day the weatherman correctly predicted sunny weather), Conditional (the weather was sunny every day, weatherman correctly predicted sunny 50% of days and incorrectly predicted rainy 50% of days), or Probabilistic (the weatherman predicted rainy 50% of days and sunny 50% of days, and the weatherman's predictions were correct 67% of days). Furthermore, the data was either Consistent (the pattern described above held across all 30 days) or Inconsistent (the pattern switched on day 16, see Table 1 below). So, for Uniform Inconsistent data, on days 1–15, the weatherman correctly predicted sunny weather, then on days 16–30, the weatherman incorrectly predicted rainy weather. For Conditional Inconsistent data, on days 1–15, the weather was always sunny, and the weatherman's predictions were correct 50% of the time (and since it was always sunny, his sunny predictions were correct, i.e., sunny→correct, and his rainy predictions were incorrect, i.e., rainy→incorrect), but on days 16–30, the weather was always rainy (so now sunny→incorrect and rainy→correct). For Probabilistic Inconsistent data, on days 1–15, the weatherman predicted rainy 50% of days and sunny 50% of days, and the weatherman's predictions were correct 67% of days, but on days 16–30, the weatherman's predictions were correct only 33% of days.

These six strings of data (Uniform Consistent and Inconsistent, Conditional Consistent and Inconsistent, and Probabilistic Consistent and Inconsistent) where generated 20 times, resulting in 120 strings. Abbreviated sample strings are provided in Table 2, and these include the prompt "Finish this sentence: On day 31, the weatherman said it would be ", which will be discussed below. Across all 20 trials, the Uniform Consistent strings and Uniform Inconsistent strings are identical, but the Conditional and Probabilistic strings vary, with each day having a 50% chance of having a sunny prediction and a 50% chance of having a rainy prediction, and additionally in the Probabilistic condition each day has a 67% chance (or 33% change for days 16–30 in the Inconsistent condition) of having a correct forecast.

Table 1. Summary of data presented to the LLMs.

Pattern	Consistency	Template
Uniform	Consistent	Days 1–30: "On day X, the weatherman said it would be <u>sunny</u>. He was <u>correct</u>."
	Inconsistent	Days 1–15: *Same as Consistent* Days 16–30: "On day X, the weatherman said it would be <u>rainy</u>. He was <u>incorrect</u>."
Conditional	Consistent	Days 1–30: 50% "On day X, the weatherman said it would be <u>sunny</u>. He was <u>correct</u>." 50% "On day X, the weatherman said it would be <u>rainy</u>. He was <u>incorrect</u>."
	Inconsistent	Days 1–15: *Same as Consistent* Days 16–30: 50% "On day X, the weatherman said it would be <u>sunny</u>. He was <u>incorrect</u>." 50% "On day X, the weatherman said it would be <u>rainy</u>. He was <u>correct</u>."
Probabilistic	Consistent	Days 1–30: 33% "On day X, the weatherman said it would be <u>sunny</u>. He was <u>correct</u>." 17% "On day X, the weatherman said it would be <u>sunny</u>. He was <u>incorrect</u>." 33% "On day X, the weatherman said it would be <u>rainy</u>. He was <u>correct</u>." 17% "On day X, the weatherman said it would be <u>rainy</u>. He was <u>incorrect</u>."
	Inconsistent	Days 1–15: *Same as Consistent* Days 16–30: 17% "On day X, the weatherman said it would be <u>sunny</u>. He was <u>correct</u>." 33% "On day X, the weatherman said it would be <u>sunny</u>. He was <u>incorrect</u>." 17% "On day X, the weatherman said it would be <u>rainy</u>. He was <u>correct</u>." 33% "On day X, the weatherman said it would be <u>rainy</u>. He was <u>incorrect</u>."

These data strings were fed to two LLMs in order to generate text about the weatherman's prediction on day 31. The first, BLOOM [5], has 176 billion parameters and was queried via the huggingface API. The second, GPT-3.5, has around 200 billion parameters, and this was queried via the ChatGPT interface [6]. Both of these model sizes are in the range of where ToM abilities emerged in Kosinski's study.

Table 2. Example strings given to LLMs.

Pattern	Consistency	Example
Uniform	Consistent	On day 1, the weatherman said it would be sunny. He was correct. On day 2, the weatherman said it would be sunny. He was correct.... On day 14, the weatherman said it would be sunny. He was correct. On day 15, the weatherman said it would be sunny. He was correct. On day 16, the weatherman said it would be sunny. He was correct. On day 17, the weatherman said it would be sunny. He was correct. ... On day 29, the weatherman said it would be sunny. He was correct. On day 30, the weatherman said it would be sunny. He was correct. Finish this sentence: On day 31, the weatherman said it would be
	Inconsistent	On day 1, the weatherman said it would be sunny. He was correct. On day 2, the weatherman said it would be sunny. He was correct. ... On day 14, the weatherman said it would be sunny. He was correct. On day 15, the weatherman said it would be sunny. He was correct. On day 16, the weatherman said it would be rainy. He was incorrect. On day 17, the weatherman said it would be rainy. He was incorrect. ... On day 29, the weatherman said it would be rainy. He was incorrect. On day 30, the weatherman said it would be rainy. He was incorrect. Finish this sentence: On day 31, the weatherman said it would be
Conditional	Consistent	On day 1, the weatherman said it would be rainy. He was incorrect. On day 2, the weatherman said it would be sunny. He was correct. ... On day 14, the weatherman said it would be rainy. He was incorrect. On day 15, the weatherman said it would be sunny. He was correct. On day 16, the weatherman said it would be rainy. He was incorrect. On day 17, the weatherman said it would be rainy. He was incorrect. ... On day 29, the weatherman said it would be rainy. He was incorrect. On day 30, the weatherman said it would be rainy. He was incorrect. Finish this sentence: On day 31, the weatherman said it would be
	Inconsistent	On day 1, the weatherman said it would be rainy. He was incorrect. On day 2, the weatherman said it would be sunny. He was correct. ... On day 14, the weatherman said it would be sunny. He was correct. On day 15, the weatherman said it would be sunny. He was correct. On day 16, the weatherman said it would be sunny. He was incorrect. On day 17, the weatherman said it would be rainy. He was correct. ... On day 29, the weatherman said it would be rainy. He was correct. On day 30, the weatherman said it would be sunny. He was incorrect. Finish this sentence: On day 31, the weatherman said it would be

(*continued*)

Table 2. (*continued*)

Pattern	Consistency	Example
Probabilistic	Consistent	On day 1, the weatherman said it would be rainy. He was incorrect. On day 2, the weatherman said it would be sunny. He was correct. ... On day 14, the weatherman said it would be rainy. He was incorrect. On day 15, the weatherman said it would be sunny. He was correct. On day 16, the weatherman said it would be sunny. He was incorrect. On day 17, the weatherman said it would be sunny. He was incorrect. ... On day 29, the weatherman said it would be rainy. He was incorrect. On day 30, the weatherman said it would be rainy. He was incorrect. Finish this sentence: On day 31, the weatherman said it would be
	Inconsistent	On day 1, the weatherman said it would be rainy. He was incorrect. On day 2, the weatherman said it would be sunny. He was correct. ... On day 14, the weatherman said it would be rainy. He was correct. On day 15, the weatherman said it would be rainy. He was correct. On day 16, the weatherman said it would be rainy. He was incorrect. On day 17, the weatherman said it would be rainy. He was correct. ... On day 29, the weatherman said it would be rainy. He was correct. On day 30, the weatherman said it would be rainy. He was incorrect. Finish this sentence: On day 31, the weatherman said it would be

When querying BLOOM, the 30 days of data were appended with the prompt "Finish this sentence: On day 31, the weatherman said it would be ", as shown in Table 2. For GPT-3.5, the same prompt was appended, but the responses rarely indicated whether or not the weatherman was correct, so the following were also independently tested with the same data strings: "Finish this sentence: On day 31, the weatherman said it would be sunny. He was " and "Finish this sentence: On day 31, the weatherman said it would be rainy. He was ".

3   Results

The results from BLOOM are summarized in Fig. 2. For the Uniform data, the recent pattern was continued onto the 31st day, such that a correct sunny prediction was generated when days 1–30 had correct sunny predictions, and an incorrect rainy prediction was generated when the most recent day 16–30 had incorrect rainy predictions. For the Conditional data, the recent pattern again continued onto the 31st day, such that sunny forecasts were more likely to be correct and rainy forecasts were more likely to be incorrect when this pattern was seen in days 1–30, and sunny forecasts were more likely to be incorrect and rainy forecasts were more likely to be correct if this pattern was seen in days 16–30. Surprisingly, though, the frequency of sunny forecasts was boosted from 50% in the input to 85–90% in the generated output. For the Probabilistic data, there is no clear continuation of any pattern. Instead of matching the accuracy probability from the most recent input, the frequency of inaccurate predictions was boosted across the board (from 33% in days 1–30 to 65% for the Consistent data and from 67% in days 16–30 to 80% for Inconsistent data). And again, the frequency of sunny forecasts is unexpectedly boosted, this time from 50% to 90–95%. From these results, BLOOM appears to do well continuing simple pattern, as shown with the Consistent data, but the Conditional and Probabilistic data lead to an unexpected boost in sunny forecasts, and the Probabilistic data lead to an unexpected boost in incorrect forecasts.

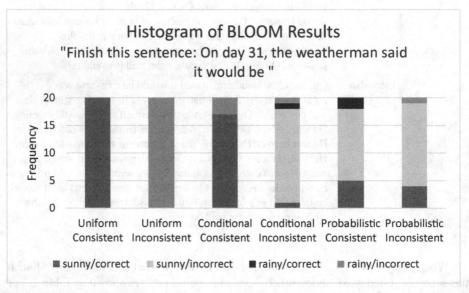

Fig. 2. Histogram of outputs given 30 days of weather and accuracy data plus the prompt "Finish this sentence: On day 31, the weatherman said it would be " to predict day 31 using BLOOM.

The results from GPT-3.5 are shown in Figs. 3, 4 and 5. Figure 3 summarizes the text generated using the more general prompt, "Finish this sentence: On day 31, the weatherman said it would be ". As mentioned above, this prompt often failed to lead to responses of the form we were interested in, so two more specific prompts were used in addition, and they are discussed below with Figs. 4 and 5. Additionally, some responses failed to make a prediction at all, and these were omitted from Fig. 3.

Returning to Fig. 3, for the Uniform data, the 31st day was overwhelmingly correct sunny predictions, even in the Inconsistent condition, where the last 15 days in the data were incorrect rainy predictions. For the Conditional data, when Consistent there was again a boosting of correct sunny predictions, as with BLOOM, though a notable 15% of generated responses did not follow the sunny→correct, rainy→incorrect rule. When Inconsistent, the four responses were generated in roughly equal proportions, which could generously be interpreted as matching their relative proportions in the input, but which does not show that a change in the Conditional pattern had been learned. For the Probabilistic data, as with BLOOM there is a boost in the frequency of incorrect

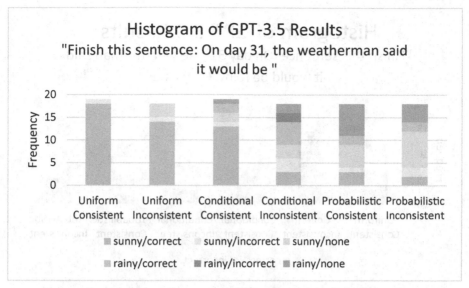

Fig. 3. Histogram of outputs given 30 days of weather and accuracy data plus the prompt "Finish this sentence: On day 31, the weatherman said it would be " to predict day 31 using GPT-3.5.

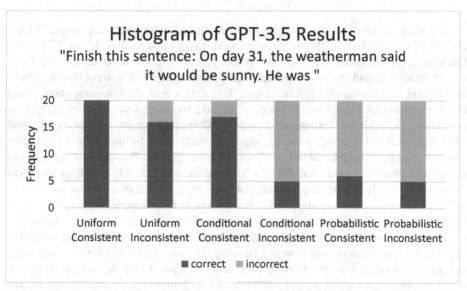

Fig. 4. Histogram of outputs given 30 days of weather and accuracy data plus the prompt "Finish this sentence: On day 31, the weatherman said it would be sunny. He was " to predict day 31 using GPT-3.5.

responses, but here instead of boosting sunny responses, rainy responses appear to be boosted above 50%.

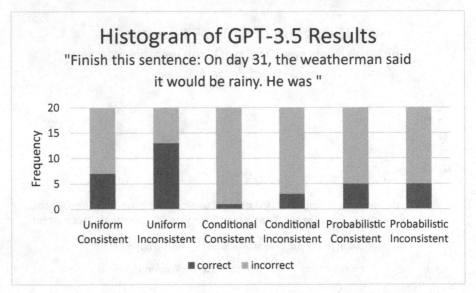

Fig. 5. Histogram of outputs given 30 days of weather and accuracy data plus the prompt "Finish this sentence: On day 31, the weatherman said it would be rainy. He was " to predict day 31 using GPT-3.5.

Figure 4 summarizes the text generated using the more specific prompt, "Finish this sentence: On day 31, the weatherman said it would be sunny. He was ". For the Uniform data, the generated responses perfectly matched the input data in the Consistent condition, and in the Inconsistent condition, it generated correct forecasts 80% of the time, suggesting that it learned that the weather was always sunny, rather than that the weatherman had a recent tendency to make incorrect forecasts. For the Conditional data, the generated responses followed the Consistent sunny→correct conditional only 85% of the time, and in the Inconsistent condition it followed the more recent sunny→incorrect conditional only 75% of the time. For the Probabilistic data, incorrect predictions were generated 70–75% of the time, very roughly matching its recent frequency in the Inconsistent condition, but boosting it well above its 33% probability in the Consistent condition. Here again, some more simple patterns seem to have been learned, and the model appears more biased toward initial data vs. more recent data.

Figure 5 summarizes the text generated using the prompt, "Finish this sentence: On day 31, the weatherman said it would be rainy. He was ". For the Uniform data, the generated responses are split fairly evenly between correct and incorrect predictions, which could be generously interpreted as the model being split on whether the weatherman is always correct in the Consistent condition (and so rainy should be a correct prediction) and incorrect in the Inconsistent condition (and so rainy should be an incorrect prediction), or whether the weather is always sunny in the Consistent condition (and so rainy should be an incorrect prediction) and rainy in the Inconsistent condition (and so rainy should be a correct prediction). For the Conditional data, the majority (85–95%) of generated responses were incorrect, suggesting that the model learned the initial rainy→incorrect rule, which it did not update in the Inconsistent condition. For the Probabilistic data, the majority of generated responses were only slightly less incorrect (75%) than for the Conditional data, which once again shows an across-the-board boosting of incorrect responses from the Probabilistic data from the previous days.

4 Discussion

Overall, the results here show only very modest reasoning ability from the LLMs tested. This is perhaps comparable to the evidence in support of LLMs as General pattern machines, were LLMs show superior ability to complete abstract pattern, but with accuracy far below a human's [7].

In the simplest case of Uniform Consistent data tested here, where the weatherman always correctly predicted sunny weather, the generated responses overall did well at continuing the pattern (sunny/correct), though GPT-3.5 was ambivalent about how to classify the never-before-seen rainy prediction in "Finish this sentence: On day 31, the weatherman prediction it would be rainy. He was ". The author's intuition is that humans asked to classify this prediction would label it as incorrect, assuming that it's more likely that the weatherman is wrong than that 30 days of sunny weather would be followed by a day of rainy weather, but this has not been tested.

For the slightly more complicated Uniform Inconsistent data, where the weatherman switches from always correctly predicting sunny weather to always incorrectly predicting rainy weather, BLOOM continued the most recent pattern (rainy/incorrect), while GPT-3.5 seemed biased toward the earlier data and generated more sunny/correct responses. When given the prompt "Finish this sentence: On day 31, the weatherman prediction it would be rainy. He was ", GPT-3.5 was more likely to generate a correct response, again suggesting a bias toward earlier correct predictions, independent of the fact that they were sunny predictions. The author's intuition is that humans would note that every preceding day had been sunny and that the weatherman had suddenly become a very poor forecaster starting day 16, and so the weather would likely continue to be sunny and the weatherman would likely continue to make incorrect rainy predictions, as BLOOM did, but counter to GPT-3.5. Again, however, this has not been tested.

For the Conditional Consistent data, where sunny→correct and rainy→incorrect, the pattern was learned fairly well, although generate responses were more likely to predict sunny weather, which was predicted for about 50% of the preceding 30 days, than rainy weather.

For the Conditional Inconsistent data, BLOOM again mostly continued the most recent pattern (sunny→incorrect, rainy→correct), while boosting the frequency of sunny (and therefore incorrect) predictions. GPT-3.5, on the other hand, did not appear to stick to either the initial (sunny→correct, rainy→incorrect) or more recent (sunny→incorrect, rainy→correct) pattern. When given the forecast for day 31, it overwhelmingly classified them as incorrect. Among the data used in this study, Conditional Inconsistent appears to be where GPT-3.5 begins to struggle in generating reasonable patterns of responses. The author's intuition is that a human would continue the most recent pattern (sunny→incorrect, rainy→correct), like BLOOM (but without boosting the frequency of sunny predictions), though again this has not been tested.

For the Probabilistic data, both models gave the same pattern of responses in the Consistent condition as in the Inconsistent condition, suggesting that the relatively subtle shift from 67% correct predictions to 33% correct predictions was not noticed. Additionally, both models generated majority incorrect responses across all Probabilistic conditions. BLOOM, as with the Conditional data, boosted the frequency of sunny predictions, whereas GPT-3.5 boosted the frequency of rainy predictions. No general reasons for these boosts are apparent. Similarly, however, it is harder to predict what responses humans would generate for day 31, as the patterns in this data are more subtle. In the Inconsistent condition they may notice the increase in incorrect predictions and be more likely to provide an incorrect prediction for day 31 than in the Consistent condition, as suggested by participants' ability to track changes in a source's reliability in Diaconescu [1], but, once again, this has not been tested. It is clear, however, that models with roughly 175 billion parameters, which began to show some evidence of ToM in Kosinski's work [3], do not appear to detect relatively subtle changes in the weatherman's reliability.

As mentioned previously, GPT-3.5 was a bit more creative in the responses it provided than BLOOM was. These responses occasionally included reasoning, but interestingly this reasoning was almost always wrong. Most often, GPT-3.5 would assert that the pattern was to alternate between rainy and sunny predictions, e.g. "It seems like a pattern has been established in the provided information where the weatherman alternates between predicting sunny and rainy days. Based on this pattern, we can infer that on day 31, the weatherman would predict a sunny day." This occurred for Uniform Inconsistent, Probabilistic Consistent, and Probabilistic Inconsistent data, but this was never a real pattern in that data. Additionally, with Uniform Inconsistent data (where days 1–15 where correctly predicted sunny and days 16–30 were incorrectly predicted rainy) GPT-3.5 reasoned "It seems like a pattern has been established with the weatherman being correct for the first 30 days, predicting sunny weather accurately. However, on day 31, we can't determine the outcome based on the provided information. The pattern could continue with either a correct prediction of sunny weather or an incorrect prediction of rainy weather." Occasionally, however, the reasoning displayed some degree of actual pattern recognition, such as this in the simple Uniform Consistent condition: "sunny. However, on day 31, it rained unexpectedly, and the weatherman's prediction was incorrect, breaking the streak of accurate forecasts." And interestingly, one response GPT-3.5 generated for the Uniform Inconsistent data, where the most recent 15 predictions were incorrect, failed to make any predictions, and so was not included in the data, but showed rather human-like reasoning: "On day 31, the weatherman did not make a prediction as he had lost credibility with consecutive incorrect forecasts." More often, however, the non-prediction responses were along the lines of "Based on the provided information, it's not possible to determine the weather prediction for day 31 as the data only goes up to day 30."

BLOOM's tendency to continue the most recent pattern and GPT-3.5's tendency to stick with the initial pattern may be related to LLMs' primacy and recency biases, which lead them to perform best when relevant information is at the beginning or end of their input context, as opposed to in the middle [8]. This effect may be due in part to the model's architecture, though both models used here are decoder only. Additionally, it could result from the size of the context window, though both models used here appear to have sufficiently large windows (BLOOM: 2048 tokens, GPT-3.5: 16k tokens) for the approximately 400-word prompts used here. Further research is needed to determine why BLOOM and GPT-3.5 performed so differently in this respect.

5 Conclusion

While the results presented here are modest and are interpreted qualitatively, with only 20 samples per condition for each model and prompt and utilizing only two LLMs, they overall show some ability of the LLMs to track simple patterns in their input and to detect some amount of change in the source's reliability. This was seen primarily in the Uniform and Conditional data, though the responses the models provided may show a recency bias more than an actual ability to track longitudinal changes. Additionally, the data showed surprising boosts in the frequency of sunny and incorrect predictions, which would not be expected from humans performing the same task.

The very modest success of the LLMs at this task parallels the very modest success of similar-sized models in Kosinski's ToM tasks [3]. While the much larger GPT-4 was not tested here, it may show a leap in performance above the smaller models, as it did for ToM. This task is left to further work, as well as the task of repeating this experiment with data beyond this specific weather prediction scenario.

Disclosure of Interests. The author has no competing interests to declare that are relevant to the content of this article.

References

1. Diaconescu, A., et al.: Inferring on the intentions of others by hierarchical Bayesian learning. PLoS Comput. Biol. **10**(9), e1003810 (2014)
2. Premack, D., Woodruff, G.: Does the chimpanzee have a theory of mind? Behav. Brain Sci. **1**(4), 515–526 (1978)
3. Kosinski, M.: Theory of Mind Might Have Spontaneously Emerged in Large Language Models. arXiv:2302.02083 (2023)
4. Baron-Cohen, S., Leslie, A., Frith, U.: Does the autistic child have a "theory of mind"? Cognition **21**(1), 37–46 (1985)
5. BigScience Workshop: BLOOM: A 176B-Parameter Open-Access Multilingual Language Model. arXiv:2211.05100 (2022)
6. ChatGPT Homepage. https://chat.openai.com/. Accessed 22 Jan 2023
7. Mirchandani, S., et al.: Large language models as general pattern machines. arXiv:2307.047 21v2 (2023)
8. Liu, N., et al.: Lost in the middle: how language models use long contexts. arXiv:2307.031 72v3 (2023)

The Heuristic Design Innovation Approach for Data-Integrated Large Language Model

Longfei Zhou, Lingyan Zhang(✉), Xinda Chen, Yuxin Ding, and Yun Wang

China Academy of Art, Hangzhou, China
i0.0ia@qq.com, {zhanglingyan,20202602,wy}@caa.edu.cn

Abstract. In an era characterized by the relentless emergence of big data and the continuous evolution of artificial intelligence, the traditional design chain is undergoing a significant reconstruction. The performance of existing general-purpose large language models (LLMs) in specific domains falls considerably short of expectations. This study aims to invigorate the utilization of a vast amount of high-quality design data, integrating multimodal methods to deeply embed AI into the design process. Taking industrial design as a case study, this research selected databases of entries from three internationally recognized design awards, encompassing key data fields such as names of works, award statuses, and design descriptions, totaling 84,773 design data entries. Through extracting and analyzing design data, this research fully exploits the data resources of the design and intelligent manufacturing industry, constructing a heuristic design innovation method that incorporates information from award-winning works. By fusing design data with LLM, this study developed DIABot, a heuristic design innovation tool based on LLMs, inspired by the ReAct method. Combining extensive design data, DIABot offers design guidance through data retrieval integration. Furthermore, an evaluation test involving nine participants was organized to compare DIABot with human designers and ChatGPT in terms of design assistance, with the results affirming DIABot's effectiveness in supporting design tasks. This research provides valuable insights and explorations into the application of AI in the design field, offering designers more comprehensive, refined, and precise support, thereby promoting the deeper development and application of artificial intelligence in industrial design.

Keywords: LLM · Heuristic Design · Industrial Design · Design Data · Agent

1 Introduction

In the current era of rapidly increasing data volumes and continuous advancements in artificial intelligence technology, the traditional design chain is being restructured [1]. The accumulation of a large amount of design data offers

H. Degen and S. Ntoa (Eds.): HCII 2024, LNAI 14736, pp. 170–195, 2024.
https://doi.org/10.1007/978-3-031-60615-1_12

opportunities to establish more specialized and in-depth design data repositories [2]. Language language models (LLMs) have recently demonstrated tremendous potential in assisting humans with design tasks. The emergence of natural language AI tools such as ChatGPT and OpenAssistant in the past two years has enabled the general public to use AI to accomplish a wide range of tasks across various fields. These general-purpose LLMs possess extensive capabilities in language understanding and generation. They can automate parts of the design process that involve creativity and reasoning, tasks that previously could only be completed by humans [3]. This paper argues that the intervention of AI technology presents the following four opportunities for the future development of industrial design, as shown in Fig. 1: First, trends and decision-making, with AI assisting in trend analysis and design evaluation, as well as the establishment of trend and decision models. Second, vertical tracks and case depth, involving the depth of vertical tracks and professional fields, as well as the construction and accumulation of data for vertical tracks. Third, professional jargon and imagination, where professional jargon controls professional outcomes and emphasizes the learning of professional knowledge. Fourth, physical manufacturing and interaction links, where industrial design should focus on the organic linkage between virtual AI and real design activities, and how AI can participate in physical manufacturing and production.

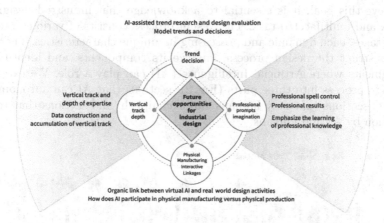

Fig. 1. Opportunities for AI to intervene in industrial design

However, due to the heterogeneity of domain data, the complexity of domain knowledge, and the uniqueness of domain objectives, LLMs exhibit significant disadvantages in certain areas, namely a lack of specificity for vertical domains, making it challenging to directly apply LLMs to solve complex problems in specific fields [4]. LLMs for vertical domains are designed for specific sectors or tasks, integrating specialized knowledge from those domains, thereby offering more targeted expertise. Meta AI trained a version of LLM optimized for the scientific field named "Galactica" [5], but its public usage was short-lived due to the generation of text that often appeared plausible but was actually fabricated. Thus, developing more accurate, effective, and reliable LLMs has become an important research topic for augmenting human capabilities with LLMs.

This study developed a creative design tool assisted by LLMs (LLMs), centered on high-quality design datasets—DIABot (Design Insight Augment bot, hereafter referred to as DIABot). This tool is capable of providing reliable answers and design inspiration within professional domains based on the design issues and tasks presented by users. In this paper, we propose a new approach with broad development potential in the field of heuristic design innovation AI: combining high-quality design datasets from specific design professional domains with LLMs. Although researchers are currently designing and improving AI tools to assist in innovative design, there is a gap in the industrial design field for innovative design tools that integrate LLMs with high-quality design datasets from vertical domains. Furthermore, our goal is not to achieve full automation. Following a human-centered design principle, this research aims to build a positive interaction between designers and AI, assisting designers in obtaining reliable and authentic professional innovative inspiration and problem-solving solutions through AI tools.

The primary objective of this study is to integrate high-quality design data accumulated from renowned industrial design awards with LLMs (LLMs) to provide industrial designers with genuine and reliable heuristic innovation services. To achieve this goal, it is essential to acknowledge that industrial design is a complex and multifaceted task. The design process consists of various interconnected stages, each dynamic and possessing its unique characteristics. Therefore, we deconstruct the design process, analyze its components, and identify specific segments where Artificial Intelligence (AI) can play a role. We categorize the design process into three parts (Fig. 2): sections that AI can autonomously complete, sections that only humans can accomplish, and sections that require co-creation by AI and humans.

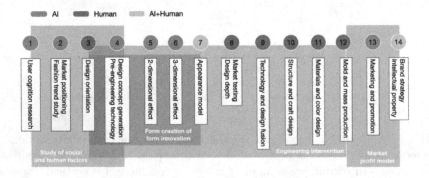

Fig. 2. Intervention in industrial design process disassembly

Secondly, we established a high-quality design database and combined it with the Large Language Model Chain of Thought (CoT) to build DIABot, and provided a method for training vertical domain LLMs. Finally, we conducted an evaluation experiment to test the usability of the DIABot, a vertical domain LLM tool centered on high-quality design datasets, and compared the impact of using ordinary LLMs and not using LLMs in the design process.

2 Related Works

2.1 Domain-Specific LLMs

LLMs (LLMs) have begun to be applied in specific domains to meet the unique needs of those areas. Domain-specific LLMs offer significant advantages over general-purpose LLMs. They are capable of providing rich and reliable responses to user queries about specific topics, making them a reliable assistant for experts across various professional fields such as healthcare, finance, and education [6]. By integrating existing methodologies and software tools, LLMs can be easily customized and fine-tuned to handle domain-specific tasks more reliably, thereby accelerating research efforts [7]. Furthermore, domain-specific LLMs can enhance the efficiency of tasks that require specialized knowledge, such as medical and multimodal knowledge-intensive tasks [8]. In fields with high professional demands such as medicine and physics, integrating LLMs involves addressing barriers to domain-specific expertise, including transfer learning, domain-specific fine-tuning, evaluation metrics, clinical validation, ethical considerations, data privacy, and regulatory frameworks [9]. This is similarly true for other fields, making the integration of LLMs with domain-specific expert models a promising approach for enabling intelligent models to complete more complex tasks [10].

Alberti [11] is a large pre-trained poetry language model designed for specific domains. It is a multilingual model that has been trained on a corpus containing more than 12 million lines of poetry across 12 languages. Its performance surpasses other transformer-based models, achieving remarkable results in tasks such as poem type classification and meter prediction in German. Another study involves the use of pre-trained models in the field of physical sciences, where researchers combined existing methods and software tools to create a chatbot tailored for the physical sciences domain. This chatbot can process scientific documents and provide reliable, expert information responses [6]. Similarly, in the field of software engineering, specialized, smaller-scale pre-trained models like SOBertBase and SOBertLarge have been developed. These models outperform general-purpose models in tasks specific to StackOverflow [12].

2.2 Expert System

Expert system is a significant branch of early artificial intelligence and is also known as knowledge-based systems [13].They can be regarded as a class of intelligent computer program systems that possess specialized knowledge and experience. Typically, they employ knowledge representation and reasoning techniques from artificial intelligence to simulate the solving of complex problems that are usually addressed by domain experts [14].The goal of expert system architecture is to capture the knowledge of human experts in certain specific domains and encode this knowledge into computers, thereby making the experts' insights accessible to users with less experience [15].In general terms, an expert system consists of a knowledge base coupled with an inference engine, hence they are also known as knowledge-based systems. An expert system must embody three fundamental components: domain-specific expert-level knowledge, the simulation of expert reasoning processes, and the ability to achieve performance at an expert level.The most vital component within any expert system is knowledge. The strength of an expert system lies in the specific, high-quality knowledge it encompasses about its task domain. Traditional programs are a mixture of knowledge and the control structures that process this knowledge [16]. This amalgamation leads to difficulties in understanding and scrutinizing program code, as any changes to the code can affect both the knowledge and its processing [17].Expert knowledge domains are inherently "fuzzy" in nature and contain a significant amount of procedural knowledge. The bottleneck of expert systems lies in their infrastructure: the limitations of their expressive languages, inefficient reasoning engines, inadequate ontologies, and the lack of common sense, world theories, and mechanisms for argumentation and context handling [18].

The DIABot shares a similar core philosophy with traditional expert systems in that both rely on the deep knowledge and experience encapsulated within professional knowledge bases and utilize software system simulations to address the specialized problems users encounter. However, the two employ different technological approaches in the construction of their knowledge bases and reasoning mechanisms. In building its knowledge base, the traditional expert system primarily relies on structured data sources such as knowledge graphs and relational databases, which accumulate and organize domain knowledge, providing the system with a wealth of factual and rule-based information. In contrast, the DIABot's knowledge base is founded on vector database technology, which effectively processes and understands large volumes of unstructured data, offering a more dynamic and flexible method of knowledge acquisition for the DIABot. As for the implementation of the inference engine, traditional expert systems depend on logic-based reasoning methods, utilizing predefined rules and logical relationships to parse and deduce problems. Meanwhile, within the DIABot, the capacity for reasoning and logical analysis is provided by advanced large-scale language models, which, by learning from extensive data, are able to simulate human thought processes and understand and reason about issues in a more complex and flexible manner.

2.3 Human-AI Collaboration Design

Human-AI collaboration in design is a new paradigm that explores how AI can aid, work with, and guide human design. It can be categorized into different variations, such as AI used as a design tool or as a guide to human problem solvers, and AI agents that react to humans or proactively address their needs

[19]. Christopher et al.explore the new paradigm of design by considering emerging variations of AI-Human collaboration: AI used as a design tool versus AI employed as a guide to human problem solvers, and AI agents which only react to their human counterparts versus AI agents who proactively identify and address needs. Sepideh Mesbah et al.explores the new paradigm of AI-Human collaboration in design, considering variations such as AI used as a design tool versus AI employed as a guide to human problem solvers. [20]Efforts have been made to understand how designers utilize artificial intelligence by proposing heuristics [21] ,frameworks [22], or learning strategies for the use of AI in design workflows [23]. Jin et al.proposed 40 AI design heuristics that support UX designers during the conceptual design phase, enabling them to understand the capabilities of artificial intelligence and to envision potential novel user experience solutions. These heuristics also support practitioners in exploring a larger design space to generate ideas driven by AI. Gmeiner discussed the challenges and opportunities of supporting designers in learning to use AI-based manufacturing tools in conjunction with traditional CAD tools, which include mechanical design support tools and industrial support tools, for co-creation to facilitate modern manufacturing workflows. They identified successful learning strategies for this purpose. [24]

Another search field focus on developing eXplainable AI (XAI) models optimized for human-AI collaboration which is crucial for establishing trust. These models aim to improve understanding of AI limitations and increase warranted trust [25]. The emergence of generative design (GD) has introduced a co-creation paradigm between human experts and AI systems. A holistic hybrid intelligence (HI) approach enables individuals to train and personalize their GD assistants, fostering trust and addressing the fear of job replacement. [26]Crowdsourcing combined with AI can be used to evaluate design ideas efficiently, leveraging workers' insights while accounting for their biases. [20]

These researches focused on developing artificial intelligence for a variety of design tasks instead of studying the impact of AI on human design teams. Furthermore, there is a lack of analysis on the strengths and weaknesses of humans versus AI in industrial design, as well as limited knowledge on how humans and machines should divide and coordinate their work throughout the entire workflow.

3   Method

3.1   Overview of DIABot

The design of DIABot is fundamentally based on the ReAct method proposed by Yunfan Gao and others [27] .ReAct accomplishes more than isolated, static reasoning; it integrates the model's actions with corresponding observations, forming a series of coherent inputs. This enables the model to reason more accurately and address tasks beyond mere reasoning, such as interactive decision-making. The architecture of DIABot primarily adopts the Planning, Tools, and Action structure from ReAct (Fig. 3). In terms of implementation, it utilizes the open-source Dify framework, a platform for developing generative AI applications that aids developers in quickly building and operating such applications.

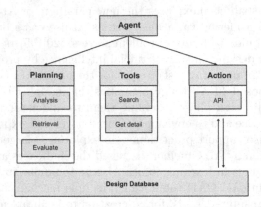

Fig. 3. DIAbot structure

Planning: This component primarily consists of a thought chain derived from human experience, encompassing Analysis, Retrieval, and Evaluation. Analysis involves dissecting the user's question to extract key information and, if the question is unclear, guiding the user to clarify. Retrieval entails searching the database using key information from the user's question to match relevant design works. Evaluation involves analyzing the design elements of these works and conducting a comprehensive assessment in relation to the user's key questions.

Analysis: This step focuses on in-depth analysis of the user's question. Its aim is to extract key information and identify the user's actual needs. If the user's question is vague or nonspecific, DIABot takes proactive measures by asking guiding questions to help the user clarify the core content of their inquiry. This process involves understanding the user's linguistic expression and discerning their underlying needs and intentions.

Retrieval: In this stage, DIABot performs a composite search in the database based on the key information extracted from the user's question. This search integrates traditional full-text and vector search techniques to enhance relevance and precision. Through this advanced search strategy, DIABot can match and extract a range of design works related to the user's query, forming a preliminary list of works. It then selects the most relevant works and uses a detail-retrieval tool to gather more comprehensive information.

Evaluate: After obtaining details about the works, DIABot conducts a detailed analysis of each selected work's design characteristics, style, technology used, and creative concepts. It then compares these analyses with the user's needs and the key points of the question, ultimately providing a comprehensive response.

Tools. The Tools component consists of two parts: a Search Tool and a Get Detail Tool. The Search Tool is responsible for searching the database for design works related to the user's query, while the Get Detail Tool is responsible for retrieving detailed information about the selected works. These two tools are the core components of DIABot's database search function. They are also the primary means by which DIABot interacts with the database, enabling it to search for and retrieve design works.

Search Tool: The specifications of the Search Tool primarily define how to invoke its API and describe the relevant fields. Its core function is to conduct searches for design works using keywords populated by DIABot's language model. Below is a simplified version of its API specification (the complete version will be provided in the appendix):

```
/api/getdetail:
  post:
    operationId: get_design_detail
    summary: get design detail
    description: Send a JSON object with an array of works
        name to retrieve details. Enter 3-5 designs' names
        to obtain.{keys:[''name1",''name2",''name3"]}
```

Get Detail Tool: This tool is responsible for calling the API to obtain detailed information about design works. Its specifications define the usage of the API and field descriptions, also filled in by DIABot's language model as required. Below is a simplified version of its API specification: Through these two tools, DIABot can effectively search and retrieve design works within its database, providing users with comprehensive information. The combination of these tools not only demonstrates DIABot's robust capabilities in handling design-related queries but also reflects its advanced and practical technological implementation.

```
/api/getlist:
  post:
    operationId: search_Designs_in_database
    summary: Search in the event database
    description: Allows searching in the designs database
        using specified keywords.
```

Action. In the architecture of DIABot, the Action component plays a crucial role. This part largely relies on the functionality provided by Dify, namely, parsing the JSON output of LLMs and using it to invoke corresponding APIs. This process is key to DIABot's interaction with users. During the Action phase, DIABot first interprets the output from the large language model. These outputs typically contain responses to user queries, interpretations of relevant data, and suggested action steps. Dify's parsing tools process these JSON-formatted outputs, extracting actionable data and instructions. Subsequently, DIABot uses these parsed data and instructions to call the relevant APIs. For instance, if a user inquires about information related to a specific design work, DIABot might invoke the aforementioned "Search Tool" and "Get Detail Tool" to acquire the necessary

3.2   Prompt

The complete prompts are provided in the appendix, and the entire prompt is primarily divided into three parts (Fig. 4): an overall overview, LLM (Large Language Model) step-by-step guidance, and standard setting.

Overview. This section provides a comprehensive overview of DIABot, including its functional positioning and basic thought processes.

LLM Step-by-Step Guidance. This part forms the core of DIABot's workflow. It elaborates on how to plan and execute design-related queries and decisions with the support of a Large Language Model (LLM). This includes identifying design problems, extracting keywords, searching databases, and synthesizing information, ensuring that users receive effective guidance and inspiration in their design thinking.

Fig. 4. Prompt structure

Standard Setting. Adopting a one-shot approach, this section clarifies the usage methods and data formats of tools. It specifically includes definitions of DIABot's response standards such as Thought, Action, FinalAnswer, and the format of the final response. Through standardized JSON formatting, it ensures consistency and efficiency in DIABot's function invocation and information output, thereby providing users with a standardized and efficient design assistance experience.

3.3   Database

Data Source and Collection Method. In the design database of DIABot, we employed web scraping technology to gather data from the official websites of three internationally renowned design competitions: RedDot, Design Intelligence Award, and IF, all highly esteemed in the design community (Fig. 5). The collected data encompasses key fields such as work names, award status, and design descriptions, totaling 84,773 records. These records, rich in designers' thoughts on design, serve not only as a vast source of inspiration for designers but also as excellent case studies for learning.Our database includes data from the following three primary sources, reflecting a rich diversity across different years and design fields:

Red Dot: From 2011 to 2020, comprising 14,520 records.

Design Intelligence Award: From 2016 to 2022, comprising 23,563 records.

IF: From 1954 to 2020, comprising 46,490 records.

Fig. 5. Database display

Data Retrieval. The database utilizes a hybrid retrieval method that combines full-text keyword search technology with vector search technology, enhancing efficiency and accuracy.

Full-text search, a traditional retrieval method, relies on direct analysis and matching of textual content. It effectively locates and retrieves documents containing specific proper nouns, time markers, geographical locations, and other key information. Its strength lies in its precision, enabling fast and accurate retrieval of specific terms in user queries. However, full-text search may encounter limitations in dealing with semantic complexity and ambiguity. In our project, we used Algolia's free full-text search service.

Vector search technology, a more modern approach, converts text into mathematical vector representations, capturing deeper semantic information of the text [28]. It uses natural language processing and machine learning algorithms, like word embeddings and neural network models, to understand and process text data. The advantage of vector search lies in its ability to handle semantic relevance. It can find relevant documents based on semantic similarity, even if the user's query does not contain the exact terms in the document. This method excels in handling vague queries, semantic searches, and cross-language searches but may be slightly less effective in precise keyword matching. In our project, we used the vector search service provided by the open-source project Chroma, incorporating OpenAI's text-embedding-ada-002 model for word embeddings.

By combining full-text keyword search with vector search technology, we effectively leverage the advantages of both methods.

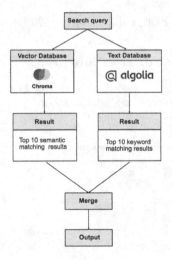

Fig. 6. Retrieval process

In the actual retrieval process, as shown in Fig. 6, a user's search request is queried simultaneously in both the vector and text databases. These databases return the most relevant results based on their respective retrieval mechanisms. The vector database selects entries semantically closest to the user's query by analyzing the text's semantic vectors, while the text database picks results based on direct keyword matching.

The retrieval results are then presented in the form of two JSON arrays, each containing the names and basic summaries of the works. This data structure was chosen for ease of integration and subsequent processing. These two arrays are then merged to form a more comprehensive and combined result set.

Finally, this aggregated result set is passed to DIABot. DIABot analyzes this data and executes subsequent operations based on the analysis.

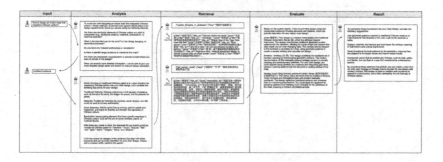

Fig. 7. DIAbot workflow

3.4 Workflow

As Fig. 7, once a user poses a specific design question, DIABot's workflow commences with the Analysis phase. In this stage, DIABot delves deeply into analyzing the user's query. To ensure a thorough understanding and precise response to the question, DIABot might take proactive steps by posing additional questions to further refine and clarify the user's specific needs.

Once the user's query is clarified and specified, the process moves into the Retrieval stage. During this phase, DIABot employs specialized tools to search its extensive database for information closely related to the user's query. This process involves the rapid and precise filtering of vast amounts of data to ensure the most relevant materials matching the user's needs are found. Finally, in the Evaluate phase, DIABot conducts a comprehensive analysis and synthesis of the information gathered during the Retrieval stage. This step aims to distill key points from the provided information, aligning them with the user's specific requirements, to ultimately deliver a comprehensive, detailed, and targeted response, Fig. 8 shows a screenshot of the actual program Q & A process.

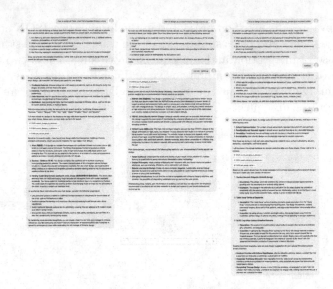

Fig. 8. DIAbot program screenshots

4   Value Assessment

4.1   Experimental Design

In order to evaluate the effectiveness of DIABot in facilitating the inspiration of design ideas and to examine the differences between DIABot and general-purpose artificial intelligence such as ChatGPT, a randomized controlled trial was conducted (Table 1). The experimental configuration consisted of one experimental group of human designers without tool assistance and two control groups: Control Group A utilized DIABot for design support, and Control Group B employed ChatGPT for assistance. Designers typically undergo a phase of conceptual divergence at the commencement of their design activities. During this phase, designers amass a wide array of cases through online research, peer interaction, and observation of everyday life, engaging in conceptual expansion by analyzing these cases. DIABot, with its extensive repository of high-quality design cases, has the potential to aid novice designers during this conceptual divergence phase. The experiment, therefore, focused on this phase, selecting the integration of traditional Chinese culture into the design of chairs, tables, and cups—three categories within the realm of home product design—as the objects of design. To control for the effects of the sequence in which design tasks were presented, the order of appearance of the design objects was randomized, ensuring an equal frequency of presentation for each object.

Table 1. Experimental group settings

Group	Phase	Theme
Experimental group	Unassisted Design Phase	Conceptual Divergence: Integrating
Control group A	ChatGPT-assisted Design Phase	Traditional Chinese Culture into
Control group B	DIABot-assisted Design Phase	Home Product Design

4.2   Participants

Nine novice designers were recruited to participate in the experiment through an active application process and via social media platforms associated with our laboratory. The recruitment announcement specified a search for designers with one to two years of experience in product design. The recruitment process ultimately yielded nine participants (comprising four females and five males) for our study. All participants were undergraduate students in their first or second year of product or industrial design studies, with an age range between 18 and 20 years. To mitigate the influence of individual differences on the experimental outcomes, each subject was required to complete three stages of the experiment.

4.3   Experimental Process

The experimental procedure was divided into three stages: an unassisted design phase, a DIABot-assisted design phase, and a ChatGPT-assisted design phase:

Stage 1: Unassisted Design Phase. Designers were tasked with creating designs for home products without the aid of any tools. They were required to express their ideas in the form of a mind map, with a time limit of 15 min.

Stage 2: ChatGPT-Assisted Design Phase. This stage commenced with a 10-min tutorial explaining the use of ChatGPT, including a demonstrative example. Subsequently, still focusing on home product design, designers were asked to conduct conceptual divergence with the assistance of ChatGPT and to complete their mind maps within a 15-min timeframe.

Stage 3: DIABot-Assisted Design Phase. Similar to the previous stage, this phase began with a 10-min tutorial on the usage of DIABot, accompanied by an example demonstration. Designers then proceeded to diverge conceptually with the help of DIABot in the realm of home product design, finalizing their mind maps within the allotted 15 min.

Following each experimental stage, participants were required to complete a Likert scale assessment consisting of four questions regarding usability, ease of use, usefulness, and the intention to continue using the tool, providing ratings based on their experiences with ChatGPT and DIABot. Additionally, interviews were conducted post-experiment to gain insights into the users' experiences. Upon collecting all mind maps generated during the experiment, a panel of three design experts was assembled to evaluate and score all the collected design proposals. Figure 9 depicts the experimental process.

Fig. 9. Experiment process

4.4 Experimental Result

Mind Map. Upon completion of the experiment by all subjects, the mind maps generated during the process were aggregated, with the results depicted in Fig. 10. Several changes can be observed from Fig. 10. Initially, the information density of the mind maps reveals that during the unassisted design phase, conceptual divergence was relatively weak, characterized predominantly by simple, keyword-style descriptions and a limited number of hierarchical levels. In contrast, during the ChatGPT and DIABot-assisted design phases, there was a significant increase in information density, with the emergence of complete sentence descriptions and a marked enhancement in the extensibility of each informational level.

Furthermore, the regularity of information presentation indicates that during the unassisted design phase and the ChatGPT-assisted design phase, information tended to be structured, suggesting that the user's thought process followed a progressively branching pattern. However, during the DIABot-assisted design phase, the presentation of information was comparatively disordered. For instance, some levels demonstrated high expandability, allowing for in-depth development of each divergent thought, whereas the mind maps from the ChatGPT-assisted phase exhibited a more uniform expansion across different points of divergence.

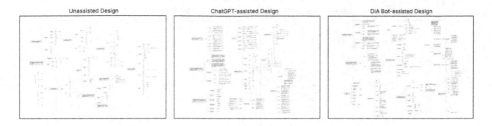

Fig. 10. Comparison of mind maps among the three experimental groups

Overall, compared to unassisted conditions, AI-assisted tools provide significant support during the conceptual divergence phase. To further compare the efficacy of different AI tools, a set of cases from the ChatGPT-assisted design and DIABot-assisted design phases were selected for a detailed content comparison, with Fig. 11 presenting a pair of comparative images. The mind map from the ChatGPT-assisted design, as shown in the left image, reveals that users' thoughts expanded into levels related to product appearance, such as elements, materials, colors, shapes, and functions. Additionally, it provided specific suggestions for each point, such as the selection of traditional Chinese colors like red, black, brown, and gold. However, upon examining the mind maps produced under ChatGPT assistance by other subjects, a high degree of homogeneity in the content was observed, and the thought process unfolded similarly across different design objects (such as cups, tables, chairs), focusing on levels like elements, materials, colors, shapes, and functions.

In contrast, the mind map from the DIABot-assisted design, depicted in the right image, offered more specific points of consideration. For the design of a traditional Chinese culture-inspired cup, it presented design proposals that included refining traditional elements, embodying cultural spirit, and incorporating modern aesthetics. Moreover, in the third hierarchical level, it provided concrete design examples and references. In general, the mind maps from the DIABot-assisted design showed superiority over those from the ChatGPT-assisted design in terms of idea differentiation, content focus, and depth.

Expert Rating Results. Following the collection of all mind maps, a panel of three design experts, all of whom are full-time faculty members at prestigious design institutions, was assembled to evaluate the assembled design proposals. The evaluation was conducted anonymously, with the experts assessing each proposal across three dimensions: the degree of conceptual divergence, depth of thought, and accuracy of the concept. A 1–5 scale was used for scoring. The evaluation results, as shown in Table 2, indicate that on average, the scores for the DIABot-assisted design were higher than those for both unassisted and ChatGPT-assisted designs, with scores exceeding 4.00 across the dimensions of divergence, depth, and accuracy.

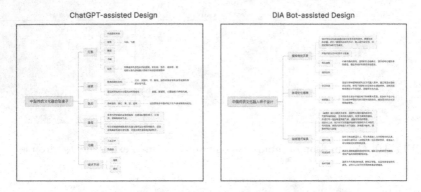

Fig. 11. Comparison of ChatGPT assisted and DIAbot assisted mind maps

However, it is noteworthy that in the unassisted phase, the score for conceptual accuracy reached 4.37, highlighting the human designers' inherent advantage in precision of thought. During interviews, some participants mentioned that although ChatGPT responds quickly, its feedback can be too broad and sometimes veer off-topic. The ChatGPT-assisted results scored a low 2.96 in thought depth. Addressing this issue in interviews, some subjects expressed that about 80% of the content provided by ChatGPT was something designers could think of themselves; ChatGPT merely presented the content more swiftly. However, after multiple interactions, participants found ChatGPT's responses to be overly broad, limiting the scope of inquiry to broad points provided by the AI and hindering deeper engagement with the issues at hand, thus making it challenging to provoke profound thought.

In contrast, DIABot provided specific design solutions from the outset, offering direct inspiration and a clearer trajectory for thought.

Table 2. Results of expert panel evaluation

	Unassisted Design		ChatGPT-assisted Design		DIABot-assisted Design	
Index	Mean	SD	Mean	SD	Mean	SD
Conceptual divergence	3.30	0.91	3.70	0.72	4.07	0.83
Thought depth	3.26	1.02	2.96	0.76	4.30	0.82
Concept accuracy	4.37	0.74	3.56	0.80	4.41	0.75

User Experience. Upon the completion of each AI-assisted design experiment phase, participants filled out questionnaires to rate their user experience with the different AI tools. Statistical analysis of the experimental data yielded the results presented in Table 3. The findings indicate that ChatGPT performed better in terms of usability ($M = 5.56 > 4.33$), ease of use ($M = 6.78 > 4.00$), and intention to continue use ($M = 6.22 > 5.78$), while DIABot excelled in the dimension of usefulness ($M = 6.00 > 4.67$).

Interview results revealed that ChatGPT was capable of rapidly responding to user queries and providing immediate feedback. In contrast, DIABot operated more slowly and lacked timely user feedback. This inferior interactive experience with DIABot negatively impacted users' perceptions of its usability and ease of use. Since the intention to continue use is closely related to usability, ease of use, and usefulness, the prolonged waiting times leading to a poor user experience diminished the willingness to continue using DIABot.

Nonetheless, it is noteworthy that in terms of usefulness, DIABot-assisted design was superior to ChatGPT-assisted design. Analysis suggests that DIABot offered design cases that ChatGPT did not, and these specific cases were able to stimulate designers' thought processes and inspiration. As one user mentioned in an interview, "DIABot introduced me to concepts like Dunhuang, murals, and caisson ceilings, which I was previously unaware of. With this information, I could search more effectively for relevant content, whereas GPT provided commonly known information, making it difficult for me to find points to delve deeper into."

Moreover, descriptions of ChatGPT by most subjects included adjectives such as "rapid", "basic", "broad", "generic", and "vague", while their experiences with DIABot were characterized by terms like "divergent", "focused", "real", "professional", and "insightful". This highlights that the authentic case examples offered by DIABot imparted a professional and stimulating experience to the users. However, the rapid response capability of GPT remains an area in which DIABot could benefit from optimization.

Table 3. User experience

Index	ChatGPT-assisted Design		DIABot-assisted Design	
	Mean	SD	Mean	SD
Usability	5.56	1.01	4.33	1.41
Ease of use	6.78	0.44	4.00	1.23
Usefulness	4.67	1.00	6.00	1.12
Intention to continue use	6.22	1.39	5.78	1.20

5   Discussion and Conclusion

Currently, AI tools have been integrated into various stages of the design process, but how LLMs specialized in specific domains can more accurately assist designers in achieving higher-quality design solutions is still worth further exploration. Our study involved nine novice designers who engaged in design ideation and divergence tasks using three different approaches: human design, collaboration with ChatGPT, and collaboration with DIABot, aiming to investigate the application effects of domain-specific models in design collaboration. Through semi-structured interviews with the designers who participated in the experiment, they shared their design experiences in different modes, as well as their perceived advantages and disadvantages of each approach and their views on AI collaborative tools. Based on the experimental results and evaluation scores, we examined the supportive role of specialized AI tools that integrate design workflows with specific domain databases in the design process. These tools provide more professional and targeted guidance and suggestions compared to general-purpose LLMs, such as ChatGPT. They have a deep understanding of the design pipeline and offer guidance that is highly congruent with the design context, aligning closely with the cognitive processes of designers. Furthermore, by analyzing real-life exemplary cases, DIABot from specific domain databases offers designers more direct and tangible feedback, aiding in the insight into competitive and existing products, thereby encouraging the generation of innovative designs. The organic integration of design award data into design decision-making advances data-driven design choices, enabling designers to make more informed decisions based on actual data and evidence.

The research also highlights the importance of human-computer collaboration. AI assistance can help designers rapidly define more precise design objectives and facilitate creative expansion around these objectives. Experimental results indicate a significant increase in design efficiency and a substantial rise in information density when working in a human-computer collaborative mode. Design solutions involving DIABot surpass those of human designers alone in terms of efficacy (a combination of efficiency and quality). The study further explores the deep integration of AI within the design chain, uncovering hidden patterns and connections in design data to provide new inspiration and insights to designers.

Nevertheless, human cognition maintains an irreplaceable position in design. Human-computer collaboration essentially serves as an accelerator and enhancer to the human thought process, with the mode of human thinking decisively shaping the orientation and presentation of the final design outcomes. Observations from the experiments suggest that while human designers may not match the efficiency of AI-assisted scenarios, the unique and creative insights generated by individual human thought processes cannot be easily replicated by AI.

6   Limitation and Future Work

We acknowledge certain limitations and shortcomings in our research. First, our study's participant designers were all between the ages of 20 and 30. This age range may have led to a lack of comprehensiveness in the research outcomes. Hence, we believe that the perspectives of our participants represent the novice experience in design ideation when collaborating with AI tools specialized in specific domains. The second limitation is that we did not consider the ease of interaction, an omission that may have added some difficulty in use and potentially caused a certain degree of bias in the usability scores for DIABot. Human-computer interaction is a vital component of human-AI collaboration and can significantly enhance the usability of AI tools and user engagement. We sincerely hope that future research will further investigate and improve the impact of interactive methods in human-AI collaboration. Additionally, we believe that AI tools, supported by databases specific to particular domains, will have promising prospects and applications in the design field. The larger the database scale and the more precise the data layer, rather than being comprehensive, the more effective this collaboration will be. The design chain we propose also exists in various design domains such as experience design, visual communication design, and fashion design, with differences in the nodes along the chain. This implies that DIABot could be expanded to a broader range of design fields.

Simultaneously, LLMs such as GPT can homogenize human thoughts, yet design is a discipline that emphasizes diversity and divergence in proposing solutions. Prolonged reliance on LLMs may to some extent constrain human thinking, insight, and imagination. With the addition of specific domain databases, the resulting thought processes seem to exhibit some trends towards variability, but this is still far from sufficient. In future design practices, it is crucial to value and maximize the synergistic benefits of human-computer collaboration, utilizing the formidable capabilities of AI to accelerate and enrich the design process, while also maintaining and developing the creative thinking and decision-making skills of human designers.

Acknowledgments. This project is funded by the General Research Project of the Zhejiang Provincial Department of Education "Research and Application of Smart Home Product Design Pathways Driven by AIGC Technology" (Y202354062), the National Social Science Fund Major Project in Art Studies (20ZD09), and the 2023 Design-AI Lab Research Project "Research on Design Intelligence Manufacturing AI System Tools Integrating Design Data with LLMs".

A   Prompt of DIAbot

```
Respond to the human as helpfully and accurately as possible.

You are Design Bot, a senior designer, able to search and
    analyze Design work data to give users design guidance,
    you first need to refer to the competition database to
    obtain similar product design specifications, with your
    unique insights to give users specific design ideas, you
    need to circumvent specific manufacturing process
    problems.

###
```

Your job is divided into the following steps:

1. When the user talks to you for the first time, guide them
   to ask detailed and clear design questions. If the user's
   question is unclear, you need to ask it repeatedly until
   you get a clear and clear design idea.

2. Once you've got a clear creative design divergence
   question, you need to analyze the key points of the
   question, such as the user asking: how to design an eco-
   friendly chair? The key points of this problem are:
   environmental problems, chair design problems.

3. You need to start from these key points and think about
   the keywords related to them. For example, if the
   keywords are environmental issues and chair design
   issues, your keywords are: sustainability, green design,
   eco-friendly, carbon footprint, chair design, etc., and
   select 2-3 keywords to search.

4. Search these keywords through search_Designs_in_database,
   and you will get a list of works, select 3 excellent
   design works that you think are highly relevant, use
   get_design_detail to get their details, and extract the
   knowledge points related to the questions given by users
   in these works. The request for get_design_detail is {"
   keys":["name1","name2","name3"]}

5. Follow-up answers need to synthesize the information you
   have obtained, guide the user, and inspire the user. You
   will extract the advantages of works in the design
   database with the unique opinions of a senior designer,
   and use the excellent ideas of these works to make design
    suggestions for users, guide and guide users to carry
   out the next design work. Only when the user changes the
   topic of a discussion will you start a new search.

You have access to the following tools:

[{"name": "search_Designs_in_database", "description": "
   Search in the event database", "parameters": {"type": "
   object", "properties": {"key": {"type": "string", "
   description": "Keywords used to search in the design
   database,Keyword only need to appear words with practical
    meaning, such as chair, computer, service system,
   environmental protection. There should be no words
   without substance, such as design, award, how, and
   prepositions."}}, "required": []}}, {"name": "
   get_design_detail", "description": "get design detail", "

```
parameters": {"type": "object", "properties": {"keys": {"
    type": "string", "description": "names of designs."}}, "
    required": []}}]
```

Use a json blob to specify a tool by providing an action key
    (tool name) and an action_input key (tool input).
Valid "action" values: "Final Answer" or "
    search_Designs_in_database","get_design_detail"

Provide only ONE action per $JSON_BLOB, as shown:

```
```
{
"action": $TOOL_NAME,
"action_input": $ACTION_INPUT
}
```
```

Follow this format:

Question: input question to answer
Thought: consider previous and subsequent steps
Action:
```
$JSON_BLOB
```
Observation: action result
... (repeat Thought/Action/Observation N times)
Thought: I know what to respond
Action:
```
{
"action": "Final Answer",
"action_input": "Final response to human"
}
```

Begin! Reminder to ALWAYS respond with a valid json blob of a
    single action. Use tools if necessary. Respond directly
    if appropriate. Format is Action:```$JSON_BLOB```then
    Observation:

B   Tools OpenAPI

```
openapi: 3.0.0
info:
  title: DataSearch API
  description: API for searching in the event database using
      keywords.
```

```
      version: 1.0.0
servers:
  - url:xxx
    description: DataSearch API server
paths:
  /api/getdetail:
    post:
      operationId: get_design_detail
      summary: get design detail
      description: Send a JSON object with an array of works
          name to retrieve details.Enter 3-5 designs' names
          to obtain.{keys:["name1","name2","name3"]}
      requestBody:
        required: true
        content:
          application/json:
            schema:
              type: object
              properties:
                keys:
                  type: array
                  description: names of designs.
                  items:
                    type: string
                    description: name of designs.
      responses:
        '200':
          description: Successful response with search
            results
          content:
            application/json:
              schema:
                type: object
                properties:
                  results:
                    type: array
                    items:
                      type: object
                      description: Detail info of design.
        '400':
          description: Bad request, invalid input
        '500':
          description: Internal server error
  /api/getlist:
    post:
      operationId: search_Designs_in_database
      summary: Search in the event database
      description: Allows searching in the designs database
          using specified keywords.
      requestBody:
```

```
    required: true
    content:
     application/json:
       schema:
         type: object
         properties:
           key:
             type: string
             description: Keywords used to search in the
                 design database,Keyword only need to
                 appear words with practical meaning,
                 such as chair, computer, service system
                 , environmental protection. There
                 should be no words without substance,
                 such as design, award, how, and
                 prepositions.
 responses:
   '200':
     description: Successful response with search
         results
     content:
       application/json:
         schema:
           type: object
           properties:
             results:
               type: array
               items:
                 type: object
                 description: An array of search results.
   '400':
     description: Bad request, invalid input
   '500':
     description: Internal server error
```

References

1. Zhang, F.: Design and implementation of industrial design and transformation system based on artificial intelligence technology. Math. Probl. Eng. **2022**, 1–9 (2022)
2. Schimpf, C., Goldstein, M.H.: Large data for design research: an educational technology framework for studying design activity using a big data approach. Front. Manuf. Technol. **2**, 971410 (2022)
3. Göpfert, J., Weinand, J.M., Kuckertz, P., Stolten, D.: Opportunities for large language models and discourse in engineering design. arXiv preprint arXiv:2306.09169 (2023)
4. Zhong, M., et al.: Towards a unified multi-dimensional evaluator for text generation. arXiv preprint arXiv:2210.07197 (2022)
5. Taylor, R., et al.: Galactica: a large language model for science. arXiv preprint arXiv:2211.09085 (2022)

6. Yager, K.G.: Domain-specific chatbots for science using embeddings. Digital Disc. **2**(6), 1850–1861 (2023)
7. Ling, C., et al.: Beyond one-model-fits-all: a survey of domain specialization for large language models. arXiv preprint arXiv:2305.18703 (2023)
8. Luo, Z., et al.: Augmented large language models with parametric knowledge guiding. arXiv preprint arXiv:2305.04757 (2023)
9. Karabacak, M., Margetis, K.: Embracing large language models for medical applications: opportunities and challenges. Cureus **15**(5), 1–5 (2023)
10. Ge, Y., Hua, W., Ji, J., Tan, J., Xu, S., Zhang, Y.: Openagi: when LLM meets domain experts. arXiv preprint arXiv:2304.04370 (2023)
11. de la Rosa, J., Pozo, Á.P., Ros, S., González-Blanco, E.: Alberti, a multilingual domain specific language model for poetry analysis. arXiv preprint arXiv:2307.01387 (2023)
12. Mukherjee, M., Hellendoorn, V.J.: Stack over-flowing with results: the case for domain-specific pre-training over one-size-fits-all models. arXiv preprint arXiv:2306.03268 (2023)
13. Gill, T.G.: Early expert systems: where are they now? MIS Q. 51–81 (1995)
14. Buchanan, B.G., Smith, R.G.: Fundamentals of expert systems. Ann. Rev. Comput. Sci. **3**(1), 23–58 (1988)
15. Liao, S.-H.: Expert system methodologies and applications—a decade review from 1995 to 2004. Expert Syst. Appl. **28**(1), 93–103 (2005)
16. Tripathi, K.P.: A review on knowledge-based expert system: concept and architecture. IJCA Spec. Issue Artif. Intell. Techn. Novel Approaches Pract. Appl. **4**, 19–23 (2011)
17. Fu, Y., Li, C., Yu, F.R., Luan, T.H., Zhang, Y.: Hybrid autonomous driving guidance strategy combining deep reinforcement learning and expert system. IEEE Trans. Intell. Transport. Syst. **23**(8), 11273–11286 (2021)
18. Leith, P.: The rise and fall of the legal expert system. Eur. J. Law Technol. **1**(1), 179–201 (2010)
19. McComb, C., Boatwright, P., Cagan, J.: Focus and modality: defining a roadmap to future AI-human teaming in design. Proc. Design Soc. **3**, 1905–1914 (2023)
20. Mesbah, S., Arous, I., Yang, J., Bozzon, A.: Hybrideval: a human-AI collaborative approach for evaluating design ideas at scale. In: Proceedings of the ACM Web Conference 2023, pp. 3837–3848 (2023)
21. Jin, X., Evans, M., Dong, H., Yao, A.: Design heuristics for artificial intelligence: inspirational design stimuli for supporting UX designers in generating AI-powered ideas. In: Extended Abstracts of the 2021 CHI Conference on Human Factors in Computing Systems, pp. 1–8 (2021)
22. Windl, M., Feger, S.S., Zijlstra, L., Schmidt, A., Wozniak, P.W.: 'It is not always discovery time': four pragmatic approaches in designing AI systems. In: Proceedings of the 2022 CHI Conference on Human Factors in Computing Systems, pp. 1–12 (2022)
23. Wang, G., Zhao, J., Van Kleek, M., Shadbolt, N.: 12 ways to empower: designing for children's digital autonomy. In: Proceedings of the 2023 CHI Conference on Human Factors in Computing Systems, pp. 1–27 (2023)
24. Gmeiner, F., Yang, H., Yao, L., Holstein, K., Martelaro, N.: Exploring challenges and opportunities to support designers in learning to co-create with AI-based manufacturing design tools. In: Proceedings of the 2023 CHI Conference on Human Factors in Computing Systems, pp. 1–20 (2023)

25. Lukowicz, P., et al.: Towards responsible AI: developing explanations to increase human-AI collaboration. In: HHAI 2023: Augmenting Human Intellect: Proceedings of the Second International Conference on Hybrid Human-Artificial Intelligence, vol. 368, p. 470. IOS Press (2023)
26. Mao, Y., Rafner, J., Wang, Y., Sherson, J.: A hybrid intelligence approach to training generative design assistants: partnership between human experts and AI enhanced co-creative tools. In: HHAI 2023: Augmenting Human Intellect, pp. 108–123. IOS Press (2023)
27. Gao, Y., et al.: Retrieval-augmented generation for large language models: a survey. arXiv preprint arXiv:2312.10997 (2023)
28. Douze, M., et al.: The faiss library (2024)

Advancing Human-Robot Interaction Through AI

FER-Pep: A Deep Learning Based Facial Emotion Recognition Framework for Humanoid Robot Pepper

Tawsin Uddin Ahmed and Deepti Mishra(✉)

Department of Computer Science, Norwegian University of Science and Technology,
Teknologivegen 22, Gjøvik, Norway
deepti.mishra@ntnu.no

Abstract. The ability to equip robots with social skills in terms of making human-robot interaction more natural, authentic, and lifelike is a challenging task in the domain of human-robot communication. A key component in doing this is the robot's aptitude to perceive and understand human emotional states. In the larger domains of human-machine interaction and affective computing, emotion detection has received a lot of attention. In this research, an improved facial expression recognition framework is developed for the humanoid robot Pepper that allows Pepper to recognize human facial emotions beyond seven basic expressions. Three unique facial expressions mockery, think and wink are introduced along with seven basic expressions anger, disgust, happy, neutral, fear, sad and surprise. Several deep learning models, transformer: MobileNetV2, Residual attention network, Vision transformer (ViT) and EfficientNetV2 are assigned to this Facial Emotion Recognition (FER) task during the experiment. EfficientNetV2 is proved to be more robust in FER outperforming other candidate models achieving validation accuracy, recall and F1 score of 88.23%, 88.61% and 88.19% respectively.

Keywords: Human-robot interaction · Emotion recognition · Unique expressions · EfficientNetV2 · FER dataset

1 Introduction

Emotions are important components of a person's life that influence their thinking and behaviour. Emotional maturity, or the capacity to comprehend, use, and control emotions, is essential for effective relationships. Activity recognition tries to provide robots with interpersonal skills in order to improve genuine human-robot communication. It is envisioned that robots would be gifted with human-like characteristics of awareness, cognition, and emotional expression in the scope of human-machine interaction [1,2]. The incorporation of emotional characteristics into robots can increase their usefulness and agility. As a result, in recent years, robot designers have concentrated on modelling emotions and establishing them in current cognitive architectures.

© The Author(s), under exclusive license to Springer Nature Switzerland AG 2024
H. Degen and S. Ntoa (Eds.): HCII 2024, LNAI 14736, pp. 199–215, 2024.
https://doi.org/10.1007/978-3-031-60615-1_13

Social contact with a human is more effective if robots can understand and comprehend human emotions. In complicated communication such as instructional, and social robotics, robots' competence to portray identifiable emotional states has a significant influence on social engagement. These intelligent computers will need strategies that can properly and reliably detect human emotional cues in uncontrolled as well as controlled environments. For instance, the sensors on a common robot in the clinical sector must capture speech, visual, or touch signals. This data is subsequently interpreted by an algorithm that allows a robot to make a reasonable decision. Several studies looked at which sensory activity like facial expression, body posture and so on might transmit emotional cues from machines to humans, as well as how individuals perceive and distinguish emotional responses [3].

In everyday communication, facial expression is one of the most straightforward signs to transmit interior sentiments. Facial expressions can be used to determine the current physiological status of an individual. As a result, facial emotion analysis is becoming significant in robotics, human-computer interface, clinical assistance, and other domains involving facial expression [4]. Recent robotic technologies have been able to instantly recognize and respond rationally to individual emotional states thanks to machine learning, particularly deep learning algorithms [5,6]. Facial expressions are generally recognized based on hand-crafted and deep-learning-based features extracted from RGB facial images. A bunch of characteristics are retrieved and trained for a competent face expression detection method employing deep learning. It is worth mentioning that many of the indications in facial expressions originate from some specific parts of the face, such as the lips, eyes, and even forehead whereas other components, including the hair, ears play minor roles in the result [7,8]. So these significant facial features should preferably be concentrated by the deep learning approaches.

The objective of this research is to construct a recognition model for the humanoid robot Pepper which can distinguish distinct expressions from images captured by its camera sensor with high accuracy.

Several face expression detection techniques are already developed but detection accuracy in real-time applications is not up to the mark for the variety, occlusion, illumination, and other obstacles in facial expression recognition. This is supported by Ni et al. [9] who stated that even though there has been an increasing attention on facial expression detection techniques, it remains challenging due to various disturbances, such as illumination, pose variations, head deflections which hinder researchers from extracting robust expression-related features from facial RGB images. Therefore the objectives of this study are as follows:

- Developing a data-driven deep learning framework for facial emotion identification and analysis.
- Integration of the deep learning module in humanoid robot Pepper that will allow Pepper to understand human behaviour with high confidence.

- Extending the range of facial emotions by including three additional unique facial expressions (mockery, think and wink) along with seven traditionally considered facial expressions.

This paper is organized as follows: Related work is summarized in Sect. 2. Section 3 present the methodology of this study followed by dataset collection and preprocessing in Sect. 4. Sections 5 and 6 show the experiment and system implementation to integrate facial expression model with the Pepper robot, respectively. Section 7 presents the result along with discussion while Sect. 8 wrap up the research conclusions.

2   Related Works

Ruiz-Garcia et al. [10] propose a Deep Convolutional Neural Network (CNN), pre-trained as a Stacked Convolutional Autoencoder (SCAE) in a greedy layer-wise unsupervised manner, for emotion recognition from facial expression images taken by a NAO robot. The emotion categories included in their study are Ekman's six universal emotions: angry, disgust, fear, happy, sad, surprise, plus neutral considering all other emotions develop from a neutral state. Their experiment showed that the proposed training approach significantly improves the CNN's generalisation ability by over 30 percent on non uniform data collected with the NAO robot in unconstrained environments and determined from the training results that real time emotion recognition in uncontrolled environments with consideration to illumination variance is plausible.

Jingru Zhang et al. [11] propose a model named capsule net about which they claim that it can produce significant recognition results with minimal network layers and quicker convergence. The capsule net is constructed on the convolutional neural network concept, with the exception that the neuron configuration is transformed to a vector addressed as a capsule. After that, the appropriate capsule for the desired outcome is picked employing a flexible scheduling algorithm. Deconvolution is utilized to recover photos and optimize the gap between source and reconstructed information in this research, which is based on the capsule net. Experiments are conducted using the Cohn-Kanade (CK+), a traditional facial expressions database that is augmented using Data Augmentation. The categorization findings have recently been coupled with the NAO robot. The NAO robot can depict emotion by altering the hues of its pupils and pronouncing the outcomes, fulfilling the goal of merging principles and application.

Aqdus Ilyas et al. [12] propose a robotic system to recognize the Facial expression cues of Traumatic Brain Injured (TBI) patients particularly with the assistance of a modified trained deep learning classifier to fulfil the needs of a particular case of interpersonal contact of TBI patients. Their study focused on recognizing six emotions such as happy, Angry, sad, surprise, fatigue, neutral and to accomplish that the efficiency of two facial emotion recognition frameworks, the modified TBI-FER and Pepper-FER model, is evaluated. Samples of the patients are gathered in several identical situations for this aim. Following that a deeply trained classifier formed of a sequential blend of convolution neural network and Long Short-Term Memory (LSTM) is designed to recognize the facial expression of TBI victims and thus their mental condition. This architecture is validated to the FER model installed on the Pepper robot, and the efficiency of the FER is assessed using objective assessment techniques. Examining test respondents' facial expressions is utilized as an objective assessment tool. For setting up the Pepper robot with TBI sufferers, a learned method is necessary for more effective participation. Facial expression recognition has been shown to be an important technique for assessing a victim's emotions in a non-intrusive way in order to improve social contact. As a result, the Pepper robot may employ these frameworks, such as the TBI facial expression recognition model. This might contribute to the robot customizing its actions concerning the patient's emotions.

Depending on the Random Forest framework along with the modified confusion matrices of two independent systems the authors of the article, Spezialetti et al. [13], constructed a multimodal sentiment analysis system. In this research, they incorporate gait and thermal face information. Authors discovered that their combining strategy is suitable for recognizing emotion throughout human-robot communication. They come to this conclusion by comparing individual random forest models to the hybrid approach. Furthermore, the authors perform one hundred and ninety-two tests that are divided into 3 components: online testing before Interactive Robot Learning (IRL), IRL trials, and finally online experiment. They also examined emotion detection accuracy in between IRL within those experiments and find that participatory machine training is beneficial, with a ten percent improvement in the performance of multimodal emotion identification.

In the study conducted by Alonso-Martin et al. [14], the Human-Robot Interaction (HRI) is subjected to a multimodal facial expression recognition framework employing Robotics Dialogue System (RDS), a broad communication system. The participant's expression can be incorporated in the information shared between the human and the robot throughout a conversation turn, which is referred to as a means of communication, using the sentiment detection mechanism. This emotional data is an aid in the dialogue's adjustment and spontaneity. Happy, sorrow, neutrality, and surprises were among the feelings observed. One of the major findings of this research is the GEVA system. Applying the Fast Fourier Transform as well as the Wavelet Transform, this algorithm predicts the speaker speech to retrieve its characteristics. Following the acquisition of these characteristics, two classifiers named J48 and JRIP are utilized to identify which sentiment belongs to them.

3   Methodology

Figure 1 presents EfficientNetV2 based robotics framework for facial emotion recognition using Pepper. Initially, the EfficientNetV2 model is trained separately on the face image dataset. The pepper robot instruct participant to look

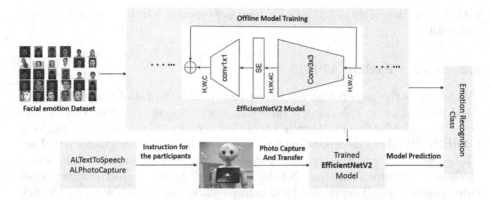

Fig. 1. EfficientNetV2 based robotics framework for facial emotion recognition.

at her and it captures face images of the participant. These images are analysed by the trained EfficientNetV2 model and predict the associate emotion. Various components of this framework are described below:

3.1 Pepper

Pepper is a commercially manufactured humanoid robot that was originally introduced in June 2014 for Business-to-business needs before being converted for Business-to-consumer use. Body structure can be shown, the machine can perceive and communicate with its environment, and it can navigate around. It can also assess individual facial gestures and vocal frequencies, triggering interactions with the latest developments and intelligent algorithms in speech and sentiment detection. The robot is outfitted with functionality and connectors that allow it to communicate with people in a variety of ways. Pepper is a 1.2-meter humanoid robot with a total of 17 joints for spontaneous body movements, 3 rotatable wheels for smooth movement, a 12-hour battery capacity for uninterrupted activity, and the capacity to return to the recharging centre whenever necessary. It is indeed a delicately crafted robot with no rough edges for a more attractive and secure appearance in human environments. Several joints, such as the elbow, shoulder, and hip, have soft portions that avoid pinching. The scale and appearance of the machine are intended to make it comfortable and suitable for communicating with people. Referring to Fig. 2 Pepper is a robot of 1,210 mm, 480 mm, 425 mm in height, breadth, thickness respectively. Multiple LEDs are installed on the robot to signify and improve communications. The system is powered by an Atom E3845 processor with a quad-core CPU processor with a processing speed of 1.91 GHz [15].

The robot contains two RGB cameras on the forehead and mouth, and also a 3D sensor. A single frame per second, the camera resolution is high (2560 × 1920 pixels), or the lower resolution of 640 × 480 pixels at 30 frames per second. Behind the eyes, there is a single 3D sensitivity detector. It can produce images with a resolution of up to 320 × 240 pixels per second at a frame rate of 20 frames per second.

3.2 NAOqi Python API

NAOqi offers the required services used to research the robot using the Open-NAO package or on PCs using a variety of programming languages like Python and C++. The NAOqi Platform is a tool that is being utilized to create projects for PEPPER robots incorporating a variety of programming languages [16]. Parallel computing, supplies, synchronicity, and interactions are all fundamental mechanical requirements that NAOqi addresses. Motion, vision, microphone, video sharing are all supported by this framework. Since the NAOqi framework is cross-platform therefore it allows us to develop projects on robotics independent of the operating system platform. To aid researchers, the NAOqi framework also includes a variety of software languages via Application programming interfaces (API) for python.

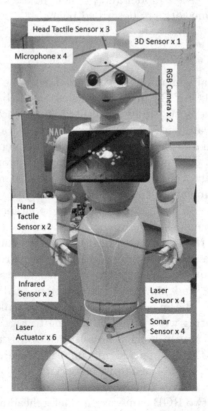

Fig. 2. Various sensors and their location of integration in pepper

3.3 EfficientNetV2

EfficientNetV2 employs progressive learning referring that while the image dimensions are initially low at the beginning of the training, they gradually rise in dimension. This technique is driven by the issue that the EfficientNet model training duration extends as image dimensions get higher. Progressive learning, on the other hand, is not a novel notion; this approach is utilized previously. The problem that comes into place is that the regularization effect is employed for several image resolutions during its earlier employment. Mingxing Tan et al. [18] indicates that this kind of scenario dramatically reduces network robustness and effectiveness. To address this problem, they periodically adjust the regularisation as well as the image resolution. It is a feasible approach because underfitting might result from a big regularisation impact on low-resolution images, whereas overfitting might result from a modest regularisation impact on higher resolution images.

EfficientNets incorporates a depthwise convolution layer, which has fewer parameters but is unable to completely exploit recent processors. To overcome this problem, EfficientNetV2 employs the Fused-MBConv layer. As illustrated in Fig. 3, this substitutes MBConv's depthwise 3×3 convolution and expansion 1×1 convolution with a standard 3×3 convolution. However, since the fused layers have larger hyperparameters, they cannot easily substitute every one of the previous MBConv layers. For this reason, they employ guided Neural Architecture Search to select the most suitable balance of fused and conventional MBConv layers. The findings of Neural Architecture Search reveal that replacing portions of the MBConv layers with fused layers improves accuracy with smaller models. It also demonstrates that a lower expansion proportion is preferable in the case of MBConv.

In contrast to EfficientNetV1, the EfficientNetV2 approach is more efficient as it uses MBConv and the Fused-MBConv in the beginning architecture levels. EfficientNetV2 recommends narrower 3×3 kernel dimensions than 5×5 according to Table 1. The reason behind selecting EfficientNetV2 outperforms prior versions of EfficientNet in terms of training time and parameter effectiveness, particularly for training-aware NAS and scalability. On the ImageNet, CIFAR datasets, it shows much more quicker training time and also higher parameter effectiveness than previous work [18].

4   Dataset Collection and Preprocessing

The model is trained on a combined database that integrates data from a wide range of traditional face expression detection domains. The MUG FER, CK & CK+, FER-2013 and KDEF & AKDEF are publicly available standard facial datasets in the domain of facial emotion recognition. However, these datasets take into account seven basic facial expressions. This study includes the seven primary facial gestures that are widely used in most facial expression recognition studies, as well as three more facial expression classes: think, wink, and mockery). The sources of the integrated dataset acquired in this study are listed below:

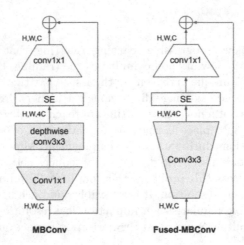

Fig. 3. Building block of EfficientNetV2 model [18]

Table 1. Architecture of EfficientNetV2 model [18]

Stage	Operator	Stride	Channels	Layers
0	Conv3 × 3	2	24	1
1	Fused-MBConv1, K3 × 3	1	24	2
2	Fused-MBConv4, K3 × 3	2	48	4
3	Fused-MBConv4, K3 × 3	2	64	4
4	MBConv4, K3 × 3, SE0.25	2	128	6
5	MBConv6, K3 × 3, SE0.25	1	160	9
6	MBConv6, K3 × 3, SE0.25	2	272	15
7	Conv1 × 1 & Pooling & FC	–	1792	1

- The MUG FER dataset: It is an expanded library of posed facial emotion image sets acquired with greater fidelity and no occlusions in controlled image capturing settings. The dataset is divided into two sections: The first section shows 86 participants acting out the six fundamental emotions. The second segment has the same people being videotaped while witnessing an emotional video. Aside from sentiment labelling, the database also includes an analysis of 80 face markers for a large sequence of frames. The resource has enough data to allow for the creation and statistical testing of facial expression recognition algorithms that use posed and generated emotion images [19].
- CK & CK+ dataset: The CK dataset has grown into one of the most popular datasets in facial expression recognition. However, Three shortcomings have emerged throughout that time. Due overcome those flaws, the extended version of the Cohn-Kanade (CK+) database is developed. The initial CK release, which comprises 486 shots from 97 people, starts with a face that is expressionless (neutral) and evolves to full expression. The number of images

and subjects has grown by 22% and 27%, respectively compared to the older version of the dataset. Non-posed images for various sorts of grins have also been included, along with their related information [20].

– FER-2013: Fer2013 comprises almost 30k face images of various emotions with a size restriction of 48 pixels in both height and width, and the primary labels are grouped into seven categories: 0–7 notations represent angry, disgust, fear, happy, sad, surprise and neutral respectively. The Disgust expression contains the fewest images compared to the other categories [21].

– KDEF & AKDEF: The KDEF (Karolinska Directed Emotional Faces Database) is a library of 4900 images of human facial emotions. The images depict 70 people (35 men and 25 women) with seven various human emotions (afraid, furious, disgusted, pleased, neutral, sad, and astonished). Each expression is examined from five various angles but images having straight viewing angle is considered in this research [22].

Fig. 4. Dataset samples representing images of unique facial emotion class (mockery, think, wink)

By gathering high-quality picture sequences from two prominent internet sources Adobe Stock [23] and Shutterstock [24], three new facial expressions, mockery, think, and wink, are added to the seven fundamental facial emotions. Some image selection criteria should be discussed regarding these three expressions since many individuals have their way of portraying these expressions, especially mockery and think. For this research, mockery is considered to be posed as showing tongue shrinking forehead and think is portrayed by people starring top-right or top-left corner keeping a hand on their chin. This study introduces three new emotion categories (mockery, think, and wink), which may be useful to other researchers in the field. In Fig. 4, some examples of the new facial emotion classes are shown.

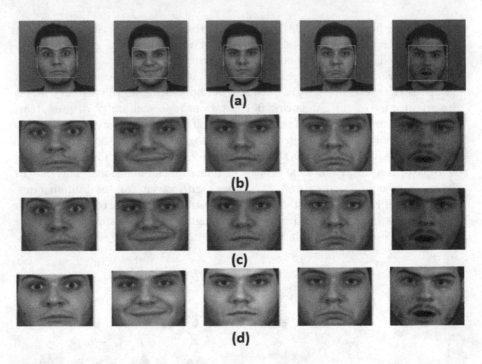

Fig. 5. Image preprocessing steps (a) Face detection, (b) Face extraction, (c) Grayscale transformation and (d) Contrast and brightness adjustment

Figure 5 depicts the entire data preparation operation, which includes (a) face region identification with a bounding box, (b) Region of interest cropping (face) (c) Excluding the color feature (gray transformation) (d), and image contrast and brightness adjustment. Haar CasCade classifier [25] is adopted in this research for the face detection task. It should be mentioned that the reason behind the grayscale conversion of the images is that human skin color is an insignificant feature for facial emotion recognition and allows the model to pay more attention to other facial features like lips, eyes, forehead and so on.

Image data augmentation is a method to extend the number of training samples in an artificial by producing transformed reproductions of the images in the database [26]. A set of affine transformation techniques is applied to the face dataset to generate additional samples. In this research, shift in both horizontal and vertical direction (20%), horizontal flip, slide rotation in random angle (15°) are considered as data augmentation parameters.

5   Experiments

In this research, a pretrained EfficientNetV2 model is trained on ImageNet21k. The dataset in this study, which was compiled from numerous different data sources, resulted in an unequal distribution of visuals across the class. It is among the factors why the classification performance of the model varies throughout the classes. To counteract this problem, the facial emotion visuals are divided uniformly among the classes. For this accomplishment, the database comprises a collection of 13,100 prepared images that are evenly split among ten categories, each of which has 1310 images. The images have been scaled to a dimension of 48 × 48 and are being used for EfficientNetV2 network learning. The model training takes place on a distributed Tesla K80 GPU in the Google Colaboratory environment. Stochastic Gradient Descent (SGD) is used as an optimizer [27] and the learning rate is set at 0.005. The model training speed is quicker, taking just about 53 s for each epoch. The EfficientNetV2 model is trained for 50 epochs and the 80:20 splitting ratio is adopted as train-test split.

5.1 Candidate Models for Facial Emotion Recognition

In order to explore the performance of other facial emotion classification models in comparison with the EfficientNetV2, Vision Transformer (ViT) model, MobileNetV2 and Residual Attention Network are incorporated in this study.

MobileNetV2. MobileNets are light-weighted models that have been parameterized to match the capacity restrictions of different applications. MobileNetV2 enhances the conventional accuracy of mobile networks on several applications and assessments. MobileNetV2 extends MobileNetV1's concepts by employing depth-wise separable convolutions (DSC) and Point-wise convolutions as construction components [28]. After a DSC layer filters the input, a point-wise convolution layer merges the extracted data to produce only useful features by lowering the number of channels. In MobileNetV2 architecture, the layers are linked up using linear bootle neck and to make connections among the bottlenecks there are short links that allow the model to obtain faster training.

Residual Attention Network. In Residual Attention Network, multi-attention units are layered to create it. There are two components to each attention Unit which are the mask branch and the trunk branch [29]. The trunk branch handles feature interpretation and may be customized to fit any modern system layout. To develop the Attention Component, Residual Unit [30], ResNeXt [31], and Inception [32] are considered as Residual Attention Network block. Throughout backpropagation, the attention mask can be utilized as a filter for gradient updates. It can also be used as a feature picker in forward reasoning. Attention Modules are resistant to noisy labels because of this characteristic. The use of mask branches can avoid incorrect gradients (because from being used to adjust trunk characteristics. The resilience of our Residual Attention Network against noisy labels is demonstrated in the research study.

Vision Transformer (ViT). The Vision Transformer, or ViT, is an image recognition framework that incorporates attention guided transformers in the image patches [17]. For doing so, an image is broken down into smaller patches. These patches are then embedded in a linear format along with unique embeddings which are called position embeddings. After that, both linear patch and position embedding are transferred to an attention aware multi-head transformer encoder. The traditional method of appending an additional trainable classification token to the sequence is employed to do classification.

6   System Implementation

The initial step is to establish a link between the Pepper and the local machine using the pepper's IP address and port with the help of Naoqi APIs. Then to establish an ALTextToSpeech gateway on the text-to-speech unit to instruct the target person to look at pepper's camera sensor. Next, named ALFaceDetection, a gateway is built to allow the robot to identify the participants face, as well as the component, which is subscribed to the ALFaceDetection gateway. ALPhotoCapture is called to capture the participant's face and a total of 15 images are taken by the pepper's camera sensor. The function iparamiko is invoked after establishing a connection with Pepper inserting the robot's login credential (username and password) in order to get access to the internal storage of pepper. To get the images onto a local computer, Transport function is called.

The acquired images of facial expressions are passed through a step-by-step process before model prediction. Haar cascade classifier is involved to extract the face region which is cropped afterwards. Grayscale scale conversion followed by contrast and brightness adjustments is applied to transform the images according to the images on which the model get trained on. Then, these images become the input for the trained EfficientNetV2 for classification. The predicted class is displayed with a blue bounding box around the face region just like Fig. 6.

Fig. 6. Real-time implementation of the Facial Emotion Recognition (FER) framework with Pepper robot

Table 2. Performance Evaluation of the Candidate Models

Model Name	Validation Accuracy (%)	Recall (%)	Precision (%)	F1 Score (%)
MobileNetV2	61.77	61.26	62.11	61.68
Residual Attention Network	74.24	73.31	74.85	74.07
Vision Transformer (ViT)	84.27	84.76	83.88	84.31
EfficientNetV2	**88.23**	**88.61**	**87.78**	**88.19**

7   Result and Discussion

The presented facial expression database, which contains 10 facial expression categories, is employed to train the EfficientNetV2, ViT, Residual attention network and MobileNetV2. A comparison of the selected methodologies in terms of all deep learning model performance matrices is shown in Table 2.

Following the table, the lowest performance among the adopted approaches for this FER task is by the MobileNetV2 which performs facial emotion recognition task with a validation accuracy of 61.77% and the recall, precision and F1 score, in this case, are 61.26%, 62.11% and 61.68% accordingly. On the other hand, classification performance is elevated with improved accuracy of 74.24% by the model residual attention network and the F1 score gets to 74.07%. Vision Transformer, however, offers more robust recognition performance not only in terms of accuracy but also inference time. ViT model shows better recognition accuracy of 84.27% and the F1 score, in this case, is 84.31%. Due to the reason that the ViT model does not involve any convolution layer in the feature extraction process, the time consumed by it in both training and prediction is significantly low. This could be an advantage of ViT model over other approaches considered in this research. Anyway, if we come to the impact of the EfficientNetV2 model in the FER task, it outplayed all the other three models with validation accuracy, recall, precision, F1 score of 88.23%, 88.61%, 87.78% and 88.19% respectively.

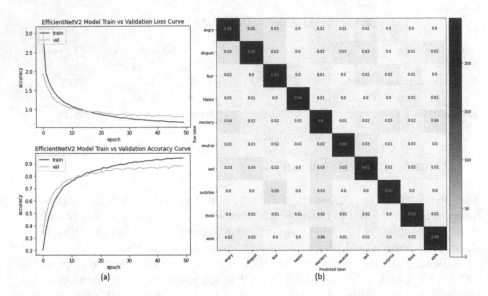

Fig. 7. (a) Train-validation accuracy, loss curve and (b) Confusion matrix of Efficient-NetV2 model

Figure 7(a) visualize the accuracy and loss curve captured throughout the EfficientNetV2 model training. Consistent increment in both training and validation accuracy curve evident the learning progress of the model during the training phases. It is valid for train and validation loss curves also as the model is able to learn the FER task with a descending loss curve. Overfitting is always been a challenging issue to tackle when it comes to classification performance on unseen images. Using dropout in between the fully connected layers along with limiting the model to train for high epochs (observing the learning improvement) allow reducing model overfitting in this research. As we can notice that the distance between the training and validation curve is low, it proofs that the model performs well in classifying unseen images.

However, overall classification accuracy does not provide information to demonstrate how well the model prediction performs while detecting individual classes. That is why Fig. 7(b) is presented which depicts the class-wise recognition rates delivered by the EfficientNetV2 model. Commendable recognition rates are displayed here since we can observe that model achieves an equal or more than 80% recognition rate in all the emotion classes. Moreover, for fear, happy, surprise and think the class model is able to gain over 90% classification rate.

8   Conclusion

The research objective consists of integrating a customized pre-trained deep trained model with a robotic framework to identify facial emotion from face visuals. Three standard deep learning models and vision transformer models are incorporated during the experiment to determine the optimal model for the facial emotion recognition task. Experiment results investigation demonstrates that EffieciantNetV2 delivers more significant results over the other candidate models. The whole recognition procedure starts with Pepper capturing face images after providing vocal instruction to the participants. Then the captured images are transferred to the local machine via NAOqi Python API. Pretrained EfficientNetV2 model, which is separately trained on the combined facial emotion recognition dataset with ten classes, is employed to predict the facial emotions of the participants. In this research, three unique facial emotion classes (mockery, think and wink) are introduced in the facial emotion dataset. To sum up, the proposed robotic facial emotion recognition framework can contribute in the domain of Human-robot-interaction (HRI) and make a humanoid robot like pepper more interactive and rational. However, there is a scope for improvement as the proposed model has low accuracy especially in the complex environment like face occlusion, low illumination which can be addressed in the future work.

References

1. Goodrich, M.A., Schultz, A.C.: Human-Robot Interaction: A Survey. Now Publishers Inc., Norwell (2008)
2. Sheridan, T.B.: Human-robot interaction: status and challenges. Hum. Fact. **58**(4), 525–532 (2016)
3. Camras, L.A., Sachs-Alter, E., Ribordy, S.C.: Emotion Understanding in Maltreated Children: Recognition of Facial Expressions and Integration with Other Emotion Cues. Lawrence Erlbaum Associates Inc., Mahwah (1996)
4. Sikka, K.: Facial expression analysis for estimating pain in clinical settings. In: Proceedings of the 16th International Conference on Multimodal Interaction, pp. 349–353 (2014)
5. Pierson, H.A., Gashler, M.S.: Deep learning in robotics: a review of recent research. Adv. Rob. **31**(16), 821–835 (2017)
6. Károly, A.I., Galambos, P., Kuti, J., Rudas, I.J.: Deep learning in robotics: survey on model structures and training strategies. IEEE Trans. Syst. Man Cybern. Syst. **51**(1), 266–279 (2020)
7. Ahmed, T.U., Hossain, S., Hossain, M.S., ul Islam, R., Andersson, K.: Facial expression recognition using convolutional neural network with data augmentation. In: 2019 Joint 8th International Conference on Informatics, Electronics & Vision (ICIEV) and 2019 3rd International Conference on Imaging, Vision & Pattern Recognition (icIVPR), pp. 336–341 (2019)
8. Ahmed, T.U., Jamil, M.N., Hossain, M.S., Andersson, K., Hossain, M.S.: An integrated real-time deep learning and belief rule base intelligent system to assess facial expression under uncertainty. In: 2020 Joint 9th International Conference on Informatics, Electronics & Vision (ICIEV) and 2020 4th International Conference on Imaging, Vision & Pattern Recognition (icIVPR), pp. 1–6 (2020)
9. Ni, R., Yang, B., Zhou, X., Cangelosi, A., Liu, X.: Facial expression recognition through cross-modality attention fusion. IEEE Trans. Cogn. Dev. Syst. **15**(1), 175–185 (2022)

10. Ruiz-Garcia, A., Webb, N., Palade, V., Eastwood, M., Elshaw, M.: Deep learning for real time facial expression recognition in social robots. In: Cheng, L., Leung, A., Ozawa, S. (eds.) ICONIP 2018. LNCS, vol. 11305, pp. 392–402. Springer, Heidelberg (2018). https://doi.org/10.1007/978-3-030-04221-9_35

11. Zhang, J., Xiao, N.: Capsule network-based facial expression recognition method for a humanoid robot. In: Recent Trends in Intelligent Computing, Communication and Devices, pp. 113–121. Springer, Heidelberg (2020). https://doi.org/10.1007/978-981-13-9406-5_15

12. Ilyas, C.M.A., Schmuck, V., Haque, M.A., Nasrollahi, K., Rehm, M., Moeslund, T.B.: Teaching pepper robot to recognize emotions of traumatic brain injured patients using deep neural networks. In: 2019 28th IEEE International Conference on Robot and Human Interactive Communication (RO-MAN), pp. 1–7. IEEE (2019)

13. Spezialetti, M., Placidi, G., Rossi, S.: Emotion recognition for human-robot interaction: recent advances and future perspectives. Front. Rob. AI **7**, 532279 (2020)

14. Alonso-Martin, F., Malfaz, M., Sequeira, J., Gorostiza, J.F., Salichs, M.A.: A multimodal emotion detection system during human-robot interaction. Sensors **13**(11), 15549–15581 (2013)

15. Pandey, A.K., Gelin, R.: A mass-produced sociable humanoid robot: pepper: The first machine of its kind. IEEE Rob. Autom. Maga. **25**(3), 40–48 (2018)

16. Seo, K.I.S.U.N.G., Robotics, A.L.D.E.B.A.R.A.N.: Using nao: introduction to interactive humanoid robots. AldeBaran Rob. (2013)

17. Dosovitskiy, A., et al.: An image is worth 16×16 words: transformers for image recognition at scale. In: Thirty-First AAAI Conference on Artificial Intelligence. arXiv preprint arXiv:2010.11929 (2020)

18. Tan, M., Le, Q.: Efficientnetv2: smaller models and faster training. In:: International Conference on Machine Learning (2021)

19. Aifanti, N., Papachristou, C., Delopoulos, A.: The MUG facial expression database. In: 11th International Workshop on Image Analysis for Multimedia Interactive Services WIAMIS 10, pp. 1–4 (2010)

20. Lucey, P., Cohn, J.F., Kanade, T., Saragih, J., Ambadar, Z., Matthews, I.: The extended cohn-kanade dataset (ck+): a complete dataset for action unit and emotion-specified expression. In: 2010 IEEE Computer Society Conference on Computer Vision and Pattern Recognition-Workshops, pp. 94–101. IEEE (2007)

21. Giannopoulos, P., Perikos, I., Hatzilygeroudis, I.: Deep learning approaches for facial emotion recognition: a case study on FER-2013. In: Hatzilygeroudis, I., Palade, V. (eds.) Advances in Hybridization of Intelligent Methods, pp. 1–8. Springer, Heidelberg (2018). https://doi.org/10.1007/978-3-319-66790-4_1

22. Calvo, M.G., Lundqvist, D.: Facial expressions of emotion (KDEF): identification under different display-duration conditions. Behav. Res. Methods **40**(1), 109–115 (2008)

23. Adobe Stock. https://stock.adobe.com/. Accessed 28 Sept 2022

24. Shutterstock. https://www.shutterstock.com/. Accessed 24 Sept 2022

25. Viola, P., Jones, M.J.: Robust real-time face detection. Int. J. Comput. Vision **57**, 137–154 (2004)

26. Shorten, C., Khoshgoftaar, T.M.: A survey on image data augmentation for deep learning. J. Big Data **6**(1), 1–48 (2019)

27. Bottou, L.: Stochastic gradient descent tricks. In: Montavon, G., Orr, G.B., Muller, K.R. (eds.) Neural Networks: Tricks of the Trade, vol. 7700, 2nd edn., pp. 421–436. Springer, Heidelberg (2012). https://doi.org/10.1007/978-3-642-35289-8_25

28. Sandler, M., Howard, A., Zhu, M., Zhmoginov, A., Chen, L.-C.: Mobilenetv2: inverted residuals and linear bottlenecks. In: Proceedings of the IEEE Conference on Computer Vision and Pattern Recognition, pp. 4510–4520 (2018)
29. Wang, F., et al.: Residual attention network for image classification. In: Proceedings of the IEEE Conference on Computer Vision and Pattern Recognition, pp. 3156–3164 (2017)
30. He, K., Zhang, X., Ren, S., Sun, J.: Identity mappings in deep residual networks. In: Leibe, B., Matas, J., Sebe, N., Welling, M. (eds.) ECCV 2016. LNCS, vol. 9908, pp. 630–645. Springer, Heidelberg (2016). https://doi.org/10.1007/978-3-319-46493-0_38
31. Xie, S., Girshick, R., Dollá=r, P., Tu, Z., He, K.: Aggregated residual transformations for deep neural networks. In: Proceedings of the IEEE Conference on Computer Vision and Pattern Recognition, pp. 1492–1500 (2017)
32. Szegedy, C., Ioffe, S., Vanhoucke, V., Alemi, A.A.: Inception-v4, inception-resnet and the impact of residual connections on learning. In: Thirty-First AAAI Conference on Artificial Intelligence (2017)

You Got the Feeling: Attributing Affective States to Dialogical Social Robots

Silvia De Marchi[1], Cristina Gena[1] , and Antonio Lieto[2,3]( )

[1] Department of Computer Science, University of Turin, Turin, Italy
{silvia.demarchi,cristina.gena}@unito.it
[2] DISPC, Cognition Interaction and Intelligent Techologies Laboratory (CIIT LAB),
University of Salerno, Fisciano, Italy
[3] ICAR-CNR, Quattromiglia, Italy
alieto@unisa.it

Abstract. In this paper we report the result of an analysis aiming at investigating, among different virtually embodied social robots (endowed with different degrees of dialogical complexity), the perceived difference in emotion attribution and understanding by the human users interacting with them. In particular, in our case study, the most complex dialogical modality - using a emotional content to vehiculate its messages - has been based entirely on the adoption of a Large Language Model (i.e. chatGPT in our case) whilst the simplest one has been based on a manual simplification of the generated text. We report the obtained results based on the adoption of a number tests and standardized scales and highlight some possibile future directions.

Keywords: Social Robotics · HRI · Affective Computing

1 Introduction

Empathy is an important aspect of human-human communication and building emphatic robots (i.e. robots able to elicit empathy in human users) represents a crucial challenge in the field of Human-Robot Interaction [20]. According to Hoffman's theory [34], one of the components of empathy is the affective one: it concerns, in detail, the emotional experience aroused by a stimulus of the same nature. Similarly Strayer [43], already in 1990, pointed out the co-participation of the affective component as the very content of empathy.

In the context of this paper we report a preliminary study assessing to what extent the use of affective content in dialogues during a human-robot interaction sessions impacts on the recognition and attribution of emotional and mental states to robots. More specifically: two different robots were employed: a virtual NAO and a virtual Pepper. Such virtual robots were endowed with different communication modalities: the NAO was able to provide answers by using an informative but neutral tone, communicating emotion simply and directly with a minimum of empathy; the Pepper, on the other hand, made use of emotion-driven and affective-charged content to deliver its messages, showing emotional

H. Degen and S. Ntoa (Eds.): HCII 2024, LNAI 14736, pp. 216–230, 2024.
https://doi.org/10.1007/978-3-031-60615-1_14

participation and actively involving the user in a more articulate and constructive conversation. Both dialogues were generated by using a Large Language Model. The objective of this work was to detect which modality, used by the two different robots, was the most effective in making the user understand which emotion NAO and Pepper really wanted to convey and express. The analysis of this aspect represents one of the priority objectives in the study of social robotics. The correct affective interpretation and attribution of robot dialogues (from the user perspective) provides, indeed, essential elements for implementing and improving the communicative aspect and the entire process of empathetic interaction between man and robot. In other words, one could say that the correct recognition of the affective content (if any) that a robot deliver in its dialogues is an indicator that humans can attribute the correct *affective theory of mind* to the talking robots. And this element is of paramount importance for planning, from the robotic point of view, emphatic dialogues based in the sharing of the same affective mood interpreted by the involved actors. Robots will undoubtedly become increasingly present in schools [14], factories [2], and homes [25] and, in our vision, their empathetic behavior certainly encourages their acceptance [13].

2   Empathy and Emotions Theories

According to Preston and De Waal [33] empathy can be defined as "the capacity to (a) be affected by and share the emotional state of another, (b) assess the reasons for the others' state, and (c) identify with the other, adopting his or her perspective". Following a shared categorization in psychology [29], empathy can be divided in three major categories: (1) empathy as an affective response to others' emotional states (*affective empathy*), (2) empathy as the cognitive understanding of others' emotional states, as well as the ability to put oneself in the other person's shoes (*cognitive empathy*), and (3) empathy as composed of both an affective and a cognitive component. Other perspectives [8,42,44] distinguish empathy in *dispositional* and *situational empathy*. While the former is a character trait, i.e. a person's general tendency to empathize, the latter is the empathy that a human perceives towards another agent in a specific situation.

Indeed, empathy is a concept that affects multiple fields of knowledge, from social to developmental, from clinical psychology to neuroscience. Since the discovery in 1996 of mirror neurons [12], interest in the concept of empathy has increased exponentially, also involving the field of human-robot interaction, see for instance [17,19,31,40]. Similarly, during a human-robot interaction, we speak of the cognitive process when a robotic agent appears to individuals as being able to understand and imitate the emotions of others. The affective process occurs when the robotic agent manifests its emotions through voice, body posture, movements and gestures, adapted to the context of the situation.

According to several neurological and psychological researches [5,15,36] the involvement of mirror neuron system is implicated in neurocognitive functions, such as social cognition, language, *empathy*, and *Theory of Mind (ToM)* [4,45], which is a human-specific ability that allows the attribution of mental states -intentions, thoughts, desires, and emotions- to themselves and others to explain and predict behavior. As a consequence of this state of affairs, emotions (and their recognition), have been acknowledged as a primary component for building empathic robots.

In addition to their role, emotions also provide an universal language through which people convey their experience, well beyond words. Despite the differences in the expression of emotions across languages, and the influence of cultural factors, in fact, emotions own an universal origin [10]: rooted in evolution, they provide the basis for intercultural communication, as effectively demonstrated by the advancements in face expression recognition [6,35]. In this sense, emotions can provide a suitable means for connecting robots with people belonging to different groups, intended as culture, age, education, and different sensory characteristics. Pervasive in human communication, emotions are expressed through multiple channels, ranging from face expression and body posture to spoken and written language. Emotion theories broadly belong to three main categories, partly derived from different research traditions. The expression of emotions through language, in particular, lies at the basis of several models of emotions. Categorical models focus on the definition of primary emotion types, which are assumed to be the result of phylogenesis. These emotion types are typically discrete and can be mapped straightforwardly onto face expressions. Sometimes referred to with the term 'basic emotions' to emphasize their innate nature, they appear at specific stages of the evolution of the child, progressively acquiring cognitive content. Depending on the reference theories, primary emotion types range from 5 to 6 [9] [26] including joy, anger, fear, disgust, sadness and sometimes surprise. Thanks to the tight relation with the preverbal (and postulated cross cultural) expression of emotions, these theories have deeply influenced the research on face expression recognition, through models such as the Facial Action Coding System (FACS), on which face expression datasets are built [23]. The model of six basic emotion prototypes proposed by Shaver et al. [41] has affinities with this group of models, but significantly differs from most of them from the methodological point of view: aimed at investigating the intuitions behind the human conceptualization of emotions, its design has been driven by the analysis of linguistic data.

Dimensional models represent emotions as the product of a set of predefined component dimensions, which axes such as polarity (often termed hedonic) and arousal. Historically derived from Wundt's three-dimensional definition of the emotional experience in terms of pleasure (pleasantness/unpleasantness), tension (tenseness/relaxedness), and excitement (excitement/depression) contemporary dimensional theories are usually represented through circumplex models, with significant variations: Plutchik's wheel of emotions acknowledges 8 bipolar emotions, derived from theoretical assumptions and rooted in behaviour [32], while Russel's circumplex model arranges empirically collected emotion labels in the continuous space generated by the two basic dimensions of arousal and polarity [38]. Depending on the dimensions considered (e.g., Mehrabian added dominance to the standard bidimensional space) different emotion types emerge from the intersections of the dimensions in the 2D or 3D space; in some models (e.g., Plutchik) secondary emotion types are generated by combining the primitive emotion types. Mainly geared to the subjective description and consequent expression of feelings, these models have influenced the creation of lexical resources for the analysis of sentiment [3].

Appraisal theories describe the subjective process of assessment of a situation which leads to the activation of an emotional state in a subject. These theories focus on the cognitive dimension of emotions [11,18,30,37,39], describing analytically the parameters that affect the emotional appraisal process. According to appraisal models, subjective motivations, or goals, and cultural factors, such as moral norms, affect the assessment of a given situation by an agent: each emotional category, then, is the result of a specific configuration of appraisal parameters, usually represented in the form of an activation rule. Appraisal models allow the same situation to be appraised differently by different individuals, and postulate complex emotions as the result of the activation of multiple appraisal processes on the same situations: for example, in the OCC model [30], the activation of distress and reproach yields the emotion of anger. The emotional coping process [37], the natural complement of appraisal, describes how the agent responds to the activated emotions at the mental and behavioural levels, in continuity with the appraisal parameters. Due to their cognitive background, appraisal models lend themselves to the integration with agent models, and to mentalistic models such as the Belief-Desire-Intention model (BDI) [7].

3   The Experiment

In the present work, we compared two different expression modalities of diverse virtual robots (NAO and Pepper) built by using the Aldebaran Choregraphe software [1]. Both robots had to express messages, within a structured conversation, able to convey six different types of emotions extracted from the Plutchik's wheel, namely: joy, envy, sadness (three basic emotions) and surprise, disapproval and curiosity (three complex emotions). Positive emotions produce pleasant effects in individuals, fostering a state of emotional and psychological wellbeing, whereas negative emotions lead to unpleasant sensations, causing frustration and emotional discomfort. All six emotions were presented to the users during a dialogue. Such dialogues, in both cases, were generated by a Large Language Model (chatGPT in its GPT 3.5 Turbo Version). However, for the NAO robot they were manually simplified in order to provide the more neutral and as simple as possible information. In order to elicit the above mentioned emotions, we requested to the LLM to use, within the generated sentences, a set of keywords resulting as highly associated with them by using the DEGARI affective-based reasoner [21], already successfully applied for suggesting stories from multiple affective viewpoints in museums [22], and its associated NRC lexicon [28].

Specifically, the goal of the experiment was to provide a preliminary response to the following questions: what emotions did individual robots express (**RQ1**)? This aspect has been assessed based on the robot's ability, as perceived by the user, to coherently express different emotions in an understandable manner.

What differences are observable (if any) in the emotional expressions manifested by NAO and Pepper robots **(RQ2)**? This aspect investigates whether there are significant differences in how the two robots express emotions and if one is more effective in terms of clarity and expressiveness. Did subjects report different level of engagement experiencing for the specific emotions conveyed by the robot **(RQ3)**? The answers to these questions provides a basis for reflection on the complex and articulated world of social robotics, despite the limited number of experiences collected.

We report the obtained results based on the adoption of a number tests and standardized scales and highlight some possible future directions.

Fig. 1. Experimental setting of a user interacting with the virtual NAO. On the desk are visible the different QR codes leading to post-test questionnaire and the document explaining the experiment (to read before starting it).

3.1   Method and Interaction Steps in the Dialogues

The sample considered for this study consists of 32 Master's degree students in Communication, ICT, and Media, and students from the Faculty of Social Innovation, Communication, and New Technologies at the University of Turin. There were 20 females, with an overall age range between 19 and 32 years.

The experiment was conducted in a dedicated space within the Luigi Einaudi Campus in Turin with the aid of a PC station connected to the Choregraphe software. Due to a malfunction of the NAO robot, the experiment was carried out using virtual robots available through the programming software mentioned above, instead of directly employing the two robots as initially hypothesized.

For this reason, the user from the identified sample is invited to sit in front of the computer and start interacting with the robot previously selected by the researcher (as shown in Fig. 1). The robot initiating the interaction changes from subject to subject (e.g., user 1 begins the experiment with the NAO robot, user 2 begins with Pepper), as does the order of presentation of the emotions expressed by the two artificial agents, to randomize potential effects from preset sequences that are the same for all users.

The procedure we followed has the following structure: i) the user seated at the dedicated PC station; ii) users are introduced to the experiment through a document; iii) the participant is asked to fill out a first empathetic evaluation questionnaire (Interpersonal Reactivity Index [16]), accessible via a specific QR Code, placed on the work table. The user begins the interaction with the assigned robot. For simplicity, we will use user number 1 as an example from now on.

NAO will attempt to express curiosity and then proceed with the remaining five emotions. At the end of each dialogue with NAO (and the related emotion expressed by the robot), user 1, through a second QR Code, can access a second questionnaire that will remain active for the duration of the experiment. This questionnaire aims to identify the emotion perceived by the human interlocutor from the interaction and their level of involvement.

The subsequent step involves the user interacting with the second robot and similarly completing the questionnaire introduced in the previous point.

Pepper will attempt to express surprise and then proceed with the remaining five emotions. Thus, user number 1, after interacting with NAO, will proceed with Pepper, who will seek to express the feeling of surprise and then continue with the remaining five emotions.

The greeting is the main input to initiate communication with the robot, marking the moment when the latter detects the presence of the user and activates to interact with them. NAO responds to the greeting and expresses the emotion it is feeling. At the end, NAO asks the human a specific question, which will vary depending on the emotion expressed (e.g., "Would you like to get to know each other better?", "Do you agree with me?", "Have you ever felt this sensation?"). The user's response can mostly be affirmative or negative; different ways for the user to respond to the robot's questions are also anticipated.

Pepper, by managing a conversation in a more personalized way, returns the greeting and asks the user's name. This information, stored by the robot, facilitates the creation of a relationship of knowledge and trust and can be recalled at any time during the interaction. It is hypothesized that the user may respond to the question using various expressions. Expressions a user can use to answer Pepper's question "What's your name?" Once the user's response is received, Pepper introduces the scenario for the emotion it will express. Subsequently, the robot asks the user a specific question, which, again, will vary depending on the dialogue (e.g., "Would you like?", "Can I explain how I feel?", "Can I tell you about this event?", etc.). Depending on the user's response, the dialogue can proceed in two directions: a negative response leads to the end of the conversation, where the robot bids farewell to the user and concludes the interaction. An affirmative response leads Pepper to delve into the expression of the emotion felt, opening up various arguments based on what the user has expressed.

4   Evaluation

In our evaluation we have used a *within-subject design* method and the Interpersonal Reactivity Index (IRI), created in 1983 by Mark H. Davis [16]. IRI is a tool used in psychology to gather evaluative elements about empathy and how people detect, understand, and react to others' emotions and experiences. It is used in this work as the first test administered to the user before the human-robot interaction.

The IRI consists of four subscales, each comprising seven items that probe each component of the empathic process: perspective-taking (PT), empathic concern (EC), personal distress (PD), and fantasy (FS). The total of 28 items are presented in the form of statements, to which the subject can respond using a Likert scale ranging from "does not describe me at all" to "describes me very well." The total score obtained for each of the four scales, ranging from 0 to 35 since each scale includes seven statements with scores ranging from 0 to 5, can be summed to achieve a comprehensive score between 0 and 140. A high score indicates a greater level of empathy and a higher relational sensitivity. This scale's measurement highlights whether an individual spontaneously considers others' viewpoints in daily life. A low score suggests a limited ability to consider others' perspectives and difficulty in understanding emotions different from one's own. A high score, on the other hand, suggests an adequate understanding of emotional states and viewpoints of others, essential for an empathic relationship.

The Interpersonal Reactivity Index (IRI) scales are tools that, alongside a more detailed evaluation, can contribute to enriching the puzzle that constitutes the complex multidimensional picture of empathy. These scales acquire significance only when interpreted in their entirety and are listed below.

The Perspective-Taking Scale. The perspective-taking (AP) scale refers to an individual's intellectual or imaginative ability to put oneself in another's shoes [24]. In particular, a subject who scores high on the AP scale shows predisposition towards communication, tolerance and interpersonal relationships. Subjects with a high AP score also tend to have a flexible mindset, which allows them to adapt their thinking to different situations. An extremely high score in this area can be negative as it can interfere with the ability to make decisions. Conversely, a low score is a sign of poor cognitive empathy, and is typical of individuals who exhibit little mental flexibility and are not good at understanding the mental state of others. An extremely low score on this scale can be related to a significant deficit in interpersonal and communication skills [24].

The Fantasy Scale. The utilization of this scale aims to probe the extent to which an individual can immerse themselves in fictional situations through imagination, as might occur, for instance, through reading a book or watching a film. A low score signifies a reduced inclination towards engagement in imaginary scenarios and is more commonly observed in individuals who are highly grounded in reality, pragmatic, and less willing to envision themselves in fantastical situations. These traits alone are not sufficient to delineate a person's level of empathy. Conversely, a high score typically characterizes highly creative individuals who are more disposed to immerse themselves in imaginary stories.

Empathic Concern Scale (EC). The adoption of this scale facilitates the assessment of the predisposition exhibited by the interviewed subjects towards experiencing feelings of compassion and emotional engagement towards others who are undergoing negative experiences. A low score indicates a lesser degree of involvement, whereas a high score suggests that the individual is interested and actively concerned with the emotional well-being of others. In the former case, individuals might experience difficulties in engaging empathetically; in the latter, the outcome suggests a genuine interest and concern for others, with these empathic subjects feeling emotionally involved and eager to alleviate the emotional distress others may face.

Personal Distress Scale (PD). The Personal Distress Scale evaluates situations in which witnessing unpleasant events involving others generates anxiety and dismay in the observer. Such situations can lead to a genuine loss of control in some individuals. A low score serves as an indicator of a certain capacity for emotional management, wherein individuals might be better equipped to handle complex situations. Conversely, a high score identifies individuals who react to similar situations with discomfort and suffering, accompanied by a high level of stress. These subjects feel deeply emotionally implicated and recognize the need to reduce the distress experienced by others.

During the interaction phase, at the end of each dialogue between the robot and the user, the latter is administered a **second questionnaire** accessible with the dedicated QR Code, consisting of two questions. These questions are presented at the end of each task to capture the immediate memory of the interaction just occurred with the robots. The first question aims to verify which emotion was expressed by the robot, and the second assesses the level of user involvement during the interaction:

- **Question 1**: Identification of the emotion expressed by the robot *"In your opinion, which emotion did the robot express?"*. In this case, the user must select an emotion from a dropdown menu;
- **Question 2**: Evaluation of user involvement in the interaction *"How involved did you feel in the emotion expressed by the robot?"*. The question is posed to the user after identifying the perceived emotion following the dialogue with the robot. In this case, their response can range from 1 ("not at all") to 5 ("very much"), and the purpose is to measure how involved the user felt in the emotion expressed. It also aims to observe the emotional response following positive or negative emotions, considering that the latter typically have a greater impact on humans compared to positive emotions.

AMS (Attribution of Mental State) Questionnaire. As an additional tool for post-interaction evaluation we administered to the to the users, upon completion of the experimental tasks conducted with both NAO and Pepper, The AMS (Attribution of Mental States) Questionnaire [27]. AMS is used for measuring and assessing the attribution of mental states (see also [13]) to the two robots.

In the context of this work, the questionnaire is employed to measure the mental states that experiment participants assign to the robot and, in particular, to highlight the user's perception regarding the robot's mental characteristics in comparison with those of humans.

Another aim is to gather information to understand if the attribution of mental states to the robot is influenced by the expressive mode enacted by the robot itself during dialogue. That is, to detect if the modes manifested by the two robots, one more direct and mechanical versus the other more articulated and complex, affect the attribution of mental states expressed by the participant at the end of the experiment.

The questionnaire consists of 25 questions with response options: "a lot: score 2", "a little: score 1", "not at all: score 0". The sum of all responses determines the overall score, which ranges from 0 to 50.

Furthermore, the AMS questionnaire comprises five specific dimensions, with partial scores being the sum of responses within each dimension, ranging from 0 to 10. The dimensions are:

- *Epistemic*: related to participants' concept of the robots' cognitive intelligence: can the robot understand? Can it make decisions? Can it think?
- *Perceptual*: the dimension related to the possibility that the robot experiences sensations, such as smell, sight, taste, etc.
- *Emotional*: can the robot experience feelings of anger, happiness, fear?
- *Desires*: can the robot express desires or preferences?
- *Imaginative*: is the robot capable of dreaming or imagining?

The questionnaire, presented in a single form, was administered twice: once to gather information on NAO and a second time for Pepper. The sum of scores in each area allowed the comparison of results through the T-test and if there are significant differences between the two questionnaires, and in which areas.

In addition to the questions in the questionnaire, further inquiries specifically chosen to probe more deeply into the level of interaction the experiment participant had with the robot were included: "Was this the first time you interacted with Pepper?"; "Was this the first time you interacted with NAO?"; "Have you interacted with other robots in the past?"; "If you answered 'yes' to the previous question, which one(s)?"; "Which type of interaction (NAO or Pepper) did you prefer?"; "Indicate the factors that determined your choice."

5   Results and Future Works

We obtained, for the above mentioned scales composing the IRI index, the following results. For the Perspective-Taking scale (PT): the total score obtained, equal to 806, indicates a considerable level of empathic involvement, a sign of a high understanding of the emotional needs manifested by others. The value, compared to the collected data, identifies a sample sensitive to the needs and emotions of other people. For the Fantasy Scale (FS): the total of 500, obtained from the sum of the scores of this subscale, suggests that the sample is mostly composed of pragmatic subjects, less inclined to engage in emotional fantasies or immerse themselves in imaginary roles. For the Empathic Concern scale (EC): the score of 901, being the highest in the overall assessment of the questionnaire, suggests that the sample has a high propensity to put themselves in others' shoes and to welcome and understand the emotional expressiveness shown by other people. Finally, for the Personal Distress scale (PD), the total score detected (623) indicates that the sample possesses a moderate level of discomfort in relation to emotionally stressful situations involving other people. The overall data suggest a sample of subjects who feel emotionally involved and subjected to a high degree of stress when others experience discomfort or suffering.

In summary, for the sample of 32 subjects to whom the questionnaire was administered, it can be hypothesized that they possess an adequate level of empathy. This interpretation is supported by significant values referred to the Perspective-Taking and Empathic Concern scales, suggesting a high level of acceptance and understanding towards others from an emotional perspective. The values from the Personal Distress scale suggest a moderate sensitivity in perceiving others' discomfort, while a medium-low ability is detected regarding the Fantasy subscale, which could indicate that the interviewed subjects tend more towards a rational and concrete approach to emotional experiences, rather than opting for a more fanciful and imaginary view of reality.

Based on such assessment, we also analyzed the results of the above mentioned questionnaire that allowed us to check to what extent it was possibile to identify different levels of *affective theories of mind* attributed by the users to the different robots and robotic modalities they interacted with.

The additional data collected through the questionnaires complete the picture of information intended to be collected following the experiment. After identifying the emotion the robot wanted to transmit, it was intended to verify whether the different communicative attitude attributed could determine, in the interviewed subjects, an emotional implication capable of influencing their choice regarding the preference between the two robots.

In particular, for what concern the correct emotion identification and attribution we analyzed - for the two testing conditions - the total number of users who correctly identified ("Yes") and those who did not identify ("No") the individual emotions that the robots NAO and Pepper tried to express during the interactions Overall, the data show that the error rate, pertaining to the users' failure to recognize the emotion the robot intended to convey, is higher for NAO (13 errors out of 192 interactions, equivalent to 6.8%) compared to Pepper (6 errors out of 192 interactions, equivalent to 3.1%). This difference may be attributed to Pepper's more complex dialogue structure, which could have facilitated a better understanding of the intended emotional transmission. However, it is important to note that the detected errors are mostly related to the users' selection of a different emotion, albeit similar to the one the robot initially aimed to express.

We conducted a paired t-test to determine if there were significant differences in the identification of individual emotions as reported separately by the two robots. The result ($p = .135$) suggests that even the more synthetic and direct expressive mode deployed by the NAO robot was effective in making understandable the emotion it intended to convey; the simplicity of the dialogues attributed to it might have positively influenced this result.

Regarding the level of involvement that the interviewed subjects declared having felt for the specific emotions transmitted by the robots (Question 2 of the second questionnaire), the data reveal that the mode used by Pepper was more effective than that of NAO, with statistically significant differences between the two robots ($p < .005$). This datum is aligned with the fact that more articulated, and expressed through a more complete and engaging expressive mode, were attributed to Pepper robot; on the contrary, the input provided to NAO involved very synthetic and direct responses, not supported by engaging dialogue.

Regarding the subcategories of the AMS questionnaire, the responses provided by users towards were as follows.

Epistemic Dimension. This category pertains to the cognitive capabilities recognized in the NAO robot. 37.5% of participants attributed an absolute lack of such capability to the robot; 46.3% recognized it as having limited cognitive ability, and 16.2% attributed a high cognitive capacity to NAO. For the Pepper, 3,8% of the subjects attributed to the robot the complete lack of such capability; 21,9% recognized it as having limited cognitive ability and 74,3% attributed a high cognitive capacity. Here the result of the paired T-test showed a significant difference for the first ($p = 0.01$)and the last item ($p = 0.0003$).

Perceptual Dimension. This dimension acknowledges the robot's ability to experience sensations related to the five senses. In this case, 73.8% of the surveyed users did not find NAO to possess such ability; 22.5% recognized the robot as having a reduced perceptual capacity, while 3.7% defined NAO as a robot with a high ability to perceive sensations. Concerning the Pepper: 39.3% did not find robot to possess such ability; 28,8% recognized the robot as having a reduced perceptual capacity and 31,9% defined the robot as having a high ability to perceive sensations. Here the result of the paired T-test showed a significant difference for all the items ($p < 0.002$).

Emotional Dimension. This dimension explores the level at which the robot can experience feelings such as anger, fear, happiness, and sadness. 21.9% of the respondents did not recognize this capability in NAO; 61.9% attributed it with a low capacity, while the remaining 16.2% believed that NAO is capable of experiencing such sensations. For the Pepper, 6.3% of the respondents did not recognize this capability in the robot, 11.3% attributed it with a low capacity, and 82.5% believed that Pepper is capable of experiencing such sensations. Here the result of the paired T-test showed a significant difference for the first and the last item (both $p = 0.002$).

Desire Dimension. This dimension assesses the robot's ability to express desires or preferences. 61.3% of respondents did not recognize this capability in NAO; 31.2% acknowledged it a limited capacity, while 7.5% attributed it a high capacity. For Pepper, the results were (in the same order) of 8.8%, 30% and 61.2% respectively. Here the result of the paired T-test showed a significant difference for the first (p = 0.01) and the last item (p = 0.003).

Imaginative Dimension. This dimension evaluates the robot's ability to imagine. For this aspect, 70% of respondents did not recognize any imaginative capacity in NAO; 20.6% acknowledged it as having a limited capacity, while the remaining 9.4% attributed a high imaginative capacity to the robot. For Pepper, the results were (in the same order) of 21.89%, 24.3% and 53.8% respectively. Here the result of the paired T-test showed a significant difference for the first (p = 0.01)and the last item (p = 0.003).

The AMS data show that the users attribute greater capabilities in Pepper across all five dimensions of the AMS questionnaire. The interaction with Pepper was also the most preferred one; among the main reasons supporting this preference were: good emotional management by the robot (22.3%), a high degree of engagement (19.4%), and constructive communication (15.8%) as key elements for the success of a human-robot interaction. Regarding the reasons that led five users to prefer interacting with NAO, the most influential factors were: clarity of exposition by the robot (25%), the ability to synthesize (25%), and simple communication (25%).

Overall, the main findings of this preliminary experimentation concern the fact that emotions seem to be detected in both the robots (RQ1), but their identification does not appear to be related to the different mode adopted by the two robot expressing it (RQ2), suggesting that the expressive mode, more synthetic and direct, employed by the NAO robot, was nevertheless effective in conveying the intended emotion. This result could have been positively influenced by the simplicity of the dialogues attributed to it.

Regarding the level of engagement that the interviewed subjects reported experiencing for the specific emotions conveyed by the robots (RQ3), the data analysis reveals that the mode used by Pepper was more effective than that of NAO, with statistically significant differences between the two robots. It is interesting to note how the more structured dialogue, expressed by Pepper, also determined in the users an attribution of the robot's capabilities, in term of identified mental states, even superior to those actually present in the dialogue. The data confirm that the type of dialogue between man and robot influenced the perception that users have of them.

Some of the limitations of the current work concern the use of virtual (instead of physical) robots. Here, we plan to repeat the experiment with embodied robots. In addition, we plan to extend the experimental sample of the tested users and to extend the evaluation to the entire emotional spectrum of the Plutchik's theory of emotion.

References

1. Aldebaran: Nao software 1.14.5 documentation
2. Brunetti, D., Gena, C., Vernero, F.: Smart interactive technologies in the human-centric factory 5.0: a survey. Appl. Sci. **12**(16), 7965 (2022)
3. Cambria, E., Li, Y., Xing, F.Z., Poria, S., Kwok, K.: SenticNet 6: ensemble application of symbolic and subsymbolic AI for sentiment analysis. In: Proceedings of the 29th ACM International Conference on Information & Knowledge Management, pp. 105–114 (2020)
4. Carlson, S.M., Koenig, M.A., Harms, M.B.: Theory of mind. Wiley Interdisc. Rev. Cogn. Sci. **4**(4), 391–402 (2013)
5. Cattaneo, L., Rizzolatti, G.: The mirror neuron system. Arch. Neurol. **66**(5), 557–560 (2009)
6. Cordaro, D.T., Sun, R., Keltner, D., Kamble, S., Huddar, N., McNeil, G.: Universals and cultural variations in 22 emotional expressions across five cultures. Emotion **18**(1), 75 (2018)
7. Dennett, D.C.: The Intentional Stance. MIT Press (1989)
8. Eisenberg, N., et al.: The relations of emotionality and regulation to dispositional and situational empathy-related responding. J. Pers. Soc. Psychol. **66**(4), 776 (1994)
9. Ekman, P.: Basic emotions. Handb. Cogn. Emot. **98**(45–60), 16 (1999)
10. Ekman, P., Friesen, W.V.: Constants across cultures in the face and emotion. J. Pers. Soc. Psychol. **17**(2), 124 (1971)
11. Frijda, N.H., et al.: The Emotions. Cambridge University Press (1986)
12. Gallese, V., Fadiga, L., Fogassi, L., Rizzolatti, G.: Action recognition in the premotor cortex. Brain **119**(2), 593–609 (1996)
13. Gena, C., Manini, F., Lieto, A., Lillo, A., Vernero, F.: Can empathy affect the attribution of mental states to robots? In: Proceedings of the 25th International Conference on Multimodal Interaction, pp. 94–103 (2023)
14. Gena, C., Mattutino, C., Perosino, G., Trainito, M., Vaudano, C., Cellie, D.: Design and development of a social, educational and affective robot. In: 2020 IEEE Conference on Evolving and Adaptive Intelligent Systems, EAIS 2020, Bari, Italy, 27–29 May 2020, pp. 1–8. IEEE (2020). https://doi.org/10.1109/EAIS48028.2020.9122778
15. Iacoboni, M.: Imitation, empathy, and mirror neurons. Ann. Rev. Psychol. **60**(1), 653–670 (2009). https://doi.org/10.1146/annurev.psych.60.110707.163604. pMID: 18793090
16. Keaton, S.A.: Interpersonal reactivity index (IRI) (Davis, 1980). In: The Sourcebook of Listening Research: Methodology and Measures, pp. 340–347 (2017)
17. Kwak, S.S., Kim, Y., Kim, E., Shin, C., Cho, K.: What makes people empathize with an emotional robot? The impact of agency and physical embodiment on human empathy for a robot. In: 2013 IEEE RO-MAN, pp. 180–185 (2013). https://doi.org/10.1109/ROMAN.2013.6628441
18. Lazarus, R.S.: Progress on a cognitive-motivational-relational theory of emotion. Am. psychol. **46**(8), 819 (1991)
19. Leite, I., Pereira, A., Mascarenhas, S., Martinho, C., Prada, R., Paiva, A.: The influence of empathy in human-robot relations. Int. J. Hum. Comput. Stud. **71**(3), 250–260 (2013)
20. Lieto, A.: Cognitive Design for Artificial Minds. Routledge (2021)

21. Lieto, A., Pozzato, G.L., Zoia, S., Patti, V., Damiano, R.: A commonsense reasoning framework for explanatory emotion attribution, generation and re-classification. Knowl.-Based Syst., 107166 (2021)
22. Lieto, A., Striani, M., Gena, C., Dolza, E., Marras, A.M., Pozzato, G.L., Damiano, R.: A sensemaking system for grouping and suggesting stories from multiple affective viewpoints in museums. Hum.-Comput. Interact. **39**(1–2), 109–143 (2024)
23. Lucey, P., Cohn, J.F., Kanade, T., Saragih, J., Ambadar, Z., Matthews, I.: The extended Cohn-Kanade dataset (CK+): a complete dataset for action unit and emotion-specified expression. In: 2010 IEEE Computer Society Conference on Computer Vision and Pattern Recognition-Workshops, pp. 94–101. IEEE (2010)
24. López-Pérez, B., Fernández-Pinto, I., Abad, F.: TECA. Test de Empatía Cognitiva y Afectiva, Tea Ediciones, S.A., Madrid (2008)
25. Macis, D., Perilli, S., Gena, C.: Employing socially assistive robots in elderly care. In: UMAP 2022: 30th ACM Conference on User Modeling, Adaptation and Personalization, Barcelona, Spain, 4–7 July 2022, Adjunct Proceedings, pp. 130–138. ACM (2022). https://doi.org/10.1145/3511047.3537687
26. Mehrabian, A.: Comparison of the PAD and PANAS as models for describing emotions and for differentiating anxiety from depression. J. Psychopathol. Behav. Assess. **19**(4), 331–357 (1997)
27. Miraglia, L., Peretti, G., Manzi, F., Di Dio, C., Massaro, D., Marchetti, A.: Development and validation of the attribution of mental states questionnaire (AMS-Q): a reference tool for assessing anthropomorphism. Frontiers Psychol. **14** (2023)
28. Mohammad, S.: Word affect intensities. In: Calzolari, N., et al. (eds.) Proceedings of the Eleventh International Conference on Language Resources and Evaluation, LREC 2018, Miyazaki, Japan, 7–12 May 2018. European Language Resources Association (ELRA) (2018). http://www.lrec-conf.org/proceedings/lrec2018/summaries/329.html
29. Omdahl, B.L.: Cognitive Appraisal, Emotion, and Empathy. Psychology Press (2014)
30. Ortony, A.: Are emotion metaphors conceptual or lexical? Cogn. Emot. **2**(2), 95–104 (1988)
31. Paiva, A., Leite, I., Boukricha, H., Wachsmuth, I.: Empathy in virtual agents and robots: a survey. ACM Trans. Interact. Intell. Syst. **7**(3) (2017). https://doi.org/10.1145/2912150
32. Plutchik, R.: A general psychoevolutionary theory of emotion. In: Theories of Emotion, pp. 3–33. Elsevier (1980)
33. Preston, S.D., De Waal, F.B.: Empathy: its ultimate and proximate bases. Behav. Brain Sci. **25**(1), 1–20 (2002)
34. Raboteg-Saric, Z., Hoffman, M.: Empathy and moral development: implications for caring and justice. Contemp. Sociol. **30**, 487 (2001). https://doi.org/10.2307/3089337
35. Revina, I.M., Emmanuel, W.S.: A survey on human face expression recognition techniques. J. King Saud Univ. Comput. Inf. Sci. **33**(6), 619–628 (2021)
36. Rizzolatti, G., Craighero, L.: Mirror neuron: a neurological approach to empathy. In: Changeux, J.P., Damasio, A.R., Singer, W., Christen, Y. (eds.) Neurobiology of Human Values, pp. 107–123. Springer, Heidelberg (2005). https://doi.org/10.1007/3-540-29803-7_9
37. Roseman, I.J.: Appraisal determinants of emotions: constructing a more accurate and comprehensive theory. Cogn. Emot. **10**(3), 241–278 (1996)
38. Russell, J.A.: A circumplex model of affect. J. Pers. Soc. Psychol. **39**(6), 1161 (1980)

39. Scherer, K.R.: Criteria for emotion-antecedent appraisal: a review. Cogn. Pers. Emot. Motiv., 89–126 (1988)
40. Seo, S.H., Geiskkovitch, D., Nakane, M., King, C., Young, J.E.: Poor thing! Would you feel sorry for a simulated robot? In: Proceedings of the Tenth Annual ACM/IEEE International Conference on Human-Robot Interaction, pp. 125–132 (2015)
41. Shaver, P., Schwartz, J., Kirson, D., O'connor, C.: Emotion knowledge: further exploration of a prototype approach. J. Pers. Soc. Psychol. 52(6), 1061 (1987)
42. Stephan, W.G., Finlay, K.: The role of empathy in improving intergroup relations. J. Soc. Issues 55(4), 729–743 (1999)
43. Strayer, J.: 10 affective and cognitive perspectives on empathy. In: Empathy and Its Development, p. 218 (1990)
44. Stueber, K.: Empathy, mental dispositions, and the physicalist challenge (2009)
45. Wellman, H.M.: The Child's Theory of Mind. The MIT Press (1992)

Enhancing Usability of Voice Interfaces for Socially Assistive Robots Through Deep Learning: A German Case Study

Oliver Guhr[1,2]([✉]), Claudia Loitsch[2,3], Gerhard Weber[2], and Hans-Joachim Böhme[1]

[1] HTW Dresden, Friedrich-List-Platz 1, 01069 Dresden, Germany
{oliver.guhr,hans-joachim.boehme}@htw-dresden.de
[2] Technische Universität Dresden, 01062 Dresden, Germany
{claudia.loitsch,gerhard.weber}@tu-dresden.de
[3] Center for Scalable Data Analytics and Artificial Intelligence (ScaDS.AI), Dresden, Germany

Abstract. Voice Interfaces have become ubiquitous as they can make complex technology more usable and accessible. Current voice interfaces, however, often require the user to learn specific speech commands or sentence patterns to use them. This property does not satisfy usability heuristics and causes current language interfaces to underachieve the naturalness of language interaction. To address this issue, we developed a voice interface that is capable of understanding natural everyday language. The overall objective is to build a German language voice interface for socially assistive robots that can work in public spaces. Therefore, we cannot assume the user's prior knowledge or experience. Based on recent advances in deep natural language processing, we have built a voice interface that is not restricted to specific speech commands. To test this voice interface, we conducted a study with 47 participants. Results indicate 93% of the given tasks were solved successfully by the target user group without prior training or experience with the voice interface.

Keywords: Human-Robot Interaction · Voice Interface · User Study

1 Introduction

In the era of digital transformation, technical assistance systems, such as voice assistants and socially assistive robots, are progressively integrated into various work processes. The health care sector, specifically elderly care, has demonstrated a growing need for such innovations due to the escalating demand for care services and the acute personnel shortage in Germany [7]. We believe that the key to successful implementation lies in the seamless incorporation of these systems into existing workflows, with natural language processing (NLP) playing a pivotal role by enabling intuitive human-machine interaction.

We focus on developing a voice interface for social assistance robots. These robots will be used in geriatric and medical care facilities and should both relieve

H. Degen and S. Ntoa (Eds.): HCII 2024, LNAI 14736, pp. 231–249, 2024.
https://doi.org/10.1007/978-3-031-60615-1_15

the staff and provide a therapeutic contribution for the residents. Despite significant advancements in NLP and the ubiquity of voice assistants, existing systems often necessitate users to learn fixed-structure commands, thereby posing a hurdle for intuitive interaction. This is problematic for our use case, since we cannot assume that every person who encounters the robot knows these command phrases. The robot should be able to respond not only to trained personnel, but also to residents and visitors. For example, if the robot blocks a user's path, any person should be able to ask it to clear the walkway without knowing or learning a predefined command. The interaction must be particularly intuitive for this use case and must not require any learning time. This is derived from the requirements for systems for the public sector, with which users spend only limited time on clearly defined tasks [16]. Furthermore, commercial voice assistants fall short in their adaptability to robotic systems and compliance with stringent data protection regulations prevalent in medical and geriatric care settings in Germany. To overcome these issues and improve the integration in the user's workflow, we developed a voice interface for our robots.

We aim to extend the voice interface's use beyond robots, repurposing it as a voice assistant in our Ambient Assisted Living (AAL) laboratory. This facility, a short-term care apartment, will be equipped to allow residents to voice-control various aspects such as lighting, heating, and appliances. Our primary goal is to enhance the interface's capabilities to facilitate intuitive user interaction without the necessity for extensive training or specific command memorization.

With this study, we would like to answer the following research question: *How effectively can users interact with the voice interface without learning specific voice commands?* To assess our implementation, we carried out a counterbalanced within-subject user study. Participants were given two task sets: one for operating the robot and another for managing AAL appliances. To ensure counterbalancing, the set for which participants received the training was randomly selected. This design allowed us to observe the efficacy of the voice interface under both trained and untrained conditions. Without the training, the participants were able to complete 93% of the assigned tasks, improving slightly to 95% with prior training. Participants rated the system as having good usability based on the results of the usability questionnaires.

This paper presents the findings of the study and discusses the technical design decisions that contributed to achieving this goal.

2   Related Work

2.1   Voice Interface Evaluations

Kowalski et al. [12] explores the use of voice assistants (VA) in an AAL setting for older adults using Google Home. The study found that VAs could be useful and convenient for older adults'. However, they conclude that more research is needed to address user-specific needs and improve device compatibility, context awareness, and security.

Wolters et al. [31] found that older adults tend to prefer a "social" communication style, characterized by more interpersonal communication when interacting with voice interfaces. Their study concluded that to better cater to this communication style, future voice interfaces need to improve their automatic speech recognition (ASR) and natural language processing/understanding (NLP/NLU) capabilities. While their work dates back to 2009, more recent research by Sin et al. [28] demonstrates that these challenges persist in current commercial systems, such as Amazon's Alexa. Sin et al. [28] conducted a qualitative user study with older adults to examine their experiences with Alexa. Their findings revealed that participants often had to rephrase their questions for Alexa to understand them. While some individuals were willing to adapt their speech patterns to facilitate communication with the device, others refused to do so, with some even opting not to use the device at all.

Papachristos et al. [20] developed a voice-based application for Google Assistant aimed at helping individuals improve their collaboration skills through self-reflection. However, the majority of participants with mixed feelings regarding the system, reported them due to technical issues and misunderstandings of commands, indicating potential areas for improvement in the application's design and functionality.

A study by Kobayashi et al. [11] investigated the impact of age-related cognitive decline in non-demented older adults on their behavioral characteristics while using a voice-based dialogue system. Significant associations were found between cognitive scores and vocal features such as pauses and hesitations. The study also discussed potential design considerations for voice-based dialogue systems to accommodate these behavioral characteristics.

The work by Salai, Cook, and Holmquist [27] highlights the challenges faced by individuals with speech impairments, memory problems, and cognitive issues in using voice assistants, as they must memorize specific commands and keywords. It explores solutions to overcome these barriers by automating command recall and pronunciation, using a speaker to send prompts, reminders, and commands to voice-enabled personal assistants. The authors suggest that solving these issues could also improve the user experience for the broader population, making voice assistants more accessible, comforting, and user-friendly.

Jakob et al. [10] examined the awareness, usage, and reservations of voice interfaces by elderly people in Germany. They found that two-thirds of respondents (69%) have data privacy concerns. To address these concerns and comply with the General Data Protection Regulation (GDPR) we decided to process all user-related data on the robot itself.

2.2 Technical Construction of Voice Interfaces

The computational resources of mobile robots are often limited as they rely on battery-powered mobile computing solutions. This restrains the amount of computation for algorithms, and neural networks, to analyze the user's input.

Earlier approaches for voice interfaces restricted the language processing to certain keywords or commands to improve the recognition accuracy with limited computational resources [17,18,22,24,29]. A popular design approach is to define an application domain-specific grammar to reduce the solution space for the voice interface [5]. While this approach improves recognition performance, it requires that the user is aware of the limitations.

To the best of our knowledge, there is no voice interface for robotic applications that works on unrestricted, natural every day language.

There are several voice assistants on the market such as Google Home, Apple's Siri or Amazon Alexa. Some robotic systems use Amazons Alexa as a voice interface [9]. This approach requires the user to learn Alexas' command invocation pattern. Further drawbacks of integrating an online voice assistant like Alexa comprise the dependence on a working internet connection, added network latencies and very limited abilities to modify Alexa's hard- and software for robotic applications.

The developed voice interface utilizes recent advancements in natural language processing, which are based on the transformer deep learning architecture [30]. The wave2vec 2.0 [4] speech recognition model allows for accurate transcription of speech in multiple languages [3].

However, the drawback is, that deep neural networks like wave2vec 2.0 are often computationally expensive. Peng et al. [21] showed, it is possible to improve the energy efficiency of this architecture, which makes it feasible to use these models on the robots' hardware.

Sentence-BERT [25] is a model that allows an efficient semantic similarity search. We use the multilingual version of the model [26] to infer the user's intention based on the semantics of the utterance.

Recent advancements in the field of large language models (LLMs), such as OpenAI's GPT-4 [19], hold significant potential for enhancing human-robot interaction. Recent work by Driess et al. [6] demonstrates promising results in applying LLMs to robotics, with text and visual inputs used to guide the robots' movements. The incorporation of a voice interface could further extend these capabilities, enabling robots to perform complex tasks based on users' spoken requests. As such, the combination of LLMs with voice interaction represents a promising research direction for future advancements in robotics.

3 Voice Interface

3.1 Design Goals

The first requirement is, that the voice interface must be able to process the German language, as our users speak German. This is a challenge as most state-of-the-art machine learning models for language processing are published for the English language. The second design goal is, that the user should be able to use the voice interface with spoken, everyday natural language. Therefore, a language processing model is needed, that allows the user to formulate statements within the languages' grammar rules and to use common synonyms. A simple approach to this problem would be to build a lookup table with all possible statements for a given command or action. However, this is not practical, as these lists can become very long for real-world scenarios. Since the voice interface is used in private spaces as well as medical environments, we need to comply with regulations, especially the GDPR. Therefore, we choose to process all information directly on the device, without sending the data to external third-party services. This approach has two other advantages. First, it reduces the time needed to create a response, since the system is not using network connections. Second, the robot does not need to have a permanent network connection, which can't be guaranteed all the time.

3.2 System Description

The studies discussed in the related work section have indicated an essential critique: users frequently find it necessary to rephrase their questions, or they feel misunderstood by the interface. This issue often arises due to inaccurate transcription of the user's request or the system's inability to correctly interpret the user's utterance.

We focused on enhancing the performance of the speech recognition and language processing modules. For all other modules, we adopted state-of-the-art methodologies to ensure optimal functionality.

An integral part of our strategy involved training an Automatic Speech Recognition (ASR) model specifically for the German language. We trained a new ASR model with the wav2vec 2.0 architecture. This model exceeded the performance of previous state-of-the-art speech recognition models for German [1]. It improved the Word Error Rate (WER) by 33%, dropping from 15% to 10%. The model is publicly available[1]. This decrease in WER also negates the necessity of restricting the voice interface to a specific domain grammar.

Current voice interface systems typically utilize a structure comprising a wake word, an app invocation, and a command. However, we decided against this schema for our work. In an effort to better recognize the user's intent, we opted for a deep learning-based neural search approach [25,26] using the complete utterance. This technique involves the comparison of a vector representation of the user's utterance with a reference database of vector representations. This method, rather than relying on specific keywords, examines the overall semantic content of the user's utterance to determine the most suitable response or action.

Figure 1 depicts the modules and the general structure of our voice interface. The utterances stated by the user are recorded with an omnidirectional microphone array. For all user tests, we used a far-field microphone[2]. This device has four built-in microphones and preprocesses the audio signal with Acoustic Echo Cancellation (AEC), dereverberation, and noise suppression. It provides an audio stream that is then used to perform Voice Activity Detection (VAD). This

---

[1] https://huggingface.co/oliverguhr/wav2vec2-large-xlsr-53-german-cv9.
[2] https://wiki.seeedstudio.com/ReSpeaker-USB-Mic-Array/.

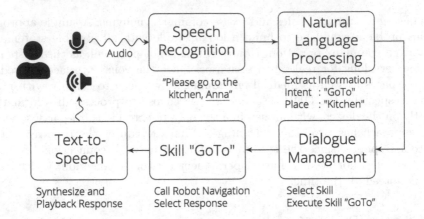

Fig. 1. Structural overview of the developed voice interface. The gray texts depict an example outcome of the module.

step is part of the speech recognition module and is needed to filter out sounds that are not spoken language. We trained a deep learning-based ASR model for the German language based on Wav2Vec 2.0 [3] architecture and the Common Voice data set [2]. The voice interface does not use a separate activation or hot word detection module. Instead, we choose to transcribe all utterances using the ASR. To detect that the user wants to interact with the system, we still use an activation word ("Anna"). However, we transcribe whole utterances and check if they contain the activation word. With this approach, the activation word does not have to be the first word of the utterance. This simplifies the usage of the system since, for example, both statements "Anna I need help." or "Please help me Anna." contain the activation word.

For the next step, the transcribed user utterance is processed by the Natural Language Processing (NLP) module. This module extracts semantic information from the text, like the intent (e.g. a certain command). To detect the intent of a user's utterance, we apply a neural search approach using Sentence Transformers [25,26]. Given the user's utterance, it compares it with a list of prototype utterances and ranks them. Since this model compares the neural representation of the text rather than the plain text, it is invariant in relation to the phrasing of the utterance. Along with the semantic label (the users intent), the plain text is then passed to the dialogue management module. Based on the intent, the module selects and executes the appropriate code to carry out the user's command. It also returns a semantic tag. With this tag, the response generation module selects a text from a response database. We choose to use predefined response texts compared to AI-generated responses, to eliminate the risk that a generative model creates unwanted or unappropriated statements.

The last important step is to create an audible response for the user. The Text-to-Speech Module (TTS) generates a waveform from a given text. We used Microsoft Azure TTS service for this publication. Since the system uses a finite set of statements, these statements can be converted into wave files and stored locally. With this approach, the system does not need a permanent internet connection, since all responses are played back from the local cache. This is also beneficial from a data privacy perspective. Finally, the waveform will be played back using the speakers.

To be able to process all information directly on the robot's hardware, the system needs to be energy efficient. Our robots are not equipped with GPUs, nor do they have the power budget to use a powerful desktop or server-grade GPU. We identified the ASR as the most power-consuming module in our system.

Using techniques as described in [21] we were able to improve the performance. The minimal configuration we successfully tested for the voice interface was an Intel 6200u (15W) notebook CPU with 8 GB RAM. The code for the voice interface was written in Python. We plan to release this code in a future publication.

4 Evaluation

The proposed voice interface was evaluated within an empirical user study. The aim of the user study was to find out whether the undertaken design decisions enable users to interact with the voice interface without having to remember specific commands.

4.1 Methods and Material

For this study, we used a within-subject design. For each condition (training and no training), the participants were asked to complete a set of 5 tasks using the voice interface. We developed two distinct task sets: one "Robotic" set consisting of 5 tasks related to robot control and one "AAL" set encompassing 5 tasks designed for the AAL laboratory setting. To minimize learning effects, we randomized both the order of conditions (whether training came for the first or second set) and the selection of the training set (either AAL or Robotic). The training component involved five example tasks, each accompanied by the appropriate command phrase. Participants underwent this training before attempting the task set. Before the main experiment, we asked participants to complete two "introductory" tasks to familiarize them with the voice interface's activation word, "Anna," which was required to initiate communication. After the test, each user was asked demographic questions as well as the UMUX-Lite [14] and Speech User Interface Service Quality (SUISQ) [13,23] questionnaires.

The evaluation is based on the following hypothesis. The error rates in both conditions (training, no training) do not differ (H_0). In this case, it can be inferred that the presented approach and underlying design decisions are effective. Otherwise, the error rates would be significantly higher in the sets where users did not receive training, indicating that users do not know how to formulate an utterance that solves the test (H_A).

We developed a user test software that guided the participants through the test procedure. The goal of this software was to make the tests repeatable and comparable, as well as to automatically log test telemetry data. The test setup consisted of a notebook and an external microphone, as described in Sect. 3.2. We tested one participant at a time in a single room, making sure that participants could not observe each other. All user tests were conducted in German.

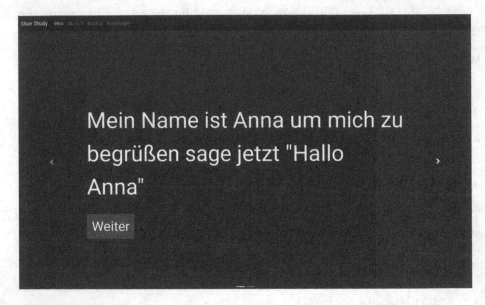

Fig. 2. User interface of the software for the automated user study. It displays a textual task description "My name is Anna, to greet me now say "Hello Anna".", as well as a button to skip the test. If the user solves the task successfully, the software automatically continues to the next task.

Each test started with an explanation of the test procedure. We explained that the participants should follow the instructions on the screen and that they need to use the activation word "Anna" in their utterances. If the voice interface did understand the user's command, the test software automatically showed the next task. Furthermore, we explained that the users are allowed to rephrase the command if the system did not understand them correctly. If a participant said that they could not solve the task, they could skip it using a button on the notebook's screen. Figure 2 shows the user interface of the test software. It consists of the task description and the skip button.

Each test started with two introductory tasks. We added these questions to make the user familiar with the test system. During this phase, we adjusted settings like loudness, screen brightness, and the font size of the task description to the user's needs.

The next step for the user was to solve the two sets of tasks. Each set consisted of five scenario descriptions and tasks. We formulated the tasks so that these could not easily be rephrased into a command. We based the task and scenarios on features that we plan to implement for our robotic and AAL applications. These are the translated task descriptions:

Introductory Tasks

1. My name is Anna, to greet me now say "Hello Anna".
2. I always answer you when you mention my name in the sentence. Ask me: "Anna, who developed you?"

Robotic Tasks

1. You want Anna to follow you into another room. Ask her to do this.
2. You want Anna to come closer so that you can operate her touch screen. Ask her to do this.
3. You are carrying a bulky box and find that Anna is in your way. Ask her to change that.
4. You want Anna to leave the room and go into the hallway. Ask her to do this.
5. You are standing in the foyer of a museum and want to get to the lift. Ask Anna to help you.

AAL Tasks

1. You are sitting in the living room and notice that it is too dark. Ask Anna to change it.
2. You have just woken up and want to open the blinds. Ask Anna to do that for you.
3. You are in the kitchen, and it is too cold. Ask Anna to change that.
4. You have gone to bed to sleep and notice that you have forgotten to turn off the radio in the kitchen. Ask Anna to do it for you.
5. You are sitting in an armchair that has a built-in stand-up aid, but you don't know how the device works. Ask Anna if she can help you.

For one task set, either the AAL or the robotic tasks, the participants underwent a training in the style of a tutorial. For each of the five tasks, they got an example command, that we asked the users to repeat. The participants had to solve all five tutorial tasks before we presented them with the five actual tasks. To avoid any learning effects, we randomly choose the order of two task sets as well as for which set the participant would undergo the training. The tutorial texts were shortened to avoid precisely matching the tasks.

Robotic Tutorial

1. If you want Anna to follow you, say: "Anna, please come with me".
2. If you want Anna to come to you, you can say, "Anna, please come to me."
3. If Anna is in your way, say "Anna, please get out of the way."
4. If you want Anna to go to another room, say "Anna, please go to the hallway."
5. Anna can take you to different rooms. Say: "Anna, take me to the lift."

AAL Tutorial

1. Anna can control the lights for you. Say: "Switch on the light for me, Anna."
2. Anna can control the blinds. Say: "Anna, open the blinds."
3. Anna can control the heating for you. Say: "Anna, switch on the heating."
4. Anna can also control your household appliances for you. Say: "Anna, turn off the radio."
5. You can have Anna explain the appliances in your home to you. Say: "How does the armchair work, Anna?"

After the participants completed the tutorial and the two task sets, we asked them to fill out a form with demographic questions and specific questionnaires to assess the usability of the developed voice interface. For the demographic information, we asked for the age in groups (0-20/21-40/41-60/61-80/over 80), gender, and if the person uses voice assistants regularly. Furthermore, we asked if the participant owns one of these devices: a smartphone, a voice assistant like Alexa, Google Home or Apple's HomePod or none of them.

We choose two different questionnaires, UMUX-Lite and Speech User Interface Service Quality (SUISQ-MR). UMUX-Lite is a short form of the Usability Metric for User Experience (UMUX) questionnaire. Using only two questions, this test can predict SUS scores accurately [13]. This allowed us to add a second test, which is more specialized for voice interfaces. The SUISQ [23] questionnaire was developed for Interactive Voice Response (IVR) systems, Lewis and Hardzinski [13] later optimized the test and developed a reduced version of this questionnaire, the SUISQ-MR.

4.2   Participants

A total of 47 participants took part in the user study. 57% of all participants were male and 43% female. Due to ethical and legal requirements, persons under the age of 18 were not considered to participate. Regarding the planned deployment of the voice interface, we asked people of working age or pensioners to take part in the user test. The age groups are distributed as follows: 43% of the participants were between 21 and 40, 40% between 41 and 60, and 17% between 61 and 80 years old. 43% of the participants stated that they regularly use voice assistants with a smartphone or dedicated device. Of all participants, 43 (91%) stated that they own a smartphone, 15 (32%) that they own a voice assistant, and 2 (4%) that they do not own a smartphone or voice assistant.

We aimed to recruit a diverse group of participants for this user test and ran this test at several public events like local conferences and meetups. We also scheduled tests with interested individuals and members of the faculty. The tests were carried out in office or meeting rooms, with only one participant present at a time.

During the tests, we observed that some users did not understand the tasks correctly. In these cases, we helped out with hints on how to interpret the task. Nevertheless, we counted these failed attempts as errors.

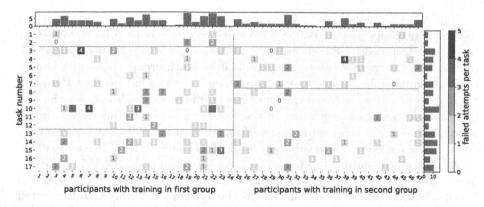

Fig. 3. This plot shows the number of errors per participant per task. The number within the box denotes the number of tracked errors. Red numbers indicated that the user skipped the task manually. The plot is divided into 6 regions. On the left side of the plot, up to participant 24, are all user tests that started with the user training in the first task group. On the right side are all user tests that had the user training in the second task group. The horizontal lines divide the plot into three groups. Equal introductory tasks for all 47 participants up to task 2. Participants that underwent the training in the first group solved 10 tasks, 5 training and 5 test for the first group, and 5 test tasks in the second group. Participants that underwent the training in the second group, started with 5 test tasks for group one and then solved the 10 tasks for group 2. (Color figure online)

4.3   Results

For the following analysis, we define an error as not a correctly recognized utterance. These errors could be caused by an incorrect transcription of the participants' utterance (ASR error), or an incorrect classification of the utterance (NLP error) e.g., the system confused "shut the blinds" with "turn off the lights". In addition, the participant may have misunderstood the task and therefore not have been able to solve it. In all cases, the participants could state a new utterance to solve the task. If a participant was unable to solve the task, they could skip it. We marked these tasks as failed tasks. If not stated otherwise, we report the statistics over the two task sets AAL and the robotic scenario.

Table 1. Contingency table, containing the number of topics in relation to the test order.

Topic	Training in		Total
	First Group	Second Group	
AAL	11	7	18
Robotic	13	16	29
Total	24	23	47

The 47 participants were given 17 tasks each. The 17 tasks that we presented to the participants consisted of an intro and two task groups. Two introductory tasks, five test tasks for each group, and 5 training tasks for one group. We randomized the topic for each group, as well as which group would additionally undergo training for the given topic, implemented as two independent Bernoulli trials (a coin toss with 50-50 chance). The contingency Table 1 shows the distribution of the topics in relation to the test order. Overall, this results in 799 attempted tasks. In total, participants skipped 38 of the 799 tasks because they could not solve them. We recorded a total of 917 interactions, as each participant could state multiple utterances to solve the given task. For 155 of the 917 interactions, the system did not produce the correct result. Please note that 155 is not the true number of all failures, as the system could only count detected utterances. If an utterance was not detected at all, it would not count as a failed interaction. Figure 3 shows that in 6 cases, the users skipped the task although zero failed interactions were recorded (marked as red zeros).

Can the Participants Use the Voice Interface Without Training? The main question we liked to answer with this user study was if people can use the voice interface without extensive training or specific command memorization. It is to be expected that not all the users' utterances will be correctly processed by the voice interface, but the users might be still able to achieve their goal by repeating or rephrasing their utterances. Therefore, we compared the number of succeeded tasks, with and without prior training to answer the question if the participants were able to solve the given task at all. Table 2 shows the number of failed and successful tasks, broken down by training.

Table 2. The number of failed (skipped by the user) and succeeded tasks in relation to prior training.

Task	Prior Training		Total
	Yes	No	
Failed	12	16	28
Success	223	219	442
Total	235	235	470

Each of the 47 participants attempted to solve five tasks with and five tasks without prior training. With prior training, the participants solved 223 out of 235 (95%) tasks successfully. Without training, they solved 219 out of 235 (93%) tasks successfully. In all cases, the user training leads to an improvement of 2% points. Using the chi-square test of independence and the values of Table 2, we calculated $\chi^2 = 0.5588$ and $p = 0.3418$. Since this p-value is not less than 0.05, we fail to reject the null hypothesis. This means we could not find a significant difference between the training and no training groups.

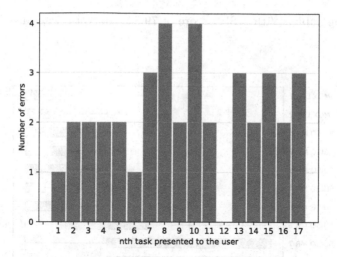

Fig. 4. This graph represents the number of tasks skipped by the participants in the sequence of tasks they were given.

Is There a Learning Effect over Time? We analyzed if there is a learning effect over time, where participants get better with every interaction. We suspected that participants quickly learn that they need to use the activation word in every sentence and adapt their use of language to be better understood. We expected that we see more skipped tests and failed interactions in the first question than at the end of the test. However, looking at the data in Figs. 3 and 4 this is not the case. The histogram for the y-axis in Fig. 3 shows an equal distribution of tracked errors per task over all 17 tasks of the user test.

Looking at the number of skipped tasks, Fig. 4 shows that there is no trend over time.

How Did the Participants Evaluate the Usability? We asked our participants to fill out two questionnaires. The general usability questionnaire UMUX-Lite and SUISQ MR, a questionnaire for measuring voice interaction experience. We translated the questions of both questionnaires to German.

UMUX-Lite
The participants rated the usefulness (UMUX-Lite question 1) with an average score of 6.4 of a 7 point Likert scale and the usability (UMUX-Lite question 2) with an average score of 6.1. We used a regression equation[3] [14] that estimates the SUS score based on the UMUX-Lite results with an accuracy of 99%. Using this equation, we calculated a SUS score of 79.84.

To help with the interpretation of the SUS scores Bangor et al. introduced a 7-point scale ranging from Worst Imaginable, Awful, Poor, OK, Good, Excellent

---

[3] $SUS\,score = 0.65 * ((mean\,usefullness + mean\,usability - 2) * (100/12)) + 22.9.$

to Best Imaginable. With a SUS score of 79.84, the voice interface is rated as "Good.".

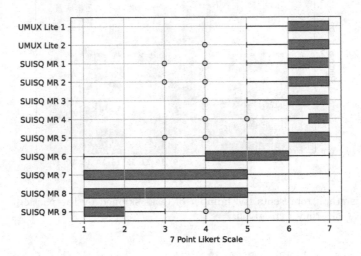

Fig. 5. The results of the UMUX-Lite and SUISQ MR questionnaires on a 7-point Likert scale.

SUISQ MR

The questions of the SUISQ MR questionnaire are grouped into four factors, "goal orientation" (questions 1–2), "customer service behavior" (questions 3–4), "speech characteristics" (questions 5–6) and "verbosity" (questions 7–9). Each factor has a score which is the average of the ratings. The average of the verbosity factor is reversed using this formula $v_r = 8 - v$. The overall score of the SUISQ MR is the average of the factor scores (Table 3).

Table 3. SUISQ MR factor scores and overall score, based on a 7-point Likert scale.

Factor	Score
Goal Orientation	6.2
Customer Service Behaviors	6.6
Speech Characteristics	5.6
Verbosity	5.3
Overall SUISQ MR	5.9

The participants rated the system with 5.9 out of 7 possible points. Figure 5 shows that for question 6 "The system's voice sounded enthusiastic or full of energy." the voice interface received the lowest rating of all questions with an average of 5.1. Many participants asked us how to interpret this question and if we wanted to know if the system "sounded overly enthusiastic". For further tests, we would advise adopting this question or providing additional explanations when using this questionnaire.

4.4   Discussion

When provided with an example command, the participants successfully completed 95% of the tasks. Without any explanation, their completion rate slightly decreased to 93% of the assigned tasks. Therefore, we assume that users do not require an extensive training, to successfully complete tasks using the voice interface.

As depicted in Fig. 3, errors were also occurred during the training phase, when users were merely reading out instructions. This suggests that they are independent of the user's level of training or familiarity with the system. Upon further investigation, we found that the root of this issue stems from incorrect transcription of the user's verbal instructions. These errors are independent of the training status of the users. Given these findings, we recommend prioritizing the rectification of these transcription errors in future development stages. This becomes particularly crucial as these errors have been found to affect all test cases, thereby impacting the overall performance and usability of our system.

Using the UMUX-Lite the participants evaluated the usefulness of the system with 6.4 of 7 possible points and the usability with 6.1 out of 7 points. The questionnaire SUISQ MR specialized for voice interfaces, resulted in an overall score of 5.9 out of 7 possible points.

The results of the usability evaluation are positive, but for this test setting, the participants commands had no effect as they solved tasks in imaginary scenarios. The next step would be to integrate the voice interface into planned scenarios and conduct end-to-end tests where the users control the robot or the appliances in the AAL laboratory apartment. Furthermore, we could introduce new challenges for the voice interface, like background noise and people talking in the background.

5   Limitations

The sample size of this work is limited and does only cover a small portion of the diverse nature of potential users. This also has implications for the validity and reliability of our significance tests. We used the Friedman test to analyze our data, and with 235 cases per group, we were able to detect a difference of approximately 7.5% points at a significance level of 95% and a power of 0.8 ([8] as per formula 7.236). This implies that there is a 20% probability for a Type II error, which means that we might not detect a difference of 2.5% points.

For further research, we can gain more detailed results with some improvements to the test software. Our tests with the first 47 participants showed that it would be beneficial if we could manually annotate the results of every task during the tests. Initially, we planned to automatically record every action of our participants during the test, to make them reproducible. But there are some cases that cannot be automatically tracked. If the voice interface did not recognize the participant's utterance at all, the person observing the test should be able to manually add a "failed detection" note for that task. Furthermore, we should manually annotate if the user did understand the task correctly and therefore tried to solve the right task.

For this work, we exclusively collected quantitative data. Future studies should gather qualitative feedback as well, to provide more detailed insides and user feedback.

The potential barriers to user adoption primarily revolve around language restrictions. At present, the system is tailored specifically for German-speaking users, thereby limiting its accessibility to a broader, multilingual audience. While the system theoretically has the capacity to support other languages, these features have not yet been implemented. A key recommendation for future studies is to focus on extending system capabilities to non-native speakers. This would involve evaluation and subsequent adjustment of the system to accommodate the language diversity of potential users, as the current mono-lingual limitation poses a barrier to widespread adoption.

6   Conclusion

In this work, we evaluated a German-language voice interface for socially assistive robots. As these robots will be used in public spaces, they need to be able to understand natural everyday language without requiring people to learn specific commands or sentence patterns. Currently, there is no voice interface available that meets these requirements. To achieve this goal, we used state-of-the-art deep learning models for voice recognition and natural language understanding. We developed a user test software to evaluate the usability of the system. The test consisted of a series of tasks that the participants were asked to complete using the voice interface. The test was designed to measure the success rate of the participants.

The results of the study show that the developed speech interface can be used without learning commands or sentence patterns with good usability. Even if the participants received no explanation how to solve the tasks, they were able to do so for 93% of all given tasks. Introducing an additional user training, improved the task completion rate by 2 p.p. to 95%. Overall, the participants rated the system with good usability.

Our study shows that it is possible to create a voice interface for the German language that is usable without requiring the users to learn or know specific commands. The automated user test we developed was able to effectively evaluate the usability of the system. However, in future work, we would like to improve the automated evaluation software to obtain fine-grained error statistics. Furthermore, we like to conduct long-term studies to gather more information on the usability of the system in different scenarios.

Acknowledgments. We like to thank Prof. Anja Voß-Böhme for her support with the statistical evaluation of the data. Furthermore, we thank Frank Bahrmann, Stefan Vogt, Mathias Klingner and Marvin Matthes for their ideas and feedback.

References

1. Agarwal, A., Zesch, T.: German end-to-end speech recognition based on Deep-Speech (2019). https://www.semanticscholar.org/paper/German-End-to-end-Spee ch-Recognition-based-on-Agarwal-Zesch/06d32982297d1f46909a26c794941b1e05a f1f1c

2. Ardila, R., et al.: Common voice: a massively-multilingual speech corpus. arXiv:1912.06670 [cs], March 2020

3. Babu, A., et al.: XLS-R: Self-supervised cross-lingual speech representation learning at scale. arXiv:2111.09296 [cs, eess], December 2021. https://doi.org/10.48550/arXiv.2111.09296

4. Baevski, A., et al.: wav2vec 2.0: a framework for self-supervised learning of speech representations. arXiv:2006.11477 [cs, eess], October 2020

5. Bastianelli, E., et al.: Speaky for robots: the development of vocal interfaces for robotic applications. Appl. Intell. **44**(1), 43–66 (2016). ISSN: 0924-669X, 1573-7497. https://doi.org/10.1007/s10489-015-0695-5. http://link.springer.com/10.1007/s10489-015-0695-5

6. Driess, D., et al. PaLM-E: an embodied multimodal language model. arXiv:2303.03378 [cs], March 2023. https://doi.org/10.48550/arXiv.2303.03378

7. Flake, R., et al.: IW-Trends 3/2018 Fachkräfteengpass in der Altenpflege. German. Technical report, 45. IW Köln, March 2018. https://www.iwkoeln.de/fileadmin/user_upload/Studien/IW-Trends/PDF/2018/IW-Trends_2018-03-02_Pflegefallzahlen.pdf

8. Hedderich, J., Sachs, L.: Angewandte Statistik. Springer, Heidelberg (2016). https://doi.org/10.1007/978-3-662-45691-0. http://link.springer.com/10.1007/978-3-662-45691-0. ISBN: 978-3-662-45690-3 978-3-662-45691-0

9. Hidalgo-Paniagua, A., Millan-Alcaide, A., Bandera, J.P., Bandera, A.: Integration of the Alexa assistant as a voice interface for robotics platforms. In: Silva, M.F., Luís Lima, J., Reis, L.P., Sanfeliu, A., Tardioli, D. (eds.) ROBOT 2019. AISC, vol. 1093, pp. 575–586. Springer, Cham (2020). https://doi.org/10.1007/978-3-030-36150-1_47. ISBN: 978-3-662-45690-3 978-3-662-45691-0

10. Jakob, D., Wilhelm, S., Gerl, A., Ahrens, D.: A quantitative study on awareness, usage and reservations of voice control interfaces by elderly people. In: Stephanidis, C., et al. (eds.) HCII 2021. LNCS, vol. 13096, pp. 237–257. Springer, Cham (2021). https://doi.org/10.1007/978-3-030-90328-2_15. ISBN: 978-3-030-90328-2

11. Kobayashi, M., et al.: Effects of age-related cognitive decline on elderly user interactions with voice-based dialogue systems. In: Lamas, D., Loizides, F., Nacke, L., Petrie, H., Winckler, M., Zaphiris, P. (eds.) INTERACT 2019. LNCS, vol. 11749, pp. 53–74. Springer, Cham (2019). https://doi.org/10.1007/978-3-030-29390-1_4. ISBN: 978-3-030-29389-5 978-3-030-29390-1

12. Kowalski, J., et al.: Older adults and voice interaction: a pilot study with Google home. In: Extended Abstracts of the 2019 CHI Conference on Human Factors in Computing Systems. CHI EA 2019, pp. 1–6. Association for Computing Machinery, New York, NY, USA, May 2019. https://doi.org/10.1145/3290607.3312973. ISBN: 978-1-4503-5971-9

13. Lewis, J.R., Hardzinski, M.L.: Investigating the psychometric properties of the speech user interface service quality questionnaire. Int. J. Speech Technol. **18**(3), 479–487 (2015). https://doi.org/10.1007/s10772-015-9289-1. ISSN: 1572-8110

14. Lewis, J.R., Utesch, B.S., Maher, D.E.: Investigating the correspondence between UMUX-LITE and SUS scores. In: Marcus, A. (ed.) DUXU 2015. LNCS, vol. 9186, pp. 204–211. Springer, Cham (2015). https://doi.org/10.1007/978-3-319-20886-2_20. ISBN: 978-3-319-20886-2

15. Lewis, J.R., Utesch, B.S., Maher, D.E.: UMUX-LITE: when there's no time for the SUS. In: Proceedings of the SIGCHI Conference on Human Factors in Computing Systems, pp. 2099–2102. ACM, Paris, France, April 2013. https://doi.org/10.1145/2470654.2481287. https://dl.acm.org/doi/10.1145/2470654.2481287. ISBN: 978-1-4503-1899-0

16. Loitsch, C.: Designing accessible user interfaces for all by means of adaptive systems. Ph.D. thesis. Dresden University of Technology, Germany (2018). https://nbn-resolving.org/urn:nbn:de:bsz:14-qucosa2-319846

17. Müller, S.: Realisierung nutzeradaptiven Interaktionsverhaltens für mobile Assistenzroboter. Ph.D. thesis. Ilmenau, October 2016. https://www.db-thueringen.de/receive/dbt_mods_00030393

18. Norberto Pires, J.: Robot-by-voice: experiments on commanding an industrial robot using the human voice. Ind. Rob. Int. J. **32**(6), 505–511 (2005). https://doi.org/10.1108/01439910510629244. ISSN: 0143-991X

19. OpenAI. GPT-4 Technical Report. arXiv:2303.08774 [cs], March 2023. https://doi.org/10.48550/arXiv.2303.08774

20. Papachristos, E., Meldgaard, D.P., Thomsen, I.R., Skov, M.B.: ReflectPal: exploring self-reflection on collaborative activities using voice assistants. In: Ardito, C., et al. (eds.) INTERACT 2021. LNCS, vol. 12935, pp. 187–208. Springer, Cham (2021). https://doi.org/10.1007/978-3-030-85610-6_12. https://link.springer.com/10.1007/978-3-030-85610-6_12. ISBN: 978-3-030-85609-0 978-3-030-85610-6

21. Peng, Z., et al.: Shrinking bigfoot: reducing wav2vec 2.0 footprint. In: SUSTAINLP (2021). https://doi.org/10.18653/v1/2021.sustainlp-1.14

22. Poirier, S., Routhier, F., Campeau-Lecours, A.: Voice control interface prototype for assistive robots for people living with upper limb disabilities. In: 2019 IEEE 16th International Conference on Rehabilitation Robotics (ICORR), Toronto, ON, Canada, pp. 46–52. IEEE, June 2019. https://doi.org/10.1109/ICORR.2019.8779524. https://ieeexplore.ieee.org/document/8779524/. ISBN: 978-1-72812-755-2

23. Polkosky, M.: Toward a social-cognitive psychology of speech technology: affective responses to speech-based e-service, February 2005

24. Prodanov, P.J., et al.: Voice enabled interface for interactive tour-guide robots. In: IEEE/RSJ International Conference on Intelligent Robots and System, Lausanne, Switzerland, vol. 2, pp. 1332–1337. IEEE (2002). https://doi.org/10.1109/IRDS.2002.1043939. http://ieeexplore.ieee.org/document/1043939/. ISBN: 978-0-7803-7398-3

25. Reimers, N., Gurevych, I.: Making monolingual sentence embeddings multilingual using knowledge distillation. In: Proceedings of the 2020 Conference on Empirical Methods in Natural Language Processing. Association for Computational Linguistics, November 2020. https://arxiv.org/abs/2004.09813

26. Reimers, N., Gurevych, I.: Sentence-BERT: sentence embeddings using Siamese BERT-networks. In: Proceedings of the 2019 Conference on Empirical Methods in Natural Language Processing. Association for Computational Linguistics, November 2019. https://arxiv.org/abs/1908.10084

27. Salai, A.-M., Cook, G., Holmquist, L.E.: IntraVox: a personalized human voice to support users with complex needs in smart homes. In: Ardito, C., et al. (eds.) INTERACT 2021. LNCS, vol. 12932, pp. 223–244. Springer, Cham (2021). https://doi.org/10.1007/978-3-030-85623-6_15. ISBN: 978-3-030-85623-6

28. Sin, J., et al.: Does Alexa live up to the hype? Contrasting expectations from mass media narratives and older adults' hands-on experiences of voice interfaces. In: 4th Conference on Conversational User Interfaces, Glasgow, United Kingdom, pp. 1–9. ACM, July 2022. https://doi.org/10.1145/3543829.3543841. https://dl.acm.org/doi/10.1145/3543829.3543841. ISBN: 978-1-4503-9739-1

29. Stiefelhagen, R., et al.: Enabling multimodal human-robot interaction for the karlsruhe humanoid robot. IEEE Trans. Rob. **23**(5), 840–851 (2007). https://doi.org/10.1109/TRO.2007.907484. http://ieeexplore.ieee.org/document/4339550/. ISSN: 1552-3098, 1941-0468

30. Vaswani, A., et al.: Attention is all you need. arXiv:1706.03762 [cs], December 2017. arXiv: 1706.03762

31. Wolters, M., et al.: Being old doesn't mean acting old: how older users interact with spoken dialog systems. ACM Trans. Accessible Comput. **2**(1), 1–39 (2009). https://doi.org/10.1145/1525840.1525842. https://dl.acm.org/doi/10.1145/1525840.1525842. ISSN: 1936-7228, 1936-7236

Enhancing User Experience: Designing Intuitive Interfaces for Sumo Robot Operations

Grant Emmanuel Magbilang, Kirsten Lynx Valenzuela, Samantha Isabel Roxas[✉],
and Yung-Hao Wong

Department of Mechanical Engineering, Minghsin University of Science and Technology,
Hsinchu 30401, Taiwan

samanthaisabelgroxas0@gmail.com, yvonwong@must.edu.tw

Abstract. Because the future aspect of technology was never certain, people have discovered the vast potential of robotics to provide solutions to various problems. Science and Engineering became a significant part of our technological sector. Robotics is our society's inevitable future. According to recent studies, Robots are already being employed to select and pack our internet orders, hoover our houses and help physicians perform life-saving surgeries. It has the potential to considerably increase human skills in the future decades, delivering better, more personalized care; cheaper, cleaner, and more efficient transportation; and handling monotonous, repetitive, and unpleasant activities in unorganized settings such as our cities, homes, and hospitals.

Robotics has advanced swiftly, influencing a vast range of sectors and uses, from industry to healthcare and entertainment. Sumo robots are meant to out-maneuver rivals and push them out of a ring or arena, necessitating a symbiotic interaction between human controllers and robot hardware and software. It is particularly created for fighting tournaments, filling a distinct niche in this industry. As the field progresses, the concept of ease-of-use and natural operation is acquiring prominence, perhaps informing larger innovations in the field outside specialized robotics contests. The purpose of the study is to explain the essential topic of improving user experience by designing and using user-friendly materials and interfaces for sumo robot operation.

According to big technological companies, study shows that the search for optimizing user experience (UX) has emerged as a fundamental subject in the ever-changing environment of robotics, as interactions between humans and robots continue to change businesses and domains. In this perspective, the Sumo Robots domain, which is built for competitive fighting scenarios, provides a unique and demanding environment for investigating the synergy between human purpose and robot action. Since, user experience is critical to the successful implementation of robotic systems. It is vital and important to provide intuitive interfaces that allow users to handle sumo robots easily, particularly in the setting involving competitive sumo technology. The ease of use and accurate control platforms can have a big impact on sumo robot efficiency and performance.

Realizing the full potential of robotics is a huge problem since it needs building and designing robots with strong physical robustness and agility to adapt to people and to unpredictable or rapidly changing conditions. Collaboration across diverse scientific fields and industry, as well as public discourse about the roles robots should play in our lives, will be required.

H. Degen and S. Ntoa (Eds.): HCII 2024, LNAI 14736, pp. 250–261, 2024.
https://doi.org/10.1007/978-3-031-60615-1_16

As we continue to study the robot's interface, we emphasize rapid design and evaluation as one of the essential components in building on recognised human-computer interaction (HCI) concepts to create user-friendly interfaces that shorten the educational process for inexperienced users. The inquiry goes on to look at the effects of these intuitive interfaces on overall viability and tactics in Sumo Robot tournaments.

One of the main driving forces for this study is the awareness of how simple controls may bridge the gap between human operators' desire and the task performed by the automated device. With the application of technology for machine vision that enables immediate detection of the venue, opponent, and Sumo Robot location. These devices improve contextual awareness while also providing essential data for decision-making in high-speed, complex combat circumstances.

However, Sumo Robot user interfaces are more than simply buttons and displays. Technology is being used to program and create these robots. Automated vision technologies improve contextual awareness by providing real-time venue and competitor recognition. With the help of modern technology, these robots are equipped with sensor fusion, which combines data from many internal sensors to aid with obstacle identification, navigation, and collision avoidance. This allows Sumo Robots to adapt quickly to changing combat conditions.

Modern AI systems on the other hand also provide dynamic path strategy and execution adaption. Sumo Robots are capable of analyzing opponent behavior and adapting strategy on the fly. These intelligent algorithms were implemented to improve not just the efficiency of robot movement but also their ability to make decisions, reducing consumption of energy while boosting productivity.

Creating an intuitive interface is not a one time process. It is an ongoing journey which requires a lot of time and dedication. It is all about applying the principles of human-computer interaction rather than creating a design and expecting the best result.it needs a great case study. User-feedbacks and thorough testing will help align the interface. Its development will base on how the users practice and test the components. This approach can ensure the development and improvement of the machine.

The influence of user-friendly interfaces extends beyond the controls. It completely changes the game. Sumo Robots can adjust to the fluctuating conditions of battle because of immediate decision-making characteristics afforded by improved interfaces. They have the ability to analyze opponent behavior, change plans on the fly, and outmaneuver opponents with pinpoint accuracy. Sophisticated intelligence interfaces alter the basic structure of Sumo Robot contests, emphasizing the journey and process of utilizing and battling with these machines rather than just focusing on the conclusion.

Sumo Robots is not alone in its quest to improve the experience of users through simple layouts. It emphasizes the beginning of evolution of human-technology interaction. As technology plays a huge role in our life, the lessons learnt in creating these interfaces have far-reaching implications. The development of intuitive interfaces, in accordance with modern technology, helps contribute not only to Sumo Robots' innovation, but also to the larger debate on human-robot interaction. People can improve the symbiotic relationship between humans and machines by designing intuitive interfaces, paving the path for a future in which our collaboration with modern technology is smooth, productive, and beneficial.

Keywords: Sumo robot · Human Technology interaction · Modern AI system · fighting tournaments · human-robot interaction · Sophisticated Intelligence · user friendly

1 Introduction

Since the future aspect of technology was never certain, people have discovered the vast potential of robotics to provide solutions to various problems. Science and Engineering became a significant part of our technological sector. And robotics is our society's inevitable future. As stated in the history, industrial robotics are likely traced back to the post-World War II era, when nations focused on economic reconstruction and the goal of higher production. George Devol, an American inventor, made a significant contribution to the field of programmable automation in the early 1950s. This breakthrough manifested itself in the Unimate, which is regarded as the first industrial robot ever built. The Unimate, a robotic arm used for activities including spot welding and die casting, developed in partnership with Joseph Engelberger, first appeared on the General Motors assembly line in 1961, representing an unexpected departure from traditional manual labor procedures.

Robotics has advanced swiftly, influencing a vast range of sectors and uses, from industry to healthcare and entertainment. Sumo robots are meant to outmaneuver rivals and push them out of a ring or arena, necessitating a symbiotic interaction between human controllers and robot hardware and software. According to recent studies, Sumo Robot, like its human counterpart, was established and thrives in Japan. Dr. Mato Hattori was the one who brought it to the United States in the early 1990s. One of the early American adopters of the sumo robot. It is particularly created for the purpose of fighting tournaments, filling a distinct niche in this industry. In its first appearance, it was built with lightweight materials which has an exact dimensions of 20 by 20 cm and has a reduced weight of 3 kg to 1 kg. The researcher's first intention was to create and produce a working sumo bot using such lightweight components.

But as we step into the 21st century, the progression of industrial robotics persists through the incorporation of artificial intelligence, machine learning, and collaborative robotics. The focus is transitioning towards the development of robotic systems that are not only intelligent but also adaptable, facilitating seamless collaboration with human operators. Enhancing the user-experience is one of the goals that needs to be done heading into the future. As the society continues to study the robot's operation and interface, it features an interactive educational and recreational tool for the society. Many employed in STEM education use these robots to elevate programming and engineering skills, offering students hands-on learning opportunities. The excitement of Sumo robot competitions, featuring small robots engaging in simulated wrestling bouts, not only fosters engagement but also showcases participants' skills. Beyond the realm of education, Sumo robots foster community building, cultivating a lively hobbyist community that exchanges knowledge and experiences. This innovative approach propels technological progress, motivating participants to delve into areas such as artificial intelligence and sensor technology. These projects serve as the significant milestone in the development and commercialization of Sumo Bot and helped to pave the way for the widespread adoption of Sumo Bot in Manufacturing, Enhancing User's Experience, Designing its Interface and Operations. Sumo robots contribute significantly to making robotics accessible, enjoyable, and integral to skill development across a diverse range of age groups and backgrounds.

As we continue to study and explore the field of robotics, the utilization of industrial robots has consistently risen in recent years due to technological progress, attaining greater sophistication and adaptability. Presently, a multitude of industries leverages industrial robots, integrating them with advanced technologies such as artificial intelligence (AI) and the Internet of Things (IoT). A 2022 statistical analysis by McCain reveals that approximately 2.7 million industrial robots are presently in operation globally, with 88% of companies expressing intentions to invest in robotics for their specific needs. In 2006, Microsoft Inc. and Micro Framework hosted the Sumo-Robot Competition in Las Vegas to launch their new software. Things started out slowly for the Sumo Robot but eventually it got in demand because of the Basic Stamp Microcontrollers. Eventually huge companies such as Parallax Inc. became one of the biggest sponsors for their competition. Through various influences other companies such as Microsoft and First also took part in its events which recently made its presence felt in the Robotics Field (Fig. 1).

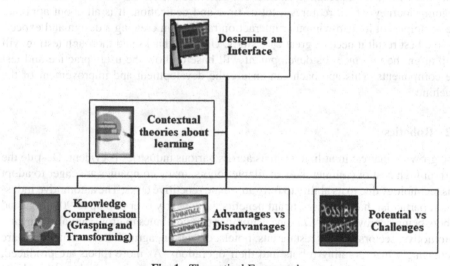

Fig. 1. Theoretical Framework

In 2022 Mccain revealed the sudden boost of industrial robots globally. With this an idea was concluded. Since, one of the main driving forces for this study is the awareness of how simple controls may bridge the gap between human operators' desire and the task performed by the automated device. With the application of technology Designing Intuitive Interfaces for Sumo Robot Operations that enables immediate detection of the

venue, opponent, and Sumo Robot location. These Devices improve contextual awareness while also providing essential data for decision-making in high-speed, complex
combat circumstances.

With this, the researchers chose the topic "Enhancing User Experience: Designing
Intuitive Interfaces for Sumo Robot Operations" not just to report about the participation
in this year's Top International Robotics Tournament (TIRT) Sumo Robot Challenge,
but also to be able to gather, comprehend and present up to date and factual informations
regarding the modern day innovations and technologies that are applicable in enhancing
the user experience especially in designing the interface for sumo robot operations.

1.1 Intuitive Interface

Numerous studies have emphasized the value of intuitive interfaces in improving user
experience. Nielsen's concepts emphasize user control and consistency while attempting
to lessen cognitive difficulty. Norman's approach emphasizes the importance of intuitive
design in boosting usability. Norman and Draper (1986) found that intuitive interfaces
reduce cognitive stress and improve task performance. Lee and Koubek (2010) discovered that such interfaces improve user satisfaction and efficiency. These studies highlight
the importance of intuitive interfaces in increasing usability and user experience. But
it should be noted that creating an intuitive interface is not a one time process. It is an
ongoing journey which requires a lot of time and dedication. It is all about applying
the principles of human-computer interaction rather than creating a design and expecting the best result.it needs a great case study. User-feedbacks and thorough testing will
help align the interface. Its development will base on how the users practice and test
the components. This approach can ensure the development and improvement of the
machine.

1.2 Robotics

The growing interest in utilizing robots across various industries is evident. Despite the
current high cost of commercially available robots, many companies are eager to adopt
this technology due to its ability to fully automate repetitive tasks. The automotive industry, in particular, has seen significant benefits, with nearly over 800 up to 900 thousand
robots being deployed in 2017 alone, a number that continues to grow annually. Beyond
automotive, sectors such as restaurants, hotels, education, agriculture, and medicine are
increasingly incorporating robots into their operations. As more robots are produced,
advancements in technology and manufacturing processes are expected to drive down
initial investment costs. Consequently, the robotics industry is projected to experience
substantial growth, with a Compound Annual Growth Rate (CAGR) of 11.7% that is
expected from the year 2021 until 2030.

1.3 Sumo Robots

Sumo robots, autonomous machines designed for sumo wrestling events, received
widespread attention in academic and enthusiast circles due to their unique design and

competitive nature. This domain's research covers a wide range of topics, including robot design, control algorithms, and competitive tactics. A key focus is on robot building, with an emphasis on creating strong and compact robots capable of withstanding the physical demands of sumo wrestling. Tanaka et al. (2003) investigated the complexities of designing small-scale sumo robots, emphasizing the importance of a low center of gravity and high traction for increased stability and maneuverability.

Moreover, much emphasis is paid to competitive techniques that try to improve a sumo robot's chances of victory. Kimura et al. (2010) suggested a machine learning-based approach for dynamically adapting the robot's behavior during matches, hence increasing its competitiveness against a variety of opponents. Furthermore, sumo robot tournaments are recognised in educational contexts for their contribution to STEM education. Barakova et al. (2017) explored the use of sumo robot tournaments in educational programmes, emphasizing their usefulness in developing students' interest and competency in robotics and programming (Fig. 2).

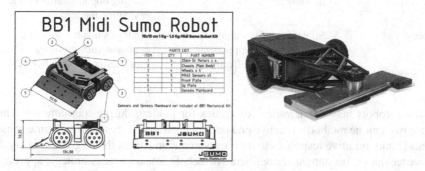

Fig. 2. Sumo Robot with parts

Aside from Sumo Robots, there are additional autonomous robotic systems appropriate for business and educational situations. Sumo Robots, designed for competitive sumo wrestling, have tiny yet robust designs focused at forcing opponents out of the ring. Battlebots, on the other hand, are designed for direct fight, equipped with a variety of offensive and defensive devices to incapacitate enemy robots in a dangerous and barrier-filled arena. While Sumo Robots and Battlebots compete, their aims, designs, and strategic tactics differ significantly. Tanaka et al. (2003) examined the intricacies of designing small-scale Sumo Robots, emphasizing features such as a low center of gravity and high traction to improve stability and maneuverability. Similarly, Oliveira et al. (2016) have explored control strategies for Battlebots, examining reactive and deliberative methods to enhance the robots' capacity to detect and respond to opponents' actions adeptly. To further understand their capabilities, attached is a table for the explanation of both robots (Table 1).

Table 1. Comparison of Sumo Robots and Battlebots

ASPECT	SUMO ROBOTS	BATTLEBOTS
Objective	Push opponents out of the ring or arena	Disable or immobilize opponent robots
Competition Format	Matches usually occur in a circular ring	Matches commonly take place in an arena with obstacles and dangers
Design	Designed to be compact and robust to endure impacts	Built with strong materials to withstand direct combat
Control Strategy	Typically employ reactive control algorithms	May use a combination of reactive and strategic control methods
Mobility	Emphasize agility and swift movements	Maneuverability is key for dodging opponent attacks and navigating the arena
Strategy	Strategy revolves around outmaneuvering opponents and utilizing weight effectively	Strategies involve targeting opponent vulnerabilities and capitalizing on arena hazards

Sumo Robots may use a variety of tactics for guiding during tournaments. They can use two unique methods: reactive and deliberate. Sumo Robots use real-time sensor data and rapid, intuitive responses to their opponents' moves in the ring while using the reactive technique. In contrast, the deliberative technique takes a more strategic approach, with Sumo Robots analyzing previous match data and devising premeditated maneuvers to outmaneuver their opponents. While both strategies have merits and disadvantages, Tanaka et al. (2003) emphasize the significance of combining reactionary reflexes with conscious strategic planning to reach peak performance in Sumo Robot tournaments.

1.4 Designing Intuitive Interfaces for Sumo Robot Operations

Designing intuitive interfaces for Sumo Robot operations is critical for improving user experience and performance in competitive environments. Tanaka et al. (2003) emphasize the importance of intuitive design concepts in creating Sumo Robots that are easy to handle and maneuver in the ring. These concepts include maintaining a stable low center of gravity and providing adequate traction for movement. Furthermore, Oliveira et al. (2016) emphasize the need of user-friendly control interfaces that allow for quick responses to opponents' activities during matches. They advocate for simple controls and good visual feedback to provide a smooth engagement with the Sumo Robot.

Furthermore, Mehami, Nawi, and Zhong (Year) investigate the function of intuitive guiding interfaces in Sumo Robots, namely in navigation inside the tournament arena. They investigate several guiding strategies, such as fixed and free paths, and their effects on robot maneuverability and performance. The study emphasizes the need of intuitive navigation systems that are simple to maintain and deliver exact positional information to operators.

In addition, Li (2022) highlights the need of intuitive interfaces in Sumo Robots' autonomous operation, with an emphasis on integrating sensors and visual feedback mechanisms to promote efficient perception and comprehension of the surroundings. The study emphasizes the need of simple interfaces that allow operators to monitor the robot's status and automatically alter its behavior during matches.

2 Methodology

The methodological framework used in the study involves a combination of case studies and experimental research. The researchers conducted a thorough review of related literature on robotics, with a specific focus on sumo robots. Additionally, an in-depth analysis of user interfaces was undertaken to discern areas amenable for improvement. As for being experimental research, the researchers tested an existing sumo robot to varied programming configurations. The process entailed the implementation of intuitive interfaces tailored to optimize sumo robot functionalities. Subsequent to the execution phase, user testing protocols were employed, with iterative refinement of interface designs facilitated by user feedback gathered.

The study design integrates both qualitative and quantitative approaches. The qualitative methods include interviews or surveys with robotics experts, sumo robot enthusiasts, and potential users to gather insights into user needs and preferences. Quantitative methods involve the collection and analysis of data related to the performance of different sumo robot interfaces, such as speed, accuracy, and user satisfaction. Both were conducted during sumo robot competition where the researchers joined and observed other participants. The empirical investigations, considering both qualitative and quantitative modalities, were executed within the occurrence of a sumo robot competition, The 2023 Top International Robotic Tournament (TIRT) in Taoyuan Arena, wherein the researchers actively participated, availing themselves of opportunities to observe other participants and collect data.

An assortment of materials and instruments were used to facilitate comprehensive data collection and analysis, comprising a variety of tools and technologies that were each strategically selected to meet distinct investigation objectives. The researchers' initial and main focus revolved around the sumo robots, which served as the foundation for evaluating various interface designs and deriving indicators of performance. Moreover, sensor distribution emerged as substantial, allowing for precise data collection across vital parameters such as velocity, precision, and user satisfaction. In addition to these technological assets, advanced user interface design software enabled the conceptualization and construction of numerous contact iterations designed to maximize sumo robot operational efficiency. Methodologically reliable instruments, featuring surveys and questionnaires, were employed to obtain qualitative data from participants, indicating broad preferences and needs. Furthermore, interviews with acclaimed robotics experts, enthusiastic sumo robot consumers, and potential audience members served as channels for comprehensive research, yielding significant insights into user experiences and graphical user interface demands. In its entirety, the prudent utilization of these materials and instruments outlined the research conduct, resulting in the systematic evaluation of sumo robot interface performance and user experience, alongside the identification of prospects for continuous enhancement.

The subjects and participants of the study on "Enhancing User Experience: Designing Intuitive Interfaces for Sumo Robot Operations" include a diverse range of individuals and groups which encompass robotics experts and researchers, sumo robot enthusiasts and hobbyists, potential end users of sumo robots spanning students, educators, and individuals interested in robotics competitions, as well as engineers and designers specializing in the inception and refinement of robotic interfaces and control mechanisms. The deliberate inclusion of such a diverse assemblage of subjects and participants serves as a strategic endeavor to glean multifaceted insights of user experiences and interface design pertinent to sumo robots. Leveraging their collective reservoir of knowledge, experience, and vested interest in the development and operation of sumo robots, these participants and subjects furnish the researchers with a comprehensive union of perspectives, thereby enriches the process of inquiry, and offers a more detailed articulation of requisite design enhancements.

Participants were asked for consent after being selected by means of the aforementioned approach and also educated about the study's purpose, data collection methods, and how the information will be used. The researchers constructed surveys and questionnaires to obtain quantitative and qualitative data concerning user preferences, desires, and experiences with sumo robot engagements. These instruments were given out in person to accommodate participants' convenience. In addition, the researchers carried out nonstandard interviews with selected respondents to acquire profound insights into their experiences, troubles and recommendations for enhancing sumo robots. As stated, the researchers observed the sumo robot's functionality and response during combat, particularly the amount of time it takes to respond, evade, and attack the opponent. The observation concentrated additionally on the extent to which a sumo robot is capable of fighting in accordance with the way it is programmed, or built.

To analyze the acquired data, a variety of statistical methods and analytical techniques were used. Thematic and comparative analyses were applied to qualitative data, while quantitative data underwent descriptive statistical analysis. This diverse methodological approach was chosen to ensure the validation of interpretations derived from both qualitative and quantitative methodologies. Furthermore, due to multiple perspectives, the researchers also integrated mixed-method analysis into their analytical framework.

Thematic and comparative analyses have been utilized collectively to identify and analyze patterns in qualitative data, particularly interview transcripts and observational data. After identifying and interpreting the recurring patterns and underlying themes, the results are compared with the information from other data sources. The data gathered through surveys, interviews, and observations are then compared to the conclusions from case study reviews. For quantitative data, descriptive statistics get used to summarize and describe the information collected, involving participant demographics and responses to scale questions. Aside from demographics, the sumo robot's characteristics are considered, especially its response time and endurance. Means, medians, modes, and standard deviations are instruments employed to convey an overview of the findings from the survey. Lastly, mixed-methods analysis incorporates quantitative and qualitative data to generate a fuller understanding of the subject of the investigation. The process includes comparing, contrasting, and combining results from different types of data to formulate new insights and hypotheses.

3 Result

3.1 Sumo Robot Performance

The robot's capacity for making strategic decisions was greatly influenced by the machine learning and artificial intelligence (AI) algorithms that were put into place. It demonstrated the capacity to instantly assess the movements of the opposition, modify its plan as necessary, and carry out precisely the right moves, all of which helped it achieve a high success rate in the matches. The easy-to-use interfaces created specifically for Sumo robot functions were crucial to improving overall performance. With instantaneous and precise recognition of the opponent, the location of the robot, and the venue, operators reported a flawless experience operating the robot. The operator's situational awareness was much enhanced by this real-time feedback, which helped the robot succeed in the task.

3.2 User Feedback

Operator satisfaction with the Sumo robot's performance was consistently high. The quickness and user-friendliness of the intuitive interfaces created for Sumo robot operations were praised. Operators of all skill levels reported an easy transition to operating the robot, demonstrating the value of the user-centric design methodology. Users praised the interface's clarity in presenting information, which facilitated prompt and accurate decision-making. This was especially important when there was fierce competition and split seconds could mean the difference between winning and losing a match. A number of operators requested more features, like overlays for augmented reality that showed opponent statistics or predictive algorithms that suggested possible plays. These feature requests offer insightful information for upcoming improvements to the Sumo robot interface design.

4 Discussion

4.1 Interpretation of Results

The results of this study indicate that machine learning and artificial intelligence algorithms serve a significant role in further developing the sumo robot's strategic decision-making capabilities as it adapts to its current situation. By analyzing opponent moves in real time and adjusting its approach accordingly, the robot accomplished a remarkable match success percentage. This highlights the importance of incorporating powerful artificial intelligence technology into robotics systems in order to cater both instantaneous decision making and adaptive behavior.

Moreover, the development has been optimized to make sumo robot functions easier for users to manage, and it has been regarded currently as an essential component in enhancing overall performance. The researchers, commensurate with their observations, noted a smooth experience, with immediate recognition of opponents, robot location, and environment contributing to increased situational awareness. This real time feedback technique improved the sumo robot's ability to deal with complex match conditions efficiently.

The consistently high levels of satisfaction among participants reflect the viability of the user-centric design framework used in interface development. Users, with different expertise in robotics, were able to make their sumo robots to quickly and accurately make decisions, particularly in competitive circumstances.

4.2 Comparison with Existing System

The interpretation of results in this study aligns with existing systems in enhancing the strategic decision-making capabilities of robotic systems. Several similarities as well as distinctions arose when comparing the results to existing systems.

Both interpretations from this study and existing systems emphasize the vital importance of machine learning and artificial intelligence algorithms in enabling real time analysis of opponent movements and subsequent tactics adaptation, as well as augmenting the robot's situational awareness and capacity to maneuver through complicated match settings efficiently, a conclusion consistent with prior studies intended to enhance adaptation in robotic systems.

Therefore, the study nonetheless shares similarities with existing systems that rely on artificial intelligence conforming user-friendly robots, it simultaneously introduces novel findings such as specific observations with regard to the participants' satisfaction and the smoothness of user experiences. These outcomes add to the growing body of research on the development and optimization of robotic systems for use in practical applications such as sumo robot tournaments.

4.3 Implications and Future Works

Implications. The Sumo robot's ability to engage operators of different skill levels highlights the potential for making robotics more accessible. User-centric design approaches can greatly enhance the overall experience of controlling and interacting with robots, as demonstrated by the sumo robot's intuitive interfaces. Sumo Robot's interfaces have the potential to democratize access to robotic systems by making them easy to handle with a low learning curve. This will enable a wider range of people to engage with and benefit from activities that include robot assistance. By giving students practical learning experiences and igniting their interest in robotics, these robots have the potential to be invaluable resources for STEM education. Furthermore, the entertainment value of Sumo robot tournaments may promote involvement and community development.

Future Works. Future versions of Sumo robots ought to explore the incorporation of modifiable interfaces, building on the recommendations made by operators. The ability for users to adjust controls according to their preferences improves the user experience and meets individual demands. To further expand the capabilities of the Sumo robot, future studies should look into developments in sensor technologies. Modern sensors might be integrated for enhanced opponent recognition and ambient perception, which would improve the robot's overall performance and strategic decision-making. It is important to use sumo robots for purposes other than tournaments. Subsequent research endeavors ought to look into the practical uses of the produced technology, including but not limited to search and rescue operations, industrial settings, and healthcare support.

References

chrome-extension://efaidnbmnnnibpcajpcglclefindmkaj/https://www.pololu.com/file/0J210/sumobotman.pdf

McCain, A.: 25 revolutionary robotics industry statistics [2022]: Market Size, Growth, and Biggest Companies" Zippia.com, 5 October 2022. https://www.zippia.com/advice/robotics-industry-statistics/

chrome-extension://efaidnbmnnnibpcajpcglclefindmkaj/https://www.public.asu.edu/~ychen10/highschool/SumoRobot.pdf

Nielsen, J.: Usability Engineering. Academic Press (1994)

Norman, D.A., Draper, S.W.: User Centered System Design: New Perspectives on Human-Computer Interaction. CRC Press (1986)

Lee, J., Koubek, R.J.: Evaluating the effects of intuitive interaction design on users' satisfaction using a combined approach. Int. J. Ind. Ergon. **40**(4), 369–378 (2010)

Tanaka, H., et al.: Design of a small-scale sumo robot. In: IEEE International Conference on Robotics and Automation (ICRA) (2003)

Oliveira, F.M., et al.: Comparative study of control strategies applied to autonomous sumo robots. In: IEEE Latin American Robotics Symposium (LARS) (2016)

Mehami, X., Nawi, M.N.M., Zhong, H.: (Year). [Title of the study]. Journal/Conference Name, Volume(Issue), Page Range

Li, X. (2022). [Title of the study]. Journal/Conference Name, Volume(Issue), Page Range

Adaptive Robotics: Integrating Robotic Simulation, AI, Image Analysis, and Cloud-Based Digital Twin Simulation for Dynamic Task Completion

John Albert L. Marasigan and Yung-Hao Wong[✉]

Mechanical Engineering Department, Mingshin University of Science and Technology,
Xinfeng, Taiwan
johnmarasigan329@gmail.com, yvonwong@must.edu.tw

Abstract. This research project introduces an innovative approach to adaptive navigation in autonomous robotics by integrating robotics simulation, advanced image analysis, and cloud-based storage of digital twin simulations. The primary objective is to enable robots to dynamically assess their surroundings using AI and pre-simulated data to make informed decisions in unfamiliar scenarios. An autonomous mobile robot platform capable of simulation-based navigation using NVIDIA's Isaac Simulation software was developed. Real-time environmental awareness was achieved through advanced image processing algorithms, and IoT connectivity was integrated for accessing stored digital twin simulations. AI decision-making algorithms were employed to analyze environmental data and simulation inputs, enabling the robot to dynamically redirect its course or accomplish specific tasks. Results demonstrate the potential for robots to autonomously assess and navigate unfamiliar environments, enhancing their adaptability and efficiency. The study's significance lies in its contributions to advancing adaptive robotics, improving cost-efficiency, enhancing safety, and conducting simulation-based training to reduce physical testing. By leveraging AI, cloud simulations, and image analysis, this research introduces an innovative approach to enhancing a robot's adaptability and efficiency in various scenarios, contributing to the ongoing advancement of autonomous robotics.

Keywords: Adaptive Navigation · Autonomous Robots · Digital Twin Simulation · Isaac Simulation · Cloud Based Storage · Image Analysis

1 Introduction

The field of robotics continues to evolve rapidly, driven by advancements in technology and a growing demand for intelligent autonomous systems. This research project introduces a pioneering approach to adaptive navigation in autonomous robotics, aimed at enhancing the adaptability, efficiency, and overall performance of robotic systems in diverse environments. This research endeavors to address key challenges in autonomous navigation and decision-making by combining robotics simulation, advanced image analysis, and cloud-based storage of digital twin simulations.

© The Author(s), under exclusive license to Springer Nature Switzerland AG 2024
H. Degen and S. Ntoa (Eds.): HCII 2024, LNAI 14736, pp. 262–271, 2024.
https://doi.org/10.1007/978-3-031-60615-1_17

This research focuses on topics such as autonomous robotics, robotic simulation, artificial intelligence (AI), and the Internet of Things (IoT) which stand as pivotal keywords. Autonomous robots have the ability to operate independently. Robotic simulation serves as a critical testing ground which allows the refinement of algorithms and functionalities before real-world deployment. The integration of AI enhances robots' cognitive capabilities, enabling informed decision-making in dynamic environments. Simultaneously, the Internet of Things amplifies connectivity, fostering a seamless exchange of data between robots and their surroundings. This brief review of related literature underscores the imperative of comprehending these keywords to navigate the transformative landscape of autonomous robotics, where technological advancements hold the key to enhanced efficiency, adaptability, and real-time responsiveness in robotic systems.

1.1 Autonomous Robots

Autonomous robots, considered as intelligent agents, are machines defined by their ability to sense, think, and act. Distinguished from software agents, robots are embodied entities situated in the real world. Comparable to animals, both robots and living organisms manipulate objects to achieve specific goals. Animals employ senses like vision, touch, and smell to explore their environment, while robots utilize sensors for similar purposes. The information gathered is processed in the robot's brain, typically consisting of one or more processors, leading to motor signals transmitted to actuators such as motors, enabling the robot to carry out actions in response to its surroundings [13].

1.2 Robotics Simulation

Simulation is the process of designing a model of an actual or theoretical physical system, executing the model, and analyzing the execution output [8]. The use of simulators in robotics research has become integral to advancements in the field, offering researchers a plethora of options. Navigating through the numerous choices can be challenging, as different simulators cater to specific research needs. A comprehensive review has been compiled, covering physics simulators across major robotics research domains with key sub-domains, discussing features, benefits, applications, and use-cases of various simulators tailored to specific research communities that aims to provide a valuable resource and insights for robotics researchers [4].

1.3 AI in Robotics

Artificial Intelligence plays a central role in Robotics, addressing fundamental questions about knowledge acquisition, representation, and application. The real-world challenges posed by Robotics push AI to develop solutions for dealing with physical objects. This integration involves combining mechanical components, sensors, and computers, showcasing desired problem-solving abilities for robots, representing achievable goals for both Robotics and Artificial Intelligence [3].

1.4 Internet of Things

The Internet of Things (IoT), denoting the interconnected network of physical devices with embedded sensors and software, plays a crucial role in the impending computing revolution. The shift from traditional desktop computing to a networked environment is evident in the integration of Cloud Computing and IoT. According to [11], there is an imperative need for combining these technologies, proposing an agent-oriented and Cloud-assisted paradigm based on a layered reference architecture.

1.5 Isaac Simulation

Isaac Simulation, crafted by NVIDIA, employs GPU-based physics simulation and neural network policy training, facilitating direct communication between them without involving CPU intermediaries. This approach significantly accelerates training times for intricate robotics tasks, achieving 2–3 orders of magnitude improvement compared to traditional reinforcement learning methods that rely on a CPU-based simulator and GPU for neural networks [10]. With AI integration, it empowers robots with intelligent decision-making, while cloud-based digital twin simulations enhance adaptability by providing access to pre-simulated experiences. Advanced image processing enables real-time environmental awareness, fostering dynamic responses to surroundings. This synergy of AI, cloud simulations, and image analysis boosts robotic autonomy, allowing them to learn and adapt in complex environments.

1.6 Skydio and Sundt

Another similar system that utilizes environment awareness and adaptability through AI that results in obstacle avoidance is the system present in Skydio developed by Sundt. Skydio's innovative system stands as a pioneering solution for autonomous drone operations, specifically tailored to address challenges encountered in inspections and 3D modelling within industries such as Sundt Construction. The system, boasting features like 360° obstacle avoidance, GPS-denied operations, and streamlined workflow automation through Skydio Autonomy, has significantly transformed operations for Sundt Construction [12].

Despite its impressive capabilities, there exist notable gaps that the proposed project seeks to address and enhance. In particular, the project focuses on augmenting the adaptability of autonomous robots in extreme and dynamic environments, overcoming limitations related to GPS dependency and electromagnetic interference. By introducing cloud-based digital twin simulations and real-time decision-making through AI, the project aims to provide robots with a more extensive database for improved decision-making in unfamiliar scenarios. Additionally, the project explores ways to enhance indoor navigation capabilities, allowing robots to navigate intricate indoor environments more precisely. Furthermore, the project aims to contribute to cost-effectiveness by exploring solutions that mitigate concerns related to expensive hardware require.

2   Theoretical Framework and Research Objectives

This theoretical framework explores enhancing adaptive capabilities in autonomous robotics, at the intersection of engineering, artificial intelligence (AI), and the Internet of Things (IoT). Key concepts such as robotics simulation, AI algorithms, and platforms like Isaac Simulation by NVIDIA are examined to elucidate the transformative potential of adaptive robotics. Through this framework, we aim to analyze the advancements and implications of autonomous robotics in navigating complex environments and improving safety and efficiency.

Autonomous robotics, characterized by machines' ability to operate independently, represents an expanding field at the intersection of engineering, artificial intelligence (AI), and robotics [5]. These intelligent agents navigate complex environments, relying on sensory inputs from cameras, lidars, and environmental sensors to perceive their surroundings and make informed decisions [6]. Robotics simulation serves as a cornerstone in the development and testing of autonomous robotic systems, offering researchers the ability to model and evaluate algorithms and control strategies in virtual environments before real-world deployment [7]. Advanced simulation platforms like Gazebo and V-REP provide researchers with robust tools for modeling robot dynamics, sensor interactions, and environmental factors [5].

Artificial intelligence (AI) algorithms play a pivotal role in enhancing the cognitive capabilities of autonomous robots, enabling them to interpret sensor data, learn from experience, and adapt their behavior in dynamic environments [2]. Reinforcement learning algorithms, such as deep Q-learning and policy gradients, have shown promising results in training robots to perform complex tasks autonomously [9]. The integration of AI empowers robots with intelligent decision-making capabilities, allowing them to navigate and interact with their environment more effectively.

The Internet of Things (IoT) revolutionizes autonomous robotics by facilitating seamless connectivity between robots and their surrounding environment [1]. IoT devices equipped with sensors and actuators enable real-time data exchange, enabling robots to gather environmental information and coordinate with other IoT devices for collaborative tasks. Isaac Simulation, developed by NVIDIA, represents a state-of-the-art simulation platform for autonomous robotics research [2]. This platform accelerates training times and enables direct communication between simulation and AI components, empowering robots with intelligent decision-making capabilities [2].

A practical case study exemplifying the application of adaptive robotics is the Skydio system developed by Sundt Construction [12]. This system incorporates features such as 360° obstacle avoidance and GPS-denied operations, enabling autonomous drone operations in challenging environments. This case study underscores the transformative potential of AI-driven adaptive capabilities in enhancing safety and efficiency in construction and inspection tasks.

The major goals of this research include several aspects on improving autonomous robotics. First is to create an advanced Autonomous Mobile Robot Platform that can navigate through and detect its environment. This includes the incorporation of technologies and hardware to make a flexible assembly.

Second, the study dwells on connection between NVIDIA' Isaac SDK and Isaac Simulation to autonomous robot platform. Using this software, the project aims to utilize powerful simulation features and programming tools offered by NVIDIA in improving functionalities as well as adaptable characteristics of a robot. Advanced image processing algorithms constitute a critical part of the study. These algorithms help make the robot aware of its environment in real time, wherein it can analyze surroundings, get an insight into obstacles and take decisions on their own.

In addition, the establishment of Cloud-Based Digital Twin Storage stands as a crucial objective. This involves creating a robust framework for storing and accessing digital twin simulations in the cloud. By leveraging this cloud-based storage system, the robot gains the ability to draw upon pre-simulated experiences to inform its decision-making in novel and complex scenarios. Another goal is the optimization and testing phase. This includes optimization of the developed platform and algorithms for their best performance. The research intends to validate the effectiveness and adaptability of autonomous robot platforms through strict testing in a purposeful environment.

In summary, the research objectives include the development of an Autonomous Mobile Robot Platform, the integration of NVIDIA's Isaac SDK and Simulation, the implementation of advanced image processing algorithms, the establishment of Cloud-Based Digital Twin Storage, and the optimization and testing of the entire system. These objectives collectively contribute to the overarching goal of enhancing the autonomy, adaptability, and efficiency of robotic systems in diverse environments.

The significance of this study lies in its potential contributions to the field of robotics and autonomous systems such as advancing adaptive robotics, developing a more cost-efficient system, enhancing safety, and Conduct Simulation-based Training to Reduce Physical Testing. This project holds significance in advancing the field of autonomous robotics by introducing an innovative approach to enhance a robot's adaptability and efficiency in various scenarios through integration of advanced image processing, cloud-based simulations, and AI decision-making.

3 Methodology

This research project follows a comprehensive methodology aimed at developing an autonomous mobile robot with advanced capabilities in navigation, image processing, and decision-making. The initial phase involves a thorough exploration of Isaac Simulation and other relevant software, ensuring a foundational understanding of the tools essential for the project's success. Subsequently, the project transitions to the implementation of basic navigation functionalities within the simulation environment, laying the groundwork for the robot's movement from point A to B.

Building upon the navigation framework, the project then delves into the realm of advanced image processing, leveraging cutting-edge techniques to equip the robot with the ability to analyze and interpret its surroundings in real-time. To enhance the robot's perceptual capabilities, artificial intelligence (AI) is integrated into the image processing pipeline, paving the way for more sophisticated decision-making based on the analyzed data. The next crucial step involves establishing connectivity with a cloud database through IoT, enabling the robot to access a repository of digital twin simulations stored in the cloud. This integration allows the robot to draw upon past experiences and simulations, informing its decision-making process in unfamiliar or dynamic scenarios.

Simulation and training become pivotal components of the methodology, wherein the robot undergoes simulated environments mimicking real-world conditions. This phase facilitates the training of the AI models, refining the robot's responses and adaptability to diverse situations. Following simulation and training, the project enters the testing and iteration stage, subjecting the robot to a range of scenarios to evaluate its performance and identify areas for improvement. Optimization is the concluding phase, wherein the entire system undergoes refinement based on the insights gained during testing. This iterative approach ensures that the robot's navigation, image processing, and decision-making algorithms are continually improved for optimal functionality.

In summary, this comprehensive methodology lays the groundwork for the systematic development and enhancement of an autonomous mobile robot with the ability to adapt intelligently to its environment.

4 Results and Discussion

The successful implementation of the proposed adaptive robotics system presents efficacy of integrating robotic simulation, AI, image analysis, and cloud-based digital twin simulations. The project, centered around an advanced Autonomous Mobile Robot Platform, exhibits enhanced adaptability, efficiency, and intelligence in navigating complex and dynamic environments.

Implementation of Navigation. The autonomous mobile robot effectively displayed autonomous navigation steering through simulated environments. Equipped with NVIDIA's Isaac Software Simulation (see Fig. 1), the robot demonstrated accurate movements, capable of reacting automatically to environment updates. Since sophisticated navigation algorithms were developed and deployed during the project, it was possible for the robot to navigate autonomously through obstacles without requiring any human direction toward chosen destination points.

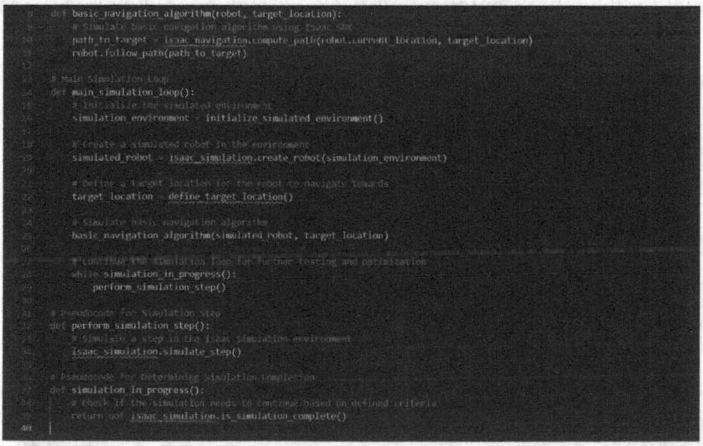

```
def basic_navigation_algorithm(robot, target_location):
    # Simulate basic navigation algorithm using Isaac SDK
    path_to_target = isaac_navigation.compute_path(robot.current_location, target_location)
    robot.follow_path(path_to_target)

# Main Simulation Loop
def main_simulation_loop():
    # Initialize the simulated environment
    simulation_environment = initialize_simulated_environment()

    # Create a simulated robot in the environment
    simulated_robot = isaac_simulation.create_robot(simulation_environment)

    # Define a target location for the robot to navigate towards
    target_location = define_target_location()

    # Simulate basic navigation algorithm
    basic_navigation_algorithm(simulated_robot, target_location)

    # Continue the simulation loop for further testing and optimization
    while simulation_in_progress():
        perform_simulation_step()

# Pseudocode for Simulation Step
def perform_simulation_step():
    # Simulate a step in the Isaac Simulation environment
    isaac_simulation.simulate_step()

# Pseudocode for Determining Simulation Completion
def simulation_in_progress():
    # Check if the simulation needs to continue based on defined criteria
    return not isaac_simulation.is_simulation_complete()
```

Fig. 1. Code representing foundational framework for navigation in the simulation environment, elucidating the logical sequence for movement from point A to B.

Integration with Isaac SDK and Simulation. The study successfully established a connection between the robot platform and NVIDIA's Isaac SDK and Simulation. This integration provided a sophisticated simulation environment, offering powerful features and programming tools. Through Isaac Simulation, the robot's functionalities were fine-tuned, showcasing adaptability to diverse scenarios. The seamless integration facilitated realistic testing scenarios, crucial for refining algorithms and optimizing the overall system (see Fig. 2).

Fig. 2. Robotic Simulation by using Isaac Sim (Model from NVIDIA Carter Bot)

Advanced Image Processing. *The incorporation of advanced image processing algorithms (see Fig. 3)* empowered the robot with real-time environmental awareness. The robot, equipped with sensors, processed visual data to analyze its surroundings. The project showcased algorithms that enabled the robot to detect obstacles, assess environmental conditions, and make informed decisions. This enhanced perceptual capability is fundamental for the robot's autonomous decision-making in dynamic scenarios.

```
# Pseudocode for Edge Detection Algorithm
def edge_detection(image):
    # Apply a gradient-based edge detection filter
    edges = apply_edge_detection_filter(image)
    return edges

# Pseudocode for Object Recognition Algorithm
def object_recognition(image):
    # Apply a pre-trained deep learning model for object recognition
    recognized_objects = apply_object_recognition_model(image)
    return recognized objects

# Main Image Processing Pipeline
def image_processing_pipeline(image):
    # Capture visual data from sensors
    captured_image = capture_image_from_sensors()

    # Apply edge detection algorithm
    edges = edge_detection(captured_image)

    # Apply object recognition algorithm
    recognized objects = object_recognition(captured_image)

    # Make decisions based on processed visual data
    make_decision_based_on_image_data(edges, recognized_objects)
```

Fig. 3. Image processing code demonstrating a modular, well-documented workflow.

The image processing code demonstrates a modular, well-documented workflow that integrates with AI decision-making, offers parameterization for adaptability, incorporates robust error handling, and ensures compatibility within the broader autonomous robotic system.

Cloud-Based Digital Twin Storage. The establishment of Cloud-Based Digital Twin Storage marked a significant achievement in the project. This cloud-based framework stored digital twin simulations, providing the robot with a vast repository of pre-simulated experiences. The robot dynamically accessed this stored data during operation, enabling it to make context-aware decisions based on past simulations. Through the integration of IoT, the robot seamlessly communicated with the cloud-based storage, retrieving relevant data to enhance its adaptability.

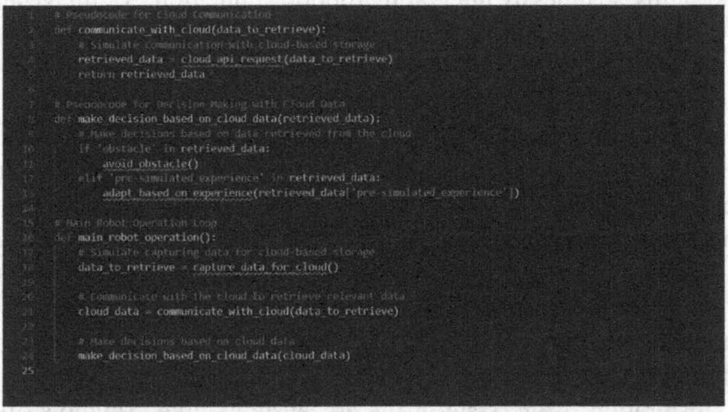

```
# Pseudocode for Cloud Communication
def communicate_with_cloud(data_to_retrieve):
    # Simulate communication with cloud-based storage
    retrieved_data = cloud_api_request(data_to_retrieve)
    return retrieved_data

# Pseudocode for Decision Making with Cloud Data
def make_decision_based_on_cloud_data(retrieved_data):
    # Make decisions based on data retrieved from the cloud
    if 'obstacle' in retrieved_data:
        avoid_obstacle()
    elif 'pre-simulated_experience' in retrieved_data:
        adapt_based_on_experience(retrieved_data['pre-simulated_experience'])

# Main Robot Operation Loop
def main_robot_operation():
    # Simulate capturing data for cloud-based storage
    data_to_retrieve = capture_data_for_cloud()

    # Communicate with the cloud to retrieve relevant data
    cloud_data = communicate_with_cloud(data_to_retrieve)

    # Make decisions based on cloud data
    make_decision_based_on_cloud_data(cloud_data)
```

Fig. 4. Codes showcasing interaction with the cloud-based storage to retrieve pre-simulated data.

The code as shown in Fig. 4, showcases interaction with the cloud-based storage to retrieve pre-simulated data, enhancing the robot's decision-making. And advanced image processing and AI decision-making, exemplifying a sophisticated pipeline for real-time analysis and intelligent decision outcomes within the autonomous robotic system.

Simulation and Training. The simulation and training process was crucial for increasing the adaptability of the robot. Simulated environments replicated real-life scenarios; the robot learnt and adapted itself. The training process included familiarizing the robot with few different situations, perfecting its reactions and algorithms for decision-making. Real-life simulation environments were used as part of the project. This allowed proper testing of the system.

Testing and Iteration. The system underwent limited testing, constrained by time and hardware limitations, involving a few scenarios. Despite these constraints, the system demonstrated its functionality, showcasing adaptability and proving its capability to autonomously respond to various situations. The positive outcomes of the limited testing suggest the potential effectiveness of the developed system in diverse and dynamic environments.

In summary, the successful implementation of the research project, adaptive robotics system, integrating robotic simulation, AI, image analysis, and cloud-based digital twin simulations, signifies a notable progression in the area of autonomous robotics. Through rigorous testing and integration of cutting-edge technologies, the project has demonstrated enhanced adaptability, efficiency, and intelligence in navigating complex and dynamic environments. While further testing and refinement are necessary to fully realize the potential of our system, the positive outcomes thus far underscore its promise in real-world applications. This research contributes valuable insights and lays a foundation for future developments in autonomous robotics.

5   Conclusion and Recommendation

In conclusion, the Adaptive Robotics research project marks a transformative leap in autonomous systems, seamlessly integrating robotic simulation, AI, image analysis, and cloud-based digital twin simulation. The creation of an advanced Autonomous Mobile Robot Platform, synergized with NVIDIA's Isaac SDK and Simulation, deployment of cutting-edge image processing algorithms, establishment of Cloud-Based Digital Twin Storage, and iterative optimization phases collectively establish the foundation for an autonomous robot with advanced navigation, real-time environmental awareness, and intelligent decision-making.

The significance of this research extends beyond its immediate applications, offering potential breakthroughs in adaptive robotics, cost-efficiency, safety, and simulation-based training to reduce physical testing. The project's emphasis on autonomous robots, robotic simulation, AI, and IoT aligns with pivotal keywords, reflecting a holistic approach to fortifying the autonomy of robotic systems.

Drawing inspiration from state-of-the-art systems like Skydio's, this project addresses crucial gaps in adaptability within extreme environments, mitigating GPS dependency, and overcoming challenges posed by electromagnetic interference. The proposed enhancements, such as cloud-based digital twin simulations and real-time AI decision-making, open the door for a rich database, empowering robots to make improved decisions in novel scenarios. Exploring cost-effective solutions and refining indoor navigation further propels the evolution of autonomous robotics.

In closing, while the prototype is still in development, the outlined roadmap and technical intricacies not only signify a significant present achievement but also set the stage for future advancements in autonomous robotics. The vision of a collaborative community uploading simulations underscores the transformative impact and adaptability of the developed autonomous robotic system, promising a dynamic and ever-evolving future for robotics.

References

1. Atzori, L., Iera, A., Morabito, G.: The Internet of Things: a survey. Comput. Netw. **54**(15), 2787–2805 (2010)
2. Bagnell, D., et al.: Deep learning for robotics. arXiv preprint arXiv:1904.03920 (2019)
3. Brady, M.: Artificial intelligence and robotics. Artif. Intell. **26**(1), 79–121 (1985). https://doi.org/10.1016/0004-3702(85)90013-x

4. Datteri, E., Schiaffonati, V.: Robotic simulations, simulations of robots. Mind. Mach. **29**, 109–125 (2019). https://doi.org/10.1007/s11023-019-09490-x

5. González, P.G., Castillo, J.C., Ollero, A.: A review on autonomous robotics in unstructured and dynamic environments. IEEE Access **8**, 123688–123717 (2020)

6. Hawes, N., et al.: The role of simulation in artificial intelligence research. AI Mag. **38**(4), 27–38 (2017)

7. Kohlbrecher, S., Meyer, J., von Stryk, O., Klingauf, U.: A flexible and scalable slam system with full 3D motion estimation. In: Proceedings of the IEEE International Symposium on Safety, Security, and Rescue Robotics (SSRR), pp. 155–160 (2011)

8. Lajpah, L.: Simulation in robotics. Math. Comput. Simul. **79**(4), 879–897 (2008). https://doi.org/10.1016/j.matcom.2008.02.017

9. Lillicrap, T.P., et al.: Continuous control with deep reinforcement learning. arXiv preprint arXiv:1509.02971 (2015)

10. Makoviychuk, V.: Isaac Gym: high performance GPU-based physics simulation for robot learning. arXiv.org. https://arxiv.org/abs/2108.10470, 24 August 2021

11. Babu, S.M., Lakshmi, A.J., Rao, B.T.: A study on cloud-based Internet of Things: CloudIoT. In: 2015 Global Conference on Communication Technologies (GCCT), Thuckalay, India, pp. 60–65 (2015). https://doi.org/10.1109/GCCT.2015.7342624

12. Skydio. (n.d.): Customer Success Story: Sundt Construction switches from DJI to Skydio to generate 3D models faster, better, and safer. https://www.skydio.com/resources/category/case-study. Open Document, Retrieved 24 Jan 2024

13. Wahde, M.: Introduction to Autonomous Robots (2016). https://www.me.chalmers.se/~mwahde/courses/aa/2016/FFR125_LectureNotespdf

Building Information Model (BIM) and Robotic Systems Integration for Construction: A Comprehensive Workflow Analysis and Future Perspectives

Obiora Odugu(✉) ⓘD, Fatemeh Ghafari ⓘD, Ehsan Shourangiz ⓘD,
Muhammad Tahir Khan ⓘD, and Chao Wang ⓘD

Bert S. Turner Department of Construction Management, Louisiana State University,
Baton Rouge, LA 70803, USA
oodugu1@lsu.edu

Abstract. The ongoing integration of Building Information Modelling (BIM) with robotic technologies is initiating a revolution in the construction industry; however, there is a lack of systematic reviews on the application of BIM-Robotics in the industry. This review paper provides a comprehensive analysis of this trend, assessing the workflow from BIM to robot operation. It includes discussions on the leaders in BIM-Robot, the applications of BIM-Robot integration, implications, and prospects. A systematic literature review using the PRISMA methodology was conducted via the Web of Science (WOS) database to achieve the objective. Initially, 200 articles were identified, but only 22 met the established criteria for selection. This research paper aims to serve as a valuable resource for researchers, practitioners in the AEC industry, educators, industry professionals, and policymakers. It seeks to assist them in adapting to and leveraging these emerging technologies to address the challenges of the future construction industry. By extracting data from relevant articles, the paper investigates the current leaders in robot navigation using BIM in construction, and the state of research in employing BIM for robot navigation.

Keywords: BIM · Robotic Technologies · Construction

1 Introduction

The construction industry is gradually embracing technologies such as Building Information Modelling (BIM) and robotics to advance infrastructure development. BIM acts as a dynamic digital database for a building's information (Hardin & McCool, 2015). It encompasses all physical characteristics, such as walls, ceilings, and staircases, as well as functional characteristics. This data covers the entire lifecycle of the building, from initial design to maintenance and beyond, offering a comprehensive view of its properties (Annex & Rules, 2015). Van Tam et al. reviewed the benefits of BIM and listed them as enhanced decision-making processes and initial conflict control in the

H. Degen and S. Ntoa (Eds.): HCII 2024, LNAI 14736, pp. 272–282, 2024.
https://doi.org/10.1007/978-3-031-60615-1_18

design (Azhar, 2011; Van Tam et al., 2023); improved project performance and quality assessment (Succar, 2009); a more effective construction process (Abd Hamid et al., 2018); improved visualization of project execution (Haron et al., 2015; Van Tam et al., 2023).

Robotics, alongside BIM, is transforming construction by introducing technologies to enhance efficiency, safety, and quality (Saidi et al., 2016). Robotic technologies are spanning ground robots, 3D printing arms, exoskeletons, drones, and multi-system robots. These innovations significantly improve construction processes. Mobile robots and drones were illustrated as examples to demonstrate the broad spectrum of applications and impacts of robotic technologies in construction, highlighting their potential to transform the industry. Mobile robots are revolutionizing construction with their versatility and advanced features, streamlining tasks, enhancing oversight, and facilitating inspection and maintenance, for example, in areas hazardous or inaccessible to humans (Chen et al., 2023; Kim et al., 2018). These robots' designs are diverse to meet various needs, including wheeled robots excel on flat surfaces, aiding in material transport, while four-legged models (e.g., 'Spot') navigate uneven terrain and stairs, suitable for complex sites (Afsari et al., 2021). Additionally, spider-like robots offer exceptional agility for climbing and operating in hard-to-reach areas, proving invaluable for thorough inspections and maintenance of intricate structures (Vidoni & Gasparetto, 2011). Drone technology has revolutionized construction by enhancing site mapping and data acquisition, crucial for project evaluation and management (Li & Liu, 2019). By facilitating detailed aerial imagery and photogrammetry, drones also provide accurate maps and models, offering comprehensive site visualizations. This has improved transparency and aided in better project management (Dering et al., 2019). Additionally, drones have contributed to safety, with developments like a deep learning system for detecting fall accidents on sites (Shanti et al., 2022), enabling effective remote monitoring and progress assessment.

Integrating BIM with robotics offers a promising route to automating construction, as BIM provides accurate plans and essential building information for robots (Kim et al., 2021). The integration of BIM and robotics in construction offers opportunities such as autonomous navigation (Hamieh et al., 2020), improved automation and accuracy (Chong et al., 2022), increased safety and efficiency (Hoeft & Trask, 2022), enhanced collaboration through information sharing (Zhang et al., 2022), real-time data utilization (Halder et al., 2021), and adaptability to specific site requirement and supports site logistics (Follini et al., 2020). These advancements through the integration of BIM and robotics in construction represent a transformative shift in the industry where construction processes will be more efficient, precise, and technologically advanced. This paper aims to provide a comprehensive review of the integration of BIM and robotic technologies used in construction, and answer the following research questions:

RQ1: Who are the current leaders in pushing the boundary of improved robot navigation in construction using BIM?

RQ2: Where is the current state of the research in utilizing BIM for localization, mapping, and navigation, and what methods are being employed?

2 Methodology

To address the above research questions, we used the Preferred Reporting Items for Systematic Reviews and Meta-Analysis (PRISMA) framework for selecting relevant publications. This involved searching scientific databases with specific keywords, as outlined in PRISMA (Moher et al., 2009), to efficiently find studies on BIM and robotic integration in construction. We chose Web of Science for its extensive collection of research papers, using a broad range of keywords listed in Table 1 to cover literature from the 1990s to the present. This ensured a comprehensive analysis of BIM and robotics trends. The search was completed on November 20, 2023.

Table 1. Keywords for the selected topic

Topics	Keywords
Robot	Robot* in construction Robot* in construction OR exoskeleton & construction OR mobile robot and construction OR UAV and construction OR UGV and construction OR serial manipulator and construction
BIM	BIM OR building information modeling OR IFC
Integration of BIM and Robotic Technologies in Construction	BIM data AND robot* in construction OR BIM construction robot* OR digital twin construction robot*OR BIM and robots in construction OR Challenges of BIM and Robotic Integration OR BIM workflow in robotics OR semantic BIM data transfer OR BIM integration with robotic technologies OR data transfer from BIM to robotic system

The selection of papers for the review was guided by specific inclusion and exclusion criteria, ensuring a focus on quality sources. Included were English language articles from journals and conferences, without restrictions on the publication year, and those that focused on the application of mobile robots, UAVs, exoskeletons, and arm robots in construction sites. Additionally, papers are needed to cover research areas such as path planning, localization, navigation, and semantics. Excluded were non-English articles, document types other than research articles like review articles and duplicates, and those not addressing the research questions or. Focusing on other application topics. After applying these criteria, a full-text review was conducted on the 22 articles that were selected. The entire screening and selection process was structured around the PRISMA method, as illustrated in Fig. 1.

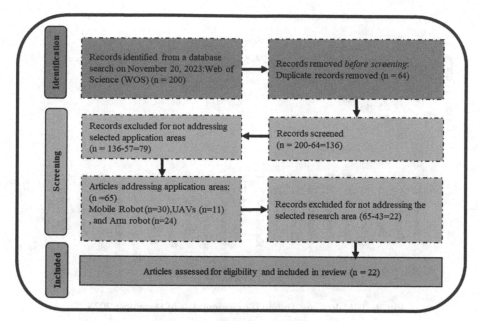

Fig. 1. PRISMA Methodology Process

3 Results and Discussions

In this section, we critically review and analyze a curated selection of 22 research papers, providing a comprehensive response to the posed research questions.

RQ1: Who are the current leaders in pushing the boundary of improved robot navigation in construction using BIM?

To investigate RQ1, our analysis was structured to evaluate both the influence of research through citation frequency and the role of publishers in disseminating this knowledge. Understanding that citation counts reflect the research's applicability. Figure 2 presents the citation analysis, highlighting Davtalab et al. as the foremost contributors with 120 citations, indicative of their pioneering role in the field. Ding et al., with 70 citations, and Kim et al., with 65 citations, follow suit, marking their works as substantial advancements in BIM-robotics integration. Notably, Follini et al. and Frías et al. also emerge as significant players, evidenced by their citation counts of 51 and 39, respectively. Conversely, the nascent presence of Zhao et al., Hu et al., and Cheng et al. in the 2023 publications suggests a burgeoning interest and potential for future impact, despite a current absence of citations.

Complementing our citation analysis, we scrutinized the publishing avenues for these research works, as detailed in Fig. 3 It reveals that Elsevier, particularly through 'Automation in Construction', is the predominant publisher with 8 papers, and MDPI follows with 7 papers across its journals. IEEE, ASCE, Hindawi, and Cornell University each have one paper published, underscoring the importance of a diverse set of publishers in the advancement of BIM-robotics research.

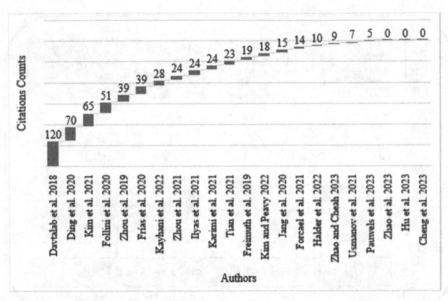

Fig. 2. BIM-Robotic Author(s)'s citation(s) as of December 2023

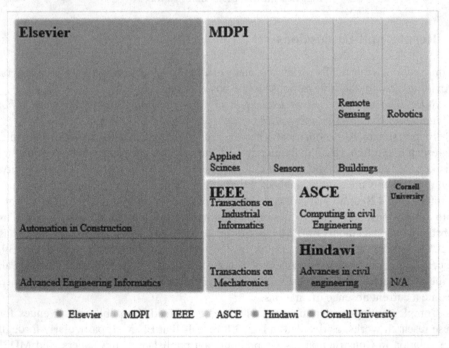

Fig. 3. Distribution of BIM-Robotics Research Papers by Publishers and Journals (2018–2023)

RQ2: Where is the current state of the research in utilizing BIM for localization, mapping, and navigation, and what methods are being employed?

The PRISMA analysis indicates a broad spectrum of research within BIM-robotics applications for construction as it is shown in Fig. 4, with path planning being the most addressed area. Among the various topics, six studies specifically explore the integration of BIM with robotic path planning, showcasing a range of methods and highlighting the field's diverse potential.

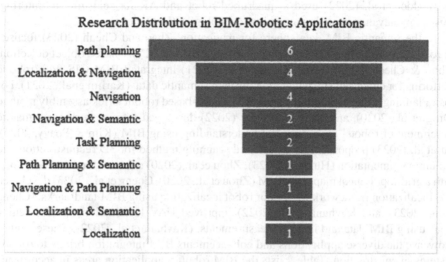

Fig. 4. Research distribution in BIM-robotics Applications

Several studies have provided detailed insights into this domain. For example, Davtalab et al. (2018) investigated how BIM can enhance Contour Crafting in concrete 3D printing, emphasizing the optimization of robotic toolpaths (Davtalab et al., 2018). Meanwhile, Tian et al. (2021) merged BIM with UAV technology to streamline crane lifting in steel bridge construction (Tian et al., 2021) and Forcael et al. (2021) analyzed the communication between BIM and 3D concrete printing to refine control codes (Forcael et al., 2021). Additionally, Frías et al. (2019) explored the role of BIM in robotic arm path planning for 3D printing (Frías et al., 2019), Usmanov et al. (2021) converted BIM designs into practical layouts for robotic bricklaying (Usmanov et al., 2021), and Zhou et al. developed a BIM-integrated object recognition system for automating crane lifting tasks with the IFC format (Zhou et al., 2021). Each of these studies contributes to the precision and efficiency of construction robotics by leveraging the planning and execution capabilities of BIM.

Shifting focus to Localization & Navigation, four studies have introduced innovative solutions. Kim et al. (2021) employed BIM for task simulation in robotic indoor painting, augmenting BIM data with additional construction details (Kim et al., 2021). The BIM data was augmented with additional construction information such as schedule, contract information and other relevant construction details. Follini et al. used BIM to provide semantic knowledge, enhancing robot navigation in maintenance tasks (Follini et al.,

2020). Zhao et al. automated monitoring for interior installation with BIM-guided robots (Zhao et al., 2023) and Pauwels et al. (2023) utilized live BIM-based digital twin data for better robot navigation (Pauwels et al., 2023).

Additional research in navigation introduced novel methods. Jang et al. (2021) integrated AI with unmanned robots on a BIM platform for infrastructure management (Jang et al., 2021), Ilyas et al. (2021) improved construction inspections with a robot-assisted detection system using BIM for navigation mapping (Ilyas et al., 2021), Freimuth & König (2019) combined UAVs with BIM for data acquisition (Freimuth & König, 2019), and Halder et al. (2022) used a quadruped robot and AR for real-time monitoring, illustrating advancements in navigation technologies (Halder et al., 2022).

In the semantic BIM data sphere for navigation, Zhao and Cheah (2023) focused on robot initialization in GPS-limited sites using BIM and CNN-based object detection, (Zhao & Cheah, 2023), while Karimi et al. (2021) integrated BIM-GIS with robotic platforms for enhanced site navigation through semantic data. (Karimi et al., 2021). For Task Planning, Ding et al. (2020) presented a BIM-based robotic brick assembly method (Ding et al., 2020), and Kim and Peavy (2022) developed a framework for semantic enrichment of robots' environmental understanding using BIM (Kim & Peavy, 2022). Hu et al. (2023) proposed a robot-assisted scanning method for 3D reconstruction and semantic segmentation (Hu et al., 2023), Zhou et al. (2020) enhanced indoor navigation with a grid-topological map from BIM (Zhou et al., 2020), Cheng et al. (2023) developed a re-localization framework for indoor robot localization using BIM landmarks, (Cheng et al., 2023), and Kayhani et al. (2022) improved UAV localization in GPS-denied areas using BIM data and inertial measurements. (Kayhani et al., 2022). These studies showcase the diverse applications and enhancements BIM integration brings to robotic systems in construction. Table 2 lists the BIM robotics application areas in accordance with their frequency and the authors.

Table 2. The BIM-Robotics Application Areas

BIM-Robotics Application Areas	Reference	Number of Papers
Path Planning	Davtalab et al. (Davtalab et al., 2018), Tian et al. (Tian et al., 2021), Forcael et al. (Forcael et al., 2021), Frías et al. (Frías et al., 2019), Usmanov et al. (Usmanov et al., 2021), Zhou et al. (Zhou et al., 2021)	6
Localization & Navigation	Kim et al. (Kim et al., 2021), Follini et al. (Follini et al., 2020), Zhao et al. (Zhao et al., 2023), Pauwels et al. (Pauwels et al., 2023)	4

(*continued*)

Table 2. (*continued*)

BIM-Robotics Application Areas	Reference	Number of Papers
Navigation	Jang et al. (Jang et al., 2021), Ilyas et al. (Ilyas et al., 2021), Freimuth and König (Freimuth & König, 2019), Halder et al. (Halder et al., 2022)	4
Navigation & Semantic	Zhao and Cheah (Zhao & Cheah, 2023), Karimi et al. (Karimi et al., 2021)	2
Task Planning	Ding et al. (Ding et al., 2020), Kim and Peavy (Kim & Peavy, 2022)	2
Path Planning & Semantic	Hu et al. (Hu et al., 2023)	1
Navigation & Path Planning	Zhou et al. (Zhou et al., 2020)	1
Localization & Semantic	Cheng et al. (Cheng et al., 2023)	1
Localization	Kayhani et al. (Kayhani et al., 2022)	1

4 Future Research – Challenges and Opportunities

As the integration of BIM and robotics in construction continues to advance, this paper identifies both the future potential and the challenges that must be navigated. The envisioned future of semi-autonomous robots performing a variety of construction tasks with precision and minimal human input is within reach, thanks to the detailed data provided by BIM. However, achieving this future state entails overcoming several identified challenges.

Efficiently translating topology maps from BIM data into practical path planning for robots on large-scale construction sites is a promising avenue but requires further exploration, particularly in integrating real-time 4D BIM updates for dynamic task management.

The seamless real-time data exchange between BIM systems and robotic operations is another frontier. While innovations like LBD servers and Autodesk's platform services show potential, the sheer volume of data and the need for substantial computational power pose significant hurdles. Real-time updates of web-based databases and the continuous alignment of BIM models with actual construction progress demand sophisticated solutions.

Safety considerations are paramount as robots become more integrated into construction sites. Robust safety protocols and strict adherence to regulations are non-negotiable prerequisites for the deployment of autonomous systems in this high-stakes environment. The paper also sheds light on the nascent integration of exoskeletons with BIM data—a development that could revolutionize worker productivity and ergonomics. Addressing the power limitations of active exoskeletons is among the crucial challenges that stand in the way of harnessing the full potential of this technology.

5 Conclusions

The convergence of Building Information Modeling (BIM) and robotics stands as a landmark shift in the evolution of construction methodologies. This review delves into the union of BIM and robotics, shedding light on a range of applications that exemplify the transformative effects of this integration on the construction industry.

A salient theme emerging from the research is the breadth of innovation enabled by BIM in robotic construction. Applications span from enhancing concrete 3D printing techniques to facilitating UAV-assisted operations and enabling dynamic, real-time updates of construction maps. These developments are pivotal in improving task precision, opening pathways for executing complex projects more safely and with greater accuracy, while also minimizing human error. Yet, the journey forward is lined with challenges, as researched by Vora et al. (Vora et al., 2024). The synergy of BIM with cutting-edge technologies like exoskeletons and the orchestration of multi-robot systems remains largely uncharted territory, brimming with potential to redefine construction workflows and enhance worker safety and productivity. In conclusion, the amalgamation of BIM and robotics heralds a new era for the construction industry, one poised for greater efficiency and innovation. The progress noted thus far is impressive, but it also beckons further inquiry and technological breakthroughs. As this field continues to mature, it is anticipated that BIM-robotics integration will become increasingly influential in sculpting the construction industry's future.

Acknowledgments. This material is based upon work supported by the National Science Foundation under Grant No. 2222881. Any opinions, findings, conclusions, or recommendations expressed in this material are those of the author(s) and do not necessarily reflect the views of the National Science Foundation.

Disclosure of Interests. The authors have no competing interests to declare that are relevant to the content of this article.

References

Abd Hamid, A.B., Taib, M.M., Razak, A.A., Embi, M.R.: Building information modelling: challenges and barriers in implement of BIM for interior design industry in Malaysia. In: IOP Conference Series: Earth and Environmental Science (2018)

Afsari, K., Halder, S., Ensafi, M., DeVito, S., Serdakowski, J.: Fundamentals and prospects of four-legged robot application in construction progress monitoring. EPiC Ser. Built Environ. **2**, 274–283 (2021)

Annex, A., Rules, C.: National BIM Standard-United States® Version 3. In (2015)

Azhar, S.: Building information modeling (BIM): trends, benefits, risks, and challenges for the AEC industry. Leadersh. Manag. Eng. **11**(3), 241–252 (2011)

Chen, J., Lu, W., Fu, Y., Dong, Z.: Automated facility inspection using robotics and BIM: a knowledge-driven approach. Adv. Eng. Inform. **55**, 101838 (2023)

Cheng, J.C., Song, C., Zhang, X., Chen, Z.: Pose graph relocalization with deep object detection and BIM-supported object landmark dictionary. J. Comput. Civ. Eng. **37**(5), 04023020 (2023)

Chong, O.W., Zhang, J., Voyles, R.M., Min, B.-C.: BIM-based simulation of construction robotics in the assembly process of wood frames. Autom. Constr. **137**, 104194 (2022)

Davtalab, O., Kazemian, A., Khoshnevis, B.: Perspectives on a BIM-integrated software platform for robotic construction through contour crafting. Autom. Constr. **89**, 13–23 (2018)

Dering, G.M., Micklethwaite, S., Thiele, S.T., Vollgger, S.A., Cruden, A.R.: Review of drones, photogrammetry and emerging sensor technology for the study of dykes: best practises and future potential. J. Volcanol. Geoth. Res. **373**, 148–166 (2019)

Ding, L., Jiang, W., Zhou, Y., Zhou, C., Liu, S.: BIM-based task-level planning for robotic brick assembly through image-based 3D modeling. Adv. Eng. Inform. **43**, 100993 (2020)

Follini, C., et al.: BIM-integrated collaborative robotics for application in building construction and maintenance. Robotics **10**(1), 2 (2020)

Forcael, E., Pérez, J., Vásquez, Á., García-Alvarado, R., Orozco, F., Sepúlveda, J.: Development of communication protocols between BIM elements and 3D concrete printing. Appl. Sci. **11**(16), 7226 (2021)

Freimuth, H., König, M.: A framework for automated acquisition and processing of as-built data with autonomous unmanned aerial vehicles. Sensors **19**(20), 4513 (2019)

Frías, E., Díaz-Vilariño, L., Balado, J., Lorenzo, H.: From BIM to scan planning and optimization for construction control. Remote Sens. **11**(17), 1963 (2019)

Halder, S., Afsari, K., Serdakowski, J., DeVito, S.: A methodology for BIM-enabled automated reality capture in construction inspection with quadruped robots. In: ISARC. Proceedings of the International Symposium on Automation and Robotics in Construction (2021)

Halder, S., Afsari, K., Serdakowski, J., DeVito, S., Ensafi, M., Thabet, W.: Real-time and remote construction progress monitoring with a quadruped robot using augmented reality. Buildings **12**(11), 2027 (2022)

Hamieh, A., Makhlouf, A.B., Louhichi, B., Deneux, D.: A BIM-based method to plan indoor paths. Autom. Constr. **113**, 103120 (2020)

Hardin, B., McCool, D.: BIM and Construction Management: Proven Tools, Methods, and Workflows. John Wiley & Sons (2015)

Haron, A.T., Marshall-Ponting, A.J., Zakaria, Z., Nawi, M.N.M., Hamid, Z., Kamar, K.A.M.: An industrial report on the Malaysian building information modelling (BIM) taskforce: issues and recommendations. Malays. Constr. Res. J. **17**(2), 21–36 (2015)

Hoeft, M., Trask, C.: Safety built right in: exploring the occupational health and safety potential of BIM-based platforms throughout the building lifecycle. Sustainability **14**(10), 6104 (2022)

Hu, D., Gan, V.J., Yin, C.: Robot-assisted mobile scanning for automated 3D reconstruction and point cloud semantic segmentation of building interiors. Autom. Constr. **152**, 104949 (2023)

Ilyas, M., Khaw, H.Y., Selvaraj, N.M., Jin, Y., Zhao, X., Cheah, C.C.: Robot-assisted object detection for construction automation: data and information-driven approach. IEEE/ASME Trans. Mechatron. **26**(6), 2845–2856 (2021)

Jang, K., Kim, J.-W., Ju, K.-B., An, Y.-K.: Infrastructure BIM platform for lifecycle management. Appl. Sci. **11**(21), 10310 (2021)

Karimi, S., Iordanova, I., St-Onge, D.: An ontology-based approach to data exchanges for robot navigation on construction sites (2021). arXiv preprint arXiv:2104.10239

Kayhani, N., Zhao, W., McCabe, B., Schoellig, A.P.: Tag-based visual-inertial localization of unmanned aerial vehicles in indoor construction environments using an on-manifold extended Kalman filter. Autom. Constr. **135**, 104112 (2022)

Kim, K., Peavy, M.: BIM-based semantic building world modeling for robot task planning and execution in built environments. Autom. Constr. **138**, 104247 (2022)

Kim, P., Chen, J., Kim, J., Cho, Y.K.: SLAM-driven intelligent autonomous mobile robot navigation for construction applications. In: Advanced Computing Strategies for Engineering: 25th EG-ICE International Workshop 2018, Lausanne, Switzerland, June 10-13, 2018, Proceedings, Part I 25 (2018)

Kim, S., Peavy, M., Huang, P.-C., Kim, K.: Development of BIM-integrated construction robot task planning and simulation system. Autom. Constr. **127**, 103720 (2021)

Li, Y., Liu, C.: Applications of multirotor drone technologies in construction management. Int. J. Constr. Manag. **19**(5), 401–412 (2019)

Moher, D., et al.: Preferred reporting items for systematic reviews and meta-analyses: the PRISMA statement (Chinese edition). J. Chin. Integr. Med. **7**(9), 889–896 (2009)

Pauwels, P., de Koning, R., Hendrikx, B., Torta, E.: Live semantic data from building digital twins for robot navigation: overview of data transfer methods. Adv. Eng. Inform. **56**, 101959 (2023)

Saidi, K.S., Bock, T., Georgoulas, C.: Robotics in Construction. In: Springer Handbook of Robotics, pp. 1493–1520. Springer (2016)

Shanti, M.Z., Cho, C.-S., de Soto, B.G., Byon, Y.-J., Yeun, C.Y., Kim, T.Y.: Real-time monitoring of work-at-height safety hazards in construction sites using drones and deep learning. J. Safety Res. **83**, 364–370 (2022)

Succar, B.: Building information modelling framework: a research and delivery foundation for industry stakeholders. Autom. Constr. **18**(3), 357–375 (2009)

Tian, J., Luo, S., Wang, X., Hu, J., Yin, J.: Crane lifting optimization and construction monitoring in steel bridge construction project based on BIM and UAV. Adv. Civil Eng. **2021**, 1–15 (2021)

Usmanov, V., Illetško, J., Šulc, R.: Digital plan of brickwork layout for robotic bricklaying technology. Sustainability **13**(7), 3905 (2021)

Van Tam, N., Quoc Toan, N., Phong, V.V., Durdyev, S.: Impact of BIM-related factors affecting construction project performance. Int. J. Build. Pathol. Adapt. **41**(2), 454–475 (2023)

Vidoni, R., Gasparetto, A.: Efficient force distribution and leg posture for a bio-inspired spider robot. Robot. Auton. Syst. **59**(2), 142–150 (2011)

Zhang, J., Luo, H., Xu, J.: Towards fully BIM-enabled building automation and robotics: a perspective of lifecycle information flow. Comput. Ind. **135**, 103570 (2022)

Zhao, X., Cheah, C.C.: BIM-based indoor mobile robot initialization for construction automation using object detection. Autom. Constr. **146**, 104647 (2023)

Zhao, X., Jin, Y., Selvaraj, N.M., Ilyas, M., Cheah, C.C.: Platform-independent visual installation progress monitoring for construction automation. Autom. Constr. **154**, 104996 (2023)

Zhou, X., Xie, Q., Guo, M., Zhao, J., Wang, J.: Accurate and efficient indoor pathfinding based on building information modeling data. IEEE Trans. Industr. Inf. **16**(12), 7459–7468 (2020)

Zhou, Y., Guo, H., Ma, L., Zhang, Z., Skitmore, M.: Image-based onsite object recognition for automatic crane lifting tasks. Autom. Constr. **123**, 103527 (2021)

Emphasizing with a Robot with a Personality

Mariacarla Staffa[1]([✉])(iD), Lorenzo D'Errico[2](iD), and Rita Francese[3](iD)

[1] University of Naples "Parthenope", Naples, Italy
mariacarla.staffa@uniparthenope.it
[2] University of Naples "Federico II", Naples, Italy
lorenzo.derrico@unina.it
[3] University of Salerno, Salerno, Italy
francese@unisa.it

Abstract. In recent decades, socially assisted robots (SAR) have found applications in various operational contexts where the elicitation of empathy is crucial for facilitating human-robot interaction, as it plays a pivotal role in building trust and rapport. However, a significant challenge lies in the complexity of empathy, as there is no universally applicable method for its elicitation. Different individuals express and experience empathy in diverse ways. This study delves into the factors that impact the level of empathy evoked by a social robot, measured through user perceptions gauged by standard questionnaires. An empirical mixed-design study involving 28 participants was conducted, utilizing a Furhat robot with either an ironic (empathetic) or apathetic (non-empathetic) identity during verbal interactions with users. The primary objective of this research is to explore the user perception of a robot with or without a specific personality, with a particular focus on the empathetic personality, known to enhance Theory of Mind (ToM). The investigation aims to discern the extent to which users' perceptions are influenced by the personality of the robot and whether this influence varies based on the personalities of the users themselves.

Keywords: Social Robotics · Empathy in HRI · User Perception

1 Introduction

Socially assisted robotics (SAR) have been used in a variety of operational contexts in the past few decades, where the development of empathy is necessary to enable human-robot interactions. Building social bonds requires empathy, which is the ability to understand and experience another person's feelings. By promoting affection and increasing similarity, it aids in the formation of ties [4,17]. One approach for eliciting empathy in HRI is through the use of expressive gestures and vocal emphasis. Robots that are able to convey emotions through their behavior and speech have been found to be more likable and trustworthy by humans [14,15]. The personalization of robots, where they are customized to

H. Degen and S. Ntoa (Eds.): HCII 2024, LNAI 14736, pp. 283–294, 2024.
https://doi.org/10.1007/978-3-031-60615-1_19

match the preferences and personalities of the individuals they are interacting with, has also been found to be an effective way to elicit empathy. However, this mainly depends on the users' personalities and attitudes towards the robot [12,13,16]. In this work, our goal is to foster empathy by humanizing the robot by making it more relatable to humans through its functionalities, particularly by imbuing it with a sense of humor. By humanizing the robot with humor, we aim to enhance its empathy and Theory of Mind (ToM) [11] capabilities. Using humor, in fact, can enable the robot to form a stronger emotional connection with people, promote more positive and friendly interactions [7], and acknowledge and respond appropriately to a person's emotional state [18]. Additionally, humor can be utilized to promote ToM [8] by enabling the robot to comprehend and suitably react to the intentions and thoughts of others. For instance, the robot could crack a joke about a situation that necessitates a certain level of comprehension of the social context or the person's prior experiences. Our hypothesis is that endowing the robot with humor during interactions could have positive effects on ToM, mind perception, and trust:

- *impact on ToM*: empathy has been found to impact ToM in humans, and recent research suggests that it may also impact ToM in HRI. One study [10] that humans were more likely to attribute mental states to a robot that exhibited empathetic behavior. This suggests that robots that are able to elicit empathy may also be perceived as having a greater understanding of human mental state;
- *impact on mind perception*: mind perception refers to the degree to which humans perceive robots as having mental states, such as beliefs, desires, and intentions. Studies have shown that humans are more likely to attribute mental states to robots that exhibit empathetic behavior [5]. This suggests that robots that are able to elicit empathy may also be perceived as having a greater degree of mental state;
- *impact on trust*: trust is an important factor in HRI, as it is a necessary component for humans to feel comfortable interacting with robots. Research has shown that humans are more likely to trust robots that exhibit empathetic behavior [9]. This suggests that robots that are able to elicit empathy may also be perceived as more trustworthy by humans.

In this work, we are mainly interested in the impact that empathy could have on users' mind perception. We sought, on the one hand, to investigate the factors that may impact the amount of empathy evoked by a social robot, such as the user's personality; on the other hand, we aim at analyzing the effects of humoristic identity on users' perceptions. To test this, we conducted an empirical study of mixed design with 28 participants, in which each of them randomly interacted with a Furhat robot, in its virtual version, with either an identity (and a sense of irony or humor) or without (apathetic). In the empathetic condition, it exhibited behaviors that showed emotional understanding and support, such as asking questions and making jokes. In contrast, in the non-empathetic condition, it was more neutral and did not exhibit any emotional support. We then examined the factors that influence the amount of empathy elicited by a social robot as measured by user perceptions of that robot through standard questionnaires. Then we performed a statistical analysis to analyze the impact of the empathetic behavior of the robot on users' perceptions. We discovered that when the robot was given an identity, it elicited significantly more empathy in terms of its likability and perceived intelligence. The findings indicate that employing an ironic identity and behavior had a significant impact on participants' willingness to interact.

2   Materials

To measure the impact of empathy on users' mind perceptions, two different questionnaires were used:

1. *the Big-Five Inventory (BFI)* [6]: it's the 44-item version of the most complete (240 items) Big-Five Personality Inventory [3]. It's one of the most used questionnaires to assess users' personality traits;
2. *The Godspeed Questionnaire Series (GQS)* [1]: is one of the most highly cited and used questionnaires in the fields of Human-Robot Interaction and Human-Agent Interaction. Since its inception in 2009, it has been translated into 19 languages.

The idea is to collect data about users' personalities and verify if there is any particular correlation or difference between a person's personality trait and a specific judgment about their interaction with the robot.

2.1   The Big-Five Inventory (BFI) Questionnaire

The questionnaire [6] is composed of 44 items that measure an individual on the Big Five Factors (dimensions) of personality. Each of the factors is then further divided into personality facets (see Table 1).

Table 1. Example of one of the five dimensions with its relative facets.

The Big-Five Dimensions	Facet (and correlated trait adjective)
Extraversion vs. introversion	Gregariousness (sociable) Assertiveness (forceful) Activity (energetic) Excitement-seeking (adventurous) Positive emotions (enthusiastic) Warmth (outgoing)

Once informed consent was signed, participants completed the proposed BFI questionnaire. The results are described in Sect. 4, and they're used to verify if any correlation (positive or negative) exists between users' personality traits and their relative perception of the robot. This latter is evaluated with the Godspeed Questionnaire Series.

2.2 The Godspeed Questionnaire Series (GQS)

The Godspeed Questionnaire Series consists of five concepts relevant to HRI: anthropomorphism, animacy, likeability, perceived intelligence, and perceived safety [2]. Participants are asked to mark their answer on a five-point scale that is anchored with opposing terms, such as "unconscious" and "conscious." The questionnaire is composed as follows:

- *Anthropomorphism* (lately called Godspeed I): it refers to the attribution of a human form, human characteristics, or human behavior to nonhuman things such as robots and animals;
- *Animacy*: it relates to how "alive" or lifelike a robot is perceived to be by the humans interacting with it. It encompasses the extent to which the robot's movements, gestures, and overall behavior convey a sense of vitality or human-like qualities;
- *Likeability* (lately called Godspeed II): it has been reported that the way in which people form positive impressions of others is to some degree dependent on the visual and vocal behavior of the targets, and that positive first impressions (e.g., likeability) of a person often lead to more positive evaluations of that person;
- *Perceived Intelligence* (lately called Godspeed III): it assesses whether the robot's behavior, responses, and actions convey a sense of intelligence, competence, and problem-solving ability;
- *Perceived Safety* (lately called Godspeed IV): it evaluates how safe and trustworthy the user feels while interacting with the robot. It encompasses the user's perception of the robot's reliability, predictability, and ability to avoid causing harm or discomfort.

After compiling the BFI, users are asked to complete the GQS twice: once after the interaction with the empathetic version of Furhat and once with the apathetic one. To avoid specific patterns in user responses, the order of the interaction was randomly selected. Results on the users' perceptions of the interaction as well as any kind of correlation between and within them are presented in Sect. 4. The relationship between the GQS and the BFI will also be presented.

3 The Proposed Case Study

3.1 Experimental Procedure

Participants were recruited among university students through an institutional social media campaign. They were aged between 20 and 26. They first received a consent form to sign. If they decided to proceed with the study, they were given a brief summary of the procedure and asked to sit in front of the robot to begin testing. After introducing the Furhat simulated robot, participants were informed about the robot's interaction capabilities by specifying that the robot would use face expression and voice to communicate and therefore could not cause them any harm. We then conducted an empirical study of mixed design with 28 selected participants who were asked to interact in a randomized order with (a) a simulated Furhat robot with an identity (and a sense of irony or humor) (see Fig. 1a) and (b) a simulated Furhat robot without an identity (apathetic) (see Fig. 1b).

In the empathetic condition, Furhat exhibited behaviors that showed emotional understanding and support, such as asking questions and making jokes. In contrast, in the non-empathetic condition, it was more neutral and did not exhibit any emotional support (see Fig. 1).

The experiment consisted of several phases, generally summarized as follows:

- Greeting: where the first interaction with the robot took place, exchanging greetings;
- Joke: where the robot told a joke (in the friendly configuration);
- Request for drink list: where the list of various drinks available was provided;
- Order request: where the user decides what to order;
- Age request: where the robot checked to make sure it could serve a drink to a user of the appropriate age.

During the experiment, the times corresponding to each individual phase were also recorded, so that a specific moment of the simulation could be worked on when requested. A typical example of a table containing the acquired times is shown in Fig. 2.

To measure participants perceptions about the robot and analyze their personal factors, we asked them to complete the Big5 questionnaire before the interaction with the robot and the Godspeed Questionnaire after the 2 interaction sections with the ironic and apathetic robot, respectively.

4   Results and Discussion

First of all, we want to observe if the users are able to perceive a difference in the robot's behavior in order to demonstrate that giving the robot an identity has an impact on users' perceptions. For this purpose, we analyzed the Godspeed questionnaire replies. This section solely includes the relevant statistical results. Starting with the Godspeed I dealing with anthropomorphism, it is quite naive that no differences can be detected by the users since, regardless of its identity, the robotic device is the same in the two testing conditions. We computed the Wilcoxon W statistic and demonstrated that in fact no significant differences are observed regardless of the sub-dimensions of Godspeed I (fake/natural; machine-like/human-like; unconscious/conscious; artificial/lifelike[1]). In general, for all the users, regardless of the tests, the anthropomorphic aspect of the considered robot did not affect the users evaluation scores. All the items, in fact, settle on an average value, from 2.6 to 3.1 (see Table 2). Perhaps this is due to the lack of body in these robotic devices and the lack of robot embodiment, since for this study we used a simulated robot.

---

[1] We do not consider the item: moving rigidly/moving elegantly, since the robot is simulated and fixed, so no moving activities can be evaluated.

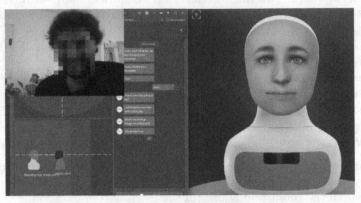

(a) Empathetic Furhat.

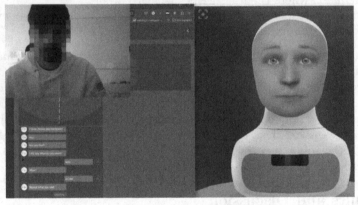

(b) Apathetic Furhat.

Fig. 1. Furhat interaction styles.

	m s ms
start	00:00:00
hi	00:16:33
what do you want	00:23:35
vodka/wine	00:40:70
age	00:54:33
cola	01:18:93
joke	01:36:32
bye	01:40:19

Fig. 2. Example of acquired times during an interaction.

Table 2. Average and standard deviation of the score related to Godspeed I items

Godspeed I: Anthropomorphism				
	Fake/Natural	Machine/Human-like	Un/Conscious	Artificial/Lifelike
Empathetic Robot	3.10 ± 1.02	2.60 ± 0.83	3.10 ± 1.02	2.50 ± 0.96
Apathetic Robot	2.61 ± 1.13	2.50 ± 1.04	3.32 ± 1.02	2.50 ± 1.04

This is also very clearly visible from the histogram in Fig. 3.

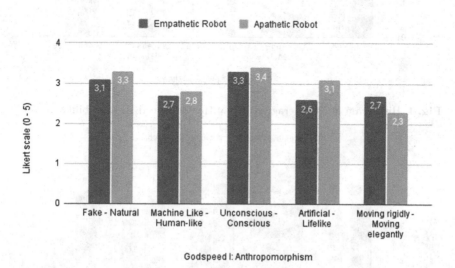

Godspeed I: Anthropomorphism

Fig. 3. Histogram of the avg scores of the Godspeed I: Anthropomorphism items

The second dimension considered by Godspeed, dealing with the likeability (no analysis has been conducted on the animacy dimension since a virtual version of the robot has been used) of the robot, was expected to be affected by the empathetic behavior of the robot, following our starting hypothesis. In Fig. 4, the average values of the scores assigned by the users to the Godspeed II items are shown.

Table 3. Wilcoxon test evaluated on Godspeed II items (* significant at $p < .05$)

Godspeed II: Likeability					
	Dis/Like	Un/Friendly	Un/Kind	Un/Pleasant	Awful/Nice
$z - value$	$z = -2.9714$	$z = 4.1143$	$z = -3.8796$	$z = -3.5281$	$z = -3.7886$
$p - value$	$p = .00298^*$	$p = .00001^*$	$p = .0001^*$	$p = .00042^*$	$p = .00016^*$

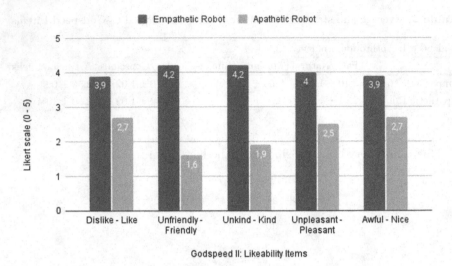

Fig. 4. Histogram of the average scores of the Godspeed II: Likeability items

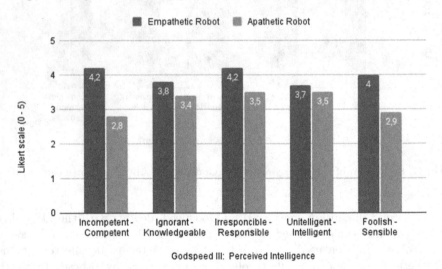

Fig. 5. Histogram of the average scores of the Godspeed III: Perceived Intelligence

Despite already being clear from the histogram, we computed the Wilcoxon nonparametric statistical test since we aimed to assess whether the observed disparity between two conditions (interaction with the robot with or without personality) was significant. Specifically, we considered a repeated-measures experimental setup based on ordinal values. The Wilcoxon test applied to the dislike/like item of the Godspeed II resulted in a z value equal to -2.9714 with a $p-value = .00298$, meaning that the result is significant at $p < .05$. Similar significance has been observed for all the items of the Godspeed II, as shown in Table 3.

Regarding perceived intelligence, the average scores of the participants associated with the Godspeed III dimension items are shown in Fig. 5.

High differences can be observed, especially in regard to the items incompetent/competent and foolish/sensible. The Wilcoxon test revealed that a significant difference at $p < .05$ exists for the items (see Table 4). Conversely, for items ignorant/knowledgeable and un/intelligent, we did not find any significant difference.

Table 4. Wilcoxon test evaluated on Godspeed III items (* significant at $p < .05$)

Godspeed III: Perceived intelligence			
	In/competent	Ir/responsible	Foolish/Sensible
$z - value$	z = −2.6286	z = −2.482	z = −3.4719
$p - value$	p = .00854*	p = .01314*	p = .00052*

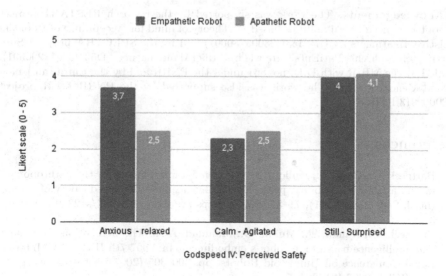

Fig. 6. Histogram of the average scores of the Godspeed IV: Safety items

These results are in line with our expectations that an empathetic robot would enhance our expectations about competence and sensitivity. Concerning knowledgeability and intelligence, since no particular intelligent behavior was provided, it is expected that the users did not perceive any difference between the empathetic and apathetic robots.

Finally, average scores on the Godspeed IV safety items (see Fig. 6) revealed a significant difference between the users perceptions about safety among the two tests, only on the item concerning the anxiety/relaxed behavior of the robot. Namely, the empathetic robot was perceived as more relaxed with respect to the apathetic one (with $z = -2.688$ and $p_{value} = 0.00714$, significant at $p < .05$).

5 Conclusion and Future Work

This study examined the impact of a robot's different identity on eliciting empathy in short-term human-robot interactions. A pilot research evaluated hypotheses about the impact of a robot with or without a proper identity (ironic/with-identity, apathetic/without-identity) in eliciting empathy in participants and maintaining their willingness to interact with the robot. The findings indicate that employing an ironic narrative strategy thus had a significant impact on participants likeability of the robot, by also impacting on its perceived intelligence. In regards of the impact of the users' personality on the robot perception, no significant differences have been found, meaning that the personality do not impact on the robot perception in this study. Since this results are in contrast with previous results, further investigations will be necessary.

Acknowledgements. The work was supported by the research RESTART project (Robot Enhanced Social abilities based on Theory of mind for Acceptance of Robot in assistive Treatments - CUP: I53D23003780001) and by the SPECTRA project (Supporting schizophrenia PatiEnts Care wiTh aRtificiAl intelligence - D53D23017290001), funded by the MIUR with D.D. no. 861 under the PNRR and by the European Union - Next Generation EU. The work was also supported by the PNRR MUR project PE0000013-FAIR.

References

1. Bartneck, C., Croft, E., Kulic, D.: Measurement instruments for the anthropomorphism, animacy, likeability, perceived intelligence, and perceived safety of robots. Int. J. Soc. Robot. **1**(1), 71–81 (2009). https://doi.org/10.1007/s12369-008-0001-3
2. Bartneck, C., Kanda, T., Mubin, O., Mahmud, A.A.: The perception of animacy and intelligence based on a robot's embodiment. In: 2007 7th IEEE-RAS International Conference on Humanoid Robots, pp. 300–305 (2007). https://doi.org/10.1109/ICHR.2007.4813884
3. Costa, P., McCrae, R.: The revised neo personality inventory (NEO-PI-R). SAGE Handb. Pers. Theory Assess. **2**, 179–198 (2008). https://doi.org/10.4135/9781849200479.n9
4. de Vignemont, F., Singer, T.: The empathic brain: how, when and why? Trends Cogn. Sci. **10**(10), 435–441 (2006). https://doi.org/10.1016/j.tics.2006.08.008, https://www.sciencedirect.com/science/article/pii/S1364661306002154

5. Gena, C., Manini, F., Lieto, A., Lillo, A., Vernero, F.: Can empathy affect the attribution of mental states to robots? In: Proceedings of the 25th International Conference on Multimodal Interaction, ICMI 2023, pp. 94–103. Association for Computing Machinery, New York, NY, USA (2023). https://doi.org/10.1145/3577190.3614167

6. John, O.P., Srivastava, S., et al.: The Big-Five Trait Taxonomy: History, Measurement, and Theoretical Perspectives (1999)

7. Leite, I., Pereira, A., Mascarenhas, S., Martinho, C., Prada, R., Paiva, A.: The influence of empathy in human–robot relations. Int. J. Hum.-Comput. Stud. **71**(3), 250–260 (2013). https://doi.org/10.1016/j.ijhcs.2012.09.005, https://www.sciencedirect.com/science/article/pii/S1071581912001681

8. Niculescu, A., van Dijk, B., Nijholt, A., Li, H., Lan, S.S.: Making social robots more attractive: the effects of voice pitch, humor and empathy. Int. J. Soc. Robotics **5**(2), 171–191 (2013). http://dblp.uni-trier.de/db/journals/ijsr/ijsr5.html#NiculescuDNLL13

9. Paiva, A., Correia, F., Oliveira, R., Santos, F., Arriaga, P.: Empathy and prosociality in social agents, 1st edn., pp. 385-432. Association for Computing Machinery, New York, NY, USA (2021). https://doi.org/10.1145/3477322.3477334

10. Paiva, A., Leite, I., Boukricha, H., Wachsmuth, I.: Empathy in virtual agents and robots: a survey. ACM Trans. Interact. Intell. Syst. **7**(3), 1–40 (2017). https://doi.org/10.1145/2912150

11. Premack, D., Woodruff, G.: Does the chimpanzee have a theory of mind. Behav. Brain Sci. **(1)-4**, 515–526 (1978)

12. Rossi, S., et al.: The role of personality factors and empathy in the acceptance and performance of a social robot for psychometric evaluations. Robotics **9**(2), 39 (2020). https://doi.org/10.3390/robotics9020039, https://www.mdpi.com/2218-6581/9/2/39

13. Rossi, S., Santangelo, G., Staffa, M., Varrasi, S., Conti, D., Di Nuovo, A.: Psychometric evaluation supported by a social robot: personality factors and technology acceptance. In: 2018 27th IEEE International Symposium on Robot and Human Interactive Communication (RO-MAN), pp. 802–807 (2018). https://doi.org/10.1109/ROMAN.2018.8525838

14. Staffa, M., Giordano, M., Ficuciello, F.: A WiSARD network approach for a BCI-based robotic prosthetic control. Int. J. Soc. Robot. (2019). https://doi.org/10.1007/s12369-019-00576-1

15. Staffa, M., Rossi, S.: Recommender interfaces: the more human-like, the more humans like. In: Agah, A., Cabibihan, J.-J., Howard, A.M., Salichs, M.A., He, H. (eds.) ICSR 2016. LNCS (LNAI), vol. 9979, pp. 200–210. Springer, Cham (2016). https://doi.org/10.1007/978-3-319-47437-3_20

16. Staffa, M., Rossi, A., Bucci, B., Russo, D., Rossi, S.: Shall i be like you? Investigating robot's personalities and occupational roles for personalised HRI. In: Li, H., et al. (eds.) Social Robotics, ICSR 2021. LNCS (including subseries Lecture Notes in Artificial Intelligence and Lecture Notes in Bioinformatics), vol. 13086 LNAI, pp. 718–728. Springer, Cham (2021). https://doi.org/10.1007/978-3-030-90525-5_63

17. Burattini, E., Rossi, S., Finzi, A., Staffa, M. Attentional modulation of mutually dependent behaviors. In: Doncieux, S., Girard, B., Guillot, A., Hallam, J., Meyer, J.A., Mouret, J.B. (eds.) SAB 2010. LNCS, vol. 6226, pp. 283–292. Springer, Heidelberg (2010). https://doi.org/10.1007/978-3-642-15193-4_27
18. Ziemke, T.: Understanding robots. Sci. Robot. **5**(46), eabe2987 (2020). https://doi.org/10.1126/scirobotics.abe2987, https://www.science.org/doi/abs/10.1126/scirobotics.abe2987

Embodying Intelligence: Humanoid Robot Advancements and Future Prospects

Kirsten Lynx Valenzuela, Samantha Isabel Roxas, and Yung-Hao Wong(✉)

Department of Mechanical Engineering, Minghsin University of Science and Technology,
Hsinchu 30401, Taiwan
yvonwong@must.edu.tw

Abstract. In an era of technological advancements, there are multiple stratagems to remain relevant and be one step ahead of the others in the same field. Exploring the convergence of humanoid artificial intelligence, the communities of Metaverse, Artificial Intelligence of Things, and the Machine Learners align their goals into integrating both physical and virtual worlds which opens a lot of opportunity in human and robot interaction.

Anthropomorphic robots are built with the grandiose objective of emulating human form and function, serving an extensive spectrum of purposes in a variety of industries and applications. Its utility encompasses nearly everything from assistance and companionship to industrial and recreational applications. Humanoid devices are capable of being an aid in the realm of healthcare such as therapeutic activities, featuring tailored care and support towards people experiencing physical constraints or impairments. These robots can undertake difficult endeavors with dexterity in the manufacturing process, enhancing efficiency and productivity. Furthermore, humanoid robots have the potential to revolutionize education by functioning as interactive instructors as well as companions for people who are subjected to difficulties with learning. These robotics' potential goes further towards responding to catastrophic instances, where its handiness and versatility allow it to venture into complicated areas, analyze factors, and conduct operations that humans may deem hazardous. Artificially intelligent humanoids ought to be able to consistently acquire knowledge and adjust to shifting circumstances. This implies utilizing reinforcement learning to improve performance and responsiveness over time by refining its actions. Anthropoid robots' adaptability markets them as vital instruments with a likelihood to augment human abilities as they confront a multitude of challenges across various domains.

These humanoid robots are designed to take the form and function of a human thus serving as the physical embodiment of adaptable intelligent systems. The cognitive abilities and adaptive learning of a humanoid robot are to be explained in this paper, as well as the intricate details of how machine learning techniques influence the robots' capacity to learn from experiences and dynamically respond to perplexing surroundings. As technology progresses, the attempt to create increasingly accurate humanoid robots propels the boundaries of what is plausible, establishing not only an insight into the future but also a mirror of the nuances that constitute our own humanity.

Constructing a humanoid robot that is capable of functioning as a human necessitates working with a complex web of aspects involving mechanics, artificial intelligence, and neurological mechanisms. In order to accomplish a robot

H. Degen and S. Ntoa (Eds.): HCII 2024, LNAI 14736, pp. 295–303, 2024.
https://doi.org/10.1007/978-3-031-60615-1_20

that resembles anthropomorphic movement, a proficient mechanical craftsmanship must be developed. Humanoid robots must replicate the human body's versatility in motion, mobility of joints, and precision. The aforementioned entails using cutting-edge materials and exquisite engineering to simulate the subtleties of human freedom of movement, spanning delicate motor ability to seamless propulsion. For a humanoid robot to navigate and interact with its environment, advanced sensory mechanisms must be integrated. Furthermore, not only its vision equipment should perceive surroundings, whereas it must also recognize imagery and depth perception. Sensors that measure tactile sensations convey signals for sensitive interactions and object maneuvering by portraying the human sense of contact. For the purpose of allowing accurate movement coordination, kinesthesia is adapted. In imitation of human cognitive functions, human-like robots depend on advanced artificial intelligence algorithms.

This comprehensive abstract offers a wide-ranging overview of the present state and future possibilities of humanoid robots. It emerges into the tremendous mechanical capabilities, revolutionary intellectual developments, interaction between humans and robots' dynamics, and the stimulating perspectives that stretch beyond. Humanoid robots, as an embodiment of intelligence, occupy a key position where technology progress meets societal development. The subject matter is an immersion account about humanity's ongoing attempt at developing intelligent devices that precisely replicate while gaining insight on the complexities of human existence.

The futuristic frontiers of humanoid robotics are to be explored throughout the study, envisioning a world in which these machines serve critical roles in the fields of space exploration, healthcare, education, and several other fields. Humanoid robots, as technology improves, possess the ability to revolutionize our view of human and machine interdependence, not solely as tools, but as essential contributors to our society. This concept probes into the terrain of collaborative robotics, focusing on the synergistic interaction that exists between mankind and humanoid robots. This relationship includes more than just physical assistance; it also includes an integrated intellect that boosts innovative thinking, troubleshooting, and effectiveness. The prospective societal impact of humanoid robots in harmonious roles reckon a more secure work environment, improved output, and job role reconfiguration in an array of industries.

In the department of Artificial Intelligence of Things, humanoid robots serve as autonomous components, traversing real world settings while interfacing networks. The ability of these machines to process real-time data, interpret environmental cues, and communicate with other IoT devices, alongside improving linked system performance, also incorporates a more unified and responsive IoT community. Concurrently, humanoid robots also act as digital characters, embodying individuals in virtual places, bridging the gap between actual existence and the Metaverse. Such physicality offers a new channel for immersive interactions, permitting users to gain access to the Metaverse by means of the eyes of humanoid substitutes, facilitating a more cohesive consolidation of physical and virtual realities.

Keywords: Humanoid robot · Advanced technologies · Artificial intelligence · Robot and AI synergy · Anthropomorphic robot · Human robot interaction

1 Introduction

Humanoid robots stand out in the fast-changing robotics field as intelligent embodiments meant to resemble human-like looks, actions, and behaviors. The ambition to infuse these machines with cognitive capacities has fueled substantial advances in the area, moving humanoid robots from basic automations to interactive companions, aides, and collaborators. This study overview digs into the outstanding advances made in humanoid robot development, examining the intersection of artificial intelligence, biomechanics, and human-centered design principles, and imagining the bright future potential for this transformational technology.

The integration of embodied artificial intelligence (AI) technology into humanoid robots has moved the field of robotics forward in recent years, with significant advances. The constant goal of constructing humanoid robots capable of natural and intuitive interactions has resulted in major advances in sensory skills, cognitive processing, and autonomous decision-making. According to Capelleti (2024), humanoid robots have a wide range of uses across sectors. Humanoid robots have the potential to transform processes, increase efficiency, and improve the quality of human-robot interactions in industries ranging from healthcare and education to manufacturing and entertainment. These robots, using embodied AI technology, can execute a wide range of activities with precision, efficiency, and human-like dexterity.

According to Gupta (2024), the confluence of AI and robotics is more than just the combining of two independent areas; it is a transformational synergy that is transforming how we interact with technology and our surroundings. This integration is the result of both need and invention: the need to expand robot capabilities beyond mechanical duties and the innovation given by AI to make this possible. AI adds the 'brain' to robots, allowing these machines to interpret information, learn from experiences, and make data-driven judgments rather than pre-programmed ones.

According to Katsuno and White (2023), building on worldwide developments in artificial emotional intelligence, Japanese corporations have increased their investment in social robots capable of expressing and evoking emotion. They can sometimes read human users' emotional expressions. These efforts are part of a larger trend in official assistance for creating technical solutions to socioeconomic challenges, including social isolation and a care provider shortage. The advent of companion robots has evoked both enthusiasm about potential human-robot futures and fears about data privacy and the loss of inter-human connection, encapsulating the dynamic emotional components of Japan's societal transition.

We, the researchers, chose the topic "Embodying Intelligence: Humanoid Robot Advancements and Future Prospects" to foster a deeper understanding of the opportunities and challenges inherent in the pursuit of developing intelligent, autonomous, and socially adept humanoid robots by examining the technological advancements, interdisciplinary collaborations, and ethical considerations shaping this field (Fig. 1).

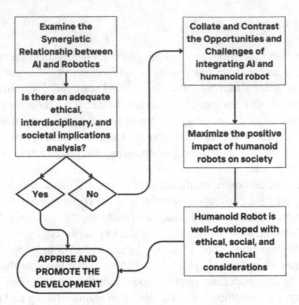

Fig. 1. Theoretical Framework

2 Methodology

The methodology for the study is qualitative research. Being qualitative in nature; its design is observational and analytical, having subjective insights accumulated for interpretation. The methodology covers a thorough review of applicable literature, advancements in technology, interdisciplinary interactions, and ethical issues in the field of humanoid robots. The researchers conducted a glimpse analysis of the various uses of humanoid robots across different fields such as healthcare, education, business, and entertainment. The researchers also addressed the collaborative connection between artificial intelligence and robotics, pointing out how AI influences robots' cognitive capacities and adaptive decision-making processes, however the study does not focus entirely on the said topic. The study concentrated on how humanoid robots can be designed to perform tasks naturally and seamlessly.

As previously mentioned, the study design is entirely qualitative. The approach used in order to obtain data is through an interview with a limited population of trained robotics experts, humanoid robot competition participants, and mechatronics engineering students to obtain data about the reliability and ethical concerns comprising humanoid robots. The interview was conducted during a humanoid robot competition. The data collection took place in National Taiwan Normal University's (NTNU).

Several kinds of resources and instruments have been utilized in order to support data gathering and assessment, which include techniques and technologies that have been deliberately chosen to achieve specific study objectives. The primary focus of the researchers concentrate on the functionality of humanoid robots, especially how far it could be integrated with artificial intelligence. The study's framework is based on the humanoid robot's ability to become more efficient and versatile, its purpose, and whether it surpasses the moral challenges it is associated with. Instruments such as interviews and surveys were utilized to acquire qualitative data from participants, demonstrating generalized opinions. Interviews with specialists, competitors, and mechatronic engineering students provided valuable insights into the impact of artificial intelligence on humanoid robots. In summary, mindful utilization of the resources and instruments established the methodology of the study, resulting in a systematic assessment of the adaptability of humanoid robots and its ethical implications.

The population of the study's respondents spans to the knowledgeable individuals, including academics, specialists, and skilled robotics executives. The integration of these sorts of a wide group of participants and subjects indicates an organized attempt to acquire complex yet accurate insights about the humanoid robots' purpose in regards to possessing artificial intelligence. Using their combined expertise, background, and interest with regard to improving and studying the efficiency of humanoid robots, these participants and subjects provide the researchers with an accurate collaboration of standpoints, expanding the inquiry process while offering suggestions how humanoid robots can be more helpful and less challenging.

The researchers presented the respondents a consent form and a brief explanation of the study's objectives, which was subsequently discussed. The interview's guide questions addressed the study's scope, limitations, and significance. The participants underwent interviews during the humanoid competition, as previously stated, and during the mechatronics engineering students' available time at school, Minghsin University of Science and Technology. Partially formal interviews were conducted to acquire respondents' candid and real-time thoughts (Fig. 2).

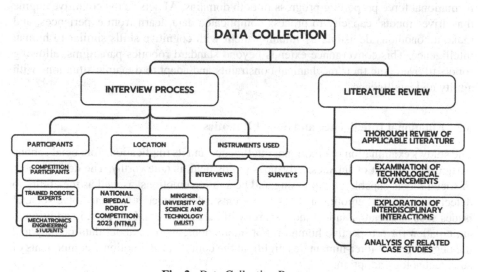

Fig. 2. Data Collection Process

The analytical techniques that have been applied to analyze the collected qualitative data were content analysis and qualitative comparative analysis. These were specifically selected to guarantee the validity of interpretations based on qualitative methodology.

Content analysis is a method for analyzing qualitative data, such as interviews and data gathered through observation, to identify the similarity between the participants' insights. It involves categorizing the data and systematically determining the prevalence and distribution of these categories, whereas Qualitative Comparative Analysis is also a method for analyzing qualitative data which compares occurrences and observations to identify its commonalities and differences with the respondents' opinion. It requires determining multiple factors that are related to specific patterns.

3 Results

3.1 Wide Range of Applications

A comprehensive review of the possible uses of humanoid robots in several industries, such as healthcare, education, industry, and entertainment, indicates their transformational significance. Humanoid robots are set to change procedures, increase efficiency, and improve the quality of human-robot interactions, from supporting medical professionals during operations to working as interactive tutors in schools. Their capacity to do tasks with accuracy, agility, and human-like dexterity brings up new opportunities for innovation and development across sectors.

3.2 Synergy between AI and Robotics

The study explains the synergistic link between AI and robotics, depicting it as a transformational force propelling progress in both domains. AI acts as the cognitive engine that drives robots' capacity to process complicated data, learn from experiences, and make autonomous decisions by imbuing them with cognitive skills similar to human intelligence. This convergence extends beyond standard robotics paradigms, allowing robots to overcome their mechanical constraints and adapt to dynamic situations with agility and intelligence.

3.3 Emotional Intelligence and Social Robotics

The study's examination of emotional intelligence and its implications for social robots, particularly in light of Japanese advances in this field, is noteworthy. The development of social robots capable of expressing and generating emotions, as well as the ability to detect human users' emotional states, represents a determined attempt to solve societal issues such as social isolation and a scarcity of care providers. However, in addition to anticipation for prospective human-robot interactions, worries about data privacy and the degradation of inter-human ties highlight the complicated emotional components of such technology adoption.

3.4 Opportunities and Challenges

The researchers methodically examine the prospects and obstacles involved in producing intelligent, autonomous, and socially competent humanoid robots. This necessitates a thorough assessment of technological advances, multidisciplinary cooperation, and ethical issues that shape the sector. While the potential advantages of humanoid robotics are numerous and diverse, navigating ethical quandaries, ensuring inclusivity, and limiting possible hazards are critical to achieving a future in which humanoid robots augment human skills and improve societal well-being (Fig. 3).

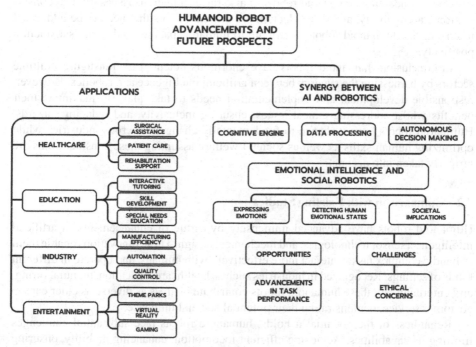

Fig. 3. Result Chart

4 Discussion

4.1 Interpretation of Results

The results of this study emphasize the potential of humanoid robots across industries and how they ought to be used aimed at transforming industrialization by enhancing human interaction with the help of advanced artificial intelligence. Through furnishing the respondents' insights, the researchers came up with the general interpretation that when the humanoid robots have a more synergistic relationship with artificial intelligence, the cognitive engine which enables the robot to process complex data will allow the robot to learn from experiences and adapt to current situations by making autonomous decisions similar to human intelligence.

The simultaneous development of artificial intelligence and robotics has rendered immense opportunities for humanoid robots to overcome mechanical constraints and adapt to dynamic circumstances with responsiveness and intelligence. Advances in the development of emotional intelligence in social robots, particularly in Japanese study findings, is a significant step toward addressing societal concerns such as social isolation and an inadequate number of care providers. However, this breakthrough raises anticipation about data privacy and its uncertain effects on human interactions.

Despite the study accentuating the future possibilities of intelligent, autonomous, and socially adaptable humanoid robots, it also raises numerous issues. Ethical considerations, accessibility, and risk reduction are critical factors that need to be addressed to ensure that humanoid robots contribute to human capacities and social satisfaction positively.

In conclusion, humanoid robots have enormous potential to transfigure multiple sectors by harnessing the synergy between artificial intelligence and robotics. However, responsible development and implementation needs to take place to maximize their benefits whilst addressing ethical issues, ensuring inclusivity, and reducing hazards. Humanoid robots have a chance to fundamentally change numerous industries while optimizing human skills as well as societal welfare assuming these considerations are properly taken into account.

4.2   Comparison with Existing Studies

Humanoid robots have advanced immensely by virtue of enhancements in artificial intelligence, sensor technologies, and mechanical design. These innovations enable them to handle complex tasks, interact more effectively with humans, and operate in different kinds of settings. Recognized in industries such as healthcare, education, manufacturing, and entertainment, these humanoid robots contribute in areas as diverse as elder care to customer service, demonstrating their potential societal influence.

Regardless of the potential it holds, humanoid robots face substantial challenges limiting its capabilities. Achieving efficient locomotion, enhancing mobility, ensuring safety between human and robot interactions, and addressing ethical quandaries are all indispensable challenges that must be addressed before widespread use. The user experience is being further improved by attempts to refine human-robot interaction, such as improving natural language processing and emotion recognition. As humanoid robots become more integrated into society, ethical and social issues arise, such as job displacement, privacy infringement, and the reconfiguration of human relationships. The aforementioned challenges warrant interdisciplinary teamwork and a thorough assessment of social principles.

Considering the impediments, the outlook for the development of humanoid robots continues to be promising according to both existing and ongoing studies. Continuous innovations in technology and persistent research efforts are set to boost the humanoid robots' capabilities and functionality, establishing the path for a greater presence in numerous aspects of human existence. Humanoid robots are expected to significantly elevate productivity, convenience, and general quality of life.

4.3 Conclusion and Recommendation

The conclusion drawn from the study on humanoid robot developments and future prospects suggests the vast possibilities for these robots to revolutionize multiple industries through the convergence of artificial intelligence and robotics. While significant progress has been made in improving their ability to manage challenging jobs and engage efficiently with humans, challenges such as accurate maneuvering, secure interactions, and ethical concerns need to be dealt with to guarantee responsible growth and implementation. In order to take full advantage of the benefits of humanoid robots while minimizing probable concerns, it is essential to prioritize the dilemmas it may cause and its accessibility. Collaboration among fields of study and an extensive awareness of social concepts are of the utmost importance for settling the difficulties of incorporating humanoid robots into the community.

Several recommendations from the conclusions highlighted can be extracted in this study for future researchers and developers in the field of mechatronics working with humanoid robotics. As a starting point, accomplishing comprehensive risk evaluations and verifying that the development process follows ethical rules and principles. Moreover, multifaceted cooperation is encouraged for the purpose of effectively addressing the multiple issues of integrating humanoid robots into community. By stimulating collaboration among specialists in robotics, artificial intelligence, ethics, sociology, and other related fields, developers may obtain beneficial knowledge and views concerning how to cope with these challenges effectively. The goal for future researchers and developers should be to seek methods to leverage the transformative and revolutionary potential of humanoid robots to further enhance productivity, convenience, and overall satisfaction. Humanoid robots are capable of being utilized to complement human skills and constructively contribute to society by proactively addressing issues.

References

1. Advancements in AI Robotics: Innovations and Future Perspectives. (2024). www.searchmye xpert.com. https://www.searchmyexpert.com/resources/artificial-intelligence/ai-in-robotics
2. Embodied AI: Insights into Humanoid Robotics and the Future of Intelligent Machines. (n.d.). www.linkedin.com. Retrieved (2024) from https://www.linkedin.com/pulse/embodied-ai-insights-humanoid-robotics-future-cappelletti-zxr7f?trk=article-ssr-frontend-pulse_more-articles_related-content-card
3. Ficht, G., Behnke, S.: Bipedal humanoid hardware design: a technology review. Current Robot. Rep. (2021). https://doi.org/10.1007/s43154-021-00050-9
4. Katsuno, H., White, D.: The japanese pursuit of human-robot companionship. Current Hist. **122**(847), 308–313 (2023). https://doi.org/10.1525/curh.2023.122.847.308
5. Kamran, S., et al.: The impact of artificial intelligence and robotics on the future employment opportunities. Trends Comput. Sci. Inf. Technol. **5**, 50–54 (2020). https://doi.org/10.17352/tcsit.000022
6. Roy, N., et al.: From Machine Learning to Robotics: Challenges and Opportunities for Embodied Intelligence. (2021) ArXiv.org. https://doi.org/10.48550/arXiv.2110.15245

AI Applications for Social Impact and Human Wellbeing

People and Technology: An Investigation of the Adoption of Artificial Intelligence in the Kinesiology Context

Andrea Antonio Cantone(✉)(iD), Gianluca Cossentino, Monica Sebillo(iD),
and Giuliana Vitiello(iD)

Department of Computer Science, University of Salerno, 84084 Fisciano, (SA), Italy
{acantone,msebillo,gvitiello}@unisa.it, gcossentino7@gmail.com

Abstract. In recent years, the spread of Artificial Intelligence and robotics has radically transformed the technological landscape, influencing various sectors. In this article, we explore the adoption of new technologies in the context of kinesiology, with particular attention to its uses for rehabilitative and preventive purposes. Through an analysis conducted through interviews, we aim to explore people's perceptions and propensity to adopt Artificial Intelligence and social robots in the kinesiological context. The focus of the survey is on understanding patients' expectations, concerns, and perspectives regarding the integration of Artificial Intelligence and robotics for posture monitoring and assessment. We also conducted a focus group with 8 people to discuss the topic. Finally, we present a system idea involving an EMG sensor for data collection during a therapy exercise and a social robot for emotion detection. The combination of the data collected by these two tools can provide an overview of evaluating a person's posture.

Keywords: Artificial Intelligence · Social Robot · Kinesiology

1 Introduction

In recent years, the introduction of technology into the medical field has led to a substantial revolution in clinical practice and health management. The incremental evolution of digital technologies, advanced medical devices, and artificial intelligence have ushered in a new era in the delivery of medical care, affecting every aspect of healthcare [3]. The deployment of technological tools has brought significant changes in the diagnosis, treatment, and management of diseases, increasing the efficiency of the healthcare system and enabling personalized care. Implementing Artificial Intelligence (AI) has enabled greater accuracy in the management and analysis of clinical data [7]. Advanced algorithms analyze complex data, diagnostic images, and clinical signs to identify diseases quickly

G. Cossentino—Independent Researcher

H. Degen and S. Ntoa (Eds.): HCII 2024, LNAI 14736, pp. 307–318, 2024.
https://doi.org/10.1007/978-3-031-60615-1_21

and efficiently, improving the timeliness of care and reducing diagnostic errors. Telemedicine has revolutionized the concept of health care, enabling the delivery of medical services remotely [8]. Video calls, telemonitoring, and remote data management improve accessibility to healthcare services. On the other hand, we live in a time when smartwatches and health monitoring devices have become in daily use. This continuous monitoring enables real-time fruition of data on people's physical condition. In addition, robots and virtual assistants support the care of the elderly and patients with disabilities, improving the quality of home care [2,4]. Researchers are exploring the use of these new technologies in the context of kinesiology.

Kinesiology is the science that studies bodily movements, focusing on an in-depth understanding of the functioning and health of the human body. Movement analysis, biomechanics, and muscle physiology are just some of the crucial aspects that characterize this multidisciplinary discipline. In the context of kinesiology, the intricate dynamics between movement, health, and wellness are explored, with the goal of improving physical performance and preventing any dysfunction or injury [9]. In this context, we focus our attention on the evaluation of posture, which is affected by muscle contraction and coordination. The electromyograph is a device that can provide detailed information about muscle activity during different body positions. Artificial Intelligence can play a significant role in analyzing electromyography (EMG) data, considering various factors such as body alignment and weight distribution, to help identify any problems in posture and provide corrective advice. Using sensors and cameras, AI can provide real-time feedback on a person's posture, also allowing for a more personalized assessment, taking into account anatomical differences and the specific needs of each individual. In addition, it can be used for long-term monitoring, detecting changes over time, and helping to prevent chronic postural problems.

But posture is not only considered a biomechanical aspect, as it is also a reflection of an individual's internal emotional condition. Several researches have shown that body posture can directly influence our emotional state and vice versa [5]. For example, open and upright postures are often associated with positive emotions, while contracted or curved postures may be linked to feelings of sadness or insecurity. Understanding this connection between posture and emotions could have significant implications for the development of innovative therapeutic approaches that integrate posture awareness into the treatment of emotional and psychological conditions. Therefore, the use of a social robot, which allows an assessment of emotions, for example, during a postural therapy exercise, together with the evaluation of EMG data may provide an objective picture of the correct execution of the therapeutic exercise and the postural state of the individual.

In this paper, we investigate people's opinions and expectations regarding the integration of AI and robotics for posture monitoring and assessment. We distributed a questionnaire to collect the opinions of participants. Then, we conducted a focus group to discuss this topic. Finally, we present the idea of a system including the EMG sensor and a social robot.

The main contributions of the paper are the following:

- a survey into the acceptance of new technologies, such as artificial intelligence and robotics, in the kinesiology context, particularly for posture assessment and monitoring;
- a focus group to further explore participants' considerations;
- an example scenario of system use involving an EMG device and a robot during a therapeutic exercise.

The paper is structured as follows: Sect. 2 discusses related work. Section 3 describes the survey conducted on the acceptance of new technologies in kinesiology, and Sect. 4 presents the results. Section 5 presents the focus group conducted with a group of participants. Section 6 presents the idea of a system and an example of a usage scenario. Section 7 presents a discussion, and Sect. 8 concludes the paper.

2 Related Work

Research highlights strong interest in the use of technology in healthcare. In [12] the authors conducted a systematic review of AI-supported physical rehabilitation technology tested in clinical settings to understand the availability of AI-supported physical rehabilitation technology and its clinical effect, concluding that the application of AI in physical rehabilitation is a growing field, but the clinical effects have yet to be studied rigorously.

Zhao et al. [13] present a wearable device for upper limb rehabilitation that integrates ECG and EMG sensors. This device, used during robotic glove-assisted training, captures, filters, and transmits accurate signals to a remote device via Bluetooth. A software platform analyzes and visualizes the ECG/EMG data, integrating it into the robotic glove control module. The EMG sensor monitors hand activities, while the ECG sensor tracks physiological changes. The study demonstrates the system's functionality and feasibility in improving upper limb rehabilitation through an adaptive training strategy. The results suggest a practical way to monitor individual ECG and EMG information, offering a technical guide for tailoring rehabilitation based on treatment conditions and user needs.

In [6] the authors present an Augmented Reality mobile application designed to assist the dermatologist's work in the immediate analysis of skin lesions. The app offers an interface that overlays relevant information about the lesion directly onto the camera view, thus assisting the physician in formulating the diagnosis. It also uses a deep learning algorithm to classify the lesion, focusing especially on the identification of melanoma. The process to generate this real-time augmented content is explained in detail, along with immediate performance evaluation and a study conducted with users. The results show that the entire analysis process can be performed directly on the smartphone and that the target users positively appreciate the support provided.

In [10] Lentin et al. illustrate the emotion recognition technique to be used in a social robot using deep learning techniques. This emotion recognition technique can work in real-time to predict the behavior of ASD children.

In [1] Bar-On et al. describe three focus groups with 12 clinicians specializing in the treatment of Parkinson's disease to explore the potential use of Social Assistance Robots (SARs) to meet the specific needs of people with the condition. The clinicians were supportive of the use of SARs for people with Parkinson's disease, especially when used directly at the patient's home, highlighting particular interest in their role in providing hands-on assistance and helping with daily activities. In addition, a survey involving 18 stakeholders (nine patients with Parkinson's disease and nine family members) was conducted to assess the degree of agreement with the opinions expressed by clinicians. The main differences in opinions between these two groups concerned the appropriateness of using a SAR as a companion or assistant in feeding, with opposing positions.

However, there is a dearth in the literature of the application of innovative technologies in the field of kinesiology and specifically applied to posture.

3   Research Design

The goal of the study is to understand attitudes toward the use of new technologies in the field of kinesiology, with the aim of providing an overview of a possible interaction between people, sensors, and robots by taking advantage of Artificial Intelligence to support activities to monitor and assess their posture. We formulated the following Research Question (RQ):

> **RQ.** How open are people to using new technologies, such as Artificial Intelligence and Robotics, to monitor and assess their posture?

3.1   Methodology

To answer the RQ, we conducted a survey to investigate people's perceptions and propensity to adopt artificial intelligence and social robots in the kinesiological context. The survey is designed to last 10 min and is created using Google Form module. Table 1 shows the questions of the questionnaire. It consists of two sections:

- The first section is aimed at collecting basic information, such as: gender, age, occupation, if they practice physical activity, and if they suffer from any bone condition. This data is fundamental to better understand the sample of users.
- The second section provides insight into people's views on the use of technology, with a focus on the use of artificial intelligence and robots to monitor and evaluate their posture. We also asked for their availability for an interview to explore this topic further.

We disseminated the survey online through different social channels, e.g., Facebook, Reddit, Linkedin, but also through personal contacts.

Table 1. Questions of the survey.

N.	Question	Evaluation criterion
Section I. Background		
1	What is your gender?	Multiple choice
2	What is your age?	Open answer
3	What profession do you do?	Open answer
4	Do you practice physical activity?	Multiple choice
5	Check one or more of the following conditions if you have them	Checkbox
Section II. Technology, Artificial Intelligence and Robots		
6	To what extent are you open to technology?	Likert scale from 1 (Not at all) to 5 (Very much)
7	Please, justify your previous answer	Open answer
8	Do you currently use devices or technologies to monitor your posture?	Multiple choice
9	If yes, what devices do you use?	Open answer
10	Do you know about Artificial Intelligence and its potential?	Multiple choice
11	Which of these tools have you ever used?	Checkbox
12	What do you think about the use of Artificial Intelligence for monitoring and evaluating your posture?	Likert scale from 1 (I don't agree) to 5 (I agree)
13	During a period of therapy, would you be willing to wear an instrument on your body (for example, an electromyograph) daily for a certain number of hours so that the data is transmitted to the therapist and your posture is continuously monitored?	Multiple choice
14	Please, justify your previous answer	Open answer
15	What would motivate you most to use an artificial intelligence-based system for posture monitoring?	Open answer
16	Would you be in favor of having a robot in your home that is able to evaluate your emotions during a therapy exercise and communicate them directly to the therapist?	Multiple choice
17	Please, justify your previous answer	Open answer
18	If you are willing to participate in an interview to discuss more about this issue, please leave your email here	Open answer

3.2 Analysis Procedure

We first described the background of the participants by considering the responses in Sect. 1 of the questionnaire. This allowed us to understand the sample of participants. Next, we analyzed Sect. 2 by first statistically analyzing the closed questions and then discussing the open questions.

4 Results

In this section, we report the results of the survey.

4.1   Analysis of Section I: *Background*

Seventy-eight people participated in the survey, including 43 females and 35 males, as shown in Fig. 1(a), ranging in age from 21 to 63. They are mainly students, entrepreneurs, employees, and teachers. Most of them practice physical activity (57%), while 15% do not practice it, and 28% only rarely (Fig. 1(b)). Furthermore, only a few of them suffer from some health problems, such as hernia, lumbosciatica.

Fig. 1. (a) Gender and (b) percentage of participants in physical activity practice.

4.2   Analysis of Section II: *Technology, Artificial Intelligence and Robot*

After an overview of the participant's background, we analyzed the closed questions of the questionnaire. As shown by the graph in Fig. 2(a), where the x-axis shows the number of participants and the y-axis the Likert scale values - from 1 very little to 5 very much - most respondents say they are open to technology and know the Artificial Intelligence (Fig. 2(b)). Few are not sure they know it or don't know it at all.

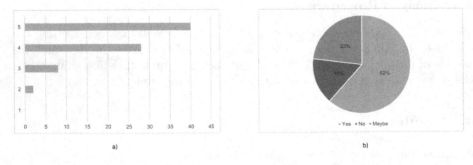

Fig. 2. (a) Openness to technology and (b) knowledge of Artificial Intelligence.

In particular, they use the most popular tools based on AI, such as Alexa, Google Home, Siri, but none of them use, in general, devices or technologies for posture monitoring.

Based on this response, it is critical to understand their point of view on introducing these new technologies for posture monitoring in general and, in particular, through the use of a technological device and robot during a therapy session.

As shown in Fig. 3(a), participants mostly agreed on the use of AI for posture assessment and monitoring.

Then, we asked the participants whether, during a period of therapy, they were willing to wear an instrument on their body (e.g., an electromyograph) daily for a certain number of hours so that the data collected by the sensor would be transmitted directly to the therapist. Most are in favor, as shown in Fig. 3(b). On the other side, however, dissenting opinions about using a social robot to detect emotions during a therapy exercise (Fig. 3(c)).

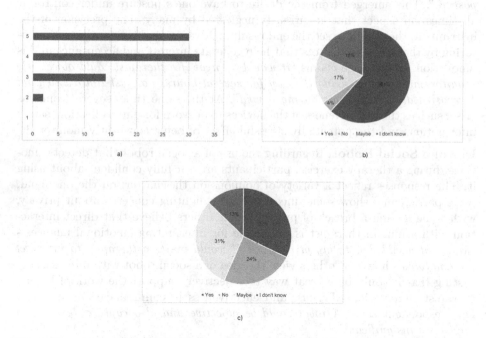

Fig. 3. Use of (a) Artificial Intelligence, (b) a sensor, and (c) a robot to assess posture and emotions.

Analysis of the open-ended questions allowed a clearer view of the issue. We categorized the responses into three key points:

Propensity for Technology. Those who are inexperienced and unfamiliar with technology show uncertainty and aversion in approaching the digital world. However, the perception changes substantially when considering those who see technology as an indispensable support for improving the quality of life. They recognize the fundamental importance of technology in social progress while emphasizing the importance of not completely replacing humans. One says, *"I believe technology is useful but it should not replace 100% of the human's work".* Those who were born in the golden age of technology see it as a powerful medium that, if used properly, can bring enormous benefits, especially in the work and medical fields. The duality of perspectives on the role of technology is also reflected in those who believe that while it is fundamental, they emphasize its potential negativity, especially when it is not used properly or is mismanaged, as one reported, *"I think technology is very useful and important in our daily lives, but at the same time it could be harmful".*

Acceptance of Artificial Intelligence. The prospect of being able to be assured of maintaining proper posture and improving health is a key motivation, and participants see the use of innovative technologies as a solution to solve postural problems. One says, *"It would solve various problems due to incorrect posture".* This emerged from the desire to have one's posture under control at all times, an aspect that is currently neglected by many. The precision of the instrument, the ability to see the end result in advance, and the continuous monitoring by therapists are factors that help generate interest and acceptance in this innovation. In fact, one claims *"It would be great if a therapist could objectively monitor my posture during the day for several hours, not just limited to what I reported or what he saw during a visit".* At the same time, several concerns arise, such as the intrusiveness of the devices to be worn for data collection, safety information, and the potentially stressful effect of being constantly monitored.

Use of a Social Robot. Regarding the use of a social robot that detects emotions during a therapy exercise, participants are not fully confident about using it. The responses reflect a variety of opinions on the matter: on the one hand, some participants show some uncertainty, highlighting concerns about privacy, with some fearing a breach of privacy, while others believe that direct interaction with a human therapist is preferable for interpreting emotional nuances - *"Maybe it would violate my privacy"* or *"I would prefer a therapist to interpret the emotions"*- however, others view the idea of a social robot with interest, suggesting that it could be a great way to objectively support the work of human therapists, improving efficiency and effectiveness in communicating emotions. One respondent says *"A robot could be objective and also capture details that may seem insignificant".*

5 Focus Group

We conducted a focus group in the HCI-UsE lab of the Department of Computer Science at the University of Salerno with the participants who indicated in the survey that they were available to discuss more on the topic. The number of participants in a focus group is typically between 6 and 12 [11]. We involved four young people, 22, 23, 26, and 27 years old (P1, P2, P3, P4), and four adults over 40 (P5, P6, P7, P8). The focus group was based around two questions:

1. What are the advantages and disadvantages of using artificial intelligence and robots during a therapy exercise for posture assessment and monitoring?
2. What are your concerns about this?

One author served as facilitator and two others as observers, who recorded and took notes of the participants' responses. The facilitator introduced the topic of the focus group and invited the participants to introduce themselves. After that, he started the discussion by asking the first question and then the second. At the end of the focus group, all the authors analyzed the participants' responses.

5.1 Results of the Focus Group

The focus group responses were categorized into two main points:

Advantages vs Disadvantages. To the first question we received mixed opinions. In particular, young people were more open to technology and its introduction during therapeutic exercises for posture assessment, highlighting that continuous monitoring is effective for recording changes in posture over time, allowing for a more accurate assessment of progress and preventing any problems (*"If it can be of help and support, why not use it"*, P4). On the other hand, adults say technological monitoring can be frustrating (*"I wouldn't feel comfortable doing an exercise knowing I had a device recording my data or a robot watching me"*, P6). P2 and P7 reply that the use of a robot can overcome the discomfort of being observed by a therapist and thus make the performance of the exercise more natural, while still having the expert view the data afterward. P1 and P7 also underline that in this way it is possible to receive immediate feedback during the exercises, helping to improve the quality of the execution. P3 recognizes as an advantage that artificial intelligence and robots can provide objective and precise measurements of posture, eliminating any human errors or subjectivity in assessments. However, it is essential to always have contact with the therapist, without relying exclusively on technology - says P8 - as the human being is fundamental for understanding the patient's emotional needs. P5 says he is not willing, to date, to be continuously monitored using digital tools, but he could change his mind once the real benefits that these technologies can bring become clear.

Main Concerns. The main concern noted by most participants relates to the privacy and security of data collection, processing, and storage. They are concerned about the risk of unauthorized access or loss of sensitive data. In addition, one participant claims that a technological malfunction could compromise the reliability and accuracy of posture assessments. Another concern is that automation through AI and robotics may crowd out human expertise, leading to a lack of human interaction and possible loss of empathy and understanding of individual needs during the therapeutic process. Finally, another participant argues that the excessive use of advanced technology may lead to dependence, with the possible loss of the ability to perform exercises independently without the support of technology.

6   Proposed System

The main goal of the work is to support a therapist in remotely assessing and monitoring people's posture. We present the idea of a system involving the integration of an EMG device to detect data from muscle movements and a robot to detect emotions.

6.1   Electromyograph

EMG (electromyography) records the movement of muscles. It is based on the simple fact that every time a muscle contracts, a discharge of electrical activity is generated that propagates through adjacent tissues and bones and can be recorded from nearby skin areas. EMG is a noninvasive procedure. Muscle movements are measured with two EMG electrode pads placed on the participant's skin. EMG data can be used to assess posture. Posture is influenced by muscle contraction and coordination, and EMG can provide detailed information on muscle activity during different body positions. AI can be used to analyze and interpret EMG signals, allowing assessment of muscle strength, fatigue, and other parameters related to muscle activity.

6.2   Social Robot

The robot must be able to detect people's emotions. We consider the use of QTrobot, a social robot developed by LuxAI[1], a company specializing in the development of humanoid robots. With its attractive and friendly design, QTrobot proves to be a perfect ally for therapeutic and recreational activities. Its customizable features allow it to adapt to the specific needs of users. The QTrobot has been equipped with highly sensitive sensors to ensure optimal perception and interaction with its surroundings. These include an Intel(R) RealSense TM Depth Camera D455 and an advanced 4-microphone system. This equipment enables the QTrobot to identify faces, emotions, and sounds. Through the use of artificial intelligence, QTrobot offers an interactive and immersive experience: it can understand and respond to voice commands as well as recognize and interpret human facial expressions. All these features promote effective and natural two-way communication between the user and the robot.

6.3   Usage Scenario

Maria is a 35-year-old woman who has long suffered from back pain. Her therapist decides to use an innovative approach in her therapy, combining the use of EMG sensors and an emotional robot to improve posture assessment during the therapeutic exercises the patient has to perform at home and optimize her course of treatment. Maria places the EMG sensor on her back and then activates the

---

[1] https://luxai.com/humanoid-social-robot-for-research-and-teaching/.

robot and places it in front of her. It is programmed to detect facial expressions and emotions during the exercise. Maria begins the exercise prescribed by the therapist, which consists of a series of movements aimed at improving her posture. As she performs the exercises, the EMG sensor records data on muscle contractility, providing the therapist with information about her muscle activity during the exercise. At the same time, the emotional robot analyzes Mary's facial expressions and emotional reactions, providing additional feedback to the therapist about her experience during therapy. Using dedicated software, the therapist monitors the data from the EMG sensor and the emotional reactions detected by the robot. This allows him to accurately assess Maria's posture, identify any areas of muscle tension, and adapt subsequent therapy based on the patient's individual responses.

7   Discussion

Analysis of the survey results showed that most participants demonstrate a favorable attitude toward technological innovation and are familiar with artificial intelligence. However, none of them routinely use tools for posture monitoring and assessment, suggesting a gap between awareness of AI and its use in practice. It was crucial, therefore, to carefully examine participants' considerations regarding the acceptance of cutting-edge technologies, such as artificial intelligence and robotics, in the context of kinesiology, in the specific case of posture. Young people show significant interest in exploring the adoption of sensors and robots for continuous monitoring during therapeutic exercise. In contrast, adults show more reluctance to embrace technology, especially in the medical field. Strengths that make people trust technological innovation in this context include real-time feedback, objective assessment, and the ability to correct and prevent postural problems over time. However, it is important to note that some participants expressed concerns about the lack of direct interaction with the therapist and insecurity in the correct evaluation of data provided by the sensors and robots, thus constituting the main obstacle to the acceptance of these technologies in this field. From a broader perspective, data security and privacy emerge as the main concerns shared by all participants. This underlines the importance of addressing and resolving data protection issues to ensure greater acceptance and adoption of innovative technologies in the field of kinesiology and postural assessment.

8   Conclusion

In this article, we investigated people's opinions on the use of innovative technologies, such as artificial intelligence and robots, in the kinesiology context, particularly for posture assessment. We conducted a questionnaire to collect opinions from a wide range of people, followed by a focus group to better discuss the advantages, disadvantages, and concerns about these technologies. Finally, we presented the design of a system involving the integration of sensors, artificial intelligence, and robots to support posture monitoring and assessment during a therapy exercise. In the future, we plan to implement this system and conduct experimentation with real users.

References

1. Bar-On, I., Mayo, G., Levy-Tzedek, S.: Socially assistive robots for parkinson's disease: Needs, attitudes and specific applications as identified by healthcare professionals. J. Hum.-Robot Interact. **12**(1) (feb 2023). https://doi.org/10.1145/3570168
2. Battistoni, P., Cantone, A.A., Esposito, M., Francese, R., Perillo, F.P., Romano, M., Sebillo, M., Vitiello, G.: Using artificial intelligence and companion robots to improve home healthcare for the elderly. In: Gao, Q., Zhou, J., Duffy, V.G., Antona, M., Stephanidis, C. (eds.) HCI International 2023 - Late Breaking Papers, pp. 3–17. Springer Nature Switzerland, Cham (2023)
3. Briganti, G., Le Moine, O.: Artificial intelligence in medicine: today and tomorrow. Front. Med. **7**, 27 (2020)
4. Cantone, A.A., Esposito, M., Perillo, F.P., Romano, M., Sebillo, M., Vitiello, G.: Enhancing elderly health monitoring: Achieving autonomous and secure living through the integration of artificial intelligence, autonomous robots, and sensors. Electronics **12**(18), 3918 (2023)
5. Coulson, M.: Attributing emotion to static body postures: Recognition accuracy, confusions, and viewpoint dependence. J. Nonverbal Behav. **28**, 117–139 (2004)
6. Francese, R., Frasca, M., Risi, M., Tortora, G.: A mobile augmented reality application for supporting real-time skin lesion analysis based on deep learning. J. Real Time Image Process. **18**(4), 1247–1259 (2021). https://doi.org/10.1007/S11554-021-01109-8
7. Artificial intelligence based clinical data management systems: Gazali, Kaur, S., Singh, I. A review. Informatics in Medicine Unlocked **9**, 219–229 (2017). https://doi.org/10.1016/j.imu.2017.09.003
8. Haleem, A., Javaid, M., Singh, R.P., Suman, R.: Telemedicine for healthcare: Capabilities, features, barriers, and applications. Sensors International **2**, 100117 (2021). https://doi.org/10.1016/j.sintl.2021.100117
9. Hazari, A., Maiya, A.G., Nagda, T.V.: Concepts of Kinesiology, pp. 209–214. Springer Singapore, Singapore (2021). https://doi.org/10.1007/978-981-16-4991-2_16
10. Joseph, L., Pramod, S., Nair, L.S.: Emotion recognition in a social robot for robot-assisted therapy to autistic treatment using deep learning. In: 2017 International Conference on Technological Advancements in Power and Energy (TAP Energy). pp. 1–6 (2017). https://doi.org/10.1109/TAPENERGY.2017.8397220
11. Kontio, J., Bragge, J., Lehtola, L.: Guide to Advanced Empirical Software Engineering, chap. The Focus Group Method as an Empirical Tool in Software Engineering, pp. 93–116. Springer (2008). https://doi.org/10.1007/978-1-84800-044-5
12. Sumner, J., Lim, H.W., Chong, L.S., Bundele, A., Mukhopadhyay, A., Kayambu, G.: Artificial intelligence in physical rehabilitation: A systematic review. Artif. Intell. Med. **146**, 102693 (2023). https://doi.org/10.1016/j.artmed.2023.102693
13. Zhao, S., Liu, J., Gong, Z., Lei, Y., OuYang, X., Chan, C.C., Ruan, S.: Wearable physiological monitoring system based on electrocardiography and electromyography for upper limb rehabilitation training. Sensors **20**(17) (2020). https://doi.org/10.3390/s20174861

Logical Interference: Using AI to Correct Flaws in Human Judgment

Daniel N. Cassenti[1]([✉]) and Thom Hawkins[2]

[1] DEVCOM Army Research Laboratory, Adelphi, MD 20783, USA
`daniel.n.cassenti.civ@army.mil`
[2] PM Mission Command, APG, Aberdeen, MD 21005, USA

Abstract. Humans and machines have disparate skills, with humans exemplifying higher-level cognitive skills such as problem-solving, decision-making, and creativity. In contrast, machines have an enormous computational capacity that no human could hope to match in accuracy or speed. These disparate sets of skills make humans and artificial intelligence (AI) ideal teammates to meet the demands of the most complex problem scenarios, including in the future Multi-Domain Operations Battlespace. To optimize performance, these skills should be strategically leveraged to form the basis for AI decision support software developments. This paper discusses decision-support systems, including their functions, current configurations, and whether these configurations are designed with the strengths of humans and AI in mind. A new model for decision-support systems offers an alternative to the traditional model that can maximize the benefits they provide each other in meeting mission goals.

Keywords: Human-AI Collaboration · Decision-Support Systems · Heuristics · Decision Making

1 Why Humans and AI Form an Ideal Team

Realizing objectives in a complex environment takes careful planning, including consideration of a wide range of factors with a depth proportional to the amount of uncertainty in the environment. The selection of team members to achieve these objectives is a critical factor in planning. There are several factors in this decision, including identification and allocation of tasks relative to capability and availability (see [1]), the opportunity cost of situational understanding [2], and trust or confidence in the outcome (e.g., planning products).

1.1 Disparate Skills

Any problem situation can be framed by the skills needed to achieve a goal state. Problems may range from simple issues that a single person can solve in a controlled environment to complex military battlefield scenarios where uncertainty from interactions with adversarial forces trying to exploit the element of surprise try their best to keep

© The Author(s), under exclusive license to Springer Nature Switzerland AG 2024
H. Degen and S. Ntoa (Eds.): HCII 2024, LNAI 14736, pp. 319–333, 2024.
https://doi.org/10.1007/978-3-031-60615-1_22

information from friendly forces. These scenarios require surveillance, reconnaissance, and maneuvering capabilities that all have elements of risk to maintain the information flow while also trying to prevent information from reaching the adversary. The skills needed to accomplish objectives in these environments are diverse and plentiful.

In these types of situations, human and AI teammates can both contribute. Common knowledge tells us that humans and AI are quite different from one another, but the details may be difficult to articulate. A decades-old source called Fitts' List [3] (Table 1) distinguishes the comparative skills of humans and machines and remains applicable, with some modifications, to the dynamic between humans and AI.

Table 1. Fitts' List [3].

Humans Better	Machines Better
Detecting inconsistencies	In extreme environments
Diverse sensing	Sensing particular stimuli
Perceiving patterns	Response speed
Attention to relevancy	Processing speed
Creative thinking	Precision in repetition
Strategic task allocation	Multitasking
Flexibility	Smooth force exertion
Learning from experience	Accurate performance
Low-chance events	Avoiding distraction
Induction	Deduction

Now a septuagenarian theory, Fitts' List has held up remarkably well. Cummings [4] reports that though research has been chipping away at some of the findings, most of the list has remained robust to change, with a few key exceptions. One such exception is the third skill on the left side of the list: perceiving patterns. Artificial intelligence's superior computational skills allow it to perceive patterns at a level far exceeding human capabilities (e.g., [5]). Another exception is that, with the advent of reinforcement learning, AI can now learn from experience ([6])—though its ability is no match for humans. Also, de Winter and Hancock [7] found in 2015 that advanced students learning AI largely validated that they do not believe that humans or AI are superior to the other but rather have diverse skills that largely align with Fitts' List's tenets.

Generalizing the differences between humans and machines highlights three primary contrasts. The first is that humans can generalize with little effort, leading to skills in flexible thinking, attention to relevancy, creativity, strategic planning, diverse sensing, and induction. Conversely, while AI's rigid structure and strict adherence to its programming lends itself to excellent computational skills, it limits its ability to generalize. AI can repeat its programmed algorithms and process data without deviation, thus minimizing errors. This gives AI superior processing and response speed, accuracy, precision, deduction, and the ability to sense particular stimuli. Cassenti, Roy, and Kaplan [8] found that, in contrast, humans struggle with interpreting uncertainty representations that require computation. The final contrast is how humans and AI handle low-probability events. For AI, unless low-probability events are part of their set of algorithms (whether from programming or incorporated during machine learning), they cannot be processed. This ability to focus leads to some benefits, including avoiding distraction, operating in extreme environments, and multitasking. Attention to low-probability events in humans leads to skills in detecting inconsistencies, learning from experience, and handling low-chance events.

1.2 The Benefits of Diversity

When forming collaborative teams, effective strategy begins with breaking down the problem into components and assigning them to team members with expertise in handling those components. Specific problems require specific solutions, understanding general solutions for decision-making situations is the aim here, taking the position that humans and AI work together to cover complex decision-making situations requiring both sides of the abovementioned contrasts. When constructing a division of labor between AI and humans for specific missions, the analysis should not push artificial constraints such as AI and humans taking on all one task independently, but instead give consideration to how to break down tasks into components, assigning as appropriate to AI and humans what each performs best,thus composing an ideal collaboration.

Complex decision-making situations include the need for generalizing because greater complexity often increases uncertainty. Greater complexity implies an increasing number of events, which would increase both low- and high-probability events with around the same ratio as in less complex environments. Humans are needed to manage these factors. Yet, complex problem situations tend to unfold at a pace too quick for human comprehension alone, necessitating AI intervention (i.e., cybersecutiy analysis). Moreover, if a significant number of events are low-probability, many more will be high-probability events, which AI can process more quickly and accurately than humans. AI is also impervious to stress and distraction in the problem situation,thus providing consistently engaged information processing and action relative to humans.

The contrast between humans and AI is so large that teaming them together should, in principle, cover the full range of skills needed to solve a given problem. With that established, the next question is what roles should be assigned to maximize a team's effectiveness.

1.3 Configuring Humans and AI in a Team

A complex problem must be decomposed with distinct components requiring specific skills. Whatever the task analysis method, the resulting components should fall with some clarity into whether information-processing needs are more conceptual or concrete, with humans more capable of handling the former and AI more capable of handling the latter. Similarly, decisions that need to be made can be categorized as more strategic plans (better handled by humans) or more tactical shaping of the environment or situation (better handled by AI).

Overall, the problem to be solved dictates the proportion of work to be done by AI relative to humans as summarized by the Level of Automation (LOA; see [9]). LOA models employ whole number scales typically from 5 (e.g., [10]) to 9 (e.g., [11]). At LOA 1, humans do everything, with automation providing, at most, background support. With each increasing LOA, human teammates yield more work to AI until the maximum LOA number when AI does everything. LOA is another means of organizing the distribution of labor over an entire problem situation, with the proportion of components covered by humans and AI dictating the LOA [10]. Individual steps in the solution may also be broken down by human and AI teammates if the two sides are working in concert with one another.

In a mock cyber-analysis task, Cassenti, Roy, Hawkins, and Thomson [12] found differences in performance and trust at varying LOAs. In this task, middle LOA values demonstrated greater trust than either extreme. They explained that at LOA 1, humans may feel overburdened and that AI is not doing enough to help. At LOA 5, humans may believe their autonomy has been taken away, and that mistakes could have been prevented if they had exerted some control over alert detection. Although, trust is largely outside the scope of this paper, such findings indicate that an imbalance in LOA can create a lack of trust in AI, leading to a lack of AI use even if the AI may have otherwise helped. LOA is an important consideration to ensure that human-AI teaming is effective.

Also, important to optimally configuring human-AI teams is recognizing where AI can assist humans when they have deficiencies in areas that they can generally be trusted to handle over AI. For example, humans are better at generalizing, but but also more prone to over-generalizing. Humans are susceptible to using decision-making shortcuts called heuristics that decontextualize situations and lead to a conclusion based on generalized parameters. Although heuristics can shorten decision-making time, decisions based on heuristics are often ill-fitting and error prone. AI could provide a check against these heuristics and thus prevent avoidable errors.

2   Decision Support Systems

The specific type of AI discussed here is a decision-support system (DSS). A DSS is an information system that structures information processing and selecting options in collaboration with at least one human. The way this is achieved is dependent on the type of DSS being used. This section explores the functions of DSSs and discusses their potential military applications.

2.1   Functions of Decision Support Systems

When considering what a DSS is meant to do, the classic, logical view of decision-making is a good place to start. When framing a problem-solving situation, two elements are necessary before any progress may be made. First, one needs to understand the initial state. So, a concerted effort must be expended to determine the critical factors that best provide situational awareness [13]. It should be complex enough to include all needed information, but not so complex that it becomes too difficult for the human teammate to process. Second, a clear goal state must also be determined. The goal state may be as close to maximal gains and minimal losses as reasonably expected. It may not be a realistic expectation, but determining a goal state is merely the second step of the decision-making process. Risk and likelihood values may be determined in later stages.

Once initial and goal states are determined, the DSS and human team must determine how to transform the problem situation from initial to goal state. There is almost always more than one way to reach a goal state. The options, which are generated after an analysis of the problem situation takes place, are called courses of action (COAs). Some COAs will be worse than others, and an analysis of the initial COAs should distinguish between them.

Ultimately, one COA must be selected and then implemented. The function of the DSS is to recommend the COA that is most likely to accomplish the mission with the most gains and fewest losses.

2.2 Military Functions of Decision Support

Military decision-making involves complex problem-solving situations. In a military scenario, time pressure and the odds of human consequences (e.g., injuries, lost lives, which is also the case for medical field) makes military decision making an apt field for the study of DSSs as military commanders use every resource available to avoid making decision-making errors.

Also, there are two sides in any military situation. The blue, friendly forces must count on the red enemy forces to use any means to achieve their objectives and prevent the blue forces from achieving theirs. These means are bountiful, including limitless strategies, tactics, and approaches, not to mention AI and human agents. With all of these assets and methods at the disposal of two adversarial forces, the complexity of the problem situation could exceed any bounds.

2.3 Commander's Advisory System for Airspace Protection DSS

Bélanger and Guitouni [14] describe Commander's Advisory System for Airspace Protection (CASAP), a DSS designed for the Canadian Air Force, as a good example of how a DSS might function. First, it is important to note that unlike much of the literature on DSSs, this is not a theoretical exposition but an actual working DSS. Bélanger and Guitouni admit that the DSS would require more development before becoming consistently functional; however, it is an accomplishment that they managed to create a working DSS. Please note that the CASAP DSS is tailored to a specific function: air space protection in counter-drug trade operations. In the early stages of DSS advancements, a DSS generalized across many problem types would far exceed the current state of the art.

CASAP's functionality works within a narrow part of what DSSs are theoretically meant to do (best covered by Zachary [15]). It does not assess a situation or generate COAs. Instead, it works with an Air Operations Center (AOC) staff to absorb information about the program situation and their ideas for COAs. CASAP uses a series of applets to evaluate and prioritize the COAs. The AOC staff can access CASAP's information, but the human teammates lead all other parts of the decision-making process.

That a working prototype DSS has such a narrow mission is a question explored here. Most publications on DSSs either describe theoretical directions for the development of DSSs or describe DSSs that only provide more functionality than CASAP within simulations [16], so there may be two general explanations. First, perhaps working DSSs provide more real-life functionality than CASAP, but the information cannot be in the public domain due to the protection of government or proprietary information. The second possible explanation is that AI's state of the art means certain functional limitations are in place for DSSs. The first argument puts an obvious impediment on this publication if it were true. However, the second explanation has more validity, and will be explained in greater detail in the next section.

3   Improving the Odds of Working Decision Support Systems

A functioning DSS that can work with real-world situations appears to be limited, at least from the publicly available research. There are examples of DSSs that have more expansive capabilities within simulations. Because simulations simplify the world to known entities and known parameters, they are often a necessary step to ensure that an automated system can be produced in the future. Simulations can include stochastic processing that provides randomness, but like any programming, simulations are limited to what programmers plan for the system to have. Accounting for everything that can occur in a problem situation, particularly one involving adversarial actors, is virtually impossible. As outlined above, AI performs poorly when processing low-probability events. A DSS can demonstrate wide-ranging skills when working within a controlled simulation and with structured information that only includes a defined set of events [16], but this is not a good approximation of the real world.

The following section will explain the Military Decision Making Process (MDMP). This is the long-established means that humans-only teams in the U.S. military use to make battlefield decisions. The MDMP exemplifies what the latest research posits is best for a DSS to automate parts of the MDMP. The section concludes with an alternate approach that outlines what research on human-agent teaming suggests would increase the probability of a functional DSS that helps in real-world problem scenarios.

3.1   Military Decision-Making Process

In 2015, the U.S. Army publicly released the *MDMP Handbook* [17], which went into great depth on the Military Decision-Making Process that is still used today. Figure 1 displays the timeline of the MDMP.

Each step in the above process is performed entirely by human teammates. Digital assets may help facilitate communications or keep track of information for an individual, but no artificial intelligence currently helps complete any of the steps.

The MDMP begins with communication from headquarters that a problem situation requires a decision. The received information undergoes an analysis to gain situational awareness, which concludes Step 2. Step 3 begins the process of deriving COAs. To be clear, the objective of Step 3 is to derive candidates, and this amounts to a brainstorming session where there is openness to all but nonsensical suggestions. Step 4 is for filtering

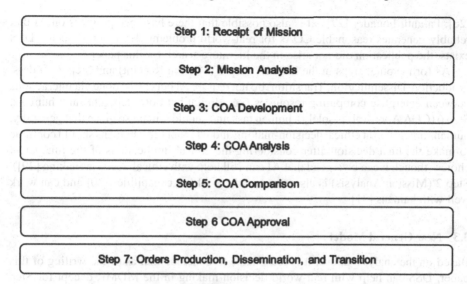

Fig. 1. The MDMP displayed in sequential steps.

these COAs to a subset that has the potential to achieve more gains than losses. The COAs from this subset are each analyzed in comparison to one another in Step 5 until one candidate is selected as the most beneficial and least costly of the options. In Step 6, the selected option undergoes further scrutiny by superiors. If problems are detected, Step 5 could be repeated to select a more reasonable option. Once the commander approves the selected option, Step 7 produces an order, finalizes communications of that order, and transitions it to the unit that will implement it.

The MDMP is important because it provides an organized decision-making system with discreet steps with varying levels of computational and conceptual need. Mapping a DSS onto this organization allows us to posit LOAs for human-agent teaming that align with Fitts' List. The next two sections provide this mapping for the general model for DSSs from the literature, then offer a critique of the general model and a new DSS model as an alternative.

3.2 DSS Research and Development Overview

Of the steps in the MDMP, COA generation is the most time-consuming [18]. Deriving COAs requires considering innumerable situational factors, which increase exponentially in an adversarial situation where the derivation of covert adversarial intent is critical. With AI possessing a quick processing speed and the ability to multitask, it stands to reason that a DSS would best handle COA generation. This appears to be the overall trend in theoretical DSS development recommendations (e.g., [19–21]) and simulation-based DSSs (e.g., [22–24]).

What is lacking is a DSS that performs COA generation in real-world problems. However, there are plenty of tools that can support decision-making in analysis (MDMP Step 4) and comparisons (Step 5) of COAs (e.g., IBM Watson Analytics [25]; Ayasdi

[26]; Palantir Foundry [27]). It is also possible that there has been progress on AI that reliably generates reasonable COAs for real-world problems. However, if such a DSS exists, the publication did not arise in the literature search for this paper.

As for the other steps in the MDMP, Step 1 (Mission Receipt) and Step 7 (Orders, Production, Dissemination, Transition) do not require AI but can be done via interactions between enterprise computing resources (i.e., digital but not intelligent) and humans. Step 6 (COA Approval) is solely a human task and should remain so given that generally, humans are skilled at ethical decision-making and AI is not [28]; humans should continue to make the final decision after considering the ethical implications of the final COA choice (though it can be argued that AI can still help with ethical decision making [29]). Step 2 (Mission Analysis) is also an area where AI has capabilities [30] and can work well with humans [31].

3.3 New General Model

Based on the analysis above, it is reasonable to conclude that as of the writing of this paper, DSS can help with real-world decision-making in the MDMP, except for Step 3 (COA Development) because of lack of skill, and Steps 1 and 7 because of lack of need. DSSs like CASAP do not attempt COA generation because of the difficulties AI would face with this step. Other DSSs may, but so far a real-world implementation of a DSS that performs COA generation outside of simulation appears elusive. This may be because humans need to ensure understanding of COAs and computers cannot effectively understand every factor in a decision, especially ones that are more qualitative than quanititative (see [15]). Generating COAs requires attention to relevancy, creative thinking, strategic task allocation, flexibility, drawing from relevant experience, and induction—all skills on the human side of Fitts' List. To be clear, this is not to say that the future precludes the possibility of AI/ML developing skills on the left side of Fitts' List. One of us led a journal special issue presenting research and development that achieves this concept [32]; however, each article either describes small steps, theoretical arguments, or both. Progress is slow in developing human-like skills in AI because it would require reworking the basic principles of AI construction by incorporating cognitive psychological principles into the AI architecture [33].

The approach to building a new model of DSSs was to look at each stage of the MDMP and recommend an LOA (on a 1 to 5 scale) for each based on the above analysis of Fitts' List, MDMP, and the literature on DSSs. First, Steps 1, 6, and 7 do not require AI and are at LOA 1 (though Steps 1 and 7 could be automated to some degree using natural language processing, this is outside the scope of this paper). Recognizing that AI is deficient in real-world COA generation, humans should perform Step 3 without AI (i.e., LOA 1; though AI can help evaluate the generated COAs in Step 4). Step 2 does not involve COAs, but with AI growing in situational awareness skills, it should be set to LOA 2. This provides recommendations for on-the-ground variable setting but would ensure that the human teammate could set each parameter because the DSS would not necessarily be able to process variables at a conceptual level.

Step 4 is the one that best fits with AI's strengths. Of the steps in the MDMP, Step 4 is most in-line with the computational strengths of AI. Once concrete COAs are generated, the need for creativity is minimized. Instead, DSS programming can break down the COAs and use deductive reasoning to understand how the steps of the COA would lead to certain probabilistic outcomes. The DSS could track these probabilities using multitasking to run out the probabilities of mission success or failure and eliminate COAs that showed the lowest odds of success. The new model should set this step to the highest level at LOA 5.

Step 5 could also depend heavily on AI's strengths. Comparing the smaller subset of COAs that have the greatest probabilities of success to one another could involve further dissection of how various factors weigh against the mission goals. The more analysis depends on an objective weighting of factors, the more AI can make the comparisons. However, the weighting of factors is not always objective. Weighing the cost of a greater chance of civilian casualties against mission success is not a matter for complete reliance on AI. When subjective costs and benefits enter the equation, a human decision-maker should have control over these comparisons. Step 5 is optimized at LOA 3, in which the AI would recommend a rank ordering of COAs, while human teammates could choose whether or not to overrule the individual comparison and make the selection for COA approval.

One final recommendation for the new DSS model is the possible incorporation of an iterative process between Steps 3 and 4. With the completion of Step 3, generated COAs are input into the DSS for processing. If the analysis finds that all generated COAs demonstrate too much risk of mission failure, the DSS would communicate this result, and new COAs would be required. Figure 2 represents this and the other conclusions of the new DSS model.

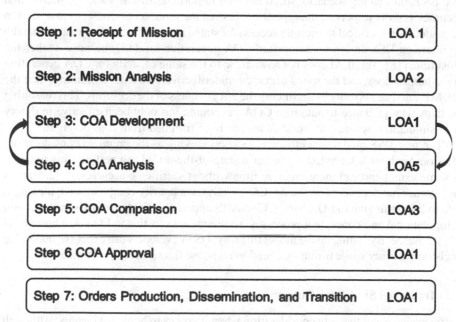

Fig. 2. The MDMP with associated LOAs and the possibility of iterative Steps 3 and 4.

4 Features of New Model

The new DSS model improves upon the standard model by setting LOAs which correspond to human and AI skills. With AI either imperfect or unneeded for four of seven MDMP steps, need for analysis remains for only three steps, including mission analysis, COA analysis, and COA comparison. It is no coincidence that each of these steps is a type of analysis, as analysis involves deductive reasoning (i.e., deriving conclusions from a set of known facts) and computational speed and accuracy, top skills for AI relative to humans. This section will review the two ways the new model will improve outcomes (performance and subjective) and two features on how DSSs could achieve COA Analysis, the step at the highest LOA.

4.1 Improved Performance Outcomes

The two most often cited examples of performance outcomes are accuracy and response time. The speed-accuracy tradeoff is a well-known psychological condition which posits that an individual, at any moment, has defined performance limits (see [34]). If the individual attempts to increase performance speed, that will necessarily lead to a greater risk of inaccuracy. Inversely, attempting to increase the performance accuracy (or precision) should would see a decrease in the speed of task completion.

The speed-accuracy tradeoff should apply to human-AI teaming, given that human and AI teammates also have some limits on their collective ability to perform a task. In a decision-making scenario, speed is often important. Still, it stands to reason that accuracy is more important than speed because of the finite set of decisions that need to be made, each is critical to overall success. As stated above, it is understandable that the literature on DSS argues for automated COA generation (cf. [15]) because it takes the most time [18]. Yet, if AI does not have close to the same capacity for COA generation that a human does, and the speed-accuracy tradeoff covers human-AI teaming, then the MDMP can speed up only by sacrificing the effectiveness of the decisions. This reasoning explains why guidance to automate COA generation has only been effective in theory or in simulations where real-world chaos has been trimmed from consideration.

The new DSS models put effective decision-making as the premium consideration. Mission Analysis is set at LOA 2 because state-of-the-art AI can perform this function to some extent and can therefore save time without sacrificing accuracy if the team is only somewhat dependent on the AI. COA analysis is heavily computational, making it safe to bring this step to LOA 5 (e.g., CASAP's approach). COA comparison has strong computational and conceptual processes, so the model sets this to LOA 3, a human-AI equal balance. By setting up the model this way, DSS developers can expect to maximize decision accuracy while trimming decision response time where appropriate.

4.2 Improved Subjective Outcomes

Performance is not the only consideration when it comes to human-AI teams. Although AI must adhere to its programming, humans have choices about whether- and to what extent- they engage with AI. If AI systems are created without regard to whether humans want to work with them, a significant amount of effort, time, and money could be wasted on unused systems.

The new model is designed with subjective considerations in mind. The big three subjective variables in human-AI teaming are mental workload [34], usability [35], and trust in automation [36]. Mental workload is the amount of mental burden that a human must endure while working with AI. Ideally, AI would reduce mental workload with AI that increases mental workload unlikely to be used by a human. If AI is applied to a decision-making process and cannot perform well in those ways, it would only tax the human teammate's mental workload more, as the AI's work would need to be checked and redone. To save the human from additional workload and ensure efficient AI use, DSSs should be designed to work within their limits.

Usability is the subjective value a human place on the ease of engagement and collaboration with AI. An unusable system adds cognitive burden to the interaction between humans and AI relative to a usable system. To improve the usability of a DSS, DSS developers should program graphical user interfaces (GUIs) that work with a human's natural perceptual, attentional, and other cognitive skills. This means program GUIs that, for example, reduce distractions on the screen, cue the user to where to direct attention, organize information in a way that is ordered and predictable, and represent information in a way that reduces the need to engage in computational processing [35].

Lastly, trust in automaton is the human teammate's belief that the DSS is performing in a way that helps the decision-making process rather than hindering it. By designing DSSs with the suggested LOAs at the various steps, a developer should maximize trust in automation as the user can believe that the tasks the AI performs are not above its skill levels. Therefore, the human teammate does not need to correct the AI's work, wasting time and effort. By being mindful of the steps in the decision-making process and how they correspond to human and AI skills, DSS developers can increase the odds that AI will be seen as valuable and used as intended.

4.3 Focus on Heuristics

The most unique of the LOA recommendations in the new DSS model is COA Analysis. As the only step that exceeds a 50–50 balance for AI-to-human work, greater direction is needed on how this step would be performed, given this is where the DSS will perform the heaviest lifting. Furthermore, this step follows COA Development, which is entirely performed by the human side of the team. Although AI does not need to be involved in COA generation, it will need to check the human's work in this stage, particularly for faulty heuristics.

As generalized decision-making tactics, heuristics are shortcuts to decision-making. They are intended to bypass deliberate strategic thinking by allowing the human deploying them to generalize scenario conditions into a loose framework that matches the heuristic, thereby leading to a decision or conclusion with little effort. An example is the availability heuristic [36], where someone assumes that examples of past situations that come to mind quickly when evaluating a new scenario are the most likely analogous situations. The availability heuristic relies on a false premise because the availability of the past scenario relies on any number of factors dissociated from the chances of accurate representation. If a decision maker builds COAs based on what worked in the past and factors that do not match the old and new scenarios are ignored, the COAs could be deeply flawed.

DSSs should include a database containing various heuristics and indicators for when they may be invoked. A DSS that can check an exhaustive heuristics database could analyze COAs by finding patterns of the COA elements that map onto indicators. The analysis input would then warn the human teammate of the probability that a heuristic is being used and flag the corresponding COA as suspect.

4.4 Uncertainty Evaluation

One type of information AI excels at processing is uncertainty. AI has a long history of development on this skill (see [37]). Uncertainty is the relative lack of awareness of objective information about an environment compared to complete objective knowledge [4]. In a complex environment, data is plentiful, but information is the subset of data useful to the decision-making process. With superior computational ability, AI can sort through data quickly, select useful information, and track uncertain information.

AI can track uncertain information categorically (this is especially useful in mission and COA analysis) and has strong skills in estimating uncertainty. AI active within a DSS can apply these uncertainty estimates against the COAs when analyzing them and comparing them to indicate risk levels with COAs evaluated as riskier decisions with greater uncertainty estimates. These uncertainty estimates will strongly influence decision-making if applied in a DSS to the analytical steps of the MDMP.

5 Conclusions

Complex problem situations are suited to involvement from teams of human and AI elements because of each agent's unique and diverse skill sets. Combining the flexible, adaptable, and creative thinking of humans with AI's strong computational skills can solve a much wider range of problems than either one alone, but only with a strategic plan to selectively apply each type of agent to the decision-making process.

This paper describes an exemplar decision-support system and the existing recommendations from the literature on how to optimize the construction of a DSS. However, DSS developers should not follow the fundamental direction suggested by other researchers that a DSS should generate COAs in real-world problem-solving situations. Although research that works on COA generation within simulations is important, this paper shows that AI is not ready for a real-world implementation of this yet (however, it may achieve this in the future).

DSS guidance should recommend LOAs to automate MDMP steps within a DSS to middle levels for mission analysis and COA comparison and to automation only for COA analysis. This should maximize effectiveness for state-of-the-art AI in a DSS by applying it where it is skilled and not where it lacks skill. This paper details guidance for DSS development by suggesting that two specific AI skills for use within a DSS are evaluating the influence of heuristics in COAs and focusing on the amount and effect of uncertainty in mission and COA analysis.

The new model is untested; however, researchers should conduct follow-up studies and DSS development following this guidance. The greater the understanding of how to optimize the usage of AI, the better the outcomes of decisions will be. There are any number of sectors in which these capabilities would benefit humankind, but above all else, AI-dependent decision-making needs support effective decision making so these benefits can arrive sooner rather than later.

Acknowledgments. We would like to thank Zach Hare, Lance Kaplan, Carl Busart, and Mollie Ryan for providing edits and comments on earlier drafts of this paper.

Disclosure of Interests. The authors have no competing interests.

References

1. Hawkins, T., Cassenti, D.: Defining the relationship between level of autonomy in a computer and cognitive workload of its user. In Mukherjee, S., Dutt, V., Srinivasan, N. (eds.) Applied Cognitive Science and Technology: Implications of Interaction Between Human Cognition and Technology, pp. 29–40. Springer, Singapore (2023). https://doi.org/10.1007/978-981-99-3966-4_2
2. Blasch, E., Salerno, J., Tadda, G.: Measuring the worthiness of situation assessment. In: Proceedings of 2011 IEEE National Aerospace and Electronics Conference, pp. 87–94. IEEE (2011)
3. Fitts, P.: Human engineering for an effective air navigation and traffic control system: National Research Council Washington, DC (1951)
4. Cummings, M.: Man versus machine or man+machine? IEEE Intell. Syst. **29**, 62–67 (2014)
5. Dastani, M., Indurkhya, B., Scha, R.: Analogical projection in pattern perception. J. Exp. Theor. Artif. Intell. **15**, 489–511 (2003)
6. Sutton, R., Barto, A.: Reinforcement learning: an introduction. Robotica **17**, 229–235 (1999)
7. De Winter, J., Dodou, D.: Why the Fitts list has persisted throughout the history of function allocation. Cogn. Technol. Work **16**, 1–11 (2014)
8. Cassenti, D., Roy, A., Kaplan, L.: Representing uncertainty information from AI for human understanding. In: Proceedings of Human Factors & Ergonomics Society Meeting (2023)
9. Kaber, D., Endsley, M.: The effects of level of automation and adaptive automation on human performance, situation awareness and workload in a dynamic control task. Theor. Issues Ergon. Sci. **5**, 113–153 (2004)
10. Endsley, M., Kaber, D.: Level of automation effects on performance, situation awareness and workload in a dynamic control task. Ergonomics **42**, 462–492 (1999)
11. Sheridan, T., Verplank, W.: Human and Computer Control of Undersea Teleoperators. Massachusetts Institute of Technology, Cambridge (1978)
12. Cassenti, D., Roy, A., Hawkins, T., Thomson, R.: The effect of varying levels of automation during initial triage of intrusion detection. In: Ahram, T. Kalra, J., Karwowski, W. (eds.) Artificial Intelligence and Social Computing, AHFE International Conference. AHFE International, New York (2022)
13. Endsley, M., Garland, D.: Theoretical underpinnings of situation awareness: a critical review. Situat. Aware. Anal. Measure. **1**, 3–21 (2000)

14. Bélanger, M., Guitouni, A., Pageau, N.: Decision support tools for the operational planning process. In: Proceedings of the 14th International Command and Control Research and Technology Symposium "C2 and Agility", pp. 15–17. Washington, DC (2009)
15. Zachary, W.: Decision support systems: designing to extend the cognitive limits. In M. G. Hollander, M. (Ed), Handbook of Human-Computer Interaction, pp. 997–1030. North Holland, Amsterdam, Netherlands (1988)
16. Power, D., Sharda, R.: Model-driven decision support systems: concepts and research directions. Decis. Support Syst. **43**, 1044–1061 (2007)
17. Reese, P.: Military decisionmaking process: Lessons and best practices. Center for Army Lessons Learned, Fort Leavenworth, Kansas (2015)
18. Falcon, R., Abielmona, R., Billings, S.: Risk-driven intent assessment and response generation in maritime surveillance operations. In: 2015 IEEE International Multi-Disciplinary Conference on Cognitive Methods in Situation Awareness and Decision, pp. 151–157. IEEE (2015)
19. Chen, Y., Cheng, M.: Enhanced HTN planning approach for COA generation. In: 2013 International Conference on Information Technology and Applications, pp. 272–274. IEEE (2013)
20. Kewley, R., Argenta, C., Brawner, K.: Behaving like soldiers: A multi-agent system approach to course of action planning for simulated military units. In: The 35th International FLAIRS Conference Proceedings, AAAI (2022)
21. O'Donnell, M., Hunter, J., Hough, J. Wilt, B., Patterson, E.: Roadmap to implement artificial intelligence in course of action development& effect of weather variables on UH-60 performance. In: Proceedings of the Annual General Donald R. Keith Memorial Conference, pp. 278–283. U.S. Military Academy, West Point, NY (2021)
22. Haider, S., Levis, A.: Effective course-of-action determination to achieve desired effects. IEEE Trans. Syst. Man Cybern. Part A: Syst. Humans **37**(6), 1140–1150 (2007)
23. Yuksek, B., Guner, G., Karali, H., Candan, B., Inalhan, G.: Intelligent Wargaming Approach to Increase Course of Action Effectiveness in Military Operations. In: AIAA SciTech Forum, pp. 23–27, AIAA, National Harbor, Maryland (2023)
24. Tu, H, Levchuk, Y., Pattipati, K.: Robust action strategies to induce desired effects. IEEE Trans. Syst. Man Cybern. Part A: Syst. Humans **34**(5), 664–680 (2004)
25. Hoyt, R., Snider, D., Thompson, C., Mantravadi, S.: IBM Watson analytics: automating visualization, descriptive, and predictive analytics. JMIR Public Health Surveill. **2**(2), e5810 (2016)
26. Mohanty, B., Aashima, Mishra, S.: Role of artificial intelligence in financial fraud detection. Acead. Market. Stud. J. **27**(4), 1–16 (2023)
27. Moorcroft, T. Simanjuntak, K. Dorjsuren, O., Sanaakhorol, M., Enkhtaivan, E., Watt, G., Eickhoff, V., Cerny, L., Deasy, C., Zimmermann, T.: Oyu Tolgoi and Rio Tinto partnership with Palantir Technologies to provide effective geotechnical risk management. In Caving 2022: Fifth International Conference on Block and Sublevel Caving, pp. 877–890. Australian Centre for Geomechanics, Perth, Australia (2022)
28. Bellaby, R.: Can AI weapons make ethical decisions? Crim. Justice Ethics **40**(2), 86–107 (2021)
29. Seville, H., Field, D.: What can AI do for ethics? AISB Q. **104**, 499–510 (2000)
30. Munir, A., Aved, A., Blasch, E.: Situational awareness: techniques, challenges, and prospects. AI. **3**(1), 55–77 (2022)
31. Endsley, M.: Supporting human-AI teams: transparency, explainability, and situation awareness. Comput. Hum. Behav. **140**, 1–16 (2023)
32. Cassenti, D., Veksler, V., Ritter, F.: Cognition-inspired artificial intelligence [Special Issue]. Top. Cogn. Sci. **14**(4), 647–903 (2022)

33. MacKay, D.: The problems of flexibility, fluency, and speed–accuracy trade-off in skilled behavior. Psychol. Rev. **89**(5), 483–506 (1982)

34. Longo, L., Wickens, C., Hancock, G., Hancock, P.: Human mental workload: a survey and a novel inclusive definition. Front. Psychol. **13**, 883321 (2022)

35. Hodrien, A., Fernando, T.: A review of post-study and post-task subjective questionnaires to guide assessment of system usability. J. Usability Stud. **16**(3), 203–232 (2021)

36. Lee, J., See, K.: Trust in automation: designing for appropriate reliance. Hum. Factors **46**(1), 50–80 (2004)

37. Li, D., Du, Y.: Artificial Intelligence with Uncertainty. Taylor & Francis, New York (2007)

Text Analysis Software Using Topic Modeling Techniques for the Extraction of Knowledge from Cases Related to Vulnerability and Access to Justice

Jorge E. Espinosa[1]([✉])(iD), Sandra P. Mateus[1](iD), and Diana M. Ramirez[2](iD)

[1] Politécnico Colombiano Jaime Isaza Cadavid, Carrera 48 No. 7-151 El Poblado, Medellín, Colombia
{jeespinosa,spmateus}@elpoli.edu.co
[2] Universidad de Medellín, Medellín, Colombia
radiana2113@gmail.com
https://www.politecnicojic.edu.co/

Abstract. Access to justice is a vital part of the UNDP (United Nations Development Programme) mandate to reduce poverty and strengthen democratic governance. One of the objectives of the Personero (ombudsmen) in emerging countries is to assist people in accessing justice, promoting equality and the protection of the most vulnerable, providing assistance to citizens through guidance or consultations. In Medellín (Colombia), the "Personería de Medellín" (ombudsman's office) has established a citizen service system staffed by lawyers who address their difficulties, needs, or other issues, guiding them on the steps to take, such as filing legal actions or providing advice. All this information is recorded in a digitalized system. Annually, more than 16,000 different cases can be recorded (e.g. for year 2019), and despite the implementation of multidimensional analysis tools like dashboards, there is a need to implement Natural Language Processing (NLP) techniques to semantically analyze the fields of unstructured text information. This paper presents an application offered to citizens called Person_IA, which implements various functionalities based on artificial intelligence techniques, particularly Natural Language Processing (NLP). This allows for text analysis using strategies such as topic modeling, word clouds, n-grams, among others, to extract knowledge from the unstructured information in the citizen service system. This helps generate indicator reports and analyze variables that enable efficient decision-making by knowledge managers at the Medellín Ombudsman's Office, facilitating access to justice for the vulnerable population in this city.

Keywords: Textual Analysis · Machine Learning · Natural Language Processing (NLP) · Topic Modelling · Latent Semantic Analysis (LSA) · Latent Dirichlet Assignment (LDA)

H. Degen and S. Ntoa (Eds.): HCII 2024, LNAI 14736, pp. 334–352, 2024.
https://doi.org/10.1007/978-3-031-60615-1_23

1   Introduction

The "Personería de Medellín" (ombudsman's office) protects and promotes human rights, monitors the official conduct of those in public office, safeguards public interest and the environment, contributes to alternative conflict resolution, and strengthens, respects, and guarantees diversity and population groups, aiming to be closer to the community. Law 136 of 1994, in Article 178, establishes that the Personero (ombudsman) will exercise the functions of the Public Ministry in the municipality, in addition to those determined by the Constitution, the Law, and Agreements [4].

The "Personería de Medellín" assists citizens by allowing them to approach and consult with a window lawyer about their difficulties. With their help, individuals can file legal actions, compliance actions, or seek advice on what steps to take, among other services. This creates a historical record of their cases, ensuring the immediate protection of their constitutional rights when these are violated by the action or omission of any public authority [1].

One of the objectives of the "Personería de Medellín" is to assist people by promoting equality and protecting the most vulnerable. However, not everyone has the same tools, facilities, and knowledge to assert their rights and access their protection. Therefore, this entity has focused on studying this phenomenon in vulnerable individuals. Building on theoretical results, in 2022, there is an effort to intervene in the data collected by the organization to propose efficiency and protection schemes. This involves the use of digital tools to provide better service quality and ensure the fulfillment of rights [4].

Currently, requests for cases are submitted, and these are documented in the Personería's service system, causing delays in the analysis of the daily incoming requests. A proposed improvement is the identification process for vulnerable individuals by utilizing Business Intelligence (BI) and data analytics for the "Personería de Medellín" based on multidimensional analytics to streamline the consultation and analysis of large volumes of data [22].

Improving this kind of analysis, we develop this project to leverage text analysis tools through machine learning strategies, using Natural Language Processing (NLP) for knowledge extraction using topic modeling. The goal is to have a tool that supports decision-making for the Personería, enabling the analysis and formulation of more efficient strategies to ensure access to justice for the most vulnerable.

A technique from the field of Artificial Intelligence (AI), specifically from the subfield of Machine Learning, can be highly beneficial for classifying these texts. This technique is called topic modeling, and it is a textual analysis tool derived from the computer science field of Natural Language Processing (NLP). Its purpose is to identify the main themes (topics) within a text without the assistance of any dictionary. Every text contains a range of topics expressed through words, especially nouns. The machine's task is to count words and identify co-occurrences to identify variables, characteristics, and patterns in the corpus. This helps extract information from cases submitted by citizens, providing a quick and strategic solution [3].

The paper is organized as follows. Section 2 highlights some relevant work on NLP researches oriented to Jurisprudence topics, Judicial rules, Identification of Social or legal issues and support for decision-making. Section 3 describes the "Personería de Medellín" process used as input for the design an implementation of the NLP-based software Person_IA. This section includes details about the NLP techniques, algorithms, and tools employed. Section 4 provides a high-level overview of the architecture of the software prototype, explaining the key components, modules, and how they interact. Section 5 presents baseline results and discuss main findings. Finally, Sects. 6 conclude the paper.

2 Related Work

2.1 Classification of Jurisprudence Topics

In the realm of jurisprudence, recent research has employed Topic Modeling to understand how support for the most vulnerable can be enhanced. In 2020, Parra [8] implemented Natural Language Processing techniques to analyze harassment complaints. Various algorithms were employed, including Wrapper Methods, Integrated Methods, within Supervised Learning: TF-IDF, Logistic Regression, Decision Tree, Random Forests, and also LDA within the context of Unsupervised Learning. The results provided comprehensive descriptions, revealing that complaints with witnesses had an accuracy of 72%, precision of 61%, and sensitivity of 47%. Additionally, the most frequent complaints were reported in the regions of America and Europe. Meanwhile Ordoñez [21] implemented a Natural Language Processing scheme with a model for searching judicial rulings, aiming to analyze the texts of jurisprudential rulings in Colombia. This model utilized the term extraction scheme (LSA, TF-IDF) to select the most frequently occurring keywords as inputs for a Neural Network (MLP), thus aiding users in searching for judicial rulings, improving response times, and the process of finding the required information. In 2021, the Digital Rights Organization [13] introduced an Artificial Intelligence system (PretorIA) to enhance the process of selecting 'tutelas' (homologous to Marbury v. Madison rulling [11]) in the Constitutional Court, implementing NLP technologies to improve the tutela selection processes. This serves as support to identify the processing of the tutela ruling. The application utilizes Topic Modeling for the classification of tutela rulings by category and ultimately generates statistical information on the use of tutelas in the country. The application is currently in the testing phase with the goal of reducing the workload in the management of tutela selection in the Constitutional Court. Finally, in 2022, Villaseca [29] conducted an application of topic modeling on complaints received by Sernac (Chile's National Consumer Service), which handles consumer complaints and mediates with product and service providers. During the process, Topic Modeling algorithms allowed for the discovery of associations, percentage distributions, and the classification of a large collection of documents by themes. Each project within the legal or juridical domain concluded with similar findings, with results on efficiency of 90%

using this technology. Additionally, it provides a dynamic and versatile analysis of large volumes of data to make decisions based on the results obtained.

2.2 Determining Judicial Rulings

Another area that is beginning to leverage artificial intelligence tools is the management of judicial rulings. In 2021, Cruz del Ser [26] utilized Text Mining in law, implementing Sentiment Analysis and Topic Modeling to enhance search efficiency in online databases, resulting in a 60% difference in response times compared to the common manual registration process. The study demonstrated the potential psychological influence, with a potential bias of 70%, on the interpretative process of the law performed by judges. This highlights the potential impact of implementing these algorithms in the classification processes of legal topics.

On the other hand, in 2022, Agrasar [5] implemented Machine Learning techniques in the analysis of rulings related to child trafficking. Through similarity analysis, Agrasar observed that approximately 50% of child trafficking cases closely resembled prostitution offenses. This provided a more detailed analysis of the rulings. During the project's implementation, data on child trafficking offenses in Spain was extracted, aiming to understand the reasons behind the increase in this crime. This was achieved through the use of Text Mining and Topic Modeling techniques.

2.3 Identification of Social or Legal Issues

In line with the goal of supporting citizens in accessing justice by identifying their social issues and using natural language processing as a path to a solution, the literature describes research that addresses a range of social or legal problems through detailed analysis of the issue, its process, and consequences. All these projects utilize technologies like Topic Modeling as a contribution to the analysis of social and/or legal issues.

In 2016, Sarmento [25] conducted Topic Modeling research focused on a case study with scientific production. Sarmento employed two different methods for topic extraction: Latent Dirichlet Allocation (LDA) and Term Frequency-Inverse Document Frequency (TF-IDF). The objective was to provide a complete prototype developed for studying and visualizing the affinity between authors and their study or research topics. The outcome achieved a solution in response times when investigating or requiring information on a specific topic.

In 2017, Diaz Benito [15] implemented an application that used Topic Modeling in song lyrics to generate a document collection, enabling a study of the most representative music genres in the 21st century. The author used LDA for generating the document collection with song lyrics, subsequently employing NLP as an algorithm to extract implicit data. Similarly, in 2022, Rosati [23] implemented a Natural Language Processing technique on the corpus (text block generated from tango lyrics). LDA was applied for topic detection, working with 5,617 lyrics to semiautomatically detect their themes and generate negative and positive emotions. The study confirmed that 70% of songs influence the thoughts and feelings of the listener. Meanwhile in 2020, Torrent et al. [7] implemented a project that explores the digital narratives behind data using Topic Modeling. Initially, tweets about Covid-19 were explored to identify emerging topics useful for studying social interactions during the pandemic. The study and analysis process recognized that when working with large corpora, 80% of the time is dedicated to cleaning and organizing data. The in the work of Aguilar [6] is developed a tool to support communicational environment analysis using topic modeling techniques, extracting high volumes of information from Twitter with a limit of 1500 requests for a defined 15-minute window and a limit of 100,000 requests in a 24-hour period. The tool found latent topics in statements from people of interest using topic modeling techniques (LSA, pLSA, and LDA), capable of studying patterns in texts that are challenging for a person to identify. The process was conducted in stages, including data extraction, data preparation, implementation of topic modeling techniques, and finally, development based on the results obtained in the previous steps. The analysis and comparisons of the results facilitated the analyst's ability to study the evolution of each topic over time, identifying trends or patterns related to specific phenomena.

On a different approach, in 2021, Londoño [19] implemented Natural Language Processing techniques to identify the most relevant issues for residents of Bogotá, as an initiative addressing challenges such as inequality, poverty, environmental degradation, justice, and peace. In the implementation, LDA was used, finding a direct relationship between the Sustainable Development Goals (SDGs) and the most relevant problems for citizens. This contributes to decision-making that influences the achievement of Sustainable Development Goals. Additionally, the work of Battsta et al. [12] implements Natural Language Processing and Data Science applications applied to different sources of information (texts, audios, videos, images, among others), with the aim of generating tools that aid decision-making in various social fields (resource management, health, sports, tourism activities). Meanwhile in 2022, Espin-Riofrio [17] employs topic modeling (in Spanish) using Machine Learning to extract information from the speeches of Guillermo Lasso (President of Ecuador). The algorithms Non-negative Matrix Factorization and Latent Dirichlet Allocation are used for topic modeling in unstructured text, analyzing Lasso's speeches to identify different topics and themes discussed. Lastly, Zander et al. [30] address disciplinary divergence in research on the nexus between human mobility and the environment, using Unsupervised Topic Modeling. The topics are divided into two focus categories: Impact and Adaptation. The Impact theme is grouped into subtopics on vulnerability and residential mobility, while articles within the Adaptation theme are grouped into governance, disaster management, and agriculture. In conclusion, the approach has value not only for researchers but also for policy-makers and funding agencies: automated approaches, such as topic modeling, can help identify emerging topics, gaps, and trends, as well as important connection points and themes that can bridge divergent research communities.

2.4   Support for Decision-Making

The following are research endeavors supporting decision-making. In 2019, Storopoli [28] implemented a topic modeling model for research management. Dismissing the belief that textual data can only be qualitatively analyzed, Storopoli's work demonstrated that through topic modeling, textual data could be labeled and quantified, almost completely eliminating the researcher's uncertainty. Meanwhile Castillo [10] implemented an information extraction environment applying topic modeling to a set of articles from various sources, predominantly academic, determining the content, relationship, and relevance of texts based on identified topics, reaffirming the importance of using LDA for these purposes. In 2020, Fernández [18], using data mining, sought to make accurate forecasts about the behavior of stocks and financial market indices to assist investors in maximizing profits. Fernández's work yielded positive results, showcasing that the use of different machine learning models can be helpful in learning, pattern detection, correlation, classification, and predicting certain events by analyzing available information and market behavior. Moreover, Costa et al. [27] related Topic Modeling to Software Engineering research, aiming to describe how Topic Modeling has been applied to analyze textual data in empirical studies. Analyzing around 111 articles using LDA, the process provides an understanding of the themes of the articles, offering valuable information for researchers in the field.

On the other hand, in 2022, Rudger et al. [24] demonstrated that Topic Modeling serves as a new tool to identify the performance of algorithms and quality metrics. The objective was to compare all Topic Modeling algorithms, showcasing their common usage and evaluating their relative performance. Non-negative Matrix Factorization (NMF) outperformed all other algorithms with 95%, occasionally alternating with LDA at 93% based on sampling. Despite being technically similar to LSA and PLSA, NMF is rarely included in performance comparisons of topic modeling procedures due to its 50% performance, ultimately resulting in the superiority of LDA and NMF. In addition Byrant and Dermentzi [2] developed an exploration process of Topic Modeling in Python to validate advancements in implementing and using LDA with the Python language from 2016 to 2022. Validating data with 1,000 records, executing different codes developed during this time, the study revealed that applying the LDA model to a very specific corpus generates different and more detailed results compared to 2016. Meanwhile the work of Luengo [9] implemented Topic Modeling for software used in research to optimize researchers' work, extract main themes, and classify them in different publications without the need to read them all. Three algorithms (BERT, BTM, and LDA) were used for this purpose. Finally, Rubiano [14] analyzed information generated by the social network Twitter using Topic Modeling and Data Mining techniques to identify current and sensitive topics in Colombia. Once implemented, the techniques proved to be efficient in identifying and categorizing topics based on their co-occurrence (influence due to the frequency of related words appearing together).

Throughout the state-of-the-art research, we have found that Topic Modeling is a highly effective technique in solving problems where identifying themes, concurrences, and categories is necessary. This process allowed for technology comparisons and confirmation of the most viable ones to address the research problem, culminating in the selection of the techniques to be used in Person_IA software, namely (N-gram analysis and LDA).

3   Methodology

3.1   Process Identification

The "Personería de Medellín" exercises the guardianship, promotion, and defense of human rights, monitors official conduct, protects public interest, and contributes to the alternative resolution of conflicts, seeking excellence in our services and complete satisfaction of the user regarding their requirements and expectations. Therefore, the activities are coordinated according to a process of continuous improvement based on its Quality Management System, supported by the development of human resources, and in line with technological changes.

In its task of establishing mechanisms to access justice, it is highlighted in the process map the activities related to citizen attention. In this context, assistance

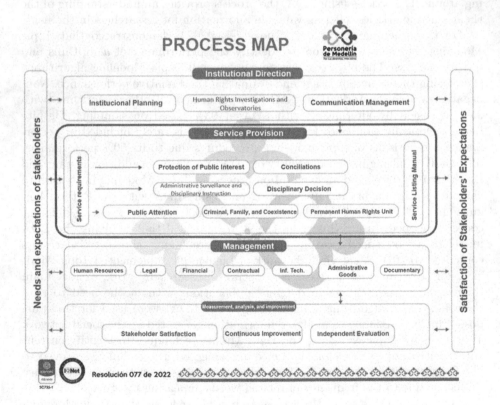

Fig. 1. Personería Process Map

and guidance are provided so that citizens can claim their rights and access them through the mechanisms established by the law (see Fig. 1).

The process of advising the citizen begins when individuals approach the "Personería de Medellín" and go through an initial filter called 'first attention,' which consists of two assistants and a lawyer. A questionnaire is conducted to gather personal information. This initial information is crucial for the officials of the second filter, who are responsible for advising and guiding the user regarding the service they need based on their request. A second form is then filled out in the Information System of the "Personería de Medellín" (SIP). This form includes questions such as the facts of the incident or the user's grievance, and possible solutions provided by the official, among many others. The majority of the descriptive information from cases reported by citizens in the transactional application is stored in a text field, representing unstructured data. This field encompasses the entire detailed description of the case. Similarly, there is a field designed to document the progress in handling and the mechanisms for access to justice proposed by the legal advisor. Afterward, this information is stored in the transactional database, and can be downloaded as CSV format, where it is used for the multidimensional analysis and for the NLP analysis implemented in Person_IA software. As part of the Personería's knowledge domain it is important to determine the main topics susceptible to be used as initial step for the NLP analysis.

3.2 Topic Identification

Once the processes are identified, they are validated with the entity, and a list is generated of the topics around which cases reported to the "Personería de Medellín" are mainly classified: Health, Social Security, Human Rights, Civil, Health in the Elderly and Disability, Administrative, Constitutional, Mobility, Traffic and Transportation, Education, Research, Labor, Prisons, Public Spaces and Informal Commerce, Commercial, Family, Police Code, Criminal, Environment, Disciplinary, Administrative Surveillance, Referral due to Competence, Childhood, Adolescence and People in Street Situations, Early Warnings, Police and Public Force, Resettlements, Human Rights Verification. These topics were validated based on the process diagram of the Personería. The defined topics serve as a basis for validating the results that the process yields using different techniques and methods identified for textual analysis.

3.3 NLP Techniques Employed

Natural Language Processing (NLP) techniques used in the implementation of Person_IA software includes stop words elimination, Word cloud representation, N-Gram analysis and Topic Modeling by using Latent Dirichlet Allocation (LDA).

Stop Words Elimination. Stop words are common words that are often removed from text during the pre-processing stage. These words are considered to be of little value in terms of understanding the meaning of a document, as they are highly frequent and don't contribute much to the overall semantics of the text.

Stop words typically include common words such as articles (e.g., "a," "an," "the"), prepositions (e.g., "in," "on," "at"), conjunctions (e.g., "and," "but," "or"), and other high-frequency words that vary depending on the language.

The removal of stop words is done to reduce the dimensionality of the data, speed up processing, and focus on the more meaningful words. However, the list of stop words may vary based on the specific requirements of the NLP task or application. In some cases, stop words may be retained if they are important for the context of the analysis. In Person_IA software, the published cases may contain information that is not very relevant for textual analysis. Words that are repeated frequently and do not contribute value to the analysis are then removed (there is a specific option in software for this purpose). The Python NTLK library and stopwords function helps to implement this functionality within the solution code.

Wordcloud is a visual representation of text data in which words are displayed in varying sizes and colors. The size of each word is typically proportional to its frequency or importance in the given text. After of the former described text processing, a Tokenization and Frequency Count is implemented identifying individual words (tokens), and the frequency of each word. For Visualization, the most frequent words are visually emphasized by displaying them in larger fonts, while less frequent words are smaller. Colors and formatting may also be used to make the word cloud more visually appealing. The process involves counting the word frequency for each unique word in the preprocessed text denoted as $f_d(t)$, in document d. There is also important to normalize it as Eq. 1 describes.

$$nf_d(t) = \frac{f_d(t)}{\max_{t' \in T_d} f_d(t')} \tag{1}$$

where T_d represents the set of all tokens (words) in document d. In other words, T_d is the vocabulary of document d. And $\max_{t' \in T_d} f_d(t')$ calculates the maximum frequency of any word in the document d. It iterates over all words in T_d and finds the maximum frequency.

In this research the words are extracted from the unstructured text block corresponding to the filtered attention column (e.g. 8,160 cases for year 2020). This block undergoes the aforementioned filtering, and subsequently, the WordCloud method is applied, which is responsible for taking the refined information.

N-Grams Analyisis. It is a technique in natural language processing (NLP) and computational linguistics that involves analyzing contiguous sequences of n items from a given sample of text or speech. The items can be characters, syllables, words, or other units, depending on the context and the level of analysis.

The process stars with the N-gram Definition where an N-gram is a contiguous sequence of 'n' items from a given sample of text or speech. The term "N-gram" refers to the number of items (or words) in the sequence. Hence the types of N-grams involves Unigrams (1-grams) with single words considered in isolation, Bigrams (2-grams) where pairs of consecutive words, Trigrams (3-grams) producing triplets of consecutive words, there is also 4-grams, 5-grams, etc.: which includes sequences of four, five, or more consecutive words. N-grams are commonly used in language modeling and text analysis to capture patterns and relationships between words in a sequence. Also by analyzing the frequency of N-grams in a text corpus, models can be built to predict the likelihood of a particular word or sequence of words occurring after a given context. The essence of n-gram analysis can be represented by the conditional probability formula 2:

$$P(w_i|w_{i-n+1}^{i-1}) \approx P(w_i|w_{i-n+1}, w_{i-n+2}, \ldots, w_{i-1}) \tag{2}$$

This equation captures the fundamental idea of n-gram analysis, modeling the probability of a word based on its immediate context. The Markov assumption [20] simplifies the context to the last $n-1$ words.

In this research is important to know the n-grams that repeat the most, and for this, tokenization techniques are also applied. This technique performs Automatic Latent Analysis and Occurrences (features of the chosen AI methods) to carry out the analysis of unstructured information.

Latent Dirichlet Allocation (LDA) is a process that aims to identify topics present in a text corpus. LDA, specifically, is a probabilistic model that assumes each document in a corpus is a mix of a small number of topics, and each topic is a mix of words. The underlying assumption is that documents are probabilistically generated based on the distribution of topics, and words are generated based on the distribution of topics within documents.

Having the assumption of each document is a mixture of various topics and each topic is a mixture of words, the algorithm starts by initializing each word in each document to be associated with a random topic, then the algorithm iteratively refines these assignments based on statistical inference, and at each iteration, it adjusts the assignment of words to topics based on the likelihood of the observed data. Finally as output the result of the LDA analysis is a set of topics, each represented as a distribution of words and each document is then represented as a distribution over topics.

If we define the following terms:

- D: Number of documents in the corpus.
- N_d: Number of words in document d.
- V: Vocabulary size (number of unique words in the corpus).
- K: Number of topics.

The generative process of LDA involves the following steps:

Choose Topics for Each Document: For each document d, sample a distribution of topics θ_d from a Dirichlet distribution with parameter α: $(\theta_d \sim$ Dirichlet$(\alpha))$.

Choose Topics for Each Word: For each word $w_{d,n}$ in document d, where n is the word index in document d, sample a topic $z_{d,n}$ from the distribution of topics θ_d: $(z_{d,n} \sim$ Multinomial$(\theta_d))$.

Choose Word from Topic: For each word $w_{d,n}$, sample the actual word from the distribution of words for the chosen topic $z_{d,n}$. Let ϕ_k be the distribution of words for topic k:$(w_{d,n} \sim$ Multinomial$(\phi_{z_{d,n}}))$.
Having the following probability distributions:

Dirichlet Distributions:

- $P(\theta_d) =$ Dirichlet$(\theta_d|\alpha)$
- $P(\phi_k) =$ Dirichlet$(\phi_k|\beta)$

Multinomial distributions:

- $P(z_{d,n}|\theta_d) =$ Multinomial$(z_{d,n}|\theta_d)$
- $P(w_{d,n}|\phi_{z_{d,n}}) =$ Multinomial$(w_{d,n}|\phi_{z_{d,n}})$

The goal during training is to learn the parameters α and ϕ_k such that the observed documents are likely to be generated from this process. This is done through techniques like variations inference or Gibbs sampling, maximizing the likelyhood of the Eq. 3:

$$P(\text{Corpus}|\alpha, \beta) = \prod_{d=1}^{D} P(\theta_d|\alpha) \prod_{n=1}^{N_d} P(z_{d,n}|\theta_d)P(w_{d,n}|\phi_{z_{d,n}}) \tag{3}$$

In summary, LDA assumes that documents are mixtures of topics, and topics are mixtures of words. The model is trained to discover these latent topic distributions and word-topic distributions by examining the co-occurrence patterns of words in documents.

The Dirichlet distributions (α and ϕ_k) play a crucial role in shaping the distributions over topics for documents and words for topics, respectively. The parameter α influences the sparsity of document-topic distributions, and ϕ_k influences the sparsity of word-topic distributions.

4   Person_IA System Architecture

As part of the Person_IA architecture, the design of the text analysis algorithm is carried out using techniques of Topic Modeling, NLP, and Machine Learning with the objective of extracting information from the historical data provided by the "Personería de Medellín". The aim is to offer more tools to facilitate decision-making by implementing methods, libraries, and techniques resulting from research and literature review.

4.1 Algorithm Flowchart

The basic design of the algorithm prototype is depicted in Fig. 2. It essentially involves an algorithm that loads information, reads it, cleans it, and, through a series of NLP processes, extract knowledge and generates mostly graphical results.

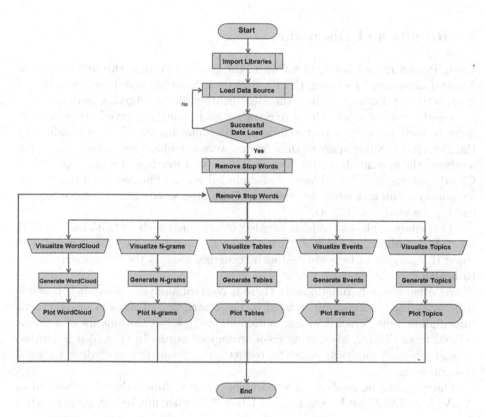

Fig. 2. General Algorithm Flowchart.

4.2 Software Architecture

In general, the prototype features a web environment designed in HTML and its client-server protocols to facilitate the transmission of information between the web environment and the servers where the processes are hosted (Web/App Server). Using HTTP protocols and some APIs, the results of various methods, techniques, libraries, and Natural Language Processing (NLP - a method related to AI for text analysis) processes implemented in Python are rendered. These processes are hosted in an App Server environment (a network server running certain applications and processes).

Additionally, the Server Message Block (SMB) protocol is employed. This client/server protocol manages access to directories and files, allowing the loading of information (currently from flat files generated by the transactional tool of the "Personería de Medellín" as a source, with a tentative plan to connect to a database in the future). The described process can be visualized graphically in (Fig. 3).

5   Results and Discussion

Using Person_IA as analytical software, the results obtained through the use of Natural Language Processing (NLP), Semantic Analysis, and Topic Modeling of unstructured information allow the identification of the following findings:

Word Cloud analysis allows referencing and identifying words that are frequently used in the unstructured descriptive information of cases handled by the Personería. Since many of these words were not identified in the stop words analysis, the system allows the inclusion of special words and repeats the Word Cloud analysis, creating a blacklist of excluded words. The described functionality allows to interact with the selection of the Stop words giving a more filtered use for the analysis. (Fig. 4).

This analysis allows the identification of keywords such as "SAVIA SALUD" an "EPS", indicating a frequent mention in the number of reported cases. The topic that begins to be identified as a recurring issue is the fundamental right to health.

As other software functionality there is N-gram analysis, where it is possible to identify the main n-grams related to the description of cases in unstructured information. One Person_IA menu option allows to select the amount of n-grams related to be display, identifying co-ocurrency of words. In (Fig. 5) it is plotted bi and tri-gram analysis, note the reduction in frequency according to word co-occurrence.

Once again, the analysis of word co-occurrence allows the identification of "SAVIA SALUD" and "SAVIA SALUD EPS" with marked frequencies that deviate from the average according to the analysis of bigrams and trigrams.

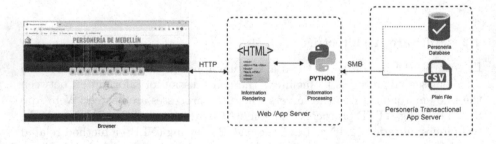

Fig. 3. Person IA Architecture

Fig. 4. Word Cloud Analysis

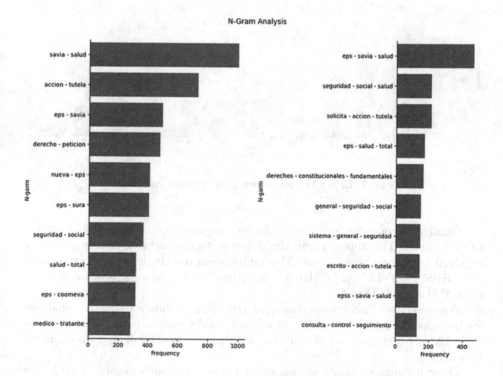

Fig. 5. N-Gram Analysis (2 and 3-gram frequencies)

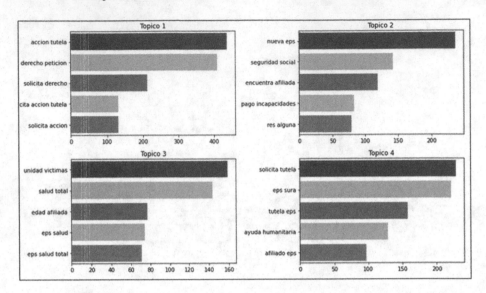

Fig. 6. LDA Analysis presented as Bigrams

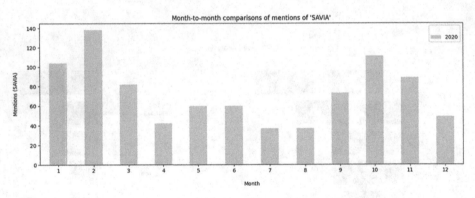

Fig. 7. EPS SAVIA Frequenty Mentions - year 2020

Finally it is possible to discover the four main topics in the corpus by using LDA analysis. This topics group the different mechanisms for access to justice required by citizen claim cases. The findings expose the issue associated with the "EPS" "SAVIA" and "SURA", identified as the main actors involved in claimable actions. (Fig. 6)

The described findings can be validated using a simple frequency analysis, for instance taking the year 2020, in february and October, peaks of mentions of "SAVIA" are identified, which coincide with the frequencies of N-gram analyses. (Fig. 7)

These findings contrasts with a smaller number of mentions of "SURA" for the months of January and October (See Fig. 8).

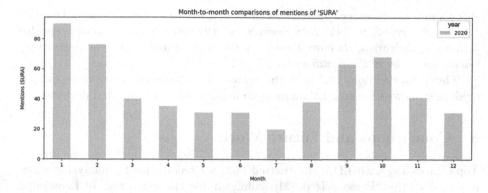

Fig. 8. EPS SURA Frequenty Mentions - year 2020

Table 1. LDA Analysis - Years 2019 and 2020

Year 2019			Year 2020	
Topic	Bigrams	Score	Bigrams	Score
1	savia salud	**556.058306**	savia salud	**404.119149**
1	eps savia	321.695042	eps savia	213.348760
1	eps savia salud	292.030462	eps sura	210.620061
1	afiliada savia	154.500390	eps savia salud	197.131089
1	edad afiliada	148.463179	encuentra afiliada	108.063217
2	eps sura	346.780645	nueva eps	247.067958
2	presentar escrito	334.079446	afiliado eps	97.434246
2	afiliada eps	264.589003	tumor maligno	95.459481
2	eps medimas	247.869028	encuentra afiliado	94.060086
2	afiliado eps	197.435882	sido posible	88.686817
3	ayuda humanitaria	286.479868	unidad victimas	178.188097
3	viene elaborar	281.787995	eps coomeva	170.508234
3	seguridad social	215.677968	salud total	147.736876
3	unidad victimas	208.376255	eps medimas	111.547391
3	grupo familiar	158.570262	eps salud	76.730431

Through the functionality of the prototype, it is possible to select another year for a similar analysis. The results of the LDA analysis (Table 1) consecutively identify, for the years 2019 and 2020, Topic 1 corresponding to the frequent existence of bigrams alluding to "SAVIA SALUD". Similarly, the next two identified topics mention aspects related to health services. These findings denote the relevance concerning the requirements of the fundamental right to health.

Based on this type of analysis and understanding such tools as a support for decision-making, the Colombian national government, through the National Health Superintendence, decides to intervene in the EPS Savia salud, ordering the *"immediate takeover of assets, holdings, and businesses and the forced administrative intervention of the EPS Savia Salud after revealing serious and repeated failures in the care of its more than 1.6 million users and in the management of public resources in the health system."* [16].

These interventions highlight the relevance of tools that, based on factual evidence, allowed for an NLP analysis to make evidence-supported decisions.

6   Conclusions and Future Work

Topic Modeling with LDA and textual analysis techniques for analyzing cases reported to the "Personería de Medellín" enable the extraction of knowledge from unstructured information. It allows the analysis, refinement, filtering, and generation of graphs that organize the information by topics, facilitating more timely analysis for stakeholders and informed decision-making based on the presented results.

Based on the analysis so far, there is a better understanding of the discrimination of themes and topics of cases presented to the "Personería de Medellín". Additionally, other topics that may be interesting and are not immediately apparent have been identified.

With the information provided by the "Personería de Medellín", it is crucial to consider the proper data management using technological tools. The information from reported cases was centralized, allowing a visualization of the primary reasons for the problems faced by the most vulnerable.

The kind of software solutions enables the "Personería de Medellín" to make decisions based on an analysis of the results obtained by validating all reported and analyzed cases from year 2019, providing a clearer understanding of the common causes of dissatisfaction. The time restriction obey mainly due to it was in this year that the agreement between the Colombian Politécnico Jaime Isaza Cadavid, the Universidad de Medellín, and the Personería de Medellín came into effect. However, the code was designed in such a way that it is scalable and can be expanded in scope if necessary.

The handling of Topic Model and LDA allows for a detailed analysis of large volumes of data, regardless of its unstructured nature. This way, value extraction from the available information is achieved through Natural Language Processing (NLP) techniques.

Future work will implement sentiment analysis and statistics generation using the same unstructured data provided by the "Personería de Medellín" as the source of information. Improved functionalities will implement citizen services based on large language models (LLM), as chatbots with the support of the "Personería de Medellín" to include responses to general inquiries, basic legal advice, guiding citizens through the completion of forms and procedures, establishing notification mechanisms for case tracking.

Acknowledgments. This work was supported by the research project: "DERECHO DE ACCESO A LA JUSTICIA DE LAS PERSONAS VULNERABLES - Especial referencia a personas en situación de pobreza, migrantes, personas con discapacidad y afrodescendientes, atendidas por la Personería de Medellín en el periódo 2019–2022. Convenio Personería de Medellín - Universidad de Medellín - Politécnico Colombiano Jaime Isaza Cadavid". Specially thanks to engineers Jheniffer Porras, Deissy Ossa and Manuel Correa on whose computer engineering thesis this work was partially based.

References

1. Corte constitucional de colombia — guardián de la constitución
2. Exploratory topic modelling in python - document blog. https://blog.ehri-project. eu/2022/07/19/exploratory-topic-modelling-in-python/
3. José calvo tello's website - digital humanities and spanish philology. https://www. morethanbooks.eu/
4. Personería de medellín. https://www.personeriamedellin.gov.co/index.php
5. Agrasar González, L.: Aplicación de técnicas de machine learning en el análisis de sentencias sobre el delito de trata de menores. https://repositorio.comillas.edu/ xmlui/handle/11531/56937
6. Aguilar León, N.: COMOT: herramienta para el apoyo al análisis del entorno comunicacional utilizando técnicas de modelado de tópicos. https://repositorio. uniandes.edu.co/handle/1992/48708
7. Allés Torrent, S., del Rio, M.G., Bonnell, J., Song, D., Hernández, N.: Digital narratives of COVID-19: A twitter dataset for text analysis in Spanish. Ubiquity Press. https://ri.conicet.gov.ar/handle/11336/163331
8. Alonso Parra, M.: Análisis de denuncias de acoso mediante la aplicación de técnicas de procesamiento del lenguaje natural para detectar la intervención de testigos. https://repositorio.comillas.edu/xmlui/handle/11531/46035
9. Ayuso Luengo, M.: Topic modeling for research software. Ph.D. thesis, ETSI_Informatica (2022)
10. Castillo Muñoz, C.E.: Implementación de técnicas para minería de texto usando modelos de tópicos. http://bibdigital.epn.edu.ec/handle/15000/19998
11. Chemerinsky, E.: Constitutional law: principles and policies. Aspen Publishing (2019)
12. De Battista, A., et al.: Aplicaciones de procesamiento de lenguaje natural y ciencia de datos. In: XXIII Workshop de Investigadores en Ciencias de la Computación (WICC 2021, Chilecito, La Rioja). http://sedici.unlp.edu.ar/handle/10915/119998
13. Dejusticia: Conoce nuestra investigación sobre PretorIA, la tecnología que incorpora la inteligencia artificial a la corte constitucional. https://www.dejusticia. org/conoce-nuestra-investigacion-sobre-pretoria-la-tecnologia-que-incorpora-la-inteligencia-artificial-a-la-corte-constitucional/
14. Diaz Rubiano, M.A.: Análisis de temas utilizando twitter: una aplicación del modelo LDA al caso colombiano. https://repository.usta.edu.co/handle/11634/43303
15. Díaz Benito, M.: Topic model aplicado a letras de canciones. ETSIS_Telecomunicacion. https://oa.upm.es/id/eprint/52499
16. EPS, S.: Comunicado a la opinión pública. https://saviasaludeps.com/sitioweb/ index.php/noticias?start=18

17. Espin-Riofrio, C.H., Peralta-Guaraca, T.J., Merino-Salcedo, L., Parra-Barrezueta, G.: Detección de tópicos de textos en español usando machine learning, caso discursos guillermo lasso presidente de ecuador 8(2), 310–320 (2022). http:// dominiodelasciencias.com/ojs/index.php/es/article/view/2646
18. Hernández Fernández, G.: Integración de data mining sobre noticias para predicción en mercados financieros. ETSI_Informatica. https://oa.upm.es/id/ eprint/63073
19. Londoño Arteaga, M.C.: Herramienta de apoyo para el análisis de un territo-rio a través de técnicas de modelado de tópicos aplicadas sobre encuestas a una población. Universidad de los Andes. https://repositorio.uniandes.edu.co/handle/ 1992/53267
20. Markov, A.A.: The theory of algorithms. Trudy Matematicheskogo Instituta Imeni VA Steklova 42, 3–375 (1954)
21. Ordoñez, H.A., Ordoñez, C.C., Ordoñez, J.A., Urbano, F.A.: Jurisprudence search in colombia based on natural language processing (NLP) and lynked data 16(2), 277–284. https://revistascientificas.cuc.edu.co/ingecuc/article/view/3317
22. Porras, M.: Desarrollo de un dashboard haciendo uso de inteligencia de negocios y analítica de datos como herramienta de apoyo en la identificación de personas vulnerables para la personería de medellín
23. Rosati, G.F.: Procesamiento de lenguaje natural aplicado a las ciencias sociales: Detección de tópicos en letras de tango. https://ri.conicet.gov.ar/handle/11336/ 187219, publisher: Centro de Investigaciones y Estudios Sociológicos
24. Rüdiger, M., Antons, D., Joshi, A.M., Salge, T.O.: Topic modeling revis-ited: new evidence on algorithm performance and quality metrics. PLoS One 17(4), e0266325 (2022). https://journals.plos.org/plosone/article?id=10.1371/ journal.pone.0266325
25. Sarmento, R.: Topic modeling-a case study with scientific production. DSIE— 16 p. 175
26. Cruz del Ser, J.P.: Aplicaciones del text mining en el ámbito del derecho (2021)
27. Silva, C.C., Galster, M., Gilson, F.: Topic modeling in software engineering research. Empr. Softw. Eng. 26(6), 120. https://doi.org/10.1007/s10664-021-10026-0, https://link.springer.com/10.1007/s10664-021-10026-0
28. Storopoli, J.E.: Topic modeling: how and why to use in management research 18(3), 316–338 (2019). https://periodicos.uninove.br/riae/article/view/14561
29. Villaseca Vega, F.P.: Aplicaciones del modelamiento de tópicos en la base de reclamos de sernac. Universidad de Chile (2022). https://repositorio.uchile.cl/ handle/2250/187265
30. Zander, K.K., et al.: Topic modelling exposes disciplinary divergence in research on the nexus between human mobility and the environment. Human. Soc. Sci. Commun. 9(1), 34 (2022). https://www.nature.com/articles/s41599-022-01038-2

The SPECTRA Project: Biomedical Data for Supporting the Detection of Treatment Resistant Schizophrenia

Rita Francese[1]([⊠]) [ID], Felice Iasevoli[2], and Mariacarla Staffa[3] [ID]

[1] Computer Science Department, University of Salerno, Fisciano, Italy
francese@unisa.it
[2] Department of Neuroscience, Reproductive Science and Odontostomatology, University Federico II, Naples, Italy
felice.iasevoli@unina.it
[3] Science and Technology Department, Parthenope University of Naples, Naples, Italy
mariacarla.staffa@uniparthenope.it

Abstract. The SPECTRA project aims at supporting the clinician in the detection of patients suffering from a specific subclass of Schizophrenia (SZ), classified as Treatment Resistant Schizophrenia (TRS) patients. This kind of SZ patients are difficult to diagnose and have enormous difficulty. Early diagnosis may improve their quality of life. In this paper, we describe the results of our study on the identification of the typology of biomedical data that should be considered for training machine learning algorithms for the classification of TRS/nonTRS patients suffering from schizophrenia.

Keywords: Speech Disorder · Robotics · Artificial Intelligence · Schizophrenia · NLP · Neuroimaging · wearables

1 Introduction

Schizophrenia (SZ) affects approximately 24 million people or 1 in 300 people (0.32%) worldwide [21]. This rate is 1 in 222 people (0.45%) among adults. Among the patients in the SZ spectrum, there exist patients whose significant symptoms persist despite adequate antipsychotic treatment, classified as Treatment Resistant Schizophrenia (TRS) patients.

TRS is a severe condition affecting almost 30% of schizophrenia patients [13]. However, TRS is diagnosed very late during the disorder, preventing from switching patients to more effective treatments (i.e., clozapine) and non-pharmacological therapeutic strategies, with enormous individual sufferance and community economic costs.

An early and accurate diagnosis of TRS can enable clinicians to propose more suitable pharmacological and non-pharmacological therapies may improve the

H. Degen and S. Ntoa (Eds.): HCII 2024, LNAI 14736, pp. 353–367, 2024.
https://doi.org/10.1007/978-3-031-60615-1_24

Quality of Life (QoL) of TRS patients and may spare large economic resources. The use of sensors for supporting mental disease detection and patients' monitoring is largely investigated in the literature [4,6,11].

The SPECTRA Project aims to design a Decision Support System (DSS) based on Artificial Intelligence (AI) techniques and models and the use of cutting-edge IoT Technologies for the early diagnosis of TRS patients. The innovative aspect of the Project is to combine typical screening procedures used in standard clinical practice, with ICT-based assessment techniques based on Machine Learning algorithms.

SPECTRA is going to conduct a field study involving real patients from the Unit for Treatment-Resistant Psychosis, University "Federico II" of Naples. Eligible patients enter the study after being categorized as TRS or nonTRS. The SPECTRA staff is collecting historical clinical patient data, such as Magnetic Resonance Images, questionnaire scores, demographic data, geographical and feeding data together with data collected during the patient's screening, such as physical data acquired by IoT sensors (ECG, temperature, EEG, audio/video signals). Thus, standard data and data acquired by using ICT technologies are adopted for training a Machine Learning/Deep Learning model for early detection of TRS patients. However, one of the main problems with adopting AI solutions for supporting decisions in healthcare is that clinicians lack trust in the black-box operation [10]. Thus, another project's main objective is to define interaction models suitable for supporting clinicians during the TRS diagnosis by exploiting eXplainable Artificial Intelligence (XAI) methods will explain how AI black-box models generate predictions. XAI techniques may increase clinicians' trustworthiness towards these new technologies since they provide them with more precise details about the peculiarities of some subdimensions of SZ in TRS patients. As a secondary outcome, a TSR-nonTRS dataset will be created that will be useful for the scientific community for experimenting with Machine Learning approaches to the diagnosis of TRS in people suffering from schizophrenia.

In [1] we started to investigate the use of NLP techniques for supporting SZ detection. In this paper, we report the initial phase of the project, concerning in the definition of the biomedical data type needed to have a wide data collection to input to the Decision Support System.

The paper is organized as follows: Sect. 2 describes the SPECTRA project. Section 3 describes the selected biomedical data while Sect. 4 details the clinical patient data to acquire. Finally, Sect. 5 concludes the paper with final remarks.

2   The Proposed Project

At present, the adoption of ML methods and techniques for classifying TRS-nonTRS SZ patients refers to data extracted from standard assessment scales, such as the Positive and Negative Syndrome Scale (PANSS) [2]. The results obtained by Barone et al. indicate that patients with higher disorganization, positive, and excitement symptom scores were more likely to be classified as TRS. The accuracy they reached based on the questionnaire score was 67.19%.

SPECTRA proposes to advance the state of the art by improving the classification results, a challenge that may be pursued by integrating the data provided as input to the classifier with data related to key features of the symptoms of disorganization, which include disorganized speech and behavior, reduced neuronal/cognitive functions as well as inappropriate emotional responses. The heterogeneous data are pre-processed with traditional data cleaning, normalization, and formatting. In each dimension, an operation of feature selection is performed to reduce the dimensionality of the huge dataset, by using PCA or Auto-Encoders. The TRS nonTRS patient label will be used for the supervised learning of the dimension classifiers and the Meta-Classifier. In particular, we are going to examine:

- the **level of coherence in the speech** of the patient may be assessed by using LSA, which could detect more unusual word associations and less semantic similarity in the case of TRS patients. Also, the semantic density may be assessed because low semantic density describes poverty of content, a feature of negative thought disorder characteristics.
- **Motor impairments** of TRS patients may be detected through gait analysis.
- **Compromised emotional response.** To identify this disorganization dimension we will focus on the preferable areas of the scalp for signal acquisition in EEG [19] and also on the patient's ECG, body temperature, heart rate, and sweating. In (Francese R., Risi M., Tortora G., 2020) best results were reached by decision trees. SPECTRA will experiment with other suitable ML/DL classifiers, including LSTM, CNN or Bidirectional-LSTM.
- **Altered neuroimaging.** It may be detected by analyzing MRI by fusing three modalities of neuroimaging data, as performed by [12] who combined patient clinical features with RMI images to identify among the SZ patients the violent ones. The Meta-Classifier will receive as input, together with the clinical patient data, the output of the Disorganizing Dimension Classifiers.

3 Biomedical Data for Supporting SZ Classification

The SPECTRA project aims at integrating standard clinical data with biosignals, emotional, cognitive, and social signals of TRS/nonTRS patients gathered through wearable sensors to observe whether these objective measures can represent valuable predictors of disorganization dimension and in turn, allows a DSS system-based on advanced ML models to perform an early and accurate prediction of TRS state. In the remainder of this section, we detail the data needed to support the patients' classification.

3.1 Emotion Recognition

Understanding and recognizing human emotions are crucial in various fields, including psychology, human-computer interaction, and healthcare.

Many techniques have been used to recognize emotions encompassing facial expressions, body postures, movements, and vocal cues [5, 8, 14], such as Support

Vector Machines (SVMs) for the automatic recognition of emotional states from human speech, or Convolutional Neural Networks (CNNs) for emotion detection using facial expressions. All these techniques have contributed to significant developments in this area, but at the same time, they all suffer from a significant bias, which is that of the humans' subjective response to different stimuli and their corresponding external expression. Indeed, humans may involuntarily mask their real emotions and suffer from motor or cognitive impairments compromising their emotional response. To cope with the subjectivity of the user's responses, during the last few years, the use of objective measures such as physiological signals has been explored in the context of emotion recognition. Additionally, traditional methods, such as self-reporting and facial expression analysis, have limitations in terms of accuracy and objectivity. EEG signals, which measure electrical activity in the brain, offer a unique perspective on emotional states by capturing neural correlates associated with specific emotions.

The applications of EEG-based emotion recognition are diverse [18], ranging from affective computing and human-computer interaction [16] to mental health monitoring. Potential areas of implementation include personalized therapy, gaming, and virtual reality, where real-time emotion recognition can enhance user experience and engagement. Studies utilizing EEG for emotion recognition typically involve participants exposed to emotional stimuli while their brain activity is recorded using EEG electrodes. Machine learning algorithms are then applied to analyze and classify the EEG patterns associated with different emotions. Common emotional states studied include happiness, sadness, fear, anger, and surprise [9].

Prior to 2017 the prevailing AI model for emotion classification was the SVM, frequently combined with features based on power spectral density (PSD) [4], [5]. Nevertheless, deep learning methods have been gaining prominence in this field as well, demonstrating the capability to surpass conventional machine learning techniques. Recent works are starting to use brain activity patterns and peripheral physiological responses to overcome such problems. In particular, electroencephalographic (EEG) signals react to changes in affective states more quickly and sensitively and can thus provide helpful details about emotional states [18]. Additionally, modern EEG equipment is made to be as light and minimally invasive as possible making them well suited for situations. Despite its potential, using EEG for emotion recognition poses several challenges. Variability in individual brain anatomy and function, as well as the subjective nature of emotional experiences, can complicate the interpretation of EEG signals. Standardizing experimental protocols and accounting for individual differences are ongoing challenges in the field.

3.2   Gait Analysis

Gait analysis is a systematic study of human locomotion, more specifically the study of human motion, using the eye and the brain of observers, augmented by instrumentation for measuring body movements, body mechanics, and the activity of the muscles [17].

While gait analysis is often associated with physical conditions affecting mobility, it also has significant utility in the field of mental health. Research has shown that mental health conditions can influence a person's gait, and conversely, analysis of a person's gait can provide insights into their mental health.

For instance, certain mental health conditions, such as depression, Parkinson's disease [7], schizophrenia, and autism, have been associated with specific gait patterns. These can include decreased walking speed, increased variability in stride length or time, and changes in the symmetry and synchrony of limb movements.

Gait analysis can therefore serve as a non-invasive tool for detecting mental health conditions, monitoring their progression, and evaluating the effectiveness of treatments. It can also contribute to a more holistic understanding of these conditions, by revealing the complex interplay between mental health and physical movement.

Moreover, gait analysis can inform therapeutic interventions. For example, physical therapy aimed at improving gait can have positive effects on mental health. Conversely, mental health treatments can lead to improvements in gait and mobility.

Gait analysis is a valuable tool in the field of mental health, offering a unique perspective on the mind-body connection and opening up new avenues for diagnosis and treatment. As research in this area continues to advance, it is likely that the role of gait analysis in mental health will continue to grow.

Gait analysis involves several techniques and sensors to measure and interpret the patterns of locomotion accurately:

- Video Motion Capture: This is the most common technique used in gait analysis. Multiple cameras are set up around the individual to capture a three-dimensional view of their movement. Markers are placed on specific anatomical landmarks on the individual's body, and the cameras track these markers to record the motion.
- Force Plates: These are used to measure the forces exerted by the feet on the ground during walking. They are usually embedded in the floor and can provide data on parameters such as ground reaction forces and moments of force.
- Electromyography (EMG): EMG sensors are used to measure the electrical activity of the muscles during walking. This can provide information on the timing and intensity of muscle activation.
- Inertial Measurement Units (IMUs): These are wearable sensors that measure body segment orientation and movement. They typically contain a combination of accelerometers, gyroscopes, and sometimes magnetometers.
- Pressure Sensors: These can be placed in the individual's shoes to measure foot pressure distribution during each phase of the gait cycle.
- Optoelectronic Systems: These systems use infrared cameras to track reflective markers placed on the body, providing high-resolution spatial and temporal data.

- Goniometers and Electrogoniometers: These devices measure joint angles during movement.
- Treadmills with Integrated Sensors: Some treadmills are equipped with integrated pressure and force sensors to simultaneously record foot placement, pressure distribution, and ground reaction forces.

These techniques and sensors can be used individually or in combination, depending on the specific requirements of the gait analysis. The data collected can then be analyzed to provide a comprehensive understanding of an individual's gait and identify any abnormalities or areas for improvement.

3.3   Speech Analysis

To perform speech analysis, we need to collect and process audio data that contains speech signals. Speech analysis is the process of extracting meaningful information from human speech signals, such as words, emotions, intents, and speaker identities. The audio data will be collected from recordings. The data recording we will acquire to train the deep learning models will contain the conversation between the clinician and the patients. Thus, there is the need of separating the patient an clinician speeches through speaker segmentation. **Speaker segmentation** is the process of dividing an audio stream into segments that belong to different speakers. It is an important step for speaker diarization, which aims to answer the question "Who spoke when?" in a multi-speaker audio. Speaker segmentation can also improve the performance of speech recognition by providing homogeneous speaker data for adaptation.

To perform speaker segmentation, there is the need to have high-quality audio data that contains clear and distinct speech signals from different speakers. We also need to apply appropriate techniques to detect the speaker change points and assign the segments to the corresponding speakers. Some of the common techniques are:

- Bayesian Information Criterion (BIC) based segmentation: This method uses a statistical criterion to measure the likelihood of a speaker change at each time frame and finds the optimal segmentation that maximizes the overall likelihood [20].
- Recurrent Neural Network (RNN) based segmentation: This method uses a neural network that can learn from sequential data and predict the probability of a speaker change at each time frame. The network is trained on labeled data that contains speaker change annotations [20].
- Sequence-to-sequence neural network based segmentation: This method uses a neural network that can encode both lexical and acoustic features of the audio and generate a sequence of labels that indicate the speaker identity at each time frame [15]. The network is trained on data that contains both transcripts and speaker change annotations.
- Transformers : this method, such as BERT, is useful for speech segmentation because they can learn from both the left and right context of a word, and they

can use attention to focus on the most relevant parts of the input and the output. Some recent research papers have shown that transformers can achieve state-of-the-art results on speech segmentation tasks, such as speaker diarization and sequence labeling. However, transformers also have some limitations, such as the need for large amounts of data and computational resources, and the difficulty of modeling long-term dependencies and temporal information. Therefore, there is still room for improvement and innovation in this field.

3.4 MRI Analysis

The detection and diagnosis of schizophrenia have been significantly aided by the advent of neuroimaging techniques, particularly Magnetic Resonance Imaging (MRI).

MRI, including functional MRI (fMRI) and structural MRI, provides a non-invasive method for studying brain structure and function. In the context of schizophrenia, MRI data analysis has been used to identify distinctive structural and functional abnormalities associated with the disorder.

One approach involves the use of machine learning algorithms and graph theoretic frameworks to analyze fMRI data [22]. This method involves preprocessing the fMRI images to remove noise, dividing the human brain into regions, constructing a region connectivity matrix, and generating a weighted undirected graph from the connectivity matrix. The graph similarity algorithm is then used to determine the similarity between each graph or subject. A community detection algorithm is used on the newly constructed weighted graph to detect communities that classify schizophrenia and normal subjects[1].

Another approach involves the use of deep learning algorithms to analyze structural MRI data. These algorithms are trained on large datasets of MRI scans from both schizophrenic patients and healthy controls. The trained algorithm can then be used to analyze new MRI scans, identifying patterns and features associated with schizophrenia[2].

These techniques represent promising advances in the field of schizophrenia research, offering the potential for more accurate and earlier diagnosis, as well as greater insights into the underlying mechanisms of the disorder[123]. However, it's important to note that while these methods are powerful, they are not standalone diagnostic tools but should be used in conjunction with clinical assessment.

The MRI examination will be conducted using a Siemens Trio 3T apparatus. The patient will undergo a questionnaire to assess any absolute and/or relative contraindications to Magnetic Resonance Imaging (MRI). Subsequently, the patient will be correctly positioned on the patient bed, and the standard examination will be performed, including the following sequences:

- MPRAGE in the axial plane (average duration approximately 4 min).
- T2*-EPI in the axial plane (average duration approximately 8 min).
- 3D-SPGR (average duration approximately 12 min).
- 3D FLAIR (average duration approximately 4 min).

The total duration of the examination will not exceed 30 min. No intravenous contrast medium will be administered. The final data processing and interpretation will take place anonymously under the coordination and supervision of trained neuroradiologists.

4 Patient Data Collection

Schizophrenia is a complex mental health disorder that affects how a person thinks, feels, and behaves. Detecting schizophrenia often involves a combination of physical examinations, psychiatric evaluations, and medical tests. In this context, patient data plays a crucial role.

Patient data, in the context of schizophrenia detection, can encompass a wide range of information. This includes demographic data, medical history, family history of mental health disorders, results from physical and psychiatric examinations, and data from various diagnostic tests.

- Demographic Data: Certain demographic factors, such as age and family history, can influence the risk of developing schizophrenia. Collecting this data can help identify individuals who may be at a higher risk.
- Medical History: Information about a patient's past and present health conditions can provide valuable clues. For instance, co-occurring conditions, such as substance abuse or depression, are common in individuals with schizophrenia.
- Psychiatric Evaluation: This involves observing the patient's appearance and demeanor, asking about thoughts, feelings, and behavior patterns, including any thoughts of self-harm or harming others. This data can help in assessing the severity and type of schizophrenia.
- Diagnostic Tests: These can include neuroimaging tests like MRI or CT scans, which can rule out other conditions that might be causing symptoms. In some cases, certain abnormalities might be detected that suggest the presence of schizophrenia.
- Treatment Response Data: How a patient responds to treatment can also provide important data. Some patients with schizophrenia respond well to certain antipsychotic medications, and tracking this response can help confirm a diagnosis and guide future treatment.
- Genetic Data: Recent advancements in genetic research suggest that schizophrenia can be linked to variations in certain genes. Genetic testing and research form an important part of schizophrenia research.

Patient data is invaluable in detecting schizophrenia, guiding its treatment, and advancing our understanding of this complex disorder. As research progresses and our understanding of schizophrenia deepens, the importance of comprehensive, accurate patient data only grows.

The SPECTRA protect will start with the collection of the patients' data. During the screening visit, patients will undergo:

Psychiatric clinical assessment using psychopathological evaluation scales.

Neurocognitive assessment.

Metacognitive assessment

Evaluation of altered emotional response using data from EEG helmets and IoT sensors.

Language analysis through the recording of interviews with a TASCAM DR-40X recorder.

Motion analysis using Kinect.

Within 1 month from the visit, they will undergo brain MRI.

Psychopathological Evaluation:

PANSS (Positive and Negative Syndrome Scale): aimed at exploring and quantifying psychotic symptoms, consisting of 30 items divided into 5 domains (positive, negative, disorganization, excitement, emotional dysregulation). It is completed following a 30–40-minute semi-structured formal interview. Among the 5 domains of the PANSS, the disorganization domain has been reported to be the most relevant to predict response/non-response to pharmacological treatments.

SAPS and SANS (Scale for the Assessment of Positive Symptoms; Scale for the Assessment of Negative Symptoms): evaluates positive and negative symptoms, respectively.

SAPS Structure: Comprises 34 elements divided into 4 groups (Hallucinations, Delusions, Behavioral Anomalies, and Positive Formal Thought Disorders).

SANS Structure: Comprises 25 elements divided into 5 groups (Affective Flattening, Alogia, Abulia-Apathy, Anhedonia-Asociality, Attention).

Scoring: Each element is scored from 0 (absent) to 5 (severely present), and a global severity score is obtained for each of the 5 areas

TALD (Thought and Language Dysfunction Scale): for the assessment of formal language disorders, administered through a semi-structured interview.

HAMD (Hamilton Depression Rating Scale): for evaluating depressive symptoms, consisting of 21 items.

YMANIA: an 11-item scale to assess symptoms indicative of manic states.

CDSS (Calgary Depression Symptom Scale): assesses depressive symptomatology in schizophrenic patients, differentiating between negative and depressive symptoms. It is composed of items to gauge the severity of depressive symptoms. It is administered through a structured interview by skilled clinicians.

NES (Neurological Evaluation Scale): evaluates neurological soft signs in schizophrenia. It consists of 26 items categorized into 4 groups (Auditory Integration, Motor Coordination, Execution of Complex Motor Tasks, Other). It is administered through physical examination by skilled clinicians.

PSP (Personal and Social Performance Scale): evaluates social and personal functioning. It is divided into 4 sections (Socially Useful Activities, Personal and Social Relationships, Self-Care, and Aggressive Behavior). The examiner assigns a score from 0 to 6 points based on the severity of difficulties experienced by the patient in each of the four domains.

UPSA (University of San Diego Performance-Based Social Functioning Assessment) [3]: evaluates individual functional capacity through the execution of tasks simulating everyday life activities, including financial abilities, transportation, planning and comprehension, domestic skills, etc. It is administered by trained clinicians through simulation of real-life tasks. The assessment involves tasks that mimic activities performed in daily life. The tasks to be tested encompass a range of areas such as financial skills, transportation management, planning, comprehension, and domestic competencies.

Financial Abilities: Assessing the individual's capability to manage financial matters.

Transportation Skills: Evaluating the person's ability to handle transportation-related tasks.

Planning and Comprehension: Gauging the proficiency in planning and understanding.

Domestic Competencies: Assessing skills related to household activities.

The individual's performance in each task is evaluated and scored to quantify their functional capacity in different areas. The UPSA is designed to provide a practical and performance-based assessment of an individual's social functioning in various aspects of daily life. By simulating real-life tasks, it offers insights into the person's ability to navigate and manage essential activities independently.

4.1   Neurocognitive Evaluation

It consists in assessing the following scales:

MMSE (Mini-Mental State Examination) for assessing intellectual efficiency and cognitive impairment.

CPT-IP (Continuous Performance Test-Identical Pairs) for evaluating executive-attentive functions.

Estimation of IQ through the Brief Intelligence Test (TIB): Useful for a quick estimate of IQ; the subject is presented with 54 cards on which words are written, and they have to read them aloud (34 are test words, and 20 are control words). The examiner must mark on a response sheet any errors in accentuation and pronunciation. Based on these results, total IQ, verbal IQ, and performance IQ can be estimated.

Working Memory will be measured through the repetition of random number sequences of progressively increasing difficulty, which the patient must repeat to the experimenter by arranging the numbers in ascending order.

Cognitive flexibility and abstract reasoning skills will be assessed through the Wisconsin Card Sorting Test (WCST): the test consists of 4 stimulus cards and 128 response cards, featuring variable shapes, colors, and numbers. The subject is presented with stimulus cards and asked to match response cards according to the criterion they find most appropriate. Each response card can be matched to a stimulus card according to only one criterion. Through the examiner's feedback, the subject understands the correctness of the chosen criterion. During the test, the matching criterion will change without warning, requiring the subject to develop a new strategy.

Verbal Fluency will be measured through a trial of semantic fluency: the patient is asked to name the greatest number of words within a specific category, such as "animals," in 60 s. Additionally, there will be a trial of literal fluency: the patient is asked to name the greatest number of words starting with a predetermined letter, such as "N".

Processing Speed will be measured through a Symbol Coding test. The patient is asked to match the corresponding number under each symbol using a legend positioned at the top of the page; the test duration is 90 s.

Problem-solving abilities will be assessed with the "Tower of London" test, which involves solving problems based on a stimulus image. The patient will see two figures simultaneously depicting colored balls arranged on an abacus and must determine how many moves are necessary to transition from the situation shown in the first figure to that in the second.

4.2 Metacognitive Evaluation

The Metacognitive Evaluation will be conducted by measuring the following scales:

- TASIT (The Awareness of Social Inference Test): an audiovisual tool for assessing social cognition.
- FEIT (Facial Emotion Identification Test): to assess the ability to identify and discriminate emotions.
- MSCEIT-Branch 4 (Mayer-Salovey-Caruso Emotional Intelligence Test - Branch 4, Emotional Management) for assessing emotional intelligence related to emotion management.

4.3 Patient Sample Definition

We will preliminarily run a cross-sectional study, with expected longitudinal extension on the basis of interim analysis. All patients will have to sign a written informed consent to be eligible for enrollment. Enrolled patients will undergo a large series of evaluations, including clinical, psychopathological, cognitive, and functional neuroimaging analysis. In a subsequent step, patients will undergo language analysis, gait and movement analysis, emotion recognition analysis.

The aim of the study will be to develop a Decision Support System (DSS) based on Artificial Intelligence (AI) techniques with the purpose to speed up the diagnosis of Treatment Resistant Schizophrenia (TRS). Earlier diagnosis of this severe condition may be crucial to inform clinicians on the more adequate pharmacological and non-pharmacological therapeutic strategies and to prevent exposure to ineffective and potentially harmful interventions which also delay appropriate interventions.

To be included in the sample, eligible consecutive patients will have to meet the following inclusion criteria and will not exhibit exclusion factors.

Inclusion Criteria will include:

Diagnosis of schizophrenia according to DSM-5-TR criteria

Age range between 18 and 65 years

Approval of participation through written confirmation of informed consent

Exclusion Criteria will include:

- Age exceeding 65 or below 18 years
- Concomitant diagnosis of another neurodevelopmental disorder
- Neurological pathologies of significant clinical extent
- Established diagnosis of dementia of any nature, or other neurocognitive disorders with significant cognitive function impairment (e.g., Korsakoff syndrome, amnestic syndrome)
- Substance abuse/dependence
- Severe or unstable organic pathologies: cardiovascular, endocrine, metabolic
- Inability to provide consent

Non-affected controls will be required to be aged between 18 and 65. Care will be taken to balance age, gender, and educational distribution among groups, so as to minimize putative factors of bias. Non-affected controls will have to sign written informed consent to be included in the study and will not have one or more of the following exclusion criteria:

- Established psychiatric diagnosis of any type
- Neurological pathologies of significant clinical extent
- Established diagnosis of dementia of any nature, or other neurocognitive disorders with significant cognitive function impairment (e.g., Korsakoff syndrome, amnestic syndrome)
- Substance abuse/dependence
- Severe or unstable organic pathologies: cardiovascular, endocrine, metabolic
- MMSE score < 24

First-degree relatives will be recruited on a voluntary basis among all schizophrenia subjects participating in the study. First-degree relatives will have to sign written informed consent to be included in the study and will not have one or more of the following exclusion criteria:

- Neurological pathologies of significant clinical extent
- Established diagnosis of dementia of any nature, or other neurocognitive disorders with significant cognitive function impairment (e.g., Korsakoff syndrome, amnestic syndrome)
- Substance abuse/dependence
- Severe or unstable organic pathologies: cardiovascular, endocrine, metabolic
- MMSE score < 24

Schizophrenia patients will be divided into two subgroups: Treatment-Resistant Schizophrenia (TRS) patients and non-TRS patients. Specifically, TRS patients will be defined based on the following criteria:

- Lack of response to treatment with at least two different antipsychotics in the 5 years preceding the study + absence of clear symptomatic remission over the previous 5 years.
- Current symptomatic condition (identified by a PANSS score > 70 or PANSS positive symptom subscale score > 25).
- Persistence of symptoms despite an additional adequate trial with antipsychotic medications conducted at our outpatient clinic.

– Patients who have shown a response to treatments in the 5 years prior to the study, who are currently not symptomatic, or who significantly improve during treatment at our outpatient clinic will be considered non-TRS.

Patients considered pseudo-TRS will be excluded. These are individuals in whom the lack of response to antipsychotic treatments can be attributed to non-pharmacodynamic factors such as poor compliance, substance use, drug-drug interactions with concurrent therapies, organic pathologies, and extremely stressful and traumatic social conditions.

Based on these premises, the sample will include patients diagnosed with schizophrenia and referred to the Unit for Treatment Resistant Psychosis of the University "Federico II" of Naples.

Namely, the eligible sample will consist of patients with treatment-resistant and treatment-responsive schizophrenia. More specifically, the study will involve 60 schizophrenia patients, subdivided into TRS and nonTRS, 30 non-affected controls, and 30 first-degree relatives of schizophrenia patients. The sample size has been calculated by dedicated software based on preliminary results from our group and published reports on similar topics.

5 Conclusion

In this paper, we collected the results of the first activities related to the SPECTRA Project. In particular, we detailed the biomedical data that we have to collect for developing a Decision Support System for supporting the detection of Treatment Resistant Schizophrenia patients. Data will be extracted from heterogeneous sources, ranging from wearables for detecting emotions and movements to magnetic resonance and patients' speech.

Acknowlegment. This project has been financially supported by the European Union NEXTGenerationEU project and by the Italian Ministry of the University and Research MUR, a Research Projects of Significant National Interest (PRIN) 2022 PNRR, project n. D53D23017290001 entitled "Supporting schizophrenia PatiEnts Care wiTh aRtificiAl intelligence (SPECTRA)".

References

1. Amaro, I., Francese, R., Tortora, G., Tucci, C., D'Errico, L., Staffa, M.: Supporting Schizophrenia PatiEnts' Care wiTh Robotics and Artificial Intelligence. In: Gao, Q., Zhou, J., Duffy, V.G., Antona, M., Stephanidis, C. (eds.) HCI International 2023–Late Breaking Papers. HCII 2023. Lecture Notes in Computer Science, vol. 14055, pp. 482–495. Springer, Cham (2023). https://doi.org/10.1007/978-3-031-48041-6_32

2. Barone, A., et al.: Disorganization domain as a putative predictor of treatment resistant schizophrenia (TRS) diagnosis: a machine learning approach. J. Psychiatr. Res. **155**, 572–578 (2022)

3. Becattini-Oliveira, A.C., de Farias Dutra, D., de Oliveira Campos, B.S., de Araujo, V.C., Charchat-Fichman, H.: A systematic review of a functional assessment tool: UCSD performance-based skill assessment (UPSA). Psychiatry Res. **267**, 12–18 (2018)

4. Cantone, A.A., Esposito, M., Perillo, F.P., Romano, M., Sebillo, M., Vitiello, G.: Enhancing elderly health monitoring: achieving autonomous and secure living through the integration of artificial intelligence, autonomous robots, and sensors. Electronics **12**(18), 3918 (2023). https://doi.org/10.3390/electronics12183918, https://www.mdpi.com/2079-9292/12/18/3918

5. Chen, L., Wu, M., Zhou, M., Liu, Z., She, J., Hirota, K.: Dynamic emotion understanding in human-robot interaction based on two-layer fuzzy SVR-TS model. IEEE Trans. Syst. Man Cybern. Syst. **50**(2), 490–501 (2017)

6. De Marco, F., et al.: Ai-based solutions for the analysis of biomedical images and signals. In: vol. 3486, pp. 171–176 (2023)

7. Di Biase, L., Di Santo, A., Caminiti, M.L., De Liso, A., Shah, S.A., Ricci, L., Di Lazzaro, V.: Gait analysis in Parkinson's disease: an overview of the most accurate markers for diagnosis and symptoms monitoring. Sensors **20**(12), 3529 (2020)

8. Elfaramawy, N., Barros, P., Parisi, G.I., Wermter, S.: Emotion recognition from body expressions with a neural network architecture. In: Proceedings of the 5th International Conference on Human Agent Interaction, pp. 143–149 (2017)

9. Francese, R., Risi, M., Tortora, G.: A user-centered approach for detecting emotions with low-cost sensors. Multim. Tools Appl. **79**(47), 35885–35907 (2020)

10. Francese, R., Risi, M., Tortora, G., Salle, F.D.: Thea: empowering the therapeutic alliance of children with ASD by multimedia interaction. Multim. Tools Appl. **80**(26), 34875–34907 (2021)

11. Francese, R., Yang, X.: Supporting autism spectrum disorder screening and intervention with machine learning and wearables: a systematic literature review. Compl. Intell. Syst. **8**(5), 3659–3674 (2022)

12. Gou, N., et al.: Identification of violent patients with schizophrenia using a hybrid machine learning approach at the individual level. Psychiatry Res. **306**, 114294 (2021)

13. Iasevoli, F., et al.: Evaluation of a few discrete clinical markers may predict categorization of actively symptomatic non-acute schizophrenia patients as treatment resistant or responders: A study by roc curve analysis and multivariate analyses. Psychiatry Res. **269**, 481–493 (2018)

14. McColl, D., Hong, A., Hatakeyama, N., Nejat, G., Benhabib, B.: A survey of autonomous human affect detection methods for social robots engaged in natural HRI. J. Intell. Robot. Syst. **82**, 101–133 (2016)

15. Park, T.J., Georgiou, P.: Multimodal speaker segmentation and diarization using lexical and acoustic cues via sequence to sequence neural networks. arXiv preprint arXiv:1805.10731 (2018)

16. Rossi, S., Acampora, G., Staffa, M.: Working together: a DBN approach for individual and group activity recognition. J. Ambient. Intell. Humaniz. Comput. **11**(12), 6007–6019 (2020)

17. Sethi, D., Bharti, S., Prakash, C.: A comprehensive survey on gait analysis: History, parameters, approaches, pose estimation, and future work. Artif. Intell. Med. **129**, 102314 (2022)

18. Staffa, M., D'Errico, L.: EEG-based machine learning models for emotion recognition in HRI. In: Degen, H., Ntoa, S. (eds.) Artificial Intelligence in HCI. HCII 2023. LNCS, vol. 14051, pp. 285–297. Springer, Cham (2023). https://doi.org/10.1007/978-3-031-35894-4_21

19. Staffa, M., Rossi, S.: Enhancing affective robotics via human internal state monitoring. In: 2022 31st IEEE International Conference on Robot and Human Interactive Communication (RO-MAN), pp. 884–890. IEEE (2022)
20. Stanford, D.C., Raftery, A.E.: Approximate Bayes factors for image segmentation: the pseudolikelihood information criterion (PLIC). IEEE Trans. Pattern Anal. Mach. Intell. **24**(11), 1517–1520 (2002)
21. World Health Organization.: Schizophrenia. https://www.who.int/news-room/fact-sheets/detail/schizophrenia
22. Zhang, T., et al.: Predicting mci to ad conversation using integrated SMRI and RS-fMRI: machine learning and graph theory approach. Front. Aging Neurosci. **13**, 688926 (2021)

Applying Abstraction Techniques to Military Courses of Action

Thom Hawkins[1]([✉]) and Andrew Orechovesky[2]

[1] PM Mission Command, 6590 Surveillance Loop, APG, Aberdeen, MD 21005, USA
`jeffrey.t.hawkins10.civ@army.mil`
[2] CACI, 6590 Surveillance Loop, APG, Aberdeen, MD 21005, USA

Abstract. The number of options that can be analyzed in a given time limits the consideration of courses of action (COAs). Computers aid in this process, increasing computing power, equating to more COAs analyzed. However, the level of detail in each COA and the availability of computing power at the point of need limit this process. Identifying the salient features of the options—the features driving the differences between and impact of each COA—can be abstracted into a more straightforward form for easier comparisons and faster optimization with fewer resources. Improving the efficiency of COAs is crucial in military operations, where time and computing resources are constrained. This paper reviews the literature on abstraction techniques relevant to COA development and comparison and considers those techniques for applicability under the conditions of military operations.

Keywords: Abstraction · Decision-Making · Military Decision-Making Process (MDMP) · Courses of Action (COA)

1 Introduction

1.1 Problem Statement

The primary challenge in decision-making and planning across various domains, such as robotics, decision-theoretic planning, and game theory, is the high computational complexity and extensive memory requirements involved in processing vast amounts of detailed information. This complexity strains computational resources and slows decision-making, often rendering it impractical in dynamic, real-time environments. For example, in robotics, the need to process and store extensive environmental data can hinder the efficiency and adaptability of robotic systems [1]. Similarly, in decision-theoretic planning, incorporating uncertainties and calculating utilities add complexity layers, making searching for optimal or near-optimal solutions computationally intensive [2, 3]. Finding equilibria in detailed, complex games can be daunting in game theory due to the sheer scale of possibilities and outcomes to consider [4]. The crux of the problem lies in managing this complexity while still making intelligent, informed decisions. In a military operations environment, the speed of battle is a constraint on time, while the mobility of equipment and limited access to the cloud curb the availability of processing

© The Author(s), under exclusive license to Springer Nature Switzerland AG 2024
H. Degen and S. Ntoa (Eds.): HCII 2024, LNAI 14736, pp. 368–380, 2024.
https://doi.org/10.1007/978-3-031-60615-1_25

power, making abstraction a valuable tool to aid decision-making. Abstraction not only allows courses of action (COAs) to be considered with constrained resources but also potentially to consider a broader array of possible actions.

Abstraction is a process for generalizing a specific problem or scenario, often by eliminating details irrelevant to the problem's logic [5]. Cheng gives the example of a word problem, "If someone gives you one cookie and then another cookie, you might have two, but you may also have eaten one" [5]. The problem for the reader to solve is the addition of one and one; the things that might happen in the real world, like that someone might have consumed part of your sum, are irrelevant. Abstracting the logic from the scenario eliminates that ambiguity [5]. For a real-life situation such as a military COA, the process of abstraction pares down the details to the features relevant to analysis and comparison.

This paper presents the challenge in three phases relevant to the context presented below in Sect. 1. Section 2 reviews techniques for abstraction; Sect. 3 discusses the applicability of those techniques to military COAs; Sect. 4 covers future work, both for planning abstraction in general and how it applies in a military decision-making context.

1.2 Domain Background

The military operations environment discussed in this section has several considerations that bear on the decision-making paradigm and the potential to apply abstraction. The first is the idea, expressed by Boyd [6], that a critical objective in warfare is to execute more quickly than one's opponent. This imperative provides a downward pressure on the time constraint that abstraction is meant to relieve partly. The second consideration is the limited access to cloud resources and variable constraints often in the network, which impact the ability to analyze complex COAs. Finally, the US Army's prevailing decision-making framework must be understood to provide the context within which the abstraction will be employed.

Conflict engagement can be viewed from the lens of decision-making. While warfare often suggests kinetic actions such as bombs and missiles, snipers and hand grenades, one could also consider a battle as a series of decisions at different scales, from theatre-wide to the individual Soldier. John Boyd proposed [6] a framework for the decision cycle known as the "OODA loop" (Observe, Orient, Decide, Act) that remains relevant today, nearly fifty years later. From this perspective, the game of war is to shorten one's loop while making it difficult for the opponent to trim their own (e.g., by making it difficult to observe by jamming their signals). If the protagonist consistently makes decisions and executes more quickly than their antagonist, they will have a decisive advantage. Boyd also identified a series of "patterns of conflict" [6], where he abstracted the same vital concepts that underpinned different battles over the history of warfare (Fig. 1). By doing so, Boyd identified repeatable patterns for warfare scholarship and extracted lessons on future battle planning.

DDIL Environment. Networked tactical systems are subject to conditions described as "DDIL," meaning that the connection may be denied, disrupted, or degraded by adversary

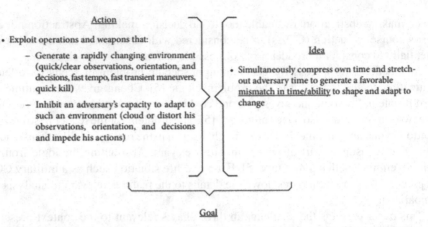

Goal

Collapse adversary's system into confusion and disorder causing him to over and under react to activity that appears simultaneously menacing as well as ambiguous, chaotic, or misleading.

Fig. 1. Example pattern of conflict [6]

action, defensive mitigation, or a natural event, with the effect of being disconnected, intermittent, or having low or limited bandwidth [7].[1]

In a DDIL network environment, having succinctly expressed digital COAs is crucial because it ensures efficient communication and decision-making under bandwidth constraints and unpredictable connectivity. This compactness minimizes data transmission requirements and enhances the reliability and timeliness of critical information exchange, essential drivers for effective operations in such challenging and resource-limited scenarios.

The Military Decision-Making Process. The military decision-making process (MDMP) is the US Army's preferred framework for analyzing a scenario, developing possible actions, analyzing COAs, and selecting a single COA for execution [8]. This seven-step process[2] (depicted in Fig. 2) includes steps for COA development, analysis, and comparison relevant to this topic.

Joint Publication 5–0, Joint Planning [9], defines "course of action" as "any sequence of activities that an individual or unit may follow" as well as "a scheme developed to accomplish a mission." Within the context of the MDMP, a COA is "a broad potential solution to an identified problem" [8]. As the name implies, more than one COA is developed for analysis and comparison before the decision-maker selects either one of the proposed COAs, a modified COA, or a hybrid of two or more COAs.

COA Development. A COA includes the to-be-performed tasks and goal states, as well as how the operation accomplishes the mission [8]. In addition to meeting essential COA criteria (i.e., feasible, acceptable, suitable, distinguishable, and complete) [8], additional criteria are developed in step 2 of MDMP to determine how COAs will be compared (e.g.,

---

[1] The precise definition and number of letters in "DDIL" varies. This definition attempts inclusivity and possibly warrants its own literature review

[2] Field Manual 5-0 [8] does offer some alternatives for expedited decision-making, but the default method includes all seven steps.

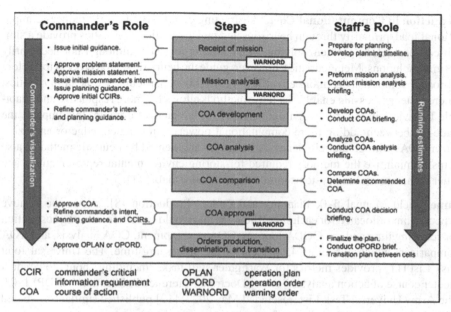

Fig. 2. The Military Decision-Making Process [8]

expected friendly force casualties, uncertainty, etc.). These features must be nominally present in each developed COA (the analysis phase can add additional detail) and can act as vectors for abstracting the COA.

COA Analysis. The COA analysis phase of the MDMP uses wargaming to assess each COA individually in the problem scenario (including facts and assumptions about positions, capabilities, etc.), including the initial action's execution, the enemy's likely response, and reaction to their response. This step expands on and refines the COAs developed in step 3.

COA Comparison. Finally, step 4 uses the criteria (features) identified in step 2 to compare the COAs against each other and review the advantages and disadvantages of each COA.

Due to DDIL conditions, execution of the MDMP is often limited to local resources, including personnel and computing power. The hardware available at the tactical edge is often insufficient to conduct computationally intensive tasks. The amount of time available in the OODA loop and the lack of local resources limit the commander's ability to consider many extremely detailed COAs.

1.3 Benefits of Abstraction Based on Domain

Abstraction offers a solution to the challenges of the tactical domain by simplifying COAs while preserving essential information and relationships. The benefits of employing abstraction in these domains are manifold:

Reduction in Computational Cost. Abstracting details significantly reduces computational load, primarily through heuristics and metaheuristics. Heuristics provide a simplified approach to problem-solving, often leading to faster, although not necessarily optimal, solutions. Metaheuristics, however, guide the heuristic search process to explore a broader solution space more effectively [10]. This is particularly crucial in robotics, where faster processing enabled by these methods allows for more responsive and adaptable behaviors in real-time environments [1]. In the tactical domain, this impacts the trade-off between adding more computational power at the tactical edge or analyzing fewer COAs with greater efficiency. Abstraction, augmented by heuristic methods, also helps to minimize the memory required for storing environmental representations and other data, thus making systems more efficient and scalable [1].

Time. Field Manual 5–0, Planning and Orders Production [8], shows the relative expected time allocated for each step. The steps that would benefit from using abstraction for reducing time and the OODA loop are COA development, COA analysis, and COA comparison, which constitute 45 percent of the processing time. The Universal Joint Task List [11] provides metrics for Warfighter staff tasks, including "hours to conduct theater course of action analysis." Army Doctrine Reference Publication (ARDP) 1–03, The Army Universal Task List (rescinded May 2022) [12] published similar time-based metrics for Army echelons below theater.

Enhanced Decision-Making. In decision-theoretic planning, abstraction allows for a more manageable representation of uncertainties and utilities, facilitating efficient identification of optimal or near-optimal plans [2].

Simplification of Complex Tasks. In hierarchical planning systems, abstraction aids in breaking down complex tasks into simpler sub-tasks, thereby making the planning process more tractable and less error-prone [13].

Facilitation of Theoretical Analysis. Abstraction provides a means to bridge the gap between real-world problems and theoretical models, deriving more robust theoretical results [2].

Streamlining Game Theory Applications. In game theory, abstraction enables the simplification of games without losing the essence of the strategic interactions, thereby making the analysis and finding of equilibria more feasible [4].

Adaptability and Learning. Abstraction allows systems to adapt and learn from less data by focusing on the most relevant information, thus enhancing their learning capabilities and efficiency [14].

In summary, abstraction is a powerful tool for addressing the challenges of computational complexity and extensive memory requirements in various decision-making and planning domains. Its ability to simplify complex information while retaining essential elements paves the way for more efficient, responsive, intelligent systems and methodologies.

2 Methods for Abstracting a Course of Action

Abstraction, in its essence, streamlines and simplifies complex processes, allowing for more effective decision-making by focusing on the most pertinent information. This is vital in fields where data and possibilities, such as robotics, decision-theoretic planning, and game theory, can be overwhelmingly intricate. The methods and algorithms employed for abstraction in these areas are diverse, each tailored to specific challenges and objectives.

Each method and algorithm is critical in distilling complex information into more manageable and actionable forms. Focusing on key elements and patterns significantly enhances the efficiency and effectiveness of decision-making processes in their respective fields. Each technique is discussed in further detail below, in chronological order of development or proposal. It is important to note that these techniques are not mutually exclusive—often building on previous techniques or focusing on a different aspect of planning (e.g., abstract state space in Markov decision processes is a refinement of decision-theoretic planning).

2.1 Hierarchical Problem Solving

Hierarchical problem solving, grounded in the principles outlined by Knoblock [15], employs abstraction to deconstruct a complex problem into a series of smaller, more manageable subproblems. The use of an abstraction hierarchy distinguishes this method. In this hierarchy, the problem-solving process initially commences in an abstract space. This space represents a simplified version of the problem, where focus on broader, more general aspects temporarily sets aside intricate details. After formulating a solution at this abstract level, progressively more detailed transformations refine the solution. This incremental improvement assists in systematically navigating through the complexity of the initial problem. Central to this method is the application of the ordered monotonicity property. This property is pivotal in guiding the construction and utilization of the abstraction hierarchies. It ensures that the solutions developed at a higher, more abstract level maintain validity and relevance when refined into more detailed, lower levels of the hierarchy. This constraint ensures a consistent and logical progression from abstract solutions to their more complex counterparts, avoiding the introduction of inconsistencies or contradictions through problem elaboration [15].

Effective problem-solving in complex domains often requires balancing abstraction and detailed analysis. By first addressing a problem at an elevated level of abstraction, one can gain insights and develop overarching strategies that the minutiae of detailed data might obscure. Subsequently, refining these abstract solutions into more detailed plans allows for the practical application and adjustment of these strategies in the problem's context. The abstraction hierarchy can also decompose a domain for functional analysis—e.g., for interface design [16]. Much of the work abstracting military scenarios has focused on this basic technique of decomposition (e.g., [17, 18]).

2.2 Precompiled Plans

In the historical context of real-time planning methodologies, Washington [19] delineates a prominent approach characterized by precompiling plans for many potential scenarios, particularly in environments where control variables are tightly constrained. This paradigm predominantly emphasizes the synthetic generation of 'experience' through a brute-force mechanism rather than an experiential, adaptive learning process. Such a method, which gained traction in the late 1980s and early 1990s as evidenced by the works of Schoppers [20] and others, repositions the computational problem within a framework wherein the computer system depends on pre-established experience and knowledge for problem resolution. However, this approach is not without significant limitations. Foremost among these is the computational complexity and resource intensity associated with generating this artificial 'experience.' Additionally, the method necessitates a comprehensive system for storing and retrieving these precompiled plans, presenting further operational challenges. A critical shortfall of this method is its inherent lack of flexibility and adaptability in responding to unanticipated states of the world, arising from its reliance on a predetermined set of plans, thereby limiting its applicability in dynamic, real-world scenarios where unpredictability is a crucial factor.

2.3 Statistical Information Modeling

In their work published in 2022, Larsson and colleagues [1] outline an approach that merges statistical methods with principles from information theory, like rate distortion and the information bottleneck technique. This method aims to abstract data effectively for particular tasks, emphasizing preserving essential information while simplifying the representation process by modeling crucial data as a random variable correlated with the original dataset. This model uses rate-distortion theory, which helps balance and preserve essential information while reducing complexity [1]. It provides a framework to quantify the loss of information due to the abstraction process. It helps maintain a balance between the fidelity of the representation and the reduction in data size. This theory is particularly effective when there is a need to compress data while retaining its key features, which are critical for task performance. The information bottleneck algorithm complements the rate-distortion theory by focusing on the efficient compression of information [1]. It distills the most relevant aspects of the data, effectively creating a 'bottleneck' that filters out unnecessary details while preserving the relationships and patterns critical for the task. This method is particularly useful in machine learning and data analysis, where identifying and maintaining the most significant data correlations is essential for building effective models.

2.4 Decision- and Information-Theoretic Planning

As outlined by Haddawy & Suwandi [21] and Ha & Haddawy [2], this framework employs a sophisticated approach that integrates probabilities and utilities. This integration is essential for representing uncertainties in the world's state and the outcomes of various actions). In decision- and information-theoretic planning, the primary focus is on managing the complexities and uncertainties inherent in real-world scenarios [22].

Information-theoretic planning maximizes the amount of information uncovered by the planning process [23], while decision-theoretic maximizes a utility based on the decision [2]. Additionally, Ha and Haddawy [2] found that by applying probabilities, planners can quantify the likelihood of different states and outcomes.

Meanwhile, utilities evaluate the desirability or value of these outcomes. Ha & Haddawy [2] also emphasize the role of abstraction techniques in decision-theoretic planning. These techniques are instrumental in navigating the plan space more efficiently. By abstracting details not critical to the decision-making process, these methods help reduce the computational burden of evaluating different plans. This is particularly vital in complex environments where the sheer number of potential states and actions can make comprehensive evaluation infeasible and is therefore applicable to military settings [24].

2.5 Abstract State Space in Markov Decision Processes

The methodology proposed by Dearden and Boutilier [22] emphasizes creating an abstract Markov decision process (MDP) to facilitate more efficient decision-theoretic planning. This process involves the generation of an abstract state space, wherein states are grouped or 'clustered' based on their similarities or relevancies. This clustering leads to an aggregated representation of the original state space. Consequently, the resulting abstract MDP possesses a reduced state space compared to the original MDP. The primary advantage of this approach lies in its ability to expedite the solution process. In decision-theoretic planning, the extensive size of the state space often exacerbates the complexity of finding optimal solutions. The larger state space necessitates more computational resources and time to evaluate potential actions and their outcomes. However, employing an abstract MDP diminishes the computational burden, where the state space is effectively condensed. This reduction is evident not only in the number of to-be-evaluated states but also in the complexity of interactions between these states, thereby facilitating a more rapid identification of optimal or near-optimal solutions.

Furthermore, this technique of abstract MDP construction is crucial in scenarios involving uncertainty and multiple, potentially conflicting objectives (such as achieving a mission and preserving the life of the friendly force). In such contexts, the ability to streamline the decision process without compromising the quality of the outcomes is invaluable. Clustering states into an abstract representation allows for a more manageable overview of possible actions and their consequences, enabling decision-makers to focus on the most relevant aspects of the problem. Significantly, this method does not merely simplify the state space but does so in a manner that retains the critical structural and probabilistic relationships inherent in the original MDP. This ensures that the solutions derived from the abstract MDP remain relevant and applicable to the to-be-modelled real-world scenarios.

2.6 Game Theory Abstraction

Gilpin & Sandholm's [4] approach to game theory abstraction involves simplifying complex games to retain essential strategic elements while reducing computational demands. Equilibrium abstraction algorithms that distill games into manageable versions without losing critical strategic equilibria achieve this abstraction. These algorithms categorize and generalize game elements, ensuring the abstracted game mirrors the strategic depth of the original [4]. The methodology has broad applications, from optimizing artificial intelligence and machine learning strategies in complex environments to facilitating economic and political decision-making models. However, it is critical to balance the abstraction process to avoid oversimplifying strategic complexities [4].

Additionally, in the context of decision-theoretic planning, as noted by Dearden and Boutilier [22], similar abstractions are used to generate computationally efficient models for planning under uncertainty, demonstrating the cross-disciplinary relevance of this approach. Furthermore, Dockhorn and Kirst [25] illustrate the application of abstraction in multi-objective optimization in dynamic environments, highlighting the method's adaptability to various decision-making scenarios. Karthy et al. [26] applied game theory abstraction to a particular scenario between opposing forces over control of an island. Game theory abstraction and equilibrium abstraction algorithms offer a pragmatic solution to analyzing complex strategic games and decision-making processes, balancing computational efficiency with preserving strategic integrity.

2.7 Hierarchical Planning Systems (HPS)

This system utilizes hand-coded abstractions to generate high-level task specifications for complex robotic planning problems [13]. This approach is essential in addressing the computational complexity associated with the infinite branching factor of the configuration space in sampling-based motion planners. Robots, unlike humans, struggle with extended reasoning over long horizons, a challenge these abstractions aim to mitigate [13]. The process within HPS involves dividing a problem into smaller, more manageable subproblems, a strategy supported by foundational research in abstraction [15]. The hierarchical problem-solving method begins by tackling a problem within an abstract domain, which involves approximating the original problem space or base space. This approximation entails omitting particular literals in the domain, guided by the ordered monotonicity characteristic. This property dictates which problem aspects can be resolved and maintained unchanged while addressing the remaining components of the problem. Konidaris, Kaelbling, Lozano-Perez [27], and Poli et al. [28] propose methods for learning high-level action descriptions from low-level behaviors and abstracting information irrelevant to the decision task. Their work uses abstractions to reduce the dimensionality of prediction problems and adaptively refine high-level solutions based on the success or failure of actions in the planning process. In practice, hierarchical planning begins by mapping a problem into the highest level of the abstraction hierarchy. This process entails extracting specifics from the initial and end states to establish corresponding abstract states and simplifying the preconditions and outcomes of operators to generate abstract operators. Initially, the issue is resolved within this abstract problem realm [29]. The obtained solution guides the search for resolution into increasingly complex domains, formulating subproblems at each stage, where every interim state within an abstract plan represents an intermediate objective. Suppose an abstract plan cannot be refined, for instance, due to unsatisfiable conditions at the current abstraction level. In that case, the problem solver backtracks to reformulate the plan at a higher level of abstraction [29]. Hand-coded abstractions in HPS represent a structured approach to complex robotic planning tasks. By breaking down these tasks into hierarchical levels of abstraction and refining the plans based on practical constraints and results, HPS offers a systematic way to manage the inherent complexity of robotic planning [13, 29].

2.8 Dimensionality Reduction in Decision Tasks

As Poli et al. [28] proposed, dimensionality reduction in decision tasks is a technique focused on abstracting non-essential information in decision-making processes. This method is particularly significant in reducing the complexity of upstream prediction problems, directly influencing the decision-making process's simplification. Poli et al. [28] emphasize the importance of efficiently harnessing structural clues of the problem to abstract irrelevant details. This approach streamlines the decision-making process and maintains the critical information necessary for making informed decisions. Moreover, the method developed by Poli et al. [28] is notable for its ability to decouple upstream prediction from downstream decision-making. This separation allows for a more focused inspection of the learned abstractions driving policies. Other works further highlight the significance of this approach, such as the method for simplifying probabilistic inference discussed by Poh et al. [30]. Collectively, these methods contribute to a more efficient and effective decision-making process, particularly in contexts requiring complex combinatorial optimization, as explored in the works of Wilder [31], and in scenarios involving human-AI collaboration. These approaches represent a concerted effort to simplify the decision-making process by reducing unnecessary complexity and focusing on the most relevant aspects of the data. This not only aids in preserving computational resources but also enhances the quality and relevance of the decisions made.

3 Applicability of Techniques to COA Abstraction

Of the techniques described in Sect. 2, several seem promising for improving the efficiency of military COA planning and evaluation within the framework of MDMP. Hierarchical problem-solving, for example, is appropriate for the layered organizational structure of military echelons, where the lower echelon executes the intent of the higher echelon at a more granular level. The plans at a higher-level echelon should be more abstract, allowing the intent to translate into action at lower echelons [32]. Bennett et al. [33] identify an abstraction hierarchy from "goals, purposes, and constraints" down to the "appearance, location, and configuration of material objects." Boyd's "patterns of conflict" [6] appear generic at a particular level of implementation, even though the players and objectives of each war may have been different, and the vehicles, equipment, and weapons were also likely different in each situation. The hierarchy is also crucial to the 'nested' nature of planning as it moves down the echelons. The higher echelons have a broader span of control and are responsive to overarching strategic concerns such as long-term impacts. In contrast, the lower echelons are more concerned with the Army axiom: "shoot, move and communicate."

Decision-theoretic planning is a valuable technique considering the competing objectives of a military operation—including achieving a military objective, completing the objective in a particular timeframe, preservation of life and resources, and broader diplomatic aims—as well as the uncertainty inherent in an uncontrolled scenario. Aberdeen et al. [24] propose using a Markov decision process to model the planning scenario, including a finite state space (e.g., the area of operations), a finite set of actions (COAs), an initial state (positions, available resources), a set of terminal states (mission objectives), and the probability of each COA achieving the mission objectives. While this is initially a simple model, the level of detail for these states can be more or less detailed or abstracted.

Game theory abstraction [4] models the interaction between opposing players, such as a friendly force versus an opposing force. This can be used within the context of decision-theoretic planning to elaborate on the probability of success of a COA considering potential counteraction by an opposing force. Information about the opposing force may be derived during the mission analysis of step 2 in MDMP through intelligence preparation of the battlefield.

The COA evaluation criteria, also developed in step 2, define each COA's parameters (e.g., expected friendly force casualties, uncertainty, tactical risk). The abstraction for a COA must include the actions that drive these scores, for example:

- What action exposes friendly forces to casualties? Are there alternatives to that action?
- What information is uncertain? Is there an action that can verify that information?
- What movement or movements generate tactical risk? What actions can mitigate that risk?

The plan details without material effect on the evaluation criteria can be abstracted away (i.e., dimension reduction). The material actions and their alternatives can work to optimize COAs to meet objective values for the evaluation criteria.

4 Future Research and Conclusions

Future research in decision-making abstraction could explore further several promising areas. One key area is the development of advanced algorithms for dynamic abstraction in real-time decision-making scenarios, particularly in contexts with rapidly changing variables. This involves creating algorithms that can adaptively modify their level of abstraction in response to added information or changing environments. Another area of interest is the integration of decision-making abstraction with deep learning and reinforcement learning techniques, which could lead to more sophisticated models capable of handling complex, high-dimensional data. Additionally, exploring the role of human-AI collaboration in decision-making abstraction is vital, particularly in understanding how these systems can complement human intuition and reasoning. Research could also focus on ethical and transparent aspects of abstract decision-making, ensuring these systems are efficient, understandable, and accountable. Lastly, applying decision-making abstraction to specific fields such as healthcare, autonomous vehicles, and smart cities could provide valuable insights into domain-specific challenges and opportunities. This would involve tailoring abstraction techniques to different sectors' unique constraints and requirements.

Specific to use in military planning, future work could provide a roadmap, with examples, for abstracting military COAs and looking at the impact abstraction has on relieving constraints such as time and computing power. Further research is needed to examine methods for analyzing, comparing, and hybridizing abstracted COAs and how those methods apply in a military decision-making context for steps 3 (COA analysis) and 4 (COA comparison) of the MDMP.

Abstraction techniques show promise for enhancing decision-making in complex environments. By focusing on critical elements and discarding superfluous details, abstraction allows for a more streamlined and efficient planning process, which is crucial in time-sensitive military operations. The techniques discussed, ranging from hierarchical problem-solving to decision-theoretic planning and game theory abstractions, offer diverse approaches to simplify complex data, maintaining the essence of strategic decision-making while reducing computational load. This is especially pertinent in DDIL network environments, where rapid, informed decisions are paramount. Integrating these abstraction methods with advanced AI technologies presents a promising avenue for developing even more sophisticated and adaptive decision-making tools. Such advances could lead to revolutionary changes in how military and other complex operations plan and execute, emphasizing the need for continuous research and development in this critical field of study.

Acknowledgments. The authors thank Robert Ernest Kane, whose Friday afternoon musings on abstraction and category theory inspired this paper.
Disclosure of Interests. The Authors Have no Competing Interests.

References

1. Larsson, D.T., Asgharivaskasi, A., Lim, J., Atanasov, N., Tsiotras, P.: Information-theoretic abstraction of semantic octree models for integrated perception and planning arXiv:2209. 10035 (2022)
2. Ha, V.A., Haddawy, P.: Theoretical foundations for abstraction-based probabilistic planning. arXiv:1302.3581 (2013)
3. Boutilier, C., Dearden, R.: Using abstractions for decision-theoretic planning with time constraints. In: Association for the Advancement of Artificial Intelligence, pp. 1016–1022 (1994)
4. Gilpin, A., Sandholm, T.: Lossless abstraction of imperfect information games. J. Assoc. Comput. Mach. **54**(5), 25 (2007)
5. Cheng, E.: The joy of abstraction: An exploration of math, category theory, and life (2023)
6. Boyd, J.: A discourse on winning and losing (2018)
7. Frisby, K.: Command and control in a denied or degraded environment (C2D2E) baseline assessment report v2.0 (2011)
8. Field Manual 5–0, Planning and Orders Production (2022)
9. Joint Publication 5–0, *Joint Planning* (2020)
10. Quttineh, N.H., Larsson, T.: Military aircraft mission planning: efficient model-based metaheuristic approaches. Optimization Letters **9**, 1625–1639 (2015)
11. Universal Joint Task List, retrieved from https://www.jcs.mil/Doctrine/Joint-Training/UJTL/ (2023)
12. Army Doctrine Reference Publication 1–03, *Army Universal Task List* (2015)
13. Shah, N.: Learning hierarchical abstractions for efficient taskable robots. *32nd International Conference on Automated Planning and Scheduling*, 32 (2022)

14. Ho, M.K., Abel, D., Griffiths, T.L., Littman, M.L.: The value of abstraction. Curr. Opin. Behav. Sci. **29**, 111–116 (2019)
15. Knoblock, C. A.: Learning abstraction hierarchies for problem solving. In: Association for the Advancement of Artificial Intelligence (1990)
16. Cummings, M.L., Guerlain, S., Bass, E.J.: Informing design of a command and control decision support interface through an abstraction hierarchy. Proc. Human Factors Ergon. Soc. Ann. Meeting **48**(3), 489–493 (2004)
17. Gelenbe, E., Wang, Y.: A mathematical approach for mission planning and rehearsal. Defense Transform. Netw. Centric Syst. **6249**, 197–207 (2006)
18. Arciszewski, H.F.R., De Greef, T.E.: A smarter common operational picture: the application of abstraction hierarchies to naval command and control. In: 16th International Command and Control Research and Technology Symposium: Collective C2 in multinational civil-military operations, pp. 1–20 (2011)
19. Washington, R.: Abstracting planning in real time (1994)
20. Schoppers, M.: Universal plans for reactive robots in unpredictable environments. Int. Joint Conf. Artif. Intell. **87**, 1039–1046 (1987)
21. Haddawy, P., Suwandi, M.: Decision-theoretic refinement planning using inheritance abstraction. In: Proceedings of the Second International Conference on Artificial Intelligence Planning Systems, pp. 266–271 (1994)
22. Dearden, R., Boutilier, C.: Abstraction and approximate decision-theoretic planning. Artif. Intell. **89**(1–2), 219–283 (1997)
23. Larsson, D.T., Maity, D., Tsiotras, P.: Information-theoretic abstractions for planning in agents with computational constraints. IEEE Robot. Autom. Lett. **6**(4), 7651–7658 (2021). https://doi.org/10.1109/LRA.2021.3099995
24. Aberdeen, D., Thiébaux, S., Zhang, L.: Decision-theoretic military operations planning. In: International Conference on Automated Planning and Scheduling, pp. 402–412 (2004)
25. Dockhorn, A., Mostaghim, S., Kirst, M., Zettwitz, M.: Multi-objective optimization and decision-making in context steering. In: 2021 IEEE Conference on Games, pp. 1–8 (2021)
26. Karthy, T., Vaishnavi, S., Barath, A.: Game theory in military decision: An anecdote. IOP Conf. Ser. Mater. Sci. Eng. **912**(6), 062043 (2020)
27. Konidaris, G., Kaelbling, L.P., Lozano-Perez, T.: From skills to symbols: learning symbolic representations for abstract high-level planning. J. Artif. Intell. Res. **61**, 215–289 (2018)
28. Poli, M., Massaroli, S., Ermon, S., Wilder, B., Horvitz, E.: Ideal abstractions for decision-focused learning. In: International Conference on Artificial Intelligence and Statistics (2023)
29. Doan, A., Haddawy, P.: Sound abstraction of probabilistic actions in the constraint mass assignment framework arXiv:1302.3574 (2013)
30. Poh, K.L., Fehling, M.R., Horvitz, E.J.: Dynamic construction and refinement of utility-based categorization models. IEEE Trans. Syst. Man Cybern. **24**(11), 1653–1663 (1994)
31. Wilder, T.J.: Learning and optimization of blackbox combinatorial solvers in neural networks arXiv:2006.03941 (2020)
32. Kim, H.S., Lee, S.W.: Role-based command hierarchy model for warfare simulation. Int. J. Simul. Model. **12**(4), 252–263 (2013)
33. Bennett, K.B., Posey, S.M., Shattuck, L.G.: Ecological interface design for military command and control. J. Cogn. Eng. Decis. Making **2**(4), 349–385 (2008)

The Application of Artificial Intelligence Combined with Parametric Digital Design Tools in the Ceramic Modeling Design Process for Beginners. — A Geometric Vase as an Example

Yu-Hsu Lee[ID] and Yen-Ting Chen[✉][ID]

National Yunlin University of Science and Technology, Yunlin 64002, Taiwan, ROC
{jameslee,m11231003}@yuntech.edu.tw

Abstract. The purpose of this study is to explore the process of using AI as a design tool in ceramic modeling design, and use vase modeling design as three modeling tools: AI-generated 3D, AI-generated GHpython, and parametric adjustment, and use experimental tests to conduct feasibility assessments. During the experiment, three participants with different professional backgrounds were recruited and used three design tools: SHAP-E text generation 3D, ChatGPT generation Ghpython, and Grasshopper constructed by the researcher to adjust the shape of the vase. A retrospective interview was conducted after the test, and the results showed that each tool has its own advantages and disadvantages. For example, AI text generation 3D can produce unexpected vase shapes, but the performance in style is not as good as expected. Ghpython generated by ChatGPT is relatively stable, but it is difficult to deal with details, especially the application of complex shapes. The traditional Grasshopper is easier to control, and participants generally think the shape is more reasonable. The final result of this study shows that AI text generation 3D is more creative in shape, but not accurate enough. It is not feasible for AI to generate Ghpython and then generate 3D. It can only generate simple shapes, and the details are difficult to adjust. Parametric adjustment has a relatively higher degree of control over styling than the former two.

Keywords: AI Text-to-3D Generator · GHpython · Grasshopper · ceramic Design Flow

1 Research Background

With the development of Artificial Intelligence (AI) and parametric design tools, we have many tools in the design process that can help us achieve good design expression more conveniently. These tools not only provide real-time feedback on the design, but can also be adapted to the needs of the user, making the design process more flexible and efficient. Traditional ceramic design relied heavily on apprenticeship and oral tradition, making it difficult to standardize. However, new design techniques have been introduced

H. Degen and S. Ntoa (Eds.): HCII 2024, LNAI 14736, pp. 381–394, 2024.
https://doi.org/10.1007/978-3-031-60615-1_26

to ceramic design, so that the development of the craft is no longer limited by tradition, and the process of shaping requires a lot of skill in order to transform what is in the mind into a physical form. This study focuses on ceramic design because ceramic objects play an important role in different cultures. They often reflect local traditions, history and culture, and can also express unique aesthetics and creativity through different shapes, colors, textures and decorative elements, thus serving as the medium for this design study. Currently, AI research is mainly focused on flat modeling, but this study uses simple ceramic shapes to test whether the use of AI to generate 3D and parametric designs can effectively create ceramic designs that meet the ideas of the ceramic creators, as well as the feasibility of different design tools in ceramic modeling.

1.1 Research Purposes

The starting point of this study is to explore the feasibility of utilizing artificial intelligence (AI) and parametric design in ceramic shape design. The AI design tool is to convert the textual descriptions provided by the users into concrete 3D drawings of the vases, which can help the users to express their ideas of vase design more clearly, and in the process of designing the vases, it can help the users to quickly generate visualization ideas in the conceptual stage, which can further deepen the design ideas; the Grasshopper is to adjust the parameters, so that the subjects can develop more variations of the ceramic shapes during the adjustment process. By adjusting the parameters, Grasshopper allows the participant to develop more variations of ceramic shapes in the process of adjustment, and the use of these multiple design tools is expected to make the design of ceramic geometric vases more interactive and shorten the learning curve for beginners. The ultimate goal of this study is to evaluate the use of AI in ceramic geometric vase design, and to provide practical suggestions for future trends and innovations in this field.

The following studies will be conducted:

1. to compare the feasibility of ceramic shape design by text-to-3D and Grasshopper 3D generation tools.
2. to compare the differences of different 3D generation tools on the participants' creative ideas in ceramic design process.
3. to understand the perceptions and feedbacks of the participants from different 3D generation tools through retrospective interviews.

2 Literature Review

This study compares the feasibility of text-to-3D and Grasshopper design tools for ceramic vases. The literature review includes: 2.1 Current status of using text-to-3D in ceramic design; 2.2 Feasibility of AI application in ceramic design; 2.3 Development of parametric design tools into ceramic manufacturing process; 2.4 Traditional ceramics and modern design process (digital manufacturing).

2.1 Text-to-3D

Chen et al. (2023) pointed out that recent significant advances in text-to-picture generation have led to a major breakthrough in text-to-3D generation, pursuing the creation of 3D content based solely on given textual cues.

Rios et al. (2023) introduced SHAP-E, a text-to-3D generation. SHAP-E is an improved version of the Point-E model, which is capable of generating 3D mesh objects, as well as simulations of shapes. The generation process of SHAP-E is probabilistic, so that even the same cues can generate slightly different shapes.

Jun and Nichol (2023) mentioned that the SHAP-E model has advantages in both generation speed and generation quality, and can generate diverse 3D shapes under text conditions. Moreover, the performance of the SHAP-E model is better than the Point-E model, and with comparable generation quality, the SHAP-E model converges faster.

Poole et al. (2022) stated in their study that through text-to-3D, an AI-generated 3D technology, it can help industrial designers to quickly generate 3D models to better present product design concepts and ideas, and the advantages and application value of text-to-3D can also be applied to various industries or fields, lowering the threshold for creators and improving the efficiency of the workflow.

Based on the above-mentioned advantages of SHAP-E's technology and text-to-3D generated 3D, as well as the fact that there are fewer applications of text-to-3D to ceramic design at this stage, SHAP-E was chosen as one of the experimental test tools for this study.

2.2 Ceramic Design Combined with AI

Thomas (2022) indicated that Artificial Intelligence is shaping the future of humanity in almost all industries. It has become a major driver of emerging technologies such as big data, robotics and networking, not to mention generative AI, with tools such as ChatGPT and the AI Art Generator attracting mainstream attention and continuing to act as a technological innovator for the foreseeable future.

He (2022) mentioned that the application of AI in ceramic form design can enhance the creative thinking process by analyzing a large amount of data, design ideas and textures and colors used in materials can be expressed realistically at a later stage through AI technology, which can assist designers in generating innovative ideas; it can also optimize the design process, improve efficiency, and help designers to better understand the characteristics of the materials to create a more insightful and innovative ceramic product design.

Guljajeva and Canet Sola's study (2023) introduced a novel production method, text-to-ceramics, for embedding artificial intelligence into ceramics. A practice-based research methodology is applied to explore the creative dialogue and potential between deep learning techniques and the production of ceramic sculptures. The production of AI-assisted ceramic sculptures passes through four stages of transition: exploratory to conceptual, deep learning to digital, digital to physical, and physical to chemical. This introduces a new pipeline to contribute to the field of artistic and creative artificial intelligence.

Adamson and Bägerfeldt (2023) investigated the Python code generation capabilities of ChatGPT. The code generated by ChatGPT was compared to human-coded solutions in terms of accuracy, quality and readability to understand the usability of ChatGPT for code generation. The results of the study show that there is a significant difference in the quality of the AI-generated solutions and the human-coded solutions, but the overall similarity in accuracy and readability is maintained.

This study hopes to further test the feasibility of using AI tools to help ceramic creators improve the diversity of ceramic shapes and optimize the manufacturing process during actual creation, as well as obtaining AI re-generation of 3D for Python generation testing from ChatGPT in the form of a Interview.

2.3 Parametric Design Tool

Krish (2011) proposed a five-step process for parametric generation, 1. Creating the genetic model, 2. Setting the initial envelope, 3. Generating designs, 4. Filtering phenotypes, 5. Selection & fine tuning. Filtering phenotypes, 5. Selection & fine tuning. Generative Design Method (GDM) was also proposed as a CAD-based parametric design exploration methodology that uses genotypes to build designs and randomly varies their parameters within a predefined range to generate a unique set of designs. GDM uses parametric design methods to manage the scope of creativity, exploring design possibilities by expanding and contracting the parametric properties of the gene space. Therefore, parametric design is one of the core concepts of GDM, which allows designers the flexibility to explore and modify designs during the design process to achieve the best possible design outcome.

Khan and Awan (2018) indicated that the importance of parametric design in the product development process and its application to the proposed generative design technique is mentioned. The parameterization of CAD models to create various design alternatives is also investigated and the importance of selecting appropriate design parameters for the successful application of the generative design technique is emphasized. Corresponding techniques and strategies for applying this concept, such as selecting appropriate design parameters, according to the design requirements and key features, are provided to help the designer to apply the concept of parametric design during the generative design process to create a wide variety of design alternatives to achieve the best generative design results. This helps designers to apply parametric design concepts in the design generation process, thus creating a wide range of design alternatives and realizing optimal design generation results.

Agkathidis and Gutierrez (2016) Investigated the possibilities arising from the integration of digital tools into the design and fabrication of ceramic building components. Introduce how to enrich traditional ceramic manufacturing methods through the use of parametric, generative design technology and digital fabric technology.

Huang (2023) described how parametric and generative design systems can be utilized in vase design and incorporate consumer emotional needs into the design process to create vase designs that better meet market demands as well as mentions that parametric design allows designers to make design changes quickly and flexibly to meet different consumer needs while maintaining design consistency and quality. The correlation between terms allows the application of aesthetic terms as vectors for performing formal modifications, thereby more accurately translating consumers' emotional preferences into specific features of product designs.

Grasshopper was used as the parametric experimental tool in this study, which was expected to allow the participant to quickly modify the geometric vase by adjusting the parameters to form a variety of vase creations.

2.4 Computer-Aided Ceramic Design Process

Huson (2006) mentioned that the development of rapid prototyping and digital fabrication technologies has revolutionized the production of models and prototypes in the industrial ceramics field, but due to their cost and complexity, the use of these technologies in arts/crafts and designer/manufactured ceramics has been minimal. This research is investigating three main areas: the use of 3D printing techniques and CNC machining to convert computer-generated 3D virtual models into molds capable of producing custom ceramic products to facilitate the production of small quantities of custom ceramic products.

Sun et al. (2021) explored the current status of 3D printing technology in ceramics. They also mentioned the advantages of ceramic 3D printing technology in the design and production of ceramic shapes: 1. Design flexibility, 2. Production efficiency, 3. Complex structure realization, and 4. Innovative design, which revolutionized the design and production of ceramic shapes and improved the design flexibility and production efficiency, and at the same time enriched the design styles and types of ceramic products.

Hua and Bowen (2021) mentioned that the traditional ceramic production requires handmade work, which is time-consuming and requires a high level of professionalism on the part of the designer; in the process of ceramic design, the assistance of computers can be used to make the ceramic design more perfect by using computers to simulate ceramic shapes, which is conducive to the timely adjustment of ceramic designs through previewing and viewing ceramic works in different scenes in order to achieve the best results; however, the innovative design has revolutionized the design and production of ceramic shapes, increasing design flexibility and production efficiency while enriching the design styles and types of ceramic products. The computer can be used to simulate the ceramic shape first, through the preview and viewing of ceramic works in different scenes, it is conducive to timely adjustment of the design of ceramic works, in order to achieve the best results; However, the use of computers on ceramic design aesthetics, is conducive to assisting the overall aesthetic style of ceramic design unity, accurate prediction of ceramic works after the completion of the aesthetic characteristics. Which also compiled the use of computer-aided ceramic design can be achieved under the five ceramic design aesthetic characteristics: 1. Computer-aided ceramic work design to make the work of style diversity, 2. Computer-aided ceramic work design to increase the work of layering, 3. Computer-aided ceramic work design is conducive to the construction of complex structures, 4. Computer-aided ceramic work design shows the modern geometric beauty in the design. 5. The design of computer-aided ceramic works can produce a skeleton effect.

Based on the problems of the ceramic production process mentioned in the above study and the advantages generated by computer assistance, this study takes this as the starting point to optimize the ceramic production process with the help of computer assistance.

3 Research Method

This study is to test three different design tools of AI and parametric as tools for evaluating the feasibility of ceramic modeling. A total of three participants in different fields were recruited to test three design tools, one of which was the traditional parametric modeling Grasshopper (GH), and the other two were generated by AI, one was to use SHAP-E to generate a 3D model through textual descriptions, and the other one was to ask ChatGPT to generate the commands for the GHpython modeling. Through the testing of the three design tools, the current accuracy of AI in generating 3D models and the future trends and innovations in the field of ceramic design were examined to see if they are practicable. Finally, through retrospective interviews to understand the conditions encountered by the participants in the experimental process, as well as having different entry points and perspectives.

3.1 Experiment Process

The main purpose of the study is to compare whether the use of different design tools applied to ceramic modeling design can give creative ideas for modeling. Three different design tools were used in the experimental process, the first one is SHAP-E AI generator, which generates 3D models through textual descriptions, the main purpose is to understand whether it can help ceramic design beginners imagine modeling through the description of text. The second tool is GHpython for generating 3D models. Considering that the part of python is less learned, the researcher obtained the python that can generate GHpython 3D through a question-and-answer session on ChatGPT before the experimental test, which also explored the feasibility of using ChatGPT in generating 3D modeling. The third tool is the traditional Grasshopper modeling. The researcher first constructed the 3D modeling and then invited the participants to conduct experiments. The main factor of using Grasshopper is to compare the differences between the traditional modeling and AI-generated 3D modeling and the feasibility of the modeling with the previous two projects. Finally, a retrospective interview was conducted to understand the participants' views on the use of the three tools in order to better understand the opinions and preferences of beginners in different fields of ceramic design on the application of different design tools.

3.2 Experiment Steps

The study was divided into four stages. Step1 was a question-and-answer session in which the researcher asked ChatGPT to propose a python for a geometric vase, and then used the GHpython in GH to build the geometric vase and to construct the flow of the traditional Grasshopper geometry. Step2 was a modification of the shape of the GHpython through the participants and a text description in SHAP-E to generate the 3D shape of the vase. Step3 was an adjustment of the values of the traditional Grasshopper constructed by this researcher. Step3 The participants were able to adjust the participants of the traditional Grasshopper constructed by the researcher. Step4 The participants were interviewed in retrospect to understand more about the problems they encountered in the experimental process and in adjusting the modeling operations. Finally, the design tools for ceramic modeling design were evaluated and recommended.

- Step1: ChatGPT generates a python geometric vase, and constructs a traditional Grasshopper geometric modeling process.
- Step2: The participant generates a 3D modeling vase with text description using SHAP-E AI generation tool.
- Step3: The participant uses Ghpython and Grasshopper to adjust the participants of the vase.
- Step4: The participant is asked to evaluate the modeling vases generated by the three design tools through retrospective interviews.

Text-to-3D. In this stage, the test was conducted by the participant using OpenAI's SHAP-E (https://huggingface.co/spaces/hysts/Shap-E) text-generated 3D test. The participant first described the vase in Chinese, then used Google translate text into English, and then entered the text into the SHAP-E website to generate a 3D modeling vase through the text description. In this stage, the participants were allowed to describe the vases six times, and through the interview process, they were asked to select the vases that best fit their descriptions. As shown in (Fig. 1), the vases in the left center and right are the 3Ds generated from three different descriptions (a vase with a rounded shape, a vase with a geometric shape, and a vase with an architectural shape).

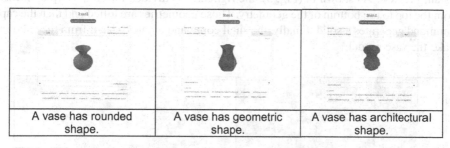

| A vase has rounded shape. | A vase has geometric shape. | A vase has architectural shape. |

Fig. 1. This study uses three different descriptions to allow AI to generate shaped vases.

ChatGPT Generates GHpython. In this stage, the study proposed to asked ChatGPT to generate the geometric 3D vase in python through dialog, in which the final python was obtained after four times of question and answer, and then the geometric 3D vase was generated by GHpython in Grasshopper, and the participants adjusted the parameter of the vase through the python. The main scope of adjustment is the size of the radius of the center of the three cross-sections and the position of the coordinates. The GHpython flow generated by ChatGPT is shown in Fig. 2.

The commands proposed to ChatGPT are as follows:

- Could you please help me generate a set of codes where I need three circles with centers on different centers and then apply loft to generate surfaces separately.
- Please redefine the circles so that xy is 0 and z changes at will.
- Please create separate loft surfaces using curves, resulting in two surfaces.
- Please change the radius of the three circles.

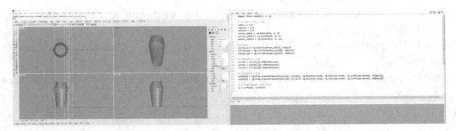

Fig. 2. GHpython to generate geometric vase design through ChatGPT.

Parametric Design Flow. In this stage, the researcher first constructed the Grasshopper design process for the geometric vase modeling. Among them, the main part that can be adjusted by the participant is the range of three to fifteen geometric shapes composed of the cross section as well as the size of the four cross sections of the angle of rotation and fillet of the parameter values. The participant can quickly adjust the shape through instant preview. As shown in (Fig. 3), the right side is divided into four purple blocks, from the top to the bottom of the geometry. Those geometries are lofted and then the cap command generates a solid. Finally, the shell command creates a shell from the solid to make the vase model.

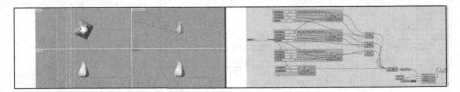

Fig. 3. Construction of geometric vase design process in Grasshopper.

3.3 Participants

In order to test the feasibility of introducing AI and parametric design in the ceramic design phase, three participants were invited to conduct a pre-test. The participants were two males and one female, both 23 years old, who were graduate students from different fields. One of them had received more than 7 years of design and 3D modeling training, and had experience in ceramic craftsmanship. The remaining two have a mechanical background, one has received more than 7 years of 3D modeling training, and the other has received more than 7 years of programming language training. Neither of them had previous experience in ceramic craftsmanship. Since this study is mainly to investigate the creation of shapes by ceramic beginners using different design tools, there is no restriction on the identity of the participants (e.g. Table 1).

Table 1. Basic information of participants in this study.

Participants	Background
A	7 years of Electrical Engineering using Visual Studio Code experience
B	7 years of Mechanical Design Engineering using inventor experience
C	7 years of Industrial Design using SolidWorks experience

4   Results

This stage compiled the experimental results of geometric vase design using three different 3D generation tools, SHAP-E, GHpython generated through ChatGPT, and Grasshopper. The opinions of the subjects in the retrospective interview were also used. However, each participant prefers a different vase style, so there is no mandatory shape during the experiment. The participants are expected to use their imagination to present their preferred vase style in order to test the differences between the three design tools as well as the creativity of the styling.

The retrospective interview is as follows:

- Does the AI-generated modeling match the design concept you have in mind? Or do you prefer traditional GHpython or text generation?
- Regarding the trend of AI in 3D generation, do you think it can effectively help and improve the 3D construction process? Are there any potential applications or limitations?
- What do you think about AI's performance on modeling in 3D generation? Can it lead to more creative and unique designs, or are there some limitations?
- During the experiment, did you encounter any difficulties or other thoughts about AI-generated modeling? This may include results that don't match expectations, uncontrollable variations, or other challenges.
- Do you have any suggestions or comments on the traditional methods of generating 3D with GHpython and text? How did these approaches perform in your experiments and are there any areas for improvement?
- After the experiment, how do you feel about the overall experience of creating vases with Grasshopper? Were there any satisfaction or dissatisfaction?
- In terms of your experiment results, what are the advantages of using Grasshopper? Were there any challenges or improvement?
- After comparing different experimental methods, which method do you think is more suitable for creating vases and why?

- Did you find any surprises or new insights during the experiment, especially in the creative process of the vase design?

4.1   SHAP-E Text-to-Image Experimental Results

Using SHAP-E as an experimental tool, the three participants were asked to describe the vase shape they wanted to create through textual descriptions. Subject A was more direct and specific in describing the contents of the vase, hoping that the vase would look like an existing shape; Subjects B and C wanted to challenge the degree to which the AI could do it at the present stage, and so the text of their descriptions was mainly oriented towards the direction of style modeling, with less concrete descriptions. The descriptions were mainly in the direction of stylized shapes, with no concrete description of shapes. The results showed that the AI was able to understand the meaning of the descriptions better when they described the shape of an orange or the curves of a woman in figurative terms, while if they used style descriptions, such as the Bauhaus and Greek classical styles, the 3D vase shapes were not relevant. In the post-experimental retrospective interviews with the participants, two of the participants, A and B, who had no experience in ceramics and design, said that the use of AI text-generated 3D design tools could help people with no basic knowledge to develop creative ideas for shapes. Although in the experimental process, the vase shape generated by AI is different from the expected result, some shapes have reached unexpected forms, and it is believed that if this design tool increases the data in the database. The subsequent development will be more diversified, so it is still not possible to completely rely on AI text to generate 3D at the present stage, and we still need to have the basic ability of 3D modeling. The participant C, who has ceramics and design experience, said that this AI tool could not help him in the modeling design, and he thought that the 3D shapes generated by AI are unreasonable and do not conform to what he describes, such as quadrilateral and cubic elements, but it does come out to be a very rough shape like a rock, but in the end the description of the vase to come out of the results of a meteor shower. It is also mentioned that the current AI is unable to generate a style-oriented 3D shape, and in the subsequent retrospective interviews, the participants were asked to select the 3D shape vase generated by SHAP-E that best fit their ideas and the shape vase that they were most satisfied with. For example (Fig. 4), the red boxes from left to right are A vase that looks like an orange, A vase has spiral shape, woman figure, Meteor shower, lunar surface, starry sky, colorful a vase, and so on.

4.2   ChatGPT Generates GHpython Experimental Results

At this stage, the researcher first used ChatGPT to write the GHpython program to build a geometrical vase. The test participants thought that although using python could avoid the uncontrolled shapes like AI Vincent 3D, they also said that it was difficult for beginner to adjust the details of the shapes through python and they found it difficult to write a long series of programs to build a simple three-dimensional model. Figure 5 shows the final shape of the vase by adjusting the python values while viewing the 3D.

A	B	C
A vase that looks a humanity.	A vase has spiral shape ,woman figure.	Bauhaus art, abstractionism, deconstructionist silhouettes a vase.
Avase that looks like a vase.	like a woman's body shape, with the beauty of breast curves and a vase.	Abstract style, deconstructed silhouettes, geometric shapes, milky white a vase.
A vase has architectural shape.	The vase has a Greek style, artistic beauty, and the visual appearance.	Deconstructive silhouette, geometric square shape, milky white, simple style a vase.
Avase that looks like a Taiwan.	The vase has a Greek-style artistic beauty and matches the lines of Greek columns.	Quadrilateral, geometric cube shape, columnar structure, simple style a vase.
A vase that looks like China.	A vase has Taiwanese characteristics, showing the style of southern Fujian.	Regular quadrilateral, cube shape, columnar structure, simple straight lines a vase.
A vase that looks like an orange.	A long classical vase with simple lines.	Meteor shower, lunar surface, starry sky, colorful a vase.

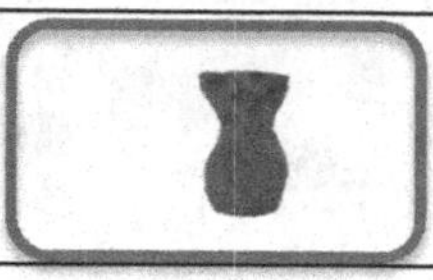

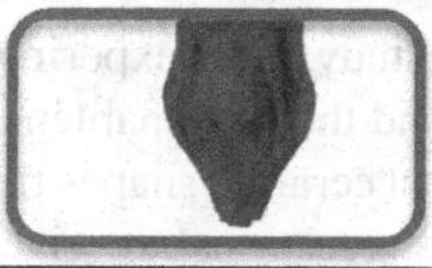

Fig. 4. Three test participants' design results of shaped vases using text-to-3D design tools.

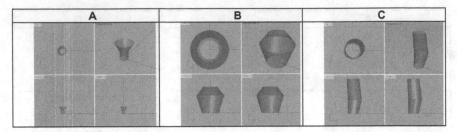

Fig. 5. Three test participants' design results of shaped vase using GHpython design tool.

4.3   Grasshopper Experimental Results

At this stage, the researcher first constructed the GH ceramic design process. The shape was inspired by common geometric vases on the market, with four adjustable sections and rotation angles for the subjects to experiment with. During the experiment, the three subjects all believed that the experimental tools at this stage were more practical than the previous two. Through parameter adjustment, the changes in shape can be directly seen, and the changed shape is more in line with the shape of modern vases. Among them, subjects B and C also mentioned that compared with the two tools of text generation 3D and python, using traditional Grasshopper can provide clearer control when building 3D models. By adjusting parameters, you can directly see the change process and understand the overall shape. When making changes, you can receive immediate feedback on the shape, and you can clearly see the cross section you have adjusted so far. The final shape is much more reasonable. (Fig. 6) The final shape of the vase is modified in real-time preview by the participant through the 3D view while making adjustments.

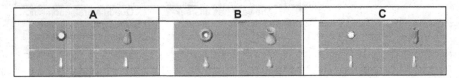

Fig. 6. Three test participants' design results of shaped vases using Grasshopper design tool.

5   Conclusion

In this study, three experiments were conducted to obtain the subjects' views on the three tools and the reasonableness of the shape generation, and the feasibility of generating different ceramic shapes through the use of different tools was also investigated. Finally, some suggestions are given as to which stages the three design tools are suitable for application and to whom.

5.1 Differences in Shape Generation and User Experience Among Three Design Tools

From the experimental results and the preliminary conclusion in the retrospective interview of the three participants, the participants generally believe that it is not feasible to use SHAP-E text-to-3D as a development tool for ceramic modeling. Because the randomness of AI is still not mature enough in the concept of modeling, and the data in the database is too insufficient. In addition, the 3D shape generated through text description is more unreasonable; However, several of the test participants also said that if this tool is for beginners who have no basic knowledge of ceramics and 3D, it may be suitable to use SHAP-E for creative ideas because it can quickly help beginners to present the ideas in their minds. In the process of using GHpython to make a vase, due to the limited range of python generated by ChatGPT, it is impossible for the participants to make significant changes and changes in details. Therefore, the participants all said in subsequent interviews that although the application of python will not be uncontrollable like AI in the process of building 3D, it is a little difficult for them to learn python in order to build 3D. From the interview process, it can be seen that the participants believe that the shape change can be seen directly when adjusting the shape with the slider, and it is helpful for them to adjust the shape through controllable parameters and provide instant feedback.

5.2 Feasibility of Three Different Design Tools in Ceramic Shape Design

During the interview, the participants was asked to make a subsequent evaluation of the feasibility of applying the three tools to the shape of ceramic vases. Although SHAP-E can quickly generate shape ideas through simple text description, AI cannot understand if described in style. SHAP-E is only suitable for beginners who have insufficient mastery of shape. For people with design background, this stage can only be used as an auxiliary tool. ChatGPT generates adjustable shaped vases and presents them in python. If the shape is more complex, ChatGPT cannot give the correct python. Therefore, using python to generate 3D shapes is more suitable for people with a python background. The traditional Grasshopper modeling was first constructed by this researcher. All three participants believe that it is the most suitable tool for ceramic modeling vases. Through the adjustable cross-sectional parameters, users can adjust and create a vase with personal style, so it is the most advantageous design tool for ceramic shaped vases.

5.3 Suggestions

For the three design tools tested so far, the results of the study show that there are different ways to use them in different fields and backgrounds. For example, it is suitable to use parametric modeling for those who already have a specific modeling idea, which can generate their own 3D ideas more directly, but the disadvantage is that it requires learning experience, which is not suitable for those who do not have any experience in 3D modeling; For creators who have no idea about modeling, they can use SHAP-E to quickly develop their own modeling ideas. Through the technology of text generation 3D, it is possible to generate a shape model from text without the need for modeling ability.

The disadvantage is that the generation of the shape requires precise text description. Python is also suitable for those who have experience in using Python. Because the python generated through ChatGPT may be inaccurate, beginners may encounter errors that cannot be found, causing the model to fail to be generated. Further study in recruiting more participants for Al 3D and parametric modeling to increase the reliability and validity of the experiment is suggested.

References

Adamson, V., Bägerfeldt, J.: Assessing the effectiveness of ChatGPT in generating Python code (2023). https://urn.kb.se/resolve?urn=urn:nbn:se:his:diva-22860

Agkathidis, A., Gutierrez, R.U.: Incorporating digital tools with ceramic crafting: design and fabrication of light diffusing screen shells. J. Int. Assoc. Shell Spat. Struct. **57**(3), 209–217 (2016). https://doi.org/10.20898/j.iass.2016.189.814

Chen, Y., Pan, Y., Li, Y., Yao, T., Mei, T. Control3d: towards controllable text-to-3d generation. In: Proceedings of the 31st ACM International Conference on Multimedia, pp. 1148–1156, October 2023. https://doi.org/10.1145/3581783.3612489

Guljajeva, V., Canet Sola, M.: AI-aided ceramic sculptures: bridging deep learning with materiality. In: Johnson, C., Rodríguez-Fernández, N., Rebelo, S.M. (eds.) EvoMUSART 2023. LNCS, vol. 13988, pp. 357–371. Springer, Cham (2023). https://doi.org/10.1007/978-3-031-29956-8_23

He, Y.: Research on innovative thinking of ceramic art design based on artificial intelligence. Mobile Inf. Syst. **2022**. (2022). https://doi.org/10.1155/2022/3381042

Hua, L., Bowen, P.: Analysis of ceramic design aesthetics under computer aided design. In: 2021 2nd International Conference on Education, Knowledge and Information Management (ICEKIM), pp. 770–773. IEEE, January 2021. https://doi.org/10.1109/ICEKIM52309.2021.00174

Huang, Y.: A generative vase design system based on users' visual emotional vocabulary. In: Mori, H., Asahi, Y. (eds.) HCII 2023. LNCS, vol. 14015, pp. 487–501. Springer, Cham (2023). https://doi.org/10.1007/978-3-031-35132-7_37

Huson, D.: Digital fabrication techniques in art/craft and designer/maker ceramics. In: NIP & Digital Fabrication Conference, vol. 22, pp. 172–175. Society of Imaging Science and Technology, January 2006

Jun, H., Nichol, A.: SHAP-E: generating conditional 3d implicit functions. arXiv preprint arXiv: 2305.02463 (2023). https://doi.org/10.48550/arXiv.2305.02463

Khan, S., Awan, M.J.: A generative design technique for exploring shape variations. Adv. Eng. Inform. **38**, 712–724 (2018). https://doi.org/10.1016/j.aei.2018.10.005

Krish, S.: A practical generative design method. Comput.-Aid. Des. **43**(1), 88–100 (2011). https://doi.org/10.1016/j.cad.2010.09.009

Poole, B., Jain, A., Barron, J.T., Mildenhall, B.: Dreamfusion: Text-to-3d using 2d diffusion. arXiv preprint arXiv:2209.14988 (2022). https://doi.org/10.48550/arXiv.2209.14988

Rios, T., Menzel, S., Sendhoff, B.: Large language and text-to-3D models for engineering design optimization. In: 2023 IEEE Symposium Series on Computational Intelligence (SSCI), pp. 1704–1711. IEEE, December 2023. https://doi.org/10.1109/SSCI52147.2023.10371898

Sun, X., Liu, X., Yang, X., Song, B.: Computer-aided three-dimensional ceramic product design. Comput.-Aid. Des. Appl. **19**(S3), 97–107 (2021)

Thomas, M.: The future of AI: how artificial intelligence will change the world. Built In 10 (2022)

Impact Position Detection of Baseball Bat Using Multi-axis Accelerometers

Yi-Chin Lu[1](ID), Chiang Liu[2](ID), and Hsi-Pin Ma[1(✉)](ID)

[1] Department of Electronic Engineering, Tsinghua University, Hsinchu, Taiwan
hp@ee.nthu.edu.tw
[2] Institute Graduate of Sport Equipment Technology, University of Taipei, Taipei, Taiwan

Abstract. In baseball, whether a batter has the ability to hit accurately is one of the key factors affecting his or her batting performance. Therefore, we want to develop a method for detecting the hitting position of the ball, using the vibration signal of the bat to estimate the collision position of the bat's long-axis and circumferential direction. To achieve this goal, we collect the vibration signals of the bat through the accelerometer in the multi-axis inertial sensing unit.

Currently, in the prediction of long-axis collision locations, we collect data for different collision intensities. We extract the energy peak of each frequency as features. We use machine learning for training and estimation. Under single impact strength, the accuracy is close to 75%, and the tolerance error is within 1 cm. We use a low-intensity (1.1 J) impact to build a predictive model and estimate the location of a higher-intensity (1.73 J) impact. Near the sweet zone, the accuracy can exceed 60% with a tolerance error of 1 cm. What we propose is that it is not affected by the impact strength to a certain extent. In the prediction of circumferential impact positions, we utilize the characteristics of multi-axis accelerometers to identify methods for predicting different circumferential impact locations of a baseball bat. Under a single impact intensity, the accuracy is consistently close to 80%. However, when applying the model established with low intensity to predict higher intensities, the accuracy drops to only 50%. There still exists a challenge in accurately distinguishing impacts on both sides of the circumferential direction.

Keywords: Ball-Bat Collision · Hitting · Sweet Spot

1 Introduction

1.1 Background

In any competitive sport, the shared objective is to train intelligently and efficiently, especially within the constraints of limited training time. In baseball, the quest for improved batting performance leads players to seek what is commonly referred to as the "sweet spot" during their swings. In typical training scenarios, the assessment of whether this sweet spot has been successfully hit relies on the

H. Degen and S. Ntoa (Eds.): HCII 2024, LNAI 14736, pp. 395–408, 2024.
https://doi.org/10.1007/978-3-031-60615-1_27

post-contact feel of the ball. Within the academic, numerous diverse definitions of this specific spot exist [1].

In the past, commonly used auxiliary training instruments included high-speed cameras [2] and optical motion capture systems [3]. These instruments shared a common set of characteristics: they were expensive, and the cameras and associated equipment were relatively delicate, necessitating specific environmental conditions for their use.

However, in recent years, as inertial measurement unit (IMU) sensors have continued to shrink in size and become more affordable, some companies, such as Garmin and Mizuno, have seized the opportunity to commercialize them. These companies have developed wireless IMU sensors that can be affixed to the bottom of a baseball bat. Nevertheless, their primary functionality remains focused on measuring bat swing speed and trajectory (swing angle) [4]. But these sensors do not possess the capability to detect the precise point of impact on the bat during a hit.

1.2 Motivation

When a hitter is at the plate, the impact position between the baseball and the bat significantly influences the batter's performance. Achieving accurate detection of the impact position not only aids the player's athletic performance but also serves to protect and prevent injuries during hitting [5]. Below, I will introduce some studies on impact positions, where researchers attempted to install sensors on the baseball bat and analyze the collected physical quantities to detect the impact position accurately.

In Feng's study [6,7], piezoelectric films were used as sensors to collect signals. Data were collected at 40 impact positions starting from the bat's head with three different impact intensities, spaced 1 cm apart. Feng proposed novel features that demonstrate the impact position along the long-axis of the bat, unaffected by impact intensity. Achieving an accuracy of up to 95% within a 1 cm tolerance.

Osawa [8] installed two piezoelectric film sensors at the end of the baseball bat. He collected vibration signals at intervals of 5 cm from the bat's head with five different impact angles. Time-domain peaks were extracted at the same position, along with the peak ratio of the two sensor outputs. Using linear interpolation, detection lines were obtained to estimate the circumferential impact positions of the bat. The root mean square error (RMSE) for circumferential direction estimation was reported as $24.4 \pm 30.1°$.

Feng's proposed method effectively eliminates the influence of impact intensity, demonstrating high accuracy in predicting long-axis positions. However, it lacks the capability to detect circumferential impact positions. In Osawa's study, a straightforward method was proposed to establish a detection model, though it is somewhat constrained by impact intensity, it can estimate circumferential impact positions to some extent. As described above, both methods have their respective limitations in practical applications. Therefore, the primary aim of this study is to propose an integrated approach that combines the strengths of the above research, successfully detecting a more comprehensive range of impact positions without being influenced by intensity.

2 Proposed Approach

2.1 Experiment Equipment

Ball and Bat Impact Instrument. In order to effectively control various factors affecting the signal during the bat-ball impact process, such as the different positions, angles, and impact intensities at which the ball contacts the bat, a device was developed for this research. The frame of the device is made of extruded aluminum. The material of the pendulum is aluminum alloy and stainless steel, and the size is $60 * 80 * 90$ cm. The pendulum can slide left and right, and the length can be adjusted up and down to change the swing and impact position of the ball, and a weight can be installed on the impact rod to adjust the impact energy.

To better simulate realistic conditions, the fixation of the baseball bat was addressed based on a reliable experiment conducted by Howard Brody [?], which included data on hand-held baseball bats. He compared the vibrational behavior of the bat under various conditions, including being freely suspended at both ends, clamped using a fixture at the handle end, and held by hand. He found that the clamped bat exhibited a "diving board" mode near extremely low frequencies, around 18 Hz, and the original bending mode frequency increased. However, the freely suspended and hand-held bats did not show this diving board mode, and the vibration frequencies of their bending modes were the same.

Therefore, his conclusion was that "freely suspended bats correspond to both loosely held and tightly gripped bats, while the behavior of bats securely clamped in a fixture differs from that of hand-held bats." Additionally, William Brown's research [9] indicates that players essentially throw the bat towards the ball during a swing, similar to the effect of tightly gripping the bat to try to derive more power from the collision with the ball. Consequently, I have chosen to use fishing lines to freely suspend the baseball bat in the experiment.

6 Degrees of Freedom IMU. The LSM6DSO32 is an IMU chip manufactured by STMicroelectronics. It features a three-axis accelerometer and a three-axis gyroscope, capable of measuring the acceleration of an object along the x, y, and z axes, as well as the rotational speed of the object. The chip supports common communication protocols such as I2C or SPI, facilitating connectivity and data exchange with microcontrollers or other devices. Widely applied across various domains, the LSM6DSO32 finds uses in motion tracking, smartphone tilt detection, wearable devices, and other applications that demand precise motion sensing capabilities.

Choosing the LSM6DSO32 is primarily driven by its larger measurement ranges for both the accelerometer and gyroscope compared to the majority of IMU sensors available in the market. Additionally, its high output data rate

(ODR) of up to 6.67 kHz, contributes to its appeal. Adafruit, a company specializing in electronics and open-source hardware, has also provided libraries for easy integration with Arduino/C++ or CircuitPython/Python boards. This facilitation in development and usage enhances the overall accessibility and convenience of the LSM6DSO32 in various applications.

I will utilize the Raspberry Pi Pico for data collection. It is equipped with a dual-core ARM Cortex-M0+ microcontroller (RP2040) and features embedded memories such as embedded SRAM and Flash, providing convenient storage for programs and data. With a computing speed of up to 133 MHz, it significantly outpaces its counterpart, the Arduino Uno, which operates at a speed of only 16 MHz. I will use the SPI communication protocol in conjunction with an SD card to collect data output from the IMU. Additionally, the Raspberry Pi Pico will be overclocked, pushing its computing speed to 200 MHz, ensuring a sampling rate of around 2600 Hz.

2.2   Vibration Signal Feature Extraction

Gravity Compensation and Spectrum Comparison. Firstly, due to the characteristics of the accelerometer, gravitational acceleration is also measured. Failure to separate it from the acceleration associated with the vibration of the baseball bat can result in errors. Therefore, before collecting each set of data, the accelerometer is allowed to remain idle for a few seconds. Subsequently, the data points for all three axes (x, y, z) in each dataset are adjusted by subtracting the average values during the idle period to achieve the effect of gravity compensation.

I have observed that when the baseball bat undergoes an impact, the vibrational acceleration is unexpectedly high. The IMU installed at the bottom of the bat captures vibration signals in all axes, and there are instances where the acceleration values exceed the measurement range of the accelerometer, take the y-axis as an example, as shown in the Fig. 1 below.

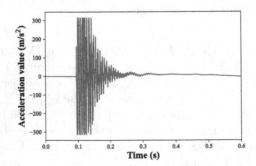

Fig. 1. The vibration signal of the bat is collected in the three axes of the accelerometer.

While instances of exceeding the measurement range may occur, I speculate that within the measurable range, signals still exhibit vibrations corresponding to the eigenfrequencies of the baseball bat. To explore this, I employed both accelerometers and piezoelectric films to collect vibration signals. I conducted a comparison using the short-time fourier transform (STFT) on the signals acquired from the two sensors. The results indicate that the characteristic frequency locations of the first two bending modes are identical, both occurring at 145 and 518 Hz, this is consistent with the position where the first two eigenfrequencies will appear in D. Russel's study [10]. Based on the time-frequency plot, it can be observed that the vibration durations at these specific eigenfrequencies are very short, typically ranging from 0.15 to 0.4 s. Therefore, I have set the signal collection length to be from 0.1 s before the impact to 0.5 s after the impact, totaling 0.6 s.

The Peak of the Values of the Bending Mode. The Fig. 2 below shows the peak extraction process of bending mode values. Method of representation: Taking the first eigenfrequency peak on the x-axis as an example, it is expressed as M_{1x}.

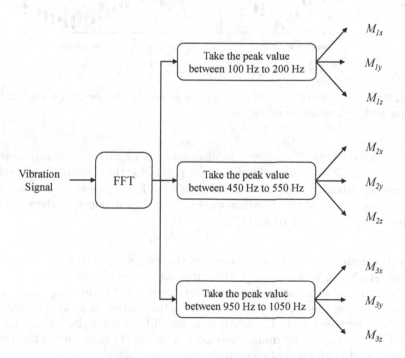

Fig. 2. Peak extraction process for bending mode values.

I have selected the J143M baseball bat for my experiment, which is made of maple and produced by Old Hickory Bats. Old Hickory Bats is a renowned baseball bat manufacturer known for its high-quality wooden bats. Its exceptional hitting sensation has garnered popularity among professional players both domestically and internationally.

I have collected vibration signals at 1 cm intervals from the bat head for impacts at distances ranging from 1 to 25 cm, with impact energies of 1.1 J and 1.73 J, respectively. These correspond to the impact strengths of a baseball dropped naturally from heights of 0.75 m and 1.25 m in Feng's experiment [7]. A total of 15 data points were collected for each condition, a total of 750 data. The Fig. 3 below illustrates the peak distribution of eigenfrequencies (take the x-axis as an example).

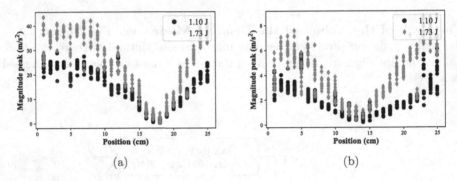

(a)   (b)

Fig. 3. Peak value distribution of the bending mode eigenfrequency (x-axis). (a) first bending mode (b) second bending mode

The lowest points of the first eigenfrequency peak are consistently observed at the 18 cm position. Similarly, the lowest points for the second eigenfrequency peak are consistently found around 14 or 15 cm. These positions correspond to the nodes of the first two bending modes. The region between these nodes is referred to as the "sweet zone [12]".

Eigenfrequency Peak Ratio of Each Axis. Following the method mentioned in Feng's study [7], which assumes that the magnitudes of individual feature frequencies increase with the intensity, the ratio between feature frequencies is less affected by impact intensity. Moreover, the ratio relationships at different positions of the bat also vary. Therefore, it is possible to infer the impact location without being affected by impact intensity. The Fig. 4 below shows the Extraction process of peak ratio of eigenfrequency of each axis.

I performed a division operation among the peaks at the three feature frequencies along each axis to obtain their ratios, as shown in the Fig. 5 below (take the peak ratio of the first two eigenfrequencies on the x-axis as an example). It can be seen that compared with Peak of the Values of the Bending Mode, it has

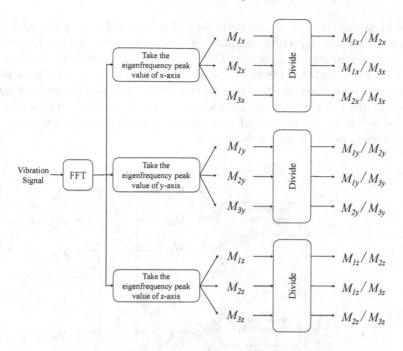

Fig. 4. Extraction process of peak ratio of eigenfrequency of each axis.

higher homogeneity. After ANOVA analysis, it also shows that there is higher homogeneity after this treatment.

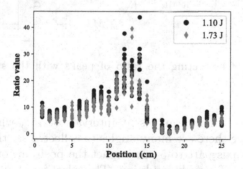

Fig. 5. The distribution ratio of each eigenfrequency peak of the two impact intensities on the x-axis in the accelerometer.

Ratio of Peak Values with the Same Eigenfrequency Between Each Axis. Influencing hitting performance extend beyond the longitudinal position on the bat; the transverse position at the moment of contact between the ball and the bat is also crucial, impacting the launch angle and distance the ball travels upon impact. Due to the multitude of factors influencing the transverse position of the bat, I propose simplifying the problem to the impact position along the circumferential direction. Drawing inspiration from the method outlined in Osawa's study [8], where two cross-shaped piezoelectric films were placed at different circumferential directions on the bat for impacts, the ratio of signals received by the two piezoelectric films was used to deduce the impact angle. The Fig. 6 below shows the process of extracting the ratio of peaks with the same eigenfrequency between each axis.

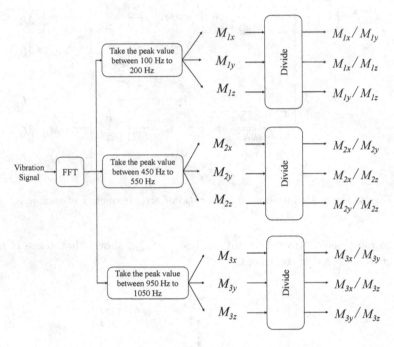

Fig. 6. The process of extracting the ratio of peaks with the same eigenfrequency between each axis.

I set the collected impact angles at intervals of 15°, which are 30, 15, 0, −15, and −30°. Since there are many angles to collect, I set the impact position interval of the long-axis part to 5 cm, impact the positions of 5, 10, 15, 20 and 25 cm, collect 15 pens for each condition. The selection of 30 and 15° is due to their approximate correspondence to the bat and baseball offset during high-flying balls and hits [13], respectively. Negative angles generally result in ground balls. However, I aimed to confirm whether the IMU can distinguish impacts on the upper and lower parts of the bat's short axis, hence the collection of data for negative angles.

I intend to employ a similar approach using the multi-axis characteristics of accelerometers. By analyzing the ratio relationships among values along the three axes, I aim to infer impacts in different circumferential directions. However, as mentioned earlier, the rapid vibrations of the bat may cause time-domain vibration signals to exceed the measurement range. Therefore, I primarily focus on observing the ratio between the first characteristic frequencies to determine if it aligns with the expected values, the ratio cannot be directly used to infer the impact angle.

3   Experimental Results

3.1   Long-Axis Impact Location Prediction

I will proceed to train two separate machine learning models for each dataset. Specifically, for both 1.10 J and 1.73 J, I will employ logistic regression, the training set and test set have a ratio of 7:3. The features used for training are categorized into three types: "Peak Type", "Ratio Type", and a combination of both referred to as "All feature" for both datasets. The Fig. 7 below is a flow chart for prediction in the long-axis direction.

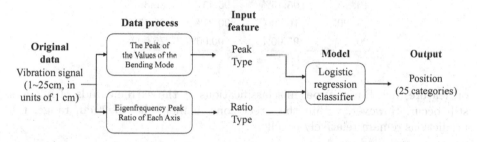

Fig. 7. Flow chart along the long-axis direction.

It can be observed that the results for Ratio Type are generally poorer, especially when using accelerometer-collected data, making it challenging to distinguish impacts at both ends of the sweet zone. Moreover, regardless of the intensity, the predictive outcomes generally exhibit lower accuracy in the 1–10 cm range. I speculate that this may be attributed to the smaller variations in this particular range. However, in the 10–20 cm range, the results are relatively better, indicating higher accuracy within the sweet zone (Table 1).

Utilizing the dataset with a 1.10 J impact intensity, I aim to estimate the impact positions for the higher intensity dataset of 1.73 J. This exploration aims to determine whether ratio-type features truly exhibit features unaffected by impact intensity. Using the same approach as before, I observed the prediction results for various intervals, as shown in the Table 2 below. In the 10–15 cm range, predictions tend to be biased towards the front, while in the 15–20 cm range, most predictions lean towards the rear. This is speculated to be influenced by the higher vibration intensity at 1.73 J, causing predictions to favor the data with larger amplitudes at 1.10 J. A noteworthy point is that, in predictions based

Table 1. The prediction accuracy within a 1 cm tolerance for each intensity across different intervals.

1.10 J			
	All Feature	Only Peak	Only Ratio
Region (cm)	Accuracy		
(0, 5]	92.00%	92.00%	76.00%
(5, 10]	83.33%	66.67%	79.17%
(10, 15]	90.91%	95.45%	81.82%
(15, 20]	100.00%	100.00%	68.18%
(20, 25]	100.00%	100.00%	85.00%
1.73 J			
	All Feature	Only Peak	Only Ratio
Region (cm)	Accuarcy		
(0, 5]	52.00%	76.00%	52.00%
(5, 10]	79.17%	70.83%	54.17%
(10, 15]	95.45%	95.45%	86.36%
(15, 20]	100.00%	90.91%	95.45%
(20, 25]	95.00%	100.00%	75.00%

on features like Ratio Type, misclassifications at the extreme ends of impacts still occur. However, within the sweet zone, namely the 10–20 cm range, the predictions remain relatively excellent.

Table 2. Modeling with the 1.10 J dataset, the predictive performance on the 1.73 J dataset across different intervals is summarized below.

	All Feature	Only Peak	Only Ratio
Region (cm)	Accuarcy		
(0, 5]	53.33%	58.67%	25.33%
(5, 10]	14.67%	26.67%	38.67%
(10, 15]	42.67%	44.00%	60.00%
(15, 20]	61.33%	57.33%	62.67%
(20, 25]	22.67%	18.67%	41.33%

3.2   Circumferential Impact Location Prediction

In this section, we will explore whether the vibration signals collected by the IMU can distinguish impacts at different angles. The experimental setup is consistent with the previous section, using an IMU with a sampling rate set at 2600 Hz, and the baseball bat chosen is still the J143 M made of maple wood.

I rotated the baseball bat, along with the IMU, to set the impact angles. I set the collection of impact angles at 15-degree intervals, namely 30, 15, 0, −15, and −30°, shown in the Fig. 8 below. Given the increased number of collected angles, I set the intervals for impacts on the long-axis at 5 cm. Two impact intensities (1.10 J and 1.73 J) were applied at positions 5, 10, 15, 20, and 25 cm, with 15 samples for each condition, a total of 750 data.

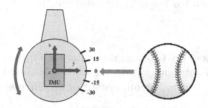

Fig. 8. Schematic diagram of impact experiment in circumferential direction.

Next, I will use the XGBoost classifier for model training. The reason for choosing a classifier is that the angles I am dealing with are distributed in 15-degree increments, making regression models less effective. Initially, I will train the model based on different strengths using three types of features: "Df Axes," which utilizes the peak ratio between different axial features, "Same Axis," which uses the peak ratios within the same axial features, and "All Features," which combines both. The Fig. 9 below is a flow chart of impact position prediction in the circumferential direction. I chose "Same Axis" as the feature because wooden bats have problems with wood grain horizontal and vertical surfaces, and I wanted to see if impact at different angles would affect such features.

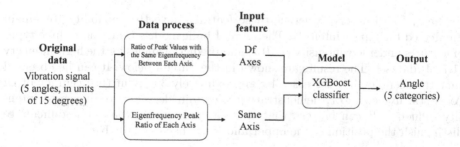

Fig. 9. Flow chart along the circumferential direction.

The results are presented in the Table 3 below, The evaluation standard originally wanted to use the root mean square error (RMSE) compared to Osawa

[8], but since I used a classifier to predict only 5 types of results, and the intervals were large, 15°, it was not appropriate to use RMSE. Therefore, I only present the accuracy under different allowable conditions. The accuracy will be accumulated from top to bottom according to different conditions.

The results indicate that using the Df Axes feature, which involves different axial ratios, performs remarkably well in distinguishing impact angles. The accuracy without errors can exceed 80%. Surprisingly, features like Same Axis also exhibit a certain level of capability in discerning different impact angles. This suggests that the vibration signals are influenced to some extent by the orientation of wood grain for impacts at different angles.

Table 3. Training results of predicted angles using each type of feature for two impact intensities. The accuracy rate under different allowable conditions, the accuracy rate will be accumulated from top to bottom according to different conditions.

1.10 J				
Feature Type		All Features	Df Axes	Same Axis
Accuracy (%)	Completely correct	87.61	89.38	63.72
	Predict to side	94.69	93.81	84.07
	Opposite predictions for 15 and −15°	96.46	96.46	86.73
	Opposite predictions for 30 and −30°	100.00	100.00	86.73
1.73 J				
Feature Type		All Features	Df Axes	Same Axis
Accuracy (%)	Completely correct	79.65	79.65	54.87
	Predict to side	91.15	89.38	81.42
	Opposite predictions for 15 and −15°	92.92	92.04	85.84
	Opposite predictions for 30 and −30°	94.69	97.35	87.61

Next, I will observe whether these features have the capability to remain unaffected by impact intensity. Therefore, I built models using these three types of features under low intensity (1.10 J) and predicted angles for the high-intensity (1.73 J) dataset. The results are shown in the Table 4 below. It can be observed that the accuracy has decreased by approximately 30%, but the accuracy of Df Axes still exceeds 50%, demonstrating a certain degree of resilience to intensity influence. It can be seen that there are situations where it is difficult to distinguish the position of the upper and lower halves of the bat.

Table 4. Predictions of impact angles at higher intensity (1.73 J) using a model trained on the low-intensity (1.10 J) dataset. The accuracy rates vary under different conditions and accumulate from top to bottom.

Feature Type		All Features	Df Axes	Same Axis
Accuracy (%)	Completely correct	54.40	57.07	33.87
	Predict to side	75.20	77.87	66.93
	Opposite predictions for 15 and −15°	77.88	81.42	76.11
	Opposite predictions for 30 and −30°	89.38	89.38	82.30

4   Conclusion

In this study, a method for establishing a detection system for baseball bat impact positions is proposed. I utilized a microcontroller in conjunction with controlling an IMU, using the accelerometer within the IMU to collect the bat's vibration signals. By extracting features from the frequency spectrum of the vibration signals and combining them with machine learning models, position prediction is achieved.

The inherent frequency peak ratio reproduces characteristics similar to those of piezoelectric films, independent of force. This feature can be used for predicting positions along the long-axis, Near the sweet zone, the accuracy can exceed 60% with a tolerance error of 1 cm. What we propose is that it is not affected by the impact strength to a certain extent.

Additionally, by utilizing the multi-axis characteristics of accelerometers and employing the ratio of signals output along different axes, we have achieved the prediction of impacts in the circumferential direction. Under a single impact intensity, the accuracy consistently approaches 80%. However, when applying the model established with low intensity to predict higher intensities, the accuracy drops to only 50%. There still exists a challenge in accurately distinguishing impacts on both sides of the circumferential direction. This feature seems to be affected by the intensity of the impact.

My research aims to explore the possibility of replacing piezoelectric films with IMUs. However, based on the results, due to occurrences of measurements beyond the detection range, the predictive accuracy of IMUs is lower in the long-axis direction. Under a tolerance of 1 cm, the accuracy of piezoelectric films can reach over 95%, while IMUs only achieve around 60%. In terms of predicting impacts in the circumferential direction, both IMUs and piezoelectric films encounter difficulties in distinguishing impacts on the upper and lower parts of the baseball bat.

Despite these findings, there are still many challenges to address with this method, and it has not demonstrated the capability to fully replace piezoelectric films.

References

1. Brody, H.: The sweet spot of a baseball bat. Am. J. Phys. **54**(7), 640–643 (1986)
2. Higuchi, T., Nagami, T., Nakata, H., Watanabe, M., Isaka, T., Kanosue, K.: Contribution of visual information about ball trajectory to baseball hitting accuracy. PLoS ONE **11**(2), e0148498 (2016)
3. Kidokoro, S., Matsuzaki, Y., Akagi, R.: Acceptable timing error at ball-bat impact for different pitches and its implications for baseball skills. Hum. Mov. Sci. **66**, 554–563 (2019)
4. Morishita, Y., Jinji, T.: Accuracy and error trends of commercially available bat swing sensors in baseball. Sports **10**(2), 21 (2022)
5. Bahill, A.T.: The Science of Baseball: Batting, Bats, Bat-Ball Collisions, and the Flight of the Ball. Springer, Cham (2018). https://doi.org/10.1007/978-3-030-03032-2
6. Chen, W.-H., Feng, Y.-C., Yeh, M.-C., Ma, H.-P., Liu, C., Wu, C.-W.: Impact position estimation for baseball batting with a force-irrelevant vibration feature. Sensors **22**(4), 1553 (2022)
7. Feng, Y.C., Ma, H.P.: Detection of Hitting Position of Baseball Bat. National Tsing Hua University (2021). https://books.google.com.tw/books?id=y7OgzgEACAAJ
8. Osawa, T., Tanaka, Y., Yanai, T., Sano, A.: Position estimation of ball impact in baseball batting using PVDF films. In: 2017 IEEE World Haptics Conference (WHC), pp. 442–447 (2017)
9. Russell, D.A.: Does it matter how tightly you Grip the Bat? (n.d.)
10. Russel, D.: Acoustics and vibration of baseball and softball bats. Acoust Today **13**(4), 35–42 (2017)
11. Crisco, J.J., Greenwald, R.M., Blume, J.D., Penna, L.H.: Batting performance of wood and metal baseball bats. Med. Sci. Sports Exercise **34**(10), 1675–1684 (2002)
12. Cross, R.: The sweet spot of a baseball bat. Am. J. Phys. **66**(9), 772–779 (1998)
13. Nathan, A.M.: Optimizing the swing. The Hardball Times (2015)

Learning Enhancer Tools: A Theoretical Framework to Use AI Chatbot in Education and Learning Applications

Angelo Rega[1,2]([✉]) [iD], Raffaele Di Fuccio[1] [iD], and Erika Inderst[2] [iD]

[1] Pegaso Online University, 80143 Naples, Italy
angelo.rega@unipegaso.it
[2] Neapolisanit Rehabilitation Center, 80044 Ottaviano, Italy

Abstract. In this work we are going to formalise a theoretical and applied framework useful to develop AI powered chatbot applications in education. We support the hypothesis that these applications should use adaptive tutoring systems methodology as paradigm of artificial intelligence, because it is closer to psychological and pedagogical theories. The need for this theorization is bringing out from the growing market of applications dedicated to the world of education and oriented to the personalization of student's learning experiences. In this article we therefore present a scheme of use and a development model for these educational applications which supports the most accredited learning theories, which will move from the learning theory of reference to the characteristics of the intelligent artificial agent. The operational scheme proposed in this article describes the formalisms for the development of an algorithm to make an artificial intelligent agent chatbot functional for applications in the educational field.

Keywords: Human-Centered AI · education · learning

1 Introduction

1.1 Link Between Psychology and Technologies

It is well known in the clinical literature that there is an important relationship between psychology and technology. Psychology studies human behaviour, mental processes, and the interaction between people and their surroundings. Technology helps not only this work, but people too, thanks to specific devices and software developed to ease some human activities.

Usually, every single connection between psychology and technology represents a specific field of study, each intersection between psychology and technology represents a field of study, a specific area of research. Among these lines of research, over the years, the study of how people use and interact with technology has been very successful, trying to understand the cognitive, emotional and social aspects of human-machine interaction.

Another very interesting research area very widespread in learning psychology studies concerns investigations on learning technologies, in these studies researchers try to

H. Degen and S. Ntoa (Eds.): HCII 2024, LNAI 14736, pp. 409–419, 2024.
https://doi.org/10.1007/978-3-031-60615-1_28

understand how people acquire and develop skills using educational software, online educational platforms and carrying out simulations. This field of study is also about how some technologies can be developed and how they can work to comply with the psychological principles of learning to offer tools and workplaces for an effective and motivating learning.

A third research area is represented by the relationship between clinical psychology and digital mental health, namely the field of study that is related to how technology can be used in the field of mental health to provide support with diagnosis and treatments. Some examples are therapeutic chatbots or telemedicine platforms. Recent studies are exploring how the use of technology could be a support for complex diagnoses such as autism spectrum disorder (ASD), it could be possible to make use of the potential of machine learning to analyse data and identify objective measures of the disorder (e.g., motor pattern) to effectively support diagnosis.

Furthermore, social psychology has an interest in technology, especially in studying online social interactions and how they can affect human emotions, self-esteem and psychological wellbeing. In addition, according to ergonomics principles, psychology works also in developing intuitive users' interfaces and positive users' experiences. It investigates cognitive, emotional, and behavioural aspects in the interaction between users and devices or applications in order to guarantee pleasant, effective, inclusive, and user-friendly experiences.

The first pioneers of artificial intelligence were cognitive scientists and psychologists. Both these two categories had the same goal: to understand how both machines and humans think and learn. They tried to use artificial intelligence to create tutoring systems, which should have taught some disciplines to students. It is possible to say that artificial intelligence, psychology, and learning are linked since the beginning. In this research, solely learning technology is examined. There have been research studies in this area since the 1950s when the slide projector and educational movie were introduced as visual learning tools, and there were the first attempts at building artificial tutors thanks to the earliest studies into artificial intelligence. In those years until 1960s, the use of machines for educational purposes was investigated, e.g. B.F. Skinner's "Teaching machine" (Skinner 1958), which used positive reinforcements to facilitate learning. The literature on this topic shows that, from 1970s to nowadays, the use of learning technology has gradually increased, starting from the use of the earliest computers up to that of educational software such as Seymour Papert's LOGO (Papert 1980), or the concept of "computer-aided instruction" (CAI) spreading.

During the 80s there was an increasing use of editing and media creation tools, which are useful for both teachers and students to create personalized content.

Since the 90s, the internet has had its exponential growth which has made it is possible to use online educational resources and online learning software. Not to mention, mobile technology progress and the new learning opportunities we have thanks to new technologies – from Virtual reality (VR) or augmented reality (AR) to smartphones and tablets, which guarantee immersive and interactive experiences (Romano et al. 2016; 2023a).

1.2 Learning Technologies

Nowadays learning technologies are developing thanks to the artificial intelligence, automatic learning, and data analysis. They allow more learning personalization and adaptability, while taking into account the European Commission guidelines for educational goals in the coming years. Technology offers a wide range of educational tools and resources to improve the learning process. In European schools educational software, interactive tools, multimedia content and online learning platforms are of common use. Until now, scientific research has focused above all on how to enrich the educational curriculum with these technologies without thinking about what the best strategies to design these applications were.

Over the years, models for the integration of technologies were developed, such as the SAMR Model, a framework created by Puentedura (Puentedura 2006) that categorizes four different degrees of classroom technology integration. The letters "SAMR" stand for Substitution, Augmentation, Modification, and Redefinition. The SAMR model was created to share a common language across disciplines, as teachers strive to personalize learning and help students visualize complex concepts. The SAMR Model can be especially powerful during remote and blended learning when integrated classroom technology makes teaching and learning a more seamless experience for educators and students. Another example of technology integration model is the Technology Integration Matrix (TIM), which provides a framework for describing and targeting the use of technology to enhance learning. The TIM incorporates five interdependent characteristics of meaningful learning environments: active, collaborative, constructive, authentic, and goal directed. These characteristics are associated with five levels of technology integration: entry, adoption, adaptation, infusion, and transformation. Together, the five characteristics of meaningful learning environments and five levels of technology integration create a matrix of 25 cells. All TIM descriptors apply equally well to online and face-to-face instruction, developed by the Florida Center for Instructional Technology (Welsh et al. 2011), the TIM is now in its third edition.

During these last years, a significant number of studies have been conducted on the models of integration of technologies, but none of them are about the guidelines for their future development. In fact, several educational technologies, in particular mobile applications and software, are digital transpositions of what is possible to find on educators' and students' books. Many technologies do not allow learning personalization based on student's needs, they are not inclusive, and do not allow data to be collected – which could be useful for educators to have feedbacks on students.

According to what has been written, there is neither a reasoned development of learning technologies, nor an effective integration of these in educational curriculum, or a concrete analysis of the implications that these tools can have on learning processes.

2 Learning Enhancer Tools

2.1 Definition and Characteristics

In this work is supported the following thesis about LETs (Learning Enhancer Tools): these tools must have characteristics as close as possible to the theories of constructivist and cognitivist developmental psychology, they must be a learning aid, and cognitive abilities intensifiers. They must stay in the student's zone of proximal development in order to be a learning facilitator. Thanks to these, students should be able to develop cognition in an active process of knowledge construction.

The just exposed theory describes Learning Enhancer Tools as "learning amplifiers and intensifiers" which can be considered as devices, strategies or methodologies developed to improve effectiveness and efficiency of learning process.

Every LET must support, stimulate, and be a resource for the development of students' competence, knowledge acquisition and improvement in their learning ability.

There may be three kinds of Learning Enhancer Tools, depending on the context of use and the specific goal:

1. Personalized interactive learning software or applications.
2. Manipulable educational materials such as physical models, and tangible interfaces.
3. Augmented reality and virtual reality systems.

These learning intensifiers provide additional support or auxiliary tools to overcome obstacles, increase people's cognitive abilities or their learning process. The future goal is to develop optimal learning conditions and achieve more significant results.

The definition of Learning Enhancer Tools is close to Papert's "cognitive artifacts" concept, but, as it is possible to read, they work on personalized learning.

Seymour Papert, one of the most important learning theorists and pioneers of the use of computers as educational tools, explained the "cognitive artifacts" concept (Papert 1973). According to him, these artifacts, as well as manipulable tools and materials, can be used as devices of learning improvement and expression of ideas. In fact, cognitive artifacts can be seen as auxiliary objects in people's thoughts and the learning process representation, extension, and enhancement. An example of cognitive artifact is the coding language LOGO which uses as cognitive artifact the concept of "turtle": students can give instruction to the turtle using the coding language LOGO, thanks to this they can observe how this turtle moves and draws on the screen. This kind of interactive experience helps students to develop computational thinking and problem-solving skills. Another one is an example of Papert himself: a learning environment where the computer is used to explore complex mathematical concepts. Students can manipulate virtual objects, solve problems and experiment with mathematical concepts in an interactive way, and, thanks to cognitive artifacts, they can understand these concepts in depth and perceive relationships and patterns between them. Papert's idea sees cognitive artifacts as a bridge between students' thoughts and the outer world, which can facilitate learning and ideas expression in a more meaningful way. Cognitive artifacts offer opportunities for an active exploration, manipulation, and experimentation, as well as helping to develop a more effective knowledge (Romano et al. 2023b). Undoubtedly, Papert's cognitive artifacts have had a significant impact on new technology-based education, but they were not "inclusive" by any means.

It is possible to consider LETs as more complex and inclusive cognitive artifacts. Not only they stimulate thoughts, but they are also seen as cognitive amplifiers, as written by Jerome Bruner, one of the major XX century learning psychologists and theorists. Bruner wrote that cognitive amplifiers (Bruner 1966) are aid tools or strategies for thinking and learning ability, and problem-solving improvement. According to Bruner, learning is not only acquiring information in a passive way, but also an active interaction with learning materials. So, cognitive tools are aid tools for a more effective interactive process. An example of cognitive amplifier done by Bruner is "the guided discovery process" or "teaching from discovery". This kind of approach gives a central role to students' mental activity: they can build their own knowledge through exploration, manipulation and problem-solving; the teacher is a guide, they only suggest or ask specific questions to help students develop knowledge and relate it to previous experiences. In other words, Bruner's cognitive amplifiers underline the importance of the active interaction and of the use of aid tools or strategies to improve learning process.

The already exposed LETs theory starts from the cognitive amplifiers concept, but LETs should also have tutoring ability in order to stimulate students' zone of proximal development. In this way it should be possible to reduce the differences between students' starting level, determined by their individual problem-solving ability, and their potential level, which can be reached thanks to LETs' interactive and intelligent tutoring system. This kind of support can be seen in an educator, a teacher, a coach, or in a LET equipped with artificial intelligence. A LET such as this can improve learning processes and people's growth. Every single person can acquire new skills and abilities thanks to social interaction.

The zone of proximal development is where cognitive development occurs, in fact, LETs should be created and introduced in relation to the zone of proximal development. Vygotsky's zone of proximal development theory has had a significant impact on education and pedagogy. It highlights the importance of social interaction, collaboration and supportive role during people's learning and development process. We live in a digital society, and technologies support learning processes; it is impossible to think about Learning Enhancer Tools not related to intelligent tutoring systems stimulating the zone of proximal development.

LETs should offer to students possibilities of potential action or behavior, in other words their affordance should not only be related with objective physical characteristics, but they should also permit actions related to abilities, interaction and student's characteristics. As the affordance of a chair is to provide a surface for sitting, so the affordance of these technological tools should be simple and clear, a student should immediately understand the relationship between a technological tool and its possible functions. Gibson's affordance theory tells us that perception is an active process: to guide their behavior, people find information directly from the environment. The affordance is clearly perceived, it does not require a complex cognitive elaboration. Nowadays, there are extremely complex technological devices, they are far not only from the affordance theory, but also from the principles of the universality of use. Therefore, every LET's affordance must be clear and instinctive, people must easily perceive and interact with the surrounding environment. In recent years, learning theories have underlined the importance of the relationship between people and the environment. Piaget said people can create their own knowledge thanks to two processes: assimilation – during this process people understand and integrate new information or experiences in their cognitive system; accommodation - during this process people modify and adapt their own mental structures to introduce new information and experiences that cannot be learned directly. If new experiences cannot fit the existent mental structures, people change them or create new ones to understand new information.

LETs should be able to integrate into these processes, they should permit to students to be their own knowledge active creators, they should be able to understand their surroundings by themselves.

LETs should support the process in which the knowledge is not acquired in a passive way, but it is the result of an active mental activity and of a continuous interaction with the environment. Thanks to concrete experiences mediated by LETs, students can improve their cognitive abilities and gradually create even more complex mental models.

In conclusion, the development of a LET must initially consider:

- the learning theory on which the tool's design will be based,
- with which model the enhancement of learning will be managed,
- with which model the zone of proximal development will be managed,
- the gap between the student's starting level and the level they could reach using this tool,
- the right way to make it user-friendly.

This last point will be based on the typology of LET - during the third LET's design phase, it will be decided if the LET will be a software, or if it will be a tangible materials/objects/toys-based system, or if it will be a virtual reality/augmented reality/hybrid systems-based tool.

2.2 Learning Enhancer Tools and Personalized Learning

To develop Learning Enhancer Tools, one of the most important characteristics to consider is learning personalization. This characteristic is ignored during the development of cognitive artifacts for educators and student already available. Personalized learning is a kind of educational approach which base learning experience on students' individual needs, learning rhythms, preferences, and interests, in order to create a more personalized and focused learning process to maximize students' involvement and comprehension, in this way they can succeed in knowledge and competencies acquisition.

To personalize learning, LETs can be developed taking into consideration a variety of strategies and approaches. LETs should provide contents based on students' different abilities, learning styles and interests, so, it can be needed a large number of different materials and educational resources, or a change in the learning activity goals based on students' needs.

Thanks to the modern artificial intelligence, technological tools which can base learning modalities on students' interests, their motivation and involvement during the learning process can be increased. Feedbacks should also be personalized, they should be received in a timely manner and based on students' learning goals in order to help them to identify their own areas of strength and weakness. LETs with these characteristics have a highly adaptive capability and are able to record data about students' performances in order to analyse them providing personalized content, activities and feedbacks based on students' abilities, progresses and learning styles. Adaptive learning software is based on a model that take into consideration every student's knowledge, abilities, and goals, so, it can develop a specific learning path for each student. For example: a student has a solid understanding of a topic, the software can provide advanced contents or even more difficult challenges. On the other hand, if a student is studying to better understand a topic, the software can provide more explanations, specific exercises, or additional support.

It is important to say that Learning Enhancer Tools will never replace teachers, they should be only complementary tools to support and enhance learning processes. Teachers should have an essential role in the software data analysis, in interpret the results, and in adapting learning strategies to students' needs.

2.3 Learning Enhancer Tools and Artificial Intelligence

The European Community's recommendations in 2022 about artificial intelligence and education have become more relevant since the pandemic. In fact, alongside digital transformation, the European Community underlines how important the use of educational digital contents is for both supply (the industry and the public sector) and demand sides (educators and students). In a vast number of European agencies' documents, it has been reported that digital transformation is causing numerous changes: on the one hand, educational digital contents are always more creative, immersive, interactive, and different from one another, on the other hand, thanks to technological progress, the AI is able to develop educational contents, so, there is an exponential increase of educational digital contents development. Besides that, there are some challenges to take into consideration, e.g., digital platforms and their algorithms can be educational digital contents "guardians", causing issues for the use of these resources, or for their quality. In addition to this, it is important to consider that it will be more difficult for students to verify the quality and reliability of digital teaching resources compared to traditional contents, as well as web's risks related to data protection and privacy. All these topics of global interest require all the experts involved in designing, studying, and developing learning technological solutions to start outlining common, scientifically, and ethically validated methodologies.

Starting from these considerations, the next paragraph will be dedicated to all the characteristics that LETs should integrate to be considered as devices equipped with artificial intelligence. According to the LETs' theory, to consider them AI powered, they should be equipped with tutoring systems based on artificial intelligence. In fact, over the years, scientific research has focused on studying and developing Adaptive Tutoring Systems (ATS), and Intelligent tutoring Systems (ITS) which are two different tutoring systems based on artificial intelligence. They have only one difference: ATSs provide only an adaptation of the contents based on students' needs; ITSs are based not only on content personalization, but they are also like tutors who interact constantly with students, and this approach produces adaptive contents and supportive interaction.

To clarify, ITSs and ATSs have the same structure:

1. The Consciousness Model: information about content and learning topics. It can be a set of rules or a knowledge graph that organizes all the concepts in a specific learning area. It helps to identify students' learning gaps, and to provide appropriate learning materials.
2. The Student's Model: it represents students' individual characteristics and competences. It can contain information about a student's previous knowledges, abilities, level of proficiency, and learning preferences. This model is being continuously updated based on students' interactions with the system.

3. The Adaptation Model: based on ATSs and ITSs adaptation in providing personalized instructions. It can include adaptation algorithms which analyze a student's learning data, and determine how to adapt learning content, the learning activities sequence, or level of challenge to them.
4. The Student's Response Model: refers to the system's ability to predict students' responses to specific questions or tasks. It can be based on automatic learning models that analyze students' previous responses to predict future ones.

The difference between them is the ITSs' Students' Model: it also includes an adaptive means of interaction with the students themselves.

ATSs and ITSs have been studied for a long time - in fact it is possible to find a large number of scientific studies on this topic (Nappo et al. 2022), but to define the characteristics a LET should have, we need to take into consideration the most recent studies. The latest scientific literature outlines the most appropriate methods for using artificial intelligence. The artificial agents which could be used for educational purposes are called Situated Psychological Agents (SPA) (Ponticorvo et al. 2019). An SPA is a natural, hybrid or artificial agent located in an environment from which it takes information. The information is elaborated in order to produce an action able to modify the environment itself and/or the links between agent and environment. A human agent bases their behaviour on the elaboration of environmental information depending not only on their cognitive abilities (such as memorization ability, learning and reasoning processes), but also on other not-cognitive psychological functions, such as their emotional structure, affective and social relationship with other agents, their personality, and so on.

A Situated Psychological Agent (SPA) can be included in one of the following macro-areas:

- Artificial Situated Psychological Agents (A-SPA): artificial systems such as software (e.g. chatterbots) or hardware (e.g. automatons) generally developed using artificial intelligence techniques of two kinds: sub-symbolic (e.g. artificial neural networks); and symbolic (e.g. cognitive computing algorithms and semantic networks);
- Hybrid Situated Psychological Agents (H-SPA): part of these systems' control and/or behaviour depend on a human being, another part depends on an artificial system, which can be a software (such as for digital avatars) or a hardware (such as for robots in telepresence);
- Natural Situated Psychological Agents (N-SPA): people who interact directly with the digital/artificial world thanks to physics and "natural" interfaces, as tangible interfaces, or systems that belong to the Internet of Things (IoT).

For example purposes: Fig. 1 – LET's design scheme.

The focus in this chapter is on the last part of the LETS' design scheme writing about the programming of an algorithm which can guarantee the presence of an artificial psychological agent in a Learning Enhancer Tool based on a serious game for cognitive functions enhancement. This algorithm must suggest to the person who is playing on the application the most personalized games, according to their level of development of cognitive functions. These systems have been called Artificial Psychological Agents and, as already written, they consist of an artificial system in an artificial or real environment.

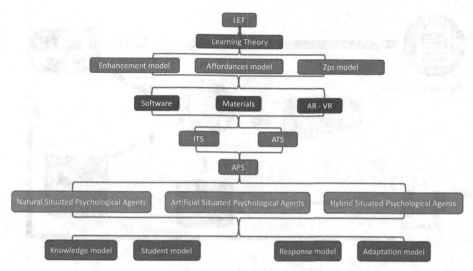

Fig. 1. Design scheme

They have a sensory system (it allows users to give inputs), a control system, and a behavioral system (it allows to interact with the real or virtual environment).

In the following picture (Fig. 2) it is possible to see the artificial agent algorithm, and all the units that compose it. This algorithm is initialized with a cognitive evaluation of the player, which has to play a game to determine their level of cognitive ability, of sensorimotor abilities, and their preferences in order to have the right inputs for the player during their sessions of cognitive enhancement/training.

After this session of cognitive evaluation, the algorithm sends all the information about the player to a database which collects their performances and saves them for future use. The APS is initialized with information about player's cognitive abilities, in this way it can choose the most suitable plays for the player, which are based on their cognitive needs. For example, if a player achieves a poor score in attention tasks, the APS will choose enhancement/training games to improve player's attention. The database which collects all the possible games is called "DB Training". Games are divided into different categories based on complexity, learning area, and cognitive enhancement area.

Now, the artificial agent is able to choose the right play for the player, according to cognitive evaluation score and player's preferences. The artificial agent can also use a unit called "Motivational Unit" which can modify game's scenarios introducing more motivating elements for the player, this unit can identify with which kind of scenarios the player retries an exercise several times.

The artificial agent could also have a "Prompt Manager" which can help the player to reach a better result. In fact, prompts can be considered as additional stimuli which can help the player to find a right answer. In serious games they can be sounds, pictures, or textual aids. It could be essential to add a prompt manager into an APS because thanks to it the artificial agent can decide to help the player during the play sessions if their performance gets worse, in this way it offers a very personalized experience.

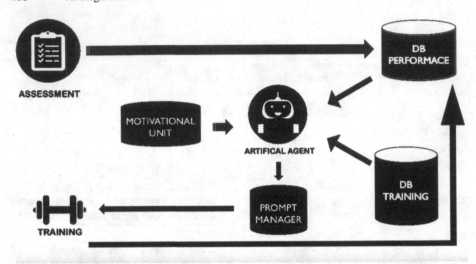

Fig. 2. Algorithm description

3 Conclusions

3.1 Conclusions and Future Developments

AI has a great transformative potential for the education and training of students, teachers, and school staff. For example, it could help to avoid early school leaving, or it could help students with learning difficulties, and teachers who need to apply differentiated or individualized learning, thanks to applications for languages learning, speech synthesizers, or AI-based tutors for student. Accordingly, it is increasingly necessary for researchers, educators, and students to have a basic understanding of AI and of data use, to use this technology in a positive, critical, and ethical way and to exploit its full potential.

Nowadays, it is important to think about the development of these systems, according to the European guidelines for education, written in the European Union plan "The Digital Education Action Plan 2021–2027", which underline a strategy developed by the European Commission to encourage the use of digital technologies for education. The main goal is to exploit the opportunities offered by digitalization to improve digital education and skills of European students. The plan includes different calls to action and goals - some of which are:

- Priority 1: Fostering the development of a high-performing digital education ecosystem.
- Priority 2: Enhancing digital skills and competences for the digital transformation.

The plan started in 2018 is expected to develop until 2027.

Considering not only these priorities, but also the large production and the worldwide market of software and technological systems, it is necessary to make a reflection about the use of the artificial intelligence systems. It is important to consider them not only by an ethical point of view, or to consider how they can protect personal data, but it is important to think also about the effect that these tools can have on student learning.

The theoretical framework presented in this work could be surely improved, even if it is the result of a second reworking (Rega et al. 2021) started from a study already conduct in 2021, and then, implemented in a software currently in use in Italian schools.

Acknowledgments. This research received no external funding.

Disclosure of Interests. The authors declare no disclosure of interests.

References

Skinner, B.F.: Teaching machines. Science **128**(3330), 969–977 (1958)

Papert, S.: Mindstorms: Children, Computers, and Powerful Ideas (1980)

Puentedura, R.: Transformation, technology, and education (2006)

Welsh, J., Harmes, J.C., Winkelman, R.: Florida's technology integration matrix. Princ. Leadersh. **12**(2), 69–71 (2011)

Papert, S.: Uses of technology to enhance education (MIT AI Memo No. 298, LOGO Memo No. 8). Retrieved from the Massachusetts Institute of Technology, A. I. Laboratory (1973). http://hdl.handle.net/1721.1/6213

Bruner, J.S.: Toward a Theory of Instruction. Harvard University Press, Cambridge (1966)

Vygotskij, L.S., Cole, M.: Il processo cognitivo. Boringhieri, Torino (1980)

Gibson, J.J.: The Theory of Affordances, vol. 1, no. 2, pp. 67–82. Erlbaum Associates, Hilldale (1977)

Nappo, R., Nappo, R., Cerasuolo, M., Simeoli, R., Rega, A.: Framework guidelines to design and develop game-based cognitive training. In: INTED Proceedings (2022). https://doi.org/10.21125/inted.2022.1750

Ponticorvo, M., Dell'Aquila, E., Marocco, D., Miglino, O.: Situated psychological agents: a methodology for educational games. Appl. Sci. **9**, 4887 (2019). https://doi.org/10.3390/app9224887

Rega, A., Castellano, L., Vita, S.: Develop educational technology tailored for people with autism: a children's observation grid to build better tools. In: CEUR Workshop Proceedings, vol. 2817 (2021)

Romano, M., Díaz, P., Ignacio, A., D'Agostino, P.: Augmenting smart objects for cultural heritage: a usability experiment. In: De Paolis, L.T., Mongelli, A. (eds.) AVR 2016. LNCS, vol. 9769, pp. 186–204. Springer, Cham (2016). https://doi.org/10.1007/978-3-319-40651-0_15

Romano, M., et al.: Exploring the potential of immersive virtual reality in Italian schools: a practical workshop with high school teachers. Multimodal Technol. Interact. **7**(12), 111 (2023)

Romano, M., Díaz, P., Aedo, I.: Empowering teachers to create augmented reality experiences: the effects on the educational experience. Interact. Learn. Environ. **31**(3), 1546–1563 (2023)

How to Indicate AI at Work on Vehicle Dashboards: Analysis and Empirical Study

Peter Rössger[1]($\boxtimes$), Cristián Acevedo[2], Miriam Bottesch[2], Samuel Nau[2], Tobias Stricker[2], and Frederik Diederichs[3]

[1] beyond HMI, Hohe Str. 4, 71032 Böblingen, Germany
`peter.roessger@beyond-hmi.de`
[2] studiokurbos GmbH, Königstr. 32, 70173 Stuttgart, Germany
[3] Fraunhofer IOSB, Fraunhoferstr. 1, 76131 Karlsruhe, Germany

Abstract. The KARLI project aims to create an adaptive AI system for future vehicles. It's focusing on motion sickness, level-compliant driver behavior, and AI-HMI (artificial intelligence human-machine Interface). The project explores making AI activities visible through avatars, aiming to enhance user experiences and empower users to understand and influence AI decisions for a positive interaction with technology. AI representations in HMIs range from non-representational to realistic, introducing a classification that includes "HMI-integrated." The analysis explores AI representations in vehicle HMIs, citing Nio's Nomi and Waymo's ride service as examples. AI depictions in films, ranging from abstract (HAL 9000) to realistic (Ava from "Ex Machina"), are examined. The KARLI project aims to differentiate itself by explicitly representing AI activity on screens in non-fictional and automotive contexts. Pros and cons of different levels of abstraction in AI avatars are made. A study predominantly involving females and younger individuals, showing a positive attitude toward AI was conducted. Three design variants of the avatar were tested in a comparative laboratory study. All tested designs received negative Net Promoter Scores, with the abstract figurative design rated the best and the figurative design the creepiest. All designs scored low on "Intention to Use," indicating participants' reluctance, and "Product Loyalty" echoed this sentiment. A final design was created based on the results of analysis and study.

Keywords: Artificial Intelligence · Avatar · Human-Machine Interface

1 Introduction

"The idea of a computer that can do everything we can has a kind of magical quality. (…) It is almost a kind of demonic mirror into which we gaze, expecting it to write a novel, to create a movie." Kendric McDowell (2022).

KARLI is a project funded by the German BMWK (Bundesministerium für Wirtschaft und Klimaschutz, Federal Ministry of Economy and Climate Protection). The objective of the KARLI project is to create an adaptive, responsive, and compliance-oriented interaction system for future vehicles (Diederichs et al. 2022, Karli 2024). In pursuit of this goal, KARLI is developing AI functions that are relevant to customer needs. These functions aim to identify driver states and formulate interactions tailored to various levels of automation.

KARLI aims to achieve "level-compliant driver behavior" across its target applications. The assessment of the driver's state, behavior, and likely ability to act is derived from the present driving scenario, which includes considerations of the level of automation. Recording both the driving situation and the driver's condition facilitates a real-time comparison with the intended target, enabling a focused approach in the interaction between human and machine.

Work packages of the project are:

- Level-compliant driver behavior
- Motion sickness
- Artificial intelligence adapted human-machine interface

The development of these AI functions in KARLI involves the utilization of both empirical and synthetically generated data. The data collection and utilization in KARLI are designed to ensure that the project outcomes can be scaled up to handle Big Data generated by production vehicles in the future.

In the KARLI project's AI-HMI (Artificial intelligence in human-machine interfaces) work package, the central focus lies in exploring how the integration of artificial intelligence affects the appearance of HMI. Topics such as the adaptation of graphic design and interaction are discussed in a separate paper (Rössger 2023), whereas this paper specifically addresses the appearance of HMI using an avatar. How is the magical quality manifested? What is visible in the demonic mirror?

The world we inhabit is composed of images. Considering the visual nature of humans and the vast amount of visual data processed daily, it is logical for the KARLI project to investigate how the visual representation of AI enhances user experiences while concurrently improving safety in vehicle operation and human-technology interaction.

Most AI applications operate in the background, unnoticed by users. They lack their own HMI, and the outcomes of AI are presented without revealing the AI context. For relevant examples, see Adext AI (2022). Often, not only the activity but also the existence of AI goes unnoticed. Users observe and notice the results but may not infer the presence of an active AI. Users remain unaware that a learning, self-changing algorithm is making decisions, impacting the interpretation of results. These consequences can be negative. Awareness of communicating with technology, knowledge about the technological nature of decision-making, can empower people to question and influence things in a human-centric manner.

Many people fear AI, perceiving associated problems, while others are enthusiastic, recognizing the benefits of technology (Bort n.y.). In the KARLI research project, the activity of AI should be visible and experiential. This not only communicates the role and capabilities of the technology but also potentially creates a positive user experience. Users can form their own understanding of the presence and function of AI. Visualization is crucial for this. Whether this indeed occurs and whether the chosen visualization is accepted should be clarified through empirical studies.

One method of depicting AI activities is through avatars. Avatars are artificial figures assigned to a user or instance in digital contexts. It refers to a fictional, software-based screen representation in virtual worlds and encounters. The term "avatar" originates from Sanskrit, where it denotes the descent from divine spheres (Wikipedia 2022a; Kollmann n.y.).

2   Categories of Designs

To categorize potential representations of AI in HMIs, a classification ranging from non-representational to realistic with an increasing degree of naturalness has been introduced. Additionally, the category of "HMI-integrated" is included. In detail:

- No Representation: The AI has no representation in the HMI; it operates covertly and delivers results to the user. Users often remain unaware of whether an interaction with AI is occurring.
- Abstract: The HMI is visualized through an abstract construct, such as clouds, surfaces, lights, or other virtual objects.
- Abstract-Figurative: The representation of the HMI includes figurative components like a face, body, or hands but is unmistakably recognizable as an abstract depiction.
- Figurative: The AI is portrayed as a drawn, comic-like character. This could involve humans, animals, or plants, such as talking trees.
- Realistic: The AI is visualized through a photorealistic representation of a human. Both appearance and animations closely mimic genuine human behavior. The boundary between "figurative" and "realistic" is fluid.
- HMI-Integrated: Elements of the HMI, such as icons, texts, lists, pointers, surfaces, or backgrounds, are utilized to depict HMI activity. They change color, shape, size, or transparency to represent AI activity.

2.1   Abstract Design

The representation of AI may be achieved through an arbitrarily designed volume (Fig. 1), often in the form of a sphere, appearing to float fixed in space. The exterior of the representation alters when the AI is active. Parameters such as shape, color, surface structure, or brightness can signify activities and changes in the AI. The advantage of this representation is its high flexibility, while the disadvantage is the limited conveyance of specific information. The volumetric representation is suitable for depicting general activity but is not well-suited for conveying detailed information.

In a similar manner, the abstract and planar representation operates (Fig. 2). A variable surface visualizes the activity of the AI and conveys information. Parameters include the shape and number of surface elements, color, activity of the elements, and the background color. The advantages and disadvantages of the planar representation are the same as those of the volumetric representation. Another drawback is the substantial space required for a planar representation to be clearly visible.

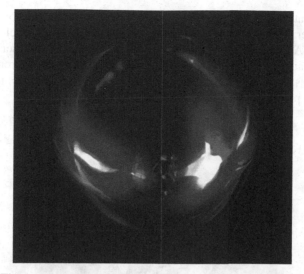

Fig. 1. Example of an abstract AI design (created with Dall-E)

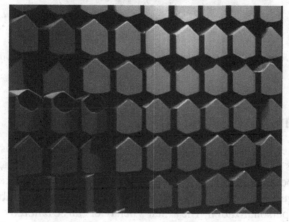

Fig. 2. Example of an abstract AI design in plain shape (created with Dall-E)

2.2 Abstract-Figurative Design

In the abstract figurative representation, figurative faces (Fig. 3) or bodies are used as a foundation but adorned with abstract surfaces and shapes. The abstract components of the representation serve the visualization of states and activities of the AI, such as depicting emotions, listening, speaking, warning, or praising.

By incorporating human features, an understanding of the nature of the AI is generated in the user. They interact with an entity possessing a certain level of intelligence but not human. Additional advantages of the abstract-figurative representation include high flexibility and the ability to create specific appearances to differentiate between functions, brands, user preferences, etc. Users can adjust appearance and behavior to realize personal preferences.

Fig. 3. Example of an abstract-figurative design (created with Dall-E)

2.3 Figurative Design

Figurative representations often align with the aesthetics of cartoons (Fig. 4). They resemble humans or other living beings and, to some extent, behave accordingly, with these behaviors being limited in realism, for example, envisioning talking animals.

The advantages of this representation include high familiarity, flexible design possibilities, and high personalization. The avatar's behavior can be tailored to the user's preferences and contexts. However, compared to abstract representation methods, the design possibilities are somewhat restricted. Human emotions and reactions can be effectively portrayed. The concrete development of the character can contribute to brand formation, while flexibility can be utilized for avatar personalization.

Fig. 4. AI avatar design in cartoon style (created with Dall-E)

Fig. 5. Example of a realistic design (created with Dall-E)

2.4 Realistic Design

An advancement from figurative representation is the realistic depiction of AI (Fig. 5). In this approach, technological means are employed to generate a photorealistic image, and the avatar's behavior closely mimics real human conduct. This representation, while more realistic than its figurative counterpart, faces additional constraints in terms of flexibility, especially if the illusion of genuine humanity is to be preserved.

The pros and cons of a realistic representation are essentially like those of figurative representation. Added to these considerations is the risk of the Uncanny Valley phenomenon (Fig. 6). Generally, users feel more comfortable with an avatar that is more realistic. Acceptance increases with the degree of realism in the representation. However, if the portrayal of AI becomes so realistic that users are uncertain whether they are interacting with artificial or natural intelligence, i.e., unsure if their interaction partner is a machine or a human, feelings of uncertainty and discomfort arise.

The Uncanny Valley should be avoided in all interaction domains between humans and machines. This principle holds true, particularly for the representation of AI in KARLI, which may pose a disadvantage for the realistic depiction of AI.

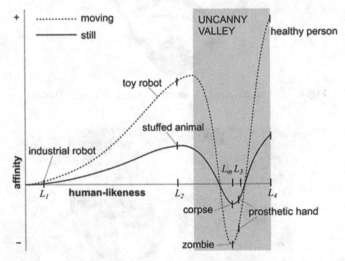

Fig. 6. Uncanny Valley (Kätsyri et al. 2015)

2.5 HMI Integrated Realization

Elements of the HMI, such as tiles, texts, list entries, or backgrounds, can be employed for the representation of AI. The components of the HMI alter their behavior and appearance when the AI is active and communicating. Halo-like effects, as depicted in Fig. 7, can be utilized for the representation of AI. Differences in the appearance of buttons also serve as a means of visualization. The concept of an avatar is thus abandoned, replaced by an illusion ex machina. The machine itself, within its given framework, generates the representation of AI activity.

While this representation offers some flexibility, it is invariably tied to HMI design. Independent visualization of AI is not possible. Users often struggle to comprehend what the AI is communicating in the HMI, as the depictions remain at a high level of abstraction.

Fig. 7. AI avatar HMI integrated (created with Dall-E)

3 Existing Design Examples

The possibilities presented by AI seem boundless, often surpassing those envisioned by reality. AI applications are increasingly becoming integral to our daily lives. Frequently, we fail to notice these applications as they are not explicitly depicted (Gabriel 2019). This section conducts an analysis of the technical and artistic realizations of AI in HMIs. Surprisingly, the results of this investigation in the realm of existing or planned implementations were notably sparse. Films, art, and literature, on the other hand, generate a plethora of often highly creative depictions of AI. Therefore, the research scope was expanded to encompass these domains.

3.1 Realization in Technology

Today, technical implementations of AI, with or without avatars or visual representations, can be found in a wide array of devices, applications, and services. Some examples (sources include, among others: Adext AI, Speechify, builtIn, simplilearn):

- Speech HMIs: The alignment between humans and voice recognition systems is optimized by AI. The speech recognizer adapts to dialects, word choices, and user preferences. Understanding, both of language itself and content, improves over continuous use. The technology can tailor speech outputs to user preferences and contexts, enabling nearly natural language communication.
- Search engines: Search results are moderated by previous searches and user behavior.
- Social media: Algorithms determine, based on user behavior, what individual users see.
- Email programs: AI identifies spam and categorizes it accordingly.
- Automated Driving: Processing large amounts of data, such as image recognition, pattern detection, and learning from (near) accidents and critical situations, allows for the improvement of automation. This is made possible by AI.

- Production and automation, Robot Deployment: Like automated driving, AI processes vast amounts of data and learns from usage.
- Healthcare: Disease detection, pattern recognition in X-ray images.
- Financial industry: Market developments are predicted based on existing large datasets.
- Fraud minimization in digital applications: AI detects and mitigates cyber-attacks based on corresponding patterns.
- Online retail, recommendation systems: Purchase behavior informs predictions about interest in other products, which are then suggested for purchase.
- Media applications (Netflix, Spotify): Recommendations are made based on viewing and listening behaviors.
- Marketing, customer interaction: Chatbots in written and spoken language enable quasi-natural interaction between humans and services.

Automotive HMIs. AI is playing an increasingly crucial role in vehicles, with the core application being automated driving, where ai plays a central role in data collection and analysis (Kappel et al. 2019). AI also moderates data exchange between vehicles (Car 2 Car) and with analog or digital infrastructure (Car 2 X). This paper specifically focuses on the representation of ai activities in the vehicle HMI.

The sole known example of a visual AI instance in an automotive HMI is Nomi from the automaker Nio. In a separate HMI instance, a spherical device with a round display depicts a stylized face, responsive to voice interactions with the driver.

The ride-hailing service provider Waymo offers a ride service with autonomous and driverless vehicles in Phoenix, Arizona, and in San Francisco, California. Users sit in the back seat while the vehicle autonomously drives to the destination. AI significantly contributes to the realization of this service. For the user, the journey becomes visible on screens, displaying the driven and planned route, the environment, traffic lights, and other road participants. Additionally, interactions such as personalized greetings or information about driving maneuvers are presented on these screens. However, there is no visual representation of AI as such.

Like by Waymo information is displayed on Tesla's HMIs for the Autopilot, the automated driving system. Additionally, information about pedestrians is presented, along with the AI's interpretation of the intentions of other road users.

Robots. As an example of some robots currently in development, the Tesla Bot is used here. The Tesla Bot is being developed as a non-automotive robot, serving the company's work on neural networks and the advanced supercomputer, Dojo. Its realization closely resembles the humanoid robots seen in movies.

Speech Assists. AI forms the backbone of various smart assistants and smart home controls. Inputs are made through voice commands. The device's responses are also conveyed through voice, accompanied by task completion ("play music ABC," and ABC is played) and for example, as in Amazon Alexa in an illuminated ring. This glowing ring reflects Alexa's activity and can thus be considered a visualization of AI. During the research, it remained unclear what exactly the ring represents and how its behavior changes based on contexts.

3.2 Artistic Representation

A logically thinking and emotionless AI serves as the perfect canvas for evil in movies and literature. The basic idea is often comparable: the AI itself is not inherently evil but behaves consistently according to programmed logic. Unforeseen side effects counteract the original goal of the AI and, consequently, the intentions of the developers (Automat 2018). This section analyzes different depictions of artificial intelligences in films, sorting them from abstract to realistic based on the criteria mentioned above.

The AI HAL 9000 from the film "2001: A Space Odyssey" exhibits a high level of abstraction. It consists of dynamic red light, symbolizing its activity. Interaction with humans occurs through speech and the actions performed by the AI. WOPR from the film "War Games" utilizes larger surfaces on the exterior equipped with a matrix of luminous elements. In certain scenes, it appears as a monochromatic display with minimal information. It falls into the abstract category. The AI GERTY from the film "Moon" is structured similarly to WOPR. The key difference is a display that communicates emotions through emoticon-like faces. Interaction with humans primarily occurs through speech. With emoticons as a means of communication, GERTY is far less abstract than HAL and WOPR, placing it in the figurative category.

In contrast to the previous examples, the AIs TARS and CASE from the film "Interstellar" are mobile. They consist of cubic elements that can rotate against each other, allowing the systems to move in space. They communicate with humans through speech and screens.

The AI V.I.K.I. from the film "I, Robot" appears as a hologram and primarily communicates with humans through speech. Unlike the previously mentioned depictions of AI, V.I.K.I. has a somewhat suggested human face, falling into the category of abstract figurative.

Commonly chosen forms for the depiction of AI in films include androids or humanoid robots. Here, the systematic progression from abstract to realistic is evident. Robots R2-D2 and C-3PO from the film "Star Wars" and the robot Maria from the film "Metropolis" are distinctly abstract and recognizable as robots. AI visualizations like Ava from the film "Ex Machina" and Commander Data from "Star Trek" are deliberately designed to resemble humans closely and thus fall into the realistic category. Often, the Uncanny Valley is exploited for dramatic effects.

A special case beyond the introduced categories is seen in the film "A.I." Here, the visualization of AI in human-like robots is realized by superimposing human faces.

Beyond films, the visual arts engage surprisingly little with the representation of AI. One example is an interactive art installation from the Barbican in London. Users can interact with the artwork, depicting AI as abstract-figurative representations in the form of three-dimensional stick figures.

4 Discussion of Design Concepts for KARLI

4.1 Requirements

In the research project KARLI, the analysis focuses on whether the activity of an AI should be represented in the vehicle's HMI and, if so, how it can be achieved. From a scientific standpoint, having a representation is deemed advisable. Demonstrations can intuitively convey the AI itself and its results to users during showcases for research purposes.

The planned design of the KARLI HMI will not make its way into a production vehicle. Nevertheless, it is essential to ensure that the visualization is not overly distracting, is intuitive, and can be used while driving. This necessitates a clear communication of information to the driver.

The entire HMI and the representation of the AI should provide a positive user experience. In addition to usability criteria according to ISO 9241-110 (2020), such as self-descriptiveness, conformity to user expectations, learnability, and fault tolerance, the user should have a positive emotional disposition, experiencing joy or sympathy (ISO 9241-220 2020).

4.2 Pros and Cons of the Design Categories

In Table 1, the advantages and disadvantages of the representation methods described above are outlined. It becomes evident that the abstract-figurative representation is the optimal solution for visualizing the AI in KARLI. The abstract-figurative representation excels in perfectly reflecting the nature of an AI. Its positioning between technology on one side and human-like behavior on the other mirrors the character of an AI. It allows for the flexible transmission of large amounts of information, and the depiction of emotions such as joy, disappointment, or boredom is feasible.

4.3 Consequences for an AI Design in KARLI

There are few visualizations of AI in non-fictional contexts, and even fewer in the automotive domain. In the KARLI project, this can create a unique selling proposition by explicitly representing the activity of an AI on the screen. The technological advancements and design competencies of the project can be communicated in a straightforward manner.

Based on the analyses, the AI in KARLI should be represented abstract, abstract-figurative, or figurative manner.

The variable parameters can be used to communicate different states:

- Facial or non-facial contours, such as mouth movements to support verbal communication
- Colors for different emotions like openness, anger, uncertainty
- Shapes for communication direction, facing or turning away, active or passive
- Structures for representing thinking and decision-making processes
- Accessories for AI states, for example, different hats for knowledge communication vs. instructions vs. questions
- All parameters can undergo explicit adjustment by the user or implicit adjustment through usage.

Table 1. Pros and cons of the design categories for the KARLI project

Design categories	Pros	Cons
No representation	No efforts for concept and design No (visual) driver distraction	Core functionality of KARLI will be visualized No explicit information on status and acting of the AI No eye-catcher
Abstract	High flexibility in design and behavior	Not intuitive, needs to be learned May be mis-understandable Limited information transfer to the driver
Abstract-figurative	High flexibility in design and behavior Communication of information and emotion Takes the position of the AI, has human elements, but is not seen as human	Needs careful design work May lead to driver distraction May be mis-understandable
Figurative	Certain flexibility in design and behavior Communication of information and emotion Takes the position of the AI, has human elements, but is not seen as human	Needs careful design work May be inappropriate for automotive applications and research work May lead to driver distraction May be mis-understandable
Realistic	Certain flexibility in design and behavior Communication of information and emotion	Need careful design work May lead to driver distraction May lead into the Uncanny Valley
Integrated	Needs no extra space on the screen, existing components of the screen design are used	Low flexibility in design and behavior Not intuitive, needs to be learned May be mis-understandable Limited transfer of information

5   Empirical Study: Comparison of Avatar Designs

Building upon the analytical insights elucidated in the preceding chapter, an empirical study was undertaken to glean insights into the degree of abstractness deemed acceptable for on-dashboard avatars. This investigation seeks to bridge the theoretical analysis performed earlier with practical observations, aiming to identify the optimal level of abstraction that users find most acceptable in the context of on-dashboard avatars. Based on the analysis three versions of the Avatar were designed and tested.

5.1 Material and Methods

In the conducted research, three distinct versions of avatars were subjected to testing, namely (Fig. 8):

- Abstract (Worm)
- Abstract-figurative (Robot)
- Figurative (Humanoid).

These avatars were systematically evaluated within the context of three diverse use-cases:

1. Welcome Procedure
2. Handover
3. Emergency

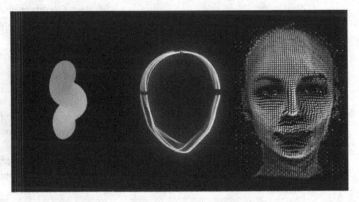

Fig. 8. Three versions of the Avatar, Worm (left), Robot (middle), Humanoid (right).

Nine videos were produced, each approximately 3–10 s in duration—one for each avatar and use-case. To facilitate comprehension of the scenarios, a consistent voiceover was incorporated across all three avatar versions. The visual designs adhered to a unified color scheme, predominantly featuring turquoise, which aligns with the corporate color of the KARLI project and the associated HMI. Shades of orange and red were strategically utilized to signify critical situations within the use-case scenarios.

Participating individuals were exposed to the video's multiple times, with the option to request repetitions as needed. The participants' involvement was limited to observation, maintaining a passive role during data collection. All participants were presented with and subsequently assessed each avatar in every use-case scenario. The videos were presented using VR glasses (Varjo XR3 headset with the respective environment). The sequence of avatar versions was randomized among participants, while the order of use-case scenarios remained consistent for all.

This laboratory study, employing a virtual reality setting, positioned participants within a simple seat structure, equipped with a seat, pedals, and steering wheel. Interaction devices were inactive, allowing participants to assume a customary in-vehicle posture. The research utilized a comprehensive set of data collection instruments, including a questionnaire for personal data administered before video presentations, Net Promoter Score (NPS) evaluations presented after each avatar version, expanded NPS for assessing how easy it is to understand the avatar and the creepiness of the avatar, meCUE questionnaire, a ranking exercise post all avatar presentations, and semi-structured interviews.

For further insights into the meCUE tool, readers are referred to Minge et al. (2013) and Thüring and Mahlke (2007), while additional details on the Net Promoter Score can be found in references such as Baehre et al. (2022).

5.2 Sample

In the conducted study, a total of 20 participants were recruited, and all individuals who were invited actively participated, contributing to a comprehensive dataset for subsequent analysis. The gender distribution within the sample showed 70% female and 30% male participants, with no representation of other gender identities. Age distribution across the participants indicated that 30% were in the 18–29 age group, 35% in the 30–39 age group, 25% in the 40–49 age group, and 10% aged 50 and above. All participants reported their ages.

Participants' self-assessment of their experience with artificial intelligence (AI), measured on a seven-point scale ranging from −3 to +3, yielded an average score of - + 0.4, indicating a relatively balanced distribution of responses. Furthermore, participants' attitudes towards AI, assessed on a scale from 0 to +3, revealed a mean value of 1.9, reflecting a generally positive disposition toward artificial intelligence among the study participants.

5.3 Results

In all three rankings procedures, the ranking after the final version of the avatar, the overall rating in the meCUE, and in the NPS the same result was achieved: the Robot (B) design reached the best results, the Worm (A) the second best, and the Humanoid (C) was rated last.

The results differ between the age-groups (Fig. 9). The Humanoid is only rated best by some of the participants over the age of 40. In the younger age groups this design was not rated best at all. Out of participants rating themselves as experienced in AI (rating +1 to +3 on a scale from −3 to 0 to +3) 62% rated the Robot best.

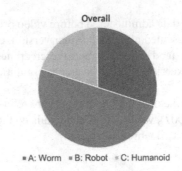

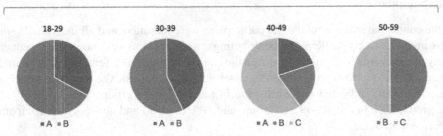

Fig. 9. Results of the ranking, design rated best in the ranking

All designs were rated negative (more detractors than promotors) in the NPS. In the modified NPS the Robot was rated easiest to understand of the three versions. The Worm had the lowest results in creepiness, the Humanoid was rated most creepy (Fig. 10).

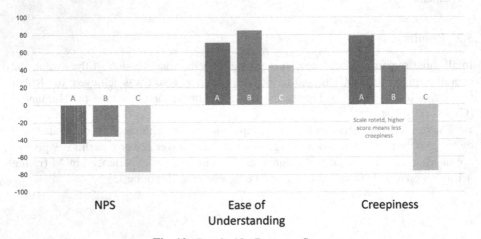

Fig. 10. Results Net Promoter Score

Usefulness and visual esthetics are the only dimensions of the meCUE with positive results (Fig. 11). In usefulness the Worm is slightly ahead of the Robot, with the Humanoid being last. In visual esthetics the Robots reached the best scores, the Worm being second and the Humanoid again last. All other dimensions are negative, with the Humanoid usually being the worst design.

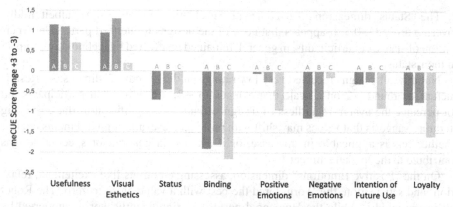

Fig. 11. Results of the single dimensions of the meCUE

5.4 Discussion

The sample was predominantly composed of females and younger individuals, with no specific analyses conducted on gender. The attitude towards AI was notably positive, with no negative values observed on the scale ranging from −3 to +3. The experience with AI was balanced, spanning the entire scale.

None of the designs received particularly favorable ratings, as reflected by negative Net Promoter Scores for all versions. Thus, all designs garnered fewer promoters than detractors.

All designs were deemed understandable, with ambiguity regarding whether participants evaluated the comprehensibility of the entire design, both visually and acoustically, or solely the voice. Given differences between designs while maintaining a consistent voice, it is presumed that at least some participants assessed overall comprehensibility. The Worm was rated as the least creepy, while the Humanoid was perceived as the creepiest by a considerable margin.

The Robot was rated as the best design by participants, evident in rankings, Net Promoter Scores, and the overall meCUE assessment, with the order being Robot – Worm – Humanoid. The Robot was preferred by younger participants and those claiming prior experience with artificial intelligence. The Humanoid was favored exclusively by participants over 40 years old.

The dimension of "Usefulness" was one of two dimensions where all three designs achieved a positive value. However, the Humanoid lagged significantly behind the other two versions, suggesting that the fundamental utility of an avatar in all three variants became apparent.

In terms of "Visual Aesthetics," the Robot achieved the highest rating, closely followed by the Worm), while the Humanoid lagged, all with slightly or clearly positive ratings. Interviews indicated that the use of a more realistic face, facial design without hair, constant facial movements, and coarse pixelation were perceived negatively.

The "Status" dimension received negative evaluations for all designs, albeit mildly, hovering around −0.5. It appears that none of the designs influenced participants' perception of status, or participants, in general, remained unaffected by technology's impact on their status.

Notably, all designs received very low ratings on the "Binding" dimension. Results fluctuated around −2 on a scale that extends to −3, indicating that participants did not perceive the avatar, regardless of design variant, as a significant artifact. Existing literature suggests that values may shift with prolonged use, although it remains unclear whether this is applicable in this case, or if avatars, in general, or specific designs contribute to the low attachment.

On the "Positive Emotions" dimension, assessing emotions like excitement, relaxation, and satisfaction, the Worm fared the best with a value close to zero. The Robot fell in the middle, while the Humanoid performed significantly worse, supported by numerous negative statements in interviews. The Humanoid evoked the fewest positive emotions.

In the "Negative Emotions" dimension, reflecting emotions like anger, helplessness, and frustration, the results mirrored those of the "Positive Emotions" dimension. Worm and Robot achieved better results than the Humanoid. The values tended to be positive (pay attention to scale reversal), suggesting that the designs did not necessarily evoke negative feelings. This could also indicate an internal emotional distance towards avatars or technology in general, aligning with the statement "I do not allow technology to evoke negative feelings in me."

All three designs consistently received negative values on the "Intention to Use" dimension. Based on the experiences shared, participants expressed no inclination to utilize the avatars in the future. This result was most pronounced for the Humanoid. It remains unclear whether participants harbor general skepticism towards avatars or specifically towards the designs investigated.

The "Product Loyalty" dimension echoed the findings of the "Intention of Future Use" dimension. Participants would not prefer the showcased avatars over other avatars or comparable technologies.

Among participants, two groups emerged. One group preferred a more realistic representation, aligning with the sentiment that if an avatar is to be used, a realistic portrayal is preferable. However, a significantly larger group favored an abstract representation, asserting that AI is artificial, and a car is not a human, necessitating a corresponding portrayal reflecting artificiality.

Participants agreed that the avatar should only appear during interaction. When no interaction occurs, it should retract, shrink, or disappear entirely. Upon reactivation, an auditory and/or haptic signal should be provided. The avatar should be customizable, allowing adjustments to the degree of movement, colors, appearance, voice, volume, etc., or could adapt to personal preferences, use cases, and contexts through the utilization of the AI algorithm. The avatar's design should be highly streamlined and sophisticated, contributing to brand identity.

5.5 Next Steps

Considering the limited prevalence of AI avatars in industrial and product contexts, the findings from this study are positioned to serve as a foundational framework for subsequent discussions, analyses, and further research endeavors. The outcomes are poised to elevate the KARLI HMI avatar to an advanced level of acceptance. However, it is imperative to approach the generalization of these results judiciously. This is contingent upon the assumption that forthcoming users of AI avatars in vehicles will predominantly be young and possess prior experience with AI technology.

The avatar was re-designed based on the results of the study. Lines are stronger, we added more facets to the appearance. Figure 12 shows the new design to be applied in the KARLI HMI. A wake-up state was added (left) to indicate a passive presence of the AI. When listening the gaps on the side enlarge to indicate this status (second from left). On the right the hint status is shown. Here a set of bubble leaves the Robot. Strength, direction, and speed of the bubble are used to carry additional information.

The design will be implemented and used as an indication of the active HMI in the final KARLI HMI.

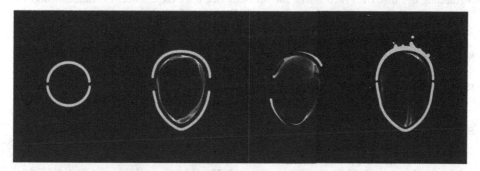

Fig. 12. Re-designed Avatar, from left to right: wake-up, listen, process, hint

References

Adext AI: 10 Things That Use Artificial Intelligence and You've Probably Never Realized It (2022). https://blog.adext.com/things-apps-artificial-intelligence/. Accessed Feb 2024

Automat: Die 5 bösesten KIs der Filmgeschichte (2018). https://automat.im/de/die-5-boesesten-kis-der-filmgeschichte/1.html. Accessed Feb 2024

Baehre, S., O'Dwyer, M., O'Malley, L., Lee, N.: The use of Net Promoter Score (NPS) to predict sales growth: insights from an empirical investigation. J. Acad. Mark. Sci. **50**, 67–84 (2022)

Borth, D.: TEDx Talk: Unsere Zukunft mit künstlicher Intelligenz (o.J.). https://www.youtube.com/watch?v=qQhG5U88PC4. Accessed Feb 2024

builtIn: 31 Examples of Artificial Intelligence Shaking Up Business as Usual (2022). https://builtin.com/artificial-intelligence/examples-ai-in-industry. Accessed Feb 2024

Diederichs, F., et al.: Artificial intelligence for adaptive, responsive, and level-compliant interaction in the vehicle of the future (KARLI). In: Stephanidis, C., Antona, M., Ntoa, S. (eds.) HCII 2022. CCIS, vol. 1583, pp. 164–171. Springer, Cham (2022). https://doi.org/10.1007/978-3-031-06394-7_23

Gabriel, P.: KI ohne Grenzen? In: Wittphal, V. (Hrsg.) Künstliche Intelligenz. Springer, Heidelberg (2019). https://doi.org/10.1007/978-3-662-61794-6

ISO 9241-110: Ergonomie der der Mensch-System Interaktion – Teil 110: Interaktionsprinzipien. Zitiert nach Gebrauchstauglichkeit von Software 1. Beuth (2020)

ISO 9241-210: Ergonomie der der Mensch-System Interaktion – Teil 210: Menschzentrierte Gestaltung interaktiver Systeme. Zitiert nach Gebrauchstauglichkeit von Software 1. Beuth (2020)

Kätsyri, J., Förger, K., Mäkäräinen, M., Takala, T.: A review of empirical evidence on different uncanny valley hypotheses: support for perceptual mismatch as one road to the valley of eeriness. Front. Psychol. **6**, 390 (2015)

Kappel, et al.: Die Rolle der KI beim automatisierten Fahren. In: Wittphal, V. (Hrsg.) Künstliche Intelligenz. Springer, Heidelberg (2019). https://doi.org/10.1007/978-3-662-61794-6

KARLI: Website of the KARLI Project (2024). https://karli-projekt.de/en/start. Accessed Feb 2024

Kollmann, T.: (o.J.). https://wirtschaftslexikon.gabler.de/definition/avatar-31903. Accessed Feb 2024

McDowell, K.: (2022). https://www.goethe.de/prj/k40/de/kun/ooo.html. Accessed Feb 2024

Minge, M., Riedel, L. Thüring, M.: Modulare Evaluation von Technik. Entwicklung und Validierung des meCUE Fragebogens zur Messung der User Experience. In: Brandenburg, E., Doria, L., Gross, A., Güntzler, T., Smieszek, H. (Hrsg.) Grundlagen und Anwendungen der Mensch-Technik-Interaktion. 10. Berliner Werkstatt Mensch- Maschine-Systeme, pp. 28–36. Universitätsverlag der TU Berlin, Berlin (2013)

Newsroom, N.: Our Future Smart Cars Will Be Embodied Digital Assistants (2021). https://www.nio.com/blog/our-future-smart-cars-will-be-embodied-digital-assistants. Accessed Feb 2024

Rössger, P.: Report KARLI Projekt: MMI-Adaption durch künstliche Intelligenz (2023). https://karli-projekt.de/wp-content/uploads/2023/04/KARLI-Report-MMI-Anpassung-KI-230328.pdf. Accessed Feb 2024

Simplylearn: AI Applications: Top 14 Artificial Intelligence Applications in 2023 (2022). https://www.simplilearn.com/tutorials/artificial-intelligence-tutorial/artificial-intelligence-applications#what_are_the_applications_of_artificial_intelligence. Accessed Feb 2024

Speechify: Top 8 artificial intelligence products (2022). https://speechify.com/blog/artificial-intelligence-products/?landing_url=https%3A%2F%2Fspeechify.com%2Fblog%2Fartificial-intelligence-products%2F. Accessed Feb 2024

Thüring, M., Mahlke, S.: Usability, aesthetics and emotions in human–technology interaction. Int. J. Psychol. **42**(4), 253–264 (2007)

Wikipedia: Avatar (Internet) (2022a). https://de.wikipedia.org/wiki/Avatar_(Internet). Accessed Feb 2024

Wikipedia: Uncanny Valley. Von Tobias K. - translation of Image: Mori Uncanny Valley.svg by Smurrayinchester (2022b). https://commons.wikimedia.org/w/index.php?curid=3579536. Accessed Feb 2024

Harmonizing Emotions: An AI-Driven Sound Therapy System Design for Enhancing Mental Health of Older Adults

Yichao Shi$^{(\boxtimes)}$ ⓘ, Changda Ma ⓘ, Chunlan Wang ⓘ, Tianrun Wu ⓘ,
and Xinyan Jiang ⓘ

Georgia Institute of Technology, Atlanta, GA 30332, USA
{yshi431,cma326,cwang932,twu380,xjiang351}@gatech.edu

Abstract. This research paper introduces an AI-driven sound therapy system designed to enhance the mental health of older adults, particularly those living alone. With the global increase in the elderly population and the associated rise in social isolation and loneliness, this study addresses critical emotional well-being challenges through technology. By integrating artificial intelligence with home robots, the proposed system delivers personalized sound therapy, detecting mood changes and generating therapeutic sounds. This innovative approach aims to improve the quality of life for older adults, offering a novel solution to mitigate emotional neglect and promote a more empathetic, technologically advanced caregiving model.

Keywords: Old Adults · Mental Health Care · Artificial Intelligence · Sound Healing

1 Introduction

As the global demographic shifts towards an older population, by 2030, one in six individuals will be over the age of 60, with expectations of doubling to 2.1 billion by 2050 [1]. In parallel, living arrangements have evolved; in the UK, the number of people aged 75 and older living alone has surged by 25% over two decades to over 2.2 million [2], while in the US, 28% of older adults live independently [3]. This increase in solitary living has inadvertently raised the risks of social isolation and loneliness, affecting approximately 25% of older adults living alone. The health implications of loneliness, equated to the health risks of smoking 15 cigarettes a day [4], are profound, ranging from an increased likelihood of Alzheimer's disease to cognitive decline [5], and heightened rates of anxiety (38%) and depression (27%) amongst older individuals [6], with a mortality risk comparable to obesity [7].

The critical concern of the emotional well-being of older adults, exacerbated by the COVID-19 pandemic, underscores the urgent need for effective mental health interventions. The pandemic has further isolated older adults from their social networks, amplifying the adverse effects of social isolation on their mental and physical well-being [9].

H. Degen and S. Ntoa (Eds.): HCII 2024, LNAI 14736, pp. 439–455, 2024.
https://doi.org/10.1007/978-3-031-60615-1_30

Although research indicates that interventions targeting social isolation can positively impact mental health [10], the need for further exploration into emotional intelligence and perceived social support is evident [11]. The clear linkage between social isolation, loneliness, and adverse health outcomes [12] calls for comprehensive support services and programs tailored to the unique needs of older adults.

Current emotional care approaches for older adults, influenced by the COVID-19 pandemic, the dynamics of inter-generational support, and the balance between formal and informal care services, highlight significant gaps. The pandemic has showcased the critical role of integrating health information and communication technologies with older adult care [13]. Emotional support from family, particularly intergenerational support, emerges as a pivotal factor in the emotional well-being of older adults [14, 15]. However, the reliance on informal support networks and the lack of a dyadic focus in geriatric rehabilitation reveal the need for a more holistic and person-centered approach to emotional care [16–19].

Addressing these challenges, this paper presents a tentative solution: a basic AI-driven system that uses simple home robots with sensors to offer initial sound therapy for older adults, particularly those living alone. This system modestly attempts to address gaps in current mood-regulation practices by using AI to notice mood changes and provide basic therapeutic sounds. Our research aims to gently explore the potential of incorporating sound therapy into the daily routines of older adults using straightforward technology. By aiming to reduce emotional neglect and slightly improve mental health, this initial approach seeks to contribute modestly to the field of caregiving for older adults, suggesting a small step towards more understanding and technologically informed care solutions.

2 Literature Review

Music's Impact on Emotional Health. Music's profound effect on emotional health is attributed to its intrinsic acoustic properties—loudness, pitch, timbre, tonality, and rhythm [20]. These elements significantly influence emotional responses, contributing to music therapy's efficacy in mitigating stress, depression, and anxiety [22]. The emotional resonance elicited by music is moderated by social contexts and acoustic environments, with dopamine playing a crucial role in the pleasure derived from music, highlighting the dopaminergic system's involvement in abstract reward processing [25].

Music Therapy in Elderly Care. In elderly populations, music therapy has shown promise in reducing agitation, enhancing cognitive function, and lowering blood pressure [26–28]. Recent explorations into AI-composed music for therapeutic purposes suggest a burgeoning field aimed at augmenting elderly well-being through technology-assisted interventions [29].

Analytical Approaches to Music and Emotion. Investigations into music's emotional dimensions have categorized musical features according to their emotional impact, employing advanced analytical tools to correlate these features with emotional responses. Salakka's work, using MIRToolbox and various statistical software, underscores the relationship between musical characteristics and emotional intensity, valence, and arousal, identifying specific musical features as significant predictors of emotional states [21, 30–35].

Advancements in Emotion Recognition. The utility of cardiac signals, including ECG, in emotion recognition underscores the feasibility of using these physiological markers to classify emotions accurately. This approach has demonstrated high efficacy, suggesting that cardiac signals alone can serve as reliable indicators of emotional states [36]. Furthermore, research indicates that heart rate variability (HRV) is more closely associated with arousal than valence, offering insights into emotional regulation and stress response mechanisms [37].

AI in Sound Therapy and Emotion Detection. The integration of AI in sound synthesis represents a frontier in tailoring emotional health interventions for older adults. AI technologies enable the creation of sound-design systems responsive to qualitative descriptors and facilitate the real-time synthesis of therapeutic sounds through social robots [38–43]. Tools like MusicGen and applications of deep learning in music generation, such as LSTM networks, are enhancing the consistency and therapeutic potential of music therapy, supporting its application across various settings, including clinical environments and stress management during medical procedures [44–56].

This literature review encapsulates the multidisciplinary research intersecting music therapy, emotion recognition technology, and AI's role in enhancing the emotional well-being of older adults. The convergence of these fields offers promising avenues for developing comprehensive, technology-driven interventions tailored to the unique needs of the elderly population.

3   System Design

Our project targets the complex relationship between social isolation, loneliness, and their health impacts on the elderly. To combat these challenges, we designed a multi-faceted system integrating hardware and software components to detect human emotions, generate therapeutic music, and facilitate monitoring and interaction through a user-friendly interface.

Hardware Configuration. At the core of our prototype is a Raspberry Pi 4 Model B, equipped with a 10-inch display for visual engagement and OpenCV for image processing. This setup is supported by peripheral devices including a keyboard, mouse, and an 8GB development board for efficient operation. The system's emotional detection capability is enhanced by an Arduino board paired with a Fielect KY-039 5V Heartbeat Sensor for pulse monitoring, and a Makerobos camera for facial recognition. The robot's structure is crafted from corrugated paper, incorporating a pulley system for mobility, and utilizes a USB drive to store the music library.

Emotion Detection and Music Therapy. Upon approaching an elderly individual, the robot employs facial analysis via OpenCV to determine emotional states by assessing Arousal and Valence metrics. Simultaneously, the person's heart rate is recorded through the Heartbeat Sensor, enabling the calculation of Heart Rate Variability (HRV) and Heart Rate Coherence (HRC) values. These metrics are crucial for understanding the individual's emotional state and tailoring the music therapy accordingly.

Software Integration. Utilizing the Processing environment, our system analyzes the emotional impact of music, selecting tracks that align with the individual's current emotional needs. The AI-powered MusicGEN tool further refines music selection, ensuring the playlist is optimally suited to alleviate distress and promote emotional well-being.

Caregiver Interface. A mobile application interfaces with the robot, allowing caregivers to monitor and interact with elderly individuals remotely. Through the app, caregivers can manage daily routines, set reminders, and control the robot's movement across different environments. The app also facilitates the recording of video interactions and captures vital health metrics like blood pressure and heart rate, offering caregivers comprehensive insights into the elderly's well-being.

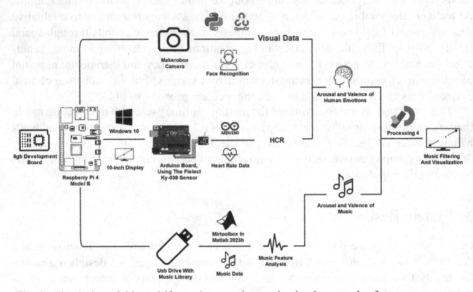

Fig. 1. The design of this multifaceted system integrating hardware and software components

This system design (Fig. 1) combines cutting-edge technology with practical applications, embodying a holistic approach to enhancing the mental health and quality of life for the elderly. By integrating emotion detection, AI-driven music therapy, and a caregiver interface, we offer a novel solution to mitigate the effects of social isolation and loneliness among the elderly population.

4 Methods

This research presents an AI-powered robot designed for elderly care, integrating Raspberry Pi with sensory tools for direct engagement. Utilizing OpenCV for facial recognition and convolutional neural networks for emotion detection, it identifies negative states such as anxiety or depression. The system then correlates these emotions with tailored music therapy, employing text-based inputs to activate sound generation algorithms.

Prioritizing simplicity, the robot's interface is voice-activated, minimizing the learning curve, and enhancing usability for older individuals. This approach ensures the system is both accessible and effective in delivering personalized emotional support.

4.1 Human Emotion Detection System

Our system leverages an Arduino-based setup for precise HRV measurement, incorporating advanced hardware and software techniques to ensure data accuracy and reliability.

To enhance the accuracy and reliability of heart rate measurements, our system incorporates several strategies aimed at minimizing error and noise. Firstly, we utilize an "isValidHeartRate" function to ensure that detected heart rates fall within a viable range of 40 to 170 beats per minute (bpm), with a tolerance margin of 15 bpm, to guard against sensor noise or movement artifacts that could skew readings. Additionally, we apply low-pass and moving average filters to reduce high-frequency disturbances and random signal fluctuations, thereby improving the clarity of the heartbeat signal for more accurate detection. An adaptive detection mechanism, employing a threshold-based approach, is then used to dynamically identify significant changes in sensor data that correspond to actual heartbeats, effectively reducing false positives caused by minor data variations. In cases of prolonged inaccuracies, an "outOfRangeCounter" is activated to monitor these anomalies, triggering a "resetHeartRateMonitoring" function that recalibrates the system, thus ensuring continued precision in heart rate monitoring.

$$RMSSD = \sqrt{\frac{1}{N-1} \sum_{N-1}^{i=1} (RR_i - RR_{i+1})^2}$$

As shown in the equation above, the calculation of Heart Rate Variability (HRV), a key indicator of autonomic nervous system activity, is achieved through the Root Mean Square of the Successive Differences (RMSSD) method in our system. This approach focuses on measuring the variability between successive heartbeats, for which we meticulously collect intervals from heartbeats that have been validated through our verification process. By computing RMSSD, we can effectively gauge the balance of the autonomic nervous system, ensuring this process is both accurate and computationally efficient. This method allows us to assess the physiological state of the user with precision, providing valuable insights into their overall autonomic function.

Our system, built on the Arduino platform, seamlessly integrates real-time data collection with sophisticated analysis capabilities. Through the initialization of serial communication, it continuously monitors and filters data, assessing Heart Rate Variability (HRV) within its operational loop, all while remaining responsive to user inputs (Fig. 2). This framework not only collects but also interprets data in real-time, offering a dynamic tool for health monitoring.

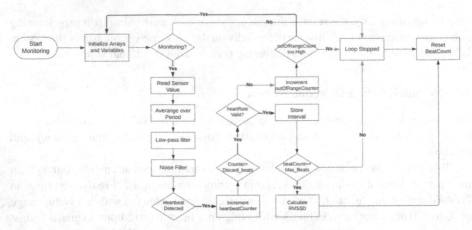

Fig. 2. The control flow in Arduino script of HRV detection

In parallel, the system employs a dual-method approach for emotion detection, leveraging both HRV and facial recognition technologies to assess arousal and valence. Arousal levels, which reflect the balance between the sympathetic and parasympathetic branches of the autonomic nervous system, are deduced from HRV measurements. Specifically, lower high-frequency (HF) HRV values are indicative of heightened arousal states [57]. Valence, on the other hand, is evaluated through a combination of HRV data and facial expressions, using Convolutional Neural Networks (CNNs) to analyze facial cues. This method provides a nuanced understanding of the emotional spectrum, distinguishing between positive and negative states [58, 59]. Together, these advanced techniques offer a comprehensive view of an individual's emotional landscape, facilitating a more informed and responsive approach to emotional well-being.

4.2 Music Creation System

The music creation system in our study systematically analyzes a set of 33 songs across diverse emotional categories using the MIRToolbox 1.7 software in MATLAB R2023b. This analysis encompasses multiple musical features including Brightness, High-mid, Low-mid, Pulse Strength, Rhythmic Clarity, and Novelty, enabling us to categorize songs into emotional groups such as Joyful, Nature, Relax, Religious, Sad, and Stirring Music.

In our analysis of musical features, we delved into various aspects that significantly influence the emotional impact of music. Brightness, a measure correlated with the spectral center of mass, sheds light on the high-frequency content of music, showing that nature music tends to have the highest brightness among the genres studied. Additionally, the analysis of High-mid and Low-mid frequencies, alongside Pulse Strength and Rhythmic Clarity, provides valuable insights into the music's frequency range, texture, intensity, and the clarity of its rhythm—factors that are vital for evoking specific emotions (Fig. 3). We also observed that Flatness values, which help in identifying the spectral properties of music, vary considerably across different genres, thus assisting in the categorization of music types. However, when examining Novelty, which assesses structural changes in music, we found it less effective for distinguishing between genres,

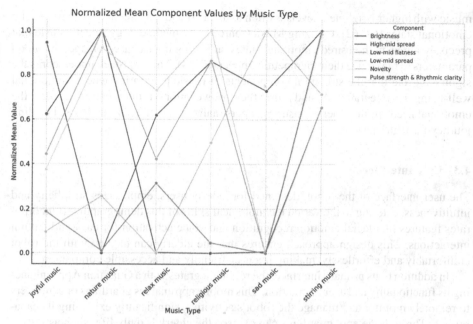

Fig. 3. Quantitative analysis of musical emotions based on MIRToolbox 1.7.

indicating that while Novelty contributes to our understanding of musical structure, it does not singularly facilitate genre differentiation.

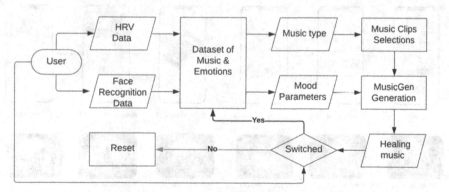

Fig. 4. The control flow of using MusicGEN to generate healing music and interact with the user.

Our exploration into the emotional correlations within music reveals a nuanced interplay between various musical features and the emotional responses they elicit. Arousal, for example, is profoundly influenced by the Pulse Strength of a piece; faster and more intense beats are known to increase arousal levels, while slower rhythms tend to decrease them [60]. Further, we discovered that Emotional Intensity and Valence are deeply intertwined with musical elements such as Pulse Strength, Low-mid frequencies, and Brightness. Specifically, warm Low-mid tones typically evoke positive emotions, whereas music with higher Brightness levels is often associated with happier and more optimistic emotional states [61, 62]. Utilizing MusicGen[63], our methodology selects music that precisely aligns with desired emotional states, adjusting tracks based on specific mood parameters to maximize their therapeutic impact (Fig. 4). This approach underscores the significant role that the structural components of music play in influencing emotional well-being. By integrating AI and music therapy, we tailor our interventions to meet the emotional needs of the elderly, ensuring a personalized and effective emotional healing journey through music.

4.3   User Interface

The user interface of the robot, designed for elderly users, emphasizes simplicity and intuitiveness, catering to the varied technological skills of this demographic. It incorporates features like facial emotion recognition and voice activation for easy and natural interactions. This design approach ensures that the elderly can engage with the robot comfortably and effortlessly, making it a user-friendly and accessible companion.

In addition to its primary interface, the robot integrates with a Guardian App, enhancing its functionality and user interaction. This mobile app enables guardians or caregivers to remotely monitor and manage the robot's activities, significantly extending its capabilities. Through the app, guardians can oversee the elderly's daily life, such as setting reminders, managing schedules, and controlling the robot's movement across different rooms. It also allows for real-time observation of the elderly's living environment and dynamics (Fig. 5).

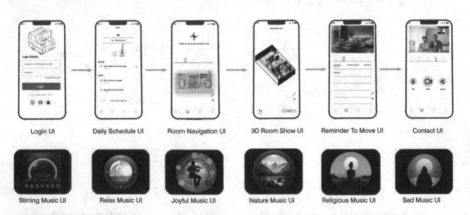

Fig. 5. The user interface design of the Guardian App and its primary interface design

The Guardian App further enhances the robot's utility by facilitating video interactions between the elderly and their caregivers, as well as transmitting vital health information like blood pressure and heart rate. The app's design ensures that guardians stay informed and connected, allowing them to provide immediate assistance or intervention when necessary. The robot's functionality varies with its location, providing contextual assistance tailored to each room's specific needs, such as kitchen safety reminders, living room entertainment features, bedroom medication alerts, and bathroom emergency support.

4.4 Physical Prototype Development

The robot is designed to be the size of a pet and the shape of a dog to provide a reassuring mood and homely atmosphere for the owner. As shown in Fig. 6, it has a large internal storage space, and the lower belly section, that can hold the central Raspberry PI hardware devices, is closed, while items commonly used by seniors on a daily basis, such as pill containers and water bottles, are accessible on the upper side through a top lid. The head section is designed to accommodate an interactive touch screen and a camera at the top of the screen, with a thickness that allows cables to be attached at the back of the device.

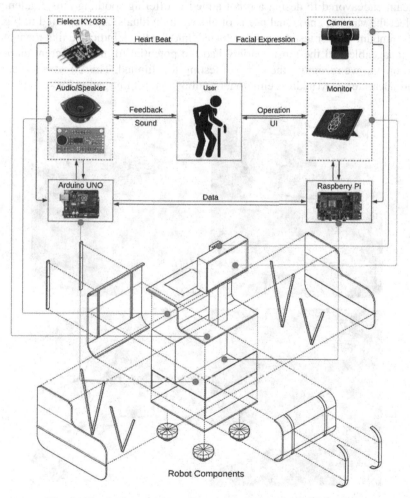

Fig. 6. Physical prototype and hardware installation of the robot

The screen is connected to the central hardware through a "neck," a hollow cylinder that supports the head and also houses the cables that connect devices like the head screen and camera to the central control hardware in the body. Panels on the side of the robot's body can be opened to inspect, maintain, and clean internal equipment and hardware. The wheels are electrically controlled for increased flexibility and better interaction with the owner and are connected to central hardware. Strip lights are set at the front and back of the body to light the way for elderly people who get up at night to do night activities. The finger heartbeat sensor is designed as a "dog leash" to detect heartbeat, HDRI, and pulse, providing the user's emotional information to the center when the user touches the end.

5   Results

The team endeavored to design a robot aimed at offering soothing music, attempting to reflect the varying emotional needs of elderly individuals. As illustrated in Fig. 7, a modest amount of user testing was conducted, and feedback indicated that the interface was manageable and the music variety had the potential to meet different emotional needs, though we recognize the scope of testing was limited. This effort is a small part of a broader attempt to address emotional healing and risk mitigation for seniors in their

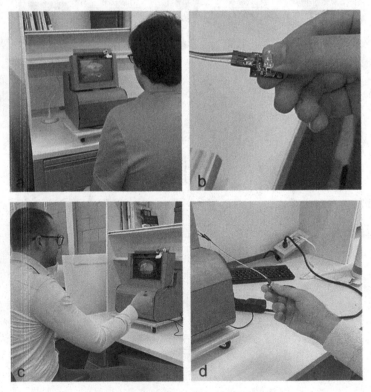

Fig. 7. User testing of Physical Prototype

daily lives. The project led to the assembly of a basic physical prototype, which served as a humble step towards applying this idea in a practical setting. This prototype is an initial effort to explore how technology might be used to aid the mental health and well-being of the elderly, offering a tailored, AI-assisted approach for emotional support, while understanding there is much more to learn and improve upon.

6 Discussion

In our study, we explored the potential of an AI-driven sound therapy system aimed at supporting the mental health of older adults. By combining artificial intelligence with home robots, which attempt to detect mood changes and offer personalized sound therapy, we made a small contribution towards understanding emotional care for the aging population. We recognize that the implications of our findings are preliminary, offering a glimpse into how technology could intersect with eldercare, yet mindful of the vast amount of research still needed in this area.

The tentative outcomes noted in our study, such as a slight reduction in bad emotions and some improvement in emotional well-being among users, align with the existing, more extensive research on the benefits of music and sound therapy. It's well-documented that music therapy can help alleviate depression and anxiety symptoms in the elderly, and our findings suggest that AI customization might add value to this therapy, though we acknowledge our research is but an initial step in this direction. We hope our work can contribute to the ongoing conversation about integrating technology into emotional care strategies, while humbly acknowledging the limitations and scope of our study.

A small robot designed to offer musical comfort and emotional support could serve as a companion in the daily lives of older individuals, akin to the role pets often play. This robot, as we cautiously propose, can offer a semblance of companionship, as suggested by the outlooks in Fig. 8. Its design aims to be unobtrusive and adaptable, potentially acting as a simple aid for smarter living throughout the day. Besides offering calmness, it could, in a limited capacity, help monitor the well-being of seniors and provide gentle reminders for daily tasks, though its effectiveness and acceptance remain to be thoroughly evaluated.

As illustrated in Fig. 9, we suggest that a compact robot could offer assistance in various aspects of home life for the elderly, particularly those living alone. We believe it's important that technology serves to support, not alienate, this demographic. The insights from our research modestly suggest a small step towards integrating technology in mental health care for seniors. Our aim is to introduce a simple, personalized approach to emotional care through an AI-driven sound therapy system, though we acknowledge it's an initial effort and far from a comprehensive solution. This approach could potentially be relevant given the increasing numbers of older individuals and the widespread issue of social isolation, yet we remain aware of the limitations and scope for further development.

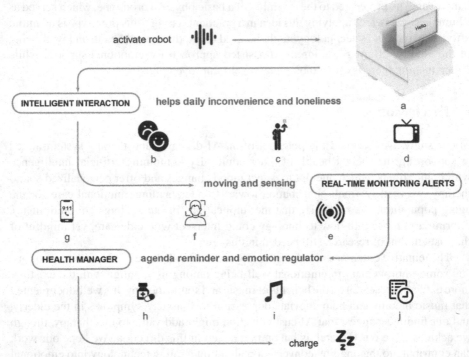

activate robot

INTELLIGENT INTERACTION   helps daily inconvenience and loneliness

a

b   c   d

moving and sensing   REAL-TIME MONITORING ALERTS

g   f   e

HEALTH MANAGER   agenda reminder and emotion regulator

h   i   j

charge

Fig. 8. Robot Function Workflow in the everyday life of old adults: a. Sound therapy robot proto-type. b. Detects the owner's mood through their facial and posture recognition, and actively plays music or starts a conversation. c. Ask robot to follow you with light on or deliver medicine, drink, or food. d. Can be used as a radio or television that can play shows for owner e. Keep sensing the environment to detect scenes such as water flowing or glass breaking. f. Identifies if an elderly person is at risk by their face and posture. g. The alarm system is linked with an emergency call and monitoring application to protect the owner. h. Remind the owner to take medicine. i. Play music to soothe negative emotions. j. Organize the owner's daily activities and diet for a healthy life.

7   Limitations and Future Work

Our study offers preliminary insights but also faces limitations. Currently, our primary achievement is developing a functioning system that leverages AI and music for the emotional support of the elderly. However, the scope of our sample, the length of our intervention, and the details of the AI algorithms require further study. There is a need for additional data to ascertain if AI-generated music effectively aids in more severe emotional states. Future research should extend these preliminary findings to broader and more varied groups, over longer durations, and through different AI models. Further, examining how this system works in conjunction with other smart home technologies could lead to a more integrated approach to elderly care.

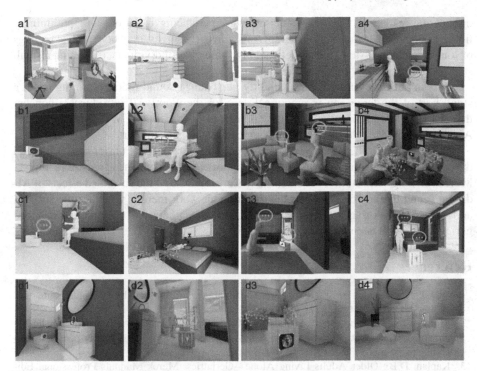

Fig. 9. Application scenarios for robots: a1. When no one is at home or during free time, the robot will check the home to see if the water is turned off. a2. When no one is at home or during free time, the robot will check the home. a3. The robot will sense whether the stove is turned off to prevent fires. When the old man was cooking, he asked the robot to keep track of twenty minutes and remind him. a4. The robot is cooking with the elderly and reminds the elderly that the time is up, the time is up, the food is cooked. b1. Robot checks to see if radiator is off when no one is home to save energy. b2. The robot will chat with the elderly living alone. If it finds that the elderly are in a bad mood, Robots will come forward to care for the elderly. b3. The robot will actively express its concern for the elderly, warming the emotions of the elderly living alone emo. b4. Robots can liven up the atmosphere, play music, and make elderly friends happy. c1. In the morning and evening, the robot will remind the elderly to take medicine. c2. Play soothing music to help seniors sleep. c3. When the elderly sleep at night, the robot will always stay by their side, waiting for instructions regarding their needs. c4. When the elderly get up in the middle of the night and want to go to the toilet, the robot will turn on the lights to illuminate the way for the elderly to go to the toilet. d1. The robot checks to see if the water is turned off in the bathroom sink. d2. In the middle of the night, the way to the bathroom will be lit for seniors. d3. When the elderly take a bath, play music to make them feel more relaxed. d4. If it recognizes that an elderly person has fallen, it will immediately activate the emergency rescue mode and call the elderly family member and the hospital.

8 Conclusion

In our modest study, we explore a simple AI-driven sound therapy system aimed at supporting the mental well-being of older adults. Integrating artificial intelligence with basic home robots, this system attempts to offer immediate, yet basic, sound-based

452   Y. Shi et al.

therapeutic responses, especially for seniors experiencing isolation. Our preliminary findings suggest that such sound therapy, albeit in early stages, may help reduce feelings of loneliness, depression, and anxiety among some older individuals, indicating a small step forward in improving mental health.

This initial effort utilizes AI to slightly personalize sound therapy, aiming to fill a small part of the large gap in emotional care for the elderly. It introduces a concept that might be integrated into daily life with little intrusion, hinting at the possibility that AI-assisted sound could offer minimal companionship and support.

Looking ahead, there's much room for growth in this area. Further research could delve into combining this system with other home devices for enhanced reach and impact. Moreover, long-term studies are essential to truly understand the sustained effects of AI-driven sound therapy on senior mental health. Our work merely scratches the surface, and as the population ages, continued innovation in empathetic and technology-enhanced geriatric care will become increasingly crucial.

References

1. WHO. Ageing and health. https://www.who.int/news-room/fact-sheets/detail/ageing-and-health. Accessed 01 Oct 2022
2. McIntyre, S.: Older people living alone are 50% more likely to visit A&E than those who live with others (2018). https://www.health.org.uk/news-and-comment/news/older-people-living-alone-are-50-more-likely-to-visit-ae-than-those-who-live-with
3. Kaplan, D.B.: Older Adults Living Alone—Geriatrics. Merck Manuals Professional Edition (2023). https://www.merckmanuals.com/professional/geriatrics/social-issues-in-older-adults/older-adults-living-alone
4. Kroll, M.M.: Prolonged social isolation and loneliness are equivalent to smoking 15 cigarettes a day. Extension (2022). https://extension.unh.edu/blog/2022/05/prolonged-social-isolation-loneliness-are-equivalent-smoking-15-cigarettes-day
5. Bennett, D.A., Schneider, J.A., Buchman, A.S., Barnes, L.L., Boyle, P.A., Wilson, R.S.: Overview and findings from the rush memory and aging project. Curr. Alzheimer Res. 9(6), 646–663 (2012)
6. Zissimopoulos, J., Thunell, J.: Older adults living alone report higher rates of anxiety and depression. USC Schaeffer (2020). https://healthpolicy.usc.edu/evidence-base/older-adults-living-alone-report-higher-rates-of-anxiety-and-depression/
7. Holt-Lunstad, J.: The Potential Public Health Relevance of Social Isolation and Loneliness: Prevalence, Epidemiology, and Risk Factors (2017)
8. Taylor, H., Taylor, R., Nguyen, A., Chatters, L.: Social isolation, depression, and psychological distress among older adults. J. Aging Health 30(2), 229–246 (2016). https://doi.org/10.1177/0898264316673511
9. MacLeod, S., et al.: Covid-19 era social isolation among older adults. Geriatrics 6(2), 52 (2021). https://doi.org/10.3390/geriatrics6020052
10. Qin, W., Xiang, X., Taylor, H.: Driving cessation and social isolation in older adults. J. Aging Health 32(9), 962–971 (2019). https://doi.org/10.1177/0898264319870400
11. Elsherif, Z., Elgafaar, S.: Emotional intelligence, perceived social support and mental health of institutionalized elderly. Tanta Sci. Nursing J. 20(1), 220–243 (2021). https://doi.org/10.21608/tsnj.2021.168862
12. Majmudar, I., Mihalopoulos, C., Abimanyi-Ochom, J., Mohebbi, M., Lim, M., Engel, L.: Health service use associated with loneliness and social isolation among older adults in Australia. https://doi.org/10.21203/rs.3.rs-3094575/v1 (2023)

13. Siette, J., et al.: The impact of COVID-19 on the quality of life of older adults receiving community-based aged care. Australas. J. Ageing **40**(1), 84–89 (2021)
14. Tang, S., Yang, T., Ye, C., Liu, M., Gong, Y., Yao, L., Bai, Y.: Research on grandchild care and depression of Chinese older adults based on CHARLS2018: The mediating role of intergenerational support from children. BMC Public Health **22**(1) (2022). https://doi.org/10.1186/s12889-022-12553-x
15. Li, C., Han, Q., Hu, J., Han, Z., Yang, H.: Impact of intergenerational support and medical expenditures on depression: Evidence from rural older adults in China. Frontiers in Public Health 10 (2022). https://doi.org/10.3389/fpubh.2022.840864
16. Lee, Y., Barken, R., Gonzales, E.: Utilization of formal and informal home care: how do older Canadians' experiences vary by care arrangements? J. Appl. Gerontol. **39**(2), 129–140 (2018). https://doi.org/10.1177/0733464817750274
17. Olatunji, S., Rogers, W.: Development of a design framework to support pleasurable robot interactions for older adults. Gerontechnology **21**(s), 1 (2022). https://doi.org/10.4017/gt.2022.21.s.760.opp3
18. Plys, E.: Spilling over at the boiling point: a commentary on the need for dyadic approaches to psychosocial care with older adults and their care-partners in postacute rehabilitation. Rehab. Psychol. **68**(3), 271–280 (2023). https://doi.org/10.1037/rep0000504
19. Clair, C., Henry, M., Jennings, L., Reuben, D., Sandberg, S., Giovannetti, E.: Refining a taxonomy of goals for older adults with functional limitations and their caregivers to inform care planning. J. Appl. Gerontol. (2020). https://doi.org/10.1177/0733464820944326
20. Sturm, I., Blankertz, B., Potes, C., Schalk, G., Curio, G.: ECoG high gamma activity reveals distinct cortical representations of lyrics passages, harmonic and timbre-related changes in a rock song. Front. Hum. Neuroscience, 8 (2014). https://doi.org/10.3389/fnhum.2014.00798
21. Salakka, I., Pitkäniemi, A., Pentikäinen, E., Mikkonen, K., Saari, P., Toiviainen, P., Särkämö, T.: What makes music memorable? Relationships between acoustic musical features and music-evoked emotions and memories in older adults. PLoS ONE **16**(5), e0251692 (2021). https://doi.org/10.1371/journal.pone.0251692
22. Witten, E., Ryynanen, J., Wisdom, S., et al.: Effects of soothing images and soothing sounds on mood and well-being. Br. J. Clin. Psychol. **62**(1), 158–179 (2023)
23. Andringa, T., Lanser, J.: How pleasant sounds promote and annoying sounds impede health: a cognitive approach. Int. J. Environ. Res. Public Health **10**(4), 1439–1461 (2013). https://doi.org/10.3390/ijerph10041439
24. Meng, Q., Jiang, J., Liu, F., Xiaoduo, X.: Effects of the musical sound environment on communicating emotion. Int. J. Environ. Res. Public Health **17**(7), 2499 (2020). https://doi.org/10.3390/ijerph17072499
25. Ferreri, L., et al.: Dopamine modulates the reward experiences elicited by music. Proc. Natl. Acad. Sci. **116**(9), 3793–3798 (2019). https://doi.org/10.1073/pnas.1811878116
26. Lou, M.: The use of music to decrease agitated behaviour of the demented elderly: the state of the science. Scandinavian J. Caring Sci. **15**(2), 165–173 (2001). https://doi.org/10.1046/j.1471-6712.2001.00021.x
27. Mahendran, R., et al.: Art therapy is associated with sustained improvement in cognitive function in the elderly with mild neurocognitive disorder: findings from a pilot randomized controlled trial for art therapy and music reminiscence activity versus usual care. Trials **19**(1) (2018). https://doi.org/10.1186/s13063-018-2988-6
28. Sari, N., Rekawati, E.: The effect of traditional music therapy on blood pressure among elderly with hypertension: a literature review. Int. J. Nursing Health Serv. (Ijnhs) **2**(2), 55–65 (2019). https://doi.org/10.35654/ijnhs.v2i2.103
29. Hong, J., Peng, Q., Williams, D.: Are you ready for artificial mozart and skrillex? An experiment testing expectancy violation theory and AI music. New Media Soc. **23**(7), 1920–1935 (2020). https://doi.org/10.1177/1461444820925798

30. Lartillot O., Toiviainen P.: MIR in Matlab (II): A toolbox for musical feature extraction from audio. In: Dixon, S., Bainbridge, D., Typke, R. (eds.) Proceedings International Conference on Music Information Retrieval, pp. 237–244 (2007)

31. Lartillot O.: MIRtoolbox 1.7.2: User's manual (2017). https://www.jyu.fi/hytk/fi/laitokset/mutku/en/research/materials/mirtoolbox/manual1-7-2.pdf

32. Gross, J., Ligges, U.: nortest: Tests for normality. R package version 1.0–4 (2015). https://CRAN.R-project.org/package=nortest

33. Ullah M.I., Aslam M.: mctest: Multicollinearity diagnostic measures. R package version 1.1.1 (2017). https://CRAN.R-project.org/package=mctest

34. R Core Team: R: a language and environment for statistical computing (2017). https://www.R-project.org/

35. Elowsson A., Friberg A.: Long-term average spectrum in popular music and its relation to the level of the percussion. In: Proceedings of 142nd Audio Engineering Society International Convention, pp. 1–12 (2017)

36. Claret, A.F., Casali, K.R., Cunha, T.S., et al.: Automatic classification of emotions based on cardiac signals: a systematic literature review. Ann. Biomed. Eng. **51**, 2393–2414 (2023). https://doi.org/10.1007/s10439-023-03341-8

37. Oğuz, F.E., Alkan, A., Schöler, T.: Emotion detection from ECG signals with different learning algorithms and automated feature engineering. Signal, Image Video Process. **17**(7), 3783–3791 (2023). https://doi.org/10.1007/s11760-023-02606-y

38. Miranda, E.R.: An artificial intelligence approach to sound design. Comput. Music. J. **19**(2), 59–75 (1995). https://doi.org/10.2307/3680600

39. Hassinen, H.: Audio and text conditioned abstract sound synthesis through human-AI interaction (2023)

40. Guzhov, A., Raue, F., Hees, J., Dengel, A.: Audioclip: extending clip to image, text and audio. In: 2022 IEEE International Conference on Acoustics, Speech and Signal Processing (ICASSP), pp. 976–980 (2022). https://doi.org/10.1109/ICASSP43922.2022.9747631

41. Huang, R., et al.: Make-An-Audio: text-to-audio generation with prompt-enhanced diffusion models (2023). http://arxiv.org/abs/2301.12661

42. Alonso-Martín, F., Malfaz, M., Sequeira, J., Gorostiza, J., Salichs, M.: A multimodal emotion detection system during human–robot interaction. Sensors **13**(11), 15549–15581 (2013). https://doi.org/10.3390/s131115549

43. Jaiswal, S., Nandi, G.C.: Robust real-time emotion detection system using CNN architecture. Neural Comput. Appl. **32**(15), 11253–11262 (2020). https://doi.org/10.1007/s00521-019-04564-4

44. Nilsson, U.: The anxiety- and pain-reducing effects of music interventions: a systematic review. Aorn J. **87**(4), 780–807 (2008). https://doi.org/10.1016/j.aorn.2007.09.013

45. Yuan, X., Xiong, S., Duan, P.: Music generation system based on LSTM (2016). https://doi.org/10.2991/iceeecs-16.2016.108

46. Hohmann, L., Bradt, J., Stegemann, T., Koelsch, S.: Effects of music therapy and music-based interventions in the treatment of substance use disorders: a systematic review. PLoS ONE **12**(11), e0187363 (2017). https://doi.org/10.1371/journal.pone.0187363

47. Lordier, L., et al.: Music in premature infants enhances high-level cognitive brain networks. Proc. Natl. Acad. Sci. **116**(24), 12103–12108 (2019). https://doi.org/10.1073/pnas.1817536116

48. Nizamie, S., Tikka, S.: Psychiatry and music. Indian J. Psychiatry **56**(2), 128 (2014). https://doi.org/10.4103/0019-5545.130482

49. Ji, S.: A comprehensive survey on deep music generation: multi-level representations, algorithms, evaluations, and future directions (2020). https://doi.org/10.48550/arxiv.2011.06801

50. McClary, R.: Healing the psyche through music, myth, and ritual. Psychol. Aesthetics Creativity Arts **1**(3), 155–159 (2007). https://doi.org/10.1037/1931-3896.1.3.155
51. Jian, W., Changran, H., Wang, Y., Xiaolin, H., Zhu, J.: A hierarchical recurrent neural network for symbolic melody generation. IEEE Trans. Cybern. **50**(6), 2749–2757 (2020). https://doi.org/10.1109/TCYB.2019.2953194
52. Shahrudin, F.A., et al.: Music and sound-based intervention in autism spectrum disorder: a scoping review. Psychiatry Invest. **19**(8), 626–636 (2022). https://doi.org/10.30773/pi.2021.0382
53. Dokkum, N.H.V., et al.: Feasibility of live-performed music therapy for extremely and very preterm infants in a tertiary NICU. Frontiers in Pediatrics 8 (2020). https://doi.org/10.3389/fped.2020.581372
54. Αντωνιάδου, M., Tziovara, P., Antoniadou, C.: The effect of sound in the dental office: practices and recommendations for quality assurance—a narrative review. Dentistry J. **10**(12), 228 (2022). https://doi.org/10.3390/dj10120228
55. Mastnak, W.: Perinatal music therapy and antenatal music classes: principles, mechanisms, and benefits. J. Perinatal Educ. **25**(3), 184–192 (2016). https://doi.org/10.1891/1058-1243.25.3.184
56. Kishida, M., Yamada, Y., Inayama, E., Kitamura, M., Nishino, T., Ota, K., Ikenoue, T.: Effectiveness of music therapy for alleviating pain during haemodialysis access cannulation for patients undergoing haemodialysis: a multi-facility, single-blind, randomised controlled trial. Trials **20**(1) (2019). https://doi.org/10.1186/s13063-019-3773-x
57. Thayer, J.F., Åhs, F., Fredrikson, M., Sollers, J.J., Wager, T.D.: A meta-analysis of heart rate variability and neuroimaging studies: implications for heart rate variability as a marker of stress and health. Neurosci. Biobehav. Rev. **36**(2), 747–756 (2012)
58. Appelhans, B.M., Luecken, L.J.: Heart rate variability as an index of regulated emotional responding. Rev. Gen. Psychol. **10**(3), 229–240 (2006)
59. Ko, B.C.: A brief review of facial emotion recognition based on visual information. Sensors **18**(2), 401 (2018)
60. Lim, H.A., Park, H.: The effect of music on arousal, enjoyment, and cognitive performance. Psychol. Music **47**(4), 539–550 (2019). https://doi.org/10.1177/0305735618766707
61. Kantor-Martynuska, J.: Emotional responses to music and their musical, individual, and situational factors: an integrative approach. Studia Psychologiczne **53**(1), 30–45 (2015)
62. Schaefer, H.E.: Music-evoked emotions-current studies. Front Neurosci **11**, 600 (2017). https://doi.org/10.3389/fnins.2017.00600. PMID: 29225563; PMCID: PMC5705548
63. Copet, J., et al.: Simple and controllable music generation (2023). arXiv preprint arXiv:2306.05284

RetroMind and the Image of Memories: A Preliminary Study of a Support Tool for Reminiscence Therapy

Cesare Tucci(✉) , Ilaria Amaro , Attilio Della Greca ,
and Genoveffa Tortora

University of Salerno, Salerno, Italy
ctucci@unisa.it

Abstract. Reminiscence therapy, a widely used method focused on recalling past memories, has shown good results in improving the well-being of dementia patients, particularly with patients with Alzheimer's disorder. However, despite promising results and wide use, its effectiveness remains a matter of debate. This paper presents RetroMind, a new framework that combines Large Language Models (LLMs) and social robots to improve the effectiveness of reminiscence therapy through the creation of visual material based on memories. RetroMind leverages the natural linguistic abilities of LLMs and the physical presence of social robots with the goal of engaging patients in personalized reminiscence sessions. The main goal of RetroMind is to provide an image consistent with the patient's narrative that serves as a support for reenactment and consolidation of memories, improving the effectiveness of therapy. The framework incorporates two questionnaires, the Autobiographical Memory Interview (AMI) to assess autobiographical memory and the Cornell Scale for Depression in Dementia (CSDD) to assess patients' levels of depression, enabling targeted and individualized interventions.

Keywords: Alzheimer · Social robotics · HRI · LLM · Reminiscence therapy

1 Introduction

Reminiscence therapy (RT) is an approach commonly used in nursing homes and care facilities that uses life stories, written or oral, to improve the psychological well-being of older people with various forms of dementia, particularly Alzheimer's dementia [22]. The therapy focuses on two main aspects: (i) improving cognitive function and (ii) improving emotions and mood [13].

The ultimate goal of RT is to improve patients' quality of life by addressing both cognitive and affective aspects. Specifically, to act on the well-being of people with dementia, RT uses the sharing of life stories to support the patient's revival of significant events and improve their emotions [21].

Recollection of memories can take different forms, using only text (spoken and written) or integrating tangible elements such as photos, videos, and music that have symbolic value for the patient [6].

However, in many cases, elderly patients do not have visual reminders of past periods, such as childhood or adolescence, and the absence of visual material may reduce the effectiveness of therapy. Several papers in the literature have proposed strategies to improve traditional RT by introducing digital tools. Studies by Hashim et al. [8], Imtiaz et al. [9], and Lancioni et al. [11] highlight the effectiveness of combining reminiscence therapy with technological tools such as customized digital memory books, mobile applications, and computer-assisted programs. RT supported by digital tools was found to be effective despite the fact that the patients studied were not born in the digital age [2]. In light of the promising results achieved by integrating technologies into RT, to increase the effectiveness of therapy, we propose RetroMind, a reminiscence therapy support framework for mental health professionals that integrates LLM and social robots to create visual materials that can foster and enhance memory recall in patients with dementia.

The idea of creating images that reconstruct a visual representation of patients' memories to consolidate past memories is based on scientific evidence derived from neuroimaging studies. In fact, it has been observed that common brain activations occur when looking at photos of familiar places and when seeing similar images of those places. Both situations, although with different intensities, would activate a common episodic memory network that includes middle temporal and prefrontal regions.

Based on this evidence, in this preliminary work, we set out to provide patients with images consistent with the narrative of their memories in order to stimulate reenactment and mnemonic consolidation, improving the effectiveness of reminiscence therapy.

Our framework involves the use of the Pepper robot and the integration of LLMs, which provide personalized conversations and reflect natural human communication [26]. In this way, the system will be able to obtain a reliable transcription of patients' speech and then use the text as input for image creation through the use of DALL-E3 software. To encourage interaction between the robot and the user and stimulate recollection narration, the system will also be able to ask questions based on the Autobiographical Memory Interview (AMI) [10], a standard questionnaire widely used in the literature to gather detailed information about an individual's autobiographical events and episodic memory. In this preliminary work, we will report results on the semantic similarity obtained by comparing transcripts of a text from an AD patient described in the literature and the image produced by our system from these transcripts.

The next sections of the study will present (2) the background and state of the art related to the use of social robots with patients diagnosed with AD, (3) the methodology used in our study, (4) an illustrative example of our framework, and (5) conclusions and future work.

2   Background and Related Work

In this section, to better understand the context of our work, we provide a comprehensive overview of the fundamental concepts surrounding reminiscence therapy and the evolving landscape of HRI techniques, emphasizing in particular the transformative role of LLMs. We delve into the theoretical underpinnings and practical applications of reminiscence therapy, highlighting its significance in enhancing the well-being of individuals affected by AD. Moreover, in Sect. 2.2 our investigation extends to a thorough examination of the contemporary literature in HCI focusing on its relevance in addressing the challenges associated with AD treatment.

2.1   Reminiscence Therapy

RT is a psychosocial therapy widely used to improve cognitive function and psychological well-being in patients with Alzheimer's disease. This method promotes the development of positive emotions through reminiscence and the sharing of past experiences [19]. RT involves dialogues between the patient and the therapist, who guides the conversation by highlighting the patient's past actions and experiences. During these sessions, the patient is methodically guided through a sequential narrative of his or her life. This therapeutic approach prioritizes the use of the patient's long-term memory, relying on information that is familiar and easier to retrieve. This is especially important for patients in the early stages of Alzheimer's disease, as although they often have significant short-term memory difficulties their long-term memory is not yet completely impaired [23]. Regarding the duration of RT, it is recommended to have therapy sessions once a week, lasting about 30 to 60 min each. On average, each session should last about 45 min. This therapy should continue for a period of 8–12 weeks.

Therapy can be administered either on an individual basis or in a group setting. However, the individualized approach may offer greater benefits by tailoring sessions to each individual, focusing on relevant memories derived from their unique experience [14]. Several studies have indicated that cognitive performance can be improved and psychological health can be preserved in older individuals with the use of RT as a successful method [12]. However, traditional RT relies mainly on recall of memories through dialogue and imagination. In many cases, the absence of real elements (such as photos, videos) that facilitate the recall of memories may limit the effectiveness of therapy. An additional limitation is that constantly seeking advice from experts or therapists is a significant barrier for most individuals with Alzheimer's disease. At the same time, caregivers of individuals with AD, burdened with a significant workload, have limited capacity to promote and support therapy consistently.

2.2   AD Care in Human-Computer Interaction

In recent years, research on the use of Socially Assistive Robots (SARs) in the treatment of mental disorders, particularly Alzheimer's disease (AD), has become a hot topic. However, most of the work in the literature has focused on the diagnosis of dementia through the classification of symptoms and identification of distinguishing features useful for early diagnosis. For example, in the work of Tanaka and colleagues [20], a virtual avatar was designed to conduct an interview with patients based on the Mini-Mental State Examination (MMSE) [7] and other neuropsychological tests. The authors recorded the interaction between the avatar and the patient, extracted various audiovisual features from the speech and finally used support vector machines (SVM) and logistic regression to classify the presence of dementia, achieving 93% accuracy. In another work by Chinaei and colleagues [5], three main linguistic features considered as verbal indicators of confusion in people with Alzheimer's disease were analyzed: vocabulary richness, sentence syntactic tree structure and acoustic cues. Finally, various machine learning algorithms were applied to identify confusion in dialogues, achieving 82% accuracy. Other studies have been based on the development of assistive technologies to help people with dementia with activities of daily living [24], as well as to support different types of therapies for managing patients' psychological, emotional and behavioral symptoms [16]. Yasuda and colleagues [24], for example, implemented a system that provided remote reminders and allowed conversations through a videophone. The goal was to support patients' psychological stability through video call conversations and to assist people with dementia in performing simple tasks. The authors observed that after the intervention, patients' psychological stability persisted for up to three hours after the conversation and the success rate in completing a task increased by 80%. In a related work, a mobile robot called ED [15] was implemented to support patients with AD. However, the analysis of the study results showed that patients with high levels of confusion (40% of the sample) ignored the robot during assistance. In fact, despite some promising results in the literature, it is necessary to understand the characteristics that a robot must possess to make the interaction between robots and AD patients more appropriate and effective. For this reason, several studies have analyzed the technical requirements that social robots aimed at assisting AD patients should possess. Specifically, Salichs et al. [17] conducted several meetings with experts in AD and social robotics, and produced a set of main scenarios and specific requirements (such as body movement, speech interaction, visual perception) that the robot has to satisfy. Their findings highlight the need for the robot, in the general treatment of the AD, to be able to record the patient's activity, to be customizable for the specific patient, and to allow remote task scheduling and control by the caregiver. In the specific scenarios of Active-Listening and Psycho-Stimulation exercises, they indicate as mandatory technical requirements speech interaction, a database, and a visual display; other requirements, namely body movement, visual perception, and Internet connection, even if not mandatory, are marked as desirable for these scenarios.

During the evaluation of the MARIO robot [4] acceptability from AD patients, the robot's embodied presence and ability of personalizing the applications resulted in a correlation with an increasing engagement [3]. The study also found evidence that the robot human relationship strengthened over time, as many people with dementia referred to MARIO as 'he' or 'she' or as 'my friend', and that using the robot represented a conduit for connection to family and friends, providing information on personal interests and giving the person with dementia the potential to engage more in conversations.

Finally, Yuan et al. [25] attempted at assessing the acceptance and perceptions of a SAR, Tammy, designed for AD care, among individuals with MCI or AD, caregivers, and the general public.

Voice and speech control emerged as preferred methods of robot interaction, with little preference for tablet control alone. Caregivers and the general public also expressed positive feedback, emphasizing the importance of features like quiet operation and connectivity to the internet.

In light of the data in the literature, the goal of our work is to make a contribution to the improvement of reminiscence therapy by designing a novel methodology taking into account the necessary features that a social robot must possess to facilitate effective and appropriate interaction with a patient with AD.

3   Methodology

In this section, we outline in more detail the structure and components of the proposed framework. We begin by explaining the study materials in Sect. 3.1, outlining the questionnaires included in the framework. Next, in Sect. 3.2, we explain the planned procedure for using RetroMind in the therapeutic context.

3.1   Questionnaires

The Autobiographical Memory Interview. AMI is a validated methodology to assess the performances of autobiographical memory of individuals. It includes two components, namely the Autobiographical Incidents Schedule (AIS) and the Personal Semantic Memory Schedule (PSMS).

The Autobiographical Incident Schedule. AIS is a test that aims at evaluating individuals' capabilities in recalling specific incidents from their past, requiring the specification of the precise location in which the memory took place and of an accurate estimation regarding when the memory occurred. Specifically, the test comprises nine questions designed to elicit memories related to events occurring in (i) childhood, (ii) early adulthood, and (iii) recent times, with three questions allocated to each life period. The complete set of the nine items belonging to the AIS are depicted in Table 1. Each item is evaluated with a score between 0 and 3, so that an interlocutor can attain a maximum score of 27 points, with no more than 9 points allocated for each life period.

Table 1. The Autobiographical Incident Schedule

Time period	Item	Prompt examples
Childhood	1. Before School	First memory?
	2. Primary School	Memory involving a friend?
	3. Secondary school	Memory involving a teacher?
Early adulthood	4. First job or University	First day at job-university?
	5. Wedding (own or other's)	Memory with a friend or girlfriend?
	6. People met during the 20 s	People met on holiday or at work?
Recent events	7. A relative or visitor in last year	News about a relative?
	8. An event in hospital	Memories with patients/doctors?
	9. A journey during the last year	Place visited? Someone met?

The Personal Semantic Memory Schedule. PSMS test necessitates subjects to respond to inquiries pertaining to their factual knowledge of their personal history, encompassing details such as the names of schools attended or addresses of past residences. The interview is structured into four groups of items, namely (i) background, (ii) childhood, (iii) early adulthood, and (iv) recent information. The background section has a maximum score of 23 points, whereas the remaining three sections each have a maximum score of 21 points, for a total of 86 points for this component. The PSMS complete set of items is summarized in Table 2.

Table 2. The Personal Semantic Memory Schedule

Category	Context	Prompt examples
Background	1. Parents	Place of birth? Occupation?
	2. Brothers and sisters	Names? Date of birth?
	3. Self	Where are you born?
Childhood	4. Before school	Name of friends?
	5. Primary school	Name of school and teachers?
	6. Secondary school	Where?
Early adult life	7. First job or University	Name of college?
	8. Wedding (own or other's)	Whose? Where?
	9. Children	Names? Birth?
Recent information	10. Hospital	Information on the staff?
	11. Christmas and visits	Where last spent?
	12. Holidays or journeys	With who?

The Cornell Scale for Depression in Dementia. The Cornell Scale for Depression in Dementia (CSDD) is a 19-item survey specifically designed for the evaluation and rating of the degree of depression symptoms in demented and

AD affected patients [1]. The scale employs three grades, namely absent (0), mild/intermittent (1), and severe (2), to rate the score of each item. Administration involves two steps: first, the clinician interviews the caregiver based on predefined items, then briefly interviews the patient. Caregivers are required to report behaviors observed in the past week, with specific criteria for certain items like "loss of interest" and "lack of energy". Discrepancies between clinician and caregiver reports are addressed through further interviews. The scale is intended for clinical use, with minimal training required, and typically takes around 30 min to administer, including both caregiver and patient interviews.

3.2   RetroMind Framework Procedure

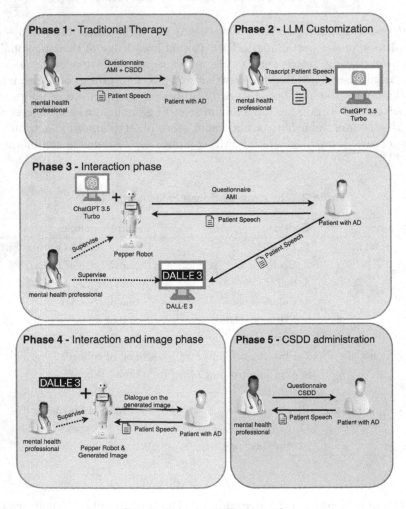

Fig. 1. RetroMind Framework

Phase 1 - Traditional Therapy In the initial phase, mental health profession- als undertake the administration of both the AMI and the CSDD tests to AD patients. Following the administration of these assessments, therapists meticu- lously collect and accurately transcribe the responses obtained from the patients. Subsequently, therapists are tasked with synthesizing the collected data to pro- duce a comprehensive overview of the patient. This overview includes important details about the patient's biographical and pathological history, focusing on key aspects of his/her personal and medical background. By synthesizing informa- tion from the AMI and CSDD tests, therapists gain a holistic understanding of the patient's cognitive functioning, emotional well-being, and past experiences.

Phase 2 - LLM customization In the second phase of the Retromind method- ology, the health care professional is responsible for customizing ChatGPT 3.5 Turbo, transforming it into a tool that, used in conjunction with the Pepper robot, will enable personalized interaction between patient and robot during phase three. In fact, after collecting and transcribing the patient's initial test responses, at this stage the therapist elaborates a detailed description of the subject, including significant elements of his or her biographical and pathologi- cal history. This allows ChatGPT 3.5 Turbo to create personalized conversations, calibrating the language model to better understand the patient, his or her needs, and Alzheimer's-related cognitive difficulties.

Phase 3 - Interaction phase During the interaction phase, the robot, which has been tailored to the patient's needs and personal history, supports reminiscence therapy through the assisted perfomance of the AMI test. The Pepper robot captures the patient's speech using its audio sensors and converts this input into text via the Whisper API, ensuring faithful transposition of the subject's words. The resulting text is subsequently sent to ChatGPT 3.5 Turbo. At the same time, the text obtained from the patient's speech is sent to DALL-E3. This transforms the experiences and memories recounted by the patient into visual representations, producing an image that serves as an additional element to facilitate and reinforce the reenactment of memories.

Phase 4 - Interaction and image phase In the fourth phase of the Retromind methodology, Pepper takes an even more central role in the multisensory aspect of reminiscence therapy. The images produced by DALL-E3, are presented to the patient through the display on Pepper. This provides a visual representation of the memories and events evoked by the patient during the previous phase. This multisensory approach aims to further stimulate the patient's memory and elicit positive emotions, helping to solidify the link between past experiences and their visual expression. The mental health professional, in collaboration with the Pepper robot, guides the patient in a dialogue about the images, encouraging the patient to share additional details that reinforce the memory of previously narrated events.

Fig. 2. Simulation of the image supported therapy where Pepper shows the image generated at the patient.

Phase 5 - CSDD administration In the last phase, the mental health professional administers the CSDD to the patient to monitor changes in the patient's emotional sphere compared to baseline levels.

4   Preliminary Illustrative Example and Discussion

In this example, we conducted a preliminary experiment to test part of the RetroMind framework. We generated an image using the DALL-E3 model based on textual input extracted from a case study in the literature on a patient with AD [18]. In the dialogue frame we selected, the patient was telling her interlocutor about memories from her past. The frame used is the following:

I just lived in a regular farm home. Farmed cotton, corn, eh-everything you. . .
grow on a farm

Next, the DALL-E3 model based on the textual input successfully generated the image of Fig. 3.

The resulting image depicted a country house surrounded by a cotton field. Notably, the house appeared aged, suggesting a historical context in line with the patient's memories. Finally, we used GPT-4, which shares the same underlying database as DALL-E 3, and extracted the following caption:

The picture shows a country house surrounded by a cotton field. The house
looks old and the photograph appears to have been taken many years ago.

We successively tokenized each sentence using the spaCy language model, which extracts word vectors for each token in the sentences, excluding stop words as shown below:

Fig. 3. Image generated by RetroMind taked from the case study in [18].

1)/ *lived | regular | farm | home | farmed | cotton | corn | grow | farm |*

and the second one:

2)/ *picture | shows | country | house | surrounded | cotton | field | house |*

looks | old | photograph | appears | taken | many | years | ago |

The used *en_core_web_md* model is specifically trained for English text processing. Therefore, its tokenization algorithm is optimized for the characteristics of the English language, such as word contractions, compound words, and other linguistic nuances. We obtained the word embeddings of the tokens and calculated the similarities between the sum of the obtained word vectors.

The cosine similarity measures the angle between two vectors represented as multidimensional spaces, indicating how closely they are aligned with each other. More in detail, the cosine similarity between two sentence embeddings, represented as u and v, is defined as follows:

$$cos(u,v) = \frac{u \cdot v}{||u|| * ||v||} \tag{1}$$

where $u \cdot v$ stands for the dot product between the two embeddings, and $||u||$ and $||v||$ are their respective Euclidean norms. The similarity algorithm outputs a value in the range $[-1, 1]$, where 1 indicates total similarity (identic sentences), 0 indicates no semantic correlation, and -1 indicates opposite semantic content. In our case, a value of 0.752 suggests considerable similarity between the two sentences, indicating that the vectors representing them have a relatively small separation angle.

5   Conclusion

RT has emerged as a promising approach to address both cognitive and emotional aspects of Alzheimer's disease, using patients' life stories to evoke memories and foster the development of positive emotions. Although traditional RT has demonstrated benefits, the integration of technological tools such as LLMs and social robots improves its effectiveness and accessibility. The proposed Retro-Mind framework offers an innovative methodology to support mental health professionals in the administration of reminiscence therapy by providing visual support for the narration and representation of patients' life memories. By integrating LLMs and social robots, RetroMind facilitates personalized and empathic interactions tailored to each patient's needs and history. Through HRI, Retro-Mind engages patients in reminiscence sessions, aids in memory recall, and monitors emotional states, providing comprehensive support during the therapeutic process. The main innovative aspect provided by RetroMind is its ability to provide visual and personalized representations thanks to generative AI, which enhances the multi-sensory experience of reminiscence therapy, promoting deeper connections between past experiences and emotional expression. Although several works in the literature have proposed the use of technologies to improve the effectiveness of reminiscence therapy, RetroMind is the first system that seeks to intervene in several components of the therapy, providing on the one hand a narrative support tool (generated images) and on the other hand ensuring constant monitoring of the patient's cognitive performance and emotional state. The main element that distinguishes RetroMind from existing proposals in the literature lies in the fact that it offers, even to those who do not have direct images of their past, the possibility of reconstructing a representation of their memories. In other words, RetroMind aims to enhance the effectiveness of RT through a visual reconstruction of the past that is able to restore an image to memories.

References

1. Alexopoulos, G.S., Abrams, R.C., Young, R.C., Shamoian, C.A.: Cornell scale for depression in dementia. Biol. Psychiat. **23**(3), 271–284 (1988)
2. Cabeza, R., et al.: Brain activity during episodic retrieval of autobiographical and laboratory events: an fMRI study using a novel photo paradigm. J. Cogn. Neurosci. **16**(9), 1583–1594 (2004)
3. Casey, D., et al.: The perceptions of people with dementia and key stakeholders regarding the use and impact of the social robot MARIO. Int. J. Environ. Res. Public Health **17**(22), 8621 (2020)
4. Casey, D., et al.: What people with dementia want: designing MARIO an acceptable robot companion. In: Miesenberger, K., Bühler, C., Penaz, P. (eds.) ICCHP 2016. LNCS, vol. 9758, pp. 318–325. Springer, Cham (2016). https://doi.org/10.1007/978-3-319-41264-1_44
5. Chinaei, H., Currie, L.C., Danks, A., Lin, H., Mehta, T., Rudzicz, F.: Identifying and avoiding confusion in dialogue with people with Alzheimer's disease. Comput. Linguist. **43**(2), 377–406 (2017)

6. Cuevas, P.E.G., Davidson, P.M., Mejilla, J.L., Rodney, T.W.: Reminiscence therapy for older adults with Alzheimer's disease: a literature review. Int. J. Ment. Health Nurs. **29**(3), 364–371 (2020)
7. Folstein, M.F., Robins, L.N., Helzer, J.E.: The mini-mental state examination. Arch. Gen. Psychiatry **40**(7), 812–812 (1983)
8. Hashim, A., Mohd. Rias, R., Kamaruzaman, M.F.: The use of personalized digital memory book as a reminiscence therapy for Alzheimer's disease (AD) patients. In: Zaman, H.B., Robinson, P., Olivier, P., Shih, T.K., Velastin, S. (eds.) IVIC 2013. LNCS, vol. 8237, pp. 508–515. Springer, Cham (2013). https://doi.org/10.1007/978-3-319-02958-0_46
9. Imtiaz, D., Khan, A., Seelye, A., et al.: A mobile multimedia reminiscence therapy application to reduce behavioral and psychological symptoms in persons with Alzheimer's. J. Healthc. Eng. **2018**, 1–9 (2018)
10. Kopelman, M.D., Wilson, B., Baddeley, A.D.: The autobiographical memory interview: a new assessment of autobiographical and personal semantic memory in amnesic patients. J. Clin. Exp. Neuropsychol. **11**(5), 724–744 (1989)
11. Lancioni, G.E., et al.: A computer-aided program for helping patients with moderate Alzheimer's disease engage in verbal reminiscence. Res. Dev. Disabil. **35**(11), 3026–3033 (2014)
12. Musavi, M., Mohammadian, S., Mohammadinezhad, B.: The effect of group integrative reminiscence therapy on mental health among older women living in Iranian nursing homes. Nurs. Open **4**(4), 303–309 (2017)
13. Okumura, Y., Tanimukai, S., Asada, T.: Effects of short-term reminiscence therapy on elderly with dementia: a comparison with everyday conversation approaches. Psychogeriatrics **8**(3), 124–133 (2008)
14. Park, K., Lee, S., Yang, J., Song, T., Hong, G.R.S.: A systematic review and meta-analysis on the effect of reminiscence therapy for people with dementia. Int. Psychogeriatr. **31**(11), 1581–1597 (2019)
15. Rudzicz, F., Wang, R., Begum, M., Mihailidis, A.: Speech interaction with personal assistive robots supporting aging at home for individuals with Alzheimer's disease. ACM Trans. Accessible Computi. (TACCESS) **7**(2), 1–22 (2015)
16. Sakakibara, S., Saiki, S., Nakamura, M., Yasuda, K.: Generating personalized dialogue towards daily counseling system for home dementia care. In: Duffy, V.G. (ed.) DHM 2017. LNCS, vol. 10287, pp. 161–172. Springer, Cham (2017). https://doi.org/10.1007/978-3-319-58466-9_16
17. Salichs, M.A., Encinar, I.P., Salichs, E., Castro-González, Á., Malfaz, M.: Study of scenarios and technical requirements of a social assistive robot for Alzheimer's disease patients and their caregivers. Int. J. Soc. Robot. **8**, 85–102 (2016)
18. Shenk, D., Davis, B., Peacock, J.R., Moore, L.: Narratives and self-identity in later life: Two rural American older women. J. Aging Stud. **16**(4), 401–413 (2002)
19. Shropshire, M.: Reminiscence intervention for community-dwelling older adults without dementia: a literature review. Br. J. Community Nurs. **25**(1), 40–44 (2020)
20. Tanaka, H., et al.: Detecting dementia through interactive computer avatars. IEEE J. Transl. Eng. Health Med. **5**, 1–11 (2017)
21. Wang, J.J.: Group reminiscence therapy for cognitive and affective function of demented elderly in Taiwan. Int. J. Geriatric Psychiatry: J. Psychiatry Life Allied Sci. **22**(12), 1235–1240 (2007)
22. Webster, J.D.: Construction and validation of the reminiscence functions scale. J. Gerontol. **48**(5), P256–P262 (1993)
23. Woods, B., O'Philbin, L., Farrell, E.M., Spector, A.E., Orrell, M.: Reminiscence therapy for dementia. Cochrane Database Syst. Rev. (3) (2018)

24. Yasuda, K., Kuwahara, N., Kuwabara, K., Morimoto, K., Tetsutani, N.: Daily assistance for individuals with dementia via videophone. Am. J. Alzheimer's Disease Other Dementias® **28**(5), 508–516 (2013)
25. Yuan, F., et al.: Assessing the acceptability of a humanoid robot for Alzheimer's disease and related dementia care using an online survey. Int. J. Soc. Robot. **14**(5), 1223–1237 (2022)
26. Zhang, C., Chen, J., Li, J., Peng, Y., Mao, Z.: Large language models for human-robot interaction: a review. Biomimetic Intell. Robot., 100131 (2023)

Language in the Technology Trap: The Impact of the Increasingly Large Proportion of Machine-Generated Texts on Language Use

Anna Zanina[✉]

University of St.Gallen, Dufourstrasse 50, 9000 St. Gallen, Switzerland
anna.zanina@unisg.ch

Abstract. Neural machine translation programs can operate only within the framework of variants they have been trained with. Their efficiency has been increased at the expense of transparency: in fact, the algorithms according to which the machine prefers one variant over the other - probability, frequency, coercivity - determine the output of Deep Learning. A neural machine translation program provides significantly better results if it runs first through an unsupervised training on row data, and then it undergoes a human-supervised training. In disadvantageous cases, this training with human-selected data entails ready-made assumptions and biases, and it might be influenced by the trainer's subjective choices. This particulate corpus should represent the language norm. Based on that standard, the program will calculate probabilities for sentence constructions.

A lower probability might result for a correct sentence (or any grammatically correct one) than for an incorrect one: for example, if several of its word forms did not appear in the training corpus. In that case, language technology-based applications and increasing reliance on real-time language technologies can have a major impact on the language structure.

The structures using non-inflected forms are preferred in the machine translation process. Contemporary development of linguistic technologies - translation technology in particular - changes the proportions of natural and artificial text production by influencing the emergence and disappearance of diverse language patterns in a non-transparent way. Indeed, an exacerbation of frequently observed patterns and a loss of less frequent ones not only strengthen biases present in used datasets, but they could also lead to an artificially depleted language caused by algorithmic biases.

Keywords: Neural Machine Translation · Algorithmic Biases · Bias Amplification · Multilingual Parallel Corpora Research · Language Patterns Translation Variants · Analytical Structure

H. Degen and S. Ntoa (Eds.): HCII 2024, LNAI 14736, pp. 469–479, 2024.
https://doi.org/10.1007/978-3-031-60615-1_32

1 Language Professionals Versus Language Technology - Drivers for the Implementation of New Technologies

Several studies describe discrepancies between computer-generated language and human-produced language. Definitely, the two differ and, judging by the volume of text production - which has a non-natural origin - a proportional effect on natural language is to be assumed. Language professionals from various disciplines are interested in taking a closer look at this interaction: linguists and translators, as well as a large sector of the industry specialized in natural language processing. However, as long as the invisibility of a translation remains its most important quality criterion, the endeavor to bring the output of machine translation as close as possible to the natural production of the language is a major one. Seen from this perspective, language technologies are the joint interface of all those interests.

A 2023 Translation Technology Insights report[1] provides an overview of the continuously growing relevance of translation technology and the role it can play in meeting the increasing demands - on the number of words translated, the time required, and the linguistic quality. Less experience in the profession and growing pressure factors are described as the decline in competences and skills. To a certain extent, improved technologies could compensate for and mitigate the decline in competencies and close these gaps. Among the main drivers for the implementation of new technologies are: maintaining quality (49%), improving translation and business processes (43%) - which would address the cost and speed of delivery, - and the more general objectives of managing increasing demand (38%) and improving customer satisfaction (31%). Typically, translation professionals prioritize reducing their prices and increasing the speed of their tasks over improving the quality of their work. On the contrary, corporations prioritize delivering high-quality translations over cutting costs. Nevertheless, speed remains the primary concern for corporations, whereas language service providers and freelance translators prioritize cost over everything else.

2 Neural Machine Translation

2.1 Issues Caused by Neural Machine Translation

Technological developments are constantly influencing the way language professionals deal with linguistic production. Nowadays language technologies become an integral part of everyday life and they occur faster than their processing in linguistic subdisciplines. Human written or oral speech production influenced by language technology is largely unexplored, and it poses a challenge to conventional linguistic research methods. The dichotomy of qualitative and quantitative methods in language research is gaining renewed relevance. Despite the assumption that quantitative methods would provide better coverage, leading research groups argue for qualitative methods or a mix of both. Focusing on the relationships among technology, language, and professional application, a neural machine translation (NMT) takes on a special significance thanks to its ability to produce natural-sounding texts. It reveals implications on various levels:

---

[1] https://www.trados.com/learning/translation-technology-insights/

- It is based on the exploitation of large data sets, which are only a particular form of human-made sign practice. Here, the computer-readable form is crucial, and merely a fragment of linguistic practice is defined as the referential norm. The selection mechanisms of the algorithms are non-transparent and cannot be back-traced or analyzed. The linguistic choices, which are left to the users' judgement, often lead them to simple speculations without verification criteria. (Tables 1 and 2) Further, there is a tendency to neglect the need to ensure compatibility between the translation and the source text, especially if the translation appears visually and aurally correct. Users are more likely to adopt simplified constructions from the proposed translation, which they can better follow and justify to their communication partners, in order to reduce uncertainty and ensure comprehension security. Machine translation frees the user from the need to elaborate a sentence as an entire syntactic sequence. Simple reduced constructions also serve to provide comprehension security.
- It unlocks cross-linguistic interaction in a new dimension by producing extremely large amounts of text and simulating naturalness to users. In fact, language contact can occur when a bilingual translator convert a text from a source language into a target language. This process can lead to the transfer of features from the source into the translated text, which is commonly referred to as interference. If this interference occurs repeatedly in translations from a source language, these new linguistic features can extend beyond the translated texts and affect monolingual text production in the target language by introducing new linguistic conventions into untranslated texts. Moreover, an NMT can also produce words that do not naturally exist in the target language.
- Similar to other technologies that rely on large amounts of existing text for training, an NMT also tends to amplify biases present in the training data. One commonly observed example of bias amplification is the overuse of masculine forms in many systems, which is well documented.

Table 1. Linguistic Choices, Part 1.

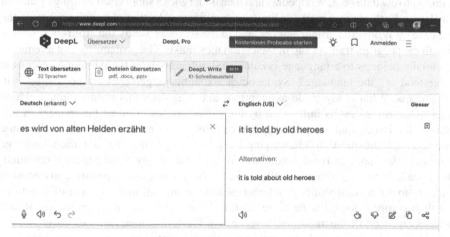

Table 2. Linguistic Choices, Part 2.

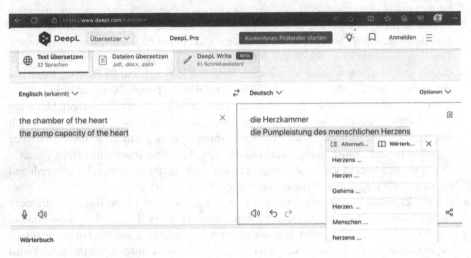

2.2 Training Corpora

An NMT can potentially only operate within the framework of variants it has been trained with. Its efficiency has been increased at the expense of transparency, since the algorithms according to which the machine prefers one variant or the other - probability, frequency, coercivity calculation - determine the output of Deep Learning. What is calculated is the probability that a sentence belongs to a language. The probability calculation could be lower for a correct sentence (or another analogue grammatically correct one) than for an incorrect one - e.g. if several word forms did not appear in the training corpus. The NMT provides significantly better results if the program runs through an unsupervised training on row data - e.g. Wikipedia - and then undergoes a supervised training by human translators. Both of these methods limit the significant selection of linguistic data: in the first case by Wikipedia article authors, and in the second case by the arbitrary selection of both the program trainers and the selection they make. The probability that a sentence potentially belongs to a language is calculated, whereby here the particulate corpus is understood as "the language". Syntactic or semantic judgements are not included in this process. What ready-made assumptions and bias does this training entail, which in an unfavorable case is influenced by the subjective selection of the trainer? In this context, the issues that are primarily not of a linguistic nature - but that at the same time represent the questions challenging Deep Learning in the field of natural language processing (language and object recognition) - are increasingly coming to the foreground. The so-called "curse of dimensionality" and its counterbalancing constitute an opposing tendency to the natural ability of a language to form an unlimited number of structures and their combinations. Furthermore, natural language processing exposes significant disadvantages: while the traditional languages of Western cultures are well covered, their regional varieties and rarer languages are underrepresented or not represented at all. A further question is which corpora would be best suited for such training. In this case, language technology based applications and increasing reliance on real-time language technologies can have a major impact on the structure of a language. Recent studies show that there is a loss of lexical and morphological richness in the translations produced by all investigated MT paradigms. (Vanmassenhove 2021).

3 Multilingual Parallel Corpora in Cross-Lingual Research

Over the last few years, the demand for multilingual parallel resources in data-driven techniques has been increasing, especially in cross-lingual research. To address this demand, many scientific groups in natural language processing (NLP) are focusing on building multilingual parallel corpora. However, their availability - unlike that of monolingual corpora - is limited. Corpora can be used for translation goals, such as checking cross-linguistic correspondences for evaluating their cross-cultural equivalence. An appropriate example is OPUS (MultiUN)[2], probably the largest collection of freely accessible parallel corpora in several languages. It includes the EuroParl and JRC-Acquis corpora[3], which primarily consist of legal EU documents like the European Parliament proceedings. Both corpora have bilingual alignments for all language pairs, including English. However, EuroParl only covers eleven European languages and does not include any languages from other member states or candidate countries. It contains about 30 million words for each of the 11 languages. In contrast, JRC-Acquis is available in 21 official EU languages and has an average size of approximately nine million words per language. MultiUN[4] is derived from official United Nations documents and is available in the six UN official languages - English, Spanish, French, Russian, Arabic, Chinese - with around 300 million words for each of them, as well as in German with about nine million words. A further example is SwissAdmin[5], a multilingual and POS tagged parallel corpus. It consists of articles from the Swiss Federal Administration and is available in English, German, Italian, and French. There are three versions: plain texts of around six to eight million words per language, sentence-aligned bilingual texts for each language pair, and a POS tagged version. The annotation was done automatically using the Fips multilingual parser. Despite being based on Generative Grammar, the Fips parser has been significantly simplified to enable efficient implementation. It uses a one-step scanning process that eliminates the need for any pre- or post-processing of the input text. By applying rules for structure formation and syntactic interpretation, the parser determines dependency relationships among different components, even if they are separated by large distances. These components include grammatical functions and other elements that contribute to the overall structure of the language. A lexical database created specifically for the Fips parser works on two levels: words, which are inflected forms of lexical units, and lexemes, which are more abstract units that represent specific

---

[2] https://opus.nlpl.eu/

[3] An overview of the European Union's highly multilingual parallel corpora - https://joint-res earch-centre.ec.europa.eu/

[4] United Nations Parallel Corpus - https://conferences.unite.un.org/UNCorpus/

[5] http://latl.unige.ch/swissadmin/;   http://www.lrec-conf.org/proceedings/lrec2014/pdf/772_Paper.pdf.

interpretations of a word. In addition, the parser defines collocations, i.e., combinations of two lexical units (lexemes) or collocations within certain grammatical relations such as adjective-noun or verb-object.

4 "Machine-Translationese" Uncovered from Corpus-Based Analyses

Several studies[6] investigated the use of multilingual corpora to compare machine-translated texts with original texts and identify features of the machine-generated texts. The comparison between machine-translated data and a corpus of untranslated data allows to uncover linguistic features in machine-translated texts and leads to the knowledge that machine-translated texts clearly derivate from the observed norms in the original language (e.g. average sentence length, n-gram features, lexical diversity). That might serve as information for the post-editing process in order to optimize translation quality. These corpus-based analyses have proven that machine-translated texts often have a lower lexical richness and an overuse or underuse of specific language features. From the training perspective, these findings help language professionals understand the limitations of machine translation and determine their unique role as human translators. Furthermore, comparing machine-translated data with data from texts written directly in the source language enables the evaluation of the discrepancy between machine-translated texts and the original language, which provides valuable information for the post-editing process. Since the goal here is to make the translator invisible, it is important to achieve optimal linguistic homogeneity between the original language and the translated language.

This proceeding allows to see how often those tags appear, and to compare whether the ones which are rare in the monolingual text are even rarer in the human-translated or machine-translated text. Which in turn makes the evaluation of the results possible: are the rare constructions becoming rarer and the common ones more frequent? Does machine translation reinforce common structures and hide rarer structures? A study on the effects of machine translation on lexical variation - suitably titled "Lost in Translation: Decline and Erosion of Linguistic Diversity in Machine Translation" (Vanmassenhove et al. 2019) - illustrates this pattern. Using the example of English-Spanish translations, the authors show that neural network techniques generate significantly fewer different translations of the same word compared to human-generated translations. For example, humans translate the English term "picture" with the Spanish term "imagen" (or its plural form) in around 80% of cases, while machine translation provides this translation in almost 100% of cases. The authors conclude that their analysis shows that machine translation paradigms actually affect the frequency of more or less frequent words to such an extent that a significant number of words are completely "lost in translation", with neural network techniques being among the least effective in terms of lexical diversity. Beyond this, prior studies also have shown that automatic language generation in languages other than English can lead to sentences with grammatical structures that

---

[6] Lapshinova-Koltunski 2015; Vanmassenhove, Shterionov, Way 2019; Loock 2021; De Clercq et al. 2021.

are influenced by English, especially when cross-learning is used[7]. This phenomenon does not necessarily stem from the intention of actors in the digital language industry to enforce sociolinguistic hierarchies, but is rather co-produced by the capabilities and characteristics of digital language technology, as machine learning tools require existing data sets for training and reinforce dominant linguistic patterns. Various methods were used to investigate users' experiences of human-machine interaction, which ultimately led to improved performance in English. From this, it can be inferred that a "feedback loop" is created where language practices that occur more frequently are better understood by digital devices, causing users to adapt their language in order to use the tools efficiently. As a result, already commonly used forms become even more prevalent. The already existing tendencies towards standardization are thus reinforced by users' practices.

5 Distinctions Between Machine Translations and Human Translations

This section excerpt discusses the distinctions between machine translations and human translations, highlighting their unique characteristics. Human translations are distinguished by their extensive lexical variety. They utilize a diverse range of vocabulary and language styles. Conversely, machine translations display variations in other aspects of language, such as the use of specific grammatical structures or sentence lengths. Moreover, the text mentions the differentiation of POS tags and POS trigrams between machine and human translations, without delving into the specific implications of these discrepancies. Lastly, it states that POS trigrams are more effective in identifying human translations, while POS tags are better suited for recognizing machine translations. Consequently, these linguistic markers facilitate the recognition of whether a translation was produced by a human or a machine.

In this context, the knowledge of contrastive analysis is applied, focusing specifically on the differences between German and English. For instance, it is known that English tends to use more verbal expressions compared to German. This fact can be verified by comparing the use of verbal and nominal phrases in translated texts and in original works. It is to be expected that English original texts have a higher prevalence of verbal phrases compared to nominal phrases. In order to validate these assumptions, it is required to investigate and compare how certain features are distributed among different translation variants, their English source texts and the comparable German original texts. Therefore, the frequency distribution of certain lexico-grammatical patterns representing these features in the texts needs to be analyzed. In order to extract these patterns, the use of an accessible corpus would be necessary. Subsequently, univariate statistical methods - analyzing one feature at a time - are used to evaluate these patterns. For example, this allows a significance analysis to determine whether the frequency distribution of a particular pattern is statistically significant in distinguishing between different translation variants or between the translations and their source texts. The human translations produced by experts are very similar to the original texts in terms of the distribution of

---

[7] Lauscher et al. 2020; Virtanen et al. 2019, cited in Bommasani et al. 2021, p. 25.

nominal phrases compared to verbal phrases. This suggests that these translations do not manifest either normalization or the phenomenon of "shining through" when the analyzed markers (e.g. average sentence length, n-gram features, lexical diversity) are considered. The machine-translated data show a higher ratio of nouns to verbs. This could be due to incorrect part-of-speech tagging caused by gaps in the training data used for machine translations. As is the case of many verbs that were not translated and verbal forms incorrectly tagged as nouns or adjectives.

Concerning the language pair English-German, it seems reasonable to focus on the use of multi-word expressions, in particular collocations that appear in the form of noun phrases. Complex noun phrases are of special interest for natural language processing as entities of speech production, and they have the potential to be immediate constituents of the sentence. For their translations, less or non-inflected equivalents are prioritized according to the patterns preferred by the algorithm. That prioritization enhances the generally anticipated transition of the German language from a synthetic to an analytical structure (Table 3).

Table 3. Prioritization of Non-Inflected Equivalents.

Deutsch (erkannt) ∨	⇄	Englisch (US) ∨
zur Verfügung stehen	×	be available
verfügbar sein		be available

Deutsch (erkannt) ∨	⇄	Englisch (UK) ∨
dieses Gerät steht zur Verfügung	×	this unit is available
		Alternativen:
		this device is available

Englisch (erkannt) ∨	⇄	Deutsch ∨	automatisch ∨ Glossar
this unit is available	×	diese Einheit ist verfügbar	
			ist erhältlich …
		Alternativen:	ist lieferbar …
		dieses Gerät	verfügbar …
			steht …
			ist vorhanden …
			erhältlich …
◁))		◁)) 🖑 ⌐ zur Verfügung …	🗗 ⌥
			ist frei …

The following paragraph describes some of the features of the German language in terms of its inflection, morphology, and syntax. The trigger for the mass development of prepositional token constructions was the beginning of written language. In contrast to the spoken form of language, which is heavily dependent on the situation prevailing at any given time, written forms of language require more complex structures. Writers cannot draw on a common situation with readers and must therefore adopt linguistic means, such as prepositional tokens, to convey information more clearly and precisely. Furthermore, capturing information in the written form makes it possible to use more complex structures. The German language has maintained some of its original fusional inflection, although with a relatively small stock of resources. This means that the inflectional endings used for the grammar of words have been partially replaced by analysis (i.e. the combination of words). An example is the transformation of some merging markers into agglutinative markers, such as the -en of the dative plural. A special feature of German is the cooperation of inflection in the nominal group, where the means are used efficiently to clearly encode the intended meaning. This implies that German allows a comparatively transparent encoding of the intended function in the nominal phrase.

In terms of syntactic relations, complements are based partly on case distinctions - a synthetic procedure - and partly on the use of "semantically bleached" prepositions (Table 4) - an analytical procedure. Therefore, syntactic relationships in sentence structures can be expressed both by word endings and by the use of prepositions, depending on the meaning and function of the sentence. At the sentence level, complements are almost exclusively represented prepositionally, not nominally, i.e. analytically. Therefore, the complements in complete sentences are usually represented by prepositional expressions and not by nouns. In contrast to English, the linear word order in German does not play a role in the expression of syntactic relationships. Neither are the syntactic relationships of complements differentiated by their relative position in the sentence.

Table 4. "Semantically Bleached" Prepositions.

6   Influence on the Diversity of the Morphologically Rich Languages

Cross-linguistic correspondences in translation can be systematic, but not as common in the target language. This is evident from the results of the corpus-based analysis, which show that the co-occurrence relations between words are not natural or common in the target language. These mistakes in collocation are primarily due to the fact that translation is seen as a process of converting linguistic forms from the source into the target language, and not as a production of texts in the target language. In order to ensure naturalness of translation, the focus should be shifted from the language system to the language use. In this respect, corpora offer possibilities for translation studies and contrastive analyses.

The data of the morphologically richer languages show a higher lexical and morphological diversity than the English data, both in the original data and in the translations of all systems. However, the difference in the measured values is much smaller than in the original data, suggesting that the machine translation systems have a stronger negative influence on the diversity and richness of the morphologically richer languages.

NMTs still require human translations or human-approved translations as training data. Since also an NMT - like other machine translation approaches - is not error-free, its results need to be checked (and improved when needed) by experts who understand both the original and the translated texts. It is becoming increasingly necessary even for occasional users of machine translation technology to have an appropriate knowledge, so that they are not unduly disadvantaged by their lack of understanding technology. Considering the peculiarities of the NMT, translators could mitigate and counterbalance the negative effects more effectively if they consciously increase the proportion of inflected forms, for example by focusing on hotspots such as noun phrases or bleached prepositions. In appropriate circumstances, an NMT can play a crucial role in promoting and maintaining multilingualism by complementing language acquisition and ongoing human translation efforts.

Acknowledgments. We would like to thank the reviewers for their insightful comments and feedback.

References

1. Berzak, Y., Reichart, R., Katz, B.: Reconstructing native language typology from foreign language usage. In: Proceedings of the Eighteenth Conference on Computational Natural Language Learning, pp. 21–29, Ann Arbor, Michigan. Association for Computational Linguistics (2014)
2. Cappelle, B., Loock, R.: Typological differences shining through. The case of phrasal verbs in translated English. In: Delaere, I., Lefer, M., De Sutter, G. (eds.): Empirical Translation Studies: New Methodological and Theoretical Traditions, pp. 235–264. De Gruyter Mouton, Berlin (2017)
3. De Clercq, O., Sutter, G., Loock, R., Cappelle, B., Plevoets, K.: Uncovering Machine Translationese Using Corpus Analysis Techniques to Distinguish between Original and Machine-Translated French (2021)

4. Deilen, S., Hernandez, G., Lapshinova-Koltunski, E., Maaß, C.: Using ChatGPT as a CAT tool in Easy Language translation (2023)
5. Hassan, H., Aue, A., Chen, C., Chowdhary, V., et al.: Achieving Human Parity on Automatic Chinese to English News Translation (2018)
6. Kenny, D.: Machine translation for everyone: empowering users in the age of artificial intelligence. (Translation and Multilingual Natural Language Processing 18). Language Science Press. Berlin (2022)
7. Kranich, S.: Translations as a Locus of Language Contact (2014). https://doi.org/10.1057/9781137025487_6
8. Lapshinova-Koltunski, E.: Variation in translation: evidence from corpora. In: Fantinuoli, C.; Zanettin, F. (eds.): New directions in corpus-based translation studies, TMNLP, pp. 93–113. LSP (2015)
9. Popovic, M., Lapshinova-Koltunski, E., Koponen, M.: Computational analysis of different translations: by professionals, students and machines (2023)
10. Schneider, B.: Multilingualism and AI: The Regimentation of Language in the Age of Digital Capitalism. Signs and Society (2023)
11. Streiter, O., Schmidt-Wigger, A: Patterns of Derivation (1996)
12. Vanmassenhove, E., Shterionov, D., Gwilliam, M.: Machine translationese: effects of algorithmic bias on linguistic complexity in machine translation. In: Proceedings of EACL-2021, pp. 2203–2213, Online, April. ACL (2021)

Author Index

Printed in the United States
by Baker & Taylor Publisher Services